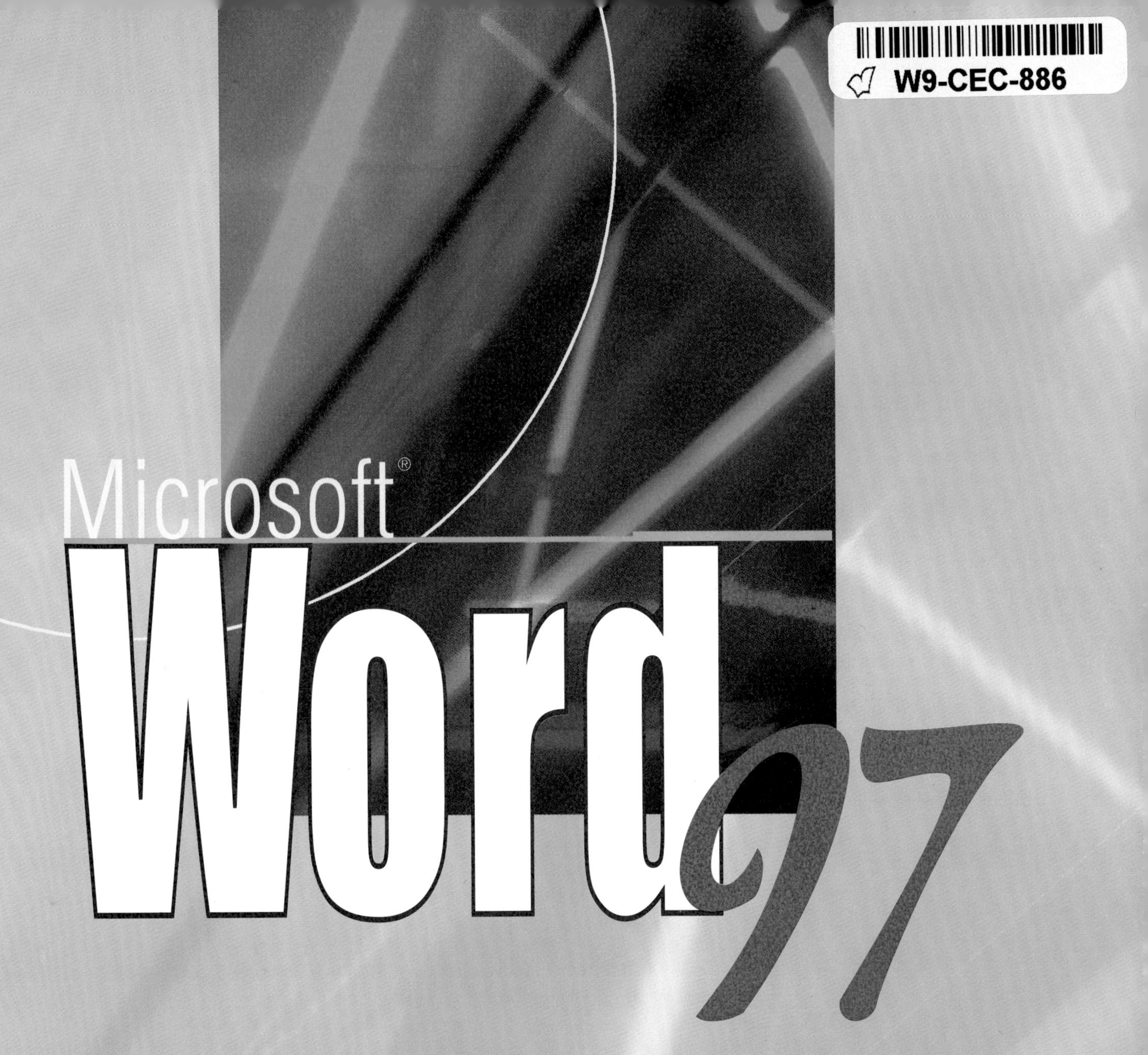

NITA HEWITT RUTKOSKY
PIERCE COLLEGE AT PUYALLUP
PUYALLUP, WASHINGTON

Developmental Editor	Michael Sander
Copy Editor	Susan Trzeciak Gibson
Proofreader	Sharon R. O'Donnell
Indexer	Nancy Sauro
Art Director	Joan Silver
Cover & Text Designer	Jennifer Wreisner
Desktop Production Specialist	Jennifer Wreisner

Permissions—Material for selected documents has been excerpted from "Exploring the Internet," by Joseph Habraken, *EMC/Paradigm Profile*, Fall 1995; *Telecommunications: Systems and Applications*, by William Mitchell, Robert Hendricks, and Leonard Sterry, published by Paradigm Publishing Inc., 1993; *Advanced WordPerfect: Desktop Publishing 6.1 for Windows*, by Nita Hewitt Rutkosky, Judy Dwyer Burnside, and Joanne Marschke Arford, published by Paradigm Publishing Inc., 1996; and *Desktop Publishing: Technology and Design*, by Holly Yasui, published by Paradigm Publishing Inc., 1989.

Acknowledgments—The author and publisher wish to thank the following reviewers for their technical and academic assistance:

- LAURA BAGLEY, Pierce College at Puyallup, Puyallup, Washington
- DEBORAH C. CLEAR, Virginia Highlands Community College, Abingdon, Virginia
- NINA M. EDGMAND, MPC, Salt Lake Community College, Salt Lake City, Utah

---

Library of Congress Cataloging-in-Publication Data

Rutkosky, Nita Hewitt.
Microsoft Word 97 / Nita Hewitt Rutkosky.
p. cm.
Includes index.
ISBN 0-7638-0070-8 (text with data disk). — ISBN 0-7638-0069-4 (text alone)
1. Microsoft Word. 2. Word processing. I. Title.
Z52.5.M52R89 1997 97-20994
652.5'536—dc21 CIP

Text + 3.5" disks: ISBN 0-7638-0070-8
Order number: 05293

Published by **EMC**Paradigm
875 Montreal Way
St. Paul, MN 55102
(800) 535-6865
E-mail: publish@emcp.com

Printed in the United States of America
10 9 8 7 6 5 4 3 2

contents

preface

When students prepare for a successful business career, they need to acquire the skills and qualifications essential to becoming a productive member of the business community. Microcomputer systems are prevalent in most business offices, and students will encounter employment opportunities that require a working knowledge of computers and computer software. Microcomputers, with the appropriate software, are used by businesses in a variety of capacities. One of the most popular uses of a microcomputer system is word processing—the creation of documents.

Word processing certainly belongs in the business world, but it is also a popular application for home computer use. People will want to learn word processing to write personal correspondence, keep personal records, provide support for a home-based business or cottage industry, write term papers and reports, and much more.

This textbook provides students with the opportunity to learn word processing for employment purposes or home use and to utilize a microcomputer as a word processor. The Word 97 program together with an IBM or IBM-compatible microcomputer system must be available for students to practice the features of the program. Word 97 needs to be installed on a hard-drive or network system. To properly install the program, please refer to the Word or Microsoft Office documentation.

This textbook instructs students in the theories and practical applications of one of the most popular word processing programs—Microsoft Word. The text is designed to be used in beginning and advanced word processing classes and provides approximately 80 to 120 hours of instruction.

The book is divided into six units. Chapters within units each contain performance objectives, material introducing and explaining new concepts and commands, step-by-step exercises completed at the computer, a chapter summary, a knowledge self-check, and skill assessment exercises (also completed at the computer).

The step-by-step exercises integrated within the chapter provide students with the opportunity to practice using the feature(s) introduced. Skill assessments at the end of each chapter require students to complete computer exercises without step-by-step instructions. In addition, simulation exercises at the end of each unit require students to make decisions about document preparation and formatting. These practical exercises provide ample opportunity to practice new features and commands as well as previously learned material. Writing activities presented at the end of each unit provide students with the opportunity to compose and format business documents.

This textbook contains a listing of SCANS (Secretary's Commission on Achieving Necessary Skills) goals covered in each unit (see the back of the first page of each unit). The SCANS report was the result of a commission from the Department of Labor. The goal of the commission was to establish the interdisciplinary standards that should be required for *all* students. SCANS skill standards emphasize the integration of competencies from the areas of information, technology, basic skills, and thinking skills. The SCANS committee agreed that all curricula can be strengthened by emphasizing classroom work that is more authentic and relevant to learners, i.e, connecting context to content. Teaching in context helps students move away from subject-specific orientation to integrative learning that includes decision making, problem solving, and critical thinking. The concepts and applications material in each unit of this book has been designed to coordinate with and reflect this important interdisciplinary emphasis. In addition, learning assessment tools implement the SCANS standards. For example, the skill assessments at the end of each chapter reinforce acquired technical skills while providing practice in decision making and problem solving. The performance assessments at the end of each unit offer simulation exercises that require students to demonstrate their understanding of the major skills and technical features taught in the unit's chapters within the framework of critical and creative thinking. The addition of writing activities at the end of each unit makes it clear that students are not just producers, but editors and writers as well.

By the time students have completed the textbook, they have mastered most of the features and commands of Word 97 and are ready to perform on the job. They will also have acquired a solid foundation in the problem-solving and communication abilities so important in the contemporary workplace.

Getting Started

Identifying Computer Hardware

As you work your way through this textbook, you will learn functions and commands for Microsoft Word 97. To do this, you will need an IBM PC or an IBM-compatible computer. This computer system should consist of the CPU, monitor, keyboard, printer, disk drive, and mouse. If you are not sure what equipment you will be operating, check with your instructor.

The computer system displayed in figure G.1 consists of six components. Each component is discussed separately in the material that follows.

figure G.1 *IBM Personal Computer System*

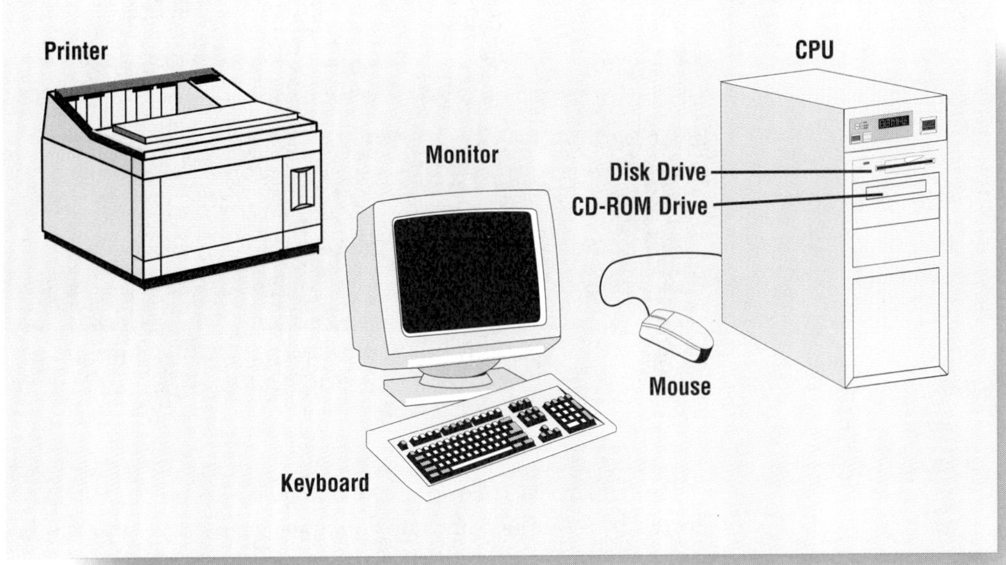

CPU

CPU stands for Central Processing Unit and is the intelligence of the computer. All the processing occurs in the CPU. Silicon chips, which contain miniaturized circuitry, are placed on boards that are plugged into slots within the CPU. Whenever an instruction is given to the computer, that instruction is processed through circuitry in the CPU.

Monitor

The monitor is a piece of equipment that looks like a television screen. It displays the information of a program and the text being input at the keyboard. The quality of display for monitors varies depending on the type of monitor and the type of resolution. Monitors can also vary in size—generally from 14 to 17 inches.

Keyboard

The keyboard is used to input information into the computer. Keyboards for microcomputers vary in the number and location of the keys. Microcomputers have the alphabetic and numeric keys in the same location as the keys on a typewriter. The symbol keys, however, may be placed in a variety of locations, depending on the manufacturer. In addition to letters, numbers, and symbols, most microcomputer keyboards contain function keys, arrow keys, and a numeric keypad. Figure G.2 shows an example of an enhanced keyboard.

G.2 **Microcomputer Enhanced Keyboard**

The 12 keys at the top of the enhanced keyboard, labeled with the letter F followed by a number, are called *function keys*. These keys can be used to perform Word functions. To the right of the regular keys is a group of *special*, or *dedicated keys*. These keys are labeled with specific functions that will be performed when you press the key. Below the special keys are arrow keys. These keys are used to move the insertion point in the document screen. In the upper right corner of the keyboard are three mode indicator lights. When certain modes have been selected, a light appears on the keyboard. For example, if you press the Caps Lock key, which disables the lowercase alphabet, a light appears next to Caps Lock. Similarly, pressing the Num Lock key will disable the special functions on the numeric keypad, which is located at the right side of the keyboard.

Disk Drive

Depending on the computer system you are using, the Word program is installed on a hard drive or as part of a network system. Whether you are using Word on a hard-drive or network system, you will need to have a disk drive available for inserting a 3.5-inch disk, on which you will open and save documents.

The memory capacity for disks varies depending on the density of the disk. Disk memory is measured in kilobytes (thousands) and megabytes (millions). The memory capacity for a 3.5-inch double density (DD) disk is 720,000 bytes (720 kilobytes, which is written as 720 Kb). The memory capacity for a 3.5-inch high density disk (HD) is 1,440,000 bytes (1.44 megabytes, which is written as 1.44 Mb).

Printer

When you create a document at the document screen, it is considered *soft copy*. If you want a *hard copy* of a document, you need to have it printed on paper. To print documents you will need to access a printer. Printers are either *impact* or *nonimpact*. Impact printers have a mechanism that strikes the paper to create text. Nonimpact printers use a variety of methods—heat, ink jet, laser—to print characters. These printers are much quieter and faster than impact printers; generally they are also more expensive than impact printers.

Mouse

Some Word functions are designed to operate more efficiently with a *mouse*. A mouse is an input device that sits on a flat surface next to the computer. A mouse can be operated with the left or the right hand. Moving the mouse on the flat surface causes a corresponding mouse pointer to move on the screen. Figure G.1 shows an illustration of a mouse. For specific instructions on how to use a mouse, please refer to "Using the Mouse" later in this section.

Properly Maintaining Disks

Two 3.5-inch student data disks containing a variety of documents accompany this textbook. You will be saving on and opening documents from these student data disks. To ensure that you will be able to retrieve information from the disks, you need to follow certain rules of disk maintenance. To properly maintain a 3.5-inch disk, follow these rules:

- Do not expose the disk to extreme heat or cold.
- Keep the disk away from magnets and magnetic fields. They can erase the information saved on the disk.
- Do not wipe or clean the magnetic surface of the disk.
- Keep the disk away from food, liquids, and smoke.
- Never remove the disk from the disk drive when the drive light is on.
- Carry the disk in a plastic case to prevent damage to the metal shutter.

The disks that you will be using for saving and opening documents have been formatted and include a number of documents. If you use Word with a blank disk, that disk will probably be formatted. Formatting is a process that establishes tracks and sectors on which information is stored and prepares the disk to accept data from the disk operating system (and erases anything previously saved on the disk). If you are using a disk that is not formatted, check with your instructor on the steps needed to format.

Using the Word Keyboard Template

Microsoft Corporation includes a Word keyboard template that identifies WordPerfect keys and the equivalent Word keys, identifies Word shortcut commands, and identifies Word function keys. This template can be folded and placed next to your computer as a quick reference guide. A keyboard template, designed by EMC/Paradigm Publishing, is included with this textbook. Use this template as a visual aid to Word functions.

Using the Mouse

Word can be operated using a keyboard or it can be operated with the keyboard and a mouse. The mouse may have two or three buttons on top, which are tapped to execute specific functions and commands. To use the mouse, rest it on a flat surface or a mouse pad. Put your hand over it with your palm resting on top of the mouse and your wrist resting on the table surface. As you move the mouse on the flat surface, a corresponding pointer moves on the screen.

When using the mouse, there are four terms you should understand—point, click, double-click, and drag. When operating the mouse, you may need to *point* to a specific command, button, or icon. Point means to position the mouse pointer on the desired item. With the mouse pointer positioned on the desired item, you may need to *click* a button on the mouse. Click means to quickly tap once a button on the mouse. To complete two steps at once such as choosing and then executing a function, *double-click* a mouse button. Double-click means to tap the left mouse button twice in quick succession. The term *drag* means to press and hold the left mouse button, move the mouse pointer to a specific location, and then release the button.

Using the Mouse Pointer

The mouse pointer will change appearance depending on the function being performed or where the pointer is positioned. The mouse pointer may appear as one of the following images:

The mouse pointer appears as an I-beam (called the *I-beam pointer*) in the document screen and can be used to move the insertion point or select text.

The mouse pointer appears as an arrow pointing up and to the left (called the *arrow pointer*) when it is moved to the Title bar, Menu bar, or one of the toolbars at the top of the screen, or when a dialog box is displayed. For example, to open a new document with the mouse, you would move the I-beam pointer to the File option on the Menu bar. When the I-beam pointer is moved to the Menu bar, it turns into an arrow pointer. To make a selection, position the tip of the arrow pointer on the File option, and then click the left mouse button. At the drop-down menu that displays, make selections by positioning the arrow pointer on the desired option, and then clicking the left mouse button.

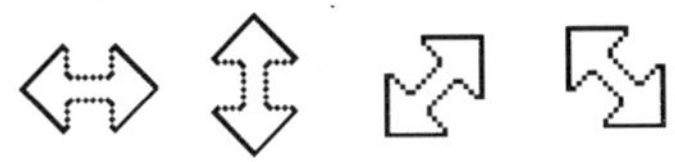

The mouse pointer becomes a double-headed arrow (pointing either left and right, up and down, or diagonally) when performing certain functions such as changing the size of a picture.

In certain situations, such as moving a picture, the mouse pointer becomes a four-headed arrow. The four-headed arrow means that you can move the object left, right, up, or down.

When Word is processing a request, or when the Word program is being loaded, the mouse pointer appears with an hourglass beside it. The hourglass image means "please wait." When the process is completed, the hourglass image is removed.

The mouse pointer also displays as a hand with a pointing index finger in certain functions, such as Help, and indicates that more information is available about that particular item.

Choosing Commands

In Word, several methods can be used to choose commands. A *command* is an instruction that tells Word to do something. You can choose a command with one of the following methods:

- Click a toolbar button with the mouse.
- Choose a command from a menu.
- Use shortcut keys.
- Use a shortcut menu.

Choosing Commands on Toolbars

Word provides several toolbars containing buttons for common tasks. Generally, two toolbars are visible on the screen (unless your system has been customized). One toolbar is called the Standard toolbar. The toolbar below the Standard toolbar is called the Formatting toolbar. To choose a command from a toolbar, position the tip of the arrow pointer on a button, and then click the left mouse button. For example, to print the document currently displayed in the document screen, position the tip of the arrow pointer on the Print button on the Standard toolbar, and then click the left mouse button.

Choosing Commands on the Menu Bar

The Menu bar at the top of the Word screen contains a variety of options you can use to format a Word document or complete file management tasks. Word features are grouped logically into options that display on the Menu bar. For example, features that allow you to work with Word files (documents) are grouped in the File option. Either the mouse or the keyboard can be used to make choices from the Menu bar or make a choice at a dialog box.

To use the mouse to make a choice from the Menu bar, move the I-beam pointer to the Menu bar. This causes the I-beam pointer to display as an arrow pointer. Position the tip of the arrow pointer on the desired option and then click the left mouse button.

To use the keyboard, press the Alt key to make the Menu bar active. Options on the Menu bar display with an underline below one of the letters. To choose an option from the Menu bar, key the underlined letter of the desired option, or move the insertion point with the left or right arrow keys to the option desired, and then press Enter. This causes a drop-down menu to display. For example, to display the File drop-down menu shown in figure G.3 using the mouse, position the arrow pointer on File on the Menu bar, and then click the left mouse button. To display the File drop-down menu with the keyboard, press the Alt key, and then key the letter F for File.

figure G.3 *File Drop-Down Menu*

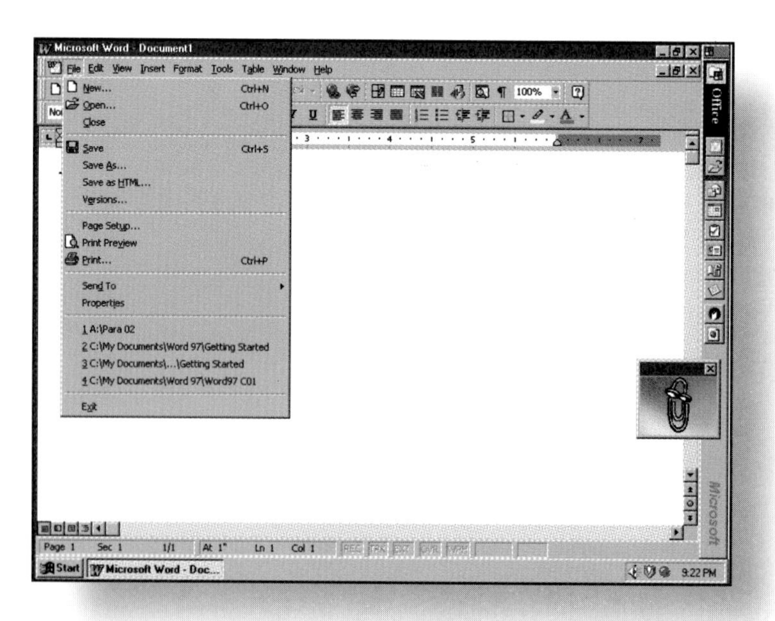

Choosing Commands from Drop-Down Menus

To choose a command from a drop-down menu with the mouse, position the arrow pointer on the desired option, and then click the left mouse button. Drag the arrow pointer to the desired option and then click the left mouse button. To make a selection from the drop-down menu with the keyboard, press the Alt key, and then key the underlined letter of the desired option. At the drop-down menu, click the underlined letter of the desired option. If you want to close a drop-down menu without making a choice, click in the document screen outside the drop-down menu; or, press the Esc key twice.

Some menu options may be gray shaded (dimmed). When an option is dimmed, it is currently not available. For example, if you choose the Edit option from the Menu bar, the Edit drop-down menu displays with several dimmed options including Cut and Copy. If text is selected before the Edit drop-down menu is displayed, these options are available and display in black.

Some menu options are preceded by a check mark. The check mark indicates that the option is currently active. To make an option inactive (turn it off) using the mouse, position the arrow pointer on the option, and then click the left mouse button. To make an option inactive (turn it off) with the keyboard, key the underlined letter of the option.

If an option from a drop-down menu displays followed by an ellipsis (...), a dialog box will display when that option is chosen. A *dialog box* provides a variety of options to let you specify how a command is to be carried out. For example, if you choose File, then Print, the Print dialog box shown in figure G.4 displays. Or, if you choose Format, then Font from the Menu bar, the Font dialog box shown in figure G.5 displays.

G.4

Print Dialog Box

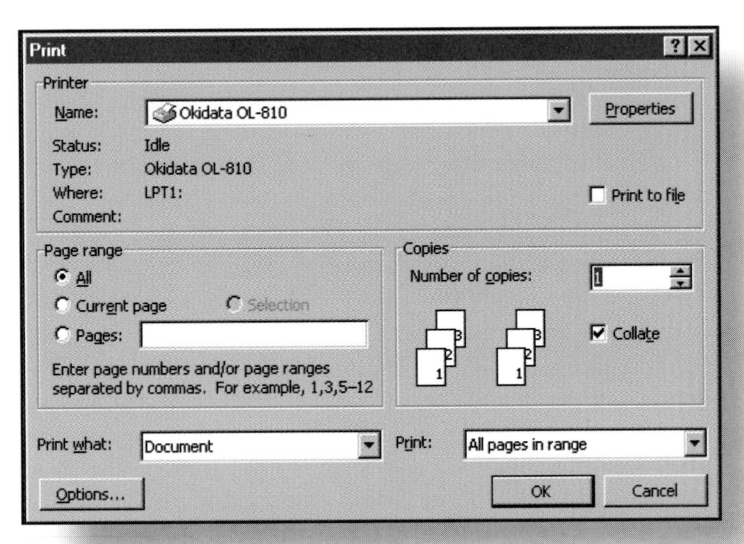

Figure G.5 Font Dialog Box

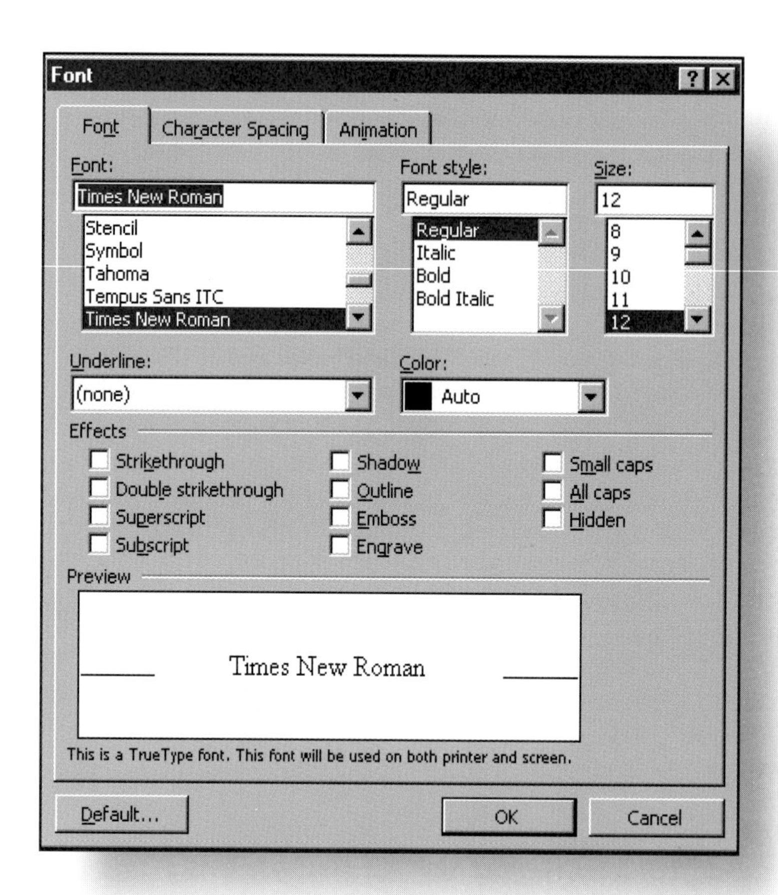

Some dialog boxes provide a set of options. These options are contained on separate tabs. For example, the Font dialog box shown in figure G.5 contains a tab at the top of the dialog box with the word Font on it. To the right of that tab are two other tabs—Character Spacing and Animation. The tab that displays in the front is the active tab. To make a tab active using the mouse, position the arrow pointer on the desired tab, and then click the left mouse button. If you are using the keyboard, press Ctrl + Tab or press Alt + the underlined letter on the desired tab. For example, to change the tab to Character Spacing in the Font dialog box, click Character Spacing, or press Ctrl + Tab, or press Alt + R.

To choose options from a dialog box with the mouse, position the arrow pointer on the desired option, and then click the left mouse button. If you are using the keyboard, press the Tab key to move the insertion point forward from option to option. Press Shift + Tab to move the insertion point backward from option to option. You can also hold down the Alt key and then press the underlined letter of the desired option. When an option is selected, it will display either in reverse video (white letters on a blue background) or surrounded by a dashed box called a *marquee*.

A dialog box contains one or more of the following elements: text boxes, list boxes, check boxes, option buttons, spin boxes, and command buttons.

Text Boxes

Some options in a dialog box require text to be entered. For example, the boxes to the right of the Find what and Replace with options at the Find and Replace dialog box shown in figure G.6 are *text boxes*. In a text box, you key text or edit existing text. Edit text in a text box in the same manner as normal text. Use the left and right arrow keys on the keyboard to move the insertion point without deleting text, and use the Delete key or Backspace key to delete text.

figure G.6 **Find and Replace Dialog Box**

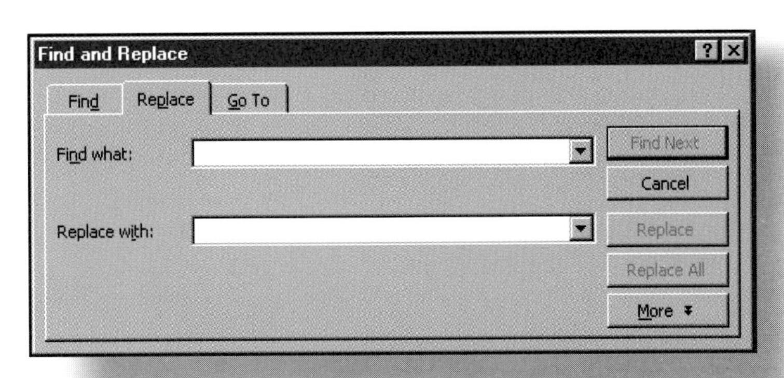

List Boxes

Some dialog boxes such as the Open dialog box shown in figure G.7 may contain a *list box*.

figure G.7 **Open Dialog Box**

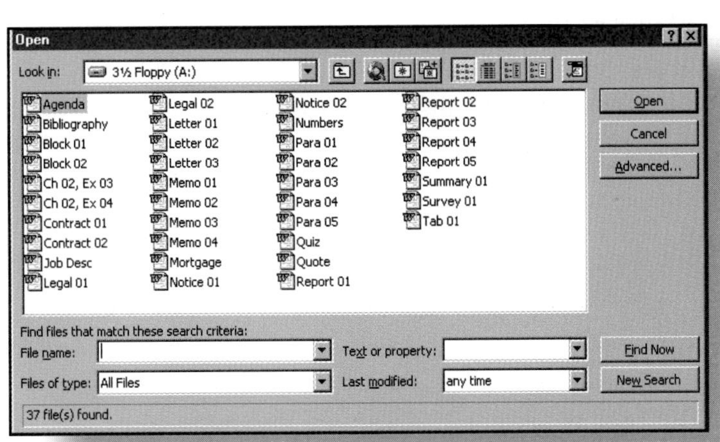

The list of files below the Look in: option is contained in a list box. To make a selection from a list box with the mouse, move the arrow pointer to the desired option, and then click the left mouse button. Some list boxes may contain a scroll bar. This scroll bar can be used to move through the list if the list is longer than the box. To move down through the list, position the arrow pointer on the down scroll triangle and hold down the left mouse button. To scroll up through the list, position the arrow pointer on the up scroll triangle and hold down the left mouse button. You can also move the arrow pointer above the scroll box and click the left mouse button to scroll up the list, or move the arrow pointer below the scroll box and click the left mouse button to move down the list.

To make a selection from a list using the keyboard, move the insertion point into the box by holding down the Alt key and pressing the underlined letter of the desired option. Press the up and/or down arrow keys on the keyboard to move through the list.

In some dialog boxes where there is not enough room for a list box, lists of options are inserted in a drop-down list box. Options that contain a drop-down list box display with a down-pointing triangle. For example, the Underline option at the Font dialog box contains a drop-down list. To display the list, click the down-pointing triangle to the right of the Underline text box. If you are using the keyboard, press Alt + U.

Check Boxes

Some dialog boxes contain options preceded by a box. A check mark may or may not appear in the box. The Font dialog box shown in figure G.5 displays a variety of check boxes within the Effects section. If a check mark appears in the box, the option is active (turned on). If there is no check mark in the check box, the option is inactive (turned off). Any number of check boxes can be active. For example, in the Font dialog box, you can insert a check mark in any or all of the boxes in the Effects section and these options will be active. To make a check box active or inactive with the mouse, position the tip of the arrow pointer in the check box, and then click the left mouse button. If you are using the keyboard, press Alt + the underlined letter of the desired option.

Option Buttons

In the Print dialog box shown in figure G.4, the options in the Page range section are preceded by *option buttons*. Only one option button can be selected at one time. When an option button is selected, a dark circle displays in the button. To select an option button with the mouse, position the tip of the arrow pointer inside the option button, and then click the left mouse button. To make a selection with the keyboard, hold down the Alt key, and then press the underlined letter of the desired option.

Spin Boxes

Some options in a dialog box contain measurements or numbers that can be increased or decreased. These options are generally located in a *spin box*. For example, the Paragraph dialog box shown in figure G.8 contains a variety of spin boxes located after the Left, Right, Before, and After options. To increase a number in a spin box, position the tip of the arrow pointer on the up-pointing triangle to the right of the desired option, and then click the left mouse button. To decrease the number, click the down-pointing triangle. If you are using the keyboard, press Alt + the underlined letter of the desired option, and then press the up arrow key to increase the number or the down arrow key to decrease the number.

G.8 Paragraph Dialog Box

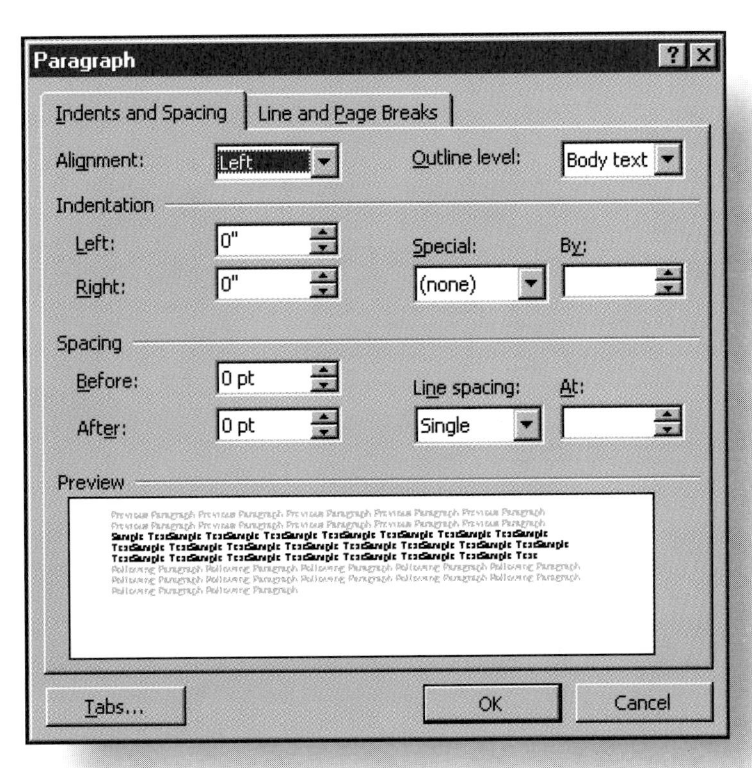

Command Buttons

In the Find and Replace dialog box shown in figure G.6, the boxes at the right side of the dialog box are called *command buttons*. A command button is used to execute or cancel a command. Some command buttons display with ellipses (...). A command button that displays with ellipses will open another dialog box. To choose a command button with the mouse, position the arrow pointer on the desired button, and then click the left mouse button. To choose a command button with the keyboard, press the Tab key until the desired command button contains the marquee, and then press the Enter key.

Choosing Commands with Shortcut Keys

At the left side of a drop-down menu is a list of options. At the right side, shortcut keys for specific options may be displayed. For example, the shortcut keys to save a document are Ctrl + S and are displayed to the right of the Save option at the File drop-down menu shown in figure G.3. To use shortcut keys to choose a command, hold down the Ctrl key, key the letter for the command, and then release the Ctrl key.

Choosing Commands with Shortcut Menus

Word includes shortcut menus that contain commands related to the item with which you are working. A shortcut menu appears right where you are working in the document. To display a shortcut menu, click the *right* mouse button or press Shift + F10. For example, if the insertion point is positioned in a paragraph of text, clicking the *right* mouse button or pressing Shift + F10 will cause the shortcut menu shown in figure G.9 to display in the document screen.

G.9 **Shortcut Menu**

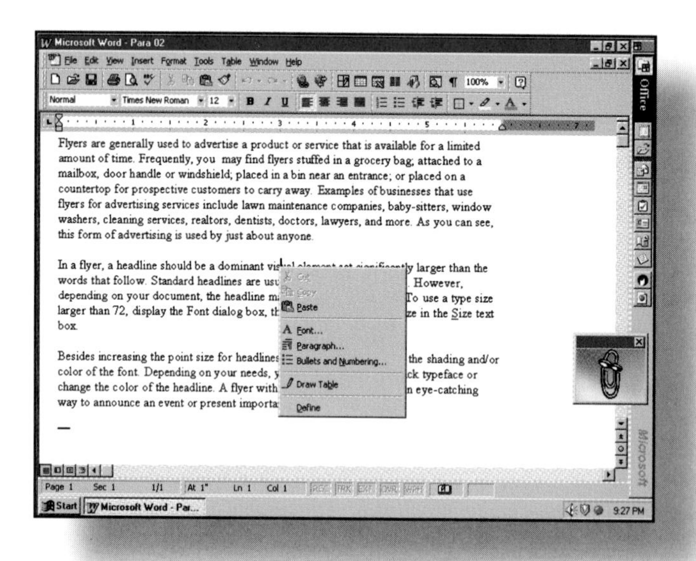

To select an option from a shortcut menu with the mouse, click the desired option. If you are using the keyboard, press the up or down arrow key until the desired option is selected, and then press the Enter key. To close a shortcut menu without choosing an option, click anywhere outside the shortcut menu or press the Esc key.

Using the Office Assistant

Microsoft Word 97 includes a new feature called the *Office Assistant*. This Assistant is a link to the on-screen Help feature that anticipates the type of help you need and suggests Help topics related to the work you are doing. The Assistant will also point out ways to perform tasks more easily and provide visual examples and step-by-step instructions for specific tasks. When you open Word, the Assistant displays, by default, in the lower right corner of the screen as shown in figure G.10. The default Assistant is named “Clippit,” and is an image of a paper clip. (This image can be changed.)

G.10

Office Assistant

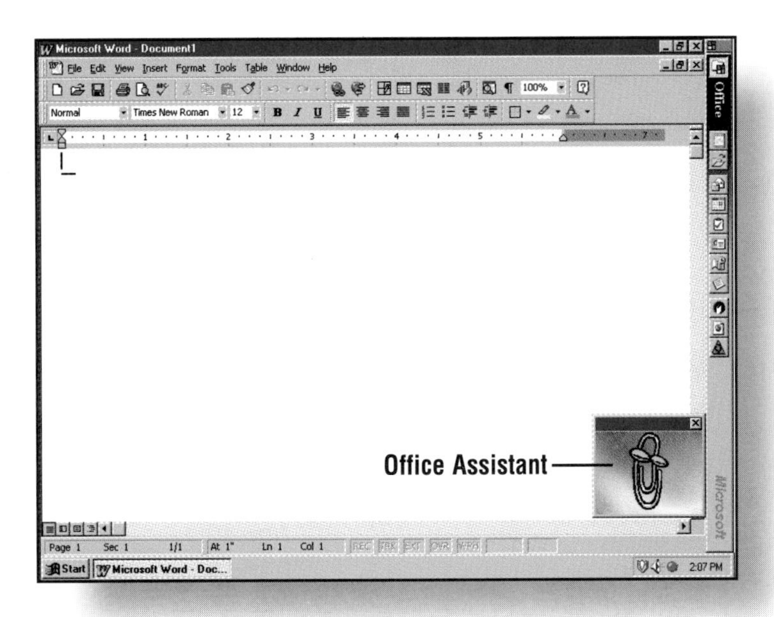

The Assistant will perform a variety of functions. For example, if you try to close a document without saving it, the Assistant will make a sound to get your attention and display a question box like the one shown in figure G.11. At this question, click the desired response.

G.11

Office Assistant Question Box

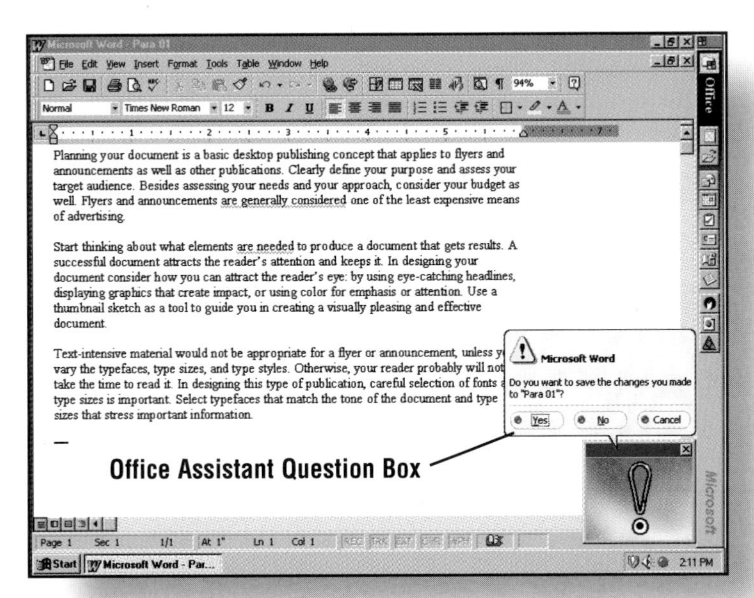

If you are completing a task that Word will automatically format, the Assistant will specify what Word is doing. For example, if you key a numbered paragraph, Word will automatically format this numbered paragraph. As you are keying the numbered paragraph, the Assistant will tell you that Word is automatically formatting the text and ask if you want to learn more about the feature.

If you are working on a task and want help, just click the Assistant. The Assistant will guess what kind of help you want and display a list of Help topics like the list shown in figure G.12. If the desired topic does not display, key a question in the text box that displays below the list of topics and then click the Search button.

Office Assistant Help Topics List Box

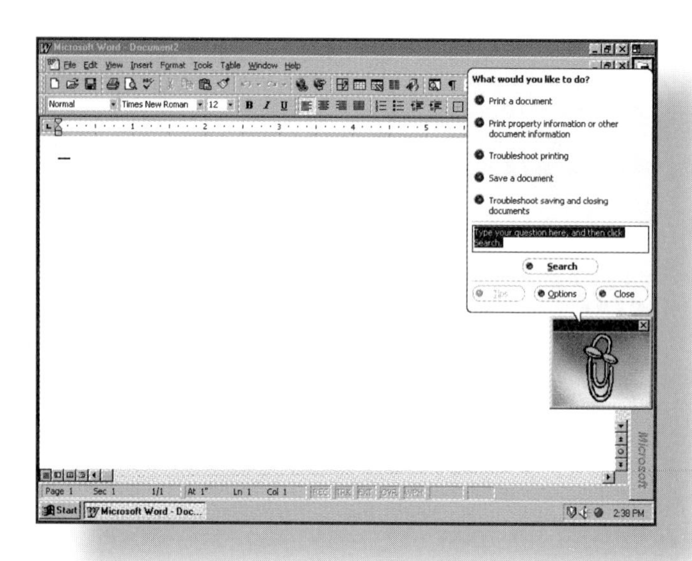

Occasionally, a light bulb will display in the Assistant box. Click this light bulb and the Assistant will display a tip about the type of work you are doing.

Turning the Assistant On/Off

Office Assistant

The Standard toolbar contains an Office Assistant button. If the Assistant is not displayed, click this button to turn it on. You can close the Office Assistant by clicking the Close button that displays at the right side of the Office Assistant Title bar.

Changing the Assistant

A variety of other assistants is available. To display and choose another Assistant, position the arrow pointer on the Assistant Title bar, and then click the *right* mouse button. At the shortcut menu that displays, click Choose Assistant. This displays the Office Assistant dialog box shown in figure G.13. At this dialog box, the current Assistant displays. To display other Assistants, click the Next button.

figure G.13 *Office Assistant Dialog Box*

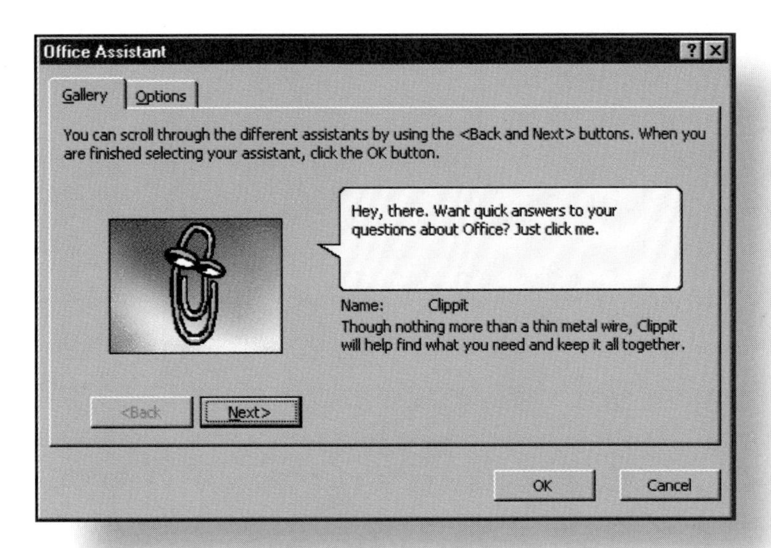

You can choose from The Dot, The Genius, Hoverbot, Office Logo, Mother Nature, Power Pup, Scribble, and Will.

You can customize the Office Assistant by clicking the Options tab at the Office Assistant dialog box. This displays a dialog box with a variety of Help options. Insert a check mark before the features you want active and remove the check mark for those features you want inactive.

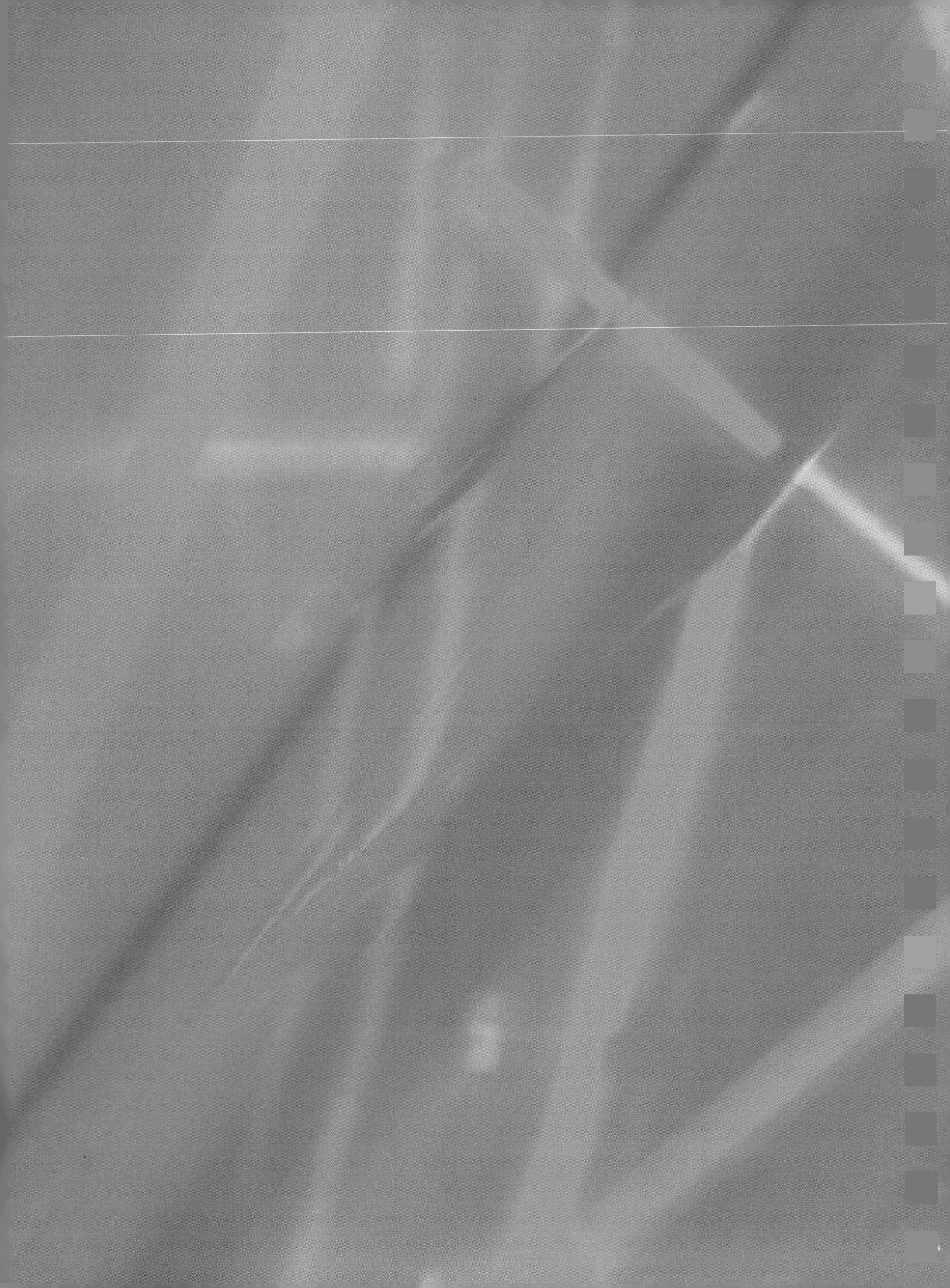

Unit one

PREPARING DOCUMENTS

In this unit, you will learn to create, edit, format, save, and print Word documents, and manage documents on disk.

s c a n s

The Secretary's Commission on Achieving Necessary Skills

DECISION MAKING

TECHNOLOGY

PROBLEM SOLVING

COMMUNICATIONS

chapter ONE

Creating, Saving, and Printing Word Documents

PERFORMANCE OBJECTIVES

Upon completion of chapter 1, you will be able to:

- **Create a Word document.**
- **Save a Word document.**
- **Open and close a Word document.**
- **Print a Word document.**

This textbook provides you with instructions on a word processing program using a microcomputer system. The program you will learn to operate is the *software*. Software is the program of instructions that tells the computer what to do. The computer equipment you will use is the *hardware*.

You will be learning to operate a software program called Word 97 on a microcomputer system. Word 97 operates within the Windows 95 program. Before continuing in this chapter, be sure to read the *Getting Started* section at the beginning of this textbook.

Creating a Word Document

Eight basic steps are completed when working with Word to create a document. The steps are:

1. Open the program.
2. Key (type) the information to create the document.
3. Save the document.
4. Proofread the document and then make any necessary edits (changes).
5. Save the revised document.
6. Print a hard copy of the document.
7. Close the document.
8. Exit the program.

In this chapter, you will be provided with the information necessary to complete all the steps except 5. As you work your way through this chapter, you will complete several exercises and practice the steps.

Opening Word

The steps to open Word may vary depending on your system setup. Generally, to open Word 97, you would complete the following steps:

1. Turn on the monitor and the CPU. (Depending on your system, you may also need to turn on the printer.)
2. After a few moments, the Windows 95 screen shown in figure 1.1 displays (your screen may vary). At the Windows 95 screen, position the arrow pointer on the Start button on the taskbar (located at the bottom left side of the screen), and then click the left mouse button. This causes the pop-up menu shown in figure 1.2 to display.
3. Position the arrow pointer on Programs (you do not need to click the mouse button). This will cause another menu to display to the right of the first pop-up menu.
4. Move the arrow pointer to *Microsoft Word* and then click the left mouse button.

Start

figure 1.1 *Windows 95 Screen*

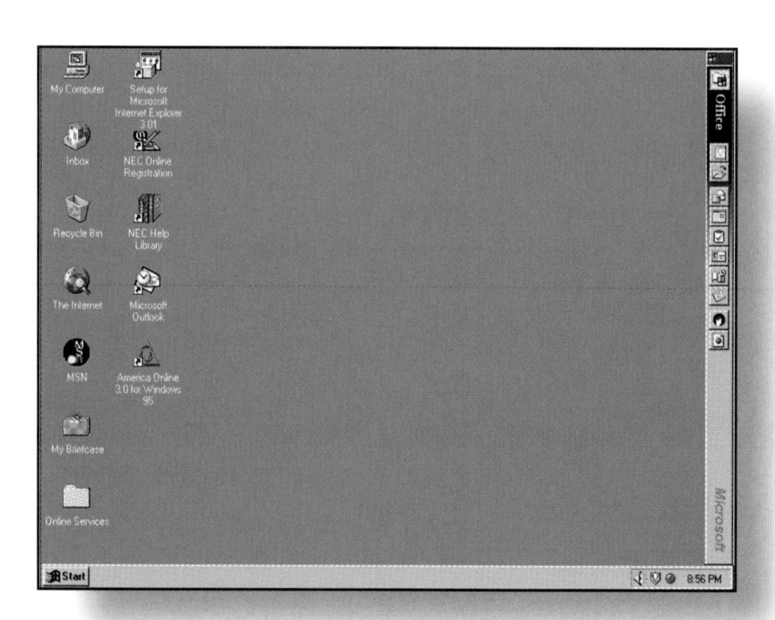

1.2

Start Pop-Up Menu

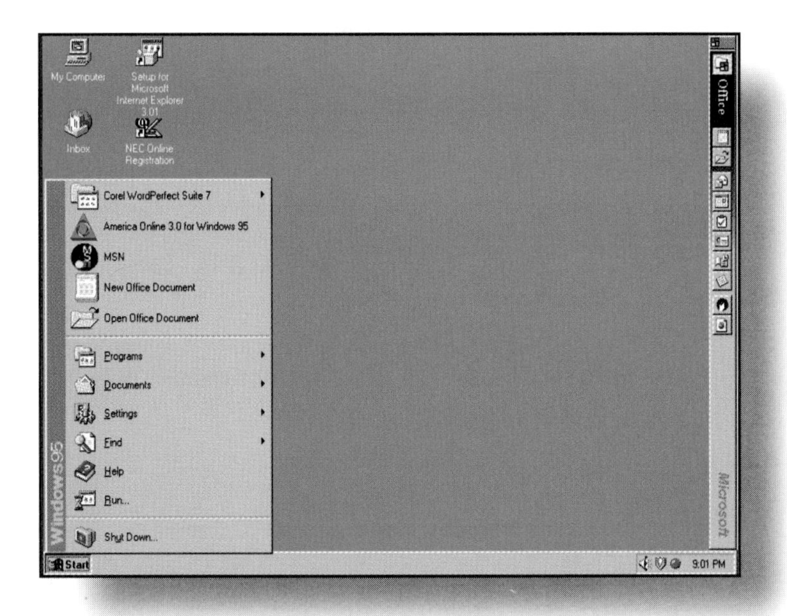

Operating Word on your computer system may vary from these instructions. If necessary, ask your instructor for specific steps to open Word and then write the steps here:

____

____

____

____

____

____

Identifying the Parts of the Word Screen

When you open Word, you will be presented with a screen that looks similar to the one shown in figure 1.3. This is referred to as the Word screen. The display of the Word screen will vary depending on whether you are running Word as one of the Microsoft Office programs or running Word independently (not within the Office program).

figure 1.3 *Word Screen*

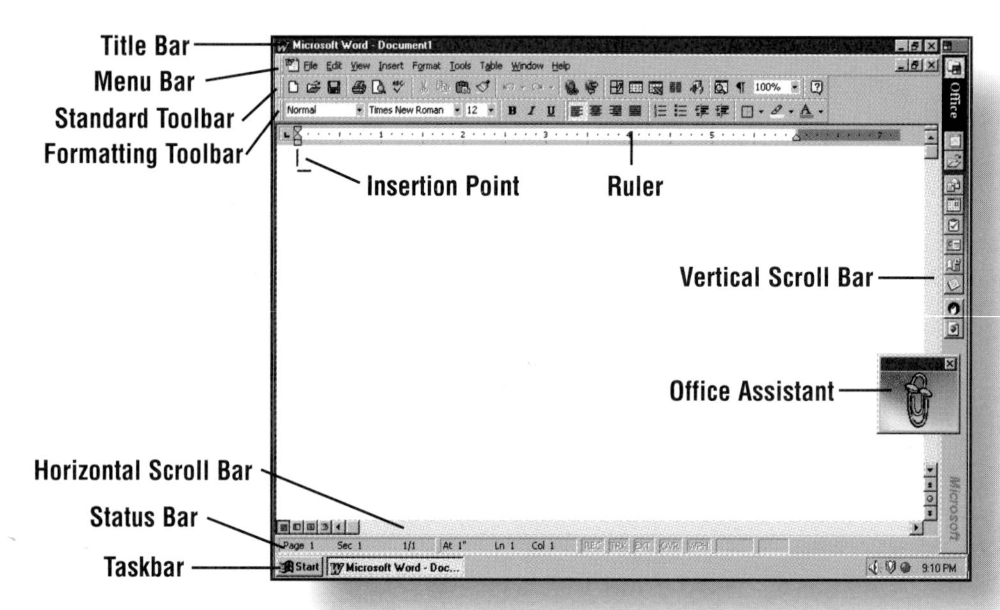

Title Bar

The top line of the Word screen is referred to as the *Title bar*. When you open Word, you are provided with a new document with the name Document1. When a document is completed, it can be saved with a new name. If you open a previously saved document to the Word screen, the document name is displayed in the Title bar.

If you are using Microsoft Word as part of the Microsoft Office suite of programs, a Shortcut bar may display at the right side of the Title bar or along the right side of the screen. This Shortcut bar provides convenient shortcuts for working with documents and Office applications.

Menu Bar

The second line of the Word screen is called the *Menu bar*. The Menu bar contains a list of options that are used to customize a Word document. Word functions and features are grouped into menu options located on the Menu bar. For example, functions to save, close, or open a new document are contained in the File option on the Menu bar.

Toolbars

Word provides two toolbars with buttons containing common Word functions. The toolbar directly below the Menu bar is called the *Standard toolbar*. The toolbar below the Standard toolbar is called the *Formatting toolbar*. These toolbars contain buttons that are shortcuts for the most popular commands. For example, the Standard toolbar contains buttons for working with documents, such as opening and saving a document. The Formatting toolbar contains buttons that can quickly apply formatting to text in a document, such as bold, italics, and underlining. The pictures (icons) on the toolbars represent functions. For example, the button to print a document contains an icon of a printer. The button containing the icon of the scissors is used to cut selected text from the document.

Word provides a *ToolTip* that shows what function the button on the toolbar will perform. To view the ToolTip, position the arrow pointer on a toolbar button. After approximately one second, the ToolTip displays. For example, if you position the arrow pointer on the Save button on the Standard toolbar, a small yellow box containing the word *Save* displays below the arrow pointer after one second.

Below the Formatting toolbar, a Ruler may display. The Ruler is used to set margins, indents, and tabs. You will learn more about the Ruler in future chapters.

The display of the toolbars and Ruler is on by default. You can turn off the display of the toolbars or Ruler using a shortcut menu or with options from the Menu bar. Information on turning on and/or off the display of toolbars or Ruler is presented later in this chapter.

Insertion Point

The blinking vertical bar, located below the Ruler at the left side of the screen, is called the *insertion point*. The insertion point indicates the location where the next character entered at the keyboard will appear.

The insertion point is positioned in the portion of the Word screen called the *document screen*. The document screen is the portion of the screen where text is entered, edited, and formatted. The underline symbol immediately to the right of the insertion point is the *end of document* marker and indicates the end of the document.

In addition to the insertion point, a mouse pointer will also display in the document screen. When the mouse pointer is positioned in the document screen, it displays as an I-beam I . This is referred to as the *I-beam pointer*. When the mouse pointer is positioned anywhere else in the Word screen, it displays as an arrow pointing up and to the left. This is referred to as the *arrow pointer.* For more information on how to use the mouse, please refer to the *Getting Started* section at the beginning of this textbook.

Scroll Bars

The gray shaded bars along the right and toward the bottom of the Word screen are called *scroll bars*. The scroll bar at the right side of the Word screen is called the *vertical scroll bar* and the scroll bar toward the bottom of the Word screen is called the *horizontal scroll bar*. Use these scroll bars to view various parts of the document. Additional information on the scroll bars is presented in chapter 2.

Status Bar

The gray bar at the bottom of the Word screen is called the *Status bar*. The Status bar displays information about the text in the document and whether certain working modes are active. The Status bar also displays the current location of the insertion point by page number, section number, line measurement, line count, and column position.

At the right side of the Status bar, working modes are displayed. When the working mode is dimmed, it is inactive. When the working mode is active, it displays in black. For example, if you want to change from the Insert mode to the Overtype mode, press the Insert key on the keyboard or double-click the OVR mode on the Status bar. This causes the OVR mode to display in black, indicating that the Overtype mode is active. To turn off the Overtype mode, press the Insert key again or double-click OVR.

Taskbar

The bottom line on the screen is the *taskbar*. The Start button displays at the left side of the taskbar and the current time displays at the right side. If a document is open, a portion of the document name displays immediately to the right of the Start button. If another program other than Word is open, the program name displays in a button on the taskbar.

Office Assistant

Word 97 includes a new feature called the *Office Assistant*. This Assistant is a link to the on-screen Help feature that anticipates the type of help you need and suggests Help topics related to the work you are doing. The Assistant will also point out ways to perform tasks more easily and provide visual examples and step-by-step instructions for specific tasks. When you open a program, the Assistant displays, by default, in the lower right corner of the screen. The default Assistant is named "Clippit," and is an image of a paper clip. For more information on the Office Assistant, refer to the *Getting Started* section at the beginning of this text.

Completing Computer Exercises

At the end of sections within chapters and at the end of chapters, you will be completing hands-on exercises. These exercises will provide you with the opportunity to practice the functions and commands presented.

Exercises in the beginning chapters present text in arranged form. Exercises in later chapters include unarranged text. This provides you with decision-making opportunities. The skill assessment exercises at the end of each chapter include general directions. If you do not remember how to perform a particular function, refer to the text in the chapter.

In the exercises in this chapter, you will be creating and saving several short documents. Press Enter only to end a paragraph or to create a blank line between paragraphs. Otherwise, let the word wrap feature wrap text to the next line within paragraphs.

The document screen displays somewhere between 19 and 24 lines of text at one time. When more lines than this are entered, the text scrolls off the top of the document screen. The text is not lost or deleted. When the document is saved, all the text is saved, not just the lines visible in the document screen.

Keying and Saving a Word Document

At a clear document screen, you can begin keying information to create a document. A document is any information you choose; for instance, a letter, memo, report, term paper, table, and so on.

Using Word Wrap

As you key (type) text to create a document, you do not need to press the Enter key at the end of each line because Word wraps text to the next line. A word is wrapped to the next line if it begins before the right margin and continues past the right margin. The only times you need to press Enter are to end a paragraph, create a blank line, or end a short line.

Using AutoCorrect

Word contains a feature that automatically corrects certain words as they are being keyed (typed). For example, if you key the word *adn* instead of *and*, Word automatically corrects it when you press the space bar after the word. There are many other automatic corrections. You will learn more about this feature in a later chapter.

Correcting Text with Spell-It

A feature called *Spell-It* automatically inserts a wavy red line below words that are not contained in the Spelling dictionary or automatically corrected by AutoCorrect. This may include misspelled words, proper names, some terminology, and some foreign words. If you key a word not recognized by the Spelling dictionary, Word inserts a red wavy line below the word. If the word is correct, you can leave it as written. If, however, the word is incorrect you have two choices—you can backspace over the word using the Backspace key and then key it correctly, or you can position the I-beam pointer on the word, click the *right* mouse button, and then click the correct spelling in the pop-up menu.

For example, if you key the word *aplication* and then press the space bar, Word inserts a wavy red line below the word. To correct it using the mouse, position the I-beam point on any character in the word *aplication*, click the right mouse button, and then click *application* in the pop-up menu that displays. If Word inserts a wavy red line below a proper name such as *Weinberg* that is spelled correctly, you can either leave it (the red line will not print) or position the I-beam pointer on any character in the name, click the right mouse button, and then click the Ignore All option in the pop-up menu.

Word also includes an automatic grammar checker. If the grammar checker detects a sentence containing a grammatical error, a wavy green line is inserted below the sentence or a portion of the sentence. At this point, leave the wavy green line. You will learn more about the grammar checker in chapter 7.

Spacing Punctuation

Word 97 uses Times New Roman as the default typeface. Times New Roman is a proportional typeface. (You will learn more about typefaces in chapter 6.) When keying text in a proportional typeface, space once (rather than twice) after end-of-sentence punctuation such as a period, question mark, or exclamation point, and after a colon. Proportional typeface is set closer together and extra white space at the end of a sentence or after a colon is not needed.

Saving a Document

When you have created a document, the information will need to be saved on your disk. When a document is keyed (typed) for the first time and is displayed in the document screen, it is temporary. If you turn off the computer or if the power goes off, you will lose the information and have to rekey it. Only when you save a document is it saved permanently.

Save

A variety of methods can be used to save a document. You can save by clicking the Save button on the Standard toolbar; by clicking File, then Save; or with the shortcut command, Ctrl + S. In this textbook, instructions will focus on the steps that are the easiest or fastest. For many features, the mouse will be emphasized. You may find that you prefer other options. At times, you may want to explore the other options for completing steps or procedures not emphasized in this textbook. (For information on using the keyboard, refer to the text in the "Choosing Commands" section in *Getting Started*.)

To save a document with the Save button on the Standard toolbar, you would complete the following steps:

1. Position the arrow pointer on the Save button (the third button from the left) on the Standard toolbar and then click the left mouse button.
2. At the Save As dialog box shown in figure 1.4, key the name of the document.
3. Click the Save button located at the right side of the dialog box or press the Enter key.

figure 1.4

Save As Dialog Box

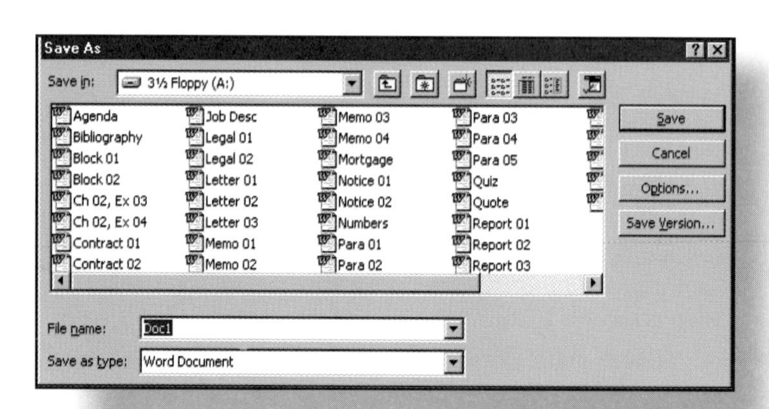

In the Save As dialog box, the beginning characters in the document are automatically inserted in the File name: text box. These characters are selected. Key the name for the document and the selected characters are automatically deleted when you press the first letter of the name you key. If you press the left or right arrow keys, the insertion point is moved and the text in the File name: text box is deselected.

In addition to the Save button on the Standard toolbar, a document can be saved using the Menu bar. To do this, you would complete the following steps:

1. Click File, then Save.
2. At the Save As dialog box, key the name of the document.
3. Click the Save button located at the right side of the dialog box or press the Enter key.

Changing the Default Folder

At the end of this and the remaining chapters in the textbook, you will be saving documents. More than likely, you will want to save documents onto your student data disk. Also, beginning with chapter 2, you will be opening documents that already have been saved on your student data disk.

To save documents on and open documents from your data disk, you will need to specify the drive where your disk is located as the default folder. Once you specify the drive where your data disk is located, Word uses this as the default folder until you exit the Word program. The next time you open Word, you will again need to specify the drive where your data disk is located.

You can change the default folder at the Open dialog box or the Save As dialog box. To change the folder to drive A at the Open dialog box, you would complete the following steps:

Open

1. Click the Open button on the Standard toolbar (the second button from the left); or click File, then Open.
2. At the Open dialog box, click the down-pointing triangle at the right side of the Look in: text box.
3. From the drop-down list that displays, click *3½ Floppy (A:)*.
4. Click the Cancel button at the right side of the dialog box.

Changing the Default Type Size

Word uses 10-point Times New Roman as the default font. (You will learn more about fonts in chapter 6.) The 10-point type size is very small and difficult to read. Exercises in this and other chapters will generally display text in 12-point size, which is easier to read. If you want to change the type size from the default of 10 points to 12, you would complete the following steps:

1. Click Format, then Font.
2. At the Font dialog box, click *12* in the Size list box.
3. Click the Default command button located at the bottom left side of the dialog box.
4. The Office Assistant displays a message box asking if you want to change the default font. Click Yes in this box.

Once the default type size has been changed in this manner, the new type size will be in effect each time you open the Word program. You only need to change the default once.

Naming a Document

A Word document name can be up to 255 characters in length, including drive letter and any folder names, and may include spaces. File names cannot include any of the following characters:

forward slash (/)	question mark (?)
backslash (\)	quotation mark (“)
greater-than sign (>)	colon (:)
less-than sign (<)	semicolon (;)
asterisk (*)	pipe symbol (|)

Canceling a Command

If a drop-down menu is displayed in the document screen, it can be removed with the mouse or the keyboard. If you are using the mouse, position the I-beam pointer in the document screen (outside the drop-down menu), and then click the left mouse button. If you are using the keyboard, press the Alt key. You can also press the Esc key twice. The first time you press Esc, the drop-down menu is removed but the menu option on the Menu bar is still selected. The second time you press Esc, the option on the Menu bar is no longer selected.

Several methods can be used to remove a dialog box from the document screen. To remove a dialog box with the mouse, position the arrow pointer on the Cancel command button, and then click the left mouse button. You can also click the Close button located in the upper right corner of the dialog box (contains the letter X). A dialog box can be removed from the document screen with the keyboard by pressing the Esc key.

Closing a Document

When a document is saved with the Save or Save As options, the document is saved on the disk and remains in the document screen. To remove the document from the screen, click File, then Close or click the Close button located at the far right side of the Menu bar. (The Close button is the button containing the X. Make sure you use the Close button on the Menu bar, not the Close button on the Title bar. The Close button on the Title bar will close the Word program.) When you close a document, the document is removed and a blank screen is displayed. At this screen, you can open a previously saved document, create a new document, or exit the Word program.

Close

When you close a document, the blank screen displays with a gray background and the Menu bar displays with just the options File and Help. At this blank screen, you can open a previously saved document, or you can create a new document. Information on creating a new document is presented later in this chapter. A new document is created at a clear screen. This is also explained later in the chapter.

exercise 1

Creating a Document

1. Follow the instructions in this chapter to open Windows 95 and Word 97.
2. At the clear document screen, change the default folder to the drive where your student data disk is located using the mouse by completing the following steps. (Depending on your system configuration, this may not be necessary. Check with your instructor before changing the default folder.)
   a. Click the Open button on the Standard toolbar.
   b. At the Open dialog box, click the down-pointing triangle to the right of the Look in: option.
   c. From the drop-down menu that displays, click *3½ Floppy (A:)* (this may vary depending on your system).
   d. Click the Cancel command button located at the right side of the dialog box.
3. At the document screen, make sure that 12-point Times New Roman is the default font. (If not, change the default type size to 12 following the directions listed in the "Changing the Default Type Size" section of this chapter; or check with your instructor.)
4. Key (type) the text in figure 1.5. If you make a mistake while keying and Spell-It inserts a wavy red line, backspace over the incorrect word using the Backspace key and then rekey the correct word. (Do not worry about doing a lot of correcting—you will learn more about editing a document in chapter 2.) Remember to space only once after end-of-sentence punctuation when keying the text.
5. When you are done keying the text, save the document and name it Ch 01, Ex 01 (for Chapter 1, Exercise 1) by completing the following steps:
   a. Click the Save button on the Standard toolbar.
   b. At the Save As dialog box, key **Ch 01, Ex 01**. (Key a zero when naming documents, not the letter O. In this textbook, the zero, 0, displays thinner than the letter O. As you key **Ch 01, Ex 01**, the selected text in the File name: text box is automatically deleted and replaced with the text you key.)
   c. Click the Save button or press the Enter key.
6. Close Ch 01, Ex 01 by clicking File, then Close, or clicking the Close button at the far right side of the Menu bar. (This displays a blank screen, rather than a clear screen.)

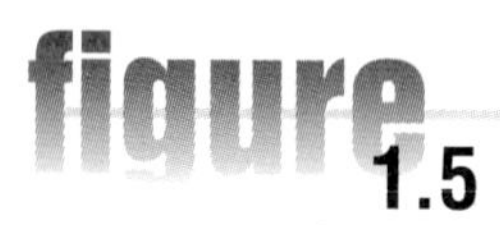
1.5

Exercise 1

The core of the Internet was created several years ago when computers from a variety of industries including universities, private institutions, and U.S. governmental agencies (particularly the Defense Department) were linked together. Now, there is a web of computers that cross international borders, transcend the possibilities of almost all other communication tools, and can potentially link every household in the world into an information-sharing network.

The Internet is several things. It is a network of computers that can maintain individual accounts for the sending and receiving of mail (called e-mail). It is a massive computer bulletin board that can be used to post information (called newsgroups). It is a pipe for the transfer of files (called FTP for file transfer protocol). The Internet is also a web of computers that can be linked together via home computers. This is referred to as the World Wide Web.

Opening a Document

When a document has been saved and closed, it can be opened at the Open dialog box. To display the Open dialog box, click the Open button on the Standard toolbar, or click File, then Open. At the Open dialog box, double-click the name of the document to be opened. You can also key the name of a document in the File name: text box and then click Open.

When a document is opened it is displayed in the document screen where you can make changes. Whenever changes are made to a document, save the document again to save the changes.

2

Opening and Closing a Document

1. At a blank screen, open the document named Ch 01, Ex 01 by completing the following steps:
   a. Click the Open button on the Standard toolbar.
   b. At the Open dialog box, position the arrow pointer on *Ch 01, Ex 01* in the list box, and then double-click the left mouse button.
2. Close Ch 01, Ex 01 by clicking File, then Close or clicking the Close button on the Menu bar.

Creating a New Document

New

When you close a document, a blank screen is displayed. If you want to create a new document, you must display a clear screen. To do this, click the New button on the Standard toolbar (the first one).

exercise 3

Creating a New Document

1. At a blank screen, create a new document by clicking the New button on the Standard toolbar (the first button).
2. At the clear screen, key the information shown in figure 1.6. (Correct any errors highlighted by Spell-It as they occur and remember to space once after end-of-sentence punctuation. When Spell-It inserts a wavy red line, either leave it or tell Spell-It to ignore all. Ignore any wavy green lines inserted by the grammar checker.)
3. Save the document and name it Ch 01, Ex 03 by completing the following steps:
   a. Click the Save button on the Standard toolbar.
   b. At the Save As dialog box, key **Ch 01, Ex 03**.
   c. Click Save or press Enter.
4. Close the document by clicking File, then Close or clicking the Close button on the Menu bar.

figure 1.6

Exercise 3

The World Wide Web seems to offer the greatest possibilities to the field of education. There are numerous web sites that can be used to get the latest information on a particular software package. Some even include exhaustive information on the use of a particular package.

To cruise the web, you need a web browser and obviously an Internet connection. A number of web browsers exist; one of the most popular is Netscape Navigator from Netscape Communications Corporation. You can download a trial copy of their latest version.

Microsoft also has its own web browser for Windows 95, and you can download a free copy from Microsoft's Web site. Microsoft also offers excellent articles on all their software packages, particularly the Microsoft Office components: Word, Excel, Access, and PowerPoint. These articles discuss advanced features and uses of the software packages that you don't find in the software documentation.

Turning On/Off the Display of Toolbars

The Standard and Formatting toolbars display below the Menu bar at the top of the screen. The display of these toolbars can be turned on and/or off using a shortcut menu or the View option from the Menu bar. To turn off or on the display of the Standard or Formatting toolbar using a shortcut menu, you would complete the following steps:

1. Position the arrow pointer anywhere in the Standard or Formatting toolbar.
2. Click the *right* mouse button.
3. At the drop-down menu that displays, click the toolbar you want turned on or off.

To turn off or on the display of the Standard or Formatting toolbar using an option from the Menu bar, you would click View, point to Toolbars, and then click the desired toolbar at the side menu that displays.

The display of the Ruler can be controlled with the Ruler option at the View drop-down menu. To turn on/off the display of the Ruler, click View, then Ruler. When the Ruler is displayed, a check mark is inserted before the Ruler option at the View drop-down menu.

Printing a Document

Print

Many of the computer exercises you have created and will be creating require that you make a hard copy of the document. (Soft copy is a document displayed in the document screen and hard copy is a document printed on paper.) A document can be sent immediately to the printer by clicking the Print button on the Standard toolbar or through the Print dialog box.

exercise 4

Printing a Document

1. Open Ch 01, Ex 01.
2. Click the Print button on the Standard toolbar.
3. After the document has printed, close Ch 01, Ex 01.

To print the current document through the Print dialog box, you would complete the following steps:

1. Open the document to be printed.
2. Click File, then Print.
3. At the Print dialog box, click the OK button.

exercise 5

Printing a Document Using the Print Dialog Box

1. Open Ch 01, Ex 03.
2. Print the document by completing the following steps:
   a. Click File, then Print.
   b. At the Print dialog box, click the OK button that displays at the bottom of the dialog box.
3. After the document is printed, close Ch 01, Ex 03.

Exiting Word and Windows

When you are finished working with Word and have saved all necessary information, exit Word by clicking File, then Exit. You can also exit the Word program by clicking the Close button on the Title bar in the upper right corner of the screen. (The Close button contains an X.) Be sure to use the Close button on the Title bar and not the Close button on the Menu bar. (Clicking the Close button on the Menu bar causes the current document to close.)

After exiting Word, you may also need to exit the Windows 95 program. To exit Windows 95, you would complete the following steps:

1. Click the Start button at the left side of the taskbar.
2. At the pop-up menu, click Shut Down.
3. At the Shut Down Windows dialog box, make sure *Shut down the computer?* is selected, and then click Yes.

exercise 6

Opening and Closing a Document, Then Exiting Word and Windows

1. At the blank screen, open Ch 01, Ex 03 by completing the following steps:
   a. Click the Open button on the Standard toolbar.
   b. At the Open dialog box, double-click *Ch 01, Ex 03.*
2. Close Ch 01, Ex 03.
3. Exit Word and Windows 95 by completing the following steps:
   a. Click File, then Exit, or click the Close button located at the far right side of the Title bar.
   b. At the Windows 95 screen, click the Start button located at the left side of the taskbar.
   c. At the pop-up menu, click Shut Down.
   d. At the Shut Down Windows dialog box, make sure *Shut down the computer?* is selected, and then click Yes.

chapter summary

- Eight basic steps are followed when creating a Word document: open the program, key the data, save the document, proofread and then make any necessary edits, save the revised document, print a hard copy of the document, close the document, and exit the program.
- The Title bar is the top line of the Word screen. The Title bar displays the name of the current document.
- The Menu bar is the second line on the screen. It contains a list of options that are used to customize a Word document.
- The Standard and Formatting toolbars display below the Menu bar and contain shortcuts for the most popular Word commands.
- The icon (picture) on each button on the toolbars represents the function each button performs. More information about each button is provided in the ToolTip that appears (after one second) when the arrow pointer is positioned on a button.
- The blinking vertical bar is called the insertion point and indicates the position in the document screen of the next character to be entered at the keyboard. The underline symbol immediately right of the insertion point is the end of document marker and indicates the end of the document.
- If a mouse is being used, the mouse pointer displays as an I-beam called the I-beam pointer or as an arrow pointing up and to the left called the arrow pointer.
- The scroll bars appear as gray shaded bars along the right and bottom of the document screen and are used to view various sections of a document.
- The Status bar appears as a gray bar below the horizontal scroll bar toward the bottom of the Word screen. It displays such information as the current location of the insertion point, whether certain modes are active, and the current time.
- Word automatically wraps text to the next line as you key information. Press the Enter key only to end a paragraph, create a blank line, or end a short line.
- Word contains a feature named AutoCorrect that automatically corrects certain words as they are keyed. For example, the error *adn* will automatically be replaced with *and*.
- When keying text, the Spell-It feature automatically inserts a wavy red line below words not contained in the Spelling dictionary. A grammar checker inserts a wavy green line below a sentence or portion of a sentence containing a grammatical error.
- In order to save on or open documents from your data disk, the default folder should be changed. Change the default folder at the Open dialog box or the Save As dialog box.
- Document names can contain a maximum of 255 characters, including the drive letter and folder names, and may include spaces. The following characters cannot be used when naming a document: / \ > < * ? " | : and ;.
- Drop-down menus and dialog boxes can be removed from the editing window with the mouse or the keyboard.

- When a document is saved on the disk using the Save or Save As options, the document remains in the document screen. To remove the document from the screen, click File, then Close, or click the Close button located at the far right side of the Menu bar.
- To print a document, open the document to be printed, and then click the Print button on the Standard toolbar or choose File, Print, then OK.
- Be sure to save all needed documents before exiting Word and Windows.

commands review

Opening Word for Windows

1. Turn on the computer.
2. At the Windows 95 screen, position the arrow pointer on the Start button on the taskbar (located at the bottom left side of the screen), and then click the left mouse button.
3. At the pop-up menu, position the arrow pointer on Programs (you do not need to click the mouse button). This will cause another menu to display to the right of the first pop-up menu.
4. Move the arrow pointer to *Microsoft Word* and then click the left mouse button.

Saving a Document

1. Click the Save button on the Standard toolbar, or click File, then Save.
2. At the Save As dialog box, key the name of the document. (The document name displays in the File name: text box.)
3. Click Save.

Changing the Default Folder

1. Click the Open button on the Standard toolbar (the second button from the left); or click File, then Open.
2. At the Open dialog box, click the down-pointing triangle at the right side of the Look in: text box.
3. From the drop-down list that displays, click *3½ Floppy (A:)*.
4. Click the Cancel button at the right side of the dialog box.

Closing a Document

1. Click File, then Close, or click the Close button located at the right side of the Menu bar.

Opening a Document

1. Click the Open button on the Standard toolbar, or click File, then Open.
2. At the Open dialog box, double-click the document name; or key the document name and then press Enter.

Printing a Document

1. Open the document.
2. Click the Print button on the Standard toolbar.

or

1. Open the document.
2. Click File, then Print.
3. At the Print dialog box, click OK or press Enter.

Exiting Word

1. Be sure all needed documents have been saved.
2. Click File, then Exit, or click the Close button on the Title bar.

Exiting Windows 95

1. Click the Start button located at the left side of the taskbar.
2. At the pop-up menu, click Shut Down.
3. At the Shut Down Windows dialog box, make sure *Shut down the computer?* is selected, and then click Yes.

check your understanding

Matching: In the space provided at the left, indicate the correct letter or letters that match each description.

A AutoCorrect
B ButtonTip
C CorrectType
D Formatting toolbar
E Horizontal scroll bar
F I-beam pointer
G Insertion point
H Menu bar
I New
J Office Assistant
K Spell-It
L Standard toolbar
M Status bar
N Title bar
O ToolTip
P Vertical scroll bar

______ 1. This toolbar contains buttons for working with documents such as the Open button and the Save button.

______ 2. This toolbar contains buttons for formatting a document such as bold, italics, and underline.

______ 3. This displays below the horizontal scroll bar and displays the current location of the insertion point.

_______ 4. This displays along the right side of the screen and is used to view various sections of a document.

_______ 5. This feature automatically corrects certain words as they are being keyed.

_______ 6. This is the second line of the Word screen and contains a list of options that are used to customize a Word document.

_______ 7. This displays at the top of the Word screen and displays the name of the currently open document.

_______ 8. This displays in the document screen as a blinking vertical bar.

_______ 9. This feature is a link to the on-screen Help feature that anticipates the type of help you need and suggests Help topics related to the work you are doing.

_______ 10. At a blank screen, click this button on the Standard toolbar to open a new blank document.

_______ 11. This appears after approximately one second when the arrow pointer is positioned on a button on a toolbar.

_______ 12. This feature inserts a wavy red line below words not contained in the Spelling dictionary.

skill assessments

Assessment 1

1. Open Windows and then open Word.
2. At the clear document screen, change the default folder to the drive where your student data disk is located. (Check with your instructor to determine if this step is necessary.)
3. At the clear document screen, key the text in figure 1.7. (Correct any errors highlighted by Spell-It as they occur and remember to space once after end-of-sentence punctuation.)
4. Save the document and name it Ch 01, SA 01.
5. Print Ch 01, SA 01.
6. Close Ch 01, SA 01.

Figure 1.7 • Assessment 1

The world economy is based on trade. The "global economy" is often mentioned when trade is discussed. The global economy refers to the relationship between the exports produced by countries and the imports brought into countries. Many business terms translate to international business.

The relationship of exports to imports is called the balance of trade. When the value of exports exceeds the value of imports, a favorable balance of trade occurs. An unfavorable balance of trade occurs when the opposite happens (value of imports exceeds value of exports).

In trade, the difference between money coming into a country from exports and the money leaving a country for imports is called the balance of payments. In addition, money that flows from other areas such as tourism, foreign aid, and military expenditures has an impact on balance of payments. The goal for a country's economy is to have more money flowing into the country than out of it.

Assessment 2

1. At the blank screen, click the New button on the Standard toolbar (the first button) to open a clear document screen.
2. At the clear document, key the text in figure 1.8. (Correct any errors highlighted by Spell-It as they occur and remember to space once after end-of-sentence punctuation.)
3. Save the document and name it Ch 01, SA 02.
4. Print Ch 01, SA 02.
5. Close Ch 01, SA 02.
6. Exit Word and then exit Windows.

Figure 1.8 • Assessment 2

In international business, selling a product in foreign countries for less than a company charges for that product in its own country is referred to as dumping. There are laws in the United States against dumping. These laws state that foreign companies must include a 10 percent overhead cost plus an 8 percent profit margin to the cost of products.

Some countries use government regulations to limit the import of goods and services. This practice is called trade protectionism. Trade protectionism is used by a country to protect their industries from foreign competition and from dumping. The idea of protectionism is to help domestic companies survive and expand, which will produce more jobs.

The value of one country's currency in relation to the currencies of other countries is referred to as the exchange rate. When a country's currency is valued high, its currency will buy more foreign goods (or trade for more foreign currency). If the currency value is lower, foreign products are more expensive.

chapter TWO

Editing a Document

PERFORMANCE OBJECTIVES

Upon successful completion of chapter 2, you will be able to:

- **Move the insertion point within a document.**
- **Scroll within a document.**
- **Edit a document.**

Many documents that are created need to have changes made to them. These changes may include adding text, called *inserting*, or removing text, called *deleting*. To insert or delete text, you need to be able to move the insertion point to certain locations in a document without erasing the text through which it passes. For example, if you key three paragraphs and then notice an error in the first paragraph, you need to move the insertion point through lines of text to the location of the error without deleting the lines. To move the insertion point without interfering with text, you can use the mouse, the keyboard, or the mouse combined with the keyboard.

Moving the Insertion Point with the Mouse

The mouse can be used to move the insertion point quickly to specific locations in the document. To do this, position the I-beam pointer at the location where you want the insertion point, and then click the left mouse button.

Scrolling with the Mouse

In addition to moving the insertion point to a specific location, the mouse can be used to move the display of text in the document screen. Scrolling in a document changes the text displayed but does not move the insertion point. If you want to move the insertion point to a new location in a document, scroll to the location, position the I-beam pointer in the desired location, and then click the left mouse button.

You can use the mouse with the *horizontal scroll bar* and/or the *vertical scroll bar* to scroll through text in a document. The horizontal scroll bar displays toward the bottom of the Word screen and the vertical scroll bar displays at the right side. Figure 2.1 displays the Word screen with the scroll bars and scroll boxes identified.

figure 2.1

Scroll Bars

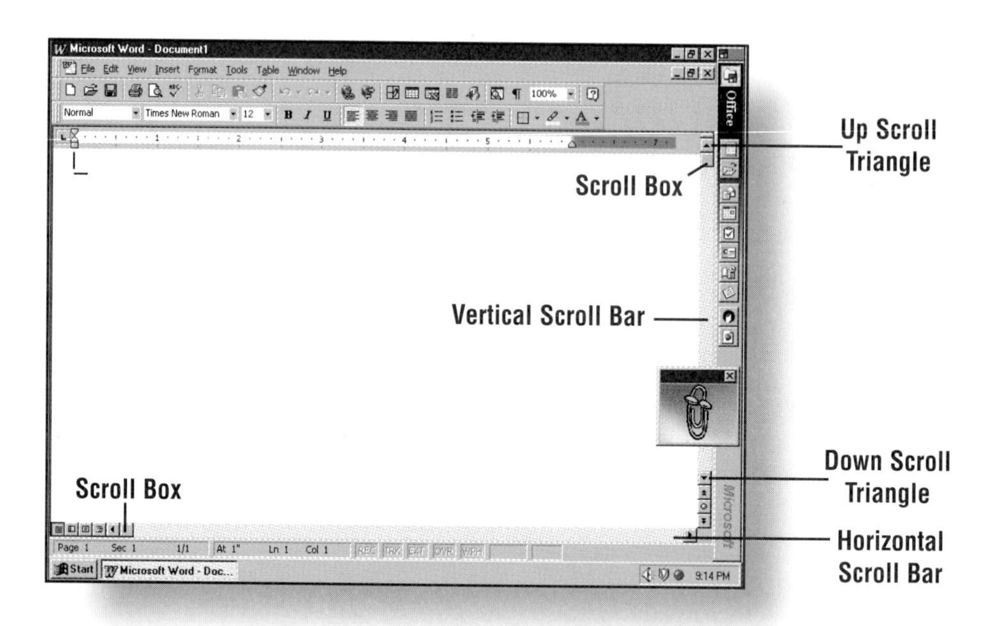

Scrolling with the Vertical Scroll Bar

An up-pointing triangle displays at the top of the vertical scroll bar. This up-pointing triangle is called the *up scroll triangle*. You can scroll up a line in the document by positioning the arrow pointer on the up scroll triangle and clicking the left mouse button. To scroll through the document continuously, position the arrow pointer on the up scroll triangle, and then hold down the left button.

The down-pointing triangle at the bottom of the vertical scroll bar is the *down scroll triangle*. Scroll down a line in the document by positioning the arrow pointer on the down scroll triangle and then clicking the left button. Hold down the left button if you want continuous action.

When you begin working in longer documents, the scroll bars will be useful for scrolling to certain areas in a document. The small gray box located in the vertical scroll bar is called the *scroll box*. This scroll box indicates the location of the text in the document screen in relation to the remainder of the document. The scroll box moves along the vertical scroll bar as you scroll through the document. You can scroll up or down through a document one screen at a time by using the arrow pointer on the scroll bar. To scroll up one screen, position the arrow pointer above the scroll box (but below the up scroll triangle) and click the left button. Position the arrow pointer below the scroll box and click the left button to scroll down a screen. If you hold down the left button, the action becomes continuous. You can also position the arrow pointer on the scroll box, hold down the left mouse button, and then drag the scroll box along the scroll bar to reposition text in the document screen. For example, if you want to scroll to the end of the document, position the arrow pointer on the scroll box in the vertical scroll bar, hold down the left mouse button, drag the scroll box to the bottom of the scroll bar, and then release the mouse button.

As you drag the scroll box along the vertical scroll bar in a longer document, the page number displays at the right side of the document screen in a yellow box. (You will notice this when completing exercise 1.)

Scrolling with the Horizontal Scroll Bar

A left-pointing triangle called the *left scroll triangle* displays at the left side of the horizontal scroll bar (after four buttons containing icons). The *right scroll triangle* displays at the right side of the horizontal scroll bar. These scroll triangles operate in the same manner as the up and down scroll triangles. Click the left scroll triangle to scroll the text to the right in the document screen. Click the right scroll triangle to scroll the text to the left in the document screen.

If you position the arrow pointer to the right of the scroll box but before the right scroll triangle and then click the left mouse button, the text scrolls an entire screen to the left. If you position the arrow pointer to the left of the scroll box but before the left scroll triangle and then click the left mouse button, the text scrolls an entire screen to the right.

You can reposition text in the document screen by positioning the arrow pointer on the scroll box, holding down the left mouse button, and then dragging the scroll box along the horizontal scroll bar.

Moving the Insertion Point to a Specific Page

Word includes a Go To option that you can use to move the insertion point to a specific page within a document. To move the insertion point to a specific page, you would complete the following steps:

1. Click Edit, then Go To, or double-click the page number at the left side of the Status bar.
2. At the Find and Replace dialog box with the Go To tab selected, as shown in figure 2.2, key the page number.
3. Click Go To or press Enter.
4. Click Close to close the Find and Replace dialog box.

If you open a previously saved document, you can move the insertion point to where the insertion point was last located when the document was closed by pressing Shift + F5.

Find and Replace Dialog Box with Go To Tab Selected

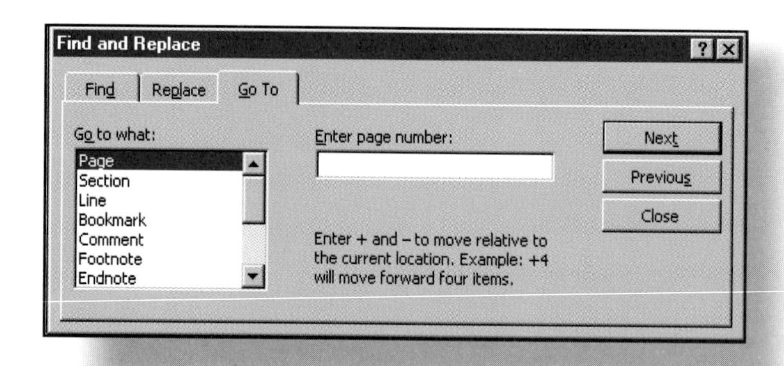

Browsing in a Document

Select Browse Object

A button located at the bottom of the vertical scroll bar contains options for browsing through a document. Click this button, called Select Browse Object, and a palette of browsing choices displays as shown in figure 2.3. Use the options on the palette to move the insertion point to various features in a Word document. Position the arrow pointer on an option in the palette and the option name displays below the options. For example, position the arrow pointer on the last option in the first row and *Browse by Page* displays below the options. When you click the Browse by Page option, the insertion point moves to the next page in the document. Use the other options in the palette to move to the next specified object in the document.

Select Browse Object Palette

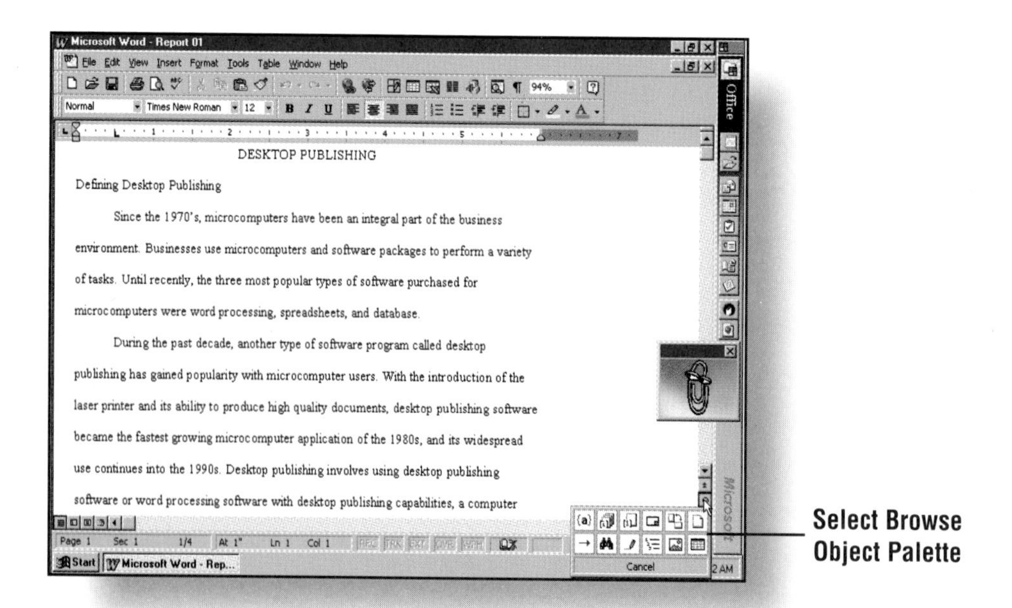

exercise 1

Scrolling, Browsing, and Moving the Insertion Point in a Document

1. Open Word following the instructions in chapter 1.
2. At a clear document screen, open Report 01. This document is located on your student data disk.
3. Practice moving the insertion point and scrolling through the document using the mouse by completing the following steps:
   a. Position the I-beam pointer at the beginning of the first paragraph and then click the left mouse button. This moves the insertion point to the location of the I-beam pointer.
   b. Position the arrow pointer on the down scroll triangle on the vertical scroll bar and then click the left mouse button several times. This scrolls down lines of text in the document. With the arrow pointer on the down scroll triangle, hold down the left mouse button and keep it down until the end of the document is displayed.
   c. Position the arrow pointer on the up scroll triangle and hold down the left mouse button until the beginning of the document is displayed.
   d. Position the arrow pointer below the scroll box and then click the left mouse button. Continue clicking the mouse button (with the arrow pointer positioned below the scroll box) until the end of the document is displayed.
   e. Position the arrow pointer on the scroll box in the vertical scroll bar. Hold down the left mouse button, drag the scroll box to the top of the vertical scroll bar, and then release the mouse button. (Notice that the document page number is displayed in a yellow box at the right side of the document screen.)
   f. Click on the title at the beginning of the document. (This moves the insertion point to the location of the mouse pointer.)
   g. Move the insertion point to page 4 by completing the following steps:
      1) Click Edit, then Go To; or double-click the page number at the left side of the Status bar.
      2) At the Find and Replace dialog box with the Go To tab selected, key **4**.
      3) Click Go To or press Enter.
      4) Click Close to close the Find and Replace dialog box.
   h. Move the insertion point to page 1 by completing the following steps:
      1) Click the Select Browse Object button located toward the bottom of the vertical scroll bar.
      2) At the palette of browsing choices that displays, click the first choice in the second row (Go To). (The location of the Go To choice may vary. It may be the first choice in the first row.)

3) At the Find and Replace dialog box with the Go To tab selected, delete the 4 in the Enter page number text box, and then key **1**.
4) Click Go To or press Enter.
5) Click Close to close the Find and Replace dialog box.

i. Move to the beginning of page 2 by completing the following steps:
1) Click the Select Browse Object button located toward the bottom of the vertical scroll bar.
2) At the palette of browsing choices that displays, click the last choice in the first row (Browse by Page). (The location of the Browse by Page choice may vary. It may be the last choice in the second row.) This moves the insertion point to page 2.
3) Click the Select Browse Object button again and then click the last choice in the first row (Browse by Page). (The location of the Browse by Page choice may vary. It may be the last choice in the second row.) This moves the insertion point to page 3.

4. Close Report 01.

Moving the Insertion Point with the Keyboard

To move the insertion point with the keyboard, use the arrow keys located to the right of the regular keyboard. (You can also use the arrow keys on the numeric keypad. If you use these keys, make sure Num Lock is off.) The illustration in figure 2.4 shows arrow keys marked with left, right, up, and down arrows.

figure 2.4 *Insertion Point Movement Keys*

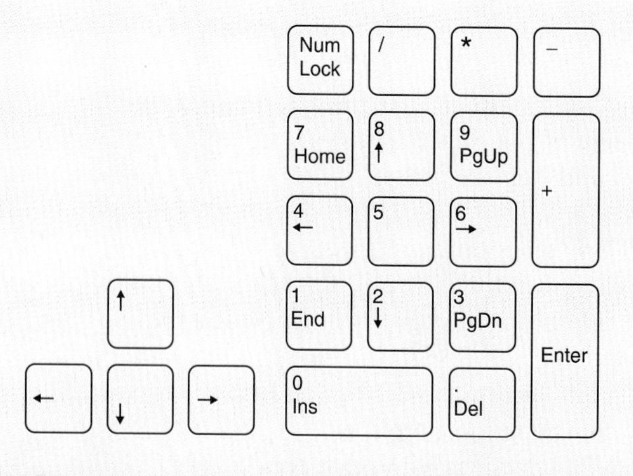

Use the arrow keys together with other keys to move the insertion point to various locations in the document as shown in figure 2.5.

2.5 ***Insertion Point Movement Commands***

To move insertion point	Press
One character left	←
One character right	→
One line up	↑
One line down	↓
One word to the left	CTRL + ←
One word to the right	CTRL + →
To end of a line	END
To beginning of a line	HOME
To beginning of current paragraph	CTRL + ↑
To beginning of next paragraph	CTRL + ↓
Up one screen	PG UP
Down one screen	PG DN
To top of previous page	CTRL + PG UP
To top of next page	CTRL + PG DN
To beginning of document	CTRL + HOME
To end of document	CTRL + END

When moving the insertion point, Word considers a word to be any series of characters between spaces. A paragraph is any text that is followed by a stroke of the Enter key. A page is text that is separated by a soft or hard page break.

exercise 2

Moving the Insertion Point Using the Keyboard

1. Open Report 01. This document is located on your student data disk.
2. Practice moving the insertion point with the keyboard, by completing the following steps:
   a. Press the right arrow key to move the insertion point to the next character to the right. Continue pressing the right arrow key until the insertion point is located at the end of the first paragraph.
   b. Press Ctrl + right arrow key to move the insertion point to the next word to the right. Continue pressing Ctrl + right arrow until the insertion point is located on the last word of the second paragraph.

c. Press Ctrl + left arrow key until the insertion point is positioned at the beginning of the document.
d. Press the End key to move the insertion point to the end of the title.
e. Press the Home key to move the insertion point to the beginning of the title.
f. Press Ctrl + Page Down to position the insertion point at the beginning of page 2.
g. Press Ctrl + Page Up to position the insertion point at the beginning of the document.
h. Position the insertion point at the beginning of page 3 using the Go To option by completing the following steps:
    1) Click Edit, then Go To, or double-click the page number at the left side of the Status bar.
    2) At the Find and Replace dialog box with the Go To tab selected, key **3**.
    3) Click Go To or press Enter.
    4) When the insertion point is positioned at the beginning of page 3, click Close to close the Go To dialog box.
i. Press Ctrl + End to move the insertion point to the end of the document.
j. Press Ctrl + Home to move the insertion point to the beginning of the document.

3. Close Report 01.

Inserting Text

Once you have created a document, you may want to insert information you forgot or have since decided to include. At the default document screen, Word moves existing characters to the right as you key additional text.

If you want to key over something, switch to the Overtype mode. You can do this by pressing the Insert key or by double-clicking the OVR mode button on the Status bar. When Overtype is on, the OVR mode button displays in black. To turn off Overtype, press the Insert key or double-click the OVR mode button.

Deleting Text

When you edit a document, you may want to delete (remove) text. Commands for deleting text are presented in figure 2.6.

figure 2.6 *Deletion Commands*

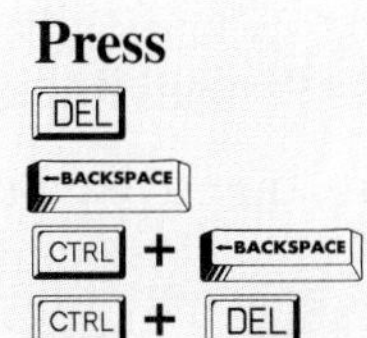

To delete	Press
Character right of insertion point	DEL
Character left of insertion point	BACKSPACE
Text from insertion point to beginning of word	CTRL + BACKSPACE
Text from insertion point to end of word	CTRL + DEL

Splitting and Joining Paragraphs

By inserting or deleting, paragraphs of text can be split or joined. To split a large paragraph into two smaller paragraphs, position the insertion point on the first character that will begin the new paragraph, and then press the Enter key twice. The first time you press Enter, the text is moved to the next line. The second time you press Enter, a blank line is inserted between the paragraphs.

To join two paragraphs into one, you need to delete the spaces between them. To do this, position the insertion point on the first character of the second paragraph and then press the Backspace key until the paragraphs join. More than likely, you will need to then press the space bar to separate the sentences. You can also join two paragraphs together by positioning the insertion point one space past the period at the end of the first paragraph and then pressing the Delete key until the paragraphs join. When you join the two paragraphs, the new paragraph will be automatically adjusted.

exercise 3

Editing a Document

1. Open Ch 02, Ex 03. This document is located on your student data disk.
2. Make the changes indicated by the proofreaders' marks in figure 2.7. (Proofreaders' marks are listed and described in Appendix A at the end of this textbook.)
3. Save the document with the same name (Ch 02, Ex 03) by using the Save option from the File menu or clicking the Save button on the Standard toolbar.
4. Print and then close Ch 02, Ex 03.

Exercise 3

Since the 1970s, microcomputers have been an integral part of the business environment. Businesses use microcomputers and software packages to perform a variety of tasks. Until recently, the three most popular types of software purchased for microcomputers were word processing, spreadsheets, and database.

During the past decade, another type of software program called desktop publishing has gained popularity with microcomputer users. With the introduction of the laser printer and its ability to produce high quality documents, desktop publishing software became the fastest growing microcomputer application of the 1980s and its widespread use continues into the 1990s. Desktop publishing involves using desktop publishing software or word processing software with desktop publishing capabilities, a computer system, and a printer to produce professional-looking documents. The phrase "desktop publishing," coined by Aldus Corporation president, Paul Brainard, means that publishing can now literally take place at your desktop.

Until the mid-1980s, graphic design depended almost exclusively on design professionals. But desktop publishing changed all that by bringing graphic design into the office and home. Faster microprocessors, improved printer capabilities, increased supply of clip art, CD ROMs, and the like continue to expand the role of desktop publishing. Everything from a flyer to a newsletter can be designed, created, and produced at a computer.

Selecting Text

The mouse and/or keyboard can be used to select a specific amount of text. Once selected, you can delete the text or perform other Word functions involving the selected text. When text is selected it displays in reverse video in the document screen as shown in figure 2.8. For example, if the document screen displays with a white background and black characters, selected text will display as white characters on a black background. The text in the second paragraph in figure 2.8 has been selected and displays with white characters on a black background.

2.8 **Selected Text**

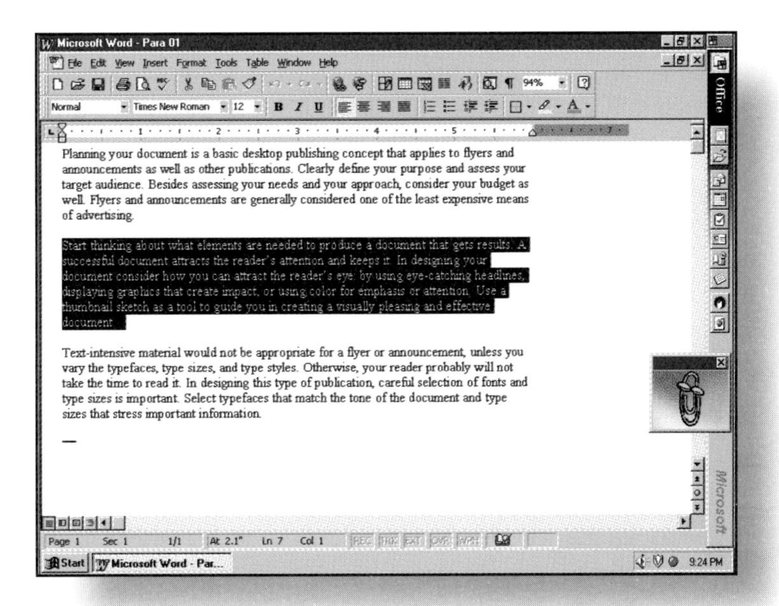

Selecting Text with the Mouse

You can use the mouse to select a word, line, sentence, paragraph, or the entire document. Figure 2.9 indicates the steps to follow to select various amounts of text. To select certain amounts of text such as a line, the instructions in the figure tell you to click in the *selection bar*. The selection bar is the space at the left side of the document screen between the left edge of the screen and the text. When the arrow pointer is positioned in the selection bar, the pointer turns into an arrow pointing up and to the right (instead of to the left).

2.9 **Selecting with the Mouse**

To select	Complete these steps using the mouse
A word	Double-click the word.
A line of text	Click in the selection bar to the left of the line.
Multiple lines of text	Drag in the selection bar to the left of the lines.
A sentence	Hold down the Ctrl key and then click anywhere in the sentence.
A paragraph	Double-click in the selection bar next to the paragraph or triple-click anywhere in the paragraph.
An entire document	Triple-click in the selection bar.

To select an amount of text other than a word, sentence, or paragraph, position the I-beam pointer on the first character of the text to be selected, hold down the left mouse button, drag the I-beam pointer to the last character of the text to be selected, and then release the mouse button. You can also select all text between the current insertion point and the I-beam pointer. To do this, position the insertion point where you want the selection to begin, hold down the Shift key, click the I-beam pointer at the end of the selection, and then release the Shift key.

To cancel a selection using the mouse, click anywhere in the document screen outside the selected text.

Selecting Text with the Keyboard

To select a specific amount of text using the keyboard, use the Extend Selection key, F8, along with the arrow keys. When you press F8, the Extend Selection mode is turned on and the EXT mode button on the Status bar displays in black letters. (You can also turn on the Extend Selection mode by double-clicking the EXT mode button on the Status bar.) As you move the insertion point through text, the text is selected. If you want to cancel the selection, press the Esc key, and then press any arrow key (or double-click the EXT mode button on the Status bar, and then press any arrow key). You can also select text with the commands shown in figure 2.10.

figure 2.10 *Selecting with the Keyboard*

To select	Press
One character to right	SHIFT + →
One character to left	SHIFT + ←
To end of word	CTRL + SHIFT + →
To beginning of word	CTRL + SHIFT + ←
To end of line	SHIFT + END
To beginning of line	SHIFT + HOME
One line up	SHIFT + ↑
One line down	SHIFT + ↓
To beginning of paragraph	CTRL + SHIFT + ↑
To end of paragraph	CTRL + SHIFT + ↓
One screen up	SHIFT + PG UP
One screen down	SHIFT + PG DN
To end of document	CTRL + SHIFT + END
To beginning of document	CTRL + SHIFT + HOME
Entire document	CTRL + A or click Edit, Select All

If you use one of the commands in figure 2.10 to select text and then decide to cancel the selection, press any arrow key.

With text selected, press the Delete key to remove the selected text from the document, or press Shift + Delete to remove it from the document and save it in temporary memory. If you want to insert the saved text in the document, move the insertion point to the desired location, and then press Shift + Insert.

exercise 4

Selecting and Deleting Text

1. Open Ch 02, Ex 04. This document is located on your student data disk.
2. Delete the name, *Dr. Jennifer Salo*, and the department, *Office Technology Department*, using the mouse by completing the following steps:
   a. Position the I-beam pointer on the *D* in *Dr.* (in the address).
   b. Hold down the left mouse button and then drag the mouse down until *Dr. Jennifer Salo* and *Office Technology Department* are selected.
   c. Release the left mouse button.
   d. Press the Delete key.
3. Position the insertion point at the left margin on the line above *Greenwater Community College* and then key the name, **Mrs. Gina Thompson**.
4. Delete *Dr. Salo* in the salutation (after the word *Dear*), then key the name **Mrs. Thompson**. (You choose the method for deleting.)
5. Delete the reference line, *Re: Desktop Publishing Course*, using the Extend Selection key, F8, by completing the following steps:
   a. Position the insertion point on the *R* in *Re:*.
   b. Press F8 to turn on select.
   c. Press the down arrow key twice. (This selects the reference line and the blank line below it.)
   d. Press the Delete key.
6. Delete the first sentence in the first paragraph using the mouse by completing the following steps:
   a. Position the I-beam pointer anywhere in the sentence, *The Southern Computer Technology conference we attended last week was very educational.*
   b. Hold down the Ctrl key and then click the left mouse button.
   c. Press the Delete key.
7. Delete the first sentence in the second paragraph (the sentence that reads, *The interest in the class has been phenomenal.*) using the keyboard by completing the following steps:

   a. Position the insertion point on the first letter of the sentence (the *T* in *The*).
   b. Hold down the Shift key and then press the right arrow key until the sentence is selected. Be sure to include the period at the end of the sentence and the space after the period.
   c. Press the Delete key.
8. Delete the third paragraph in the letter using the mouse by completing the following steps:
   a. Position the I-beam pointer anywhere in the third paragraph (the paragraph that begins, *The instructor for the course...*).
   b. Triple-click the left mouse button.
   c. Press the Delete key.
   d. Press the Delete key again to delete the extra blank lines before the last paragraph.
9. Save the document with the same name (Ch 02, Ex 04) by using the Save option from the File menu or clicking the Save button on the Standard toolbar.
10. Print and then close Ch 02, Ex 04.

Using the Undo and Redo Buttons

Undo

Redo

If you make a mistake and delete text that you did not intend to, or if you change your mind after deleting text and want to retrieve it, you can use the Undo or Redo buttons on the Standard toolbar. The Undo button is the eleventh button from the left on the Standard toolbar and the Redo button is the twelfth. For example, if you just keyed text and then click the Undo button, the text will be removed. Word removes text to the beginning of the document or up to the point where text had been previously deleted. You can undo text or commands. For example, if you add formatting such as bolding to text and then click the Undo button, the bolding is removed.

If you use the Undo button and then decide you do not want to reverse the original action, click the Redo button. For example, if you select and underline text, and then decide to remove underlining, click the Undo button. If you then decide you want the underlining back on, click the Redo button. Many Word actions can be undone or redone. Some actions, however, such as printing and saving cannot be undone or redone.

In addition to the Undo and Redo buttons on the Standard toolbar, you can use options from the Edit drop-down menu to undo and redo actions. The first two options at the Edit drop-down menu will vary depending on the last action completed. For example, if you just clicked the Numbering button on the Formatting toolbar, and then displayed the Edit drop-down menu, the first option displays as Undo Number Default. The second option displays as Repeat Number Default. If you decide you do not want the numbering option on, click Edit, then Undo Number Default. You can also just click the Undo button on the Standard toolbar.

Word maintains actions in temporary memory. If you want to undo an action performed earlier, click the down-pointing triangle to the right of the Undo button. This causes a drop-down menu to display as shown in figure 2.11.

figure 2.11 **Undo Drop-Down List**

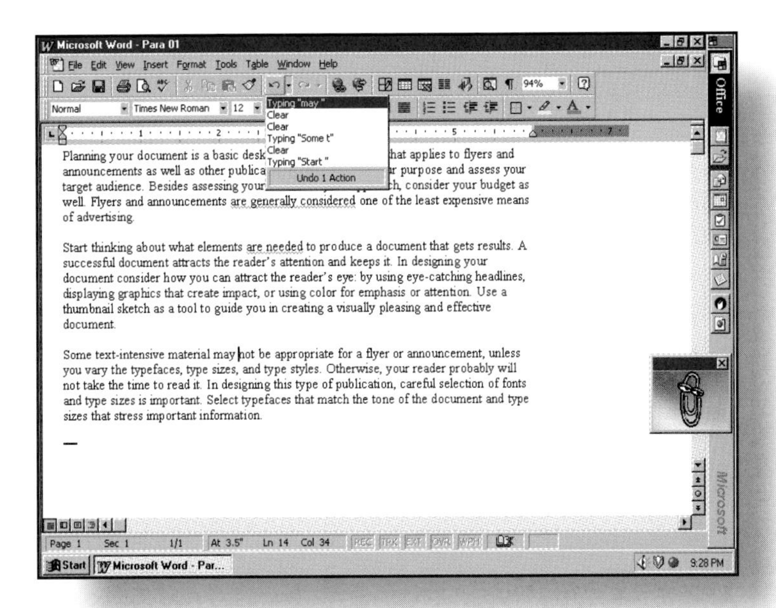

To make a selection from this drop-down menu, click the desired action. Any actions preceding a chosen action are also undone. You can do the same with the actions in the Redo drop-down list. To display the Redo drop-down list, click the down-pointing triangle to the right of the Redo button. To redo an action, click the desired action. Any actions preceding the chosen action are also redone. Multiple actions must be undone or redone in sequence.

exercise 5

Deleting and Restoring Text with the Undo Button

1. Open Para 01. This document is located on your student data disk.
2. Move the insertion point to the end of the document. Press the Backspace key until the last seven words of the document (*and type sizes that stress important information.*) are deleted. Be sure to delete the space before *and*.
3. Undo the deletion by clicking the Undo button on the Standard toolbar.
4. Redo the deletion by clicking the Redo button on the Standard toolbar.
5. Key a period after the word *document* to end the sentence.
6. Select the first sentence in the first paragraph and then delete it.
7. Select the second paragraph in the document and then delete it.
8. Undo the two deletions by completing the following steps:

a. Click the down-pointing triangle to the right of the Undo button.
b. Click the *second* Clear listed in the drop-down menu. (This will redisplay the first sentence in the first paragraph and the second paragraph. The first sentence will be selected.)

9. With the first sentence of the paragraph selected, press the Delete key.
10. Save the document with the same name (Para 01) by using the Save option from the File menu or clicking the Save button on the Standard toolbar.
11. Print and then close Para 01.

Saving Documents

In chapter 1, you learned to save a document with the Save button on the Standard toolbar or the Save option from the File drop-down menu. The File drop-down menu also contains a Save As option. The Save As option is used to save a previously created document with a new name.

For example, suppose you created and saved a document named *Memo*, and then opened it later. If you save the document again with the Save button on the Standard toolbar or the Save option from the File drop-down menu, Word will save the document with the same name. You will not be prompted to key a name for the document. This is because Word assumes that when you use the Save option on a previously saved document, you want to save it with the same name. If you open the document named *Memo*, make some changes to it, and then want to save it with a new name, you must use the Save As option. When you use the Save As option, Word displays the Save As dialog box where you can key a new name for the document. To save a document with Save As, complete the following steps:

1. Click File, then Save As.
2. At the Save As dialog box, key the document name.
3. Click Save or press Enter.

In many of the computer exercises in this textbook, you will be asked to open a document from your student data disk, and then save it with a new name. You will be instructed to use the Save As option to do this.

exercise 6

Editing, Then Saving a Document with Save As

1. Open Para 02. This document is located on your student data disk.
2. Save the document with the name Ch 02, Ex 06 using Save As by completing the following steps:
   a. Click File, then Save As.
   b. At the Save As dialog box, key **Ch 02, Ex 06**.
   c. Click Save or press Enter.
3. Make the changes indicated by the proofreaders' marks in figure 2.12.
4. Save the document again with the same name (Ch 02, Ex 06). To do this, click the Save button on the Standard toolbar or click File, then Save.
5. Print and then close Ch 02, Ex 06.

2.12 *Exercise 6*

Flyers are generally used to advertise a product or service that is available for a limited amount of time. ~~Frequently, you may find~~ flyers may be found stuffed in a grocery bag; attached to a mailbox, door handle or windshield; placed in a bin near an entrance; or placed on a countertop for prospective customers to carry away. Examples of businesses that use flyers for advertising services include lawn maintenance companies, babysitters, window washers, cleaning services, realtors, dentists, doctors, lawyers, and more. ~~As you can see, this form of advertising is used by just about anyone.~~

~~In a flyer,~~ a headline in a flyer should be a dominant visual element, set significantly larger than the words that follow. Standard headlines are usually 36 to 48 points in size. However, depending on your document, the headline may ~~even~~ exceed 72 points. ~~To use a type size larger than 72, display the Font dialog box, and then key the desired point size in the Size text box.~~

no ¶ Besides increasing the point size for headlines, you may want to change the shading and/or color of the ~~font~~ text. Depending on your needs, you may choose a large, thick typeface or change the color of the headline. A flyer with a large, color headline ~~is an eye-catching way to~~ effectively announce(s) an event or present(s) important information.

chapter summary

- The insertion point can be moved throughout the document without interfering with text by using the mouse, the keyboard, or the mouse combined with the keyboard.
- The insertion point can be moved by character, word, screen, or page and from the first to the last character in a document.
- Switch to the Overtype mode if you want to key over something. When Overtype is on, the OVR mode button in the Status bar displays in black.
- Text can be deleted by character, word, line, several lines, or partial page using specific keys or by selecting text using the mouse or the keyboard.
- The horizontal/vertical scroll bars and the mouse can be used to scroll through a document. The scroll box indicates the location of the text in the document screen in relation to the remainder of the document.
- A paragraph can be split into two paragraphs by pressing the Enter key. Join two paragraphs into one by deleting spaces between the paragraphs.
- A specific amount of text can be selected using the mouse or the keyboard. That text can then be deleted or manipulated in other ways using Word functions.
- The selection bar can be used to select specific units of text such as a line. The selection bar is the space at the left side of the document screen between the left edge of the screen and the text.
- Use the Undo button on the Standard toolbar if you change your mind after keying, deleting, or formatting text and want to undo the deleting or formatting. Use the Redo button to redo something that had been undone with the Undo button.
- The Save As option is used to save a previously created document with a new name.

commands review

Scrolling Review

Changing the Display Using the Mouse and the Vertical Scroll Bar

Up one line	Click the up scroll triangle on the vertical scroll bar
Up several lines	Position the arrow pointer as above and then hold down left button
Down one line	Click the down scroll triangle on the vertical scroll bar
Down several lines	Position the arrow pointer as above and then hold down left mouse button
Up one screen	Click with arrow pointer above the scroll box on the scroll bar
Up several screens	Position the arrow pointer as above and then hold down left mouse button

Down one screen	Click with the arrow pointer below the scroll box on the scroll bar
Down several screens	Position the arrow pointer as above and then hold down left mouse button
To beginning of document	Position the arrow pointer on the scroll box, hold down the left mouse button, drag the scroll box to the beginning of the scroll bar, and then release the mouse button
To end of document	Position the arrow pointer on the scroll box, hold down left mouse button, drag the scroll box to the end of the scroll bar, then release the mouse button

Changing the Display Using the Mouse and the Horizontal Scroll Bar

One screen to the right	Position the arrow pointer to the right of the scroll box on the horizontal scroll bar and then click the left mouse button
One screen to the left	Position the arrow pointer to the left of the scroll box on the horizontal scroll bar and then click the left mouse button
Reposition text horizontally in the document screen	Position the arrow pointer on the scroll box on the horizontal scroll bar, hold down the left mouse button, then drag the scroll box along the scroll bar

Insertion Point Movement Review

Moving the Insertion Point Using the Mouse

To move to a specific location: Move arrow pointer to desired location and then click left mouse button

To move to a specific page:

1. Click Edit, Go To; or double-click the page number at the left side of the Status bar.
2. Key the page number.
3. Click Go To or press Enter.
4. Click the Close command button.

Moving the Insertion Point Using the Keyboard

To move insertion point	Press
One character left	←
One character right	→
One line up	↑
One line down	↓
One word to the left	CTRL + ←
One word to the right	CTRL + →
To end of line	END
To beginning of a line	HOME
To beginning of current paragraph	CTRL + ↑
To beginning of next paragraph	CTRL + ↓
Up one screen	PG UP

Down one screen	PG DN
To top of previous page	CTRL + PG UP
To top of next page	CTRL + PG DN
To beginning of document	CTRL + HOME
To end of document	CTRL + END
To last location when document was closed	SHIFT + F5

Deletion Commands Review

To delete	Press
Character right of insertion point	DEL
Character left of insertion point	BACKSPACE
Word before insertion point	CTRL + BACKSPACE
Word after insertion point	CTRL + DEL

Selecting Text Review

Selecting Text Using the Mouse

To select text	Position I-beam pointer at the beginning of text to be selected, hold down left mouse button, drag the I-beam pointer to the end of text to be selected, then release the mouse button
To select	**Complete these steps**
A word	Double-click the word
A line of text	Click in the selection bar to the left of line
Multiple lines of text	Drag in the selection bar to the left of lines
A sentence	Hold down Ctrl key and then click anywhere in the sentence
A paragraph	Double-click in the selection bar next to paragraph or triple-click anywhere in the paragraph
Multiple paragraphs	Drag in the selection bar
An entire document	Triple-click in the selection bar
To cancel a selection	Click anywhere outside the selected text in the document screen

Selecting Text Using the Keyboard

To select	Press
One character to right	SHIFT + →
One character to left	SHIFT + ←
To end of word	CTRL + SHIFT + →
To beginning of word	CTRL + SHIFT + ←
To end of line	SHIFT + END
To beginning of line	SHIFT + HOME
One line up	SHIFT + ↑
One line down	SHIFT + ↓
To beginning of paragraph	CTRL + SHIFT + ↑
To end of paragraph	CTRL + SHIFT + ↓
One screen up	SHIFT + PG UP
One screen down	SHIFT + PG DN
To end of document	CTRL + SHIFT + END
To beginning of document	CTRL + SHIFT + HOME
Entire document	CTRL + A or click Edit, Select All
To cancel a selection	Press any arrow key

Deleting Selected Text

Select and then permanently delete selected text	Select text, press DEL
Select and then remove text to temporary memory	Select text, press SHIFT + DEL
Insert text from temporary memory into document	Position insertion point, press SHIFT + INS

Other Commands Review

Turn on Overtype	Double-click the OVR mode button on the Status bar, or press the Insert key
Undo option	Click the [Undo] button on the Standard toolbar; or click the down-pointing triangle to the right of the Undo button; or click Undo from the Edit drop-down menu
Redo option	Click the [Redo] button on the Standard toolbar; or click the down-pointing triangle to the right of the Redo button; or click Repeat from the Edit drop-down menu
Save As	1. Click File, then Save As. 2. At the Save As dialog box, key the document name. 3. Click Save or press Enter.

check your understanding

Completion: In the space provided at the right, indicate the correct term, command, or number.

1. Use this keyboard command to move the insertion point to the beginning of the previous page. __________
2. When Overtype is on, this mode button displays in black on the Status bar. __________
3. To delete the word after the insertion point, use this keyboard command. __________
4. To join two paragraphs into one, position the insertion point on the first character of the second paragraph, and then press this key until the paragraphs join. __________
5. Complete these steps using the mouse to select one word. __________
6. Text in the document screen can be adjusted to the right or left using this scroll bar. __________
7. Use this keyboard command to select text to the end of the line. __________
8. If you click this button on the Standard toolbar, text you just keyed will be removed. __________
9. Use this keyboard command to move the insertion point to the end of the document. __________
10. Move the insertion point to a specific page in a document by keying the page number in the Find and Replace dialog box with this tab selected. __________
11. Use this keyboard command to select text to the end of the paragraph. __________
12. To select various amounts of text using the mouse, you can click in this bar. __________
13. Choose this option from the File drop-down menu to save the currently open document with a new name. __________

skill assessments

Assessment 1

1. Open Para 03. This document is located on your student data disk.
2. Save the document with Save As and name it Ch 02, SA 01.
3. Make the changes indicated by the proofreaders' marks in figure 2.13.
4. Save the document again with the same name (Ch 02, SA 01).
5. Print and then close Ch 02, SA 01.

Figure 2.13 • Assessment 1

Flyers are typically one of the least expensive forms of advertising. The primary basic goal of a flyer is to communicate a message at a glance. so the message should be brief and to the point. For the flyer to be effective, the basic layout and design should be free of clutter, and The flyer should not contain too much text or too many graphics. Have the information arranged so it is easy to understand.

no ¶ When creating a flyer, use white space generously to set off an image or text. In a flyer, Also, consider directional flow in placing elements on a page. The left corner is usually read first. Consider your audience when choosing type sizes. The older your audience, the larger the print might need to be. Most important, always prepare a thumbnail sketch before beginning the project.

A graphics element, such as a watermark, can be very effective in a flyer. When using a watermark, try to find a graphic or text that matches the tone or theme of your message. The watermark can be used to add more emphasis, color, and excitement to a flyer.

Assessment 2

1. Open Para 04. This document is located on your student data disk.
2. Save the document with Save As and name it Ch 02, SA 02.
3. Make the changes indicated by the proofreaders' marks in figure 2.14.
4. Save the document again with the same name (Ch 02, SA 02).
5. Print and then close Ch 02, SA 02.

Figure 2.14 • Assessment 2

for Windows

Word~~, one of the best-selling word processing programs for microcomputers,~~ includes a wide variety of desktop publishing features. The ~~scope and~~ capabilities of these features have expanded with each new Word for Windows version. Some of the desktop publishing features include a ~~wide~~ variety of fonts and special symbols, drawing, charting, text design capabilities, graphic manipulation, templates, and much more.

no ¶ ing with design.

Design can be learned by studying ~~design~~ and ~~by~~ experiment~~ation~~. Collect and study designs that are attractive and visually interesting. Analyze what makes the design and layout unique and try using the same principles ~~or variations~~ in your publications. ¶ Take advantage of the special design and layout features that Word for Windows has to offer. Take the time to design an attractive publication. Layout and design is a lengthy process of revising, refining, and making adjustments. Start with small variations from the default formats to create designs that are attractive and visually interesting.

Assessment 3

1. At a clear document screen, compose a paragraph explaining when you would use the Save As command when saving a document and the advantages to Save As.
2. Save the document and name it Ch 02, SA 03.
3. Print and then close Ch 02, SA 03.

chapter THREE

Formatting Characters

PERFORMANCE OBJECTIVES

Upon successful completion of chapter 3, you will be able to:

- **Key text in all capital letters.**
- **Apply bold, italic, and underline formatting to characters.**
- **Change the case of letters.**
- **Use Word's Help feature.**

As you work with Word, you will learn a number of commands and procedures that affect how the document appears when printed. The appearance of a document in the document screen and how it looks when printed is called the *format*. Formatting can include such elements as all caps, line spacing, indenting, even or uneven margins, tabs, bolding, underlining, and much more.

Creating Text in All Caps

To key text in all uppercase letters, activate the Caps Lock feature by pressing the Caps Lock key. Press Caps Lock again to deactivate the uppercase feature. When Caps Lock is activated, a green mode indicator light usually appears at the upper right side of the keyboard.

Using the Tab Key

The Word program contains a variety of default settings. A *default* is a preset standard or value that is established by the program. One default setting in Word is a tab line that contains tab stops every 0.5 inch. In a later chapter, you will learn how to change the default tab stops. For now, use the default tab stops to indent text from the left margin. To indent text, press Tab. The Tab key on a microcomputer keyboard is generally located above the Caps Lock key.

Formatting Text

Text can be formatted to emphasize text, elicit a particular feeling from the text, or draw the reader's eyes to a particular word or words. Text can be accentuated in a variety of ways such as bolding, italicizing, and underlining. Text can be bolded, italicized, or underlined with buttons on the Formatting toolbar or with shortcut commands. (You can also bold, italicize, or underline text at the Font dialog box. You will learn more about this dialog box in chapter 6.)

Bolding Text

Bold

The Bold button on the Formatting toolbar or the shortcut command, Ctrl + B, can be used to bold text. When text is bolded, it appears darker than surrounding text in the document screen and also on the printed page. Text can be bolded as it is being keyed, or existing text can be bolded. To bold text as it is being keyed, click the Bold button on the Formatting toolbar or press Ctrl + B. Key the text to be bolded and then click the Bold button again or press Ctrl + B. To bold existing text, select the text first, and then click the Bold button on the Formatting toolbar or press Ctrl + B.

Before Completing Exercise 1

In exercise 1 and other exercises in the text, you will be required to create memos. Please refer to Appendix B at the end of this text for the correct placement and spacing of a traditional-style memo. Unless otherwise instructed by your teacher, use this format when creating memos. The initials of the person keying the memo usually appear at the end of a memo. In this text, the initials will appear in the exercises as XX. Key your initials where you see the XX. Identifying a document name is a good idea because it lets you find and open the document quickly and easily at a future date. In this text, the document name is identified after the reference initials.

Note: The typist's initials are generally keyed in lowercase letters. Word's AutoCorrect feature by default, however, automatically changes the first letter to an uppercase. For this reason, uppercase letters are used for the initials. (If you want to key initials in lowercase letters, consider turning off the Capitalize first letter of sentence option at the AutoCorrect dialog box. To display the AutoCorrect dialog box, click Tools, then AutoCorrect.)

1

Bolding Text as It Is Keyed

1. At a clear document screen, key the memo shown in figure 3.1 in the traditional memo format. Use Caps Lock to key the memo headings—*DATE*, *TO*, *FROM*, and *SUBJECT*. To align the information after *DATE:*, key **DATE:**, press the Tab key twice, and then key **June 3, 1998**. (Press the Tab twice after TO: and once after FROM: and SUBJECT: to properly align the text.) Bold the populations as shown in the memo as they are being keyed by completing the following steps:
   a. Press Ctrl + B.
   b. Key the population number.
   c. Press Ctrl + B.
2. Save the memo and name it Ch 03, Ex 01.
3. Print and then close Ch 03, Ex 01.

figure 3.1

Exercise 1

DATE:		June 3, 1998

TO:		Stephanie Branson, President

FROM:	Paul O'Shea, Development Manager

SUBJECT:	TAHOMA PROJECT

The Tahoma region the company is interested in purchasing is characterized by a series of rivers, valleys, and forests creating a distinctive natural landscape. Settlement in the region has been in small, compact villages that are linked together with a system of farm to market roads. West Creek was incorporated in 1918 and has **19,000** residents; Grandfield in 1931 with **8,500** residents; Dunbar in 1948 with **7,800** residents; Wagoner in 1952 with **3,600** residents; and Overbrook in 1922 with **1,400** residents.

Development expansion has been on the increase with new large communities under way near Stillwater. Southern Manufacturing is planning an operation nearby. Grandfield and Dunbar have recently extended their municipal boundaries through annexation. The Coleman Development Corporation is situated to play a major role in the future development and expansion of this region.

XX:Ch 03, Ex 01

Text that has already been keyed in a document can be made bold by selecting the text first and then using the Bold button on the Formatting toolbar, or the shortcut command, Ctrl + B. In chapter 2 you learned various methods for selecting text with either the mouse or the keyboard. For a review of how to select text, please refer to chapter 2.

exercise 2

Bolding Previously Keyed Text

1. Open Ch 03, Ex 01.
2. Save the memo with Save As and name it Ch 03, Ex 02.
3. With Ch 03, Ex 02 displayed, bold the words *West Creek* in the first paragraph by completing the following steps:
   a. Select *West Creek*. (Do this with either the mouse or the keyboard.)
   b. Click the Bold button on the Formatting toolbar.
4. Bold *Grandfield* in the first paragraph of the memo by positioning the insertion point on any letter in *Grandfield* and then clicking the Bold button on the Formatting toolbar.
5. Bold the following text in the memo:
   a. *Grandfield* (in the second paragraph)
   b. *Dunbar* (in the first and second paragraph)
   c. *Wagoner*
   d. *Overbrook*
   e. *Stillwater* (in the second paragraph)
   f. The heading *DATE:*. (When bold is applied to *DATE:*, *June 3, 1998* is moved to the right and is no longer aligned with the other text after headings. To realign *June 3, 1998* after *DATE:*, position the insertion point immediately left of the *J* in *June*, and then press the Backspace key.)
   g. The heading *TO:*.
   h. The heading *FROM:*.
   i. The heading *SUBJECT:*.
6. Change the document name after your initials from Ch 03, Ex 01 to Ch 03, Ex 02.
7. Save the memo again with the same name (Ch 03, Ex 02).
8. Print and then close Ch 03, Ex 02.

To remove bolding from text, select the text containing the bold formatting, and then click the Bold button on the Formatting toolbar, or press Ctrl + B. You can remove *all* character formatting from selected text by pressing Ctrl + spacebar. This command removes all character formatting that has been applied to the selected text. For this reason, you may want to remove bold formatting with the Bold button on the Formatting toolbar or Ctrl + B.

exercise 3

Removing Bold Formatting from Text

1. Open Ch 03, Ex 02.
2. Save the memo with Save As and name it Ch 03, Ex 03.
3. Remove bold from the heading *DATE:* by completing the following steps:
   a. Position the insertion point on any character in the word *DATE:*.
   b. Click the Bold button on the Formatting toolbar or press Ctrl + B. (You may need to realign *June 3, 1998* after *DATE:*.)
4. Complete steps similar to those in 3 to remove bold formatting from the headings *TO:*, *FROM:*, and *SUBJECT:*.
5. Change the document name after your initials from Ch 03, Ex 02 to Ch 03, Ex 03.
6. Save the memo again with the same name (Ch 03, Ex 03).
7. Print and then close Ch 03, Ex 03.

Italicizing Text

Word's italics feature can be used in documents to emphasize specific text such as the names of published works. Text can be italicized using the Italic button on the Formatting toolbar or the shortcut command, Ctrl + I. Text identified with italics will appear in italics in the document screen.

Italic

exercise 4

Italicizing Text as It Is Keyed

1. At a clear document screen, key the text shown in figure 3.2. Italicize the text shown as it is being keyed by completing the following steps:
   a. Press Ctrl + I.
   b. Key the text.
   c. Press Ctrl + I.
2. Save the document and name it Ch 03, Ex 04.
3. Print and then close Ch 03, Ex 04.

3.2

Exercise 4

Arvelo, Carlos J. (1996). *Communications for the 90's* (pp. 89 -92). Newark, NJ: Orion Publishing.

Creson, Marla S. (1997). *Business Documents.* Montreal, Quebec, Canada: St. Jean Press.

Dresslor, Donald A. and Richardson, Jacob C. (1997). *Communicating in Business* (pp. 5-18). Baltimore, MD: D&D Publishing.

Gilliardi, Terry M. (1998). *Practical Communications.* Los Angeles, CA: Western Shores Publishing House.

Text that has already been keyed in a document can be italicized by selecting the text first. You can italicize a single word by positioning the insertion point on any letter of the word (make sure the letter is not selected) and then clicking the Italic button on the Formatting toolbar or pressing Ctrl + I.

exercise 5

Italicizing Previously Keyed Text

1. Open the document named Bibliography from your student data disk.
2. Save the document with Save As and name it Ch 03, Ex 05.
3. Select and italicize the title, *The Art of Communicating*, by completing the following steps:
   a. Select *The Art of Communicating*. (For a review of how to select text, please refer to chapter 2.)
   b. Click the Italic button on the Formatting toolbar.
4. Select and italicize the following titles in the document:
   a. *Fundamentals of Written Communications* in the second paragraph.
   b. *A Resource Guide to Business Documents* in the third paragraph.
   c. *Improving Business Communications* in the fourth paragraph.
5. Save the document again with the same name (Ch 03, Ex 05).
6. Print and then close Ch 03, Ex 05.

Underlining Text

Text can be underlined using the Underline button on the Formatting toolbar or the shortcut command, Ctrl + U.

Underline

exercise 6

Underlining Text as It Is Keyed

1. At a clear document screen, key the text shown in figure 3.3. Underline the text shown as it is being keyed by completing the following steps:
   a. Press Ctrl + U.
   b. Key the text.
   c. Press Ctrl + U.
2. Save the document and name it Ch 03, Ex 06.
3. Print and then close Ch 03, Ex 06.

Exercise 6

Benjamin, Phoebe A. (1996). Creative Communications. Salt Lake City, UT: Purcell & Gibbs Publishing.

Crosby, Gene G. (1996). Business Communications: Theory and Application. Albany, NY: Northeastern Publishing, Inc.

Ewing, Stanley K. (1997). Writing at the Word Processor. New Orleans, LA: Robicheaux Publishing House.

Laramore, Jamie C. (1998). Adding Emphasis to Business Documents. San Diego, CA: Westside Publishers.

Text that has already been keyed in a document can be underlined by selecting the text first and then clicking the Underline button on the Formatting toolbar or pressing Ctrl + U. You can underline a single word by positioning the insertion point on any letter of the word (make sure the letter is not selected) and then clicking the Underline button on the Formatting toolbar or pressing Ctrl + U.

exercise 7

Underlining Previously Keyed Text

1. Open Ch 03, Ex 05.
2. Save the document with Save As and name it Ch 03, Ex 07.
3. Remove the italics from the book titles. To do this, select a title, and then click the Italic button on the Formatting toolbar or press Ctrl + I.
4. Select and underline the title *The Art of Communicating*, by completing the following steps:
   a. Select *The Art of Communicating*.
   b. Click the Underline button on the Formatting toolbar.
5. Select and underline the following titles in the document:
   a. *Fundamentals of Written Communications* in the second paragraph.
   b. *A Resource Guide to Business Documents* in the third paragraph.
   c. *Improving Business Communications* in the fourth paragraph.
6. Save the document again with the same name (Ch 03, Ex 07).
7. Print and then close Ch 03, Ex 07.

The Underline button on the Formatting toolbar and the shortcut command, Ctrl + U, underline words, spaces between words, and spaces created with the Tab key. If you want just words underlined, use the shortcut command, Ctrl + Shift + W. Use this command either as you are keying text or on selected text.

exercise 8

Underlining Words but Not Spaces in a Document

1. Open Notice 01. This document is located on your student data disk.
2. Save the document with Save As and name it Ch 03, Ex 08.
3. Select and underline the words *as soon as possible* in the first paragraph by completing the following steps:
   a. Select *as soon as possible* in the first paragraph (do not include the exclamation point at the end of the sentence).
   b. Press Ctrl + Shift + W.
4. Select and underline the following text in the document (use Ctrl + Shift + W; only the words will be underlined, not the spaces between words):
   a. *a thousand toys* in the second paragraph.
   b. *Bring your appetite* in the third paragraph.
   c. *fun-filled evening with your family* in the fourth paragraph.
5. Save the document again with the same name (Ch 03, Ex 08).
6. Print and then close Ch 03, Ex 08.

Double Underlining

Text can be formatted with double underlining. To double underline text, use the shortcut command, Ctrl + Shift + D. There is no button on the Formatting toolbar for double underlining.

exercise 9

Double Underlining Text in a Document

1. Open Numbers. This document is located on your student data disk.
2. Save the document with Save As and name it Ch 03, Ex 09.
3. Select and underline the number *214.98* in the first column.
4. Select and underline the number *159.88* in the second column.
5. Select and double underline the total *751.88* by completing the following steps:
   a. Select *751.88*.
   b. Press Ctrl + Shift + D.
6. Select and double underline the total *744.76*.
7. Save the document again with the same name (Ch 03, Ex 09).
8. Print and then close Ch 03, Ex 09.

Changing the Case of Letters

With Word's Change Case feature, you can change the case of selected text. Change the case of selected text at the Change Case dialog box or with the shortcut command, Shift + F3. To change the case of selected text, click Format, then Change Case. At the Change Case dialog box, shown in figure 3.4, click the desired style of case, and then click OK or press Enter.

figure 3.4

Change Case Dialog Box

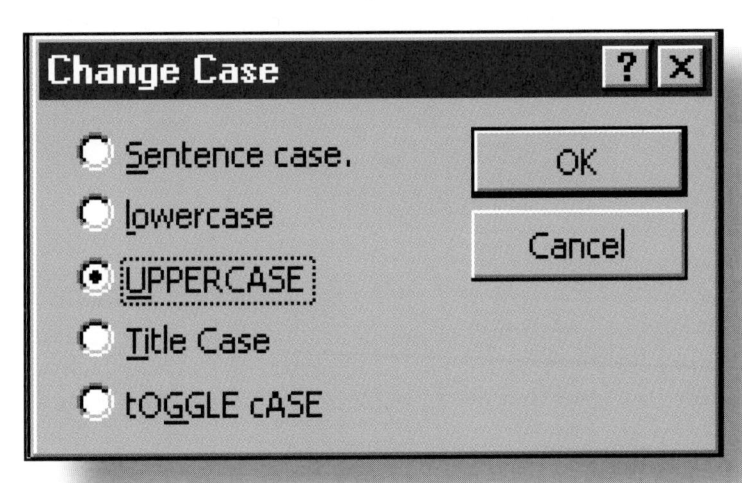

If you choose the *Sentence case.* option from the Change Case dialog box, selected text displays with the first letter of the sentence in an uppercase letter and the remaining letters in lowercase. The *lowercase* option changes selected text to all lowercase letters. Choose *UPPERCASE* if you want all selected letters to change to uppercase. The *Title Case* option changes the first letter of each selected word to uppercase. The last option, *tOGGLE cASE* causes selected lowercase letters to change to uppercase and selected uppercase letters to change to lowercase.

The shortcut command, Shift + F3, can also be used to change the case of selected text. Each time you press Shift + F3, the selected text reflects the changes. The changes match three options at the Change Case dialog box—Sentence case., lowercase, and UPPERCASE. Continue pressing Shift + F3 until the selected text displays with the desired cases and then deselect the text.

exercise 10

Changing Case

1. Open Report 01. This document is located on your student data disk.
2. Save the document with Save As and name it Ch 03, Ex 10.
3. Select and bold the title, DESKTOP PUBLISHING.
4. Change the case of the heading, *Defining Desktop Publishing*, to uppercase letters by completing the following steps:
   a. Select *Defining Desktop Publishing*.
   b. Click Format, then Change Case.
   c. At the Change Case dialog box, click UPPERCASE.
   d. Click OK or press Enter.
5. Change the case of the heading, *Initiating the Desktop Publishing Process* (located toward the top of the second page), to uppercase letters by completing the following steps:
   a. Select *Initiating the Desktop Publishing Process.*
   b. Press Shift + F3 (until the heading displays in all uppercase letters).
6. Select the heading, *Planning the Publication* (located near the middle of the second page), and change the case to all uppercase letters.
7. Select the heading, *Creating the Content* (located near the middle of the third page), and change the case to all uppercase letters.
8. Save the document again with the same name (Ch 03, Ex 10).
9. Print and then close Ch 03, Ex 10.

Using Help

Word's Help feature is an on-screen reference manual containing information about all Word features and commands. Access the Help feature with options from the Help drop-down menu or with the Office Assistant.

Using the Help Drop-Down Menu

Access information about Word by clicking the Help option on the Menu bar and then clicking Contents and Index at the drop-down menu. This displays the Help Topics dialog box shown in figure 3.5.

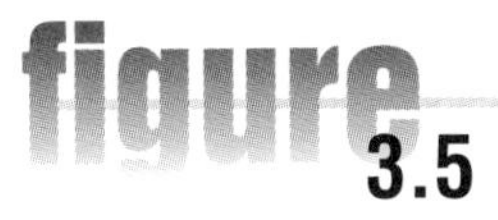

3.5 Help Topics Dialog Box

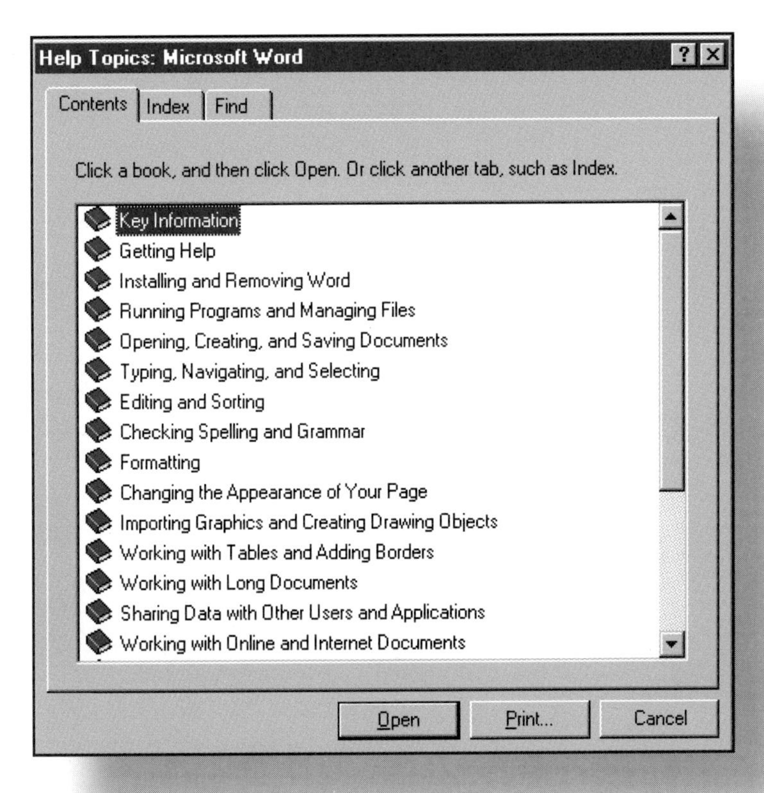

The Help Topics dialog box displays a variety of categories, each preceded by the icon of a closed book. Most of these categories contain additional categories. To display these additional categories, double-click a category. This causes the closed book icon to change to an open book icon and the additional categories to display below the selected category. Some of these additional categories may be preceded by an icon containing a question mark. If you choose one of these categories, Word will display a help screen containing information about the topic. Some of these screens may display with text in a yellow box or icons representing features or buttons. Move the arrow pointer to one of these yellow boxes (the pointer turns into a hand) and then click the left mouse button. This causes information about the topic to display on the screen. Move the arrow pointer to an icon representing a feature or button (the pointer turns into a hand), click the left mouse button, and an explanation of the feature or a definition of the button displays in the screen.

exercise 11

Using Help to Read about Formatting Characters

1. At a blank screen, use Word's Help feature to read information about bolding characters by completing the following steps:
   a. Click Help, then Contents and Index.
   b. At the Help Topics dialog box, make sure the Contents tab is selected. (If it is not, position the arrow pointer on the Contents tab at the top of the dialog box, and then click the left mouse button.)
   c. Position the arrow pointer on *Formatting* and then double-click the left mouse button.
   d. From the list of additional categories that displays, double-click *Formatting Characters*.
   e. From the next list of topics, double-click *Apply bold formatting to text or numbers*.
   f. Read the information displayed in the yellow box and then click the button that displays immediately preceding the text *Show me*. (This button contains the image of an arrow pointing up and to the left.)
   g. After Word shows you where the Bold button is on the Formatting toolbar and reading the information presented in the yellow box, click anywhere in the document screen.
2. Use Word's Help feature to read information about underlining characters by completing the following steps:
   a. Click Help, then Contents and Index.
   b. At the Help Topics dialog box, make sure the Contents tab is selected. (If it is not, position the arrow pointer on the Contents tab at the top of the dialog box, and then click the left mouse button.)
   c. Position the arrow pointer on *Formatting* and then double-click the left mouse button.
   d. From the list of additional categories that displays, double-click *Formatting Characters*.
   e. From the next list of topics, double-click *Underline text or numbers*.
   f. Read the information displayed in the yellow box and then click the button that displays immediately preceding the text *Show me*.
   g. After Word shows you where the Underline button is on the Formatting toolbar, click anywhere in the document screen.

Using the Index

With the Index tab selected at the Help Topics dialog box, a list of topics displays in alphabetical order. Key the first few letters of the topic you want to display and then double-click the desired topic. You can also click the desired topic once and then click Display at the bottom of the dialog box. When you choose a topic, another dialog box may display with a list of additional topics. Continue choosing topics until the specific information you desire is displayed.

When Help displays information about a particular feature, buttons display at the top of the yellow box. The Options button can be used to print a copy of the help topic. To do this, click Options, then click Print Topic. At the Print dialog box, click OK to send the information to the printer.

exercise 12

Using Help to Read and Print Information about Selecting Text

1. At a blank screen, use Word's Help feature to read and print information about selecting text using the mouse by completing the following steps:
   a. Click Help, then Contents and Index.
   b. At the Help Topics dialog box, click the Index tab at the top of the dialog box.
   c. Key **sel** in the text box below the *Type the first few letters of the word you're looking for* option.
   d. Double-click the option *selecting text and graphics.*
   e. At the next dialog box, double-click *Select text and graphics by using the mouse.*
   f. Read the information that displays in the yellow box at the right side of the screen. (To read all the information, you will need to scroll down the screen.)
2. After reading the information in the yellow box, print the information by completing the following steps:
   a. Click Options, then Print Topic.
   b. At the Print dialog box, click OK.
3. Close the yellow box by clicking the Close button in the upper right corner of the box (the button containing the X).

Finding Special Words or Phrases

At the Help Topics dialog box with the Find tab selected, you can search for specific words or phrases in help topics rather than searching for information by category. The first time you use this feature, Windows must create a list containing every word from the help files. Before using this feature, please check with your instructor.

Getting Help from the Office Assistant

The Office Assistant will provide information about specific topics. To get help using the Office Assistant, click the blue bar at the top of the Office Assistant box or click Help, then Microsoft Word Help. This causes a box to display above the Office Assistant as shown in figure 3.6.

figure 3.6 **Office Assistant Help Box**

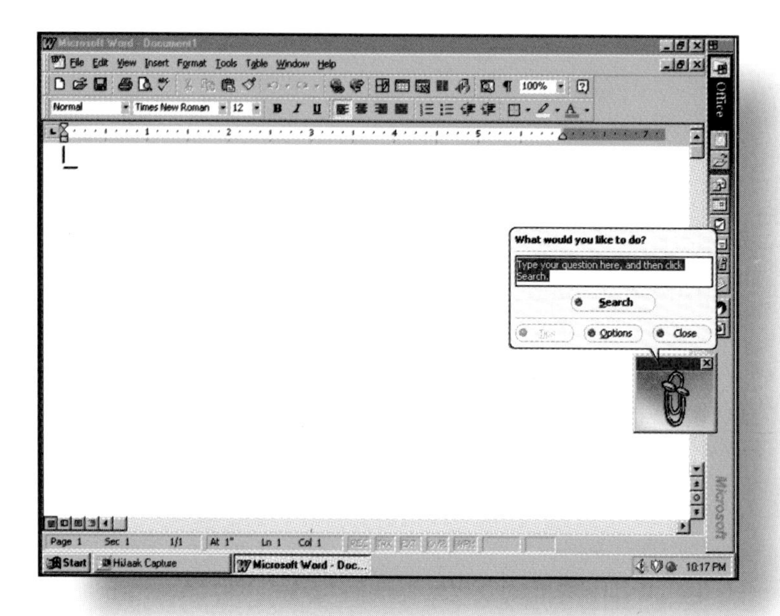

When the help box displays above the Office Assistant, the text *Type your question here, and then click Search* displays in the text box below the question *What would you like to do?* This text is already selected, so key a question about a specific Word feature, and then click the Search button. The Office Assistant will display a list of related topics. At this list, click the desired topic and information will display in a yellow dialog box. After reading the information, click the Close button located in the upper right side of the yellow dialog box.

exercise 13

Using the Office Assistant to Read Information on Saving Documents

1. At a blank screen, use the Help feature to read information about saving documents by completing the following steps:
   a. Click the blue bar located at the top of the Office Assistant box.
   b. At the yellow box that displays above the Office Assistant, key **How do I keep a previous version of a document when I save?**
   c. Click the Search button.
   d. At the list that displays in the yellow box, click *Save a document*.
   e. At the yellow dialog box that displays, read the information presented on saving documents. Be sure to scroll to the end of the document.
   f. After reading the information, click *Save a copy of a document* that displays toward the end of the yellow box in the *What do you want to do?* section. (When you position the arrow pointer on the topic, the pointer turns into a hand.)
   g. Read the information about saving a copy of a document and then click the Back button located at the top of the dialog box. (This takes you back to the information on saving documents.)
   h. Scroll to the end of the text in the yellow box and then click *Save all open documents at the same time* in the *What do you want to do?* section.
   i. Read the information displayed and then click Back.
2. Click the Close button in the upper right corner of the dialog box (the one containing the X).

Using Additional Help Features

If you have been a WordPerfect user and would like information on how to carry out a command in Word, click Help, then WordPerfect Help. The last option, About Microsoft Word, displays information such as the release date, license number, and system information. You can also display information about Microsoft's technical support.

Using ScreenTips

Word includes a ScreenTips feature that is available in every dialog box and displays as a button containing a question mark. This button displays in the upper right corner of dialog boxes. To use the ScreenTips feature, click the ScreenTips button, and then click an item in the dialog box. Word will display an explanation about the particular item.

ScreenTips

exercise 14

Using ScreenTips

1. At a blank screen, read information about Word by completing the following steps:
   a. Click Help, then About Microsoft Word.
   b. At the About Microsoft Word dialog box, click System Info.
   c. At the Microsoft System Info dialog box, read the information, and then click the Close button. (This button is located in the upper right corner of the dialog box and contains an X.)
   d. At the About Microsoft Word dialog box, click Tech Support.
   e. At the Help Topics: Technical Support dialog box with the Contents tab selected, look at the information, and then click the Index tab.
   f. After looking at information in the Help Topics: Technical Support dialog box with the Index tab selected, click the Find tab.
   g. Read the information in the Find Setup Wizard dialog box and then click the Cancel button.
   h. At the Help Topics: Technical Support dialog box, click the Cancel button.
   i. At the About Microsoft Word dialog box, click OK.
2. Read information about specific items in the Open dialog box by completing the following steps:
   a. Display the Open dialog box by clicking the Open button on the Standard toolbar.
   b. Click the ScreenTips button. (This button is located in the upper right corner of the dialog box and contains a question mark.)
   c. Move the arrow pointer (displays with a question mark attached) anywhere in the Look in: text box and then click the left mouse button. (This causes a box to display containing information about looking in different drives.)
   d. Click the ScreenTips button and then click anywhere in the File name: text box.
   e. Close the Open dialog box.

chapter summary

- To key text in all uppercase letters, press the Caps Lock key. Press Caps Lock again to deactivate the uppercase feature.
- The default or preset tab stops are set every 0.5 inch from the left margin. Press the Tab key to indent text 0.5 inch.
- Text can be bolded, italicized, and underlined with buttons on the Formatting toolbar or with shortcut commands. Do this as text is keyed or apply the formatting later by selecting the text and then choosing the desired formatting.
- Text can be underlined without underlining the spaces between the words with the shortcut command Ctrl + Shift + W.
- Double underline text with the shortcut command Ctrl + Shift + D.
- You can remove all character formatting from selected text by pressing Ctrl + spacebar.
- Change the case of selected text at the Change Case dialog box or with the shortcut command Shift + F3. You can choose to change text from/to uppercase/lowercase.
- Word's Help feature is an on-screen reference manual containing information about all Word features and commands. The Help Topics dialog box contains three tabs: Contents, Index, and Find. Use these tabs to read about and print specific features or commands.
- The Office Assistant can provide help. To use the Office Assistant, click the blue bar at the top of the Office Assistant box, key a question related to a specific topic, and then click the Search button.
- Use the ScreenTips button in any dialog box to read information about specific items in the dialog box.

commands review

	Mouse (Formatting Toolbar)	**Keyboard**
Bold	Click the B	CTRL + B
Italics	Click the I	CTRL + I
Underline (including spaces)	Click the U	CTRL + U
Underline (not including spaces)		CTRL + SHIFT + W
Double underline		CTRL + SHIFT + D
Remove all character formatting from selected text		CTRL + SPACE
	Mouse (Menu bar)	**Keyboard**
Change Case	Click Format, Change Case	SHIFT + F3
Uppercase function		CAPS LOCK
Help Topics dialog box	Click Help, Contents, and Index	

check your understanding

Completion: In the space provided at the right, indicate the correct term, command, or number.

1. This is the shortcut command to bold text. ________________
2. This is the shortcut command to underline text. ________________
3. This is the shortcut command to double underline text. ________________
4. This command removes all character formatting from selected text. ________________
5. Change the case of selected text at the Change Case dialog box or with this shortcut command. ________________
6. Remove underlining only from selected text with this shortcut command. ________________
7. Press this key to indent text to the next tab stop. ________________
8. Click here and the Office Assistant will display a yellow box containing the question *What would you like to do?* ________________
9. This is the name of the button in any dialog box that can be used to display information about specific items in the dialog box. ________________
10. Click this tab at the Help Topics dialog box to display an alphabetic list of Word topics. ________________

skill assessments

Assessment 1

1. At a clear document screen, key the memo shown in figure 3.7. Bold and underline the text as shown.
2. Save the memo and name it Ch 03, SA 01.
3. Print and then close Ch 03, SA 01.

Figure 3.7 • Assessment 1

DATE: November 4, 1997

TO: Linda Schillar

FROM: Christy Edmonds

SUBJECT: DESKTOP PUBLISHING COURSE

After reviewing a number of desktop publishing textbooks, I have chosen Desktop Publishing Business Documents for use in **OT 223, Desktop Publishing**. The bookstore manager has ordered the book for next semester.

The class was to be held in **Room 154**. Due to computer requirements, the class has been moved to **Room 106**. The classroom can accommodate 25 people. Therefore, the class enrollment has been changed from 30 to 25.

XX:Ch 03, SA 01

Assessment 2

1. Open Memo 01. This document is located on your student data disk.
2. Save the memo with Save As and name it Ch 03, SA 02.
3. Make the following changes:
   a. Select the book title, *The ABC's of Business Communications*, remove the underlining, and then add italics.
   b. Select the book title, *Communications for the Business Office*, remove the underlining, and then add italics.
   c. Select the book title, *Basics of Business Communications*, remove the underlining, and then add italics.
   d. Select the book title, *Communicating with Style*, remove the underlining, and then add italics.
   e. Select and bold the headings *DATE:*, *TO:*, *FROM:*, and *SUBJECT:*. (If necessary, realign the date, *October 26, 1998*, after *DATE:*.)
   f. Insert your initials at the end of the document where you see the "XX." Change the document name after your initials from Memo 01 to Ch 03, SA 02.
4. Save the document again with the same name (Ch 03, SA 02).
5. Print and then close Ch 03, SA 02.

Assessment 3

1. Open Ch 03, SA 01.
2. Save the document with Save As and name it Ch 03, SA 03.
3. Make the following changes:
   a. Remove the bold and underline codes from the text.
   b. Select and italicize the book title, *Desktop Publishing Business Documents.*
   c. Select and double underline *Room 154* and *Room 106*.
   d. Select and bold the two occurrences of the number 25 in the second paragraph and the number 30 in the second paragraph.
   e. Change the document name after your initials from Ch 03, SA 01 to Ch 03, SA 03.
4. Save the document again with the same name (Ch 03, SA 03).
5. Print and then close Ch 03, SA 03.

Assessment 4

1. Open Notice 01. This document is located on your student data disk.
2. Save the document with Save As and name it Ch 03, SA 04.
3. Make the following changes:
   a. Select the title, EMERALD HEIGHTS ELEMENTARY SCHOOL CARNIVAL, and then change the case to Title Case at the Change Case dialog box.
   b. Select *Friday, April* (in the first paragraph) and change the case to uppercase.
   c. Select *a thousand toys* (in the second paragraph) and change the case to uppercase.
   d. Select *Bring your appetite* (in the third paragraph) and change the case to uppercase.
4. Save the document again with the same name (Ch 03, SA 04).
5. Print and then close Ch 03, SA 04.

chapter FOUR

Formatting Paragraphs

PERFORMANCE OBJECTIVES

Upon successful completion of chapter 4, you will be able to:

- **Display nonprinting characters.**
- **Change the alignment of text in paragraphs.**
- **Indent text in paragraphs.**
- **Create numbered and bulleted paragraphs.**
- **Change line spacing.**

In Word, a paragraph is any amount of text followed by a paragraph mark. A paragraph mark is inserted in a document each time the Enter key is pressed. By default, this paragraph mark is not visible. When changes are made to a paragraph, the formatting changes are inserted in the paragraph mark. If the paragraph mark is deleted, the formatting in the mark is eliminated and the text returns to the default.

Displaying Nonprinting Characters

When you begin formatting text by paragraph, you may find it useful to display some nonprinting characters. As mentioned earlier, Word inserts paragraph formatting into the paragraph mark. If you want to remove paragraph formatting from text, delete the paragraph mark.

To display the paragraph mark and other nonprinting characters, use the Show/Hide ¶ button on the Standard toolbar, a shortcut command, or selections from the Options dialog box.

Show/Hide ¶

To display nonprinting characters using the Standard toolbar, click the Show/Hide ¶ button. You can also display nonprinting characters by pressing Shift + Ctrl + *. Either of these methods causes nonprinting characters to display as shown in the document in figure 4.1

To turn off the display of nonprinting characters, click the Show/Hide ¶ button on the Standard toolbar or press Shift + Ctrl + *.

figure 4.1 Document with Nonprinting Symbols Displayed

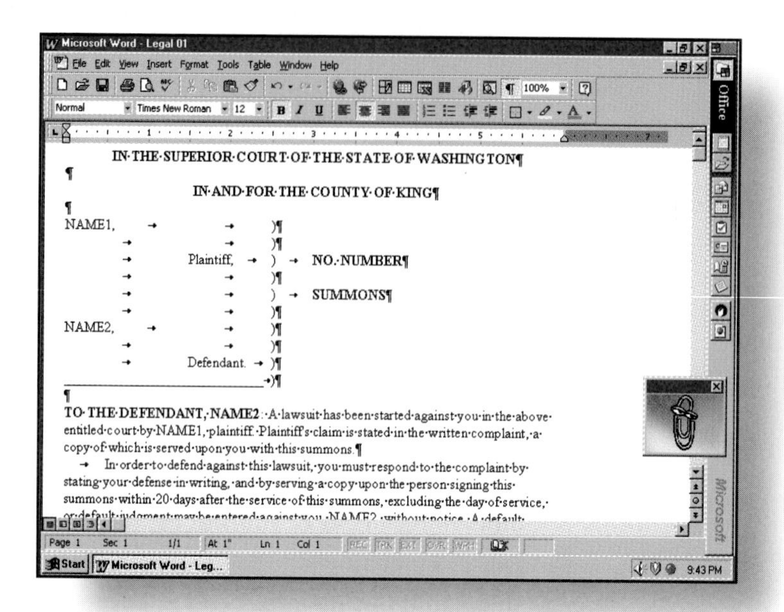

The Show/Hide ¶ button on the Standard toolbar and Shift + Ctrl + * turn on the display of all nonprinting characters. To control which nonprinting characters display, use the Options dialog box shown in figure 4.2. To display this dialog box, click Tools, then Options. (Make sure the View tab is displayed.)

figure 4.2 Options Dialog Box with View Tab Selected

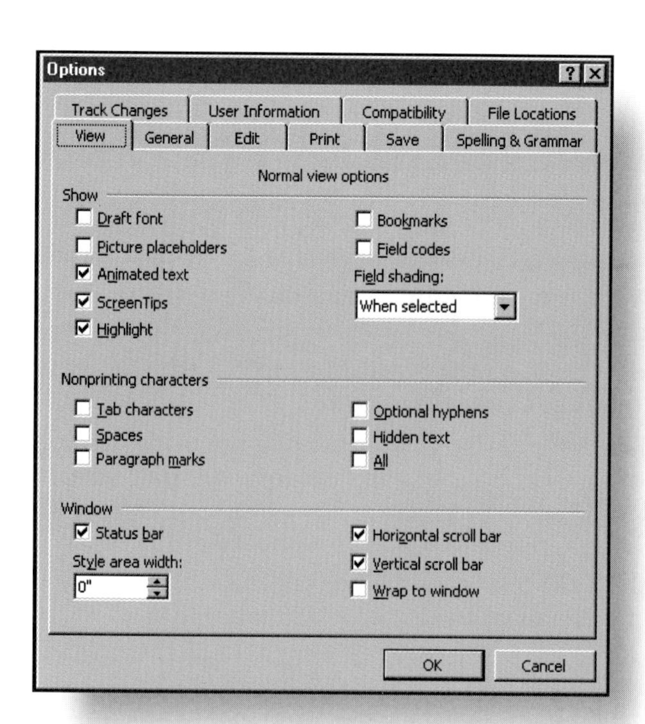

Choose options from the Nonprinting characters section of the Options dialog box to determine what nonprinting symbols you want displayed in the document. Click the All option if you want all nonprinting characters displayed. After making changes to the Options dialog box, click OK or press Enter.

exercise 1

Displaying Nonprinting Characters

1. Open Legal 01. This document is located on your student data disk.
2. Turn on the display of nonprinting characters by clicking the Show/Hide ¶ button on the Standard toolbar.
3. Scroll through the document to see how the document appears with nonprinting characters displayed.
4. Position the insertion point at the beginning of the document and then turn off the display of nonprinting characters by clicking the Show/Hide ¶ button on the Standard toolbar.
5. Turn on the display of only tab and paragraph marks by completing the following steps:
   a. Click Tools, then Options.
   b. At the Options dialog box, make sure the View tab is displayed.
   c. Click Tab characters and then Paragraph marks from the Nonprinting characters section of the Options dialog box.
   d. Click OK or press Enter.
6. Scroll through the document to see how the document appears with tab and paragraph marks visible.
7. Turn off the display of tab and paragraph marks by completing steps 5a through 5d.
8. Close Legal 01 without saving it.

Changing the Alignment of Text in Paragraphs

By default, paragraphs in a Word document are aligned at the left margin and ragged at the right margin. This default alignment can be changed with buttons on the Formatting toolbar or with shortcut commands. Text in a paragraph can be aligned at the left margin, between margins, at the right margin, or to the left and right margins. Figure 4.3 illustrates the different paragraph alignments.

figure 4.3

Paragraph Alignments

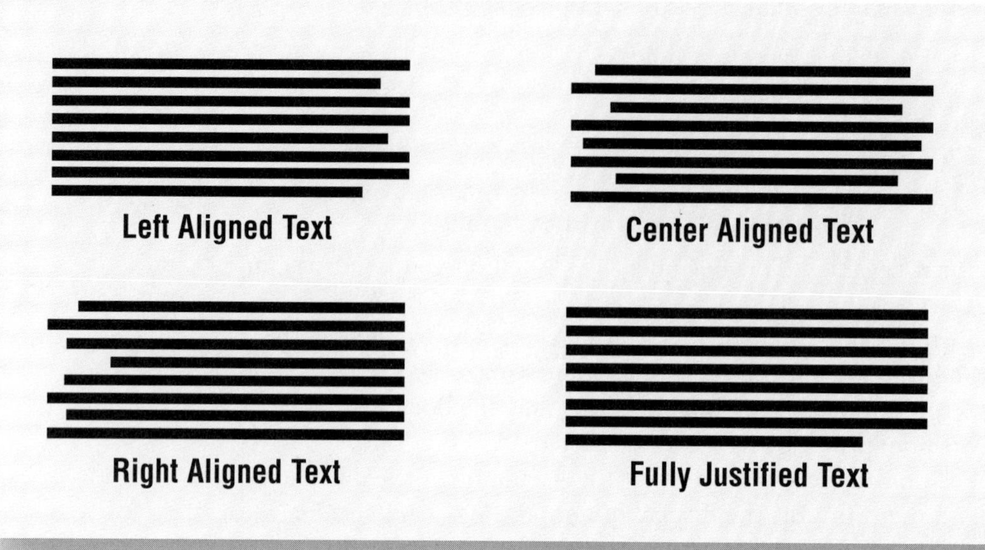

Use the buttons on the Formatting toolbar or the shortcut commands shown in figure 4.4 to change the alignment of text in paragraphs.

figure 4.4

Paragraph Alignment Buttons and Commands

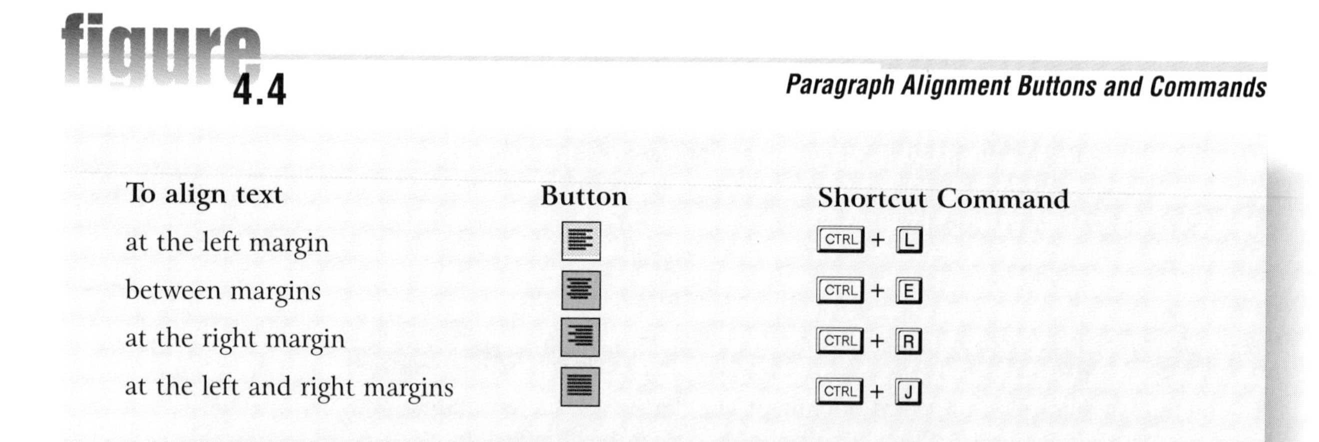

To align text	Button	Shortcut Command
at the left margin		CTRL + L
between margins		CTRL + E
at the right margin		CTRL + R
at the left and right margins		CTRL + J

You can change the alignment of text in paragraphs before you key the text or you can change the alignment of existing text. If you change the alignment before keying text, the alignment formatting is inserted in the paragraph mark. As you key text and press Enter, the paragraph formatting is continued. For example, if you press Ctrl + E to turn on center aligning, key text for the first paragraph and then press Enter, the center alignment formatting is still active and the insertion point displays in the middle of the left and right margins.

To return paragraph alignment to the default (left aligned), click the Left Align button on the Formatting toolbar or press Ctrl + L. You can also return all paragraph formatting to the default by pressing Ctrl + Q. This shortcut command returns all paragraph formatting (not just alignment) to the default settings.

Left Align

To change the alignment of existing text in a paragraph, position the insertion point anywhere within the paragraph. The entire paragraph does not have to be selected. To change the alignment of several adjacent paragraphs in a document, select a portion of the first paragraph through a portion of the last paragraph. Only a portion of the first and last paragraphs needs to be selected.

If you want to apply paragraph formatting to several paragraphs that are not adjacent, you can use the Repeat key, F4; the shortcut command, Ctrl + Y; or the Repeat option from the Edit drop-down menu. For example, if you apply center alignment to a paragraph and then want to repeat it for another paragraph, position the insertion anywhere in the next paragraph, and then press F4; press Ctrl + Y; or click Edit, then Repeat Paragraph Alignment.

exercise 2

Changing Paragraph Alignment to Center

1. At a clear document screen, key the text shown in figure 4.5.
2. After keying the text, select all the text and then turn on bold. (*Hint: You can quickly select the entire document with Ctrl + A; or position the arrow pointer in the invisible selection bar, hold down the Ctrl key, and then click the left mouse button.*)
3. With the entire document selected, change the alignment of paragraphs to center by pressing Ctrl + E.
4. Save the document and name it Ch 04, Ex 02.
5. Print and then close Ch 04, Ex 02.

figure 4.5

Exercise 2

OT 250, BUSINESS COMMUNICATIONS

Monday through Friday

8:00 a.m. to 8:50 a.m.

Room 106

exercise 3

Changing Paragraph Alignment to Justified

1. Open Para 02. This document is located on your student data disk.
2. Save the document with Save As and name it Ch 04, Ex 03.
3. Change the alignment of the text in paragraphs to justified by completing the following steps:
   a. Select the entire document.
   b. Click the Justify button on the Formatting toolbar.
4. Save the document again with the same name (Ch 04, Ex 03).
5. Print and then close Ch 04, Ex 03.

Justify

Changing Alignment at the Paragraph Dialog Box

Paragraph alignment can also be changed at the Paragraph dialog box shown in figure 4.6. To change the alignment of text in a paragraph, display the Paragraph dialog box by clicking Format, then Paragraph. At the Paragraph dialog box, click the down-pointing triangle at the right side of the Alignment text box. At the drop-down list that displays, click the desired alignment option and then click OK or press Enter.

Paragraph Dialog Box

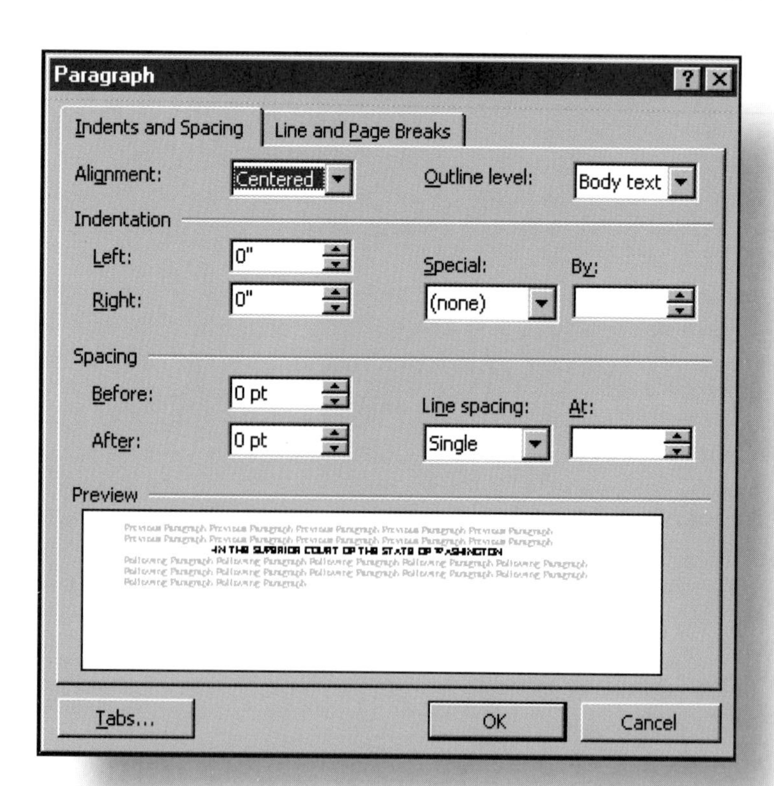

exercise 4

Changing Paragraph Alignment to Justified Using the Paragraph Dialog Box

1. Open Para 04. This document is located on your student data disk.
2. Save the document with Save As and name it Ch 04, Ex 04.
3. Change the alignment of text in paragraphs to justified using the Paragraph dialog box by completing the following steps:
   a. Select the entire document.
   b. Click *Format*, then *Paragraph*.
   c. At the Paragraph dialog box, click the down-pointing triangle at the right of the Alignment text box, and then click *Justified*.
   d. Click OK or press Enter.
4. Save the document again with the same name (Ch 04, Ex 04).
5. Print and then close Ch 04, Ex 04.

Using Shortcut Menus

Word provides shortcut menus that can be used to display commands related to the text or item of selected text or where the insertion point is positioned. Use shortcut menus to format documents. You learned to use a shortcut menu in chapter 1 to turn on and/or off the display of toolbars. You can use a shortcut menu to display the Paragraph dialog box shown in figure 4.6. To do this, you would complete the following steps:

1. Position the insertion point in the text that you want formatted with an option from the Paragraph dialog box.
2. Click the *right* button on the mouse. This causes a shortcut menu to display at the location of the insertion point as shown in figure 4.7.
3. Click *Paragraph* to display the Paragraph dialog box.
4. Make changes to the Paragraph dialog box as needed and then click OK or press Enter.

Shortcut Menu

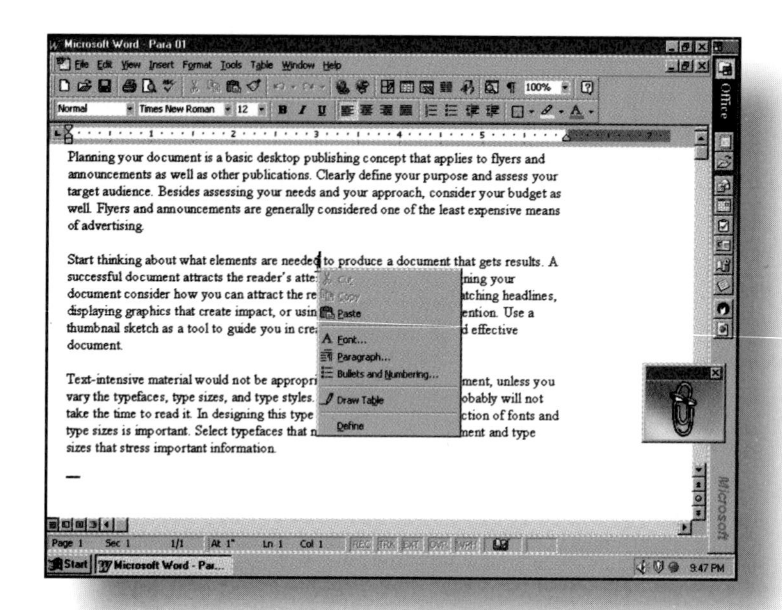

Some keyboards include a Shortcut Menu key located in the bottom row of the keyboard (to the right of the space bar—contains an image of a menu). When pressed, this key will display a shortcut menu with the Paragraph option.

exercise 5

Changing Paragraph Alignment to Right Using a Shortcut Menu

1. At a clear document screen, turn on the display of nonprinting characters.
2. Change the alignment of text to Right by completing the following steps:
   a. Position the I-beam pointer anywhere in the document screen and then click the *right* mouse button.
   b. At the shortcut menu that displays, click *Paragraph*.
   c. At the Paragraph dialog box, change the Alignment to *Right*.
   d. Click OK or press Enter.
3. Key the first line of text shown in figure 4.8 and then press Enter.
4. Key the remaining lines of text. (Each time you press Enter, the formatting from the previous paragraph is carried to the next paragraph.)
5. Select and then bold the entire document.
6. Save the document and name it Ch 04, Ex 05.
7. Print Ch 04, Ex 05.
8. Turn off the display of nonprinting characters.
9. Close Ch 04, Ex 05.

4.8 *Exercise 5*

Coleman Development Corporation
3451 Classen Boulevard
Oklahoma City, OK 76341
(801) 555-4500

Indenting Text in Paragraphs

By now you are familiar with the word wrap feature of Word which ends lines and wraps the insertion point to the next line. To indent text from the left margin, the left and right margin, or create numbered items, use indent buttons from the Formatting toolbar, shortcut commands, options from the Paragraph dialog box, or markers on the Ruler.

With markers on the Ruler you can indent text in a paragraph. The Ruler displays below the Formatting toolbar as shown in figure 4.9. The indent markers on the Ruler are identified in figure 4.9. (If the Ruler is not displayed, you can turn it on by clicking View, then Ruler.)

4.9 *Ruler and Indent Markers*

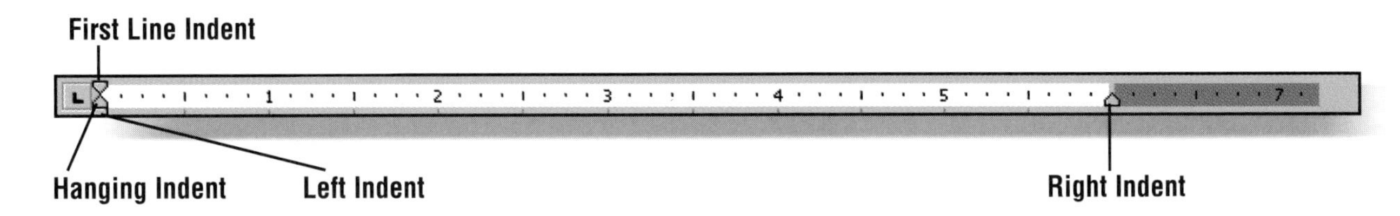

Indenting the First Line of Text in a Paragraph

When creating certain documents, you may want to indent the first line of a paragraph to identify where a new paragraph begins. You can indent the first line of a paragraph by pressing the Tab key, with an option from the Paragraph dialog box, or with the First Line Indent marker on the Ruler.

If you use the Tab key to indent the first line of a paragraph, the insertion point is indented to the first tab stop. By default, Word contains a tab stop every 0.5 inch. Therefore, if the insertion point is positioned at the left margin and you press the Tab key, the insertion point is moved 0.5 inch from the left margin.

You can also indent the first line of text in a paragraph with an option from the Paragraph dialog box shown in figure 4.6. To display this dialog box, click Format, then Paragraph. At the Paragraph dialog box, you can specify a measurement to which you want the text indented. Additionally, if you indent the first line of text in a paragraph with the Paragraph dialog box, each paragraph you key will have the first line of text indented. To indent the first line of text in a paragraph using the Paragraph dialog box, you would complete the following steps:

1. Click Format, then Paragraph.
2. At the Paragraph dialog box, click the down-pointing triangle to the right of the Special text box.
3. At the drop-down menu that displays, click *First line*.
4. Click OK or press Enter.

By default, Word indents the text in the first paragraph 0.5 inch. At the Paragraph dialog box, you can change the first indent measurement. To change the indent measurement, key the desired measurement in the By text box in the Paragraph dialog box.

exercise 6

Indenting the First Line of Paragraphs Using the Paragraph Dialog Box

1. Open Para 03. This document is located on your student data disk.
2. Save the document with Save As and name it Ch 04, Ex 06.
3. Indent the first line of each paragraph 0.3 inch by completing the following steps:
   a. Select the entire document.
   b. Click Format, then Paragraph.
   c. At the Paragraph dialog box, click the down-pointing triangle to the right of the Special text box.
   d. At the drop-down menu that displays, click *First line*.
   e. Click the down-pointing triangle to the right of the By text box until *0.3* displays.
   f. Click OK or press Enter.
4. Save the document again with the same name (Ch 04, Ex 06).
5. Print and then close Ch 04, Ex 06.

The first line of text in a paragraph can also be indented with the First Line Indent marker on the Ruler. The First Line Indent marker is identified in figure 4.9. To indent with this marker, position the arrow pointer on the First Line Indent marker, hold down the left mouse button, drag the marker to the desired location on the Ruler, and then release the mouse button.

Indenting the First Line of Paragraphs Using the Ruler

1. Open Para 04. This document is located on your student data disk.
2. Save the document with Save As and name it Ch 04, Ex 07.
3. Indent the first line of all paragraphs in the document approximately 0.5 inch by completing the following steps:
   a. Make sure the Ruler is displayed. (If not, click View, then Ruler.)
   b. Select the entire document.
   c. Position the arrow pointer on the First Line Indent marker on the Ruler.
   d. Hold down the left mouse button, drag the First Line Indent marker to the 0.5-inch mark on the Ruler, and then release the mouse button.
4. With the document still selected, change the paragraph alignment to justified.
5. Save the document again with the same name (Ch 04, Ex 07).
6. Print and then close Ch 04, Ex 07.

Indenting Text from the Left Margin

All lines of text in a paragraph can be indented to a tab stop or to a specific measurement from the left margin. All lines of text in a paragraph can be indented using a shortcut command, a button on the Formatting toolbar, an option from the Paragraph dialog box, or the Left Indent marker on the Ruler.

To indent all lines of text in a paragraph or selected paragraphs with a shortcut command, position the insertion point in the paragraph to be indented or select the paragraphs to be indented, and then press Ctrl + M. When you press Ctrl + M, text is indented to the first tab stop from the left margin. By default, this tab stop is 0.5 inch from the left margin. If you press Ctrl + M again, the text is indented to the next tab stop, which is 1.0 inch from the left margin by default.

You can also indent all lines of text in a paragraph or selected paragraphs by clicking the Increase Indent button on the Formatting toolbar. (This button is located toward the right side of the Formatting toolbar.) You can indent all lines of text in a paragraph to a specific measurement from the left margin using the Left option at the Paragraph dialog box. You can key a measurement in the Left text box, or you can click the up- or down-pointing triangles to the right of the Left text box to increase or decrease the left indent measurement.

Increase Indent

To indent all lines of text in a paragraph or selected paragraphs with the Ruler, position the arrow pointer on the Left Indent marker on the Ruler, hold down the left mouse button, drag the marker to the desired position on the Ruler, and then release the mouse button.

exercise 8

Indenting Text from the Left Margin

1. Open Memo 02. This document is located on your student data disk.
2. Save the document with Save As and name it Ch 04, Ex 08.
3. Indent the second paragraph in the document (containing the book title) to the first tab setting by completing the following steps:
   a. Position the insertion point anywhere in the second paragraph.
   b. Press Ctrl + M.
4. Indent the third paragraph by completing the following steps:
   a. Position the insertion point anywhere in the third paragraph.
   b. Click the Increase Indent button on the Formatting toolbar.
5. Indent the fourth paragraph by completing the following steps:
   a. Position the insertion point anywhere in the fourth paragraph.
   b. Click Format, then Paragraph.
   c. At the Paragraph dialog box, key **0.5** in the Left text box. (The **0**" measurement in the Left text box is automatically selected when you first display the Paragraph dialog box.)
   d. Click OK or press Enter.
6. Indent the fifth paragraph in the document by completing the following steps:
   a. Make sure the Ruler is displayed. (If not, click View, then Ruler.)
   b. Position the insertion point anywhere in the fifth paragraph.
   c. Position the arrow pointer on the Left Indent marker on the Ruler, hold down the left mouse button, drag the marker to the 0.5-inch mark on the Ruler, and then release the mouse button.
7. Save the document again with the same name (Ch 04, Ex 08).
8. Print and then close Ch 04, Ex 08.

Decreasing the Indent

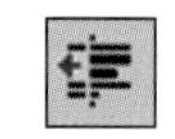

Decrease Indent

You can decrease the indent of text in a paragraph with the shortcut command, Ctrl + Shift + M, or with the Decrease Indent button on the Formatting toolbar. When you press Ctrl + Shift + M or click the Decrease Indent button on the Formatting toolbar, the lines of text in the paragraph or selected paragraphs are moved to the previous tab stop or the left margin. To decrease the indent using the Ruler, drag the Left Indent marker to the left on the Ruler. You can also decrease the left margin indent by decreasing the number in the Left text box at the Paragraph dialog box.

Indenting Text from the Left and Right Margins

Text in paragraphs can be indented from the left and the right margins with options at the Paragraph dialog box or with the Left Indent marker and the Right Indent marker on the Ruler. Indent text from the left and right margins for text that you want set off from other text in a document, such as a quotation. To indent text from the left and right margins, increase the measurement in the Left and Right text boxes at the Paragraph dialog box. To indent text from the left and right margins using the Ruler, drag the Left Indent marker and drag the Right Indent marker to the desired measurements on the Ruler.

exercise 9

Indenting Text from the Left and Right Margins

1. At a clear document screen, key the document shown in figure 4.10. Bold and center align the title as shown.
2. After keying the document, indent the third paragraph of the document from the left and right margins by completing the following steps:
   a. Make sure the Ruler is displayed. (If not, click View, then Ruler.)
   b. Position the insertion point anywhere in the third paragraph.
   c. Position the arrow pointer on the Left Indent marker on the Ruler, hold down the left mouse button, drag the marker to the 0.5-inch mark on the Ruler, and then release the mouse button.
   d. Position the arrow pointer on the Right Indent marker on the Ruler, hold down the left mouse button, drag the marker to the 5.5-inch mark on the Ruler, and then release the mouse button.
3. Indent the fifth paragraph in the document from the left and right margins by completing the following steps:
   a. Position the insertion point anywhere within the fifth paragraph.
   b. Click Format, then Paragraph.
   c. At the Paragraph dialog box with the Indents and Spacing tab selected, key **0.5** in the Left text box.
   d. Select the current measurement in the Right text box and then key **0.5**.
   e. Click OK or press Enter.
4. Select all the paragraphs in the document (excluding the title) and then change the paragraph alignment to justified.
5. Save the document and name it Ch 04, Ex 09.
6. Print and then close Ch 04, Ex 09.

Exercise 9

DESKTOP PUBLISHING

Desktop publishing is the use of a microcomputer-based system to produce publication materials that includes typeset or near-typeset quality text and graphics integrated on a page. These materials can include memos, correspondence, notices, fliers, posters, certificates, office forms, brochures, schedules, catalogues, reports, manuals, newsletters, newspapers, magazines, or books.

In her book, *Desktop Publishing Technology and Design*, Holly Yasui states:

What makes desktop publishing different from traditional publishing is that equipment small enough to fit on a person's desktop can provide all the resources needed to prepare and assemble pages.

In a later section of her book, Holly Yasui makes the following statement about desktop publishing technology:

In the graphic arts world, desktop publishing is considered a *prepress* technology, that is, the desktop publishing system itself is generally not used to produce the final multiple copies of a publication, but rather to produce masters for reproduction.

Creating a Hanging Paragraph

Hanging paragraphs such as bibliographic references shown in figure 4.11 can be created in a document. Hanging paragraphs are also useful when creating enumerated items or any text you want flagged or marked with a specific character. In a hanging paragraph, the first line of the paragraph remains at the left margin, while the remaining lines are indented to the first tab stop.

Hanging Paragraphs

Esterhaus, Sandra (1997). *Office Communications*. Vancouver, British Columbia, Canada: Frazier Valley Publishing House.

Hunter, Regina M. (1998). *International Communications* (pp. 102-108). Portland, OR: Columbia Press.

Hanging paragraphs can be created with the shortcut command, Ctrl + T, or with options from the Paragraph dialog box. To create a hanging paragraph or paragraphs using the shortcut command, position the insertion point in the paragraph to be hanging indented or select the paragraphs, and then press Ctrl + T.

To create a hanging paragraph or paragraphs using options from the Paragraph dialog box, position the insertion point in the paragraph to be hanging indented or select the paragraphs, and then click Format, then Paragraph. At the Paragraph dialog box, key the desired indent measurement in the Left text box. (You can also click the up-pointing triangle to the right of the Left text box to increase the indent measurement.) Click Special and then click *Hanging* at the drop-down menu.

exercise 10

Creating Hanging Paragraphs

1. Open Bibliography. This document is located on your student data disk.
2. Save the document with Save As and name it Ch 04, Ex 10.
3. Create a hanging indent for the first two paragraphs by completing the following steps:
   a. Select at least a portion of the first and second paragraphs.
   b. Press Ctrl + T.
4. Create a hanging indent for the third and fourth paragraphs by completing the following steps:
   a. Select at least a portion of the third and fourth paragraphs.
   b. Click Format, then Paragraph.
   c. At the Paragraph dialog box with the Indents and Spacing tab selected, click the down-pointing triangle at the right side of the Special text box (contains the word *(none)*).
   d. At the drop-down menu that displays, click *Hanging*.
   e. Click OK or press Enter.
5. Save the document again with the same name (Ch 04, Ex 10).
6. Print and then close Ch 04, Ex 10.

Creating Numbered and Bulleted Paragraphs

If you key **1.**, press the space bar, key a paragraph of text, and then press Enter, Word will hang indent the paragraphs approximately 0.25 inch from the left margin and also insert *2.* at the beginning of the next paragraph. This is part of Word's AutoFormat feature. (If this feature is not activated, you can turn it on by clicking Tools, then AutoCorrect. At the AutoCorrect dialog box, click the AutoFormat As You Type tab. Click in the Automatic numbered lists check box to insert a check mark, and then click OK.) Continue keying numbered items and Word will insert the next number in the list. To turn off numbering, press the Enter key twice or click the Numbering button on the Formatting toolbar. (You can also remove all paragraph formatting from a paragraph, including automatic numbering, by pressing Ctrl + Q.)

Numbering

If you press the Enter key twice between numbered paragraphs, the automatic number is removed. Key the next number in the list (and the period) followed by a space, key the paragraph of text, and then press Enter. Word will automatically hang indent the text approximately 0.25 inch from the left margin.

exercise 11

Creating Numbered Paragraphs

(Note: In this exercise and other exercises in the text, you will be required to create business letters. Please refer to Appendix C at the end of this text for the correct placement and spacing of a block-style and modified block-style business letter.)

1. At a clear document screen, key the text shown in figure 4.12 in an appropriate business letter format. When keying the numbered paragraphs, complete the following steps:
   a. Key **1.** and then press the space bar.
   b. Key the paragraph of text and then press the Enter key twice.
   c. Key **2.** and then press the space bar.
   d. Key the paragraph of text and then press the Enter key twice.
   e. Key **3.** and then press the space bar.
   f. Key the paragraph of text and then press the Enter key twice.
   g. Key the remaining text of the document.
2. Save the letter and name it Ch 04, Ex 11.
3. Print and then close Ch 04, Ex 11.

4.12

Exercise 11

May 27, 1998

Ms. Stephanie Branson
Coleman Development Corporation
3451 Classen Boulevard
Oklahoma City, OK 76341

Dear Ms. Branson:

The development summary for the Tahoma region was completed recently. It analyzes the economic and demographic outlook for the region for the next two decades. Three basic conclusions are reached in the summary:

1. Significant *quantitative* growth is headed in the direction of the Tahoma region, exceeding forecasts made in the recent past.

2. The growth that will be experienced in the Tahoma region has important *qualitative* potential, created by the types of jobs and personal income that will be added to the area's economic base.

3. To fully capture this qualitative potential, managers of the Tahoma region will need to utilize self-contained communities and other planned developments.

A community meeting has been planned for June 17, 1998, at 7:30 p.m. in the West Creek Community Center. Representatives from local cities are interested in the findings of the summary and will be attending this meeting.

Sincerely,

Dean Talmadge
Tahoma Regional Manager

XX:Ch 04, Ex 11

If you do not want automatic numbering in a document, turn the feature off at the AutoCorrect dialog box with the AutoFormat As You Type tab selected as shown in figure 4.13. To display this dialog box, click Tools, then AutoCorrect. At the AutoCorrect dialog box, click the AutoFormat As You Type tab. To turn off automatic numbering, remove the check mark from the option *Automatic numbered lists*.

figure 4.13 ***AutoCorrect Dialog Box with AutoFormat As You Type Tab Selected***

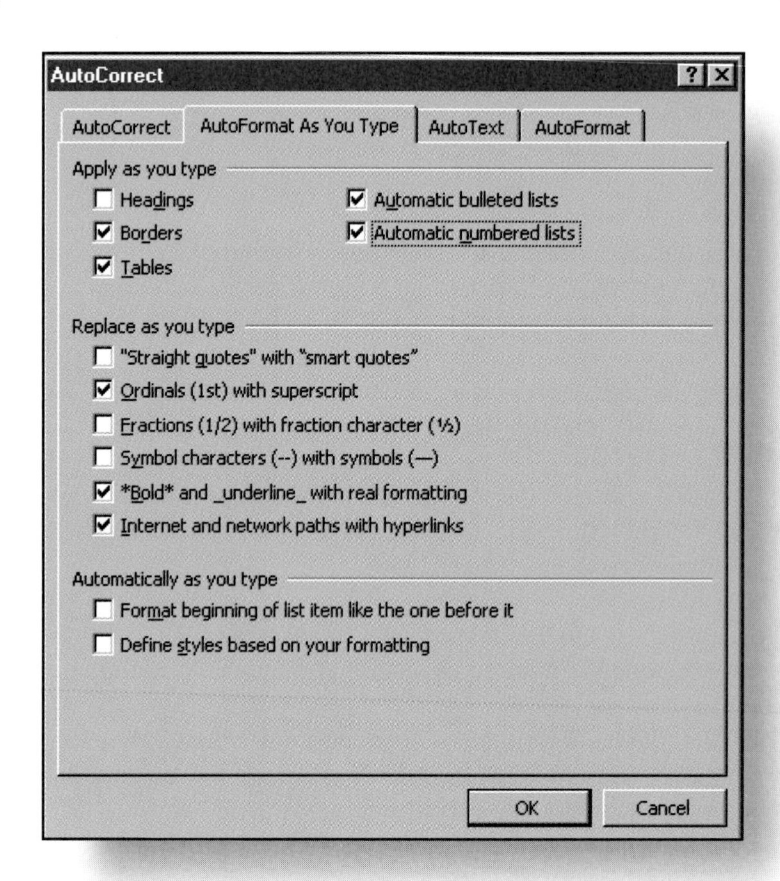

You can also automate the creation of numbered paragraphs with the Numbering button on the Formatting toolbar. To use this button, key the text (do not key the number) for each paragraph to be numbered, select the paragraphs to be numbered, and then click the Numbering button on the Formatting toolbar. Numbered paragraphs can be inserted or deleted from text.

exercise 12

Inserting Paragraph Numbering

1. Open Quiz. This document is located on your student data disk.
2. Save the document with Save As and name it Ch 04, Ex 12.
3. Insert paragraph numbering before all paragraphs in the document (except the title) by completing the following steps:
   a. Select all paragraphs in the document (except the title).
   b. Click the Numbering button on the Formatting toolbar.
4. Add the paragraph shown in figure 4.14 between paragraphs 5 and 6 by completing the following steps:
   a. Position the insertion point immediately to the right of the question mark at the end of the fifth paragraph.
   b. Press Enter.
   c. Key the paragraph shown in figure 4.14
5. Delete the second question (paragraph) by completing the following steps:
   a. Select the text of the second paragraph (you will not be able to select the number).
   b. Press the Delete key.
6. Save the document again with the same name (Ch 04, Ex 12).
7. Print and then close Ch 04, Ex 12.

figure 4.14

Exercise 12

Cellular mobile telephone service was offered for the first time in the 1980s. What role will this technology most likely play in the future?

In addition to automatically numbering paragraphs, Word's AutoFormat feature will create bulleted paragraphs. (If this feature is not activated, you can turn it on by clicking Tools, then AutoCorrect. At the AutoCorrect dialog box, click the AutoFormat As You Type tab. Click in the *Automatic bulleted lists* check box to insert a check mark and then click OK.) You can also create bulleted paragraphs with the Bullets button on the Formatting toolbar.

Bullets

Figure 4.15 shows an example of bulleted paragraphs. Bulleted lists with hanging indents are automatically created when a paragraph begins with *, o, >, -, or any symbol character. Key one of the symbols, press the space bar, key text, and then press Enter, and the AutoFormat feature inserts a bullet and indents the text following the bullet 0.25 inch. The type of bullet inserted depends on the type of character entered. For example, if you use the asterisk (*) symbol or lowercase O (o) symbol, a round bullet is inserted as shown in figure 4.15. If you use a hyphen (-) symbol, a square bullet is inserted. An arrow bullet is inserted if the greater than symbol (>) is used.

figure 4.15 *Bulleted Paragraphs*

- This is a paragraph preceded by a bullet. A bullet is used to indicate a list of items or topics.
- This is another paragraph preceded by a bullet. Bulleted paragraphs can be easily created by keying certain symbols before the text or with the Bullets button on the Formatting toolbar.

The automatic bulleting feature, like the numbering feature, can be turned off at the AutoCorrect dialog box with the AutoFormat As You Type tab selected. To display this dialog box, shown in figure 4.13, click Tools, then AutoCorrect. At the AutoCorrect dialog box, click the AutoFormat As You Type tab. To turn off automatic bulleting, remove the check mark from the *Automatic bulleted lists* option.

exercise 13

Creating Bullets

1. At a clear document screen, key the text shown in figure 4.16. Bold and center the title in uppercase letters as indicated. Create the bulleted paragraphs by completing the following steps:
   a. With the insertion point positioned at the left margin of the first paragraph to contain a bullet, key the greater than symbol (>).
   b. Press the space bar once.
   c. Key the text of the first bulleted paragraph (*What is the intent of the document?*).
   d. Press the Enter key once, then continue keying the text after the bullets.
2. After keying the last bulleted paragraph, press the Enter key twice (this turns off bullets), and then key the last paragraph shown in figure 4.16.
3. Save the document and name it Ch 04, Ex 13.
4. Print and then close Ch 04, Ex 13.

figure 4.16

Exercise 13

DESIGNING A DOCUMENT

A well-planned and relevant design sets one document apart from another. Just as people may be judged by their appearance, a publication may be judged by its design. Design also helps organize ideas so the reader can find information quickly and easily. Whether you are creating a business flyer, letterhead, or newsletter, anything you create will look more attractive, more professional, and more convincing if you take a little extra time to design it. When designing a document, you need to consider many factors:

- ➢ What is the intent of the document?
- ➢ Who is the intended audience?
- ➢ What is the feeling the document is meant to elicit?
- ➢ What is the most important information and how can it be emphasized?
- ➢ What different types of information are to be presented and how can these elements be distinguished and kept internally consistent?
- ➢ How much space is available?
- ➢ How will the document be distributed?

Answering these questions will help you determine the design and layout of your communication.

Bulleted paragraphs can also be created with the Bullets button on the Formatting toolbar. To create bulleted paragraphs using the Bullets button, key the text (do not key the bullet) of the paragraphs, select the paragraphs, and then click the Bullets button on the Formatting toolbar.

exercise 14

Inserting Bullets Using the Bullets Button

1. Open Quiz. This document is located on the student data disk.
2. Save the document with Save As and name it Ch 04, Ex 14.
3. Insert bullets before the quiz questions by completing the following steps:
   a. Select the text in the document (excluding the title and the blank line below the title).
   b. Click the Bullets button on the Formatting toolbar.
4. Save the document again with the same name (Ch 04, Ex 14).
5. Print and then close Ch 04, Ex 14.

In addition to the Bullets button on the Formatting toolbar, you can also use options from the Bullets and Numbering dialog box shown in figure 4.17 to number paragraphs or insert bullets. To display this dialog box, click Format, then Bullets and Numbering.

figure 4.17 ***Bullets and Numbering Dialog Box with Bulleted Tab Selected***

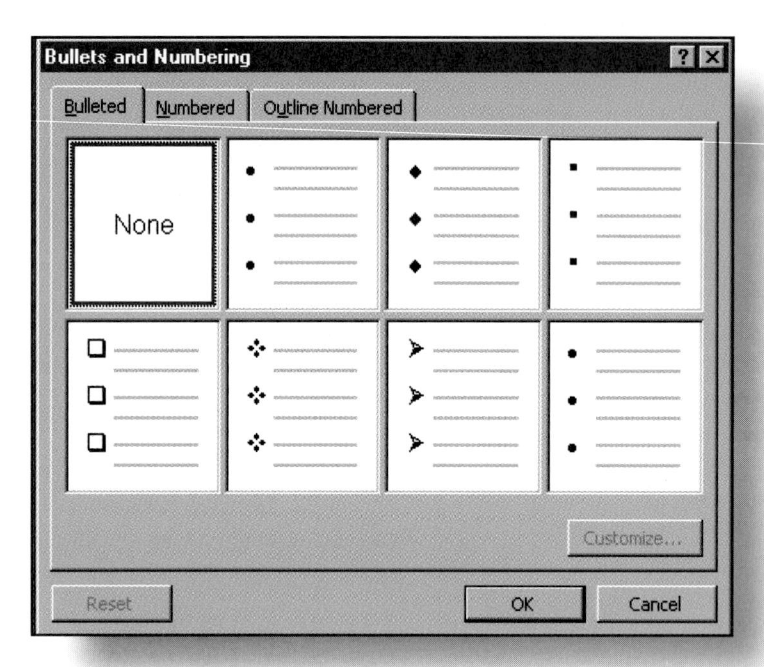

The Bullets and Numbering dialog box contains three tabs: Bulleted, Numbered, and Outline Numbered. Display the Bulleted tab if you want to insert bullets before selected paragraphs. Display the Numbered tab if you want to insert numbers before selected paragraphs. When you click Outline Numbered, the dialog box displays as shown in figure 4.18.

figure 4.18 *Bullets and Numbering Dialog Box with Outline Numbered Tab Displayed*

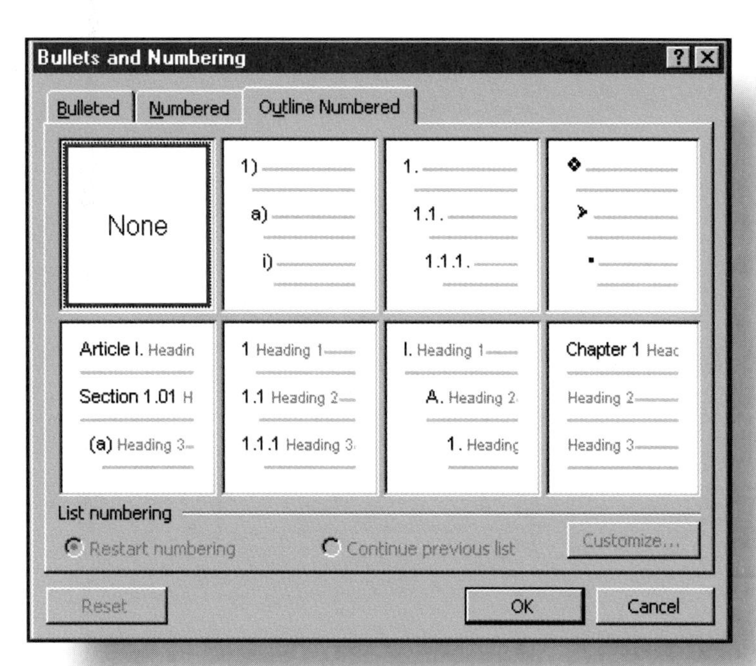

At the Bullets and Numbering dialog box with the Outline Numbered tab displayed, you can specify the type of numbering for paragraphs at the left margin, first tab stop, second tab stop, etc. (The options that display with *Heading 1*, *Heading 2*, or *Heading 3* are not available unless the text to be numbered has been formatted with a Heading style.)

exercise 15

Numbering Paragraphs Using the Bullets and Numbering Dialog Box

1. Open List. This document is located on your student data disk.
2. Save the document with Save As and name it Ch 04, Ex 15.
3. Number the paragraphs in the document using the Bullets and Numbering dialog box by completing the following steps:
   a. Select the paragraphs in the document (excluding the title and the blank lines below the title).
   b. Click Format, then Bullets and Numbering.
   c. At the Bullets and Numbering dialog box, click the Numbered tab.
   d. Click the second numbering option box in the first row.
   e. Click OK or press Enter.
4. Add *Annuity Contracts* between paragraphs 4 and 5 by completing the following steps:

a. Position the insertion point immediately to the right of the last *t* in *Role of Account*.
b. Press Enter. (This moves the insertion point a double space below the previous paragraph.)
c. Key **Annuity Contracts**.

5. Select and then delete *Investment Practices of the Account* (paragraph 2).
6. Save the document again with the same name (Ch 04, Ex 15).
7. Print and then close Ch 04, Ex 15.

Creating Ordinals

Word's AutoFormat feature automatically formats ordinal numbers. For example, if you key *1st* and then press the space bar, Word will correct it to *1st*. Word automatically changes the font size of the *st* and formats the letters as superscript text. This automatic feature will change other ordinal numbers such as 2nd, 3rd, 4th, etc.

exercise 16

Keying a Document with Ordinals

1. At a clear document screen, key the text shown in figure 4.19. Let Word's AutoFormat feature insert the arrow bullets and automatically change the formatting of the ordinal numbers.
2. Save the document and name it Ch 04, Ex 16.
3. Print and then close Ch 04, Ex 16.

4.19

Exercise 16

DATE: April 16, 1998

TO: Barry Langstrom

FROM: Mona Brown

SUBJECT: DEVELOPMENT CONTRACT

After reading the contract prepared by the Coleman Development Corporation, I would like to see the following changes made:

➢ Delete the 2nd paragraph in the 4th section.
➢ Add a paragraph between the 3rd and 4th paragraphs in the 5th section that fully describes the responsibilities of the development corporation.
➢ Remove the words *and others* in the 1st paragraph of the 6th section.

I have also made additional changes on the enclosed copy of the contract. Please contact me as soon as you have read the contract.

XX:Ch 04, Ex 16

Changing Line Spacing

By default, the word wrap feature single spaces text. There may be occasions when you want to change to another spacing, such as line and a half or double. Line spacing can be changed with shortcut commands or options from the Paragraph dialog box. Figure 4.20 illustrates the shortcut commands to change line spacing.

4.20

Line Spacing Shortcut Commands

Press	To change line spacing to
CTRL + 1	single spacing
CTRL + 2	double spacing
CTRL + 5	1.5 line spacing

exercise 17

Changing Line Spacing

1. Open Para 02. This document is located on your student data disk.
2. Save the document with Save As and name it Ch 04, Ex 17.
3. Change the line spacing for all paragraphs to 1.5 line spacing by completing the following steps:
   a. Select the entire document.
   b. Press Ctrl + 5.
4. Change the alignment of all paragraphs to justified.
5. Save the document again with the same name (Ch 04, Ex 17).
6. Print and then close Ch 04, Ex 17.

Line spacing can also be changed at the Paragraph dialog box. At the Paragraph dialog box, you can change line spacing with the Line spacing option or the At option. If you click the down-pointing triangle at the right side of the Line spacing text box at the Paragraph dialog box, a drop-down list displays with a variety of spacing options. For example, to change the line spacing to double you would click *Double* at the drop-down list. You can key a specific line spacing measurement in the At text box at the Paragraph dialog box. For example, to change the line spacing to 1.75, key **1.75** in the At text box.

exercise 18

Changing Line Spacing at the Paragraph Dialog Box

1. Open Quiz. This document is located on your student data disk.
2. Save the document with Save As and name it Ch 04, Ex 18.
3. Insert bullets before the test questions.
4. Change the line spacing to 1.75 using the Paragraph dialog box by completing the following steps:
   a. Select the paragraphs in the document (excluding the title and the blank line below the title).
   b. Click Format, then Paragraph.
   c. At the Paragraph dialog box, make sure the Indents and Spacing tab is selected, click inside the At text box, and then key **1.75**. (This text box is located to the right of the Line spacing text box.)
   d. Click OK or press Enter.
5. Save the document again with the same name (Ch 04, Ex 18).
6. Change the line spacing to double using a shortcut command by completing the following steps:
   a. Select the paragraphs in the document (excluding the title and the blank line below the title).
   b. Press Ctrl + 2.
7. Save the document again with the same name (Ch 04, Ex 18).
8. Print and then close Ch 04, Ex 18.

chapter summary

- In Word, a paragraph is any amount of text followed by a paragraph mark (press of the Enter key).
- Word inserts into the paragraph mark any paragraph formatting that is turned on before the text is keyed. If you want to remove paragraph formatting from text, delete the paragraph mark. You can also use the shortcut command Ctrl + Q to remove all formatting from a paragraph.
- To turn on or off the display of nonprinting characters such as paragraph marks, click the Show/Hide ¶ button on the Standard toolbar.
- By default, paragraphs in a Word document are aligned at the left margin and ragged at the right margin. This default alignment can be changed at the Formatting toolbar, at the Paragraph dialog box, or with shortcut commands to left, center, right, or fully aligned.
- You can change the alignment of text in paragraphs before you key the text or you can change the alignment of existing text. To change the alignment of existing text in a paragraph, position the insertion point anywhere within the paragraph, and then choose the desired alignment.
- If you want to apply paragraph formatting to several paragraphs that are not adjacent, you can use the Repeat key, F4; the shortcut command, Ctrl + Y; or the Repeat option from the Edit drop-down menu.
- The first line of text in a paragraph can be indented by pressing the Tab key, with an option from the Paragraph dialog box, or with the First Line Indent marker on the Ruler.
- All lines of text in a paragraph can be indented to a tab stop or to a specific measurement from the left margin using a shortcut command, an option from the Paragraph dialog box, or the Left Indent marker on the Ruler.
- Text in paragraphs can be indented from the left and the right margins with options at the Paragraph dialog box or with the Left Indent and Right Indent markers on the Ruler.
- In a hanging paragraph, the first line of the paragraph remains at the left margin, while the remaining lines are indented to the first tab stop. Hanging paragraphs can be created with a shortcut command or with options from the Paragraph dialog box.
- Word's AutoFormat feature will automatically format numbered and bulleted lists as well as create ordinal numbers.
- Bulleted lists with hanging indents are automatically created when a paragraph begins with *, o, >, -, or any symbol character. Key one of the symbols, followed by a space, key text, then press Enter, and Word automatically inserts a bullet. The type of bullet inserted depends on the type of character entered.
- Paragraphs can also be numbered with the Numbering button on the Formatting toolbar and bullets can be inserted before paragraphs with the Bullets button. Numbers or bullets can also be inserted with options at the Bullets and Numbering dialog box.
- Line spacing can be changed with shortcut commands or options from the Paragraph dialog box.

commands review

	Mouse	Keyboard
Turn on/off display of nonprinting characters	Click Tools, Options; or click ¶ button on Standard toolbar	Tools, Options; or SHIFT + CTRL + *
To align text...	**Formatting toolbar buttons**	
at the left margin	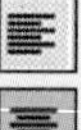	CTRL + L
between margins		CTRL + E
at the right margin		CTRL + R
at the left and right margins		CTRL + J
Return paragraph alignment to normal (left aligned)		CTRL + L
Return all paragraph formatting to normal		CTRL + Q
Repeat formatting command for several paragraphs	Position insertion point in paragraph, click Edit, Repeat Paragraph Alignment	F4; or CTRL + Y
Paragraph dialog box	Format, Paragraph; or position insertion point in paragraph, click *right* mouse button, click Paragraph	Format, Paragraph
Turn on/off display of the Ruler	View, Ruler	View, Ruler
Indent first line of a paragraph	At the Paragraph dialog box click Special, then First Line; or with arrow pointer on First Line Indent marker on Ruler, hold down left mouse button and drag marker to desired measurement	TAB
Indent left margin of all lines of of text in a paragraph or selected paragraphs	At the Paragraph dialog box, key indent measurement in the Left text box; or drag the Left Indent marker on the Ruler to desired measurement; or click on Formatting toolbar	CTRL + M
Decrease indent of text in a paragraph	Decrease number in the Left text box at the Paragraph dialog box; or drag Left Indent marker on the Ruler to desired measurement; or click the Decrease Indent button on the Formatting toolbar	CTRL + SHIFT + M

Indent left and right margins of paragraph	At the Paragraph dialog box, key indent measurement in the Left and Right text boxes; or with the arrow pointer on the Left Indent maker on the Ruler, drag the marker to the desired measurement and then drag the Right Indent marker to the desired measurement	
Create a hanging paragraph	At the Paragraph dialog box, key the desired indent measurement in the Left text box, click Special, then Hanging; or drag Hanging Indent marker on Ruler to desired measurement	CTRL + T
Create numbered/bulleted paragraphs	Select paragraphs, click Numbering/Bullets button on Formatting toolbar; or display the Bullets and Numbering dialog box	
Bullets and Numbering dialog box	Format, Bullets and Numbering	Format, Bullets and Numbering
Change to single spacing		CTRL + 1
Change to double spacing		CTRL + 2
Change to 1.5 line spacing		CTRL + 5
Change line spacing at Paragraph dialog box	Click the up/down-pointing triangle to right of At box; or click Line spacing	

check your understanding

Completion: In the space provided at the right, indicate the correct term, command, or number.

1. Word inserts paragraph formatting into this mark. ____________
2. If the insertion point is positioned at the left margin, the insertion point is moved to this measurement from the left margin when you press the Tab key. ____________
3. To turn on or off the display of nonprinting characters, click this button on the Standard toolbar. ____________
4. You can return all paragraph formatting to normal with this keyboard command. ____________
5. This is the default paragraph alignment. ____________
6. Click this button on the Formatting toolbar to align text at the right margin. ____________

7. To indent right and left margins in a paragraph, display this dialog box. ____________
8. Indent the left margin of a paragraph with this shortcut command. ____________
9. In this kind of paragraph, the first line remains at the left margin and the remaining lines are indented to the first tab stop. ____________
10. The number, 2nd, is referred to as this. ____________
11. Automate the creation of bulleted paragraphs with the Bullets button located on this toolbar. ____________
12. The Bullets and Numbering dialog box contains three tab options: Bulleted, Numbered, and this. ____________
13. At the Paragraph dialog box, change line spacing with the Line spacing option or this. ____________
14. This is the default line spacing. ____________
15. This is the shortcut command to change line spacing to 2. ____________

In the space provided below, list the steps you would complete to format paragraphs in a document as hanging paragraphs.

____

____

In the space provided below, list the steps you would complete to change the line spacing to 1.25.

____

____

skill assessments

Assessment 1

1. Open Memo 01. This document is located on your student data disk.
2. Save the document with Save As and name it Ch 04, SA 01.
3. Turn on the display of nonprinting characters.
4. Make the following changes to the memo:
   a. Bold the headings, DATE:, TO:, FROM:, and SUBJECT:. (If necessary, realign the text after DATE:.)
   b. Change the line spacing to 1.5 for the three paragraphs in the body of the memo.
   c. Change the paragraph alignment to justified for the three paragraphs in the body of the memo.

5. Turn off the display of the nonprinting characters.
6. Save the document again with the same name (Ch 04, SA 01).
7. Print and then close Ch 04, SA 01.

Assessment 2

1. At a clear document screen, key the memo shown in figure 4.21 with the following specifications:
   a. Bold text as indicated.
   b. Center text as indicated.
   c. Change the alignment of paragraphs in the body of the memo to justified.
2. Save the memo and name it Ch 04, SA 02.
3. Print and then close Ch 04, SA 02.

Figure 4.21 • Assessment 2

DATE: March 12, 1998

TO: Administrative Support Staff

FROM: Sheila Arnold, Training and Education

SUBJECT: BUSINESS COMMUNICATIONS CLASSES

Plains Community College administrative support staff will have the opportunity to complete classes in written business documents. This training is designed for any support staff who wishes to improve the grammar, punctuation, style, and clarity of his or her business documents.

The business communications classes will be held in Room 120 from 3:30 p.m. to 5:30 p.m. on the following days:

Monday, April 6
Wednesday, April 7
Tuesday, April 21
Thursday, April 23

The training sessions are limited to 15 employees. To register, please call Training and Education at extension 575.

XX:Ch 04, SA 02

Assessment 3

1. At a clear document screen, key the memo shown in figure 4.22. Indent the second paragraph in the body of the memo from the left and right margins.
2. Save the memo and name it Ch 04, SA 03.
3. Print and then close Ch 04, SA 03.

Figure 4.22 • Assessment 3

DATE: December 3, 1998

TO: Richard Polk, College Relations

FROM: Christy Edmonds, OT Department

SUBJECT: BUSINESS COMMUNICATIONS COURSE

The desktop publishing course, BUS 250, has been a great success this semester. Because of the interest in the course, we have decided to offer it again in the spring semester. Please include the following description for the course in the spring schedule:

> Students in Business Communications, BUS 250, will learn to recognize basic barriers to effective communication; plan and prepare oral communications; follow a process for preparing business documents; and evaluate and improve presentation skills.

I would like to see the course advertised not only in the spring schedule but also in the school newspaper. Would you help me write an advertisement for the newspaper? You can contact me at extension 405.

XX:Ch 04, SA 03

Assessment 4

1. At a clear document screen, create the document shown in figure 4.23 with the following specifications:
   a. Change the line spacing to double.
   b. Center, bold, and italicize text as indicated.
   c. Create hanging paragraphs as indicated.
   d. Change the alignment of paragraphs to justified.
2. Save the document and name it Ch 04, SA 04.
3. Print and then close Ch 04, SA 04.

Figure 4.23 • Assessment 4

BIBLIOGRAPHY

Aiken, Charles A. (1996). *Oral Communications*, 3rd edition (pp. 24-33). Salt Lake City, UT: Blue Ridge Publishing Company.

Florez, Lisa M. (1997). *Computerized Business Documents* (pp. 19-22). Boston, MA: Northampton Publishers.

Greenfield, Noel E. (1998). *Complete Business Forms* (pp. 43-51). Philadelphia, PA: Greenleaf Press.

Ketchum, Marilyn A. (1997). *Oral and Written Communications*, 2nd edition (pp. 38-42). New Orleans, LA: Pontchartrain Publishing, Inc.

Assessment 5

1. Open Memo 02. This document is located on your student data disk.
2. Save the document with Save As and name it Ch 04, SA 05.
3. Make the following changes to the memo:
   a. Insert bullets before paragraphs two through five (the paragraphs containing the book titles).
   b. Change the alignment of paragraphs in the body of the memo to justified.
4. Save the document again with the same name (Ch 04, SA 05).
5. Print and then close Ch 04, SA 05.

Assessment 6

1. Open Job Desc. This document is located on your student data disk.
2. Save the document with Save As and name it Ch 04, SA 06.
3. Bold and center the title, JOB DESCRIPTION, and subtitle, REGISTERED NURSE.
4. Select the text paragraphs in the document and then make the following changes:
   a. Change the line spacing to double.
   b. Change the alignment to justified.
   c. Insert numbers at the beginning of each paragraph. (*Hint: Use the Numbering button on the Formatting toolbar.*)
5. Delete the fifth paragraph.
6. Add the paragraph shown in figure 4.24 between the fourth and fifth paragraph. (This paragraph will be numbered 5.)
7. Save the document again with the same name (Ch 04, SA 06).
8. Print and then close Ch 04, SA 06.

Figure 4.24 • Assessment 6

Supervises, trains, and monitors licensed practical nurses and nurses aides.

chapter FIVE

Managing Documents

PERFORMANCE OBJECTIVES

Upon successful completion of chapter 5, you will be able to:

- **Create a folder.**
- **Copy, move, rename, delete, and print documents.**
- **Open a document as read-only.**
- **Display document properties.**
- **Create a shortcut to a document.**

Almost every company that conducts business maintains a filing system. The system may consist of documents, folders, and cabinets; or it may be a computerized filing system where information is stored on tapes and disks. Whatever type of filing system a business uses, daily maintenance of files is important to a company's operation. Maintaining files (documents) in Word can include such activities as copying, moving, renaming, and printing documents as well as creating additional file folders.

Maintaining Documents

Many file (document) management tasks can be completed at the Open dialog box (and some at the Save As dialog box). These tasks can include copying, moving, printing, and renaming documents; opening multiple documents; and opening a document as read-only. In addition, a new folder can be created at the Save As dialog box. To display the Open dialog box, click the Open button on the Standard toolbar or click File, then Open. To display the Save As dialog box click File, then Save As.

Creating a Folder

In Word, documents are grouped logically and placed in *folders*. A folder can be created within a folder. The main folder on a disk or drive is called the *root* folder. Folders can be created as a branch of this root folder.

Document Icon

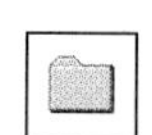

Folder Icon

Create New Folder

At the Open or Save As dialog boxes, documents display in the list box preceded by a document icon and a folder is preceded by a folder icon. More than likely, your data disk will not contain a folder since you have not created additional folders on the data disk.

A new folder can be created with the Create New Folder button at the Save As dialog box. (A new folder cannot be created at the Open dialog box.) To create a new folder, you would complete the following steps:

1. Display the Save As dialog box.
2. Click the Create New Folder button at the top of the dialog box.
3. At the New Folder dialog box shown in figure 5.1, key a name for the folder.
4. Press Enter or click OK.
5. Close the Save As dialog box. To do this, click the Cancel button at the right side of the dialog box.

A folder name can contain a maximum of 255 characters. Numbers, spaces, and symbols can be used in the folder name except those symbols explained in chapter 1 in the "Naming a Document" section.

figure 5.1 *New Folder Dialog Box*

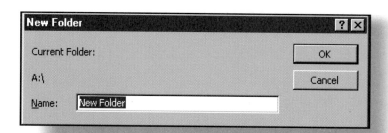

exercise 1

Creating a Folder

1. Create a folder named *Memos* on the data disk by completing the following steps:
   a. Click the New button on the Standard toolbar to display a clear editing window.
   b. Display the Save As dialog box. (Make sure the drive where your data disk is located is the active folder.)
   c. Click the Create New Folder button (located toward the top of the dialog box).
   d. At the New Folder dialog box, key **Memos**.
   e. Press Enter or click OK.
2. Close the Save As dialog box. To do this, click the Cancel button at the right side of the dialog box.

New

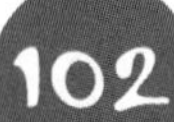

Selecting Documents

Document management tasks can be completed on one document or selected documents. For example, you can move one document to a different folder, or you can select several documents and move them at one time. Selected documents can be deleted, copied, moved, or printed.

To select one document, display the Open dialog box, and then click the desired document. To select several adjacent documents (documents displayed next to each other) using the mouse, you would complete the following steps:

1. Display the Open dialog box.
2. Click the first document to make it active.
3. Position the arrow pointer on the last document to be selected, hold down the Shift key, and then click the left mouse button.

To select several adjacent documents using the keyboard, you would complete the following steps:

1. Display the Open dialog box.
2. Press Shift + Tab. (This selects the first document in the list.)
3. Press the up or down arrow key until the first document you want selected is active.
4. Hold down the Shift key, press the down arrow key until all desired documents are selected, and then release the Shift key.

You can also select documents that are not adjacent in the Open dialog box. To do this with the mouse, you would complete the following steps:

1. Display the Open dialog box.
2. Click the first document to make it active.
3. Hold down the Ctrl key.
4. Click each document you want selected.
5. When all desired documents are selected, release the Ctrl key.

Deleting Documents

At some point, you may want to delete certain documents from your data disk or any other disk or folder in which you may be working. If you use Word on a regular basis, you should establish a system for deleting documents. The system you choose depends on the work you are doing and the amount of folder or disk space available. To delete a document, display the Open or Save As dialog box, right-click the document to be deleted (position the arrow pointer on the document to be deleted and then click the *right* mouse button), and then click Delete at the shortcut menu. At the dialog box asking you to confirm the deletion, click Yes.

exercise 2

Deleting a Document

1. Delete documents by completing the following steps:
   a. Display the Open dialog box.
   b. Position the arrow pointer on *Ch 02, Ex 03*, click the *right* mouse button, and then click Delete.
   c. At the question asking if you want to delete the selected document, click Yes.
2. Close the Open dialog box.

exercise 3

Deleting Selected Documents

1. Delete all documents you created that begin *Ch 01*, *Ch 02*, and *Ch 03* by completing the following steps:
   a. Display the Open dialog box.
   b. Click *Ch 01, Ex 01*. (This should be the first document in the list for chapter 1.)
   c. Hold down the Shift key and then click *Ch 03, SA 04*. (This should be the last document in the list for chapter 3. If not, click the last document name listed for chapter 3.)
   d. Position the arrow pointer on one of the selected documents and then click the *right* mouse button.
   e. From the shortcut menu that displays, click Delete.
   f. At the question asking if you are sure you want to delete all selected documents, click Yes.
2. Close the Open dialog box.

A folder and all its contents can be deleted at the Open or Save As dialog box. To delete a folder and its contents, right-click the folder, and then click Delete. At the question asking if you are sure you want to delete the folder and all its contents, click Yes. You will be deleting a folder in a later exercise in this chapter.

Deleting to the Recycle Bin

Documents deleted from your data disk are deleted permanently. (There are recovery programs, however, that will help you recover deleted text. If you accidentally delete a document or documents from a disk, do not do anything more with the disk until you can run a recovery program.) Documents deleted from the hard drive are automatically sent to the Windows Recycle Bin. If you accidentally delete a document to the Recycle Bin, it can be easily restored. To free space on the disk or drive, empty the Recycle Bin on a periodic basis. Restoring a document from or emptying the contents of the Recycle Bin is done at the Windows 95 screen (not in Word). To empty the Recycle Bin, you would complete the following steps:

1. Display the Windows 95 screen. (If you are just beginning, turn on the computer, and Windows 95 will load. If you are currently working in Word, click the Minimize button at the right side of the Title bar. (The Minimize button contains the single underline symbol (_). Be sure to click the Minimize button on the Title bar and not the one just below it on the Menu bar.)
2. At the Windows 95 screen, double-click the Recycle Bin icon (located at the left side of the screen).
3. At the Recycle Bin dialog box, click File, then Empty Recycle Bin.
4. At the question asking if you are sure you want to empty the Recycle Bin, click Yes.

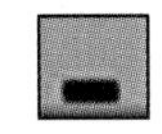

Minimize

Recycle Bin Icon

If you want to empty only specific documents from the Recycle Bin, hold down the Ctrl key while clicking the documents to be emptied. Position the arrow pointer on one of the selected documents, click the *right* mouse button, and then click the left mouse button on Delete. At the question asking if you want to delete the selected documents, click Yes.

If you minimized the Word program by clicking the Minimize button, you can maximize (display the Word screen) the Word program at the Windows 95 screen by clicking the Microsoft Word - (document name) button located on the taskbar (at the bottom of the screen).

A document or selected documents can also be restored from the Recycle Bin. To do this, you would complete the following steps:

1. At the Windows 95 screen, double-click the Recycle Bin icon.
2. At the Recycle Bin dialog box, click the document to be restored. (If you are restoring more than one document, hold down the Ctrl key while clicking the desired documents.)
3. Click File, then Restore.

At the Recycle Bin dialog box, you can also restore a document by positioning the arrow pointer on the document to be restored, clicking the *right* mouse button, and then clicking the left mouse button on Restore.

Copying Files

In previous chapters, you have been opening a document from your data disk and saving it with a new name on the same disk. This process makes an exact copy of the document, leaving the original on the disk. You have been copying documents and saving the new document in the same folder as the original document. You can also copy a document into another folder and use the document's original name or give it a different name, or select documents at the Open or Save As dialog boxes and copy them to the same folder or into a different folder. To copy a document into another folder, you would complete the following steps:

1. Open the document you want to copy.
2. Display the Save As dialog box.
3. At the Save As dialog box, change to the desired folder. To do this, click the down-pointing triangle to the right of the Save in text box, and then click the desired folder at the drop-down menu.
4. Click the Save button at the right side of the dialog box.

Up One Level

The Open and Save As dialog boxes contain an Up One Level button. Use this button if you want to change to the folder that is up one level from the current folder. You can also press the Backspace key to change to the folder that is one level up from the current folder.

exercise 4

Saving a Copy of an Open Document

1. Open Memo 01.
2. Save the document with Save As and name it Books. (Make sure the drive containing your data disk is the active folder.)
3. Save a copy of the Books document in the *Memos* folder by completing the following steps:
   a. With Books still open, display the Save As dialog box.
   b. At the Save As dialog box, change to the *Memos* folder. To do this, double-click *Memos* at the beginning of the list box (folders are listed before documents).
   c. Click the Save button at the right side of the dialog box.
4. Close Books.
5. Change the folder back to the main folder for drive A by completing the following steps:
   a. Display the Open dialog box.
   b. Click the Up One Level button toward the top of the Open dialog box, or press the Backspace key.
   c. Click Cancel to close the Open dialog box.

A document can be copied to another folder without opening the document first. To do this, use the Copy and Paste options from a shortcut menu at the Open (or Save As) dialog box. To copy a document from one folder to another without opening it first, you would complete the following steps:

1. Display the Open (or Save As) dialog box.
2. Position the arrow pointer on the document to be copied and then click the *right* mouse button.
3. From the shortcut menu that displays, click Copy.
4. Change to the desired folder. (To do this, click the down-pointing triangle to the right of the Look in: text box, and then click the desired folder. Or, click the Up One Level button if this displays the desired folder.)
5. Position the arrow pointer in any white area in the list box (containing the names of the documents in the folder), click the *right* mouse button, and then click Paste at the shortcut menu.

exercise 5

Copying a Document at the Open Dialog Box

1. Copy Memo 02 to the *Memos* folder by completing the following steps:
   a. Display the Open dialog box.
   b. Position the arrow pointer on *Memo 02*, click the *right* mouse button, and then click Copy.
   c. Change to the *Memos* folder. To do this, double-click *Memos* located at the beginning of the list box.
   d. Position the arrow pointer in any white area (not on a document name) in the list box, click the *right* mouse button, and then click Paste.
2. Change back to the root folder for the data disk. To do this, click the Up One Level button located toward the top of the dialog box, or press the Backspace key.
3. Close the Open dialog box.

A document or selected documents can be copied into the same folder. When you do this, Word names the document(s) *"Copy of xxx"* (where xxx is the current document name). You can copy one document or selected documents into the same folder.

exercise 6

Copying Selected Documents into the Same Folder

1. Copy documents into the same folder by completing the following steps:
   a. Display the Open dialog box.
   b. Select *Para 01*, *Para 02*, and *Para 03*. (To do this, click *Para 01*, hold down the Shift key, and then click *Para 03*.)
   c. Position the arrow pointer on one of the selected documents, click the *right* mouse button, and then click the left mouse button on Copy.
   d. Position the arrow pointer in any white area in the list box, click the *right* mouse button, and then click Paste. (In a few moments, Word will redisplay the Open dialog box with the following documents added: *Copy of Para 01, Copy of Para 02*, and *Copy of Para 03*.)
2. Close the Open dialog box.

Documents can also be copied into a different folder. To do this, select and then copy the desired documents, switch to the desired folder and then paste the selected documents.

exercise 7

Copying Selected Documents into a Different Folder

1. Copy several memo documents to the *Memos* folder by completing the following steps:
   a. Display the Open dialog box.
   b. Select *Memo 01, Memo 03,* and *Memo 04* by completing the following steps:
      1) Click *Memo 01*.
      2) Hold down the Ctrl key, click *Memo 03,* click *Memo 04,* and then release the Ctrl key.
   c. Position the arrow pointer on one of the selected documents, click the *right* mouse button, and then click Copy with the left mouse button.
   d. Double-click the folder named *Memos*. (This folder is located at the beginning of the list box.)
   e. When the *Memos* folder is displayed, position the arrow pointer in any white area in the list box, click the *right* mouse button, and then click Paste.
   f. Change back to the root folder for the data disk by clicking the Up One Level button located toward the top of the dialog box, or pressing the Backspace key.
2. Close the Open dialog box by clicking the Cancel button.

Sending Documents to a Different Drive or Folder

With the Copy and Paste options from the shortcut menu at the Open or Save As dialog box, you can copy documents to another folder or drive. With the Send To option, you can send a copy of a document to another drive or folder. To use this option, position the arrow pointer on the document you want copied, click the *right* mouse button, and then position the arrow pointer on Send To. This causes another pop-up menu to display. At this pop-up menu, click the desired drive or folder.

Cutting and Pasting a Document

A document can be removed from one folder or disk and inserted in another folder or on a disk using the Cut and Paste options from the shortcut menu at the Open dialog box . To do this you would display the Open dialog box, position the arrow pointer on the document to be removed (cut), click the *right* mouse button, and then click the left mouse button on Cut. Change to the desired folder, position the arrow pointer in a white area in the list box, click the *right* mouse button, and then click the left mouse button on Paste.

exercise 8

Cutting and Pasting a Document

1. Save and move a document into a different folder by completing the following steps:
   a. Open Memo 04.
   b. Save the document with Save As and name it Emp Survey.
   c. Close Emp Survey.
   d. Move Emp Survey to the *Memos* folder by completing the following steps:
      1) Display the Open dialog box.
      2) Position the arrow pointer on *Emp Survey*, click the *right* mouse button, and then click the left mouse button on Cut.
      3) Double-click *Memos* to make it the active folder. (The *Memos* folder name is located at the beginning of the list.)
      4) Position the arrow pointer in the white area in the list box, click the *right* mouse button, and then click the left mouse button on Paste.
   e. Click the Up One Level button to make the main folder for the data disk the active folder.
2. Close the Open dialog box.

Renaming Documents

At the Open or Save As dialog boxes, you can use the Rename option from the shortcut menu to give a document a different name. The Rename option changes the name of the document and keeps it in the same folder. To use Rename, position the arrow pointer on the document to be renamed, click the *right* mouse button, and then click the left mouse button on Rename. This causes a black border to surround the document name and the name to be selected. Key the desired name and then press Enter.

exercise 9

Renaming a Document

1. Rename a document located in the *Memos* folder by completing the following steps:
   a. Display the Open dialog box.
   b. Double-click *Memos* to make it the active folder.
   c. Position the arrow pointer on *Memo 01*, click the *right* mouse button, and then click the left mouse button on Rename.
   d. Key **Nguyen** and then press the Enter key.
   e. Complete steps similar to those in 1b through 1d to rename *Memo 02* to *St. Claire*.
   f. Click the Up One Level button.
2. Close the Open dialog box.

Deleting a Folder and Its Contents

As you learned earlier in this chapter, a document or selected documents can be deleted. In addition to documents, a folder (and all its contents) can be deleted. Delete a folder in the same manner as you delete a document.

Deleting a Folder and Its Contents

1. Delete the *Memos* folder and its contents by completing the following steps:
   a. Display the Open dialog box.
   b. Position the arrow pointer on *Memos*, click the *right* mouse button, and then click Delete.
   c. At the question asking if you want to delete the folder and its contents, click Yes.
2. Close the Open dialog box.

Opening Documents

A document or selected documents can be opened at the Open dialog box. To open one document, display the Open dialog box, position the arrow pointer on the desired document, click the *right* mouse button, and then click the left mouse button on Open. To open more than one document, select the documents in the Open dialog box, position the arrow pointer on one of the selected documents, click the *right* mouse button, and then click the left mouse button on Open.

If more than one document is open, all open documents can be closed at the same time. To do this, hold down the Shift key, click File, then Close All. Holding down the Shift key before clicking File causes the Close option to change to Close All.

exercise 11

Opening and Closing Several Documents

1. Open several documents by completing the following steps:
   a. Display the Open dialog box.
   b. Select *Memo 01, Memo 02, Memo 03,* and *Memo 04.*
   c. Position the arrow pointer on one of the selected documents, click the *right* mouse button, and then click the left mouse button on Open.
2. Close the open documents by completing the following steps:
   a. Hold down the Shift key.
   b. Click File, then Close All.

A document can be opened that is read-only. With a read-only document, you can make changes to the document but you cannot save those changes with the same name. Word protects the original document and does not allow you to save the changes to the document with the same name. You can, however, open a document as read-only, make changes to it, and then save the document with a different name. To open a read-only document, display the Open dialog box, position the arrow pointer on the desired document, click the *right* mouse button, and then click the left mouse button on Open Read-Only. With a read-only document displayed, clicking the Save button, or choosing File, then Save causes the Save As dialog box to display where you can key a new name for the document.

exercise 12

Opening a Read-Only Document

1. Open a document as read-only by completing the following steps:
   a. Display the Open dialog box.
   b. Position the arrow pointer on *Notice 01*, click the *right* mouse button, and then click the left mouse button on Open Read-Only.
2. With Notice 01 open, make the following changes:
   a. Change *EMERALD HEIGHTS* (in the title) to *LIBERTY FALLS*.
   b. Change *Emerald Heights* (in the first paragraph) to *Liberty Falls*.
   c. Change *April 17* (in the first and the fourth paragraphs) to *May 15*.
   d. Change *6:00* (in the first paragraph) to *6:30*.
   e. Change *Mike Shelton* (in the first paragraph) to *Christine Long*.
3. Save the document by completing the following steps:
   a. Click the Save button on the Standard toolbar.
   b. At the Microsoft Word information box, click OK.
   c. At the Save As dialog box, key **Ch 05, Ex 12**, and then press Enter.
4. Print and then close Ch 05, Ex 12.

Printing Documents

Up to this point, you have opened a document and then printed it. With the Print option from the shortcut menu at the Open dialog box, you can print a document or several documents without opening them. To use this option, display the Open dialog box, position the arrow pointer on the document to be printed, click the *right* mouse button, and then click the left mouse button on Print. To send several documents to the printer, select the documents first. Position the arrow pointer on one of the selected document, click the *right* mouse button, and then click the left mouse button on Print.

13

Printing Documents

1. Display the Open dialog box.
2. Select *Para 01, Para 02,* and *Para 03*.
3. Position the arrow pointer on one of the selected documents, click the *right* mouse button, and then click the left mouse button on Print.

Displaying Document Properties

Word will provide specific details about a document with the Properties option from the Open or Save As dialog boxes shortcut menus. To display information about a document, display the Open dialog box (or Save As dialog box), position the arrow pointer on the desired document, click the *right* mouse button, and then click the left button on Properties. This displays a Properties dialog box similar to the one shown in figure 5.2.

figure 5.2 ***Properties Dialog Box***

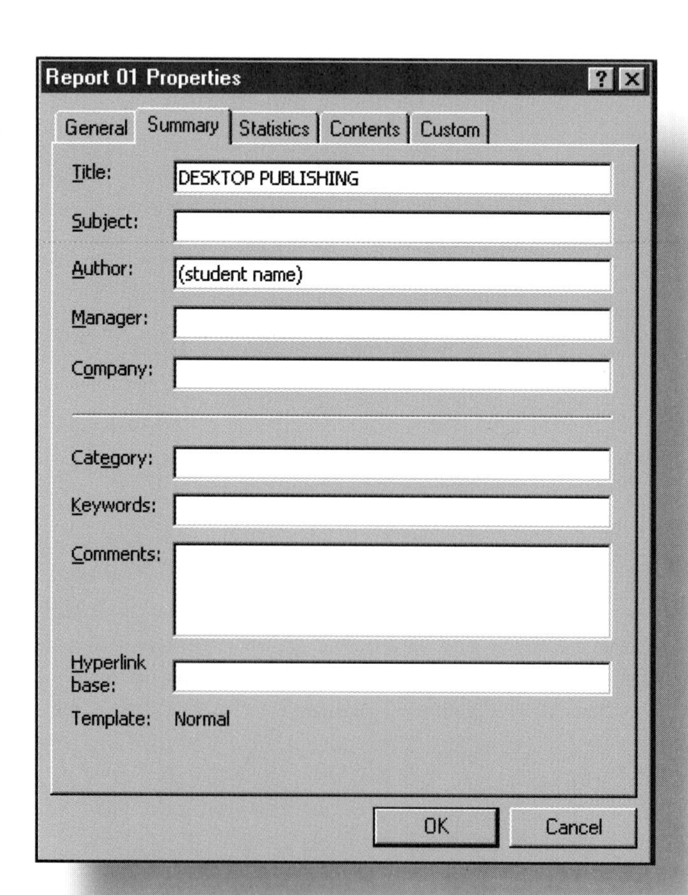

By default (this may vary), the Summary tab is selected and fields such as title, subject author, keywords, and commands display. Some of these fields may contain information, while others are blank. You can key specific information in each of these fields to describe the document. To move the insertion point to the next field, press the Tab key. To move the insertion point to the previous field, press Shift + Tab. Key information in the fields desired and then click OK to close the Properties dialog box.

Other tabs can be selected at the Properties dialog box to view additional information about the document. If you click the General tab, information about the document type, size, and location is displayed. Click the Statistics tab to view information such as the number of pages, paragraphs, lines, words, characters, and bytes included in the document. You can view the document without bringing it to the document screen by clicking the Contents tab. This displays a portion of the document in a viewing window. Click the Custom tab if you want to customize the properties of a document.

exercise 14

Displaying Document Properties

1. Display information about Report 01 by completing the following steps:
   a. Display the Open dialog box.
   b. Position the arrow pointer on *Report 01*, click the *right* mouse button, and then click the left mouse button on Properties.
   c. Read the information displayed in the Properties dialog box and then click the General tab.
   d. Read the information displayed with the General tab selected and then click the Statistics tab.
   e. Read the information displayed with the Statistics tab selected and then click the Contents tab.
   f. Read the information displayed with the Contents tab selected.
   g. Click the Cancel button to remove the Properties dialog box.
2. At the Open dialog box, display the Properties dialog box for the document named Report 02.
3. Display information for the document named Report 03.
4. Close the Open dialog box.

Changing the Display Options

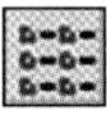
List

When the Open dialog box or Save As dialog box is displayed, the list of documents in the active folder is displayed. This display can be changed with buttons at the top of the dialog box. The List button is the active button. The button to the right of the List button is the Details button. Click the Details button and additional information displays about documents such as the size, type, and last date the document was modified. Click the Properties button

Details

Properties

(located to the right of the Details button) and information about the currently selected document displays to the right of the list box. This information includes the title, author, and revision date of the document along with information such as the number of pages, words, and characters in the document.

Preview

The Open dialog box, but not the Save As dialog box, contains a Preview button located to the right of the Properties button. Click this button and Word displays a portion of the currently selected document in a window to the right of the list box. This option is helpful if you are searching for a specific document and cannot remember the name of the document.

exercise 15

Changing the Display at the Open Dialog Box

1. Change the display at the Open dialog box by completing the following steps:
   a. Display the Open dialog box.
   b. Click the Details button at the top of the dialog box.
   c. Scroll through the list of documents and view the information on the size and type of the document and the last modification date.
   d. Click the Properties button at the top of the dialog box.
   e. Read the properties information for the selected document and then click the next document in the list. Continue clicking the next document in the list and reading the properties information. Do this approximately four or five times.
   f. Click the Preview button at the top of the dialog box.
   g. Click the document named Report 01 and then preview a portion of the document in the viewing window to the right of the list box.
   h. Click the document named Report 02 and then preview a portion of the document in the viewing window.
   i. Click the List button at the top of the dialog box to return the display of the list of documents to the default.
2. Close the Open dialog box.

Creating Shortcuts

When working with a disk or in a drive where many folders and folders within folders have been created, the Create Shortcut option from the Open or Save As dialog boxes shortcut menus can be very useful. With the Create Shortcut option, you create a shortcut document name that "points" to the original document. This shortcut name does not contain the original document, it is simply a marker that lets you quickly open the document.

For example, suppose you have a disk in drive A with the following folders: Contracts, Insurance, and Liability. Liability is a folder within Insurance, which is a folder within Contracts. You have saved a document named *Auto Insurance* in the Liability folder. You use this document on a consistent basis and would like to open the document without always having to change to the Liability folder. To do this, you can create a shortcut document name that displays in the main folder for drive A. A shortcut document name is created in the folder where the original document is located and then cut and pasted to a different folder. Exercise 16 covers the steps to create and then cut and paste a shortcut document name.

exercise 16

Creating a Folder, Then Creating a Shortcut Document Name

1. Display the Save As dialog box and then make the following changes:
   a. Create a folder named *Tests* on the data disk.
   b. Copy the document named Quiz to the *Tests* folder.
   c. Change to the *Tests* folder.
   d. Rename *Quiz* to *Telecommunications Test*.
   e. Create a shortcut document name in the main folder for the data disk that "points" to the original document by completing the following steps:
      1) Position the arrow pointer on *Telecommunications Test* and then click the right mouse button.
      2) At the pop-up menu that displays, click the left mouse button on Create Shortcut. (This inserts the name *Shortcut to Telecommunications Test* in the *Tests* folder.)
      3) Position the arrow pointer on *Shortcut to Telecommunications Test* and then click the right mouse button.
      4) At the pop-up menu that displays, click the left mouse button on Cut.
      5) Click the Up One Level button to return to the original folder for the data disk.
      6) Position the arrow pointer in the white area in the Save As dialog box Save in list box and then click the *right* mouse button.
      7) From the pop-up menu that displays, click the left mouse button on Paste.
2. Cancel the Save As dialog box.
3. Display the Open dialog box and then open Telecommunications Test by double-clicking *Shortcut to Telecommunications Test*. (This opens the original document that is located in the *Tests* folder.)
4. Close Telecommunications Test.
5. Remove the *Tests* folder and all its contents.
6. Delete the *Shortcut to Telecommunications Test* document.

chapter summary

- Word documents are grouped logically into folders. A new folder can be created at the Save As dialog box.
- One document or several documents can be selected at the Open dialog box. A document or selected documents can be copied, moved, renamed, deleted, printed, or opened.
- A copy of a document can be made by opening the document and then saving it with a different name. A document can also be copied with the Copy option from the Open dialog box shortcut menu. A document or selected documents can be copied to the same folder or to a different folder. If a document is copied to the same folder, Word adds *Copy of* before the document name.
- Use the Cut and Paste options from the Open dialog box shortcut menu to move a document from one folder to another.
- Use the Rename option from the Open dialog box shortcut menu to give a document a different name.
- Documents and/or folders can be deleted with the Delete option from the Open dialog box shortcut menu. Documents deleted from the hard drive are sent to the Windows Recycle Bin. Documents can be emptied or recovered from the Recycle Bin at the Windows 95 screen.
- Several documents can be opened at one time at the Open dialog box. All open documents can be closed at the same time by holding down the Shift key, clicking File, then Close All.
- A document can be opened as read-only. A read-only document must be saved with a different name from the original.
- A document or selected documents can be printed at the Open dialog box.
- Display information about documents with the Properties option from the Open dialog box shortcut menu.
- Additional information about documents can be displayed at the Open or Save As dialog box by clicking different buttons toward the top of the dialog box. In addition to a list of documents, information such as the type and size of the document can be displayed; information about the properties of each document can be displayed; and a portion of each document can be displayed to the right of the list box.
- A shortcut document name can be created in a different folder than the original document that "points" to the original document. This shortcut name does not contain the original document; it is simply a marker that lets you quickly open the document.

commands review

	Mouse/Keyboard
Open dialog box	File, Open; or click the Open button on Standard toolbar
Save As dialog box	File, Save As
Minimize Word	Click Minimize button at right side of Title bar
Close all open documents	Hold Shift key, click File, Close All

check your understanding

Completion: In the space provided at the right, indicate the correct term, command, or number.

1. A new folder can be created with this button at the Save As dialog box. ________
2. Click this button at the Open or Save As dialog box to change to the folder that is one level up from the current folder. ________
3. To select documents at the Open dialog box that are not adjacent using the mouse, hold down this key while clicking the desired documents. ________
4. A document can be copied to another folder without opening the document using the Copy option and this option from the Open dialog box shortcut menu. ________
5. To close all open documents at once, hold down this key, click File, then Close All. ________
6. When a document or selected documents are deleted from the hard drive, the documents are sent to this bin. ________
7. Click this tab at the Properties dialog box to view information about the document type, size, and location. ________

In the space provided, list the steps you would complete to create a folder named *Finances* on the data disk.

____

____

In the space provided, list the steps you would complete to open several consecutive documents at one time.

____

____

skill assessments

Assessment 1

1. Create a new folder named *Letters*.
2. Copy (be sure to use the Copy option and not the Cut option) all documents beginning with *Letter* into the *Letters* folder.
3. With the *Letters* folder as the active folder, rename the following documents:
   a. Rename *Letter 01* to *Donovan*.
   b. Rename *Letter 02* to *Omura*.
4. Make the root folder for the drive the active folder. (This should display the documents contained on the data disk.)

Assessment 2

1. Display the Open dialog box and then find the following properties for the specified document (write the information on a piece of paper):
   a. Find out how many pages, paragraphs, lines, and words are contained in Report 01. (You will need to scroll down the list of properties to discover all the information.)
   b. Find out the size (in bytes) of the following documents:
      1) Memo 01
      2) Letter 01
      3) Report 01
2. Close the Open dialog box. (Check with your instructor to determine if you should hand in the page containing the specified properties for the documents.)

Assessment 3

1. Display the Open dialog box and then delete the *Letters* folder and all documents contained within it.
2. Close the Open dialog box.

Assessment 4

(Note: Check with your instructor before completing this exercise. Before deleting the documents in this assessment, make sure any assignments handed in from chapter 4 have been returned and you do not need to make any changes to the documents.)

1. Display the Open dialog box and then delete all documents you created in chapter 4 that begin *Ch 04*.
2. Close the Open dialog box.

Unit one

PERFORMANCE ASSESSMENTS

DEMONSTRATING YOUR SKILLS

Assessment one

1. At a clear document screen, key the text shown in figure U1.1 in an appropriate memo format. Indent the second paragraph 0.5 inch from the left and right margins.
2. Change the alignment to justified for the body of the memo.
3. Save the document and name it Unit 1, PA 01.
4. Print and then close Unit 1, PA 01.

DATE: January 6, 1998

TO: Allen DeMarco

FROM: Jo Margolis

SUBJECT: ANNUAL REPORT

I have reviewed the first two sections of the draft of the 1997 Annual Report. Only a few minor changes need to be made to the first section. I made those changes on the attached copy. The second section looks great. The only suggestion I have is to add the following paragraph to page 5 below the fourth paragraph:

> The Fund's high performance during the first and second quarters of 1997 compensated for the low performance during the third and fourth quarters. The

Fund's strength in the first two quarters was due primarily to our decision to increase the overall maturity of the portfolio. Our strategic country weightings allowed us to participate in five of the six best performing markets in local currency terms for the six-month period.

This paragraph should help stockholders understand the upward and downward trend of the Fund. Whenever possible, please add explanatory paragraphs such as this to the remaining sections of the report.

XX:Unit 01, PA 01

Attachment

Figure U1.1 • Assessment 1

Assessment two

1. At a clear document screen, key the document (but not the bullets) shown in figure U1.2.
2. After keying the document, complete the following steps:
   a. Insert the bullets before the paragraphs of text as shown in figure U1.2.
   b. Select the title, PLANNING THE PUBLICATION, and then turn on bold.
   c. Select the first sentence of each bulleted item and then turn on bold.
   d. Change the alignment to justified for all paragraphs in the document except the title.
3. Save the document and name it Unit 1, PA 02.
4. Print and then close Unit 1, PA 02.

PLANNING THE PUBLICATION

Initial planning is probably one of the most important steps in the desktop publishing process. During this stage, the following items must be addressed:

- Clearly identify the purpose of your communication. The more definite you are about your purpose, the easier it will be to organize your material into an effective communication. Are you trying to provide information? Are you trying to sell a product? Are you announcing an event?

- Assess your target audience. Whom do you want to read your publication? Are they employees, clients, friends, or family? What will your target audience expect from your publication? Do they expect a serious, more conservative approach, or an informal, humorous approach?

- Determine in what form your intended audience will be exposed to your message. Will your message be contained in a brochure in a packet of presentation materials for a company seminar? Will your message be in the form of a newspaper advertisement, surrounded by other advertisements? Will your message be in the form of a business card that is to be distributed when making sales calls? Will your message be tacked on a bulletin board?

- Decide what you want your readers to do after reading your message. Do you want your readers to ask for more information? Do you want some kind of a response? Do you want your readers to be able to contact you in person or over the telephone?

- Collect examples of effective designs. Decide what you like and do not like. Try to determine why one design is more appealing than another. What elements attract your attention? Let the designs you like be a catalyst for developing your own ideas.

Figure U1.2 • Assessment 2

Assessment three

1. At a clear document screen, key the text shown in figure U1.3 in an appropriate business letter format. Center and bold the three paragraphs (each contains only one sentence) of text as shown in the figure.
2. Save the document and name it Unit 1, PA 03.
3. Print and then close Unit 1, PA 03.

November 9, 1998

Mr. and Mrs. Rudy Blake
10293 Southeast 42nd Street
Boise, ID 87432

Dear Mr. and Mrs. Blake:

You are now eligible to receive a Traveler Plus card that earns you one free mile for every dollar you charge in purchases.

You will be able to earn free miles immediately!

Consider how often you use a credit card now and imagine if the amount of your usual monthly purchases was also credited to your Traveler Plus account in free miles. Why not get started immediately.

Reply now and collect two bonus certificates.

Your card will be issued with this generous line of credit…one that allows you to charge major purchases like air travel and hotel bills without fear of going over a spending limit.

Your preapproved status expires 02-01-99.

Please take a moment to complete and return the enclosed form. Your new Traveler Plus card will be on its way in no time.

Very truly yours,

Veronica Kazinsky
Senior Vice President

XX:Unit 1, PA 03

Enclosure

Figure U1.3 • Assessment 3

Assessment four

1. At a clear document screen, create the document shown in figure U1.4 with the following specifications:
   a. Center and bold the text as indicated.
   b. Use the automatic bullet feature to create the arrow bullets. (*Hint: To create the arrow bullet, key >, press the space bar once, and then key the text following the bullet.*)
2. Save the document and name it Unit 1, PA 04.
3. Print Unit 1, PA 04.
4. Select the bulleted paragraphs and change to numbers (use the Numbering button on the Formatting toolbar).
5. Save the document again with the same name (Unit 1, PA 04).
6. Print and then close Unit 1, PA 04.

PERFORMANCE CHALLENGE

Group Project

Select an organization that is familiar to the group members. Selections might include your school, a local business, or a government agency. Make an assessment of what telecommunications services the organization uses and their applications. The assessment will require a variety of means for collecting information. Examples of how data may be collected include:

➢ interviewing individuals within the organization
➢ conducting observations
➢ constructing questionnaires for administrators or staff members to complete
➢ meeting with vendors who market telecommunications systems and services to the organization
➢ reviewing current business periodicals that address telecommunications
➢ talking with people who do business with the organization

Summarize your findings. Based on what was presented in Unit 1, identify technological developments and trends in telecommunications that would help the organization to more effectively conduct its day-to-day business operations.

Prepare a report that includes a title page, table of contents, introduction, methods used in collecting information, summary of findings, identification of telecommunications technology and trends that would favorably affect the organization's operations, and a general summary.

Individual Project

Prepare a report that includes the job you will be pursuing after completing your current educational program. What telecommunications systems and services will be used in conjunction with this job? Identify technological changes and trends in telecommunications systems and services that will most likely affect this field. What areas of telecommunications do you need to strengthen relative to the job you plan to pursue?

Figure U1.4 • Assessment 4

CREATING ORIGINAL DOCUMENTS

The following activities give you the opportunity to practice your writing skills along with demonstrating an understanding of some of the important Word features you have mastered in this unit. Follow the steps explained below to improve your writing skills.

The Writing Process

Plan: Gather ideas, select which information to include, and choose the order in which to present the information.

Checkpoints

What is the purpose?

Who is the audience and what do you want them to do?

What information do the readers need to reach your intended conclusion?

Write: Following the information plan and keeping the reader in mind, draft the document using clear, direct sentences that say what you mean.

Checkpoints

What are the subpoints for each main thought?

What is the simplest way to state the key ideas and supporting information?

How can you connect paragraphs so the reader moves smoothly from one idea to the next?

Revise: Improve what is written by changing, deleting, rearranging, or adding words, sentences, and paragraphs.

Checkpoints

Is the meaning clear?

Do the ideas follow a logical order?

Have you included any unnecessary information?

Have you built your sentences around strong nouns and verbs?

Edit: Check spelling, sentence construction, word use, punctuation, and capitalization.

Checkpoints

Can you spot any redundancies or cliches?

Can you reduce any phrases to an effective word (for example, change *the fact that* to *because*)?

Have you used commas only where there is a strong reason for doing so?

Did you proofread the document for errors that your spell checker cannot identify?

Publish: Prepare a final copy that could be reproduced and shared with others.

Checkpoints

Which design elements—for example, bolding and different fonts— would help highlight important ideas or sections?

Would charts or other graphics help clarify meaning?

Use correct grammar, appropriate word choices, and clear sentence constructions.

Assessment five

Situation: You are Shannon Gibson, public relations officer for the Coleman Development Corporation. Prepare an announcement with the following information:

- Stephanie Branson has been appointed president by the Board of Trustees.
- She has 25 years of experience in the land management field and has spent the past 10 years as president of Lancaster, Inc.
- The selection process began over six months ago and included several interviews and visitations to Lancaster by several board members.
- An open house is planned for August 19, 1998, from 1:30 to 5:00 p.m. in the corporation's conference room.

Include a title for the announcement. Name the announcement Unit 1, PA 05. Print and then close Unit 1, PA 05.

Assessment six

Situation: You are an employee for the Washington County Department of Emergency Management. Prepare a letter to Vicki Fortino, superintendent of Bakersville School District, thanking her for the inquiry about earthquake preparedness. In the letter, talk about the importance of earthquake preparedness for all schools. Tell her that a basic earthquake survival kit includes the following items:

Water (two quarts to one gallon per person per day)
First-aid kit and first-aid books
Food (packaged, canned, no-cook, baby food, and foods for special diets)
Can opener (non-electric)
Blankets or sleeping bags
Portable radio, flashlight, spare batteries
Essential medicines and glasses
Fire extinguisher (A-B-C type)
Food and water for pets
Cash or currency

Send the letter to:

Vicki Fortino, Superintendent
Bakersville School District
6600 Northside Drive
Bakersville, OR 99702

Use your own name in the complimentary close. (Since you are writing the letter, you do not need to include typist's initials at the end of the document—just the document name.) When the letter is completed, save it and name it Unit 1, PA 06. Print and then close Unit 1, PA 06.

Unit two

PRODUCING ENHANCED AND CUSTOMIZED DOCUMENTS

In this unit, you will learn to enhance documents with writing tools such as Spelling, Thesaurus, and Grammar; produce business documents with customized features such as fonts and templates; and prepare form documents with personalized information.

scans

The Secretary's Commission on Achieving Necessary Skills

DECISION MAKING

TECHNOLOGY

PROBLEM SOLVING

COMMUNICATIONS

6 Changing Fonts

PERFORMANCE OBJECTIVES

Upon successful completion of chapter 6, you will be able to:

- **Enhance the visual display of text in documents by changing the font.**
- **Apply formatting effects to text such as strikethrough, superscript, subscript, small caps, and hidden text.**
- **Format text with Format Painter.**
- **Insert symbols in a document.**

Word 97 uses the Times New Roman font as the default. This font can be changed to a variety of other fonts provided by the Word program as well as the printer you are using. In this chapter, you will learn how to change the font for text. You will also learn how to apply formatting effects to text, format with Format Painter, and insert symbols in a document.

Choosing a Typeface

A font consists of three parts: typeface, type style, and type size. A *typeface* is a set of characters with a common design and shape. Typefaces may be decorative or plain and are either *monospaced* or *proportional*. (Word refers to typeface as font.) A monospaced typeface allots the same amount of horizontal space for each character. Courier is an example of a monospaced typeface. Proportional typefaces allot a varying amount of space for each character. The space allotted is based on the width of the character. For example, the lowercase *i* will take up less space than the uppercase *M*.

Proportional typefaces are divided into two main categories: *serif* and *sans serif*. A serif is a small line at the end of a character stroke. Traditionally, a serif typeface is used with documents that are text intensive (documents that are mainly text) because the serifs help move the reader's eyes across the page. Figure 6.1 shows examples of serif typefaces.

A sans serif typeface does not have serifs (*sans* is French for *without*). Sans serif typefaces are often used for headlines and advertisements that are not text intensive. Figure 6.2 shows examples of sans serif typefaces.

6.1 Serif Typefaces

Arrus
Bookman Light
Garamond
Goudy Old Style
New Century Schoolbook
Palatino
Times New Roman (TT)

figure 6.2 Sans Serif Typefaces

Arial
AvantGarde
Helvetica
Tahoma
Univers

Spacing Punctuation

As mentioned earlier in chapter 1, space once after end-of-sentence punctuation and after a colon when text is set in a proportional typeface. Proportional typeface is set closer together and extra white space at the end of a sentence or after a colon is not needed.

Choosing a Type Size

Typefaces can be set in different sizes. The size of text is measured vertically in units called *points*. A point is approximately 1/72 of an inch. The higher the point size, the larger the characters. Examples of different point sizes in the Arial typeface are shown in figure 6.3.

6.3 Different Point Sizes in Arial

8-point Arial
12-point Arial
18-point Arial
24-point Arial

Choosing a Type Style

Within a typeface, characters may have a varying style. There are four main categories of type styles:

1. regular
2. bold
3. italic
4. bold italic

Figure 6.4 illustrates the four main type styles in 12 point.

6.4 *Four Main Type Styles*

Tahoma regular	Times New Roman regular
Tahoma bold	**Times New Roman bold**
Tahoma italic	*Times New Roman italic*
Tahoma bold italic	***Times New Roman bold italic***

The term *font* describes a particular typeface in a specific style and size. Some examples of fonts include *10-point Arial, 12-point Garamond bold, 14-point Tahoma italic,* and *18-point Times New Roman bold italic.*

Choosing a Font

Fonts are provided by Word and also by the printer you are using. Word provides a number of soft fonts called True Type. The printer you are using also contains fonts. These printer fonts can be supplemented with cartridges. A font cartridge that adds fonts can be inserted directly into some printers. To install a font cartridge, refer to the documentation that comes with the cartridge. The types of fonts you have available with your printer depend on the printer you are using, the amount of memory installed with the printer, and any font cartridges that have been added.

True Type fonts are *graphically* generated (generated by the software) while printer fonts are *printer* generated. Graphically generated fonts usually take longer to print than printer generated fonts.

Using the Font Dialog Box

The fonts available with your printer are displayed in the Font list box at the Font dialog box. To display the Font dialog box, shown in figure 6.5, click Format, then Font. You can also display the Font dialog box with a shortcut menu. To do this, position the I-beam pointer anywhere within the document screen, click the *right* mouse button, and then click the left mouse button on Font.

6.5 Font Dialog Box

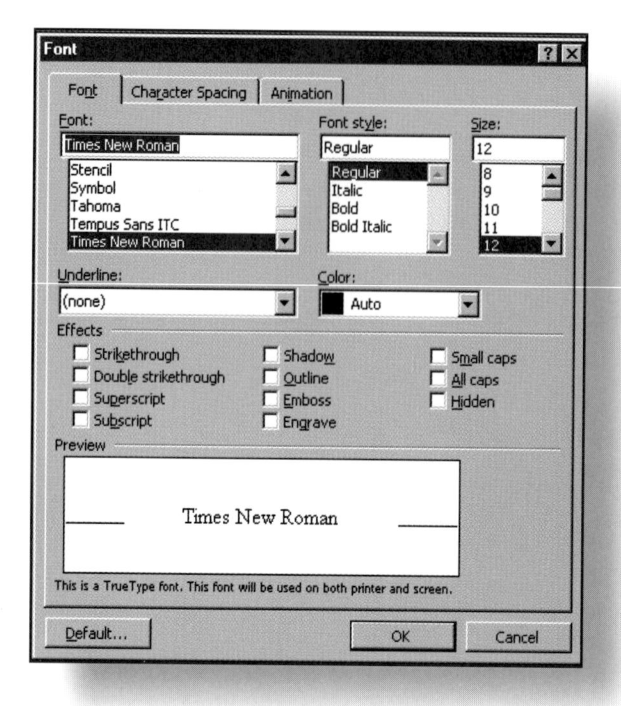

Font

The Font list box at the Font dialog box displays the typefaces (fonts) available with your printer. Figure 6.5 shows the typefaces available with a laser printer (the fonts displayed with your printer may vary from those shown). To select a typeface, click the desired typeface in the Font list box, and then click OK. When a typeface is selected, the Preview box at the bottom of the dialog box displays the appearance of the selected typeface.

exercise 1

Changing Typeface at the Font Dialog Box

1. Open Para 02.
2. Save the document with Save As and name it Ch 06, Ex 01.
3. Change the typeface to Century Schoolbook by completing the following steps:
   a. Select the entire document by pressing Ctrl + A.
   b. Display the Font dialog box by clicking Format, then Font.
   c. At the Font dialog box, click *Century Schoolbook* in the Font list box. (You will need to scroll up the list to display this typeface. If Century Schoolbook is not available, select another typeface such as Garamond or Rockwell.)
   d. Click OK.

4. At the document screen, deselect the text to see how it looks set in Century Schoolbook.
5. Save the document again with the same name (Ch 06, Ex 01).
6. Print and then close Ch 06, Ex 01.

In addition to using the Font dialog box to select a typeface, you can use the Font button on the Formatting toolbar. The Font button displays a font name followed by a down-pointing triangle. For example, if your default typeface is Times New Roman, that names displays in the Font button. If you click the down-pointing triangle after the Font button, a drop-down menu displays as shown in figure 6.6 (your drop-down menu may vary).

Font

Font Drop-Down Menu

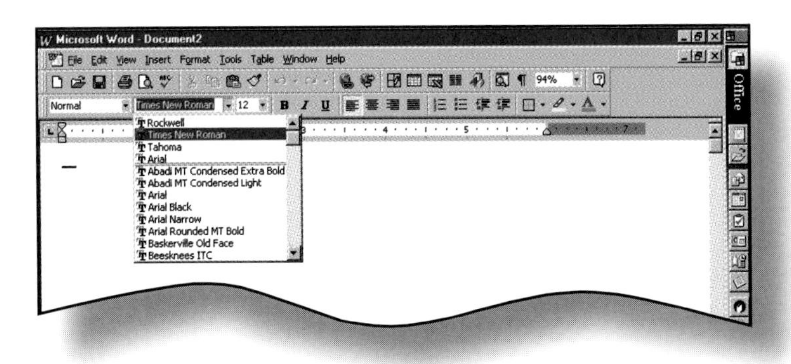

To select a typeface, position the arrow pointer on the desired typeface, and then click the left mouse button.

exercise 2

Changing Typeface Using the Font Button on the Formatting Toolbar

1. Open Para 03 as a read-only document. (For a review on how to open a read-only document, refer to chapter 5.)
2. Change the typeface to Arial using the Font button on the Formatting toolbar by completing the following steps:
   a. Select the entire document by pressing Ctrl + A.
   b. Click the down-pointing triangle to the right of the Font button.
   c. From the drop-down menu that displays, click *Arial.* (You may need to click the up or down triangle in the scroll bar to display Arial.)

3. Deselect the text to see what it looks like set in Arial.
4. Save the document with Save As and name it Ch 06, Ex 02.
5. Print and then close Ch 06, Ex 02.

Size

The Size list box at the Font dialog box displays a variety of common type sizes. Decrease point size to make text smaller or increase point size to make text larger. To select a point size with the mouse, click the desired point size. To view more point sizes, click the down-pointing triangle in the Size scroll bar. If you are using the keyboard, press Alt + S for Size, and then press the down arrow key until the desired point size is selected.

You can also key a specific point size. To do this with the mouse, select the number in the Size text box, and then key the desired point size. If you are using the keyboard, press Alt + S, and then key the desired point size.

Word also provides shortcut commands that can be used to increase or decrease the point size of selected text. To increase the point size of text, select the text, and then press Ctrl +]. Each time you press Ctrl +], the point size increases by one point. To decrease the point size of text, select the text, and then press Ctrl + [until the text displays in the desired size.

exercise 3

Changing Typeface and Size Using the Font Dialog Box

1. Open Para 04 as a read-only document.
2. Change the font to 10-point Bookman Old Style using the Font dialog box by completing the following steps:
   a. Select the entire document.
   b. Display the Font dialog box.
   c. At the Font dialog box, click *Bookman Old Style* in the Font list box. (You will need to scroll up the list to display this typeface.)
   d. Click the *10* that displays in the Size list box.
   e. Click OK.
3. With the document still selected, change alignment of paragraphs to justified.
4. Deselect the text to see what it looks like set in 10-point Bookman Old Style.
5. Save the document with Save As and name it Ch 06, Ex 03.
6. Print and then close Ch 06, Ex 03.

In addition to the Font dialog box, you can use the Font Size button on the Formatting toolbar to change type size. The Font Size button contains the current point size followed by a down-pointing triangle. To change the type size with the Font Size button, position the arrow pointer on the down-pointing triangle that displays after the point size, and then click the left mouse button. From the drop-down menu that displays, click the desired type size.

12

Font Size

exercise 4

Changing Typeface and Size Using the Formatting Toolbar

1. Open Para 02 as a read-only document.
2. Change the font to 11-point Tahoma using the Formatting toolbar by completing the following steps:
   a. Select the entire document.
   b. Click the down-pointing triangle to the right of the Font button on the Formatting toolbar.
   c. From the drop-down menu that displays, click *Tahoma*.
   d. Click the down-pointing triangle to the right of the Size button on the Formatting toolbar and then click *11* at the drop-down list.
3. Deselect the text to see what it looks like set in 11-point Tahoma.
4. Save the document with Save As and name it Ch 06, Ex 04.
5. Print and then close Ch 06, Ex 04.

Font Style

The Font style list box at the Font dialog box displays the styles available with typefaces. Choose from a variety of type styles such as regular, bold, italic, or bold and italic.

exercise 5

Changing Typeface and Style Using the Font Dialog Box

1. Open Para 03 as a read-only document.
2. Change the typeface to Century Schoolbook and the style to Bold Italic by completing the following steps:
   a. Select the entire document.
   b. Display the Font dialog box.
   c. At the Font dialog box, click *Century Schoolbook* in the Font list box. (You will need to scroll up the list to display this typeface.)
   d. Click *Bold Italic* in the Font style list box.
   e. Click OK.

3. Deselect the text to see what it looks like set in Century Schoolbook bold italic.
4. Save the document with Save As and name it Ch 06, Ex 05.
5. Print and then close Ch 06, Ex 05.

Underline Options

When underlining is turned on, Word will underline words and spaces between words with a single line. With Underline options at the Font dialog box, you can underline words and spaces between words with a single line, a double line, or a dotted line. You can also tell Word to underline words only and not the spaces between words.

exercise 6

Underlining Text Using an Underlining Option

1. Open Notice 01 as a read-only document.
2. Underline the words *Friday, April 17, 1998* in the first paragraph with a dotted line by completing the following steps:
   a. Select *Friday, April 17, 1998*.
   b. Display the Font dialog box by clicking Format, then Font.
   c. Click the down-pointing triangle at the right side of the Underline text box and then click *Dotted* at the drop-down list.
   d. Click OK.
3. Select the words *6:00 p.m.* in the first paragraph and then underline them with a Dotted line.
4. Select the words *9:30 p.m.* in the first paragraph and then underline them with a Dotted line.
5. Select the words *20 new gadgets* in the second paragraph and then underline them with a Dotted line.
6. Select the words *in advance* in the third paragraph and then underline them with a Dotted line.
7. Select the words *exciting and fun-filled evening* in the last paragraph and then underline them with a Dotted line.
8. Save the document with Save As and name it Ch 06, Ex 06.
9. Print and then close Ch 06, Ex 06.

Color Options

With the Color option from the Font dialog box, you can specify a color for text or selected text. If you do not have access to a color printer, text identified with color will print in black or shades of gray.

exercise 7

Changing the Font and Text Color

1. Open Notice 02 as a read-only document.
2. Make the following changes to the document:
   a. Select the entire document.
   b. Display the Font dialog box.
   c. Change the font to 14-point Bookman Old Style bold.
   d. With the Font dialog box still displayed, change the text color to Blue by clicking the down-pointing triangle at the right side of the Color text box and then clicking *Blue* at the drop-down list.
   e. Click OK.
   f. Deselect the text.
3. Save the document with Save As and name it Ch 06, Ex 07.
4. Print and then close Ch 06, Ex 07.

Effects

The Effects section of the Font dialog box contains a variety of options that can be used to create different character styles.

The Strikethrough option lets you show text that needs to be deleted from a document. Strikethrough prints text with a line of hyphens running through it. This feature has practical application for some legal documents in which deleted text must be retained in the document. The hyphens indicate that the text has been deleted. Strikethrough text looks like this:

~~This is Strikethrough text.~~

exercise 8

Using Strikethrough

1. Open Legal 01
2. Save the document with Save As and name it Ch 06, Ex 08.
3. Make the following changes to the document:
   a. Select the entire document and then change the font to 12-point Garamond. (If this typeface is not available, use another typeface such as Century Schoolbook or Bookman Old Style.)
   b. Deselect the text.
   c. Select the last sentence in the second paragraph (the one that begins "A default judgment is one where the plaintiff..."), and identify it for strikethrough by completing the following steps:
      1) Select the sentence.
      2) Display the Font dialog box.

3) Click the Strikethrough check box.
4) Click OK.

d. Select the last paragraph (one sentence) that begins "This Summons is issued pursuant..." and then identify it for strikethrough following step 3c.

4. Save the document again with the same name (Ch 06, Ex 08).
5. Print and then close Ch 06, Ex 08.

With the Superscript option, you can create text that is raised slightly above the line. Some mathematical expressions are written with superscripted numbers. For example, the mathematical expression 4 to the second power is written as 4^2. You can create superscripted text as you key text or you can superscript selected text. Create superscripted text with the Superscript option at the Font dialog box. Superscripted text can also be created at the keyboard with Ctrl + Shift + =.

With the Subscript option from the Font dialog box, you can create text that is lowered slightly below the line. Some chemical formulas require the use of subscripted characters. For example, the formula for water is written as H_2O. You can create subscripted text as you are keying text or you can subscript selected text. Subscripted text can also be created at the keyboard with Ctrl + =.

exercise 9

Changing the Font and Superscripting and Subscripting Text

1. At a clear document screen, key the memo shown in figure 6.7 in an appropriate memo format (refer to Appendix B for a review of memo formatting) with the following specifications:
   a. Change the font to 12-point Century Schoolbook.
   b. Indent and italicize text as indicated.
   c. Create the superscripted numbers in the memo by completing the following steps:
      1) Key text to the point where superscripted text is to appear.
      2) Display the Font dialog box.
      3) At the Font dialog box, click the Superscript check box.
      4) Click OK.
      5) Key the superscripted text.
      6) Repeat steps 2) through 4) to turn off superscript.
   d. Create the subscripted numbers in the memo by completing the following steps:
      1) Key text to the point where subscripted text is to appear.
      2) Press Ctrl + =.

3) Key the subscripted text.
4) Press Ctrl + =.

2. Save the memo and name it Ch 06, Ex 09.
3. Print and then close Ch 06, Ex 09.

figure 6.7 *Exercise 9*

DATE: February 2, 1999; TO: Gerald Ramey; FROM: Yolanda Whitten; SUBJECT: STATISTICAL ANALYSIS

The research and analysis you are conducting on product marketing is very important to the project planning. As you complete your analysis, please address the following areas:

- What is the relationship between the indices *C*, *D*, and *I* to both r^1 and r^2?
- What is the improvement when $r^1 = .55$ and r^2 is nearly .79?
- What is the main effect on the scores of X_1, X_2, and X_3?

When these areas have been addressed, please give me a copy of the analysis.

XX:Ch 06, Ex 09

With the Hidden option from the Font dialog box, you can include such items as comments, personal messages, or questions in a document. These items can be displayed, printed, or hidden. Hidden text will display in the document screen only if the display of nonprinting characters has been turned on. Hidden text displays in the screen with a dotted underline below. To turn the display of nonprinting characters on or off, click the Show/Hide ¶ button on the Standard toolbar. Press Ctrl + Shift + H to create hidden text with the keyboard.

By default, hidden text does not print. If you want to print hidden text, display the Print dialog box, and then click Options. At the Options dialog box, click the Hidden text check box, and then click OK. At the Print dialog box, click OK. If you decide you do not want hidden text to print, complete similar steps to remove the check mark from the Hidden text check box at the Options dialog box.

exercise 10

Creating Hidden Text

1. Open Memo 01.
2. Save the document with Save As and name it Ch 06, Ex 10.
3. Create hidden text at the end of the document by completing the following steps:
   a. Move the insertion point to the end of the document.
   b. Key **bcc Carlton Waters, Dean**
   c. Select *bcc Carlton Waters, Dean*.
   d. Display the Font dialog box.
   e. At the Font dialog box, click the Hidden check box.
   f. Click OK.
4. Save the document again with the same name (Ch 06, Ex 10).
5. Print the memo and the hidden text by completing the following steps:
   a. Display the Print dialog box.
   b. Click the Options button that displays in the bottom left corner of the Print dialog box.
   c. At the Options dialog box, click the Hidden text check box. (This will insert a check mark in the check box. If the box already contains a check mark, skip this step.)
   d. Click OK.
   e. At the Print dialog box, click OK.
6. After the memo is printed, remove the check mark from the Hidden text check box at the Options dialog box by completing the following steps:
   a. Display the Print dialog box.
   b. Click the Options button that displays in the bottom left corner of the dialog box.
   c. At the Options dialog box, click the Hidden text check box (this removes the check mark).
   d. Click OK.
   e. At the Print dialog box, click Close.
7. Close Ch 06, Ex 10.

The Effects section of the Font dialog box contains additional options for creating special effects. Click the Shadow option to add a shadow behind and to the right of text. Make text display the inner and outer borders of each character by choosing the Outline option. Apply the Emboss option to text to make it appear raised off the page. Choose the Engrave option to make text appear to be imprinted on the page. Use the Small caps option to make text display in small capital letters or choose the All caps option to make text display in all capital letters.

Changing Text to Small Caps

1. Open Memo 01.
2. Save the document with Save As and name it Ch 06, Ex 11.
3. Make the following changes to the document:
   a. Select the entire document and then change the font to 12-point Rockwell. (If this typeface is not available, choose another typeface such as Century Schoolbook, Garamond, or Bookman Old Style.)
   b. With the document still selected, change the text in the document to Small caps by completing the following steps:
      1) Display the Font dialog box.
      2) Click the Small caps check box.
      3) Click OK.
   c. If necessary, realign text after the headings at the beginning of the memo.
4. Save the document again with the same name (Ch 06, Ex 11).
5. Print and then close Ch 06, Ex 11.

Formatting with Format Painter

The Standard toolbar contains a button that can be used to copy character formatting to different locations in the document. This button is called the Format Painter and displays on the Standard toolbar as a paintbrush.

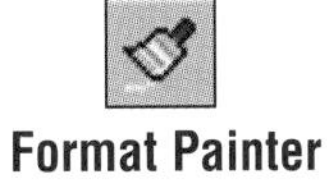
Format Painter

To use the Format Painter button, position the insertion point on a character containing the desired character formatting, click the Format Painter button, and then select text to which you want the character formatting applied. When you click the Format Painter button, the mouse I-beam pointer displays with a paintbrush attached. If you want to apply character formatting a single time, click the Format Painter button once. If, however, you want to apply the character formatting in more than one location in the document, double-click the Format Painter button. If you have double-clicked the Format Painter button, turn off the feature by clicking the Format Painter button once.

exercise 12

Formatting Text with the Format Painter

1. Open Bibliography.
2. Save the document with Save As and name it Ch 06, Ex 12.
3. Make the following changes to the document:
   a. Select the book title, *The Art of Communicating*, and then click the Italic button on the Formatting toolbar.
   b. Use the Format Painter to change the other book titles to italic by completing the following steps:
      1) Position the insertion point on any character in the italicized book title, *The Art of Communicating*.
      2) Double-click the Format Painter button on the Standard toolbar.
      3) Select the book title *Fundamentals of Written Communications*. (This applies the italic formatting.)
      4) Select the book title *A Resource Guide to Business Documents*. (This applies the italic formatting.)
      5) Select the book title *Improving Business Communications*. (This applies the italic formatting.)
      6) Click once on the Format Painter button on the Standard toolbar. (This turns off Format Painter.)
4. Save the document again with the same name (Ch 06, Ex 12).
5. Print and then close Ch 06, Ex 12.

exercise 13

Formatting Headings with the Format Painter

1. Open Report 01 as a read-only document.
2. Make the following changes to the document:
   a. Select the entire document and then change the font to 12-point Century Schoolbook.
   b. Select the title, *DESKTOP PUBLISHING*, and then change the font to 14-point Arial bold.
   c. Use the Format Painter button to center and change the font of the four headings to 14-point Arial bold by completing the following steps:
      1) Position the insertion point on any character in the title *DESKTOP PUBLISHING*.
      2) Double-click the Format Painter button on the Standard toolbar.
      3) Select the heading, *Defining Desktop Publishing*.

4) Select the heading, *Initiating the Desktop Publishing Process*.
5) Select the heading, *Planning the Publication*.
6) Select the heading, *Creating the Content*.
7) Click once on the Format Painter button on the Standard toolbar.

3. Save the document and name it Ch 06, Ex 13.
4. Print and then close Ch 06, Ex 13.

Inserting Symbols

Many of the typefaces (fonts) include special symbols such as bullets, publishing symbols, and letters with special punctuation (such as É, ö, and ñ). To insert a symbol, display the Symbol dialog box shown in figure 6.8 by clicking Insert, then Symbol. At the Symbol dialog box with the Symbols tab selected, double-click the desired symbol, and then click Close; or click the desired symbol, click Insert, and then click Close.

6.8

Symbol Dialog Box with Symbols Tab Selected

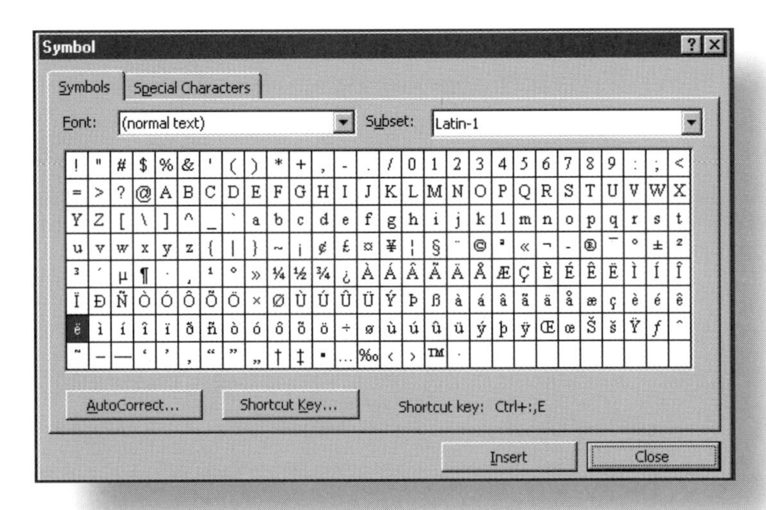

Changing the Font for Symbols

At the Symbol dialog box, you can change the font with the Font option. When you change the font, different symbols display in the dialog box. To change the font, display the Symbol dialog box, click the down-pointing triangle at the right side of the Font text box, and then click the desired font at the drop-down list.

exercise 14

Creating Special Symbols

1. At a clear document screen, create the memo shown in figure 6.9 in an appropriate memo format by completing the following steps:
   a. Key the text in the memo to the point where the ë is to be inserted and then complete the following steps:
      1) Click Insert, then Symbol.
      2) At the Symbol dialog box with the Symbols tab selected, make sure *(normal text)* displays in the Font text box. (If not, click the down-pointing triangle at the right side of the Font text box, and then click *(normal text)*. This font displays at the beginning of the list.)
      3) Double-click the ë symbol (first symbol from the left in the seventh row).
      4) Click Close.
   b. Key the text in the memo to the point where the ô is to be inserted and then complete the following steps:
      1) Click Insert, then Symbol.
      2) At the Symbol dialog box with the Symbols tab selected, make sure *(normal text)* displays in the Font text box. (If not, click the down-pointing triangle at the right side of the Font text box, and then click *(normal text)*.)
      3) Double-click the ô symbol (tenth symbol from the left in the seventh row).
      4) Click Close.
   c. Key the text in the memo to the point where the degree (°) symbol is to be inserted and then complete the following steps:
      1) Click Insert, then Symbol.
      2) At the Symbol dialog box with the Symbols tab selected, make sure *(normal text)* displays in the Font text box, and then double-click the ° symbol (eighth symbol from the left in the fifth row).
      3) Click Close.
      4) Repeat these steps for the second occurrence of the degree (°) symbol.
   d. Key the text in the memo to the point where the ® symbol is to be inserted and then complete the following steps:
      1) Click Insert, then Symbol.
      2) At the Symbol dialog box with the Symbols tab selected, make sure *(normal text)* displays in the Font text box, and then double-click the ® symbol (twenty-fourth symbol from the left in the fourth row).
      3) Click Close.
   e. Key the text in the memo to the point where the first bullet (⇨) is to be inserted and then complete the following steps:

1) Click Insert, then Symbol.
2) At the Symbol dialog box with the Symbols tab selected, click the down-pointing triangle at the right side of the Font text box, and then click *Wingdings*. (You will need to scroll down the list to display *Wingdings*.)
3) Double-click the ⇨ symbol (thirteenth symbol from the left in the last row).
4) Click Close.

f. Press Tab, key the text following the first bullet, and then press Enter. (If the automatic bulleting feature is on, Word inserts another bullet.)
g. Key the remaining text following the bullets. (The bullets will be inserted automatically.)
h. After keying the text following the last bullet, press Enter twice. (This turns off the automatic bullets.)
i. Key the remainder of the text in the memo.

2. Save the memo and name it Ch 06, Ex 14.
3. Print and then close Ch 06, Ex 14.

6.9

Exercise 14

DATE: January 15, 1999; TO: Sylvia Raphaël; FROM: Michelle Sloan; SUBJECT: DISTRICT NEWSLETTER

The layout for the February newsletter looks great! John Pacôme said that the image on the second page can be rotated either 90° or 270°. What would you prefer?

John plans to offer an informal workshop on some of the graphic capabilities of Word for Windows®. He plans to address the following topics:

⇨ adding borders
⇨ inserting pictures
⇨ drawing shapes
⇨ creating charts

If you want him to address any other topics, please give me a call by the end of this week.

XX:Ch 06, Ex 14

chapter summary

- A font consists of three parts: typeface, type style, and type size.
- A typeface is a set of characters with a common design and shape. Typefaces are either monospaced or proportional. A monospaced typeface, such as Courier, allots the same amount of horizontal space for each character. A proportional typeface, such as Times New Roman, allots a varying amount of space for each character.
- A type style is a variation of style within a certain typeface. There are four main kinds of type styles: regular, bold, italic, and bold italic.
- Type size is measured in point size, which is a vertical measurement—the higher the point size, the larger the characters.
- The kinds of fonts you have available with your printer depends on the type of printer you are using, the amount of memory installed with the printer, and what supplemental fonts you have.
- Change the font at the Font dialog box or use the Font button on the Formatting toolbar. To use the Font button, click the down-pointing triangle to the right of the font name, and then click the desired font at the drop-down list.
- The fonts available with your printer are displayed in the Font list box at the Font dialog box. At this dialog box, changes can also be made to the font size, font style, underline options, and text color.
- The Effects section of the Font dialog box contains the following options that can be used to create different character styles: Strikethrough, Superscript, Subscript, Hidden text, and Small caps.
- Use the Format Painter button to copy character formatting already applied to text to different locations in the document.
- Many of the typefaces (fonts) include special symbols such as bullets and publishing symbols. Insert a symbol in a document at the Symbol dialog box.

commands review

	Mouse	Keyboard
Font dialog box	Format, Font; or with I-beam in the document screen, click *right* mouse button, then click Font at drop-down list	Format, Font
Increase point size of selected text		CTRL +]
Decrease point size of selected text		CTRL + [
To use Format Painter button	Position insertion point on a character with desired formatting, click Format Painter button, drag through the text to which you want the formatting applied, then release mouse button	
Symbol dialog box	Insert, Symbol	Insert, Symbol

check your understanding

Matching: In the space provided at the left, indicate the correct letter or letters that match each description.

A Arial
B bold
C bold italic
D Century Schoolbook
E font
F italic
G normal
H point
I proportional
J regular
K sans serif
L serif
M subscript
N superscript
O Times New Roman
P type size
Q type style
R typeface

_______ 1. Kinds of type styles.
_______ 2. This kind of typeface does not have a small line at the end of each character stroke.
_______ 3. A particular typeface in a specific style and size.
_______ 4. A set of characters with a common design and shape.
_______ 5. Text that is lowered slightly below the regular line of text.

_________ 6. With this type of measurement, the higher the number, the larger the characters.

_________ 7. Examples of different typefaces.

_________ 8. Text that is raised slightly above the regular line of text.

Completion: In the space provided at the right, indicate the correct term, number, or command.

1. Use this feature to apply formatting to several locations in a document. _________
2. Choose this option at the Font dialog box to show text that needs to be deleted from a document. _________
3. Choose this option at the Font dialog box to specify text that has been added to a legal document. _________
4. A point is approximately this size. _________
5. Use this button on the Formatting toolbar to change type size. _________
6. Choose this option at the Font dialog box to set text in small capital letters. _________

In the space provided below, list the steps that you would complete to insert ñ in a document.

____

____

skill assessments

Note: Before completing the skill assessments, make sure you have deleted all documents created in chapter 4. (You may have already done this in chapter 5.) Check with your instructor before deleting these documents.

Assessment 1

1. Open Report 02 as a read-only document.
2. Make the following changes to the document:
   a. Select the entire document and then change the font to 12-point Century Schoolbook.
   b. Select the title, *DESKTOP PUBLISHING DESIGN*, and then change the font to 14-point Arial bold.
   c. Use Format Painter to center and change the formatting to 14-point Arial bold for the two headings *Designing a Document* and *Creating Focus*. (The *Creating Focus* heading is located toward the middle of the second page.)
3. Save the document with Save As and name it Ch 06, SA 01.
4. Print and then close Ch 06, SA 01.

Assessment 2

1. Open Legal 02.
2. Save the document with Save As and name it Ch 06, SA 02.
3. Make the following changes to the document:
   a. Select the title, *IN DISTRICT COURT NO. 4, KING COUNTY, STATE OF WASHINGTON*, and then change the font to 14-point Times New Roman bold.
   b. Select the words *the Sixty-Day Rule* toward the end of the first paragraph and identify them as strikethrough text.
   c. Select the punctuation and words*, if any, and a copy of the alcohol influence report form* at the end of the second numbered paragraph and identify them as strikethrough text.
   d. Select the words *upon the satisfactory examination of the inspection data heretofore requested* toward the end of the fourth numbered paragraph and identify them as strikethrough text.
4. Save the document again with the same name (Ch 06, SA 02).
5. Print and then close Ch 06, SA 02.

Assessment 3

1. At a clear document screen, create the document shown in figure 6.10 with the following specifications:
   a. Center the text and add bullets as shown. (If Word converts the first character after a bullet to a capital letter, delete the capital letter and key the letter again in lowercase.)
   b. Select the entire document and then change the font to 12-point Century Schoolbook.
   c. Select the title, *IDENTIFYING THE PURPOSE OF LETTERHEAD*, and then change the font to 14-point Arial bold.
   d. Select the heading, *Conveying Information*, and then change the font to 14-point Arial bold.
   e. Use Format Painter to change the font to 14-point Arial bold for the remaining headings: *Establishing an Identity* and *Projecting an Image*.
2. Save the document and name it Ch 06, SA 03.
3. Print and then close Ch 06, SA 03.

Figure 6.10 • Assessment 3

IDENTIFYING THE PURPOSE OF LETTERHEAD

Conveying Information

Consider all the necessary information you want to include in your letterhead. Also, consider what items your readers expect to find in your letterhead. Although the information provided may vary, letterheads commonly contain the following:

- name of company or organization
- logo
- very brief business philosophy statement, marketing statement, or slogan address
- shipping or mailing address, if different from street address
- telephone number, including area code (include actual numbers if your phone number incorporates a catchy word as part of the number; include extra phone numbers, such as a local number and/or an 800 number, if any)
- fax number, including area code

The information in a letterhead supplies the reader with a means of contacting you in person, by phone, or by mail. Leaving out an important component in your letterhead can affect your company's business and project a careless attitude.

Establishing an Identity

Oftentimes a business relationship is initiated through one or more business letters. A letterhead with a specific design and layout helps to establish your organization's identity. When readers are exposed to the same pattern of consistent elements in your letterhead over a period of time, they soon begin to establish a certain level of familiarity.

Projecting an Image

Along with establishing an identity, you need to think about the image that identity projects to your readers. Assess your target audience. Who are your readers? Whom do you want to be your readers? What image do you want to project and what image do your readers expect you to project?

Assessment 4

1. At a clear document screen, key the memo shown in figure 6.11 in an appropriate memo format with the following specifications:
   a. Indent, italicize, superscript, and subscript text as shown.
   b. After keying the document, select the entire document, and then change the font to 12-point Century Schoolbook.
2. Save the memo and name it Ch 06, SA 04.
3. Print and then close Ch 06, SA 04.

Figure 6.11 • Assessment 4

DATE: February 10, 1999; TO: Yolanda Whitten; FROM: Gerald Ramey; SUBJECT: STATISTICAL ANALYSIS

I have been running an analysis on the areas mentioned in your February 2 memo. Completing the computations has brought up the following questions:

- With smaller section ratios of r^1 and r^2 (.10 to .25)[1], what will be the yield increase?

- What is the interaction effect on the scores of X_1, X_2, and X_3?

I will try to report on the findings to these questions by the end of next week.

XX:Ch 06, SA 04

Assessment 5

1. At a clear document screen, key the memo shown in figure 6.12 in an appropriate memo format. (The é can be found toward the right side in the sixth row at the Symbol dialog box with the *(normal text)* font selected.) To create the bullets, key the symbol >, press the space bar, and then key the first paragraph. Word will automatically insert the arrow bullet. Press Enter and Word inserts the next bullet. After keying the last bulleted paragraph, press the Enter key twice, and then continue keying the remainder of the memo.
2. Save the memo and name it Ch 06, SA 05.
3. Print and then close Ch 06, SA 05.

Figure 6.12 • Assessment 5

DATE: March 3, 1999; TO: Chris St. Léon; FROM: Maureen Hanford; SUBJECT: TELECOMMUNICATIONS TEST

I have made many changes to the attached Telecommunications test. Please revise the test according to the proofreaders' marks and add the following questions.

- From the end user's perspective, what is the value of deregulation in the telecommunications industry?
- What were the previous obstacles to the growth of video teleconferencing? What has happened to eliminate these obstacles?
- What is X.400, and what impact does it have on telecommunications?
- Compare analog and digital transmission. Are we moving to one or the other? Why or why not?

Please intersperse these questions with the existing questions. If possible, I would like this test to fit on one page.

XX:Ch 06, SA 05

7 Using Writing Tools

PERFORMANCE OBJECTIVES

Upon successful completion of chapter 7, you will be able to:

- **Complete a spelling check on text in a document.**
- **Improve the grammar of text in a document using the grammar checker.**
- **Add words to and delete words from the AutoCorrect dialog box.**
- **Display synonyms and antonyms for specific words using Thesaurus.**
- **Display information about a document such as the number of pages, words, characters, paragraphs, and lines.**

Word 97 includes writing tools to help create a thoughtful and well-written document. One of these writing tools, a spelling checker, finds misspelled words and offers replacement words. It also finds duplicate words and irregular capitalizations. A grammar checker finds grammar and style errors in documents and provides possible corrections. Another tool, Thesaurus, provides a list of synonyms, antonyms, and related words for a particular word.

Checking the Spelling and Grammar of a Document

Two tools for creating thoughtful and well-written documents include a spelling checker and a grammar checker. The spelling checker finds misspelled words and offers replacement words. It also finds duplicate words and irregular capitalizations. When you spell check a document, the spelling checker compares the words in your document with the words in its dictionary. If a match is found, the word is passed over. If there is no match for the word, the spelling checker will stop and select:

- a misspelled word when the misspelling does not match another word that exists in the dictionary
- typographical errors such as transposed letters
- double word occurrences (such as *and and*)

- irregular capitalization
- some proper names
- jargon and some technical terms

A small number of words in the spelling checker dictionary are proper names. You will find that many proper names will not appear in this dictionary. The spelling checker will not find a match for these proper names and will select the words for correction. The spelling checker may not stop, however, at all proper names. For example, the spelling checker would assume the first name *June* is spelled correctly and pass over it because June would appear in its dictionary as a month.

The grammar checker will search a document for errors in grammar, style, punctuation, and word usage. The spelling checker and the grammar checker can help you create a well-written document but do not replace the need for proofreading.

Before checking the spelling or grammar of a document, save the document currently displayed or open a document. You would complete the following steps to check a document for spelling or grammar errors:

Spelling and Grammar

1. Click the Spelling and Grammar button on the Standard toolbar or click Tools, then Spelling and Grammar.
2. If a spelling error is detected, the misspelled word is selected and a Spelling and Grammar: English (United States) dialog box, similar to the one shown in figure 7.1, displays. The sentence containing the misspelled word is displayed in the Not in Dictionary: text box. If a grammatical error is detected, the sentence containing the error is selected and the Spelling and Grammar: English (United States) dialog box, similar to the one shown in figure 7.2, displays.
3. If a misspelled word is selected, replace the word with the correct spelling, tell Word to ignore it and continue checking the document, or add the word to a custom dictionary. If a sentence containing a grammatical error is selected, the grammar checker displays the sentence in the top text box in the Spelling and Grammar: English (United States) dialog box. Choose to ignore or change errors found by the grammar checker.
4. When the spelling and grammar check is completed, the Office Assistant displays the message *The spelling and grammar check is complete*. Click anywhere in the document screen outside the message box to remove the box.

figure 7.1 *Spelling and Grammar: English (United States) Dialog Box with Spelling Error Selected*

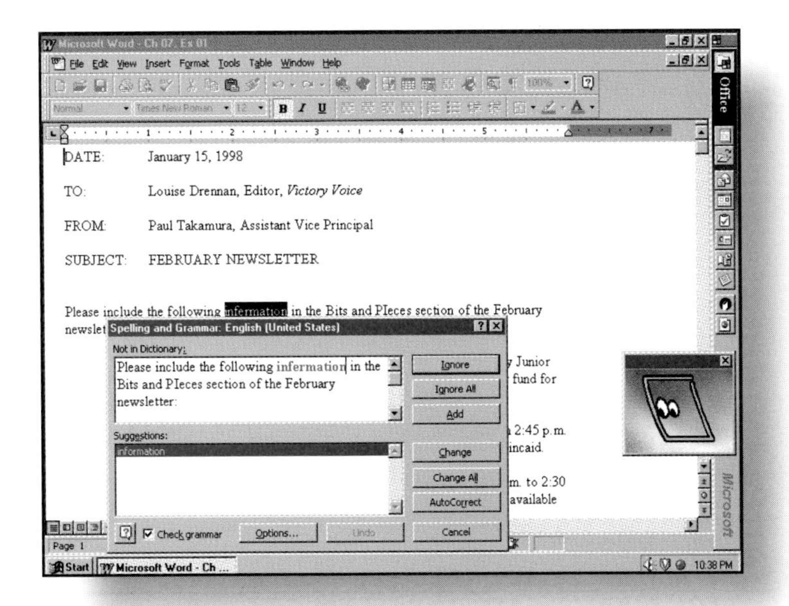

figure 7.2 *Spelling and Grammar: English (United States) Dialog Box with Grammar Error Selected*

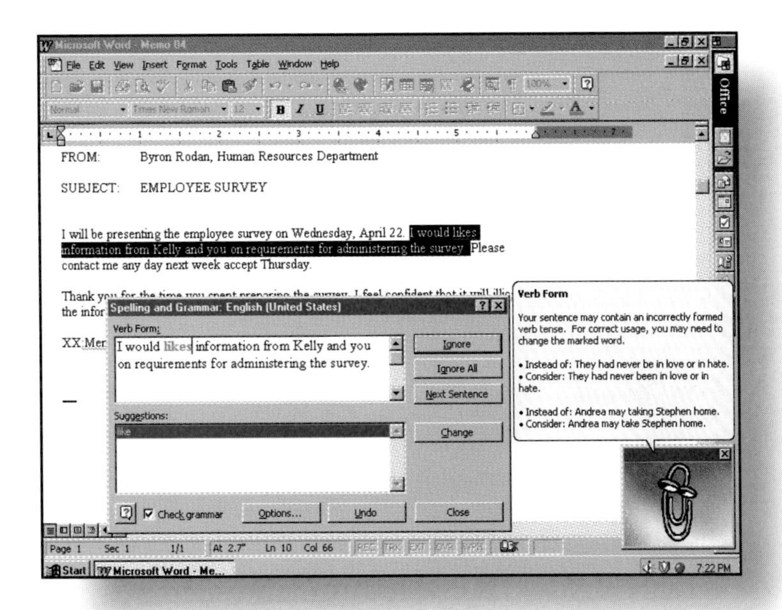

Using Spell Checking Buttons

When a word is selected during a spelling and grammar check, you need to determine if the word should be corrected or if it should be ignored. Word provides buttons at the right side and bottom of the Spelling and Grammar: English (United States) dialog box to make decisions.

Ignore and Ignore All

In some situations, the spelling checker will select a word for correction that you want to leave alone. This may happen with words such as proper names or abbreviations. To leave the word as written, click the Ignore button or the Ignore All button. If you click Ignore, the spelling checker will skip that occurrence of the word but will select occurrences in other locations in the document. If the word appears in other locations in the document and you want it skipped in those locations also, click Ignore All. This tells the spelling checker to skip all occurrences of that particular word.

Change and Change All

When the spelling checker encounters a word that is not in its dictionary, the sentence containing the word is displayed at the top of the dialog box in the Not in Dictionary: text box and suggestions for the correct spelling are listed in the Suggestions list box. To replace the selected word in the sentence with the selected word in the Suggestions list box, click Change. If you want to replace the selected word in the sentence with one of the other words displayed in the Suggestions list box, double-click the desired replacement word in the list box.

If you want to correct the same word in other locations in the document, click the Change All button rather than the Change button.

Add

Besides the spelling checker dictionary, a custom dictionary is available in which you can add words. For example, you may want to add your name, a company name, or any other word (or words) that you use in documents that is not currently found in the main spelling checker dictionary. To add a selected word to the custom dictionary, click the Add button.

Undo

When the Spelling and Grammar: English (United States) dialog box first displays, the Undo button is dimmed. Once a spelling or grammar change is made, the Undo button becomes active. Click this button if you want to reverse the most recent spelling and grammar action.

AutoCorrect

In chapter 1, you learned that Word 97 includes an AutoCorrect feature that automatically changes certain words in a document. For example, if you key *teh* and then press the space bar, AutoCorrect changes this to *the*. You can add misspelled words with the correct spelling to the AutoCorrect list. When the spelling checker selects a misspelled word during a spelling check, make sure the proper spelling is selected in the Suggestions list box, and then click AutoCorrect. The misspelling of the word and the correct spelling of the word are inserted in the AutoCorrect dialog box. The next time you key the incorrect word in a document, AutoCorrect will automatically correct it with the proper spelling.

exercise 1

Spell Checking a Document

1. Open Memo 03.
2. Save the document with Save As and name it Ch 07, Ex 01.
3. Perform a spelling check by completing the following steps:
   a. Click the Spelling and Grammar button on the Standard toolbar (the sixth button from the left).
   b. The spelling checker selects the name *Drennan*. This is a proper name, so click Ignore All to tell the spelling checker to leave the name as written.
   c. The grammar checker selects the text on the TO: line. Click Ignore All to leave the text on the TO: line as written.
   d. The spelling checker selects the name *Takamura*. This is a proper name, so click Ignore All to tell the spelling checker to leave the name as written.
   e. The grammar checker selects the text on the FROM: line. Click Ignore All to leave the text on the FROM: line as written.
   f. The spelling checker selects *infermation*. The proper spelling is selected in the Suggestions list box, so click Change All.
   g. The spelling checker selects *PIeces*. The proper capitalization is selected in the Suggestions list box, so click Change All (or Change).
   h. The spelling checker selects *colected*. The proper spelling is selected in the Suggestions list box, so click Change All (or Change).
   i. The spelling checker selects *fom*. Select the proper spelling (*from*) in the Suggestions list box by clicking the down-pointing triangle at the right side of the list box until *from* is visible, and then clicking *from*. With *from* selected, click Change All.
   j. The spelling checker selects *the*, which is a duplicate word. Click the Delete button to delete the selected *the*.
   k. The spelling checker selects the name *Kincaid*. This is a proper name, so click Ignore All to tell the spelling checker to leave the name as written.
   l. The spelling checker selects *XX:Memo*. Click Ignore All to leave this as written.
   m. The grammar checker selects *XX:Memo 03*. Click Ignore All to leave this as written.
   n. The Office Assistant displays the message, *The spelling and grammar check is complete*. Click in the document screen outside this message to remove the message.
4. Save the document again with the same name (Ch 07, Ex 01).
5. Print and then close Ch 07, Ex 01.

Options

If you click the Options button at the Spelling and Grammar: English (United States) dialog box, the Spelling & Grammar dialog box displays as shown in figure 7.3.

7.3 **Spelling & Grammar Dialog Box**

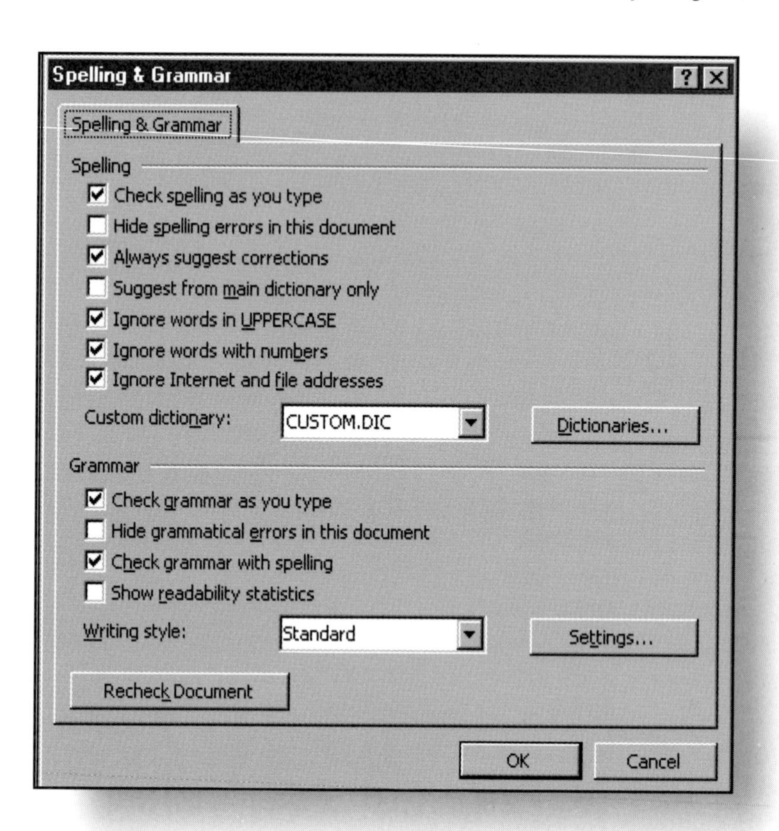

Figure 7.4 describes the options available in the Spelling section of the Spelling & Grammar dialog box. (The Grammar options are explained in the "Checking the Grammar and Style of a Document" section of this chapter.)

Spelling Options at the Spelling & Grammar Dialog Box

Choose this option...	and Word will...
Check spelling as you type	check words in a document as they are being keyed by inserting a wavy red line below words not contained in the spelling dictionary.
Hide spelling errors in this document	remove the wavy red line below words not contained in the spelling dictionary.
Always suggest corrections	always suggest corrections. Make this option inactive if you do not want suggestions (spelling checker will work faster).
Suggest from main dictionary only	provide suggestions only from the main dictionary, not from any custom dictionaries.
Ignore words in UPPERCASE	ignore words in all uppercase letters.
Ignore words with numbers	ignore words that include numbers.
Ignore Internet and file addresses	ignore Internet addresses (such as http://www.company.com), file names, and electronic mail addresses.

At the Spelling & Grammar dialog box, you can also create or edit a custom dictionary. Custom dictionaries can be created for specialized terms or a specific profession. Refer to Word's Help feature for more information on custom dictionaries.

You can also display the Spelling & Grammar dialog box by clicking Tools, then Options. At the Options dialog box, click the Spelling & Grammar tab.

Editing While Spell Checking

When spell checking a document, you can temporarily leave the Spelling and Grammar: English (United States) dialog box, make corrections in the document, and then resume spell checking. For example, suppose while spell checking you notice a sentence that you want to change. To correct the sentence, move the I-beam pointer to the location in the sentence where the change is to occur, click the left mouse button, and then make changes to the sentence. To resume spell checking, click the Resume button, which was formerly the Ignore button.

exercise 2

Spell Checking a Document with Words in Uppercase and with Numbers

1. Open Letter 01.
2. Save the letter with Save As and name it Ch 07, Ex 02.
3. Review spell checking options by completing the following steps:
   a. Click Tools, then Options.
   b. At the Options dialog box, click the Spelling & Grammar tab.
   c. Make sure there is a check mark in the Ignore words in UPPERCASE check box. (If there is no check mark, click in the check box before Ignore words in UPPERCASE to insert one.)
   d. Make sure there is a check mark in the Ignore words with numbers check box. (If there is no check mark, click in the check box before Ignore words with numbers to insert one.)
   e. Click OK or press Enter to close the dialog box.
4. Perform a spelling check by completing the following steps:
   a. Click the Spelling and Grammar button on the Standard toolbar.
   b. The spelling checker selects the name *Garcetti*. This is a proper name, so click Ignore All to tell the spelling checker to leave the name as written.
   c. The spelling checker selects *atached*. The proper spelling is selected in the Suggestions list box, so click Change (or Change All).
   d. The spelling checker selects *reprasenting*. The proper spelling is selected in the Suggestions list box, so click Change (or Change All).
   e. The spelling checker selects *correspondances*. The proper spelling is selected in the Suggestions list box, so click Change (or Change All).
   f. The spelling checker selects *suld* and does not offer the correct spelling (which is *should*). To correct the word in the Not in Dictionary: text box, move the insertion point immediately left of the *u* in *suld*, key *ho*, and then click the Change button.
   g. The spelling checker selects *Streat*. The proper spelling is selected in the Suggestions list box, so click Change (or Change All).
   h. The spelling checker selects *XX:Letter*. Click Ignore to leave this as written.
   i. The grammar checker selects *XX:Letter 01* and the Office Assistant displays information on spacing. Click Ignore to leave this as written.
   j. When the spell check is completed, click outside the Office Assistant message box to remove the message box.
5. Save the document again with the same name (Ch 07, Ex 02).
6. Print and then close Ch 07, Ex 02.

Checking the Grammar and Style of a Document

Word includes a grammar checking feature that you can use to search a document for grammar, style, punctuation, and word usage. Like the spelling checker, the grammar checker does not find every error in a document and may stop at correct phrases. The grammar checker can help you create a well-written document, but does not replace the need for proofreading.

To complete a grammar check (as well as a spelling check) on a document, click the Spelling and Grammar button on the Standard toolbar or click Tools, then Spelling and Grammar. The grammar checker selects the first sentence with a grammatical error and displays the sentence in the top text box in the dialog box. The grammar rule that is violated is displayed above the text box and the Office Assistant displays information about the grammar rule. Choose to ignore or change errors found by the grammar checker. When the grammar checker is done, the open document is displayed in the screen. The changes made during the check are inserted in the document. You can save the document with the same name, overwriting the original; or, you can save the document with a different name, retaining the original.

By default, a spelling check is completed on a document during a grammar check. If a word is found in the document that does not match a word in the spelling dictionary, the word is selected and the sentence containing the error is displayed in the Not in Dictionary: text box. Make spelling corrections at the Spelling and Grammar: English (United States) dialog box as described earlier in this chapter.

If a grammar error is detected while completing a grammar and spelling check, the Spelling and Grammar: English (United States) dialog box displays as shown earlier in this chapter in figure 7.2. In figure 7.2 the grammar checker selected the sentence, *I would likes information from Kelly and you on requirements for administering the survey.*, and displayed *like* in the Suggestions list box.

Making Changes

When an error is detected during a grammar check, replacement word(s) may be displayed in the Suggestions list box. If you agree with the suggested change, click the Change button. If the grammar checker does not offer a replacement word or words, you can temporarily leave the grammar checker and edit the text. To do this, position the I-beam pointer in the document screen (outside the Spelling and Grammar: English (United States) dialog box), and then click the left mouse button. Edit the text in the document and then click the Resume button (previously the Ignore button). When you click the Resume button, the grammar (and spell) checking is resumed at the location of the insertion point after you edited the document.

In some situations, the grammar checker will insert a sentence containing a grammatical error in the Spelling and Grammar: English (United States) dialog box. You can edit this sentence as needed and then click the Next Sentence button to resume grammar checking.

Ignoring Text

At times, the grammar checker will select text that you want left as written. Click the Ignore button to tell the grammar checker to ignore the selected text and move to the next error.

The grammar checker checks a document for a variety of grammar and style errors. In some situations, you may want the grammar checker to ignore a particular grammar or style rule. To do this, click the Ignore Rule button the first time the grammar checker displays text breaking the particular grammar or style rule you want ignored.

If the grammar checker selects a sentence in a document containing a grammar or style error and you want that sentence left as written, click the Next Sentence button. This tells the grammar checker to leave the current sentence unchanged and move to the next sentence.

exercise 3

Checking Grammar in a Document

1. Open Memo 04.
2. Save the document with Save As and name it Ch 07, Ex 03.
3. Perform a grammar check by completing the following steps:
   a. Click the Spelling and Grammar button on the Standard toolbar.
   b. The spelling checker selects the name *Rodan*. This is a proper name, so click Ignore All to tell the spelling checker to leave the name as written.
   c. The grammar checker selects the sentence *I would likes information from Kelly and you on requirements for administering the survey.* and displays *like* in the Suggestions list box. The Office Assistant displays information on Verb Form. Read this information and then click Change.
   d. The grammar checker selects the sentence *I feel confident that it will illicit the information needed to determines employee requirements.* and displays *elicit* in the Suggestions list box. The Office Assistant displays information on Commonly Confused Words. Read this information and then click Change.
   e. The grammar checker selects the same sentence again: *I feel confident that it will elicit the information needed to determines employee requirements.* and displays *determine* in the Suggestions list box. The Office Assistant displays information on Verb Form. Read this information and then click Change.
   f. The grammar checker selects *XX:Memo 04* and the Office Assistant displays information on Spacing. Read this information and then click Ignore.
   g. The Office Assistant displays a message box telling you that the spelling and grammar check is completed. Click in the document screen outside this box to remove the box.
4. Save the document again with the same name (Ch 07, Ex 03).
5. Print and then close Ch 07, Ex 03.

Changing Grammar Checking Options

If you click the Options button in the Spelling and Grammar: English (United States) dialog box, the Spelling & Grammar dialog box displays as shown earlier in figure 7.3. You can also display this dialog box by clicking Tools, then Options. At the Options dialog box, click the Spelling & Grammar tab. The options in the Spelling section were discussed earlier in this chapter. Additional options display in the Grammar section. Figure 7.5 identifies the check box options in the dialog box and what will occur if the option is active.

7.5

Grammar Options

Make this option active...	To do this...
Check grammar as you type	Check grammar automatically and mark errors with wavy green line as you key text.
Hide grammatical errors in this document	Hide the wavy green line under possible grammatical errors in the document.
Check grammar with spelling	Check both spelling and grammar in a document. (Remove the check mark from this option if you want to check spelling in a document but not grammar.)
Show readability statistics	Display readability statistics about the document when grammar checking is completed.

If you make the Show readability statistics option active (insert a check mark), readability statistics about the document will display when grammar checking is completed. Most of the readability information is self-explanatory. The last two statistics, however, are described in figure 7.6.

Figure 7.6 *Readability Statistics*

Flesch Reading Ease	The Flesch reading ease is based on the average number of syllables per word and the average number of words per sentence. The higher the score, the greater the number of people who will be able to understand the text in the document. Standard writing generally scores in the 60-70 range.
Flesch-Kincaid Grade Level	This is based on the average number of syllables per word and the average number of words per sentence. The score indicates a grade level. Standard writing is generally written at the seventh or eighth grade level.

Changing Writing Style

At the Spelling & Grammar dialog box (as well as the Options dialog box with the Spelling & Grammar tab selected), you can specify a writing style. The default writing style is *Standard*. This can be changed to *Casual, Formal, Technical*, or *Custom*. Choose the writing style that matches the document you are checking. For example, if you are checking a scientific document, change the writing style to *Technical*. If you are checking a short story, consider changing the writing style to *Casual*. To change the writing style, click the down-pointing triangle at the right of the Writing style text box, then click the desired style at the drop-down list.

exercise 4

Changing Grammar Checking Options and Then Grammar Checking a Document

1. Open Para 02.
2. Save the document with Save As and name it Ch 07, Ex 04.
3. Change grammar checking options by completing the following steps:
   a. Click Tools, then Options.
   b. At the Options dialog box, click the Spelling & Grammar tab.
   c. At the Options dialog box with the Spelling & Grammar tab selected, click the Show readability statistics. (This inserts a check mark in the option.)
   d. Click the down-pointing triangle at the right of the Writing style text box and then click *Formal* at the drop-down list.
   e. Click OK to close the dialog box.

4. Complete a grammar check on the document by completing the following steps:
   a. Click the Spelling and Grammar button on the Standard toolbar.
   b. The grammar checker selects the sentence *Flyers are generally used to advertise a product or service that is available for a limited amount of time.* and the Office Assistant displays information on Passive Voice. Read this information and then edit the sentence displayed in the dialog box by completing the following steps:
      1) Delete the words *are, used,* and *to* (located in the dialog box) so that the sentence reads *Flyers generally advertise a product or service that is available for a limited amount of time.*
   c. Click the Next Sentence button to continue grammar checking.
   d. The grammar checker selects the sentence *As you can see, this form of advertising is used by just about anyone.* and the Office Assistant displays information on Passive Voice. Edit the sentence in the dialog box so it reads *As you can see, many people use this form of advertising.*
   e. Click the Next Sentence button to continue grammar checking.
   f. The grammar checker selects the sentence *In a flyer, a headline should be a dominant visual element set significantly larger than the words that follow.* and the Office Assistant displays information on Too Many Nouns. Read this information and then click the Ignore button to leave the sentence as written.
   g. The grammar checker displays the Readability Statistics dialog box for the document. Read the statistics and then click OK to close the dialog box.
5. Change the checking options back to the default by completing the following steps:
   a. Click Tools, then Options.
   b. At the Options dialog box, click the Spelling & Grammar tab.
   c. At the Options dialog box with the Spelling & Grammar tab selected, click the Show readability statistics. (This removes the check mark from the check box.)
   d. Click the down-pointing triangle at the right of the Writing style text box and then click *Standard* at the drop-down list.
   e. Click OK to close the dialog box.
6. Save the document again with the same name (Ch 07, Ex 04).
7. Print and then close Ch 07, Ex 04.

Customizing AutoCorrect

Earlier in this chapter, you learned that a selected word can be added to AutoCorrect during a spelling check. You can add, delete, or change words at the AutoCorrect dialog box. To display the AutoCorrect dialog box with the AutoCorrect tab selected as shown in figure 7.7, click Tools, then AutoCorrect.

figure 7.7 AutoCorrect Dialog Box

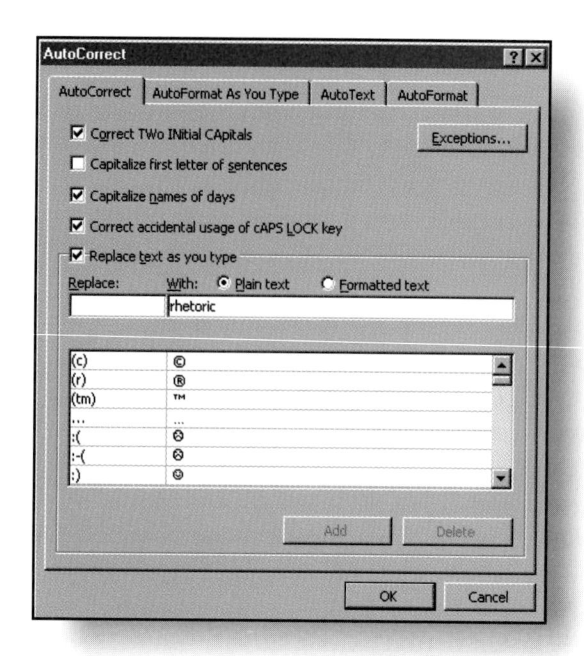

Several options display at the beginning of the AutoCorrect dialog box. If a check appears in the check box before the option, the option is active. Figure 7.8 describes what will occur if the option is active.

The AutoCorrect feature will automatically correct the capitalization of the first letter in a sentence as well as correct two initial capitalizations. There are some abbreviations that you may not want corrected. For example, you may want to start a list with *a.* and not want the letter corrected to a capital. The AutoCorrect feature contains exceptions to what capitalizations will be corrected. To view these exceptions, click the Exceptions button at the AutoCorrect dialog box. This displays the AutoCorrect Exceptions dialog box. At this dialog box, you can add to the list abbreviations you do not want corrected or delete from the list those abbreviations that you want corrected.

figure 7.8 AutoCorrect Options

If this option is active...	Word will...
Correct TWo INitial CApitals	change the second capital to a lowercase letter.
Capitalize first letter of sentences	capitalize the first letter of a word beginning a sentence.
Capitalize names of days	capitalize the first letter of days of the week.
Correct accidental use of cAPS LOCK key	correct instances in which the Caps Lock key is used incorrectly.
Replace text as you type	replace misspelled word with correct spelling as displayed in the list box at the bottom of the AutoCorrect dialog box.

Adding a Word to AutoCorrect

Commonly misspelled words or typographical errors can be added to AutoCorrect. For example, if you consistently key *oopen* instead of *open*, you can add *oopen* to AutoCorrect and tell it to correct it as *open*. To do this, you would display the AutoCorrect dialog box, key *oopen* in the Replace text box, key *open* in the With text box, and then click the Add button. The next time you key *oopen* and then press the space bar, AutoCorrect changes it to *open*.

Deleting a Word from AutoCorrect

A word that is contained in AutoCorrect can be deleted. To delete a word, display the AutoCorrect dialog box, click the desired word in the list box (you may need to click the down-pointing triangle to display the desired word), and then click the Delete button.

exercise 5

Adding Text to and Deleting Text from AutoCorrect

1. At a clear document screen, add words to AutoCorrect by completing the following steps:
   a. Click Tools, then AutoCorrect.
   b. At the AutoCorrect dialog box with the AutoCorrect tab selected, make sure the insertion point is positioned in the Replace text box. If not, click in the Replace text box.
   c. Key **dtp**.
   d. Press the Tab key (this moves the insertion point to the With text box) and then key **desktop publishing**.
   e. Click the Add button. (This adds *dtp* and *desktop publishing* to the AutoCorrect and also selects *dtp* in the Replace text box.)
   f. Key **particuler** in the Replace text box. (When you begin keying *particuler*, *dtp* is automatically deleted.)
   g. Press the Tab key and then key **particular**.
   h. Click the Add button.
   i. With the insertion point positioned in the Replace text box, key **populer**.
   j. Press the Tab key and then key **popular**.
   k. Click the Add button.
   l. With the insertion point positioned in the Replace text box, key **tf**.
   m. Press the Tab key and then key **typeface**.
   n. Click the Add button.
   o. Click OK or press Enter.
2. Key the text shown in figure 7.9. (Key the text exactly as shown. AutoCorrect will correct words as you key.)

3. Save the document and name it Ch 07, Ex 05.
4. Print Ch 07, Ex 05.
5. Delete the words you added to AutoCorrect by completing the following steps:
   a. Click Tools, then AutoCorrect.
   b. At the AutoCorrect dialog box, click *dtp* in the list box. (Click the down-pointing triangle in the list box scroll bar until *dtp* is visible, then click *dtp*.)
   c. Click the Delete button.
   d. Click the *particuler* option in the list box.
   e. Click the Delete button.
   f. Click the *populer* option in the list box.
   g. Click the Delete button.
   h. Click the *tf* option in the list box.
   i. Click the Delete button.
   j. Click OK or press Enter.
6. Close Ch 07, Ex 05.

7.9

Exercise 5

CHOOSING A TYPEFACE

A tf is a set of characters with a common general design and shape. One of teh most important considerations in establishing a particuler mood or feeling in a document is the tf. For example, a decorative tf may be chosen for invitations or menus, while a simple block-style tf may be chosen for headlines or reports. Choose a tf that reflects the contents, your audience expectations, and the image you want to project.

There are many typefaces, adn new designs are created on a regular basis. The most populer tf for typewriters is Courier. There are a variety of typefaces populer with dtp programs including Arial, Bookman, Century Schoolbook, Garamond, Helvetica, and Times New Roman.

Using Thesaurus

Word offers a Thesaurus program that can be used to find synonyms, antonyms, and related words for a particular word. Synonyms are words that have the same or nearly the same meaning. When using Thesaurus, Word may display antonyms for some words. Antonyms are words with opposite meanings. With Thesaurus, you can improve the clarity of business documents.

To use Thesaurus, position the insertion point next to any character in the word for which you want to find a synonym or antonym, click Tools, point to Language, then click Thesaurus. At the Thesaurus: English (United States) dialog box shown in figure 7.10, select the desired synonym (or antonym) in the Meanings list box, and then click the Replace button.

figure 7.10 *Thesaurus: English (United States) Dialog Box*

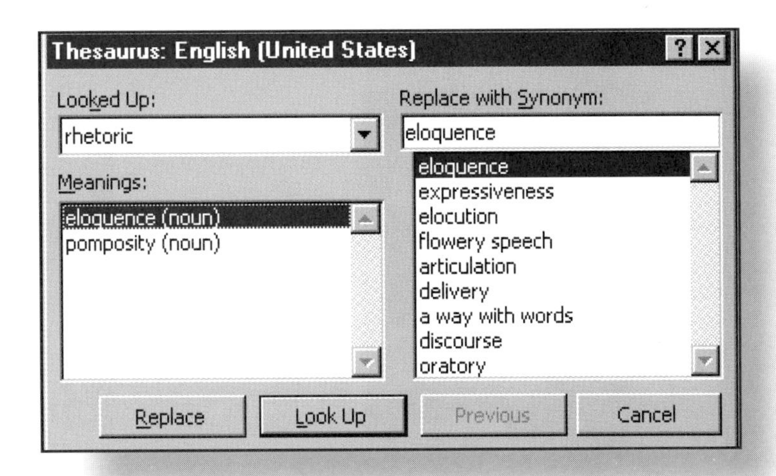

At the Thesaurus: English (United States) dialog box, a list of words displays in the Meanings list box. Depending on the word you are looking up, the words in the Meanings list box may display followed by *(noun)* or *(adj)*. You might also see the words *Antonym*, and *Related Words*. The first word in the Meanings list box is selected by default and synonyms for that word are displayed in the Replace with Synonym list box.

You can view synonyms in the Replace with Synonym list box for the words shown in the Meanings list box by clicking the desired word.

exercise 6

Finding Synonyms Using Thesaurus

1. At a clear document screen, look up synonyms for the word *rhetoric* by completing the following steps:
   a. Key **rhetoric**.
   b. With the insertion point positioned in the word or immediately after the word, click Tools, point to Language, then click Thesaurus.
   c. After viewing the synonyms for *rhetoric*, close the Thesaurus: English (United States) dialog box by clicking the Cancel button.

2. Look up synonyms for the word *subtle* by completing steps similar to those in 1a through 1c.
3. Look up synonyms for the word *insipid* by completing steps similar to those in 1a through 1c.
4. Close the document without saving it.

Using Buttons

Use the buttons at the bottom of the Thesaurus: English (United States) dialog box to replace a word, look up a different word, or display the previous word.

Replace: Click the Replace button to replace the word in the document with the word displayed in the Replace with Synonym list box.

Look Up: You can look up synonyms for words displayed in either the Meanings list box or the Replace with Synonym list box. To do this, click the word for which you want to look up synonyms, and then click the Look Up button. If you are using the mouse, you can also double-click the word for which you want synonyms displayed.

Cancel: Click the Cancel button to remove the Thesaurus: English (United States) dialog box from the document screen without making a change.

Previous: Click the Previous button to display the previous word you looked up.

exercise 7

Changing Words Using Thesaurus

1. Open Memo 01.
2. Save the memo with Save As and name it Ch 07, Ex 07.
3. Change the word *discovered* in the first paragraph to *located* using Thesaurus by completing the following steps:
   a. Position the insertion point in the word *discovered*.
   b. Display the Thesaurus: English (United States) dialog box.
   c. At the Thesaurus: English (United States) dialog box, click *located*, and then click the Replace button.
4. Follow similar steps to make the following changes using Thesaurus:
   a. Change *excellent* in the first paragraph to *superior*.
   b. Change *retail* in the third paragraph to *sell*.
5. Save the memo again with the same name (Ch 07, Ex 07).
6. Print and then close Ch 07, Ex 07.

Displaying Word Count

With the Word Count option from the Tools menu, the number of pages, words, characters, paragraphs, and lines in a document can be displayed. To use this option, open the document for which you want the word count displayed, click Tools, then Word Count. Read the information displayed in the Word Count dialog box, then click Close or press Enter.

exercise 8

Displaying Word Count

1. Open Letter 01.
2. Display a word count for the document by completing the following steps:
   a. Click Tools, then Word Count.
   b. After reading the statistics in the Word Count dialog box, click the Close button.
3. Close Letter 01 without saving changes.
4. Open Report 01.
5. Display the word count for the document by completing step 2.
6. Close Report 01 without saving changes.

chapter summary

- Word includes a spelling and grammar checker.
- The spelling checker matches the words in your document with the words in its dictionary. If a match is not found, the word is selected and possible corrections are suggested.
- While the spelling checker is at work, these buttons are available: Ignore and Ignore All, Change and Change All, Add, or AutoCorrect. Several other options are available at the Options dialog box.
- When checking the spelling and/or grammar in a document, you can temporarily leave the Spelling and Grammar: English (United States) dialog box, make corrections in the document, and then resume checking.
- With the grammar checker, you can search a document for correct grammar, style, punctuation, and word usage.
- While the grammar checker is at work, these buttons are available: Ignore, Ignore All, Next Sentence, and Change.
- When a grammar error is detected, the Office Assistant displays information about the specific error.
- Words can be added to AutoCorrect during a spelling check, as well as at the AutoCorrect dialog box.
- Use Thesaurus to find synonyms and antonyms for words in your document.
- While Thesaurus is at work, these buttons are available: Replace, Look Up, Cancel, and Previous.
- With the Word Count option from the Tools menu, the number of pages, words, characters, paragraphs, and lines in a document can be displayed.

commands review

	Mouse/Keyboard
Spelling and Grammar: English (United States) dialog box	Click [button] on Standard toolbar; or click Tools, Spelling and Grammar
Options dialog box	Tools, Options
AutoCorrect dialog box	Tools, AutoCorrect
Thesaurus dialog box	Tools, Language, Thesaurus
Word Count dialog box	Tools, Word Count

check your understanding

Completion: In the space provided at the right, indicate the correct term, symbol, or command.

1. Display the Spelling and Grammar: English (United States) dialog box by clicking the Spelling and Grammar button on this toolbar. ____________
2. This is the default writing style that the grammar checker uses when checking grammar in a document. ____________
3. Choose this writing style when checking a business letter. ____________
4. Use this program to find synonyms for a word. ____________
5. Click this option at the Tools drop-down menu to display information about the document such as the number of pages, words, characters, paragraphs, and lines. ____________
6. When an error is detected during a grammar check, replacement word(s) may be displayed in this list box. ____________
7. To display the AutoCorrect dialog box with the AutoCorrect tab selected click this option on the Menu bar and then click AutoCorrect. ____________
8. This term refers to words with similar meanings. ____________
9. This term refers to words with opposite meanings. ____________

Underline the words in the paragraph below that the spelling checker would highlight for correction.

The cost for a larje nubmer of listings is assessed monthly. The number of companys in your business category should be determined, if posssible. Try too learn what percentge of there business each month comes form people who have located them through the yellow pages. This percentage can range from 6 to 50 percent.

Using the same paragraph above, underline twice the incorrect words that the spelling checker would not highlight.

skill assessments

Note: Before completing the skill assessments, display the Open dialog box, and then select and delete documents created in chapter 5 that begin Ch 05 and Unit 1 performance assessments that begin Unit 1. You may want to check with your instructor before deleting these documents.

Assessment 1

1. Open Summary 01.
2. Save the document with Save As and name it Ch 07, SA 01.
3. Complete a spell check on the document. (The words *duplexing* and *codecs* are spelled correctly.)
4. After completing the spell check, insert bullets before each paragraph (except the title).
5. Save the document again with the same name (Ch 07, SA 01).
6. Print and then close Ch 07, SA 01.

Assessment 2

1. Open Letter 02.
2. Save the letter with Save As and name it Ch 07, SA 02.
3. Complete a spelling and grammar check on the document.
4. After the spelling and grammar check is completed, proofread the letter and make necessary changes. (There is a mistake that the spelling and grammar checker will not select.)
5. Save the letter again with the same name (Ch 07, SA 02).
6. Print and then close Ch 07, SA 02.

Assessment 3

1. Open Letter 03.
2. Save the document with Save As and name it Ch 07, SA 03.
3. Change the grammar check option to *Formal* and then complete a spelling and grammar check. (Proper names are spelled correctly; leave passive sentences as written.)
4. After completing the grammar check, proofread the letter and make necessary changes. (There are mistakes in the letter that the grammar checker will not select.)
5. Change the grammar check option back to *Standard*.
6. Save the letter again with the same name (Ch 07, SA 03).
7. Print and then close Ch 07, SA 03.

Assessment 4

1. Open Para 02.
2. Save the document with Save As and name it Ch 07, SA 04.
3. Use Thesaurus to make the following changes:
   a. Change *prospective* in the first paragraph to *future*.
   b. Change *significantly* in the second paragraph to *considerably*.
   c. Change *desired* in the second paragraph to *preferred*.
   d. Change *way* in the third paragraph to *method*.

4. Save the document again with the same name (Ch 07, SA 04).
5. Print and then close Ch 07, SA 04.

Assessment 5

1. Open Para 05.
2. Save the document with Save As and name it Ch 07, SA 05.
3. This document overuses the words *producing* and *produce*, as well as *newsletters* and *designing*. Use Thesaurus to make changes to some of the occurrences of *producing*, *produce*, and *designing*. Also, consider rewriting some of the sentences to reduce the number of times *newsletters* appears in the document.
4. Save the document again with the same name (Ch 07, SA 05).
5. Print and then close Ch 07, SA 05.

chapter EIGHT

Formatting with Special Features

PERFORMANCE OBJECTIVES

Upon successful completion of chapter 8, you will be able to:

- **Add text quickly to a document with the AutoText feature.**
- **Edit and delete an AutoText entry.**
- **Increase the spacing between paragraphs.**
- **Insert a nonbreaking space between words in a document.**
- **Automatically insert the date in a document.**
- **Create a drop cap in a document.**
- **Highlight text in a document.**
- **Create documents using Word templates.**

In this chapter, you will learn to use a variety of Word features that can automate the creation of documents and enhance the visual appeal of text in documents. Use Word's AutoText feature to simplify inserting commonly used words, names, or phrases in a document. Increase the visual appeal of a document by spacing above and below certain headings or paragraphs, by adding drop caps to the document, and by inserting nonbreaking spaces between words that are to be kept together as a unit. Word has included a number of *template* documents containing formatting for producing a variety of documents such as memos, letters, reports, invoices, and résumés. Word also includes Wizards that guide you through the creation of documents.

Using AutoText

Word's AutoText feature is similar to the AutoCorrect feature you learned about in a previous chapter. With AutoCorrect, the text is automatically inserted in a document when the space bar is pressed. For example, if you assigned the letters *HC* to *Hartland Corporation*, when you key **HC**, and then press the space bar, *Hartland Corporation* is automatically inserted in the document. If you use text on a less frequent basis and do not want it automatically inserted in the document when you press the space bar, use Word's AutoText feature. An AutoText entry is inserted in the document with an option from the AutoText side menu or the shortcut key, F3.

Saving an AutoText Entry

The AutoText feature is useful for items such as addresses, company logos, lists, standard text, letter closing, or any other text that you use on a frequent basis. To save an AutoText entry, key the desired text, applying any necessary formatting, select the text, and then click Insert, point to AutoText, and then click New. At the Create AutoText dialog box shown in figure 8.1, key a short name for the text, then click OK.

When you save selected text as an AutoText entry, the formatting applied to the text is also saved. If you are saving a paragraph or paragraphs of text that have paragraph formatting applied, make sure you include the paragraph mark with the selected text. To make sure the paragraph mark is included, turn on the display of nonprinting characters before selecting the text.

An AutoText entry name can contain a maximum of 32 characters and can include spaces. Try to name the AutoText something that is short but also gives you an idea of the contents of the entry.

8.1

Create AutoText Dialog Box

Inserting an AutoText Entry

An AutoText entry can be inserted in a document by keying the name of the AutoText and then pressing the Enter key or the shortcut key, F3; with an option from the AutoText side menu; or at the AutoCorrect dialog box with the AutoText tab selected. An AutoText entry name must be at least four characters in length to display the AutoText with the Enter key. The shortcut key, F3, can be used on an AutoText entry name of any length. To insert an AutoText entry with the Enter key, key the name given (at least four characters) to the AutoText entry (the full entry displays in a yellow box above the insertion point), and then press the Enter key. To insert an AutoText entry with the shortcut key, key the name given the AutoText entry, and then press F3.

To insert an AutoText entry with the AutoText side menu, click Insert, point to AutoText, point to Normal at the side menu, and then click the desired AutoText entry at the second side menu.

You can also insert an AutoText entry into a document at the AutoCorrect dialog box with the AutoText tab selected. To display this dialog box, shown in figure 8.2, click Insert, point to AutoText, then click AutoText. At the AutoCorrect dialog box with the AutoText tab selected, key the name you gave the AutoText entry in the Enter AutoText entries here text box, and then click the Insert button.

8.2

AutoCorrect Dialog Box with AutoText Tab Selected

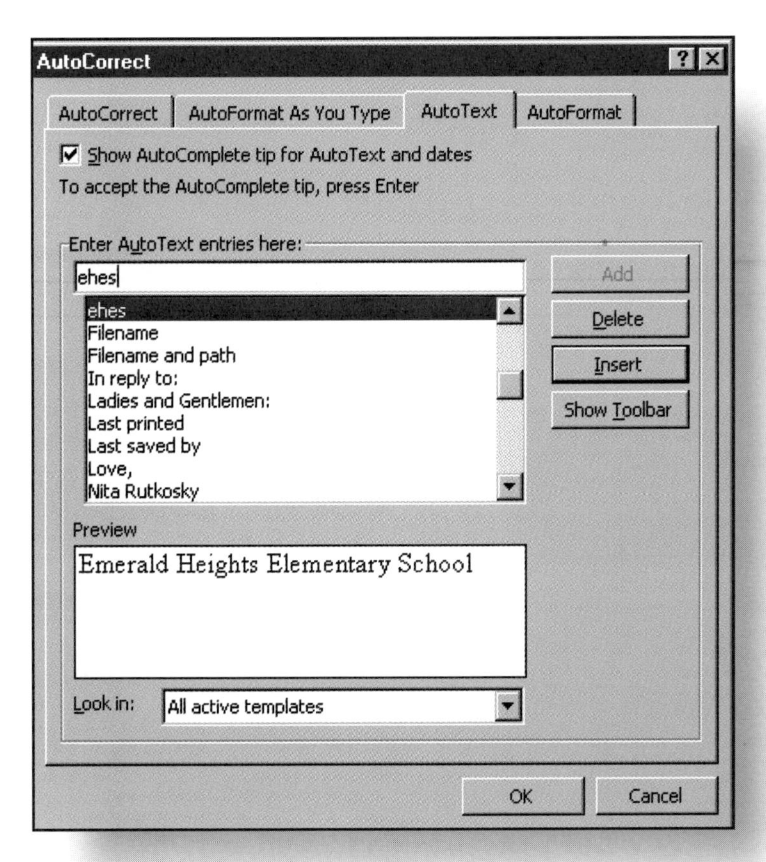

At the AutoCorrect dialog box with the AutoText tab selected, the Preview box displays the contents of the entry. This is useful if you cannot remember the name of the desired entry. Click each entry in the list box that displays below the Enter AutoText entries here text box and view the contents in the Preview box.

exercise 1

Creating AutoText Entries

1. At a clear document screen, create an AutoText entry for Emerald Heights Elementary School, by completing the following steps:
   a. Key **Emerald Heights Elementary School**.
   b. Select *Emerald Heights Elementary School*. (Be sure you do not include the paragraph symbol when selecting text. You may want to turn on the display of nonprinting characters.)
   c. Click Insert, point to AutoText, then click New.
   d. At the Create AutoText dialog box, key **ehes**.
   e. Click OK.
   f. Deselect the text.
   g. Close the document without saving it.
2. At a clear document screen, create an AutoText entry for the letter complimentary closing shown in figure 8.3 by completing the following steps:
   a. Key the text as shown in figure 8.3. (Insert your initials where you see the *XX*.)
   b. Select the text.
   c. Click Insert, point to AutoText, then click New.
   d. At the Create AutoText dialog box, key **cc**.
   e. Click OK.
   f. Deselect the text.
3. Close the document without saving it.
4. At a clear document screen, create the letter shown in figure 8.4 with the following specifications:
   a. While keying the letter, insert the *ehes* AutoText by keying **ehes** (this displays *Emerald Heights Elementary School* in a yellow box above the insertion point), and then pressing the Enter key.
   b. Insert the *cc* AutoText entry at the end of the letter by keying **cc** and then pressing F3.
5. When the letter is completed, save it and name it Ch 08, Ex 01.
6. Print and then close Ch 08, Ex 01.

figure 8.3

Exercise 1

Very truly yours,

Blaine Dowler
Principal

XX:

8.4

Exercise 1

September 2, 1998

Dear Parents:

The 1998 ehes Open House will be held Thursday, September 24. A short program explaining ehes opportunities and activities will be presented in the school gym. After the program, you can visit your student's classroom and speak with teachers. The program begins at 6:30 p.m. and the classroom visitations begin at 7:00 p.m.

During the school year, you can help make your student's school year a success by considering the following suggestions:

- Schedule a teacher conference within the first month of school and during each major grading period.
- Ask the teacher for expectations.
- Be sure you oversee your child's work and review any graded tests.
- Help your child set a time and place for homework. Be sure to provide support, materials, and encouragement.

During the classroom visitation, ask about each teacher's planning hour so you can schedule a private visitation when needed. Each of us at ehes looks forward to a great year!

cc

Editing an AutoText Entry

An AutoText entry can be edited by inserting the entry in a document, making any necessary changes, and then saving it again with the same AutoText entry name. When the Office Assistant asks if you want to redefine the AutoText entry, click Yes.

Deleting an AutoText Entry

An AutoText entry can be removed from the AutoCorrect dialog box with the AutoText tab selected. To do this, display the AutoCorrect dialog box with the AutoText tab selected, select the entry to be deleted, and then click the Delete button.

exercise 2

Editing AutoText Entries

1. At a clear document screen, edit the *cc* AutoText entry by completing the following steps:
   a. Key **cc**.
   b. Press F3. (This inserts the complimentary close text.)
   c. Delete the name *Blaine Dowler* and then key **Linda Shing**.
   d. Delete the title *Principal* and then key **Superintendent**.
   e. Select the complimentary close text.
   f. Click Insert, point to AutoText, then click New.
   g. At the Create AutoText dialog box, key **cc**.
   h. Click OK.
   i. At the message *Do you want to redefine the AutoText entry?*, click Yes.
   j. Deselect the text.
2. Close the document without saving it.
3. At a clear document screen, create an AutoText entry named *KSD* that includes the text shown in figure 8.5 by completing the following steps:
   a. Click the Center button on the Formatting toolbar.
   b. Key **KENTWOOD SCHOOL DISTRICT**.
   c. Press Enter.
   d. Key **200 Walton Boulevard**.
   e. Press Enter.
   f. Key **Kentwood, MI 48930**.
   g. Press Enter.
   h. Click the Align Left button on the Formatting toolbar.
   i. Press Enter.
   j. Select the text and the hard returns below the text.
   k. Change the font to 18-point Arial bold.
   l. With the text still selected, click Insert, point to AutoText, then click New.

m. At the Create AutoText dialog box, key **KSD**.
n. Click OK.

4. Close the document without saving it.
5. At a clear document screen, create an AutoText entry named *ores* for Oak Ridge Elementary School.
6. Close the document without saving it.
7. At a clear document screen, create the letter shown in figure 8.6. Insert the AutoText entry where you see the AutoText entry name.
8. After creating the letter, save it and name it Ch 08, Ex 02.
9. Print and then close Ch 08, Ex 02.
10. At a clear document screen, delete the *ehes* AutoText entry by completing the following steps:
    a. Click Insert, point to AutoText, then click AutoText.
    b. At the AutoCorrect dialog box with the AutoText tab selected, click *ehes* in the list box below the Enter AutoText entries here text box (you will need to scroll down the list to display *ehes*).
    c. Click Delete.
    d. Complete steps similar to those in 10b and 10c to delete the following AutoText entries: *cc, KSD,* and *ores*.
    e. Click Close to close the AutoCorrect dialog box with the AutoText tab selected.
11. Close the document.

8.5 *Exercise 2*

KENTWOOD SCHOOL DISTRICT
200 Walton Boulevard
Kentwood, MI 48930

figure 8.6

Exercise 2

KSD

March 23, 1999

Dear Parents:

Child Psychologist, Dr. Sandra White, from the University of Michigan will be speaking at ehes and ores. Her topic is "Preparing all students for success in the 21st Century." Dr. White will speak at ehes Tuesday, April 13, from 7:00 to 8:30 p.m. in the multipurpose room. She will speak Thursday, April 15, from 7:30 to 8:30 p.m. in the gym at ores.

After speaking, Dr. White will accept questions from the audience. She will address the following issues:

- What knowledge, skills, attitudes, and maturity will be required of our students in the future world of work.
- The areas of education that need to be reconsidered to better prepare students for a future of fluctuating economy and global competition.
- The need for a comprehensive, integrated approach to education.

We are excited to have Dr. White as our guest speaker. The information she provides will help us and you make sound educational decisions.

cc

Spacing Between Paragraphs

Space can be added before and after a paragraph by pressing the Enter key. If you want more control over the spacing above or below paragraphs, use the Before and/or After options at the Paragraph dialog box with the Indents and Spacing tab selected.

If spacing before or after a paragraph is added at the Paragraph dialog box, the spacing is part of the paragraph and will be moved, copied, or deleted with the paragraph. If a paragraph, such as a heading, contains spacing above it, and the paragraph falls at the top of a page, the spacing is ignored.

Spacing above or below paragraphs is added in points. For example, to add 9 points of spacing below selected paragraphs you would display the Paragraph dialog box with the Indents and Spacing tab selected, select the current measurement in the After text box, and then key **9**. You can also click the up-pointing or down-pointing triangles to increase or decrease the amount of spacing before or after paragraphs. With the shortcut command, Ctrl + 0 (zero), you can add 12 points of space before a paragraph.

exercise 3

Changing the Spacing after Paragraphs

1. Open Job Desc.
2. Save the document with Save As and name it Ch 08, Ex 03.
3. Make the following changes to the document:
   a. Select the title *JOB DESCRIPTION*, and the subtitle, *REGISTERED NURSE*, and then change the paragraph alignment to center and turn on bold.
   b. Select the text from the paragraph that begins *Provides direct and indirect patient care...*, to the end of the document.
   c. With the text selected, click the Bullets button on the Formatting toolbar.
   d. With the text still selected, change the spacing after the paragraphs to 6 points by completing the following steps:
      1) Click Format, then Paragraph.
      2) At the Paragraph dialog box, make sure the Indents and Spacing tab is selected. If not, click Indents and Spacing.
      3) Click once the up-pointing triangle at the right of the After text box. (This inserts *6pt* in the After text box.)
      4) Click OK or press Enter.
   e. Deselect the text.
4. Save the document again with the same name (Ch 08, Ex 03).
5. Print and then close Ch 08, Ex 03.

Inserting a Nonbreaking Space

As you key text in a document, Word makes line-end decisions and automatically wraps text to the next line. In some situations, word wrap may break up words or phrases on separate lines that should remain together. For example, a name such as *Daniel C. Lagasa* can be broken after, but should not be broken before, the initial *C.* The phrase *World War II* can be broken between *World* and *War*, but should not be broken between *War* and *II*.

To control what text is wrapped to the next line, a nonbreaking space can be inserted between words. When a nonbreaking space is inserted, Word considers the words as one unit and will not divide them. To insert a nonbreaking space between words, key the first word, press Ctrl + Shift + space bar, then key the second word.

If nonprinting characters are displayed, a normal space displays as a dot and a nonbreaking space displays as a degree symbol. To turn on the display of nonprinting characters, click the Show/Hide ¶ button on the Standard toolbar.

exercise 4

Inserting Nonbreaking Spaces

1. At a clear document screen, turn on the display of nonprinting characters (click Show/Hide ¶ button on the Standard toolbar), and then key the memo shown in figure 8.7. Insert nonbreaking spaces between the commands in the memo (for example, between *Ctrl* + *B* and *Ctrl* + *I*). Insert a nonbreaking space by pressing Ctrl + Shift + space bar before and after the plus symbol in all the shortcut commands.
2. Save the memo and name it Ch 08, Ex 04.
3. Turn off the display of nonprinting characters.
4. Print and then close Ch 08, Ex 04.

figure 8.7

Exercise 4

DATE: January 20, 1999

TO: All Administrative Assistants

FROM: Jolene Risse

SUBJECT: SHORTCUT COMMANDS

The transition to Word 97 is almost complete. During the transition, I will continue offering helpful hints to all administrative assistants. Word offers a variety of shortcut keys and commands that you can use to quickly access certain features and functions. For example, to bold text press Ctrl + B, key text to be bolded, then press Ctrl + B again to turn off bold. To underline text use the command Ctrl + U, and to italicize text use Ctrl + I.

In addition to the shortcut commands for applying character formatting, you can use shortcut commands to display certain dialog boxes. For example, use the command Ctrl + F to display the Find and Replace dialog box. Display the Open dialog box by pressing Ctrl + O. The command Ctrl + G will display the Find and Replace dialog box with the Go To tab selected.

If you have any questions regarding Word features, please call me at extension 710. I will be available between 9:00 a.m. and 12:00 noon and also between 1:00 p.m. and 4:30 p.m.

XX:Ch 08, Ex 04

Inserting the Date and Time

The current date and/or time can be inserted in a document with options from the Date and Time dialog box shown in figure 8.8. To display the Date and Time dialog box, click Insert, then Date and Time.

8.8 *Date and Time Dialog Box*

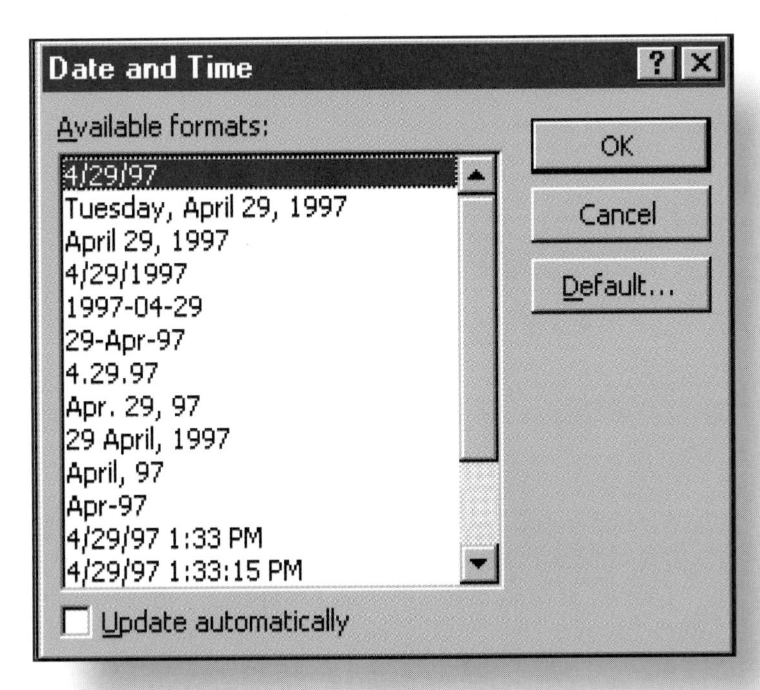

The Date and Time dialog box contains a list of date and time options in the Available formats list box. Click the desired date or time format, then click OK or press Enter.

The date can also be inserted in a document with the shortcut command, Alt + Shift + D. When you press Alt + Shift + D, the date is inserted in figures (such as 01/20/99). Press Alt + Shift + T to insert the current time in the document. The time is inserted in figures followed by AM or PM (such as 2:33 PM).

The date and/or time is inserted in the document as regular text. The date and/or time can also be inserted in a document as a field. If a date is inserted in a document as a field, the date is automatically updated if the document is opened on a different day. If the time is inserted as a field, the time is automatically updated when the document is opened again. To insert the date and/or time as a field, click the Update automatically check box that displays at the bottom of the Date and Time dialog box.

exercise 5

Inserting the Date Automatically

1. Open Memo 01.
2. Save the document with Save As and name it Ch 08, Ex 05.
3. Delete the date *October 26, 1998* and then insert the current date by pressing Alt + Shift + D.
4. Print Ch 08, Ex 05.
5. Delete the current date you just inserted and then insert the current date in a different format by completing the following steps:
   a. Click Insert, then Date and Time.
   b. At the Date and Time dialog box, click the fourth option in the Available formats list box.
   c. Click OK or press Enter.
6. Save the document again with the same name (Ch 08, Ex 05).
7. Print and then close Ch 08, Ex 05.

Creating a Drop Capital Letter

In publications such as magazines, newsletters, brochures, etc., a graphic feature called *drop caps* can be used to enhance the appearance of text. A drop cap is the first letter of the first word of a paragraph that is set into a paragraph. Drop caps identify the beginning of major sections or parts of a document.

Drop caps look best when set in a paragraph containing text set in a proportional font. The drop cap can be set in the same font as the paragraph text or it can be set in a complimentary font. For example, a drop cap can be set in a sans serif font while the paragraph text is set in a serif font.

Figure 8.9 illustrates three paragraphs with different types of drop caps. The paragraph text and the drop cap in the first paragraph are set in Times New Roman. The drop caps in the second paragraph are set in Bookman Old Style and the paragraph text is set in Times New Roman. The drop cap in the third paragraph is set in Desdemona and the paragraph text is set in Times New Roman. The first paragraph shows the first letter of the paragraph as the drop cap. The first word of the paragraph is set as drop caps in the second paragraph. The first letter of the third paragraph is a drop cap that displays in the left margin of the paragraph.

Paragraphs with Drop Caps

On the most apparent level, graphics and the content of the text communicate characteristics such as humor, elegance, and warmth. Red and yellow are warm, while blue and purple are cool. Illustrations and color should be chosen for their appropriateness in terms of the content of the publication.

On the most apparent level, graphics and the content of the text communicate characteristics such as humor, elegance, and warmth. Red and yellow are warm, while blue and purple are cool. Illustrations and color should be chosen for their appropriateness in terms of the content of the publication.

On the most apparent level, graphics and the content of the text communicate characteristics such as humor, elegance, and warmth. Red and yellow are warm, while blue and purple are cool. Illustrations and color should be chosen for their appropriateness in terms of the content of the publication.

Drop caps in Word are created through the Drop Cap dialog box shown in figure 8.10. To display this dialog box, click Format, then Drop Cap. At the Drop Cap dialog box, click the desired drop cap option, and then click OK or press Enter. When you create a drop cap, Word automatically changes the viewing mode from Normal to Page Layout.

figure 8.10 *Drop Cap Dialog Box*

exercise 6

Creating Drop Caps

1. Open Para 02.
2. Save the document with Save As and name it Ch 08, Ex 06.
3. Create a drop cap for the first paragraph by completing the following steps:
   a. Position the insertion point anywhere in the first paragraph.
   b. Click Format, then Drop Cap.
   c. At the Drop Cap dialog box, click Dropped in the Position section.
   d. Click OK or press Enter.
   e. Deselect the drop cap. (To do this with the mouse, click anywhere in the document screen outside the drop cap.)
4. Complete steps similar to those in 3 to create a drop cap for the second paragraph and then the third paragraph.
5. Save the document again with the same name (Ch 08, Ex 06).
6. Print and then close Ch 08, Ex 06.

If you want more than the first letter of a paragraph to be set in drop caps, you must select the word before displaying the Drop Cap dialog box.

exercise 7

Creating a Drop Cap on the First Word of a Paragraph

1. Open Para 05.
2. Save the document with Save As and name it Ch 08, Ex 07.
3. Create a drop cap for the first word of the first paragraph and change the font of the word by completing the following steps:
   a. Select the first word (*The*) of the first paragraph.
   b. Click Format, then Drop Cap.
   c. At the Drop Cap dialog box, click Dropped in the Position section.
   d. Click the down-pointing triangle at the right of the Font text box and then click *Desdemona* at the drop-down menu. (If Desdemona is not available, choose a similar decorative typeface.)
   e. Click OK or press Enter.
   f. Deselect the drop cap.
4. Save the document again with the same name (Ch 08, Ex 07).
5. Print and then close Ch 08, Ex 07.

To remove drop caps from a paragraph, position the insertion point in the paragraph, click Format, then Drop Cap. At the Drop Cap dialog box, click None in the Position section of the dialog box, and then click OK or press Enter.

exercise 8

Removing a Drop Cap

1. Open Ch 08, Ex 06.
2. Save the document with Save As and name it Ch 08, Ex 08.
3. Remove the drop cap from the second paragraph by completing the following steps:
   a. Position the insertion point anywhere in the second paragraph.
   b. Click Format, then Drop Cap.
   c. At the Drop cap dialog box, click None in the Position section of the dialog box.
   d. Click OK or press Enter.
4. Complete steps similar to those in 3 to remove the drop cap from the third paragraph.
5. Save the document again with the same name (Ch 08, Ex 08).
6. Print and then close Ch 08, Ex 08.

Highlighting Text

As people read information in books, magazines, periodicals, papers, and so on, they may highlight important information with a highlighting pen. A highlighting pen creates a colored background through which the text can be read. This colored background draws the reader's eyes to the specific text.

Word provides a button on the Formatting toolbar that lets you highlight text in a document using the mouse. With this highlighting feature, you can select and highlight specific text in a document with a variety of colors.

Highlight

To use this feature, click the Highlight button on the Formatting toolbar, and then select the desired text using the mouse. When the Highlight button is activated, the I-beam pointer displays with a pen attached. Continue selecting text you want highlighted and when completed, click once on the Highlight button to deactivate it.

The default highlighting color is yellow. You can change this color by clicking the down-pointing triangle to the right of the Highlight button. From the drop-down list of colors that displays, click the desired color. This changes the color of the small square below the pen on the Highlight button. If you are using a noncolor printer, highlighted text will print with a gray background. To remove highlighting from text, change the highlighting color to *None*, activate the Highlight button, and then select the highlighted text.

exercise 9

Highlighting Text in a Document

1. Open Report 01.
2. Save the document with Save As and name it Ch 08, Ex 09.
3. Change the highlighting color and then highlight text in the document by completing the following steps:
   a. Click the down-pointing triangle to the right of the Highlight button on the Formatting toolbar.
   b. From the drop-down list of colors, click the light blue color.
   c. Select the sentence, *Desktop publishing involves using desktop publishing software or word processing software with desktop publishing capabilities, a computer system, and a printer to produce professional-looking documents.*, that displays at the end of the second paragraph.
   d. Select the sentence, *With the use of desktop publishing software, one person may be performing all of the tasks necessary to complete a project, greatly reducing the costs of publishing documents.*, that displays in the fourth paragraph.
   e. Select the sentence, *The beginning process of creating a publication involves two steps—planning the publication and creating the content.*, that displays in the first paragraph of the *Initiating the Desktop Publishing Process* section of the document.
   f. Select the sentence, *During this stage, clearly identify the purpose of your communication.*, that displays in the first paragraph of the *Planning the Publication* section of the document.

g. Select the sentence, *Create a document that communicates the message clearly to your intended audience.*, that displays at the end of the first paragraph in the *Creating the Content* section of the document.
h. Select the sentence, *Clear and organized content combined with an attractive layout and design contribute to the effectiveness of your message.*, that displays at the end of the document.
i. Click the Highlight button to deactivate it.

4. Save the document again with the same name (Ch 08, Ex 09).
5. Print and then close Ch 08, Ex 09.
6. Deselect text in the document by completing the following steps:
   a. Click the down-pointing triangle to the right of the Highlight button on the Formatting toolbar.
   b. From the drop-down list that displays, click *None*.
   c. Select the sentence, *Desktop publishing involves using desktop publishing software or word processing software with desktop publishing capabilities, a computer system, and a printer to produce professional-looking documents.*, that displays at the end of the second paragraph.
   d. Select the sentence, *During this stage, clearly identify the purpose of your communication.*, that displays in the first paragraph of the *Planning the Publication* section of the document.
   e. Click the Highlight button to deactivate it.
   f. Return the highlight color to yellow.
7. Save the document again with the same name (Ch 08, Ex 09).
8. Print and then close Ch 08, Ex 09.

Using Templates

Word has included a number of *template* documents that are formatted for specific uses. Each Word document is based on a template document with the *Normal* template the default. With Word templates, you can easily create a variety of documents such as letters, memos, and awards, with specialized formatting. Along with templates, Word also includes *Wizards*. Wizards are templates that do most of the work for you. *(Note: During a typical installation, not all templates may be installed. Before completing the template exercises, check to see if the templates described in figure 8.13 are available. For information on installing templates, refer to the "Getting Started" section of this textbook.)*

Templates and Wizards are available at the New dialog box. To display this dialog box, shown in figure 8.11, click File, then New. The New dialog box contains several tabs for displaying a variety of templates and Wizards. If the default tab, General, is selected as shown in figure 8.11, the *Blank Document* template displays. To view other templates and Wizards, click a different tab at the top of the New dialog box. For example, if you click the Memos tab, the following templates and Wizard display: *Contemporary Memo, Elegant Memo, Memo Wizard,* and *Professional Memo*.

8.11

New Dialog Box

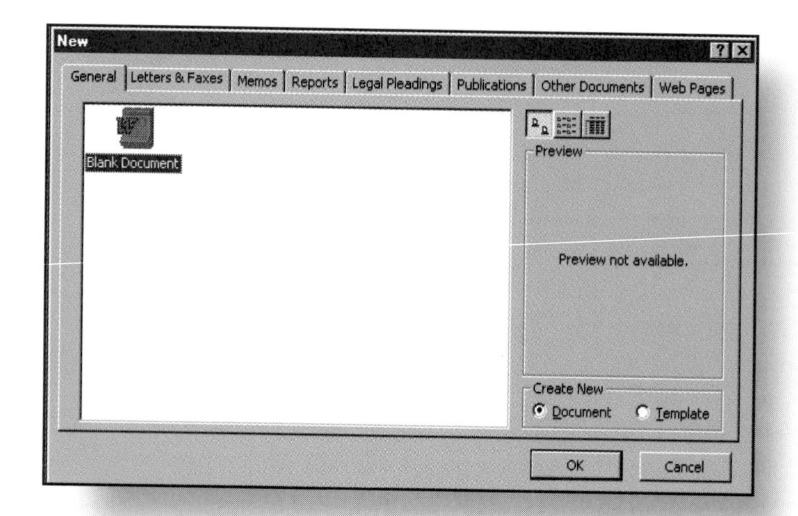

To create a document based on a different template, click the desired template, and then click OK, or double-click the desired template. If you click once on the desired template, a sample template displays in the Preview box at the right side of the dialog box. When you double-click a template, a template document is opened with certain formatting already applied. Specific information is then entered in the template document. After all information has been entered, the template document is saved in the normal manner. If, for example, you opened the *Contemporary Memo* template, the template document shown in figure 8.12 would display (you would see a portion of the top of the memo).

figure 8.12

Contemporary Memo Template

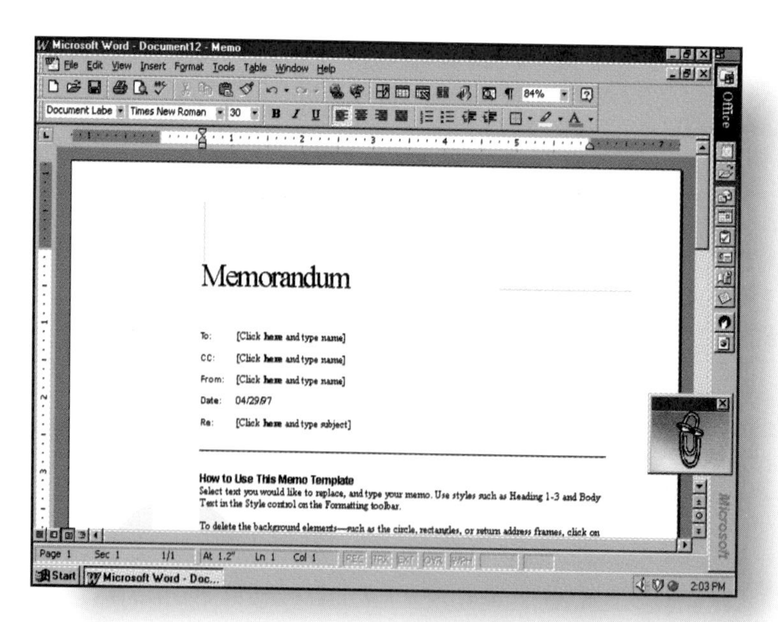

At the *Contemporary Memo* template, text in brackets identifies where specific information is to be entered. For example, text after *To:* displays as *[Click **here** and type name]*. The word *here* displays in bold. Position the I-beam pointer on the word *here*, and then click the left mouse button. This selects the bracketed text. Key the name of the person receiving the memo. When you begin keying the person's name, the selected bracketed text is automatically deleted. Continue in this manner to insert the appropriate text after the headings. Before keying the text for the body of the memo, select and then delete the existing text (below *Re:*).

Use other template documents in a similar manner. The formatting and text will vary for each template document. Figure 8.13 shows the template documents available with each tab at the New dialog box.

figure 8.13 ***Template Documents***

Tab	Template
General	Blank Document
Letters & Faxes	Contemporary Fax Contemporary Letter Elegant Fax Elegant Letter Envelope Wizard Fax Wizard Letter Wizard Mailing Label Wizard Professional Fax Professional Letter
Memos	Contemporary Memo Elegant Memo Memo Wizard Professional Memo
Reports	Contemporary Report Elegant Report Professional Report
Legal Pleadings	Pleading Wizard
Publications	Newsletter Wizard
Other Documents	Contemporary Wizard Elegant Resume More Templates and Wizards Professional Resume Resume Wizard
Web Pages	Blank Web Page More Cool Stuff Web Page Wizard

exercise 10

Creating a Memo with a Memo Template

1. Use the *Contemporary Memo* template to create a memo by completing the following steps:
   a. Click File, then New.
   b. At the New dialog box, click the Memos tab.
   c. At the New dialog box with the Memos tab selected, double-click *Contemporary Memo*.
   d. At the *Contemporary Memo* template document, complete the following steps to key the text in the memo:
      1) Position the I-beam pointer on the word *here* in the bracketed text *[Click **here** and type name]* after *To:*, click the left mouse button, and then key **Stephanie Branson, President**.
      2) Position the I-beam pointer on the word *here* in the bracketed text *[Click **here** and type name]* after *CC:*, click the left mouse button, and then key **Brandon Kent, Vice President**.
      3) Position the I-beam pointer on the word *here* in the bracketed text *[Click **here** and type name]* after *From:*, click the left mouse button, and then key **Paul O'Shea, Development Manager**.
      4) Position the I-beam pointer on the word *here* in the bracketed text *[Click **here** and type subject]* after *Re:*, click the left mouse button, and then key **Tahoma Region Project**.
      5) Select and then delete the text in the memo from ***How To Use This Memo Template*** to the end of the document.
      6) Key the text shown in figure 8.14 pressing Enter only once to end a paragraph. (The template contains automatic spacing between paragraphs.)
2. Save the memo and name it Ch 08, Ex 10.
3. Print and then close Ch 08, Ex 10. (This memo template will print with several graphics including horizontal and vertical lines as well as lightened images.)

8.14

Exercise 10

Anita Stratten, a city council member from West Creek, recently requested that a representative from Coleman Development Corporation attend the next city council meeting. Ms. Stratten indicated that the city council would like to hear more about the development proposed by Coleman.

The development proposal is almost completed. What do you think about the information being presented at the West Creek city council meeting next month? Either I or someone from my department could make the presentation. Please let me know if you feel a presentation to the community is appropriate at this time.

Using Wizards

Wizards are template documents that do most of the work for you. When you select a Wizard template document, Word asks you questions and gives you choices about what type of formatting you want applied to the document. Follow the steps provided by the Wizard to complete the document.

chapter summary

- Text that is used frequently can be saved as an AutoText entry and then inserted in a document. An AutoText entry is inserted in the document with the Enter key, the shortcut key F3, or at the AutoCorrect dialog box with the AutoText tab selected.
- Additional spacing, measured in points, above or below selected paragraphs can be added at the Paragraph dialog box with the Indents and Spacing tab selected.
- When a nonbreaking space is inserted between words, Word considers these words as one unit and will not divide them. Insert a nonbreaking space with the shortcut command, Ctrl + Shift + space bar.
- The current date and/or time can be inserted in a document with options from the Date and Time dialog box or with shortcut commands.
- A drop cap can be used to identify the beginning of major sections of a document. Create a drop cap at the Drop Cap dialog box.
- With the Highlight feature, you can highlight specific text in a document using the mouse. A variety of highlighting colors is available.
- With Word templates, you can easily create a variety of documents such as letters, memos, and awards, with specialized formatting.
- Wizards are templates that do most of the work for you.
- The templates and Wizards provided by Word are available at the New dialog box.

commands review

	Mouse	Keyboard
AutoCorrect dialog box with AutoText tab selected	Insert, AutoText, AutoText	Insert, AutoText, AutoText
Insert 12 points of space above paragraph	Format, Paragraph; with Indent and Spacing tab selected, click up-pointing triangle after Before until *12* pt displays	CTRL + 0 (zero)
Insert a nonbreaking space		CTRL + SHIFT + spacebar
Insert date/time	Insert, Date and Time, click desired selection, click OK	ALT + SHIFT + D (for Date) ALT + SHIFT + T (for Time)
Drop Cap dialog box	Format, Drop Cap	Format, Drop Cap
Activate Highlight feature	Click Highlight button on Formatting toolbar	
New dialog box	File, New	File, New

check your understanding

Completion: In the space provided at the right, indicate the correct term, command, or number.

1. When increasing the space before or after paragraphs, be sure this tab is selected at the Paragraph dialog box. __________
2. If an AutoText entry name is less than four characters in length, key the AutoText entry name and then press this key on the keyboard to insert the full text. __________
3. This is the shortcut command from the keyboard to insert a nonbreaking space. __________
4. This shortcut command will add 12 points of space before a paragraph. __________
5. This feature simplifies the insertion of frequently used text. __________
6. This is the shortcut command to insert the current date. __________
7. Display the Drop Cap dialog box by clicking this option on the Menu bar and then clicking Drop Cap at the drop-down menu. __________
8. This is the default color for the Highlight feature. __________
9. The Highlight button is located on this toolbar. __________
10. Choose a template or Wizard at this dialog box. __________

In the space provided below, write the steps you would complete to create an AutoText entry for *Kellerman Manufacturing Corporation* with the name *kmc*.

____

____

skill assessments

Note: Before completing the skill assessments, display the Open dialog box, and then select and delete documents created in chapter 6 that begin Ch 06. You may want to check with your instructor before deleting these documents.

Assessment 1

1. Open Quiz.
2. Save the document with Save As and name it Ch 08, SA 01.
3. Make the following changes to the document:
   a. Set the title in 14-point Times New Roman bold.
   b. Select the text in the body of the report (everything except the title) and then make the following changes:
      1) Change the font to 12-point Century Schoolbook. (If your printer does not support Century Schoolbook, choose a similar serif typeface.)
      2) Click the Numbering button on the Formatting toolbar.
      3) Change the spacing after paragraphs to 12 points.
4. Save the document again with the same name (Ch 08, SA 01).
5. Print and then close Ch 08, SA 01.

Assessment 2

1. At a clear document screen, create the memo shown in figure 8.15. Insert the current date at the Date and Time dialog box or with a shortcut command. Insert nonbreaking spaces between the shortcut commands.
2. Save the document and name it Ch 08, SA 02.
3. Print and then close Ch 08, SA 02.

Figure 8.15 • Assessment 2

DATE: (current date)

TO: Administrative Assistants

FROM: Cynthia Stophel

SUBJECT: SHORTCUT COMMANDS

Shortcut commands can be used to format text, display dialog boxes, and insert special characters. For example, you can insert a nonbreaking space in text with Ctrl + Shift + space bar. You can insert a nonbreaking hyphen in a document with Ctrl + Shift + -. Shortcut commands can also be used to insert symbols. Press Alt + Ctrl + C to insert a copyright symbol. Insert a registered trademark with Alt + Ctrl + R.

A Word 97 training session has been scheduled for next month. At this training, additional shortcut commands will be introduced.

XX:Ch 08, SA 02

Assessment 3

1. Open Para 03.
2. Save the document with Save As and name it Ch 08, SA 03.
3. Create a drop cap for the first letter of each paragraph.
4. Save the document again with the same name (Ch 08, SA 03).
5. Print and then close Ch 08, SA 03.

Assessment 4

1. Use the *Contemporary Letter* template (displays when the Letters & Faxes tab is selected at the New dialog box) to create a business letter. Select the text in brackets, delete it, and then key the information as shown below each bracketed item:

    *[Click **here** and type return address]* (This text is located in the upper right corner of the template. You may want to change the percentage of display to a larger number to see the text.)

    1201 James Street
    St. Louis, MO 62033

    Select ***Company Name Here*** and then key the following:

    GOOD SAMARITAN HOSPITAL

[Click **here** *and type recipient's address]*
Ms. Mariah Jackson
300 Blue Ridge Boulevard
Kansas City, MO 63009

Select *Dear Sir or Madam:* and then key **Dear Ms. Jackson:**

Select the text *Type your letter here. For more details on modifying this letter template, double-click ✉ . To return to this letter, use the Windows menu.*, and then key the following (press Enter only once between the paragraphs):

> Thank you for the registered nurse job description. I will be including the additional job requirements listed in your letter.
>
> A committee spent several months designing a recruitment plan. A copy of that plan is attached. The plan is very thorough and will help us recruit highly qualified nurses. I will contact you after the eight registered nursing positions have been filled.

[Click **here** *and type your name]*
Victor Durham

[Click **here** *and type job title]*
Director of Nursing

[Click **here** *and type slogan]* (This is located at the bottom.)
Community health needs

2. After creating the letter, save it and name it Ch 08, SA 04.
3. Print and then close Ch 08, SA 04.

Assessment 5

1. Use a memo template of your choosing and compose a memo to your instructor describing three Word shortcut features you have learned up to this point.
2. When the memo is completed, save it and name it Ch 08, SA 05.
3. Print and then close Ch 08, SA 05.

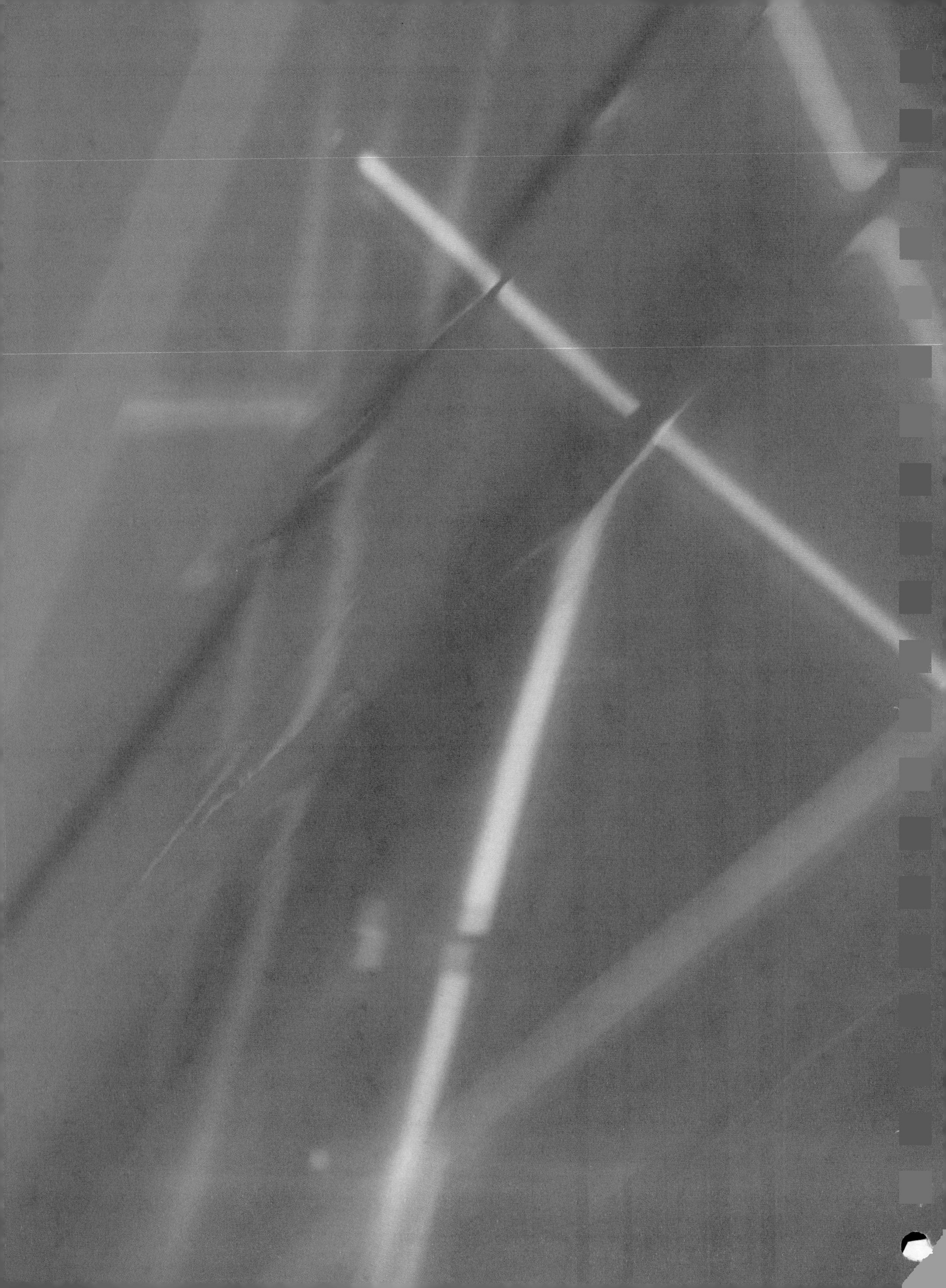

chapter NINE

9 Manipulating Tabs

PERFORMANCE OBJECTIVES

Upon successful completion of chapter 9, you will be able to:

- **Set left, right, center, and decimal tabs on the Ruler and at the Tabs dialog box.**
- **Move, clear, and delete tabs from the Ruler.**
- **Set leader tabs.**
- **Reset default tabs.**
- **Visually align columns of text.**

When you work with a document, Word offers a variety of default settings such as margins and line spacing. One of these defaults is tab stops every 0.5 inch. In some situations, these default tab stops are appropriate; in others, you may want to create your own tab stops. Two methods exist for setting tabs. Tabs can be set on the Ruler or at the Tabs dialog box.

Manipulating Tabs on the Ruler

The Ruler can be used, together with the mouse, to set, move, and/or delete tabs. The Ruler displays below the Formatting toolbar as shown in figure 9.1. If the Ruler is not displayed, click View, then Ruler.

The Ruler displays left tabs set every 0.5 inch. These default tabs are indicated by tiny vertical lines along the bottom of the Ruler. With a left tab, text aligns at the left edge of the tab. The other types of tabs that can be set on the Ruler are center, right, and decimal.

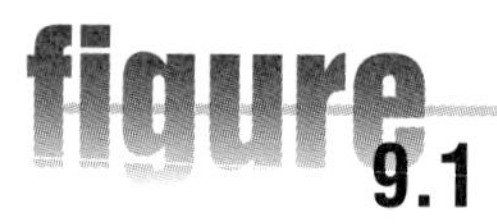

figure 9.1

Ruler

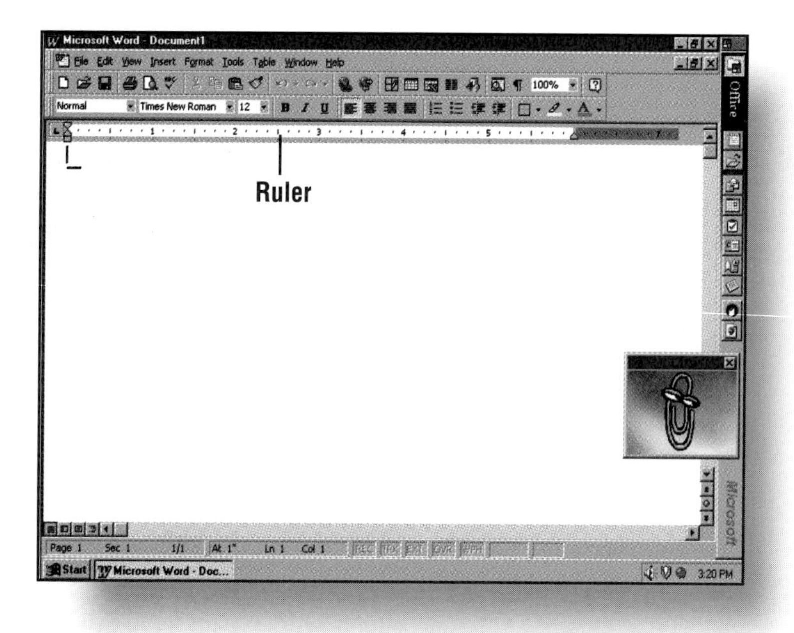

The small button at the left side of the Ruler is the Tab Alignment button. The name of this button changes depending on the tab type selected. Click this button to display the various tab alignment options. Each time you click the Tab Alignment button, a different tab alignment symbol displays. Figure 9.2 shows each symbol and what kind of tab it will set.

Tab Alignment

figure 9.2

Tab Alignment Symbols

└	=	left alignment tab
┴	=	center alignment tab
┘	=	right alignment tab
┴.	=	decimal alignment tab

The columns displayed in figure 9.3 show text aligned at different tabs. The text in the first column in figure 9.3 was keyed at a left tab. The second column of text was keyed at a center tab, the third column at a right tab, and the fourth column at a decimal tab.

figure 9.3 *Types of Tabs*

Mathews	British Columbia	Victoria	34.565
Angleton	Saskatchewan	Regina	2,314.0888
Carras	Alberta	Edmonton	368.9

Setting Tabs

To set a left tab on the Ruler, make sure the left alignment symbol L displays in the Tab Alignment button. Position the arrow pointer just below the tick mark (the marks on the Ruler) where you want the tab symbol to appear, and then click the left mouse button. When you set a tab on the Ruler, any default tabs to the left are automatically deleted by Word.

Set a center, right, or decimal tab on the Ruler in a similar manner. Before setting a tab on the Ruler, click the Tab Alignment button at the left side of the Ruler until the appropriate tab symbol is displayed, and then set the tab.

If you change the tab symbol on the Tab Alignment button, the symbol remains until you change it again or you exit Word. If you exit then reenter Word, the tab symbol returns to the default of left tab.

You can set the tabs first and then key the text or key the text at the default tab stops and then set tabs. If you set tabs and then key text, the tab formatting is inserted in the paragraph mark. As you press the Enter key, the paragraph mark is copied down to the next line and the tab formatting is carried with the paragraph mark.

Turning on the display of nonprinting characters is useful when creating tabbed text. With nonprinting characters turned on, the paragraph mark that contains the tab formatting displays. Also, when the Tab key is pressed, a right-pointing arrow displays in the document screen. To turn on the display of nonprinting characters, click the Show/Hide ¶ button on the Standard toolbar or press Shift + Ctrl + *.

exercise 1

Setting Left Tabs on the Ruler

1. At a clear document screen, key the document shown in figure 9.4 by completing the following steps:
   a. Key the heading **TRAINING DEPARTMENT**, centered and bolded.
   b. Press Enter twice.
   c. Return the paragraph alignment back to left and turn off bold.
   d. Set left tabs at the 1-inch mark and the 3.5-inch mark on the Ruler by completing the following steps:
      1) Click the Show/Hide ¶ button on the Standard toolbar to turn on the display of nonprinting characters.
      2) Make sure the Ruler is displayed. (If the Ruler is not displayed, click View, then Ruler.)
      3) Make sure the left tab symbol displays on the Tab Alignment button at the left side of the Ruler.
      4) Position the arrow pointer below the 1-inch mark on the Ruler and then click the left mouse button.
      5) Position the arrow pointer below the 3.5-inch mark on the Ruler and then click the left mouse button.
   e. Key the text in columns as shown in figure 9.4. Press the Tab key before keying each column entry. (Make sure you press Tab before keying the text in the first column as well as the second column.)
   f. Click the Show/Hide ¶ button on the Standard toolbar to turn off the display of nonprinting characters.
2. Save the document and name it Ch 09, Ex 01.
3. Print and then close Ch 09, Ex 01.

figure 9.4

Exercise 1

TRAINING DEPARTMENT

Robert Ludlow	Director
Jessie Mundell	Trainer Supervisor
Rose Paolino	Trainer Specialist
Dale Barlow	Trainer Specialist
Marion Cummings	Administrative Assistant
Alfred King	Administrative Assistant

When you press the Enter key, the insertion point is moved down to the next line and a paragraph mark is inserted in the document. Paragraph formatting is stored in this paragraph mark. For example, if you make changes to tab stops, these changes are inserted in the paragraph mark. In some situations, you may want to start a new line but not a new paragraph. To do this, press Shift + Enter. Word inserts a line break symbol (visible when nonprinting characters have been turned on) and moves the insertion point to the next line.

If you change tab stops and then create columns of text using the New Line command, Shift + Enter, the tab formatting is stored in the paragraph mark at the end of the columns. If you want to make changes to the tab stops for text in the columns, position the insertion point anywhere within the columns (all the text in the columns does not have to be selected), and then make the changes.

If you set tabs for existing text, you must press the Tab key before keying each column entry. After the text is keyed, select the lines of text you want to be formatted with the new tab stops, and then set the tabs on the Ruler.

If you want to set a tab at a specific measurement on the Ruler, hold down the Alt key, position the arrow pointer at the desired position, and then hold down the left mouse button. This displays two measurements on the Ruler. The first measurement displays the location of the arrow pointer on the Ruler in relation to the left margin. The second measurement is the distance from the location of the arrow pointer on the Ruler to the right margin. With the left mouse button held down, position the tab symbol at the desired location, and then release the mouse button and then the Alt key.

exercise 2

Setting Left, Center, and Right Tabs on the Ruler

1. At a clear document screen, key the document shown in figure 9.5 by completing the following steps:
   a. Key the heading **TRAINING SCHEDULE AND COSTS**, centered and bolded.
   b. Press Enter three times.
   c. Return the paragraph alignment back to left and turn off bold.
   d. Set a left tab at the 0.5-inch mark, a center tab at the 3.5-inch mark, and a right tab at the 5.5-inch mark by completing the following steps:
      1) Click the Show/Hide ¶ button on the Standard toolbar to turn on the display of nonprinting characters.
      2) Make sure the Ruler is displayed and then make sure the left tab symbol displays on the Tab Alignment button.
      3) Position the arrow pointer below the 0.5-inch mark on the Ruler and then hold down the Alt key and then the left mouse button. Make sure the first measurement on the Ruler displays as 0.5" and then release the mouse button and then the Alt key.

4) Position the arrow pointer on the Tab Alignment button at the left side of the Ruler and then click the left mouse button until the center tab symbol ⊥ displays.
5) Position the arrow pointer below the 3.5-inch mark on the Ruler and then hold down the Alt key and then the left mouse button. Make sure the first measurement on the Ruler displays as 3.5" and then release the mouse button and then the Alt key.
6) Position the arrow pointer on the Tab Alignment button at the left side of the Ruler and then click the left mouse button until the right tab symbol ┘ displays.
7) Position the arrow pointer below the 5.5-inch mark on the Ruler and then hold down the Alt key and then the left mouse button. Make sure the first measurement on the Ruler displays as 5.5" and then release the mouse button and then the Alt key.

e. Key the text in columns as shown in figure 9.5. Press the Tab key before keying each column entry and press Shift + Enter twice after keying the text in the third column. (This moves the insertion point a double space below the text and inserts the New Line command. *Note: You* ***must*** *use the New Line command, Shift + Enter, to move the insertion point to the next line in the columnar text because you will be using this document again in exercise 3.*)

2. Save the document and name it Ch 09, Ex 02.
3. Print and then close Ch 09, Ex 02.

figure 9.5 ***Exercise 2***

TRAINING SCHEDULE AND COSTS

Supervision	October 15	$125
Document Preparation	October 30	150
Accessing the Internet	November 4	140
Ethics in Business	November 24	95

Moving Tabs

After a tab has been set on the Ruler, it can be moved to a new location. To move a single tab, position the arrow pointer on the tab symbol on the Ruler, hold down the left mouse button, drag the symbol to the new location on the Ruler, and then release the mouse button.

exercise 3

Moving Tabs on the Ruler

1. Open Ch 09, Ex 02.
2. Save the document with Save As and name it Ch 09, Ex 03.
3. Move the text in columns by completing the following steps:
   a. Position the insertion point on any character in the first column of text.
   b. Position the arrow pointer on the left tab symbol on the Ruler, drag the symbol to the 1-inch mark, and then release the left mouse button.
   c. Position the arrow pointer on the right tab symbol on the Ruler, drag the symbol to the 5-inch mark, and then release the left mouse button.
4. Save the document again with the same name (Ch 09, Ex 03).
5. Print and then close Ch 09, Ex 03.

Deleting Tabs

A tab can be removed from the Ruler. To delete a tab from the Ruler, position the arrow pointer on the tab symbol you want deleted, hold down the left mouse button, drag the symbol down into the document screen, and then release the mouse button.

exercise 4

Moving and Deleting Tabs on the Ruler

1. Open Tab 01. This document is located on your student data disk.
2. Save the document with Save As and name it Ch 09, Ex 04.
3. Move the tab stops so the columns are more balanced by completing the following steps:
   a. Select the text in columns.
   b. Position the arrow pointer on the left tab symbol at the 0.5-inch mark, hold down the left mouse button, drag the left tab symbol to the 1.25-inch mark on the Ruler, and then release the mouse button. *(Hint: Use the Alt key to help you precisely position the tab symbol.)*
   c. Position the arrow pointer on the decimal tab symbol at the 3.5-inch mark, hold down the left mouse button, drag the

decimal tab symbol into the document screen, and then release the mouse button. (This deletes the tab and merges the second column of text with the first column.)

d. Click the Tab Alignment button at the left side of the Ruler until the right tab symbol displays.

e. Position the arrow pointer on the 4.75-inch mark on the Ruler and then click the left mouse button. *(Hint: Use the Alt key to help you precisely position the tab symbol.)*

f. Deselect the text.

4. Save the document again with the same name (Ch 09, Ex 04).
5. Print and then close Ch 09, Ex 04.

Manipulating Tabs at the Tabs Dialog Box

Use the Tabs dialog box shown in figure 9.6 to set tabs at a specific measurement. You can also use the Tabs dialog box to set tabs with preceding leaders and clear one tab or all tabs. To display the Tabs dialog box, click Format, then Tabs.

9.6 *Tabs Dialog Box*

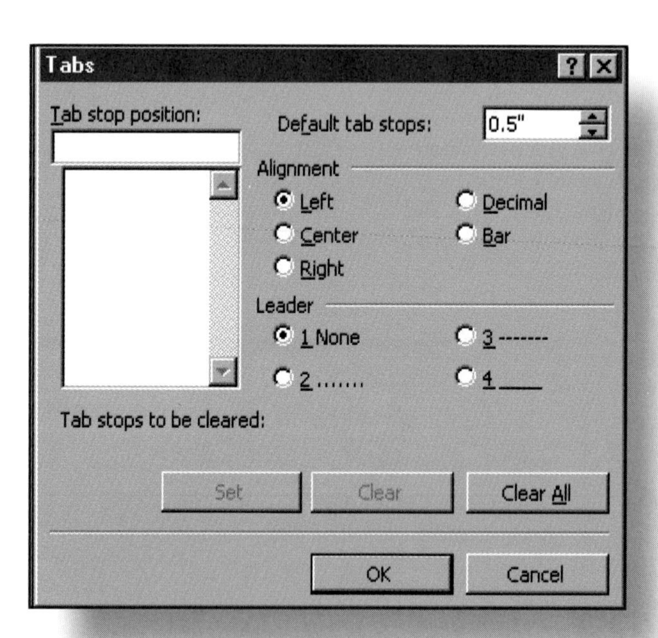

Clearing Tabs

At the Tabs dialog box, you can clear an individual tab or all tabs. To clear all tabs, click the Clear All button. To clear an individual tab, specify the tab stop position, and then click the Clear button.

Setting Tabs

At the Tabs dialog box, you can set a left, right, center, or decimal tab as well as a vertical bar. (For an example of a vertical bar, refer to figure 9.8.) You can also set a left, right, center, or decimal tab with preceding leaders. To change the type of tab at the Tabs dialog box, display the dialog box, and then click the desired tab in the Alignment section.

The Tab stop position option at the Tabs dialog box is used to identify the specific measurement where the tab is to be set. To set a tab, click the desired tab alignment, click in the Tab stop position text box, and then key the desired measurement.

exercise 5

Setting Left Tabs at the Tabs Dialog Box

1. At a clear document screen, key the document shown in figure 9.7 by completing the following steps:
   a. Key the headings in the memo and the first paragraph, and then center and bold the title **OCTOBER ACTIVITIES**. (Be sure to return the paragraph alignment back to left and turn off bold.)
   b. With the insertion point a double space below the title, *OCTOBER ACTIVITIES*, use the Tabs dialog box to set a left tab at the 1-inch mark and the 2.2-inch mark by completing the following steps:
      1) Click Format, then Tabs.
      2) At the Tabs dialog box click the Clear All button.
      3) Make sure Left is selected in the Alignment section of the dialog box. (If not, click Left in the Alignment section.)
      4) Key **1**. (The insertion point should automatically be positioned in the Tab stop position text box. If not, click in the Tab stop position text box.)
      5) Click Set.
      6) Key **2.2** (in the Tab stop position text box).
      7) Click Set.
      8) Click OK or press Enter.
   c. Key the text in columns as shown in figure 9.7. Press the Tab key before keying each column entry. (Make sure you press Tab before keying the text in the first column as well as the second column.)
2. Key the remaining text in the memo.
3. Save the memo and name it Ch 09, Ex 05.
4. Print and then close Ch 09, Ex 05.

9.7

Exercise 5

DATE: September 9, 1998

TO: Louise Drennan, Editor

FROM: Denise Quincy

SUBJECT: OCTOBER NEWSLETTER

A variety of exciting activities are planned for October. Please include the following information in the October newsletter.

OCTOBER ACTIVITIES

October 1	Back-to-school luncheon for teachers
October 8	Skating party
October 13	Open house
October 23	Walk-a-thon (fund raiser)
October 27	Fall performance

The Activities Committee is busy planning the school carnival. If the final schedule for the carnival is ready before the publication date of the October newsletter, I will fax it to you.

XX:Ch 09, Ex 05

exercise 6

Setting Left and Vertical Tabs at the Tabs Dialog Box

1. At a clear document screen, key the document shown in figure 9.8 by completing the following steps:
   a. Key the title, **MONROE FAST PITCH SOFTBALL**, bolded and centered, and then press the Enter key twice.
   b. Key the subtitle, **At-Home Games for the Chargers**, bolded and centered, and then press the Enter key three times. (Be sure to return the paragraph alignment to left and turn off bold.)

c. Display the Tabs dialog box, then set left tabs at the 1.25-inch mark, the 2.75-inch mark, and the 4.25-inch mark; set vertical bar tabs at the 2.25-inch mark and the 3.75-inch mark by completing the following steps:
   1) Click Format, then Tabs.
   2) At the Tabs dialog box, click the Clear All button.
   3) Make sure Left is selected in the Alignment section of the dialog box. (If not, click Left.)
   4) Key **1.25**. (The insertion point should automatically be positioned in the Tab stop position text box. If not, click in the Tab stop position text box.)
   5) Click Set.
   6) Key **2.75**.
   7) Click Set.
   8) Key **4.25**.
   9) Click Set.
   10) Key **2.25**.
   11) Click Bar.
   12) Click Set.
   13) Key **3.75**.
   14) Click Set.
   15) Click OK or press Enter.

d. Key the text in columns as shown in figure 9.8. Press the Tab key before keying each column entry. (The vertical lines between columns of numbers will appear automatically. You need only key the dates. Do not press Enter after keying the date *June 23*.)

2. Save the document and name it Ch 09, Ex 06.
3. Print and then close Ch 09, Ex 06.

9.8

Exercise 6

MONROE FAST PITCH SOFTBALL

At-Home Games for the Chargers

April 7	May 5	June 3
April 14	May 12	June 10
April 21	May 20	June 16
April 28	May 27	June 23

Setting Leader Tabs

The four types of tabs can also be set with leaders. Leaders are useful in a table of contents or other material where you want to direct the reader's eyes across the page. Figure 9.9 shows an example of leaders. The text in the first column was keyed at a left tab. The text in the second column was keyed at a right tab with leaders.

figure 9.9 *Leader Tabs*

British Columbia .... Victoria
Alberta .... Edmonton
Saskatchewan .... Regina
Manitoba .... Winnipeg
Ontario .... Toronto
Quebec .... Montreal

Leaders can be periods (.), hyphens (-), or underlines (_). To add leaders to a tab, click the type of leader desired in the Leader section of the Tabs dialog box.

exercise 7

Setting a Left Tab and a Right Tab with Dot Leaders

1. At a clear document screen, create the document shown in figure 9.10 by completing the following steps:
   a. Change the font to 12-point Helvetica. (If your printer does not support Helvetica, choose a similar sans serif typeface such as Universe or Univers.)
   b. Center and bold the title, *TABLE OF CONTENTS*.
   c. Press Enter three times. (Be sure to return the alignment of the paragraph back to left and turn off bold.)
   d. Set a left tab at the 0.5-inch mark and a right tab with dot leaders at the 5.5-inch mark by completing the following steps:
      1) Click Format, then Tabs.
      2) At the Tabs dialog box, click the Clear All button.
      3) Make sure Left is selected in the Alignment section of the dialog box. (If not, click Left.)
      4) Make sure the insertion point is positioned in the Tab stop position text box and then key **0.5**.

5) Click Set.
6) Key **5.5**.
7) Click Right in the Alignment section of the dialog box.
8) Click 2....... in the Leader section of the dialog box.
9) Click Set.
10) Click OK or press Enter.

e. Key the text in columns as shown in figure 9.10. Press the Tab key before keying each column entry.

2. Save the document and name it Ch 09, Ex 07.
3. Print and then close Ch 09, Ex 07.

9.10

Exercise 7

TABLE OF CONTENTS

exercise 8

Setting a Left Tab and Right Tab with Leaders at the Tabs Dialog Box

1. At a clear document screen, key the document shown in figure 9.11 by completing the following steps:
   a. Key the letter through the first paragraph.
   b. With the insertion point a double space below the first paragraph, set a left tab at the 1-inch mark and a right tab with hyphen leaders at the 5-inch mark by completing the following steps:
      1) Click Format, then Tabs.
      2) At the Tabs dialog box, click the Clear All button.
      3) Make sure Left is selected in the Alignment section of the dialog box. (If not, click Left.)
      4) Make sure the insertion point is positioned in the Tab stop position text box and then key **1**.
      5) Click Set.
      6) Key **5**.
      7) Click Right in the Alignment section of the dialog box.
      8) Click 3 --------- in the Leader section of the dialog box.
      9) Click Set.
      10) Click OK or press Enter.
   c. Key the text in columns as shown in figure 9.11. Press the Tab key before keying each column entry.
   d. After keying the column text, press the Enter key twice, and then key the remaining text of the letter.
2. Save the document and name it Ch 09, Ex 08.
3. Print and then close Ch 09, Ex 08.

9.11

Exercise 8

November 4, 1998

Mr. and Mrs. Donald Sturgis
1519 South Fourth Avenue
Salem, OR 99023

Dear Mr. and Mrs. Sturgis:

Hotel reservations for your trip to the Hawaiian Islands have been finalized. As you requested, all hotel reservations have been made at Grand Palace hotels. Reservations have been confirmed for the following dates:

Maui Grand Palace - - - - - - - - - - - - - - - - - -December 4-8
Grand Palace Resort - - - - - - - - - - - - - - - - -December 9-12
Grand Palace Seaside - - - - - - - - - - - - - -December 13-15
Honolulu Grand Palace - - - - - - - - - - - - -December 16-18

Your airline reservations have not been confirmed. I am still waiting for a reduction in price. I have heard that airlines will be lowering their rates during the next two weeks. As soon as the airfare is reduced below $500, I will make your flight reservations.

Will you need a car while you are vacationing in Hawaii? Please let me know if you would like me to reserve a car for you at each island.

Sincerely,

Frank Truman

XX:Ch 09, Ex 08

Resetting Default Tab Stops

Word sets left tabs every 0.5 inch by default. If you set a tab on the Ruler or at the Tabs dialog box, any tabs to the left are automatically deleted. The interval between default tabs can be changed with the Default tab stops option at the Tabs dialog box. For example, if you want to set tabs every 1 inch, you would key **1** in the Default tab stops text box.

Visually Aligning Columns

Columns of text or data in a document are usually centered between the left and right margins to provide a balanced look. If you do not know the measurements for setting tabs for columns of text, try visually centering columns of text using the Ruler. To do this, you would follow these basic steps:

1. Display the Ruler.
2. Press the Tab key and then key the text for the first row.
3. Press the Tab key and then key the text for the second row. (Continue in this manner for any additional rows of text. Text may not align; this will be corrected in a later step.)
4. Select the text in the columns.
5. Make sure the correct tab alignment symbol is displayed at the left side of the Ruler, position the arrow pointer on the Ruler at the desired location for the first tab, and then click the left mouse button.
6. Set additional tabs on the Ruler as needed. Be sure to change to the proper tab alignment symbol before setting a tab.
7. With the text in columns still selected, drag each tab symbol on the Ruler until the text in the columns displays visually centered between the left and right margins.

exercise 9

Setting Left Tabs for Existing Text

1. At a clear document screen, key the document shown in figure 9.12 by completing the following steps:
   a. Key the title, **COLEMAN DEVELOPMENT CORPORATION**, centered and bolded.
   b. Press the Enter key three times. (Be sure to return the alignment of the paragraph back to left and turn off bold.)
   c. Press the Tab key and then key **President**.
   d. Press the Tab key and then key **Stephanie Branson**.
   e. Press the Enter key twice, press the Tab key, and then key **Vice President**.
   f. Press the Tab and then key **James Zenger**.
   g. Continue keying the remaining text in columns as shown in figure 9.12. Press Tab before each column entry. (The text in the second column will not align.)

h. After all column text is keyed, select the text in the columns.
i. Make sure the left tab alignment symbol is displayed at the left side of the Ruler. Position the arrow pointer on the Ruler at approximately the 1-inch mark on the Ruler and then click the left mouse button.
j. Position the arrow pointer on the Ruler at approximately the 4-inch mark on the Ruler and then click the left mouse button.
k. If the columns of text do not look balanced, drag each left tab symbol to a more desirable location on the Ruler.

2. Save the document and name it Ch 09, Ex 09.
3. Print and then close Ch 09, Ex 09.

9.12

Exercise 9

COLEMAN DEVELOPMENT CORPORATION

President	Stephanie Branson
Vice President	James Zenger
Manager of Land Development	Paul O'Shea
Director of Training	Robert Ludlow
Director of Finances	Pamela Sturman

Keying Column Headings

If the column heading is the longest line in the column, use the heading to determine tab stops. Column headings that are shorter than the column entries can be visually centered above the entries. To do this, key the column entries first, leaving blank lines above the columns for the headings. After the column entries have been keyed, move the insertion point above the columns, visually determine the center of the columns, and then key the headings.

Some businesses are accepting column headings aligned at the tab stops rather than centered. Keying column headings at the tab stop takes less time than centering headings.

exercise 10

Setting Left and Right Tabs for Existing Text

1. At a clear document screen, key the document shown in figure 9.13 by completing the following steps:
   a. Key the title, **SUPERVISION CLASS**, centered and bolded.
   b. Press the Enter key three times. (Be sure to return the alignment of the paragraph back to left.)
   c. Press the Tab key and then key **Name**
   d. Press the Tab key and then key **#1**.
   e. Press the Tab key and then key **#2**.
   f. Press the Tab key, key **#3**, and then turn off bold.
   g. Press the Enter key twice, press the Tab key, and then key **Annie Long**.
   h. Press the Tab key and then key **78**.
   i. Press the Tab key and then key **80**.
   j. Press the Tab key and then key **84**.
   k. Press the Enter key and then continue keying the remaining text in columns as shown in figure 9.13. Press Tab before each column entry. (The text in the second, third, and fourth columns will not align.)
   l. After all column text is keyed, select the text in the columns (including the column headings).
   m. Make sure the left tab alignment symbol is displayed at the left side of the Ruler. Position the arrow pointer on the Ruler at approximately the 1-inch mark on the Ruler and then click the left mouse button.
   n. Change to the right tab alignment symbol, position the arrow pointer on the Ruler at approximately the 3.5-inch mark on the Ruler, and then click the left mouse button.
   o. Set a right tab at the 4.5-inch mark and another at the 5.5-inch mark on the Ruler.
   p. If the columns of text do not look balanced, drag each tab symbol to a more desirable location on the Ruler.
2. Save the document and name it Ch 09, Ex 10.
3. Print and then close Ch 09, Ex 10.

figure 9.13

Exercise 10

SUPERVISION CLASS

Name	**#1**	**#2**	**#3**
Annie Long	78	80	84
Gretchen Bittner	75	80	78
Lennart Soderstrom	88	95	93
Steven Quarles	68	73	70
Nobuo Yoshihara	100	94	97
Jeffrey Gehring	64	74	82
Christine Kirby	97	89	100
Marilee Metcalf	74	85	78
Alisa Shepherd	98	100	94

chapter summary

- By default, tab stops are set every 0.5 inch. These settings can be changed on the Ruler or at the Tabs dialog box.
- Use the Tab Alignment button located at the left side of the Ruler to select a left, right, center, or decimal tab. When you set a tab on the Ruler, any tabs to the left are automatically deleted.
- You can set tab stops before or after keying text. If you set them before, the tab formatting is inserted in the paragraph mark. As you press the Enter key, the tab formatting is copied to the next paragraph mark. If you set tab stops after keying text, select the lines of text you want to be formatted with the new tab stops, and then set the tabs on the Ruler or at the Tabs dialog box.
- Turning on the display of nonprinting characters, such as those for paragraphs and tabs, is useful when creating tabbed text.
- After a tab has been set on the Ruler, it can be moved or deleted using the mouse pointer.
- At the Tabs dialog box, you can set any of the four types of tabs as well as a vertical bar at a specific measurement. You can also set tabs with preceding leaders and clear one tab or all tabs.
- Preceding leaders can be periods, hyphens, or underlines.
- The 0.5-inch interval between default tabs can be changed with the Default tab stops option at the Tabs dialog box.

commands review

	Mouse	Keyboard
Display the Ruler	View, Ruler	View, Ruler
Display nonprinting characters	Click ¶ on Standard toolbar	SHIFT + CTRL + *
Tabs dialog box	Format, Tabs	Format, Tabs
New Line command		SHIFT + ENTER

check your understanding

Completion: In the space provided at the right, indicate the correct command, term, or number.

1. By default, each tab is set apart from the other by this measurement. __________
2. These are the four types of tabs that can be set on the Ruler. __________ __________ __________ __________
3. This is the default tab type. __________
4. Tabs can be set on the Ruler or here. __________
5. To remove all previous tabs, click this button at the Tabs dialog box. __________
6. Press these keys on the keyboard to insert a New Line command. __________
7. Click this button on the Standard toolbar to turn on the display of nonprinting characters. __________
8. This is the name for the line of periods that can run between columns of text. __________
9. Tab formatting is inserted in this symbol if you set tabs before keying text. __________
10. To display the Tabs dialog box, click this option on the Menu bar, and then click Tabs. __________

skill assessments

Note: Before completing the skill assessments, display the Open dialog box, and then select and delete documents created in chapter 7 that begin Ch 07. You may want to check with your instructor before deleting these documents.

Assessment 1

1. At a clear document screen, change the font to 12-point Arial, and then key the document shown in figure 9.14. (Be sure to bold the title.) Before keying the text in columns, set left tabs at the 0.5-inch mark, the 3.25-inch mark, and the 4.75-inch mark on the Ruler.
2. Save the document and name it Ch 09, SA 01.
3. Print and then close Ch 09, SA 01.

Figure 9.14 • Assessment 1

FINANCIAL PLANNING WORKSHOPS

Estate Planning	02/02/99	6:30 - 8:30
Saving for College	02/09/99	7:00 - 8:30
Preparing for Retirement	03/03/99	6:00 - 8:00
High-Yield Investments	03/10/99	7:00 - 8:30

Assessment 2

1. At a clear document screen, key the memo shown in figure 9.15. Before keying the text in columns, display the Tabs dialog box, clear all tabs, and then set a left tab at the 0.8-inch mark, and right tabs at the 2.9-inch mark, the 4-inch mark, and the 5.1-inch mark.
2. After keying the memo, save the document and name it Ch 09, SA 02.
3. Print and then close Ch 09, SA 02.

Figure 9.15 • Assessment 2

DATE: November 19, 1998

TO: Louise Drennan, Editor

FROM: Vicki Fortino, Superintendent

SUBJECT: SCHOOL LEVY

With the recent passing of the school levy, I would like the following information presented in the next newsletter to help community members understand how levy dollars are utilized.

The operations levy will raise $6.3 million in 1999 and $6.9 million in 2000. The computer levy will raise $4 million over three years. The bus levy will raise $1 million over two years. The bond was approved by voters in 1997.

The following information shows the projected tax rates per $1,000 of assessed property value for 1999, 2000, and 2001.

	1999	**2000**	**2001**
Operations	$3.98	$3.95	$0.00
Computers	1.04	0.98	0.77
Bus	0.31	0.28	0.00
Bond	3.12	3.12	3.12

Money from the school bus levy will help purchase new school buses. These new buses will save taxpayers thousands of dollars through lower maintenance and fuel cost. The computer levy will purchase computers, printers, and related hardware and software for student use. Computers and communications technology are an essential part of ensuring that every student who graduates has the skills to compete in the job market. Every school in the district will receive equipment funded by the computer levy.

XX:Ch 09, SA 02

Assessment 3

1. At a clear editing window, key the document shown in figure 9.16 with the following specifications:
   a. Change the font to 12-point Century Schoolbook.
   b. Bold and center the title as shown.

c. Before keying the text in columns, display the Tabs dialog box, and then set left tabs at the 1-inch mark and the 1.5-inch mark, and a right tab with dot leaders at the 5-inch mark.
2. Save the document and name it Ch 09, SA 03.
3. Print and then close Ch 09, SA 03.

Figure 9.16 • Assessment 3

TABLE OF CONTENTS

Assessment 4

1. Open Ch 09, SA 03 as a read-only document.
2. Select the text in columns and then move the tab symbols on the Ruler as follows:
   a. Move the left tab symbol at the 1-inch mark to the 0.5-inch mark.
   b. Move the left tab symbol at the 1.5-inch mark to the 1-inch mark.
   c. Move the right tab symbol at the 5-inch mark to the 5.5-inch mark.
3. Save the document with Save As and name it Ch 09, SA 04.
4. Print and then close Ch 09, SA 04.

Assessment 5

1. At a clear document screen, key the document shown in figure 9.17. You determine the tab settings for the text in columns. (Align the first column at a left tab and the second column at a right tab.)
2. Save the document and name it Ch 09, SA 05.
3. Print and then close Ch 09, SA 05.

Figure 9.17 • Assessment 5

LAND DEVELOPMENT DEPARTMENT

Paul O'Shea	Manager
Tamara Langston	Assistant Manager
Daniel Roarke	Environmental Specialist
Jeanne Beeler	Legal Aide
Carl Wassal	Administrative Assistant
Ching Ney	Administrative Assistant

Assessment 6

1. At a clear document screen, key the text shown in figure 9.18 in an appropriate business letter format. You determine the tab settings for the text in columns.
2. After keying the letter, save it and name it Ch 09, SA 06.
3. Print and then close Ch 09, SA 06.

Figure 9.18 • Assessment 6

October 8, 1998

Mr. and Mrs. George Sedgwick
2033 Regents Boulevard
Salem, OR 99022

Dear Mr. and Mrs. Sedgwick:

The travel experts at Travel Advantage have specially chosen the most exciting and inviting vacation destinations for you and your family. This month, we are offering a package travel plan to St. Thomas, a dazzling Caribbean island. At St. Thomas, you will be able to enjoy boating, swimming, sailing, wind surfing, scuba diving, golfing, and tennis.

The St. Thomas package includes round-trip airfare, seven nights' hotel accommodations, and round-trip airport transfers. The prices for this exciting vacation vary depending on the city of departure. Sample prices are shown below.

	Regular	**TA Price**
Los Angeles	$1,320	$1,088
Dallas	1,220	930
Chicago	1,250	980
New York	1,040	880

This package offer includes a bonus of 2-for-1 pricing on sightseeing tours, a diving course at Bolongo Bay, and a full-day or half-day catamaran cruise. Call us now to make your reservations for beautiful St. Thomas. All prices are firm through the end of April. After that, prices may vary depending on hotel availability.

Sincerely,

TRAVEL ADVANTAGE

Lisa Wellington
Travel Consultant

XX:Ch 09, SA 06

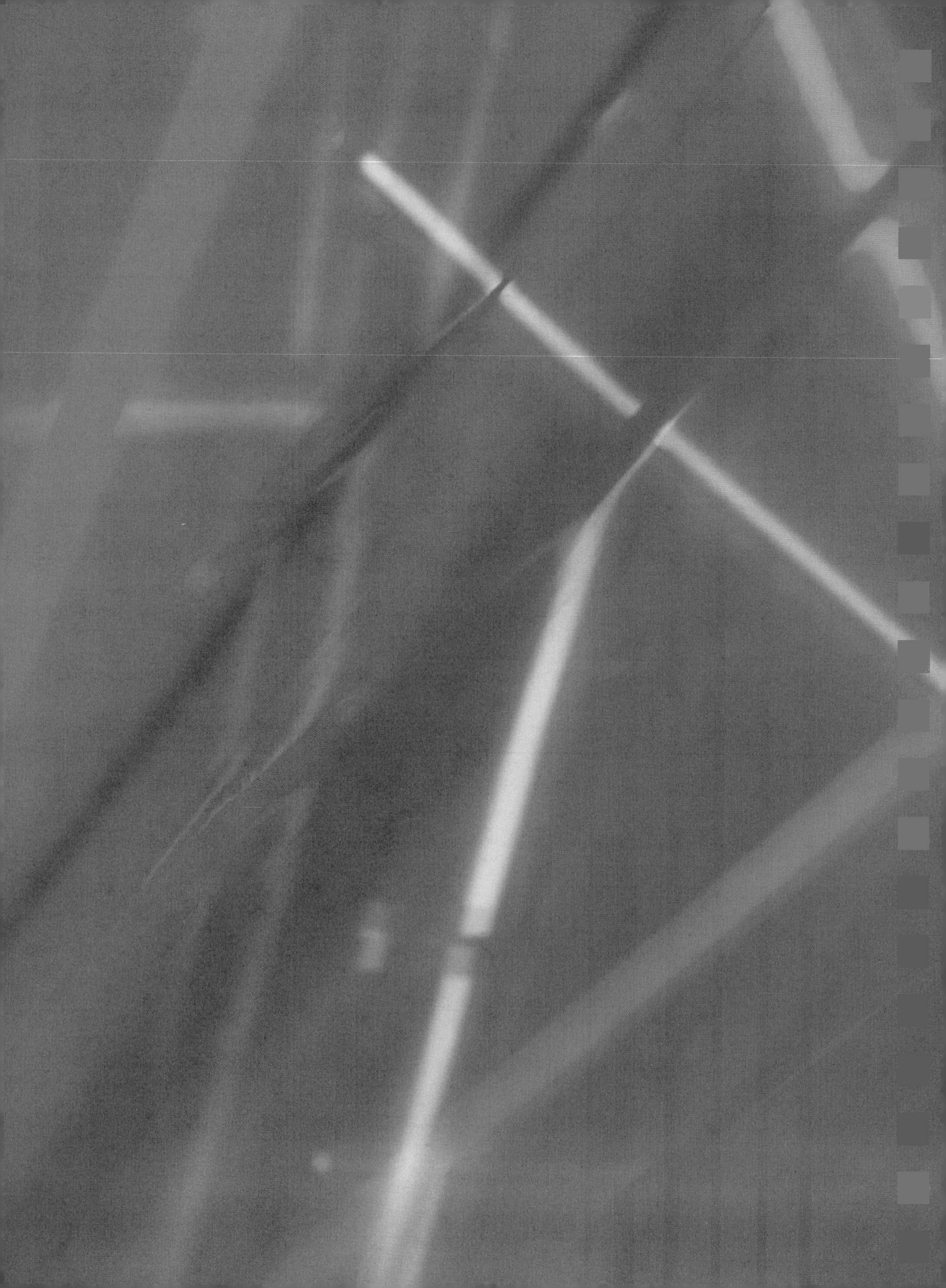

chapter TEN

Printing

PERFORMANCE OBJECTIVES

Upon successful completion of chapter 10, you will be able to:

- **Print specific pages in a document.**
- **Print multiple copies of a document.**
- **Print selected text.**
- **Print odd and/or even pages in a document.**
- **Create and print envelopes.**
- **Create and print labels.**

In chapter 1, you learned to print the document displayed in the document screen at the Print dialog box. By default, one copy of all pages is printed of the currently open document. In this chapter, you will learn to customize a print job with selections from the Print dialog box.

Using the Print Dialog Box

To display the Print dialog box shown in figure 10.1, click File, then Print; or press Ctrl + P.

Selecting Printers

The name of the selected printer is displayed in the Name text box in the Printer section of the Print dialog box. When Word 97 was installed on the hard drive or network, a printer was selected. The printer displayed in the Name text box should be the printer you are using. If other printers are installed, you can display a list of installed printers by clicking the down-pointing triangle at the right side of the Name text box. At this drop-down list, click the desired printer.

10.1

Print Dialog Box

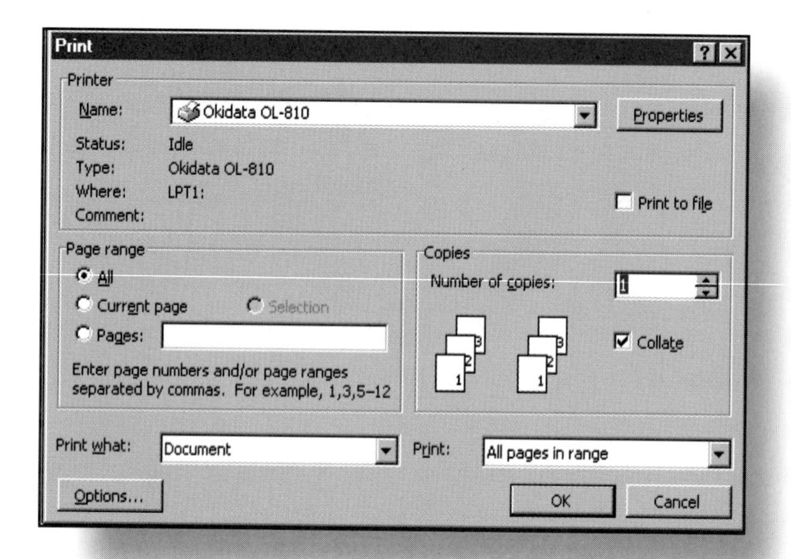

Each printer has a set of properties that can be viewed by clicking the Properties button at the Print dialog box. The options at the Properties dialog box will vary with each printer. At the Properties dialog box, you are able to set such options as paper size, layout, orientation, paper source, and print quality. If a color printer is selected, color options can also be set.

If you want to cancel the current print job, double-click the Print Status icon on the Status bar (located at the far right side). Depending on how much of the document has been sent to the printer, this may or may not stop the printing of the entire document.

Printing to a File

Use the Print to file option at the Print dialog box to print a document to a file. This is useful if you want to print a document from a computer that does not have Word 97 installed. Switching printers can change page breaks and font spacing in a document.

Printing Specific Text or Pages

The Page range section of the Print dialog box contains settings you can use to specify the amount of text you want printed. At the default setting of All, all pages of the current document are printed. Click the Current page option to print the page where the insertion point is located. Click the Selection option if you have selected text in a document and want only the selected text printed. (This option is dimmed unless text is selected in the document.)

With the Pages option, you can identify a specific page, multiple pages, and/or a range of pages. If you want specific multiple pages printed, use a comma (,) to indicate *and* and use a hyphen (-) to indicate *through*. For example, to print pages 2 and 5, you would key **2,5** in the Pages text box. To print pages 6 through 10, you would key **6-10**. Figure 10.2 illustrates options for printing pages (X, Y, and Z denote page numbers). As illustrated in the last entry in the figure, the hyphen and comma can be used in the same print job.

figure 10.2 ***Page Printing Options***

Entry	Action
X	Page X printed
X,Y	Pages X and Y printed
X-	Pages X to end of document printed
X-Y	Pages X through Y printed
-X	Beginning of document through page X printed
X-Y,Z	Pages X through Y and page Z printed

exercise 1

Printing Specific Pages

1. Open Report 03.
2. Print pages 1 and 4 by completing the following steps:
   a. Display the Print dialog box by clicking File, then Print.
   b. At the Print dialog box, click Pages.
   c. Key **1,4**.
   d. Click OK or press Enter.
3. Close Report 03.

Printing Multiple Copies

If you want to print more than one copy of a document, use the Number of copies option from the Print dialog box. To print more copies of the document, increase the number in the Number of copies text box.

If you print several copies of a document containing multiple pages, Word prints the pages in the document collated. For example, if you print two copies of a three-page document, pages 1, 2, and 3 are printed and then the pages are printed a second time. Printing pages collated is helpful but takes more printing time. To speed up the printing time, you can tell Word to not print the pages collated. (However, time is required to manually arrange the pages into sets.) To do this, remove the check mark from the Collate option at the Print dialog box. With the check mark removed, Word will print all copies of the first page, then all copies of the second page, and so on.

exercise 2

Printing Multiple Copies of a Document

1. Open Memo 01.
2. Print three copies of the memo by completing the following steps:
   a. Display the Print dialog box.
   b. Key **3**. (This inserts 3 in the Number of copies text box.)
   c. Click OK or press Enter.
3. Close Memo 01.

Printing Specific Parts of a Document

By default, Word prints the document currently displayed in the document screen. With Print what options you can print various parts of a document. If you click the down-pointing triangle after the Print what text box, a drop-down list displays with the options *Document*, *Document Properties*, *Comments*, *Styles*, *AutoText entries*, and *Key assignments*. As you learn about these options, you can print these sections by clicking the desired option.

Printing Odd and/or Even Pages

If you are printing on both sides of the paper, the Odd Pages and Even Pages selections from the Print option are useful. For example, you can print all odd pages in the document, turn the pages over, then print all even pages on the back side. To print odd or even pages, display the Print dialog box. At the Print dialog box, click the down-pointing triangle at the right side of the Print text box, and then click Odd Pages or Even Pages.

exercise 3

Printing Odd-Numbered Pages

1. Open Report 03.
2. Print only odd-numbered pages by completing the following steps:
   a. Display the Print dialog box.
   b. At the Print dialog box, click the down-pointing triangle at the right side of the Print text box, and then click *Odd Pages* at the drop-down list.
   c. Click OK or press Enter.
3. Close Report 03.

Changing Print Options

Clicking the Options button at the Print dialog box causes the Print dialog box with the Print tab selected to display as shown in figure 10.3.

figure 10.3

Print Dialog Box with Print Tab Selected

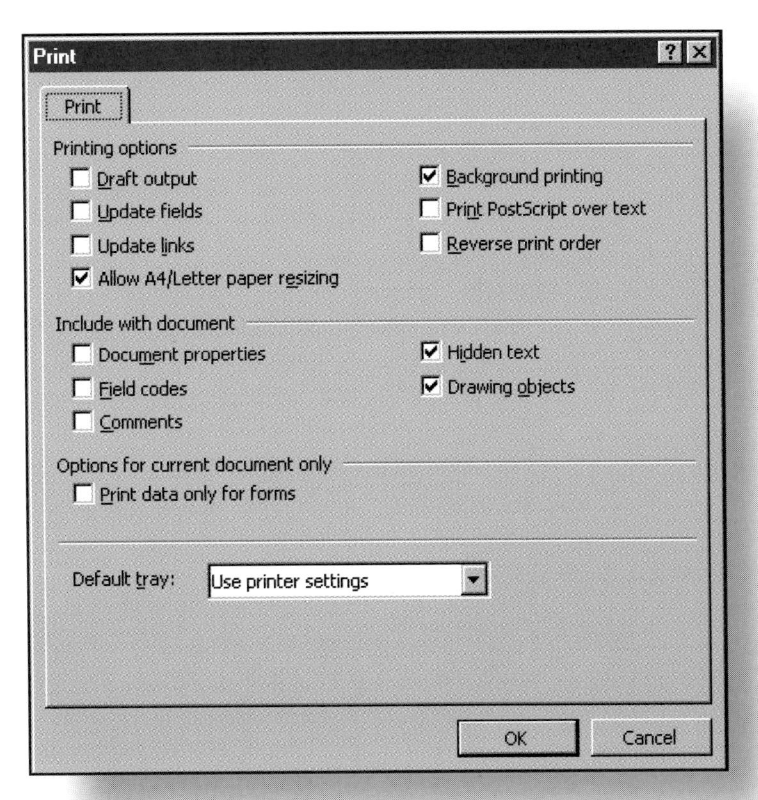

With the selections from the Printing options section, you can print the document in draft, reverse the print order (last pages first, etc.), and update fields and links. With the *Include with document* options, you can identify what additional information or text you want printed with the document, such as the document properties information, comments, or hidden text.

exercise 4

Printing a Document in Reverse Order

1. Open Report 04.
2. Print this document in reverse order by completing the following steps:
   a. Display the Print dialog box.
   b. Click the Options button.
   c. At the Print dialog box with the Print tab selected, click Reverse print order. (This inserts a check mark in the check box.)
   d. Click OK or press Enter.
   e. At the Print dialog box, click OK or press Enter.
3. After the document is printed, remove the check mark from the Reverse print order check box by completing the following steps:
   a. Display the Print dialog box.
   b. Click the Options button.
   c. At the Print dialog box with the Print tab selected, click Reverse print order. (This removes the check mark from the check box.)
   d. Click OK or press Enter.
   e. At the Print dialog box, click Close.
4. Close Report 04.

Printing Envelopes

With Word's envelope feature you can create and print an envelope. You can use the delivery address in the current document or enter the delivery address and return address at the Envelopes and Labels dialog box.

Creating an Envelope at a Clear Document Screen

To create an envelope document at a clear document screen using the envelope feature, display the Envelopes and Labels dialog box shown in figure 10.4. To display this dialog box, click Tools, then Envelopes and Labels. At the Envelopes and Labels dialog box with the Envelopes tab selected, key the delivery address. (When the Envelopes and Labels dialog box is displayed, the insertion point is automatically positioned in the Delivery address text box.) Press the Enter key to end each line in the address. Click in the Return address text box and then key the return address. Press the Enter key to end each line in the address. Click the Print button to print the envelope or click the Add to Document button to insert the envelope delivery address and return address in the current document screen formatted for an envelope.

10.4

Envelopes and Labels Dialog Box with Envelopes Tab Selected

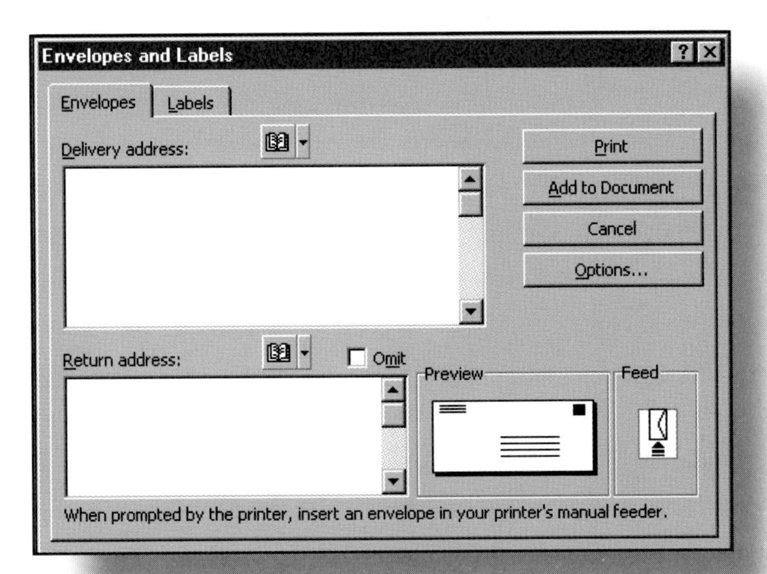

If you entered a return address, before printing the envelope, the Office Assistant will display the question, *Do you want to save the new return address as the default return address?* At this question, click Yes if you want the current return address available for future envelopes. Click No if you do not want the current return address used as the default.

When you send the envelope text to the printer, you may be prompted to insert the envelope in the printer. This is dependent upon the printer you are using.

If a default return address displays in the Return address section of the dialog box, you can tell Word to omit the return address when printing the envelope by clicking Omit. This inserts a check mark in the Omit check box.

The Envelopes and Labels dialog box contains a Preview sample box and a Feed sample box. The Preview sample box shows how the envelope will appear when printed, and the Feed sample box shows how the envelope is to be inserted into the printer.

exercise 5

Printing an Envelope

1. At a clear document screen, create an envelope that prints the delivery address and return address shown in figure 10.5 by completing the following steps:
   a. Click Tools, then Envelopes and Labels.
   b. At the Envelopes and Labels dialog box with the Envelopes tab selected, key the delivery address shown in figure 10.5 (the one containing the name *Mrs. Roseanne Moore*). (Press the Enter key to end each line in the name and address.)

c. Click in the Return address text box.
d. Key the return address shown in figure 10.5 (the one containing the name *Mr. Thomas Aniston*). (Press the Enter key to end each line in the name and address.)
e. Click the Add to Document button.
f. At the message displayed by the Office Assistant, *Do you want to save the new return address as the default return address?*, click No.

2. Save the document and name it Ch 10, Ex 05.
3. Print and then close Ch 10, Ex 05.

10.5

Exercise 5

Mr. Thomas Aniston
1210 South Alameda
Santa Fe, NM 77342

Mrs. Roseanne Moore
321 Aurora Boulevard
Santa Fe, NM 78329

Creating an Envelope with an Existing Document

If you open the Envelopes and Labels dialog box in a document containing a name and address, the name and address are automatically inserted in the Delivery address section of the dialog box. To do this, open a document containing a name and address, and then display the Envelopes and Labels dialog box.

In exercise 5, you added the envelope to the current document. At the Envelopes and Labels dialog box, you can send the envelope directly to the printer without inserting it in the document. To do this, click the Print button instead of the Add to Document button. When you click the Print button, the envelope is sent directly to the printer (but not the text in the document).

exercise 6

Creating an Envelope in an Existing Document

1. Open Letter 01.
2. Create and print an envelope for the document by completing the following steps:
   a. Click Tools, then Envelopes and Labels.
   b. At the Envelopes and Labels dialog box (with the Envelopes tab selected), make sure the delivery address displays properly in the Delivery address section.
   c. If any text displays in the Return address section, insert a check mark in the Omit check box, which is located to the right of the Return address option. (This tells Word not to print the return address on the envelope.)
   d. Click the Print button.
3. Close Letter 01 without saving the changes.

Changing Envelope Options

If you click the Options button at the Envelopes and Labels dialog box, the Envelope Options dialog box with the Envelope Options tab selected displays as shown in figure 10.6.

figure 10.6 *Envelope Options Dialog Box with Envelope Options Tab Selected*

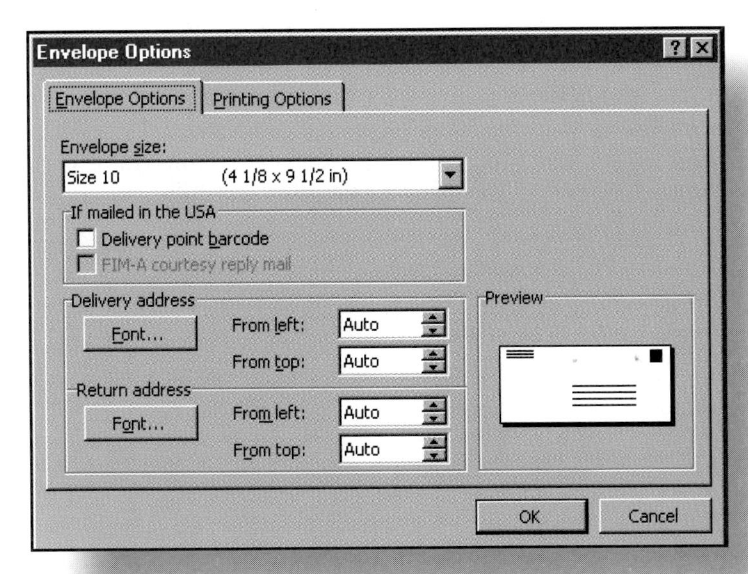

Word provides a variety of envelope sizes from which you can choose. To view the list of envelope sizes, click the down-pointing triangle at the right side of the Envelope size text box.

You can include a delivery point bar code for the delivery address at the Envelope Options dialog box. The bar code is a machine-readable representation of the Zip Code and speeds mail sorting, increases the accuracy of delivery, and reduces postage costs.

To create a delivery point bar code for the delivery address, click Delivery point barcode at the Envelope Options dialog box. Word automatically converts the Zip Code displayed in the Delivery address section of the Envelopes and Labels dialog box into vertical lines that create the bar code.

The Envelope Options dialog box also contains a FIM-A courtesy reply mail option. This option is dimmed unless the Delivery point barcode option is selected. A FIM (Facing Identification Mark) identifies the front (face) of the envelope during presorting. A courtesy reply envelope is provided as a service to the recipient and is preprinted with the sender's name and address. To add a FIM to an envelope, click the FIM-A courtesy reply mail option at the Envelope Options dialog box.

The delivery address and the return address will print with the default font. If you want to change the delivery address font, click the Font button at the Envelope Options dialog box. This displays the Envelope Address dialog box with the Font tab selected. The options at the Envelope Address dialog box with the Font tab selected are the same as the options available at the Font dialog box. At this dialog box, choose the desired font and then click OK or press Enter. This returns you to the Envelope Options dialog box.

To change the font for the return address, click the Font button at the Envelope Options dialog box. This displays the Envelope Address dialog box with the Font tab selected. Choose the desired font at this dialog box and then click OK or press Enter.

Word automatically determines the location of the delivery and return addresses from the top and left edges of the envelope. If you want to control where the delivery address is printed on the envelope, enter the desired measurement in the From left text box at the Envelope Options dialog box. Enter the desired top measurement in the From top text box. Enter the desired measurements in the From left and From top text boxes for the return address.

The Preview box at the Envelope Options dialog box displays how the envelope will appear when printed. The Preview box changes as changes are made to the dialog box.

If you click the Printing Options tab at the Envelope Options dialog box, the dialog box displays as shown in figure 10.7.

10.7

Envelope Options Dialog Box with Printing Options Tab Selected

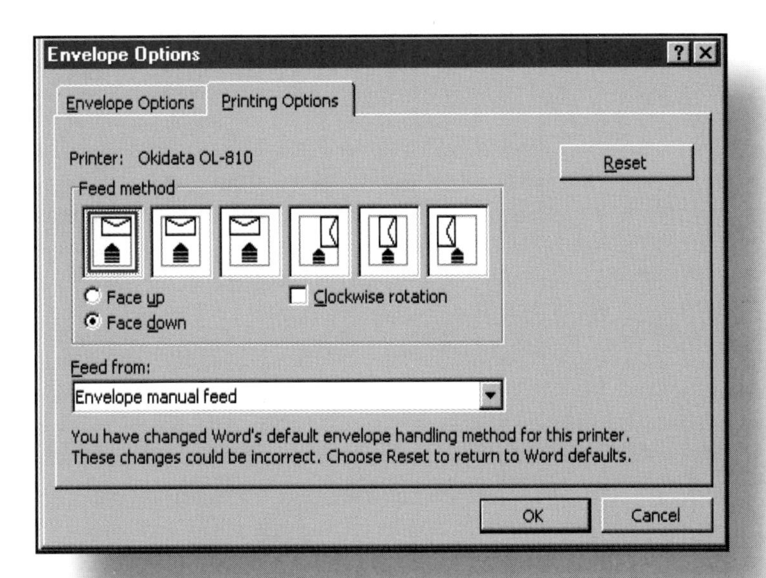

Word determines the feed method for envelopes and the feed form. If this method does not work for your printer, choose the correct feed method and feed form at the Envelope Options dialog box with the Printing Options tab selected. Feed methods are visually displayed at the dialog box. You can also determine if the envelope is fed into the printer face up or face down.

exercise 7

Creating an Envelope with a Delivery Point Barcode and a FIM

1. Open Letter 02.
2. Save the document with Save As and name it Ch 10, Ex 07.
3. Select the entire letter, change the font to 12-point Century Schoolbook, and then deselect the letter.
4. Create an envelope for the letter, add a delivery point bar code and a FIM to the envelope, and change the font of the delivery address by completing the following steps:
   a. Click Tools, then Envelopes and Labels.
   b. At the Envelopes and Labels dialog box (with the Envelopes tab selected), delete any text that may display in the Return address text box.
   c. Click the Options button.
   d. At the Envelope Options dialog box with the Envelope Options tab selected, click Delivery point barcode. (This inserts a check mark in the check box.)

e. Click FIM-A courtesy reply mail.
f. Click the Font button (immediately below Delivery address).
g. At the Envelope Address dialog box with the Font tab selected, click *Century Schoolbook* in the Font list box. (You will need to scroll up the list box to display this font.)
h. Make sure *12* displays in the Size list box.
i. Click OK or press Enter.
j. At the Envelope Options dialog box, click OK or press Enter.
k. At the Envelopes and Labels dialog box, click the Add to Document button.

5. Save the document again with the same name (Ch 10, Ex 07).
6. Print and then close Ch 10, Ex 07.

Printing Labels

Use Word's labels feature to print text on mailing labels, file labels, disk labels, or other types of labels. Word includes a variety of predefined labels that can be purchased at an office supply store. To create a sheet of mailing labels with the same name and address using the default options, click Tools, then Envelopes and Labels. At the Envelopes and Labels dialog box, click the Labels tab. At the Envelopes and Labels dialog box with the Labels tab selected, as displayed in figure 10.8, key the desired address in the Address text box. Click the New Document button to insert the mailing label in a new document or click the Print button to send the mailing label directly to the printer.

10.8 ***Envelopes and Labels Dialog Box with Labels Tab Selected***

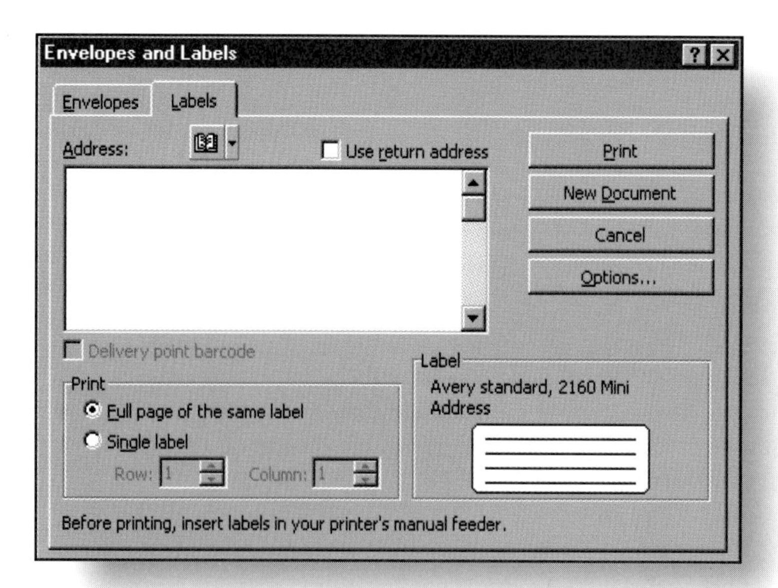

If you open the Envelopes and Labels dialog box (with the Labels tab selected) in a document containing a name and address, the name and address are automatically inserted in the Address section of the dialog box. To enter different names in each of the mailing labels, you would start at a clear document screen, then click Tools, then Envelopes and Labels. At the Envelopes and Labels dialog box, click the Labels tab, and then click the New Document button. When you click the New Document button, the Envelopes and Labels dialog box is removed from the screen and the document screen displays with label forms. The insertion point is positioned in the first label form. Key the name and address in this label and then press the Tab key to move the insertion point to the next label. Pressing Shift + Tab will move the insertion point to the preceding label. Because labels are designed primarily for merging with the data source (covered in chapter 11) or for one name and address, the first label has a different format than the other labels.

exercise 8

Creating Mailing Labels

1. Open Letter 02.
2. Create mailing labels with the delivery address by completing the following steps:
   a. Click Tools, then Envelopes and Labels.
   b. At the Envelopes and Labels dialog box, click the Labels tab.
   c. Make sure the delivery address displays properly in the Address section.
   d. If there is a check mark in the Delivery point barcode check box, click Delivery point barcode to remove the check mark.
   e. Click the New Document button.
3. Save the mailing label document and name it Ch 10, Ex 08.
4. Print and then close Ch 10, Ex 08.
5. Close Letter 02 without saving the changes.

Changing Label Options

If you click the Options button at the Envelopes and Labels dialog box with the Labels tab selected, the Label Options dialog box shown in figure 10.9 displays.

In the Printer information section of the dialog box, the type of printer you are using is displayed. If you are using a laser printer, you can specify where labels are located. The default setting depends on the selected printer.

The Label products option lets you choose from options such as Avery standard, Avery A4 and A5 sizes, and Other. This list will vary depending on the selected printer. The list of labels in the Product number list box will change depending on what label product you select.

figure 10.9

Label Options Dialog Box

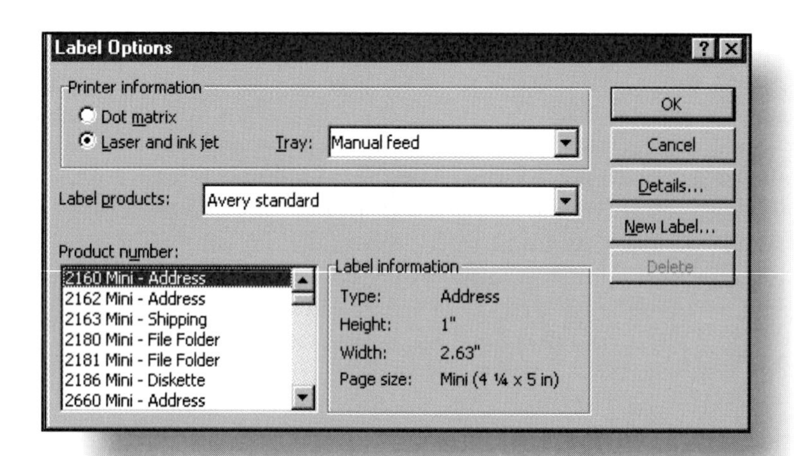

To select a different label product number, click the desired label in the Product number list box. When you select a label, information about that label is displayed in the Label information section of the Label Options dialog box, including the type, height, width, and page size. When you select a label, Word automatically determines label margins. If, however, you want to customize these default settings, click the Details button at the Label Options dialog box.

exercise 9

Creating Customized Mailing Labels

1. At a clear document screen, create mailing labels by completing the following steps:
   - a. Click Tools, then Envelopes and Labels.
   - b. Make sure the Labels tab is selected. (If not, click Labels.)
   - c. Click the Options button.
   - d. At the Label Options dialog box, make sure *Avery standard* displays in the Label products text box.
   - e. Click the down-pointing triangle at the right side of the Product number list box until *5662 - Address* is visible and then click *5662 - Address*.
   - f. Click OK or press Enter.
   - g. At the Envelopes and Labels dialog box, click the New Document button.
   - h. At the document screen, key the first name and address shown in figure 10.10 in the first label. (This label will contain different formatting than the other labels.)

i. Press Tab to move the insertion point to the next label and then key the second name and address shown in figure 10.10. Continue in this manner until all names and addresses have been keyed.

2. Save the document and name it Ch 10, Ex 09.
3. Print and then close Ch 10, Ex 09.
4. At the clear document screen, close the document screen without saving changes.

figure 10.10

Exercise 10

Ms. Barbara Peralt 9832 Meander Way Harrisburg, PA 34201	Mr. Paul Tsukamoto 12032 North 32nd Street Hershey, PA 32102
Mrs. Darlene Emerson 10293 Margate Drive Carlisle, PA 34102	Mr. and Mrs. Marc Cross 7543 160th Street East Harrisburg, PA 34095

chapter summary

- The options available at the Print dialog box can help to customize a print job.
- To cancel a print job, double-click the Print Status icon on the Status bar (located at the far right side).
- The printer displayed after the Name option in the Printer section should be the printer you are using.
- If you want to print a document from a computer that does not have Word 97 installed, use the Print to file option at the Print dialog box.
- The Page range section of the Print dialog box contains settings you can use to specify the amount of text you want printed. With the Pages option, you can identify a specific page for printing, multiple pages, and/or a range of pages. You can also specify a section to be printed or pages within a section for printing.
- You can select text and then print only the selected text.
- If you want to print more than one copy of a document, use the Number of copies option at the Print dialog box.

- With Print what options, you can print various parts of a document.
- The Odd Pages and Even Pages selections from the Print option are useful if you are printing on both sides of the paper.
- With Word's envelope feature you can create and print an envelope at the Envelopes and Labels dialog box. This dialog box contains a Preview sample box, which shows how the envelope will appear when printed, and a Feed sample box, which shows how the envelope will be fed into the printer.
- If you open the Envelopes and Labels dialog box in a document containing a name and address, that information is automatically inserted in the Delivery address section of the dialog box.
- You can include a delivery point bar code for the delivery address at the Envelope Options dialog box.
- These additional options are available at the Envelope Options dialog box: Envelope size, FIM-A courtesy reply mail, delivery and return address fonts, and options to change the top and left measurements for the delivery and return addresses.
- Use Word's labels feature to print text on mailing labels, file labels, disk labels, or other types of labels.
- These additional options are available at the Label Options dialog box: Printer information, Label products (to choose the type of label), and Details (to change label margins).

commands review

	Mouse	Keyboard
Print dialog box	File, Print	CTRL + P
Envelopes and Labels dialog box	Tools, Envelopes and Labels	Tools, Envelopes and Labels

check your understanding

Completion: In the space provided at the right, indicate the correct term, symbol, or command.

1. This is the keyboard shortcut command to display the Print dialog box. ________
2. This section of the Print dialog box contains settings for specifying the amount of text to be printed. ________
3. When specifying a range of pages to be printed, this character indicates *and*. ________

4. When specifying a range of pages to be printed, this character indicates *through*. ________________
5. Key this in the Pages text box at the Print dialog box to print pages from the beginning of the document through page 6. ________________
6. Key this in the Pages text box at the Print dialog box to print pages 2, 4, and 6 through 12. ________________
7. To display the Envelopes and Labels dialog box, click this option on the Menu bar, and then click Envelopes and Labels. ________________
8. If you open the Envelopes and Labels dialog box in a document containing a name and address, the name and address are automatically inserted in this section of the dialog box. ________________
9. Include this bar code on an envelope to speed mail sorting, increase the accuracy of delivery, and reduce postage costs. ________________
10. The letters FIM in FIM-A courtesy reply mail stand for this. ________________

skill assessments

Note: Before completing the skill assessments, display the Open dialog box, and then select and delete documents created in chapter 8 that begin Ch 08. You may want to check with your instructor before deleting these documents.

Assessment 1

1. Open Report 01.
2. Print two copies of page 2, displaying the Print dialog box only once.
3. Close Report 01.

Assessment 2

1. Open Report 03.
2. Save the document with Save As and name it Ch 10, SA 02.
3. Make the following changes to the document:
   a. Select the entire document and then change the font to 13-point Century Schoolbook.
   b. Change the top and bottom margins to 1.5 inches
   c. Bold the two titles and all the headings in the document.
4. Save the document again with the same name (Ch 10, SA 02).
5. Print pages 2 through 4 of the report.
6. Close Ch 10, SA 02.

Assessment 3

1. At a clear document screen, create an envelope that prints the delivery address and return address shown in figure 10.11. Include the delivery point bar code and the FIM. Add the envelope to the document.
2. Save the envelope document and name it Ch 10, SA 03.
3. Print and then close Ch 10, SA 03.

Figure 10.11 • Assessment 3

Ms. Gina McCammon
2003 Rydale Drive
Boston, MA 20192

Mr. Matthew Williams
5554 Kensington Place
Boston, MA 20843

Assessment 4

1. Open Letter 03.
2. Create mailing labels with the delivery address.
3. Save the labels as a new document and name it Ch 10, SA 04.
4. Print and then close Ch 10, SA 04.
5. Close Letter 03 without saving the changes.

chapterELEVEN

11 Merging Documents

PERFORMANCE OBJECTIVES

Upon successful completion of chapter 11, you will be able to:

- **Create a data source.**
- **Create a main document.**
- **Merge a data source and a main document to create personalized documents.**
- **Edit a data source.**
- **Create envelopes during a merge.**
- **Create an envelope main document and merge it with a data source.**
- **Create a label main document and merge it with a data source.**
- **Create a list main document and merge it with a data source.**
- **Input text during a merge.**

Word includes a mail merge feature that you can use to create letters and envelopes and much more, all with personalized information. There are two documents that need to be created for merging. One document, which Word calls the *data source*, contains the variable information. The second document contains the standard text along with identifiers showing where variable information (information that changes) is to be inserted. Word refers to this as the *main document*. After these documents are created, they are merged to produce personalized documents such as letters and envelopes.

A data source is a document that contains variable information about customers, clients, companies, and so on. This may include such information as names, addresses, telephone numbers, and products. The variable information included is determined by the person creating the data source. When creating a data source, consider present and future needs.

Text in a data source is inserted in cells in a table. A table contains cells that are intersections between rows and columns. Fields in a data source are entered in *cells* within a table. In this manner, each field in a cell is easily identified.

Creating a Data Source with Mail Merge Helper

Generally, a merge takes two documents—the *data source* and the *main document.* These documents can be created in any order, but you might find it more logical to create the data source first and then the main document.

The data source contains the variable information that will be inserted in the main document. Before creating a data source, determine what type of correspondence you will be creating and the type of information you will need to insert in the correspondence. Word provides predetermined field names that can be used when creating the data source. Use these field names if they represent the data you are creating.

Variable information in a data source is saved as a *record*. A record contains all the information for one unit (for example, a person, family, customer, client, or business). A series of fields make one record, and a series of records make a data source.

Word's Mail Merge Helper feature can be used to create a data source. For example, suppose the customer service manager of Lifetime Annuity Association wants to introduce a new sales representative to all customers in the Phoenix, Arizona, area. The manager determines that a personal letter should be sent to all customers in the greater Phoenix area. Figure 11.1 shows one way this letter can be written.

The date, body of the letter, and the complimentary close are standard. The variable information—information that will change with each letter—is the name, job title, company name, address, city, state, ZIP code, and salutation.

figure 11.1 ***Sample Letter***

February 24, 1999

(Name)
(Job Title)
(Company)
(Address)
(City, State Zip)

Dear (Name):

At Lifetime Annuity Association, we are committed to providing insurance and financial planning services for employees of our customers. To provide continuing service to you, a new customer representative has been hired. The new customer representative, Mr. Raymond

Miller, began his employment with Lifetime Annuity Association on February 1. He comes to our company with over 10 years' experience in the employee benefits and insurance industry.

Mr. Miller will be in the Phoenix area during the third week of March. He would like to schedule a time for a visit to your company, and will be contacting you by telephone next week.

Sincerely,

Evelyn Colwell, Manager
Customer Service Department

Before creating the letter as a main document, the data source is created. This document includes the variable information for each customer of Lifetime Annuity Association. In exercise 1, you will use the Mail Merge Helper to create a data source containing the customers of Lifetime Annuity Association who will receive the form letter.

When naming the data source, you may want to add the letters *ds* to the name to identify it as a data source document. For example, in exercise 1, you are instructed to name the data source document *Cust ds* (for *customer data source*).

Creating a Data Source

1. At a clear document screen create a data source named *Cust ds* containing the information shown in figure 11.2 by completing the following steps:
   a. Click Tools, then Mail Merge.
   b. At the Mail Merge Helper dialog box shown in figure 11.3, click Create (below Main document).
   c. At the drop-down list that displays, click Form Letters.
   d. At the dialog box asking if you want to use the active document or a new document window, click Active Window.
   e. Click Get Data and then click Create Data Source at the drop-down list.
   f. At the Create Data Source dialog box shown in figure 11.4, the fields provided by Word are shown in the Field names in header row list box. These fields are needed for the data source except *Country* and *HomePhone*. Scroll down the Field names in header row list box until *Country* is visible, click *Country*, and then click the Remove Field Name button.

g. With *HomePhone* selected in the Field names in header row list box, click the Remove Field Name button.
h. Click OK.
i. At the Save As dialog box, key **Cust ds**, and then click Save or press Enter.
j. At the dialog box containing the warning that the data source contains no data, click Edit Data Source. This displays the Data Form dialog box shown in figure 11.5.
k. At the Data Form dialog box, key the title, **Mrs.**, of the first customer shown in figure 11.2, and then press the Enter key or the Tab key.
l. Continue keying the information in figure 11.2 for the customer, *Mrs. Sara Kerrick*, in the appropriate fields. Press the Enter key or the Tab key to move to the next field or press Shift + Tab to move to the preceding field.
m. After entering all the information for *Mrs. Sara Kerrick*, click Add New. (You can also press Enter after keying the work phone.) This saves the information and displays a blank Data Form dialog box. Continue keying the information for each person in this manner until all records shown in figure 11.2 have been created.
n. After creating the last record for the data source, click View Source.
o. At the data source document, click File, then Save.

2. Print and then close *Cust ds*.
3. Close the clear document screen without saving the changes.

figure 11.2 *Exercise 1*

Title	=	Mrs.
FirstName	=	Sara
LastName	=	Kerrick
JobTitle	=	Manager
Company	=	Rayman Corporation
Address1	=	209 Tapps Drive
Address2	=	Suite 330
City	=	Phoenix
State	=	AZ
PostalCode	=	86744
WorkPhone	=	(602) 555-3409

Title	=	Mr.
FirstName	=	Gerald
LastName	=	Jorgenson
JobTitle	=	Director
Company	=	Baxter Manufacturing
Address1	=	1203 North 24th Street
Address2	=	(leave this blank)
City	=	Phoenix
State	=	AZ
PostalCode	=	86342
WorkPhone	=	(602) 555-9800

Title	=	Ms.
FirstName	=	Linda
LastName	=	White
JobTitle	=	Assistant Manager
Company	=	Broadway Builders
Address1	=	8700 Broadway Avenue
Address2	=	(leave this blank)
City	=	Phoenix
State	=	AZ
PostalCode	=	86745
WorkPhone	=	(602) 555-3344

figure 11.3

Mail Merge Helper Dialog Box

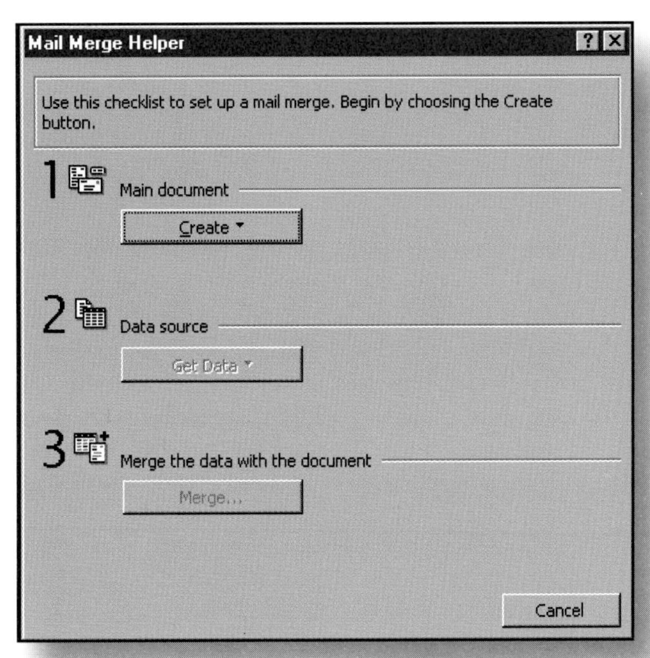

figure 11.4 *Create Data Source Dialog Box*

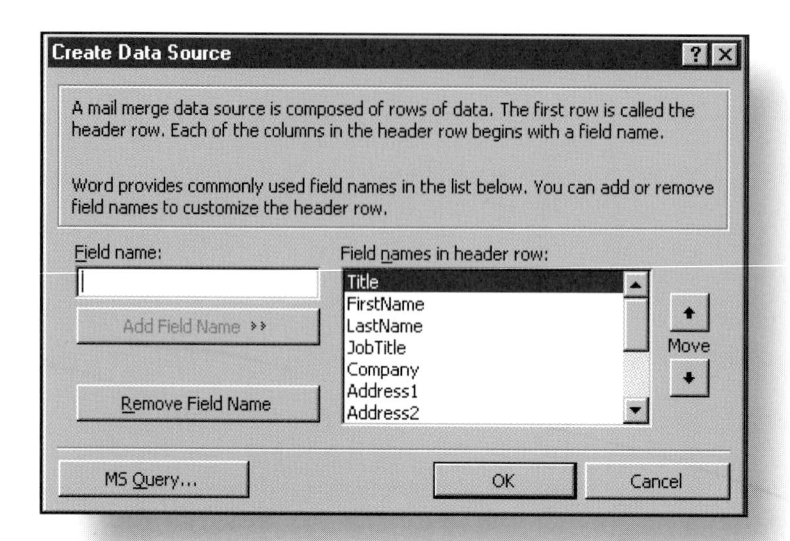

figure 11.5 *Data Form Dialog Box*

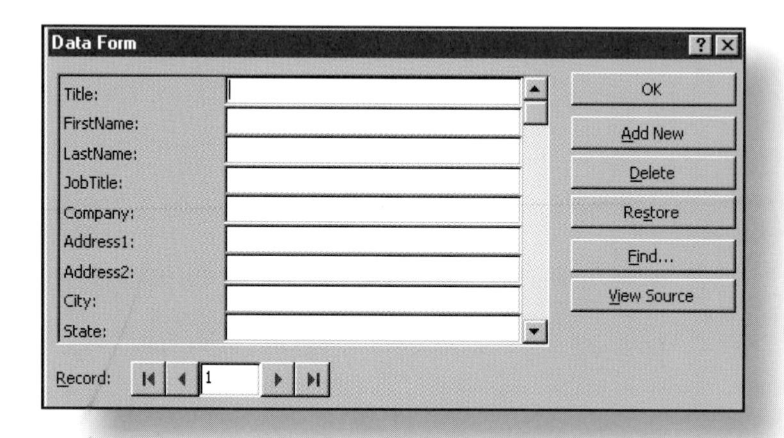

In the printed *Cust ds* data source document, the first row of the table is called the *header row* and identifies the names of the fields. These field names are important in identifying where variable information will be inserted in a main document. Text in the table may wrap within a cell. The text will be inserted properly, however, in the main document. Some fields in a data source may not contain text. For example, in the second and third records in the *Cust ds* data source, there is no data for the *Address2* data field.

Creating the Main Document

When you have determined the fields and field names and created the data source, the next step is to create the main document. When the main document is completed and the fields have been inserted in the proper locations, it will look similar to the letter shown in figure 11.6. To create the main document shown in figure 11.6, complete exercise 2.

When naming a main document, you may want to add the initials *md* to indicate that it is a main document. Notice that in figure 11.6 there is a space between the fields. Spaces are inserted between fields as if there were text; then, when the variable information is inserted, it is spaced correctly. This is also true for punctuation. Insert punctuation in a main document as you would a normal document. For example, key the comma immediately after the ‹‹City›› field in the address and key a colon (:) immediately after the ‹‹LastName›› field in the salutation. The ‹‹Title›› and ‹‹LastName›› fields are used more than once in the main document in figure 11.6. Fields can be used in a main document as often as needed.

exercise 2

Creating a Main Document

1. At a clear document screen, create the main document shown in figure 11.6 and name it *Cust md* by completing the following steps:
   a. Click Tools, then Mail Merge.
   b. At the Mail Merge Helper dialog box, click Create (below Main document), and then click Form Letters at the drop-down list.
   c. At the question asking if you want to use the active document window or a new document, click Active Window.
   d. At the Mail Merge Helper dialog box, click Get Data (below Data source) and then click Open Data Source at the drop-down list.
   e. At the Open Data Source dialog box, double-click *Cust ds* in the list box.
   f. At the Microsoft Word dialog box telling you that Word found no fields in your main document, click Edit Main Document.
   g. At the clear document screen with the Mail Merge toolbar displayed above the Ruler, key the date at the beginning of the letter shown in figure 11.6, press the Enter key five times, and then insert the first field by completing the following steps:
      1) Click the Insert Merge Field button on the Mail Merge toolbar (first button from the left).
      2) From the drop-down menu that displays, click *Title*.
   h. Press the space bar once and then insert the *FirstName* data field by completing steps similar to those in 1g. Continue in this manner until all data fields have been entered as shown

Insert Merge Field

in figure 11.6. (Be sure to press the Enter key to end a text line as shown in the figure. Also, be sure to key the comma after the «City» field.)

i. Key the remaining text in the main document, proofread the document, and then click File, then Save.
j. At the Save As dialog box, key **Cust md**, and then click Save or press Enter.

2. Print and then close *Cust md*.

figure 11.6

Exercise 2

February 24, 1999

‹‹Title›› ‹‹FirstName›› ‹‹LastName››
‹‹JobTitle››
‹‹Company››
‹‹Address1››
‹‹Address2››
‹‹City››, ‹‹State›› ‹‹PostalCode››

Dear ‹‹Title›› ‹‹Last Name››:

At Lifetime Annuity Association, we are committed to providing insurance and financial planning services for employees of our customers. To provide continuing service to you, a new customer representative has been hired. The new customer representative, Mr. Raymond Miller, began his employment with Lifetime Annuity Association on February 1. He comes to our company with over 10 years' experience in the employee benefits and insurance industry.

Mr. Miller will be in the Phoenix area during the third week of March. He would like to schedule a time for a visit to your company, and will be contacting you by telephone next week.

Sincerely,

Evelyn Colwell, Manager
Customer Service Department

XX:Cust md

Merging Files

Once the data source and the main document have been created and saved, they can be merged. Merged documents can be saved in a new document or they can be sent directly to the printer. There are several ways to merge a data source with a main document. A main document and a data source can be merged with buttons on the Mail Merge toolbar or options at the Merge dialog box.

When a main document is open, the Mail Merge toolbar shown in figure 11.7 displays below the Formatting toolbar and above the Ruler. Figure 11.7 identifies each button on the Mail Merge toolbar.

figure 11.7 *Buttons on the Mail Merge Toolbar*

Insert Merge Field ▾ | Insert Word Field ▾ | «» ABC | 1

Insert Merge Field
Insert Word Field
View Merged Data
First Record
Previous Record
Go to Record
Next Record
Last Record
Mail Merge Helper
Check for Errors
Merge to New Document
Merge to Printer
Mail Merge
Find Record
Edit Data Source

Merging to a New Document

To merge a main document with a data source to a new document using a button on the Mail Merge toolbar, open the main document, and then click the Merge to New Document button. During a merge, if a field contains no data, Word removes the blank line. For example, in the data source shown in figure 11.2, two records do not contain data for *Address2*. Instead of printing a line with no data, Word removes the blank line. At the Merge dialog box shown in figure 11.8, the *Don't print blank lines when data fields are empty* option is selected. If you do not want the blank line removed, click the *Print blank lines when data fields are empty* option. To display the Merge dialog box, click the Mail Merge button on the Mail Merge toolbar.

Merge to New Document

Mail Merge

Merge Dialog Box

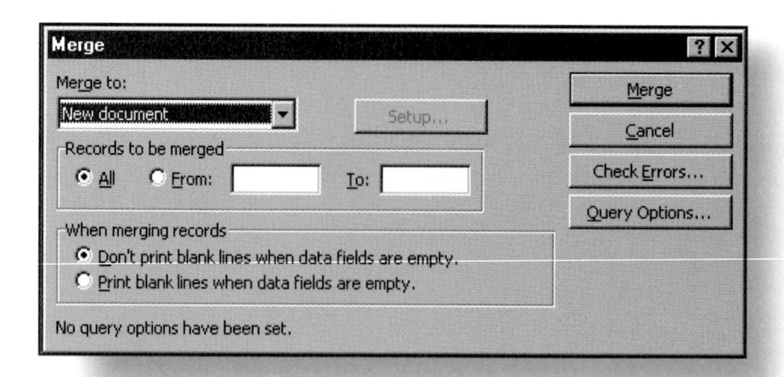

exercise 3

Merging Documents

1. Merge *Cust md* with *Cust ds* by completing the following steps:
   a. Open *Cust md*.
   b. Click the Merge to New Document button on the Mail Merge toolbar.
   c. When the main document is merged with the data source, save the document and name it Ch 11, Ex 03.
2. Print and then close Ch 11, Ex 03.
3. Close *Cust md* without saving the changes.

Merging to the Printer

In the steps in the preceding section, the records in the data source are merged with the main document and then inserted in a new document. You can also merge the records in a data source with a main document and send the merged documents directly to the printer. To do this, open the main document and then click the Merge to Printer button on the Mail Merge toolbar.

Merge to Printer

Viewing Merged Records in the Main Document

When the main document is open, the data fields, such as «Title» and «FirstName», display in the document as shown in figure 11.6. With buttons on the Mail Merge toolbar, you can view the main document with the fields merged with the data source.

View Merged Data

Click the View Merged Data button on the Mail Merge toolbar to view the main document merged with the first record in the data source. After viewing the main document merged with a record in the data source, click the View Merged Data button again to return the display to fields. When the

View Merged Data button is active, it displays with a lighter gray background than the other buttons on the Mail Merge toolbar.

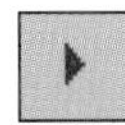

Next Record

If you click the View Merged Data button, Word displays the main document merged with the first record in the data source. If you want to see the main document merged with the next record in the data source, click the Next Record button on the Mail Merge toolbar.

First Record

Click the First Record button to view the document merged with the first record in the data source, or click the Last Record button to view the document merged with the last record in the data source. If you want to view the document merged with a specific record in the data source and you know the number of the record, key that number in the Go to Record box on the Mail Merge toolbar.

Last Record

exercise 4

Creating a Main Document with a Data Source Attached

1. At a clear document screen, create the letter shown in figure 11.9 and attach it to the *Cust ds* document by completing the following steps:
   a. Click Tools, then Mail Merge.
   b. At the Mail Merge Helper dialog box, click Create (below Main document), and then click Form Letters at the drop-down list.
   c. At the question asking if you want to use the active document window or a new document, click Active Window.
   d. At the Mail Merge Helper dialog box, click Get Data (below Data source), and then click Open Data Source at the drop-down list.
   e. At the Open Data Source dialog box, double-click *Cust ds* in the list box.
   f. At the Microsoft Word dialog box telling you that Word found no fields in your main document, click Edit Main Document.
   g. At the clear document screen with the Mail Merge toolbar displayed above the Ruler, key the letter shown in figure 11.9. Insert the fields as indicated. (Use the Insert Merge Field button to do this.)
   h. After keying the entire main document, click File, then Save.
   i. At the Save As dialog box, key **Cust ltr2 md**, and then click Save or press Enter.
2. Position the insertion point at the beginning of the document and then click the View Merged Data button on the Mail Merge toolbar to view the main document merged with the first record in the data source.
3. Click the Next Record button on the Mail Merge toolbar to view the main document merged with the second record in the data source.

4. Click the Last Record button on the Mail Merge toolbar to view the main document merged with the last record in the data source.
5. Click the View Merged Data button on the Mail Merge toolbar. (This redisplays the main document with the fields.)
6. Print and then close *Cust ltr2 md* without saving the changes.

figure 11.9 **Exercise 4**

(current date)

‹‹Title›› ‹‹FirstName›› ‹‹LastName››
‹‹Address1››
‹‹City››, ‹‹State›› ‹‹PostalCode››

Dear ‹‹Title›› ‹‹LastName››:

A few weeks ago, we shared with you the exciting news that you are preapproved for the First Choice credit card. This card offers you the ability to earn one MilesPlus mile for every purchase dollar you charge.

Now is the time to take us up on this incredible offer. Just accept your preapproved First Choice credit card and we will credit your MilesPlus account with 5,000 bonus miles after your First Choice account has been opened.

All you need to do to accept your First Choice credit card is to mail your enclosed Acceptance Form in the postage-paid envelope provided or you can call our toll-free number, 1-800-555-8900. In addition to the miles you will earn, you will also enjoy cash advances available 24 hours a day, traveler's message service, and toll-free customer service.

Sincerely,

Walter Chamberlin
Marketing Manager

XX:Cust ltr2 md

Attachment

Checking for Errors

For a merge to operate smoothly, no errors can occur in the main document or the data source. Word includes a helpful feature you can use to check for errors in the main and data source documents. This provides you with the opportunity to correct errors before completing the merge.

To correct errors, open a main document, and then click the Check for Errors button on the Mail Merge toolbar. When you click the Check for Errors button, the Checking and Reporting Errors dialog box shown in figure 11.10 displays.

Check for Errors

figure 11.10 *Checking and Reporting Errors Dialog Box*

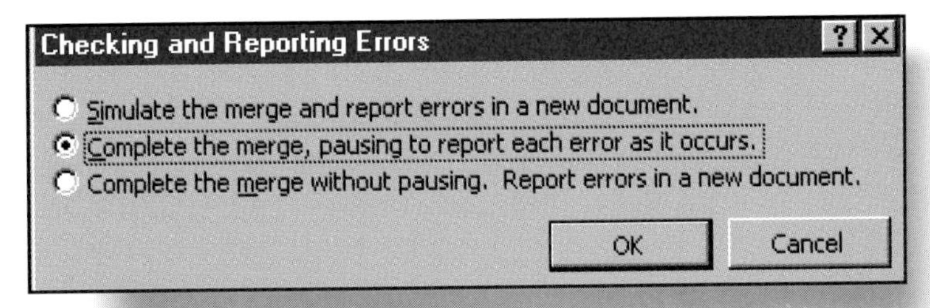

The Checking and Reporting Errors dialog box contains three options. You can tell Word to simulate the merge, then report errors in a new document; complete the merge, pausing to report each error as it occurs; or complete the merge without pausing, then report errors in a new document. If you are going to merge a main document with a data source containing a large number of records and you expect there may be errors, click the *Simulate the merge and report errors in a new document* option. The steps to check will vary depending on the options you choose. Consider the following guidelines and you will reduce or eliminate errors in the merge:

- Field names must be unique, begin with a letter, and contain no spaces. (If you let Word choose the field names for you when creating the data source, this will not be a problem.)
- Field names must be in one row at the beginning of the data source.
- Each field (column) must have a field name.

exercise 5

Checking for Errors in a Main Document

1. Open *Cust ltr2 md*.
2. Check for errors in the main document and data source document by completing the following steps:
   a. Click the Check for Errors button on the Mail Merge toolbar.
   b. At the Checking and Reporting Errors dialog box, make sure *Complete the merge, pausing to report each error as it occurs* is selected, and then click OK or press Enter.

c. If Word finds any errors, make the necessary corrections. If no errors are found, the main document is merged with the data source and the merged document is displayed in the document screen.

3. Save the merged document and name it Ch 11, Ex 05.
4. Print and then close Ch 11, Ex 05.
5. Close *Cust ltr2 md* without saving the changes.

Editing the Data Source

Edit Data Source

With the main document displayed, you can edit records in a data source with the Edit Data Source button on the Mail Merge toolbar. When you click the Edit Data Source button, Word displays the Data Form dialog box containing the information for the record number displayed in the Go to Record box on the Mail Merge toolbar.

With the Data Form dialog box displayed, make changes to the text in the record as required. Press the Tab key to move to the next field; press Shift + Tab to move to the previous field. Use the arrow buttons at the bottom left side of the Data Form dialog box to display the first record, next record, previous record, or last record in the data source.

To delete a record from the data source, display the desired record then click Delete. If you edit a record and then decide you want to return the record to its original state before editing, click Restore.

If you want to make edits to the data source, click View Source. This displays the data source document in the table format. When the data source is displayed, the Database toolbar displays below the Formatting toolbar and above the Ruler. Figure 11.11 identifies the buttons on the Database toolbar and what you can perform with each button.

figure 11.11 *Buttons on the Database Toolbar*

Choose this button	Named	To do this...
	Data Form	display the Data Form dialog box where you can add or delete records or edit existing records.
	Manage Fields	display the Manage Fields dialog box where you can add, remove, or rename field names in the header row.
	Add New Record	add a new record at the location of the insertion point in the table.
	Delete Record	remove a record at the location of the insertion point in the table.

Button	Name	Description
	Sort Ascending	sort the records in the table in ascending order on the current field.
	Sort Descending	sort the records in the table in descending order on the current field.
	Insert Database	display the Database dialog box where you can insert a file containing a database.
	Update Field	update fields in the document.
	Find Record	display the Find in Field dialog box where you can search for a specific record.
	Mail Merge Main Document	open the main document attached to the current data source.

With the buttons on the Database toolbar as described in figure 11.11, you can easily manage the data source document. If you want to add or remove field names from the header row in the data source, display the Manage Fields dialog box shown in figure 11.12 by clicking the Manage Fields button on the Database toolbar.

Manage Fields

figure 11.12 *Manage Fields Dialog Box*

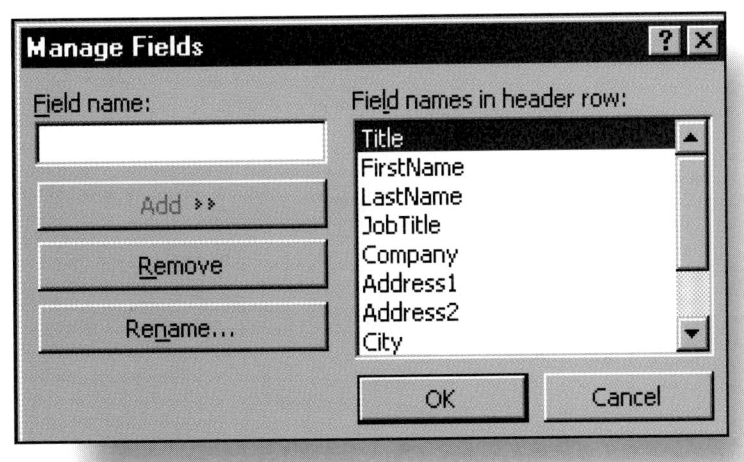

At the Manage Fields dialog box, you can add a data field to the data source and remove or rename a data field. To add a data field, key the new data field name in the Field name text box, and then click Add. Word adds the new field name to the end of the list in the Field names in header row list box and adds a new column at the right side of the table in the data source document. Key information in the cells in the new column as needed.

exercise 6

Editing a Data Source Document

1. Edit the *Cust ds* document by completing the following steps:
   a. Open *Cust md*.
   b. Click the Edit Data Source button on the Mail Merge toolbar.
   c. At the Data Form dialog box, click once on the button containing the right-pointing triangle immediately right of the Record text box. (This displays the second record in the data source containing the name *Gerald Jorgenson*.)
   d. Press the Tab key until *1203 North 24th Street* is selected, and then key **4133 Monta Vista**.
   e. Press the Tab key until *Phoenix* is selected and then key **Scottsdale**.
   f. Press the Tab key until *86342* is selected and then key **87332**.
   g. Click View Source. (This displays the data source document.)
   h. At the data source document, click the Add New Record button on the Database toolbar.

Add New Record

   i. With the insertion point positioned in the first cell of the new row, key the text after *Title*, and then press the Tab key. Continue keying the text as indicated below:

Title	=	Mrs.
FirstName	=	Barbara
LastName	=	Houston
JobTitle	=	Director
Company	=	CR Electrical
Address1	=	7903 South 122nd
Address2	=	Building C
City	=	Scottsdale
State	=	AZ
PostalCode	=	87923
WorkPhone	=	(602) 555-5050

   j. Save the data source document with the same name (*Cust ds*).
   k. Close *Cust ds*.
   l. Click the Merge to New Document button on the Mail Merge toolbar.
2. Save the merged document and name it Ch 11, Ex 06.
3. Print and then close Ch 11, Ex 06.
4. Close *Cust md* and save the changes.

Merging Envelopes

If you create a letter as a main document and then merge it with a data source, more than likely you will need an envelope properly addressed in which to send the letters. An envelope can be created that contains data fields that are then merged with a data source. In this way, you can quickly prepare envelopes. In exercise 7 you will prepare envelopes for the customers in the data source document named *Cust ds*.

exercise 7

Creating an Envelope Main Document

1. At a clear document screen, create a main document for envelopes with the *Cust ds* data source document attached by completing the following steps:
   a. Click Tools, then Mail Merge.
   b. At the Mail Merge Helper dialog box, click Create (below Main document) and then click Envelopes at the drop-down list.
   c. At the question asking if you want to use the active document window or a new document, click Active Window.
   d. At the Mail Merge Helper dialog box, click Get Data (below Data source), and then click Open Data Source at the drop-down list.
   e. At the Open Data Source dialog box, double-click *Cust ds* in the list box.
   f. At the Microsoft Word dialog box telling you that Word needs to set up your main document, click Set Up Main Document.
   g. At the Envelope Options dialog box with the Envelope Options tab selected, make sure the correct envelope size is displayed, and then click OK.
   h. At the Envelope address dialog box, click the Insert Merge Field button, and then click *Title* from the drop-down list. (This inserts «Title» in the Sample envelope address section of the dialog box.) Continue choosing fields from the Insert Merge Field drop-down list as shown in figure 11.13.
   i. When all fields have been entered in the Sample envelope address section of the dialog box as shown in figure 11.13, click OK to close the Envelope address dialog box.
   j. At the Mail Merge Helper dialog box, click Merge.
   k. At the Merge dialog box, make sure *New document* displays in the Merge to text box, and then click the Merge button.
2. Save the merged document and name it Ch 11, Ex 07.
3. Print and then close Ch 11, Ex 07.
4. At the envelope main document, save it and name it *Env md*.
5. Close *Env md*.

11.13

Exercise 7

«Title» «FirstName» «LastName»
«Address1»
«City», «State» «PostalCode»

When you click the Merge button at the Merge dialog box, the records in the data source are merged with the envelope and then the merged envelopes are inserted in a document. Print this document in the normal manner. If you want to send the merged envelopes directly to the printer, change the Merge to option at the Merge dialog box to Printer, and then click the Merge button.

If you want to save the merged envelopes, save the document in the normal manner, and then close it. This displays the envelope main document. If you think you will need this envelope main document in the future, save it with a name that includes the letters *md* to identify it as a main document.

At the Envelope address dialog box, you can specify that a postal bar code be inserted on the envelope and also a FIM (Facing Identification Marker). Mail coming into the Post Office is scanned and, if a postal bar code is found, the mail is sent to a bar code sorter rather than an OCR (Optional Character Recognition) scanner. This speeds up the sorting process and gets the envelope delivered more quickly. A FIM is a bar code that is printed on the front of a courtesy reply envelope identifying the front (face) of the envelope. To include a postal bar code and a FIM for an envelope, click the Insert Postal Bar Code button. At the Insert Postal Bar Code dialog box, specify the *PostalCode* field in the Merge field with ZIP code text box. Click the FIM-A courtesy reply mail if you want a FIM included on the envelope.

Merging Mailing Labels

Mailing labels can be created for records in a data source in much the same way that you create envelopes. Complete steps similar to those for creating envelopes for records in a data source. By default, records in a data source are merged with a mailing label, then the merged labels are inserted in the document screen. Print a mailing label document in the normal manner. If you want to send merged labels directly to the printer, change the Merge to option at the Merge dialog box to Printer, and then click the Merge button.

If you want to save merged labels, save the document in the normal manner, and then close it. This displays the label main document. If you think you will need this label main document in the future, save it with a name that includes the letters *md* to identify it as a main document.

exercise 8

Creating Mailing Labels

1. At a clear document screen, create mailing labels for Avery 5163 shipping labels using the records in the *Cust ds* data source document by completing the following steps:
   a. Click Tools, then Mail Merge.
   b. At the Mail Merge Helper dialog box, click Create (below Main document), and then click Mailing Labels at the drop-down list.
   c. At the question asking if you want to use the active document window or a new document, click Active Window.
   d. At the Mail Merge Helper dialog box, click Get Data (below Data source), and then click Open Data Source at the drop-down list.
   e. At the Open Data Source dialog box, double-click *Cust ds* in the list box.
   f. At the Microsoft Word dialog box telling you that Word needs to set up your main document, click Set Up Main Document.
   g. At the Label Options dialog box, scroll down the Product number list box until *5163 - Shipping* is visible and then click it.
   h. Click OK to close the Labels Options dialog box.
   i. At the Create Labels dialog box, click the Insert Merge Field button, and then click *Title* at the drop-down list. (This inserts «Title» in the Sample label box.)
   j. Press the space bar once and then insert the «FirstName» data field by completing steps similar to those in step 1i.
   k. Continue entering the data fields in the Sample label box until all necessary fields are entered. (Fields should be inserted in the location where you want the data to appear on the label.)
   l. Add a delivery point bar code to the label by completing the following steps:
      1) Click the Insert Postal Bar Code button.
      2) At the Insert Postal Bar Code dialog box, click the down-pointing triangle at the right side of the Merge field with ZIP code text box, scroll down the list until *PostalCode* is visible, and then click it.
      3) Click OK to close the Insert Postal Bar Code dialog box.
   m. At the Create Labels dialog box, click OK.
   n. At the Mail Merge Helper dialog box, click Merge.
   o. At the Merge dialog box, make sure *New document* displays in the Merge to text box, and then click the Merge button.
2. Save the merged document and name it Ch 11, Ex 08.
3. Print and then close Ch 11, Ex 08.
4. At the labels main document, save it and name it *Cust Label md.*
5. Close *Cust Label md.*

Creating Lists with Merge

When merging form letters, envelopes, or mailing labels, a new form is created for each record. For example, if there are eight records in the data source that is merged with a form letter, eight letters are created. If there are twenty records in a data source that is merged with a mailing label, twenty labels are created. In some situations, you may want merged information to remain on the same page. This is useful, for example, when creating a list such as a directory or address list.

A merge document can be created that inserts records on the same page by using the Catalog option from the Create drop-down list at the Mail Merge Helper dialog box. For example, suppose you want to create a list of the employees in a company by name, department, and extension. The first step is to create the data source using the Mail Merge Helper. In this example, the data source contains three fields: *Name*, *Department*, and *Extension*. After the data source is created, the next step is to create the main document and link it to the data source. In exercise 9, you will create a main document and link it to a data source to create a list.

exercise 9

Creating a List with Text from a Data Source Document

1. At a clear document screen, create a list containing the name, company name, and title for the customers in the *Cust ds* data source by completing the following steps:
   a. Click Tools, then Mail Merge.
   b. At the Mail Merge Helper dialog box, click Create (below Main document), and then click Catalog at the drop-down list.
   c. At the question asking if you want to use the active document window or a new document, click Active Window.
   d. At the Mail Merge Helper dialog box, click Get Data (below Data source) and then click Open Data Source at the drop-down list.
   e. At the Open Data Source dialog box, double-click *Cust ds* in the list box.
   f. At the Microsoft Word dialog box telling you that Word found no fields in your main document, click Edit Main Document.
   g. At the clear document screen, complete the following steps:
      1) Set left tabs at the 2-inch mark and the 4-inch mark on the Ruler.
      2) Insert the *FirstName* field at the left margin by clicking the Insert Merge Field button on the Mail Merge toolbar and then clicking *FirstName*.

3) Press the space bar and then insert the *LastName* field.
4) Press the Tab key and then insert the *JobTitle* field.
5) Press the Tab key and then insert the *Company* field.
6) Press the Enter key twice.

h. Click the Merge to New Document button on the Mail Merge toolbar.

2. At the merged document, complete the following steps:
   a. Position the insertion point at the beginning of the document.
   b. Press the Enter key three times.
   c. Move the insertion point back to the beginning of the document.
   d. Turn on bold and then key **Customer**.
   e. Press the Tab key and then key **Title**.
   f. Press the Tab key and then key **Company**.
3. Save the merged list document and name it Ch 11, Ex 09.
4. Print and then close Ch 11, Ex 09.
5. Save the list main document and name it *Cust List md*.
6. Close *Cust List md*.

Inputting Text During a Merge

Word's Merge feature contains a large number of Word fields that can be inserted in a main document. In this chapter, you will learn about the *Fill-in* field that is used for information that is input at the keyboard during a merge. For more information on the other Word fields, please refer to the on-screen help.

Situations may arise in which you do not need to keep all variable information in a data source. For example, there may be variable information that changes on a regular basis such as a customer's monthly balance, a product price, etc. Word lets you input variable information into a document during the merge using the keyboard. A fill-in field is inserted in a main document by clicking the Insert Word Field button on the Mail Merge toolbar and then clicking Fill-in at the drop-down list. A document can contain any number of Fill-in fields.

To insert a Fill-in field, open a main document and position the insertion point at the location in the document where you want the field to display. Click the Insert Word Field button on the Mail Merge toolbar and then click Fill-in at the drop-down list that displays. At the Insert Word Field: Fill-in dialog box shown in figure 11.14, key a short message indicating what should be entered at the keyboard, and then click OK. At the Microsoft Word dialog box with the message you entered displayed in the upper left corner, key text you want to display in the document, and then click OK. When the Fill-in field or fields are added, save the main document in the normal manner.

Insert Word Field ▾

Insert Word Field

11.14 Insert Word Field: Fill-in Dialog Box

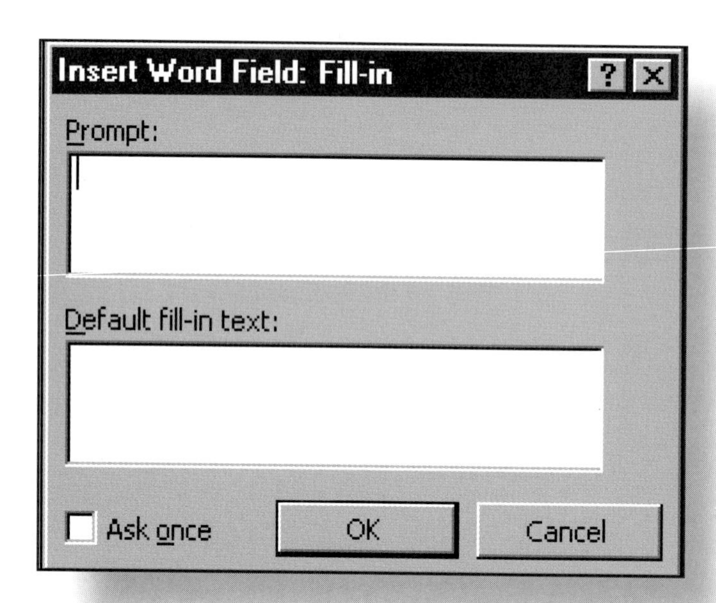

To merge the main document with the data source, click the Merge to New Document button on the Mail Merge toolbar or the Merge to Printer button. When Word merges the main document with the first record in the data source, the Microsoft Word dialog box displays with the message you entered displayed in the upper left corner. Key the required information for the first record in the data source and then click the OK button. If you are using the keyboard, key the required information, press the Tab key to make the OK button active, and then press Enter.

Word displays the dialog box again. Key the required information for the second record in the data source, and then click OK or press the Tab key and then press Enter. Continue in this manner until the required information has been entered for each record in the data source. Word then completes the merge.

exercise 10

Adding Fill-in Fields to a Document

1. Edit the *Cust ltr2 md* main document so it includes Fill-in fields by completing the following steps:
   a. Open *Cust ltr2 md*.
   b. Change the third paragraph in the document to the paragraph shown in figure 11.15. Insert the first Fill-in field (displays in the paragraph in parentheses) by completing the following steps:

1) Click the Insert Word Field button on the Mail Merge toolbar.
2) At the drop-down menu that displays, click Fill-in.
3) At the Insert Word Field: Fill-in dialog box, key **Insert rep name**.
4) Click OK.
5) At the Microsoft Word dialog box with *Insert rep name* displayed in the upper left corner, key **(representative's name)**, and then click OK.

c. Complete steps similar to those in 1b to insert the second Fill-in field, except key **Insert phone number** at the Insert Word Field: Fill-in dialog box and key **(phone number)** at the Microsoft Word dialog box.

2. When the paragraph is completed, save the document with Save As and name it *Cust ltr3 md*.
3. Merge the main document with the data source by completing the following steps:
   a. Click the Merge to New Document button on the Mail Merge toolbar.
   b. When Word merges the main document with the first record, a dialog box displays with the message *Insert rep name*. At this dialog box, key **Charles Noland**, and then click OK.
   c. At the dialog box with the message *Insert phone number*, key **(206) 555-3443**, and then click OK.
   d. At the dialog box with the message *Insert rep name*, key **Denise Nickel** (over *Charles Noland*), and then click OK.
   e. At the dialog box with the message *Insert phone number*, key **(206) 555-3430** (over the previous number), and then click OK.
   f. At the dialog box with the message *Insert rep name*, key **Andrew Christie** (over *Denise Nickel*), and then click OK.
   g. At the dialog box with the message *Insert phone number*, key **(206) 555-3456** (over the previous number), and then click OK.
   h. At the dialog box with the message *Insert rep name*, key **Nicole Gelmann** (over *Andrew Christie*), and then click OK.
   i. At the dialog box with the message *Insert phone number*, key **(206) 555-3422** (over the previous number), and then click OK.
4. Save the merged document and name it Ch 11, Ex 10.
5. Print and then close Ch 11, Ex 10.
6. Close *Cust ltr3 md* and save the changes.

11.15 *Exercise 13*

All you need to do to accept your First Choice card is to mail your enclosed Acceptance Form in the postage-paid envelope provided or call our service representative, **(representative's name)**, at **(phone number)**. In addition to the miles you will earn, you will also enjoy cash advances available 24 hours a day, traveler's message service, and toll-free customer service.

chapter summary

- Word includes a mail merge feature that you can use to create letters and envelopes and much more, all with personalized information.
- Two different documents are usually required for merging. The *data source* document contains the variable information. The *main document* contains the standard text along with identifiers showing where variable information is to be inserted.
- Use Word's Mail Merge Helper to assist you in creating the data source. At the Mail Merge Helper, Word provides predetermined field names that can be used when creating the data source.
- Variable information in a data source is saved as a *record*. A record contains all the information for one unit. A series of fields make one record, and a series of records make a data source.
- After determining what information you want in the main document, you need to determine what fields from the data source you will need and where they should be inserted in the main document.
- When creating a main document, you need to identify what data source will be used for the variable information. This is done at the Mail Merge Helper dialog box.
- Once the data source and the main document have been created and saved, they can be merged. Merged documents can be saved in a new document or sent directly to the printer.
- When the main document is open, you can use buttons on the Mail Merge toolbar to view how the document will look after merging with the first record, the next record, the last record, or a specific record from the data source.
- With the Check for Errors button on the Mail Merge toolbar, you can check the data source and the main document for errors before merging.
- With the Edit Data Source button on the Mail Merge toolbar, you can edit records in a data source. With buttons on the Database toolbar, you can easily manage the data source document.
- An envelope can be created that contains data fields that are then merged with a data source. Mailing labels can be created for records in a data source in much the same way.

- A merge document can be created that inserts records on the same page by using the Catalog option from the Create drop-down list at the Mail Merge Helper dialog box.
- Word lets you input variable information with the keyboard into a document during the merge. This fill-in field is inserted in a main document by clicking the Insert Word Field button on the Mail Merge toolbar, and then clicking Fill-in at the drop-down list.

commands review

	Mouse/Keyboard
Display Mail Merge Helper dialog box	Tools, Mail Merge

check your understanding

Fill in the Blank: In the space provided, indicate the correct term, command, or number.

1. At the ____________________ dialog box, predetermined fields are provided by Word.
2. The first row of a data source table is called a ____________________ and identifies the names of the fields.
3. Before creating the main document, determine what information will remain the same and what information will ____________________.
4. When creating a main document, you need to identify what ____________________ will be used for the variable information.
5. The data source and the main document can be merged to a new document or to the ____________________.
6. A series of fields makes a ____________________.
7. Click the ____________________ button on the Mail Merge toolbar to view the main document merged with the first record in the data source.
8. With the main document displayed, you can edit records in a data source with the ____________________ button on the Mail Merge toolbar.
9. To begin creating envelopes for the names and addresses in a source document, click ____________________ at the Mail Merge Helper dialog box.
10. So that merged information remains on the same page, click the ____________________ option at the Create drop-down list at the Mail Merge Helper dialog box.
11. A field that is used for information that is input at the keyboard during a merge is called a(n) ____________________ field.

skill assessments

Note: Before completing the skill assessments, display the Open dialog box, and then select and delete documents created in chapter 9 that begin Ch 09. You may want to check with your instructor before deleting these documents.

Assessment 1

1. Look at the letter in figure 11.17 and the information in figure 11.16. Determine the fields you need for the main document and the data source. Create the data source and name it *Self-Study Ltr ds*. Create the main document shown in figure 11.17, and then merge it with *Self-Study Ltr ds* to a new document.
2. Save the merged document and name it Ch 11, SA 01.
3. Print and then close Ch 11, SA 01.
4. Save the main document and name it *Self-Study Ltr md*.
5. Close *Self-Study Ltr md*.

Figure 11.16 • Assessment 1

Mr. and Mrs. Charles Vuong
10421 Fifth Avenue
Petersburg, ND 76322

Ms. Julie Combs
309 Fawcett Drive
Petersburg, ND 76322

Mr. John Stahl
4707 North Oakes
Apartment 4C
Petersburg, ND 76322

Mr. and Mrs. Darrell Wren
21883 South 43rd
Petersburg, ND 76322

Mrs. Rhonda Visell
5404 North Foster
Apartment 206
Petersburg, ND 76322

Figure 11.17 • Assessment 1

(current date)

Name
Address
City, State Zip

Dear (Name):

The results of the parent self-study are attached. As you read through the information, you will find there are several areas that will become a focus for change. Your input was extremely valuable and is being used to develop our student learning improvement plan and to apply for a legislative student learning improvement grant.

A concern that was mentioned repeatedly in the survey was the lack of computers. The reason new schools have access to the networking system and computers is that it is built into the entire new school package that is impacted by state matching funds. One of the levy components is computer technology to bring existing schools in line with the technology currently experienced in new buildings. We hope that the voter registration drive currently under way will impact the number of voters going to the polls in November.

Thank you for your input and for being an integral partner with us in your child(ren)'s education. If you would like to discuss the results further or have additional comments, please give me a call.

Sincerely,

Kathryn Rosell, Principal
Stewart Elementary School

XX:Self-Study Ltr md

Attachment

Assessment 2

1. Look at the letter in figure 11.19 and the information in figure 11.18. Determine the fields you need for the main document and the data source. Create the data source and name it *MP Cust ds*. Create the main document shown in figure 11.19 and then merge it with *MP Cust ds* to a new document.
2. Save the merged document and name it Ch 11, SA 02.
3. Print and then close Ch 11, SA 02.
4. Save the main document and name it *MP Cust md*.
5. Close *MP Cust md*.

Figure 11.18 • Assessment 2

Mr. and Mrs. Dennis Haynes
1810 23rd Avenue
Seattle, WA 98221

Ms. Deborah Burke
17420 Vander Road
Federal Way, WA 98045

Mr. Kevin Jergens
10605 Lakeside Drive
Seattle, WA 98188

Mr. and Mrs. Lloyd Rienhart
818 Vista Drive
Redmond, WA 98013

Dr. Janice Crivello
8905 West 50th Street
Seattle, WA 98041

Figure 11.19 • Assessment 2

(current date)

Name
Address
City, State Zip

Dear (Name):

We would like to introduce you to a great way to earn free travel to Alaska, Hawaii, Europe, and Asia, and hundreds of other places. Because you are a valued MilesPlus member, (Name), you have been preapproved for the First Choice credit card with a credit line of $3,000. This is the only credit card that offers you the ability to earn one MilesPlus mile for every purchase dollar you charge.

You can use your First Choice card for all kinds of purchases at over 10 million locations throughout the world. Every purchase you make brings you closer to your next free flight to Seaview Airlines destinations. You can also enjoy a 30-day, interest-free grace period on your purchases when you pay your previous balance in full by the due date.

Take advantage of this special opportunity to earn more miles and fantastic free travel by accepting your preapproved First Choice card today.

Sincerely,

Walter Chamberlin
Marketing Manager

XX:MP Cust md

Assessment 3

1. Edit the *MP Cust ds* document and make the following changes:
   a. Delete the fourth record in the data source.
   b. Make the following changes to the third record in the data source:
      1) Change the address from *10605 Lakeside Drive* to *3402 North 45th*.
      2) Change the city from *Seattle* to *Bellevue*.
      3) Change the Zip code from *98188* to *98065*.

c. Add a new record with the following information:

Ms. Megan Soltis
10234 South Issaquah Road
Bellevue, WA 98047

2. Save the data source document with the same name (*MP Cust ds*).
3. Close *MP Cust ds*.
4. Click the Merge to New Document button on the Mail Merge toolbar.
5. Save the merged document and name it Ch 11, SA 03.
6. Print and then close Ch 11, SA 03.
7. Close *MP Cust md* and save the changes.

Assessment 4

1. Create an envelope main document for the records in the *MP Cust ds* data source.
2. Merge the envelope main document with *MP Cust ds* to a new document.
3. Save the merged document and name it Ch 11, SA 04.
4. Print and then close Ch 11, SA 04.
5. Save the envelope main document and name it *MP Cust Env md*.
6. Close *MP Cust Env md*.

Assessment 5

1. Create a mailing label main document for the records in the *Self-Study Ltr ds* data source. (Use the 5163 - Shipping mailing labels.)
2. Merge the mailing labels main document with the *Self-Study Ltr ds* data source to a new document.
3. Save the merged document and name it Ch 11, SA 05.
4. Print and then close Ch 11, SA 05.
5. Save the label main document and name it *Self-Study Labels md*.
6. Close *Self-Study Labels md*.

Assessment 6

1. Open *MP Cust md*.
2. Change the third paragraph in the letter *MP Cust md* so it reads as shown in figure 11.20. Include the Fill-in field as shown in parentheses in figure 11.20. (Key the message *Insert customer number* at the Insert Word Field: Fill-in dialog box.)
3. Save the edited main document with Save As and name it *MP Cust2 md*.
4. Merge the records to a new document. At the dialog boxes asking for the customer number, key the following:

Record 1	=	MP-875
Record 2	=	MP-231
Record 3	=	MP-110
Record 4	=	MP-877
Record 5	=	MP-234

5. Save the merged document and name it Ch 11, SA 06.
6. Print and then close Ch 11, SA 06.
7. Close *MP Cust2 md,* saving the changes.

Figure 11.20 • Assessment 6

We have assigned you customer number (**customer's number**). To accept this special offer, call our toll-free number at 1-800-555-3440 and tell the representative your customer number. It's as simple as that! You will have your new card within a few days!

Unit two

PERFORMANCE ASSESSMENTS

DEMONSTRATING YOUR SKILLS

Assessment one

1. At a clear document screen, key the text shown in figure U2.1 with the following specifications:
   a. Change the font to 18-point Goudy Old Style bold (or a similar typeface).
   b. Change the line spacing to 1.5.
2. Save the document and name it Unit 2, PA 01.
3. Print and then close Unit 2, PA 01.

Volunteer Appreciation Luncheon
Friday, December 11, 1998
11:30 a.m. - 1:30 p.m.
Madison's Resort
2315 West Lake Boulevard
(Please make reservations by December 2.)

Figure U2.1 • Assessment 1

Assessment two

1. At a clear document window, key the text shown in figure U2.2 in an appropriate business letter format with the following specifications:
   a. Change the font to 12-point Century Schoolbook.
   b. After the keying the letter, change the alignment of the paragraphs within the body of the letter to justified.
   c. After keying the letter, complete a spelling check. (Proper names are spelled correctly. Ignore sentences selected by the grammar checker.)
   d. Use Thesaurus to find appropriate synonyms for the following words:
      1) *growth* in the first paragraph
      2) *best* in the first paragraph
      3) *many* in the last paragraph
      4) *choosing* in the last paragraph
   e. Make sure the letter fits on one page. (If it does not, consider deleting a few blank lines before the date, or a few blank lines between the date and the inside address.)
2. Save the letter and name it Unit 2, PA 02.
3. Print and then close Unit 2, PA 02.

April 15, 1999

Mr. Alan Erickson
103 Tenth Street Northeast
Juneau, AK 99065

Dear Mr. Erickson:

As the next stage in the growth of Seaview Airlines Frequent Traveler program, I am plaesed to anounce a new program, AIR MILES, affective May 1, 1999. In designing this new program, Seaview relied on thorough reserch to make key business decesions and provide you with a program, which you will discover to be the best in the industry. Here are some of the highlights you have to look forward to in 1999:

- a free ticket for traval within the continental United States has been reduced from 30,000 to 25,000 miles;
- unlike some other carriers, miles earned in Seaview's new program will never expire, just take one qualifing Seaview flight every 2 years;
- an enhanced elite level program with new qualafication levels, a streamlined upgrade program, and richer rewards.

Our thanks to the many Frequent Traveler program members we invited to help us design the new program. Seaview Airlines is committed to providing you with the best programs and becoming your airline of choice. Thank you for choosing Seaview. We look forward to serving your futere travel needs.

Sincerely,

Amanda Lindberg
Senior Vice President

XX:Unit 2, PA 02

Figure U2.2 • Assessment 2

Assessment three

1. At a clear editing window, key the memo shown in figure U2.3 with the following specifications:
   a. Change the font to 12-point Century Schoolbook.
   b. You determine the tab settings for the two columns of text in the letters.
2. Complete a grammar check on the document. (Proper names are spelled correctly. When the grammar checker highlights a sentence in passive voice, tell it to ignore the sentence.) You determine what to change and what to ignore.
3. Save the memo and name it Unit 2, PA 03.
4. Print and then close Unit 2, PA 03.

DATE: April 12, 1999

TO: College Faculty and Staff

FROM: Phoebe O'Dell

SUBJECT: COLLEGE TRANSFER DAY

Its that time of year when our students begin thinking about transferring to a four-year college. Riverside Community College are hosting college transfer day on May 5. Representatives from local four-year colleges and universities will answer specific question about admission and transfer requirement. Please encourages students to attend if they are planning to transfer to a four-year college.

The college and university representatives will provide information and answer questions in the atrium area on Wednesday, May 5, 1999, from 9:30 a.m. to 2:00 p.m. The following schools will be participating:

Mountain University	University of Colorado
Colorado State College	Whitman College
Riger Women's College	East Colorado University
Chapman University	West Colorado University

You is invited to meet with the representatives during an informal coffee time from 9:00 a.m. to 9:30 a.m. in the conference room. Please stop by if you're schedule permits.

XX:Unit 2, PA 03

Figure U2.3 • Assessment 3

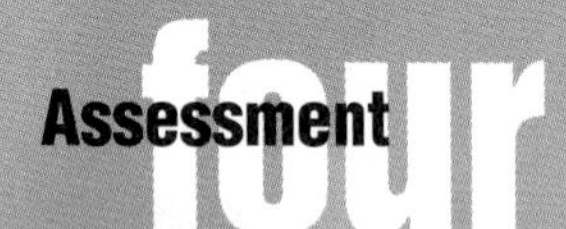

Assessment four

1. At a clear document screen, create the document shown in figure U2.4 with the following specifications:
   a. Change the font to 12-point Garamond (or a similar typeface).
   b. Bold and center text as indicated in the figure.
   c. You determine the tab stops for the text in columns.
2. Save the document and name it Unit 2, PA 04.
3. Print and then close Unit 2, PA 04.

MANORWOOD SCHOOL DISTRICT

Enrollment Comparisons

School	1998	1999
Meeker Senior High	1,160	1,033
Rollings Senior High	890	993
Lakeview Middle School	690	587
Oakridge Middle School	681	801
Cedar Middle School	702	745
Stewart Elementary	521	498
Overman Elementary	386	404
Grant Elementary	478	512
Curtiss Elementary	403	455

Figure U2.4 • Assessment 4

1. Look at the letter in figure U2.6 and the information in figure U2.5. Determine the fields you need for the main document and the data source. Create the data source and name it *Sound ds*. Create a main document with the text shown in figure U2.6 (make sure it fits on one page), and then merge it with *Sound ds*.
2. Save the merged document and name it Unit 2, PA 06.
3. Print and then close Unit 2, PA 06.
4. Save the main document and name it *Sound md*.
5. Close *Sound md*.

Mrs. Antonio Mercado
3241 Court G
Tampa, FL 33623

Ms. Alexandria Remick
909 Wheeler South
Tampa, FL 33620

Mr. Curtis Iverson
10139 93rd Court South
Tampa, FL 33654

Ms. Kristina Vukovich
1120 South Monroe
Tampa, FL 33655

Mr. Minh Vu
9302 Lawndale Southwest
Tampa, FL 33623

Mrs. Holly Bernard
8904 Emerson Road
Tampa, FL 33620

Figure U2.5 • Assessment 5

December 10, 1998

Name
Address
City, State Zip

Dear (Name):

Sound Medical is switching hospital care in Tampa to St. Jude's Hospital beginning January 1, 1999. As mentioned in last month's letter, St. Jude's Hospital was selected because it meets our requirements for high-quality, customer-pleasing care that is also affordable and accessible. Our physicians look forward to caring for you in this new environment.

Over the past month, staff members at Sound Medical have been working to make this transition as smooth as possible. Surgeries planned after January 1 are being scheduled at St. Jude's Hospital. Mothers delivering babies any time after January 1 are receiving information about delivery room tours and prenatal classes available at St. Jude's. Your Sound Medical doctor will have privileges at St. Jude's and will continue to care for you if you need to be hospitalized.

You are a very important part of our patient family, (name), and we hope this information is helpful. If you have any additional questions or concerns, please call our hospital transition manager, Jeff Greenswald, at (813) 555-9886, between 8:00 a.m. and 4:30 p.m.

Sincerely,

SOUND MEDICAL

Jody Tiemann
District Administrator

XX:Sound md

Figure U2.6 • Assessment 5

Assessment six

1. Create a main document for envelopes that has the *Sound ds* data source document attached and then merge the envelope main document.
2. Save the merged document and name it Unit 2, PA 06.
3. Print and then close Unit 2, PA 06.
4. Close the envelope main document without saving the changes.

CREATING ORIGINAL DOCUMENTS

The following activities give you the opportunity to practice your writing skills along with demonstrating an understanding of some of the important Word features you have mastered in this unit. When composing the documents, use correct grammar, appropriate word choices, and clear sentence construction.

Assessment seven

Situation: You are the administrative assistant for Linda Shing, Superintendent of the Kentwood School District. She has asked you to compose a memo to all elementary school principals telling them that an accreditation team will visit their school on the following days and times:

Oak Ridge Elementary	January 12	1:30 p.m.
Madison Creek Elementary	January 14	9:30 a.m.
Bell Valley Elementary	February 9	2:00 p.m.
South Bend Elementary	February 17	9:00 a.m.
Myers Heights Elementary	March 3	1:30 p.m.

When composing the memo, set the school names, days, and times in balanced columns. Save the memo and name it Unit 2, PA 07. Print and then close Unit 2, PA 07.

Assessment eight

Situation: You are Shawn Wingard, volunteer coordinator for the Kentwood School District. Compose a letter to the new reading volunteers listed below thanking them for their interest in volunteering for the reading literacy program and invite them to an orientation on Thursday, October 8, 1998, from 7:00 to 8:30 p.m. During this orientation, volunteers will learn more about the reading program such as the goals of the program, the students who will be served by the program, the various reading levels within the program, the time commitment required of volunteers, and the materials needed for the program. Create a data source with the names and addresses below that is attached to the main document, which is the letter to the volunteers. You determine the names for the data source and the main document. After creating the data source and the main document, merge the data source with the main document. Save the merged document as Unit 2, PA 08. Print and then close Unit 2, PA 08.

Ms. Karen Lyons
9023 South 42nd Street
Kentwood, MI 48933

Mr. Richard Ulrich
453 Silverdale Road
Kentwood, MI 48930

Mr. Juan Nunez
8329 Branchwood Drive
Kentwood, MI 48933

Mr. Bryan Hamilton
11023 12th Northeast
Kentwood, MI 48920

Mrs. Lindsay Childers
8931 133rd Place Northwest
Kentwood, MI 48933

Ms. Lisa Taua
1129 Military Road South
Kentwood, MI 48930

Unit three

PREPARING AND ENHANCING LONG DOCUMENTS

In this unit, you will learn to create multipage documents with elements such as headers, footers, footnotes, and endnotes; and to prepare, enhance, and improve documents such as notices, announcements, memos, and letters.

scans

The Secretary's Commission on Achieving Necessary Skills

DECISION MAKING

TECHNOLOGY

PROBLEM SOLVING

COMMUNICATIONS

chapter TWELVE

Preparing Multiple Page Documents

PERFORMANCE OBJECTIVES

Upon successful completion of chapter 12, you will be able to:

- **Change margins in a document.**
- **Insert a section break.**
- **Turn on/off the widow/orphan control feature.**
- **Insert a hard page break.**
- **Change the paper size.**
- **Center text on the page.**
- **Preview a document.**

Word assumes that you are using standard-sized paper, which is 8.5 inches wide and 11 inches long. By default, a Word document contains 1-inch top and bottom margins and 1.25-inch left and right margins. With the default top and bottom margins of 1 inch, a total of 9 inches of text will print on a page (1 inch for the top margin, 9 inches of printed text, and then 1 inch for the bottom margin). As you create long documents, you will notice that when the insertion point nears 9.8 inches (or approximately Line 45 [this number may vary]) a page break is inserted in the document. The page break is inserted at the next line (at the 10" measurement). The line below the page break is the beginning of the next page.

The display of the page break will change depending on the viewing mode. Word provides more than one viewing mode. By default, the Normal viewing mode is selected. At this viewing mode, a page break displays as a row of dots. If you change to the Page Layout viewing mode, a page break displays as an actual break in the page. Figure 12.1 shows an example of a page break in a document in the Normal viewing mode and another in the Page Layout viewing mode.

12.1

Page Break in Normal Viewing Mode

publication project. This may be costly and time-consuming. With the use of desktop publishing software, one person may be performing all of the tasks necessary to complete a project, greatly reducing the costs of publishing documents. The two approaches have a great deal in common. Both approaches involve setting goals, planning and organizing content, analyzing layout and design, arranging design elements, typesetting, printing, and distributing the project.

Page Break in Page Layout Viewing Mode

publication project. This may be costly and time-consuming. With the use of desktop publishing software, one person may be performing all of the tasks necessary to complete a project, greatly reducing the costs of publishing documents. The two approaches have a

great deal in common. Both approaches involve setting goals, planning and organizing content, analyzing layout and design, arranging design elements, typesetting, printing, and

Page Layout View

Normal View

To change to the Page Layout viewing mode, click View, then Page Layout or click the Page Layout View button at the left side of the horizontal scroll bar. (The Page Layout View button is the third button from the left side of the screen before the horizontal scroll bar.) To change back to the Normal viewing mode, click View, then Normal or click the Normal View button at the left side of the horizontal scroll bar. (The Normal View button is the first button from the left.)

When you are working in a document containing more than one page of text, the Status bar displays the page where the insertion point is positioned and will also display the current page followed by the total number of pages in a document. For example, if the insertion point is positioned somewhere on page 3 of a 12-page document (with one section), the left side of the Status bar will display *Page 3 Sec 1 3/12*. The *3/12* indicates that the insertion point is positioned on page 3 in a document containing 12 pages.

While Word's default settings break each page near Line 10", there are several features that can affect the location of page breaks within text in a document.

Changing Margins

The default margin settings are displayed in the Page Setup dialog box shown in figure 12.2. To display the Page Setup dialog box, click File, then Page Setup. You can also display the Page Setup dialog box by double-clicking on the gray area at the top of the Ruler. At the Page Setup dialog box, make sure the Margins tab is selected.

12.2

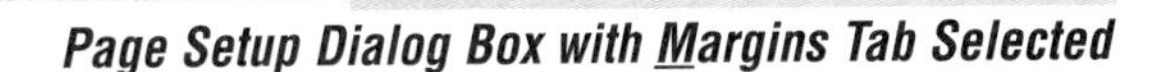

Page Setup Dialog Box with Margins Tab Selected

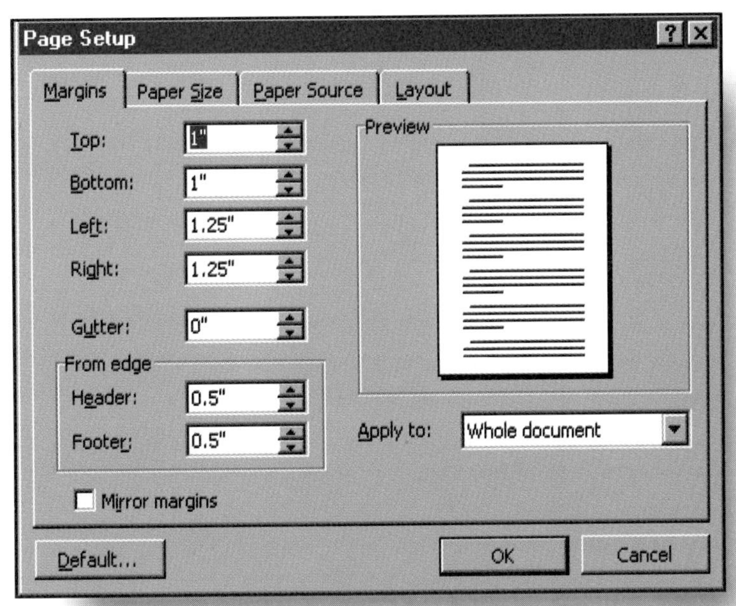

To change margins in a document, display the Page Setup dialog box, select the current measurement in either the Top, Bottom, Left, or Right text box, and then key the new measurement for the margin. You can also increase a measurement by clicking the up-pointing triangle at the right side of the text box. Decrease a measurement by clicking the down-pointing triangle. As you make changes to the margin measurements at the Page Setup dialog box, the sample page in the Preview box illustrates the affects of the margins.

If you want the new margins to affect the entire document, position the insertion point anywhere within the document, then make margin changes at the Page Setup dialog box. If you want margin changes to affect only a portion of the document, divide the document into sections. You will learn more about sections later in this chapter. You can also specify that margin changes affect the text in a document from the position of the insertion point to the end of the document. To do this, click the down-pointing triangle at the right side of the Apply to text box at the Page Setup dialog box. At the drop-down menu that displays, click *This point forward*.

exercise 1

Changing Margins

1. Open Report 01.
2. Save the report with Save As and name it Ch 12, Ex 01.
3. Change the top margin to 1.5 inches and the left and right margins to 1 inch by completing the following steps:
   a. Click File, then Page Setup.
   b. At the Page Setup dialog box, make sure the Margins tab is selected.
   c. Click the up-pointing triangle after the Top option until *1.5"* displays in the Top text box.
   d. Click the down-pointing triangle after the Left option until *1"* displays in the Left text box.
   e. Click the down-pointing triangle after the Right option until *1"* displays in the Right text box.
   f. Click OK or press Enter to close the dialog box.
4. Make the following changes to the document:
   a. Select the title, *DESKTOP PUBLISHING*, and then change the font to 18-point Arial bold.
   b. Select the heading, *Defining Desktop Publishing*, and then change the font to 14-point Arial bold.
   c. Use Format Painter to change the formatting to 14-point Arial bold for the headings, *Initiating the Desktop Publishing Process*, *Planning the Publication*, and *Creating the Content*.
5. Save the document again with the same name (Ch 12, Ex 01).
6. Print and then close Ch 12, Ex 01.

Changing Margins with the Ruler

You can change margins at the Page Setup dialog box as you did in exercise 1 or with the Ruler. At the Page Setup dialog box, you can enter specific margin measurements; at the Ruler, you can visually set margins. (If the Ruler is not displayed, click View, then Ruler.)

Word provides more than one viewing mode. By default, the Normal viewing mode is selected. At this viewing mode, a horizontal ruler displays below the Formatting toolbar. You can change paragraph indents with this ruler in the Normal viewing mode, but you cannot make changes to the left and right margins. If you want to make changes to the left, right, top, or bottom margins using rulers, change to the Page Layout viewing mode. At this viewing mode, the horizontal ruler displays below the Formatting toolbar and a vertical ruler displays along the left side of the screen. Figure 12.3 shows a document in the Page Layout viewing mode and identifies the horizontal and vertical rulers.

12.3 ***Page Layout Viewing Mode***

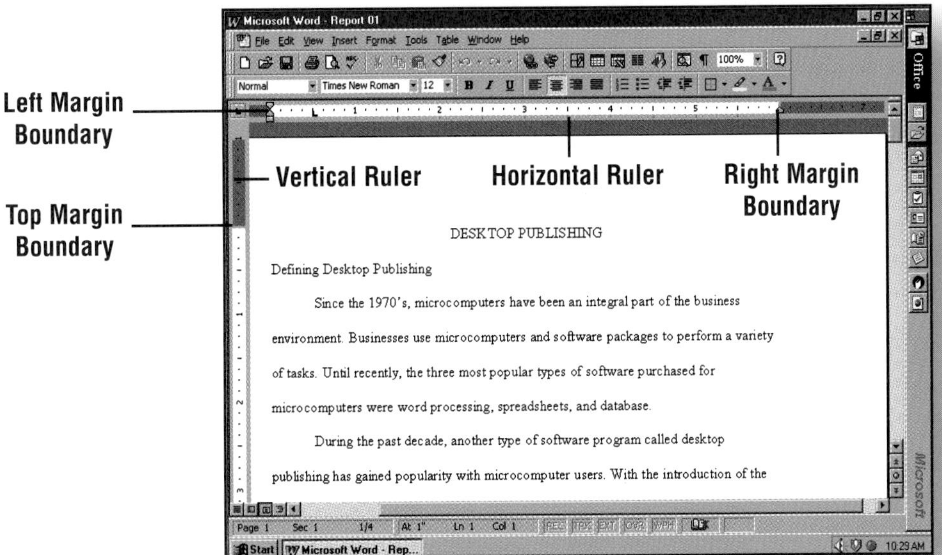

The horizontal and vertical rulers each contain a gray area and a white area. The gray area indicates the margin while the white area indicates the space between margins. The edge between the gray and white area is called the *margin boundary*.

To change margins using the Ruler in the Page Layout viewing mode, position the arrow pointer on the margin boundary. This causes the arrow pointer to turn into a double-headed arrow. Hold down the left mouse button, drag the margin boundary to the desired location, and then release the mouse button.

exercise 2

Increasing Margins Using the Horizontal Ruler

1. Open Para 02.
2. Save the document with Save As and name it Ch 12, Ex 02.
3. Increase the left and right margins in the document approximately 0.5 inch using the Ruler by completing the following steps:
   a. Make sure the Ruler is displayed. If it is not, click View, then Ruler.
   b. Change the viewing mode to Page Layout by clicking View, then Page Layout; or clicking the Page Layout View button at the left side of the horizontal scroll bar.
   c. Position the arrow pointer on the margin boundary at the left side of the horizontal ruler until the pointer turns into a

double-headed arrow pointing left and right. (A yellow box containing *Left Margin* will display.)

   d. Hold down the left mouse button, drag the margin boundary to the right approximately 0.5 inch, and then release the mouse button. (As you drag the margin boundary, a dashed vertical line appears in the document screen. Use this to help you position the left margin. When you drag the margin boundary, the entire horizontal ruler moves.)
   e. Position the arrow pointer on the margin boundary at the right side of the horizontal ruler until it turns into a double-headed arrow pointing left and right. (A yellow box containing *Right Margin* will display.) (If the margin boundary at the right side of the horizontal ruler is not visible, position the arrow pointer on the scroll box in the horizontal scroll bar, hold down the left mouse button, drag the scroll box to the right edge of the horizontal scroll bar, and then release the mouse button.)
   f. Hold down the left mouse button, drag the margin boundary to the left about 0.5 inch, and then release the mouse button. (When you drag the right margin boundary, the horizontal ruler is stationary and the margin boundary moves along it.)
4. Change the viewing mode back to Normal by clicking View, then Normal; or clicking the Normal View button at the left side of the horizontal scroll bar.
5. Save the report again with the same name (Ch 12, Ex 02).
6. Print and then close Ch 12, Ex 02.

Make changes to the top and bottom margins in a document using the vertical ruler by completing similar steps.

exercise 3

Changing Margins Using the Horizontal and Vertical Rulers

1. Open Legal 01.
2. Save the document with Save As and name it Ch 12, Ex 03.
3. Change the top margin to 2 inches and the left and right margins to 1 inch using the horizontal and vertical rulers by completing the following steps:
   a. Click View, then Page Layout; or click the Page Layout View button at the left side of the horizontal scroll bar.
   b. Make sure the horizontal and vertical rulers are displayed. (If they are not displayed, click View, then Ruler.)

c. Position the arrow pointer on the left margin boundary on the horizontal ruler until the pointer turns into a double-headed arrow pointing left and right (and a yellow box containing *Left Margin* displays).
d. Hold down the left mouse button, drag the margin boundary to the left until the left edge of the page displays, drag the mouse to the right until the gray 1-inch mark is positioned at the left edge of the horizontal ruler, and then release the mouse button.
e. Display the right margin boundary.
f. Position the arrow pointer on the right margin boundary until it turns into a double-headed arrow pointing left and right (and a yellow box containing *Right Margin* displays).
g. Hold down the left mouse button, drag the right margin boundary to the 6.5-inch mark on the horizontal ruler, and then release the mouse button.
h. Position the arrow pointer on the top margin boundary on the vertical ruler until it turns into a double-headed arrow pointing up and down (and a yellow box containing *Top Margin* displays).
i. Drag the top margin boundary down until the 2-inch gray mark displays at the top of the vertical ruler.

4. Change the viewing mode back to Normal.
5. Save the document again with the same name (Ch 12, Ex 03).
6. Print and then close Ch 12, Ex 03.

When you move the left margin boundary on the horizontal ruler or the top margin boundary on the vertical ruler, the entire ruler moves. If you want to move margin boundaries to a precise measurement, you can use the Alt key when dragging a margin boundary. If you position the arrow pointer on a margin boundary on the horizontal ruler, hold down the Alt key, and then hold down the left mouse button, the width of the text line displays in the horizontal ruler. If you position the arrow pointer on a margin boundary on the vertical ruler, hold down the Alt key, and then hold down the left mouse button, the length of the top margin (or bottom margin) displays in the vertical ruler.

exercise 4

Changing Margins to Specific Measurements Using the Horizontal and Vertical Rulers

1. Open Legal 02.
2. Save the document with Save As and name it Ch 12, Ex 04.
3. Change the top margin to 1.5 inches and the left and right margins to 1 inch by completing the following steps:

a. Click View, then Page Layout; or click the Page Layout View button at the left side of the horizontal scroll bar.
b. Make sure the horizontal and vertical rulers are displayed. (If they are not displayed, click View, then Ruler.)
c. Position the arrow pointer on the left margin boundary, hold down the Alt key and the left mouse button, drag the margin boundary to the left until *1"* appears in the gray area and *6.25"* appears in the white area on the horizontal ruler, and then release the mouse button and then the Alt key.
d. Position the arrow pointer on the right margin boundary until it turns into a double-headed arrow pointing left and right.
e. Hold down the Alt key and the left mouse button, drag the right margin boundary to the right until *6.5"* displays in the white area and *1"* displays in the gray area on the horizontal ruler, and then release the mouse button and then the Alt key.
f. Position the arrow pointer on the top margin boundary on the vertical ruler until it turns into a double-headed arrow pointing up and down.
g. Hold down the Alt key and the left mouse button, drag the top margin boundary down until *1.5"* displays in the gray area on the vertical ruler, and then release the mouse button and then the Alt key.

4. Change the viewing mode back to Normal.
5. Save the document again with the same name (Ch 12, Ex 04).
6. Print and then close Ch 12, Ex 04.

Creating Mirror Margins

The Page Setup dialog box contains the option, Mirror margins. If this option is active (a check mark appears in the check box), the measurements for left and right margins are applied to odd-numbered pages and reversed for even-numbered pages. For example, if you change the left margin to 2.5 inches and the right margin to 1 inch, odd-numbered pages will have these margins but even-numbered pages will have a left margin of 1 inch and a right margin of 2.5 inches.

exercise 5

Creating Mirror Margins

1. Open Report 01.
2. Save the document with Save As and name it Ch 12, Ex 05.
3. Make the following changes to the document:
   a. Select the title, *DESKTOP PUBLISHING*, and then change the font to 14-point Arial bold.
   b. Select the heading, *Defining Desktop Publishing*, and then change the font to 14-point Arial bold.

c. Use Format Painter to apply 14-point Arial bold to the remaining headings: *Initiating the Desktop Publishing Process*, *Planning the Publication*, and *Creating the Content*.
d. Change the left margin to 2 inches and the right margin to 1 inch.
e. Create mirror margins by completing the following steps:
   1) Click File, then Page Setup.
   2) At the Page Setup dialog box, make sure the Margins tab is selected.
   3) Click Mirror margins. (This inserts a check mark in the check box.)
   4) Click OK or press Enter.

4. Save the document again with the same name (Ch 12, Ex 05).
5. Print and then close Ch 12, Ex 05.

Adding a Gutter Margin

Use the Gutter option at the Page Setup dialog box to create gutter margins for bound material. The default setting for gutter margins is 0 inches. When creating a document that is to be bound and printed on both sides, such as a report or manual, change the gutter margin measurement to properly position text on the page. In addition, the Mirror margins option must be active.

For left-bound material to properly display on the page, change the gutter margins to approximately 0.5 inch, and turn on the Mirror margins option. When you make these changes, Word adds the 0.5 inch of extra margin to the right margin on even pages and to the left margin on odd pages. When the material is bound, even-numbered pages are generally located at the left and odd-numbered pages are generally located at the right. The 0.5-inch gutter margin allows room for the binding. Change gutter margins in a document with the Gutter option at the Page Setup dialog box.

exercise 6

Changing Left, Right, and Gutter Margins

1. Open Report 02.
2. Save the document with Save As and name it Ch 12, Ex 06.
3. Make the following changes to the document:
   a. Select the entire document and then change the font to 12-point Century Schoolbook.
   b. Set the title, *DESKTOP PUBLISHING DESIGN*, in 14-point Arial bold as well as the headings *Designing a Document* and *Creating Focus*.
   c. Change the left and right margins to 1 inch and the gutter margin to 0.5 inch and turn on the Mirror margins option by completing the following steps:

1) Click File, then Page Setup.
2) At the Page Setup dialog box, make sure the Margins tab is selected, and then change the left and right margins to 1 inch.
3) Click Mirror margins. (This inserts a check mark.)
4) Click the up-pointing triangle at the right side of the Gutter option until *0.5*" displays.
5) Click OK or press Enter.

4. Save the document again with the same name (Ch 12, Ex 06).
5. Print and then close Ch 12, Ex 06.

Inserting a Section Break

By default, changes made to margins in a document are applied to all text in the document. If you want margin changes to apply to specific text in a document, select the text first. Text in a document can also be divided into sections. When a document is divided into sections, each section can be formatted separately. For example, different margin settings can be applied to each section in a document.

A section can insert a page break in a document or a continuous section can be created that does not insert a page break. To insert a continuous section break in a document, position the insertion point at the location in the document where you want the new section to begin, and then click Insert, then Break. At the Break dialog box shown in figure 12.4, click Continuous, and then click OK or press Enter.

12.4

Break Dialog Box

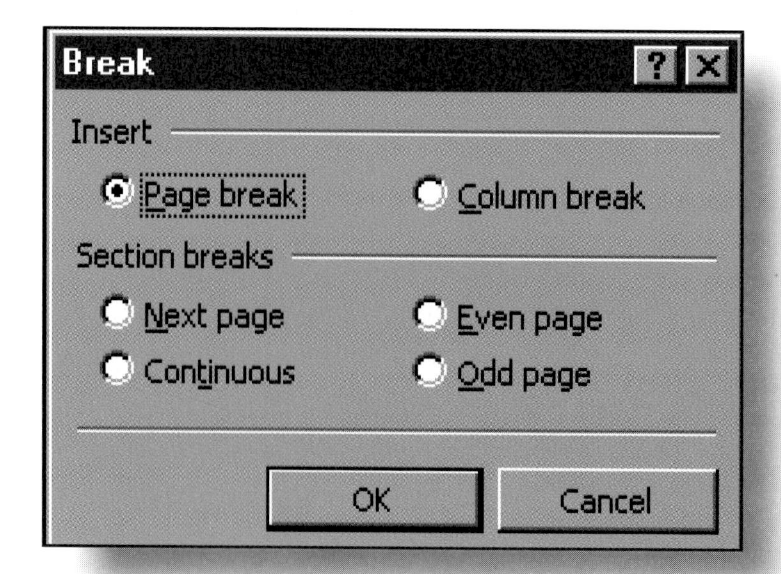

A section break displays in the Normal viewing mode as a double line of dots across the screen with the words *Section Break (Continuous)* inserted in the middle. In the Page Layout viewing mode, a section break does not display on the screen. However, the section number where the insertion point is located displays in the Status bar as *Sec* followed by the number.

To create a section break and begin a new page, position the insertion point at the location in the document where you want the new section to begin, click Insert, then Break. At the Break dialog box, click Next page, and then click OK or press Enter.

In the Normal viewing mode, a section break that begins a new page displays as a double row of dots across the screen with the words *Section Break (Next Page)* inserted in the middle. In the Page Layout viewing mode, a section break that begins a new page displays as a new page.

At the Break dialog box, click Even page if you want to insert a section break and begin the next page with an even number. Click Odd page if you want to insert a section break and begin the next page with an odd number. For example, if you position the insertion point somewhere in the middle of page 4 and then insert a section break with the Even page option, a section break is inserted and the page below the section break is page 6.

If you change margins in a section of text, the Apply to option at the Page Setup dialog box will have the default setting of *This section*.

exercise 7

Inserting Section Breaks

1. Open Quote.
2. Save the document with Save As and name it Ch 12, Ex 07.
3. Make the following changes to the document:
   a. Insert a section break between the first two paragraphs by completing the following steps:
      1) Position the insertion point on the blank line between the first and second paragraph.
      2) Click Insert, then Break.
      3) At the Break dialog box, click Continuous in the Section breaks section.
      4) Click OK or press Enter.

   b. Insert a section break between the second and third paragraphs by completing steps similar to those in step 3a.

   c. Insert a section break between the third and fourth paragraphs by completing steps similar to those in step 3a.

   d. Position the insertion point anywhere in the second paragraph and then change the left and right margins to 1.75 inches. (To change the margins, display the Page Setup dialog box with the Margins tab selected, select *1.25"* in the Left text box, and then key **1.75**. Complete similar steps to change the right margin. Make sure the default setting at the Apply to option is *This section*.)

e. Position the insertion point anywhere in the fourth paragraph and then change the left and right margins to 1.75 inches. (At the Page Setup dialog box, make sure the default setting at the Apply to option is *This section.*)

4. Save the document again with the same name (Ch 12, Ex 07).
5. Print and then close Ch 12, Ex 07.

Affecting Text Flow

There are several options from the Paragraph dialog box with the Line and Page Breaks tab selected that will affect the position of page breaks within a document. With the Line and Page Breaks tab selected, the Paragraph dialog box displays as shown in figure 12.5.

12.5 ***Paragraph Dialog Box with Line and Page Breaks Tab Selected***

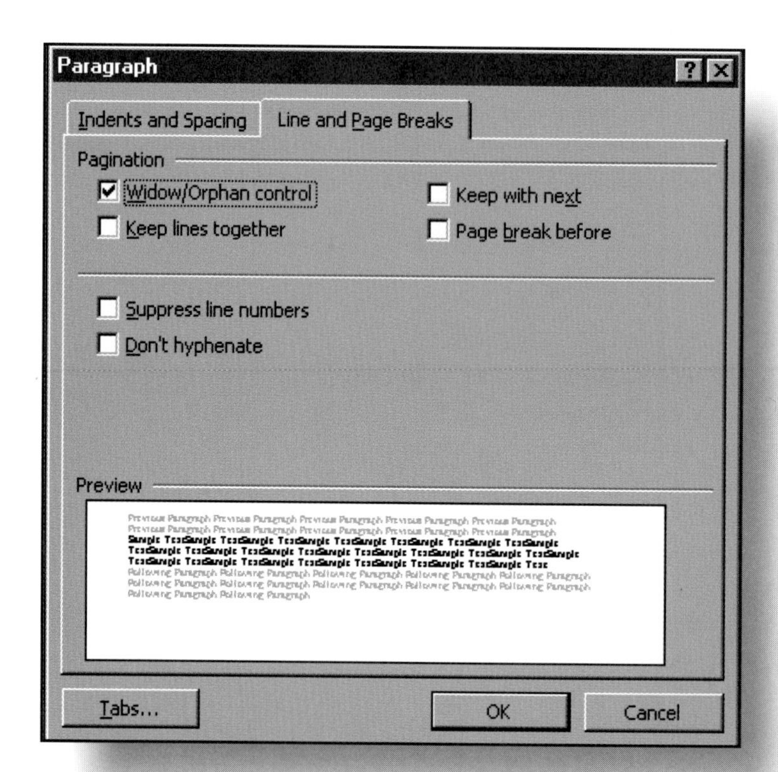

Turning Widow/Orphan Control On/Off

In a long document, you will want to avoid creating widows or orphans. A widow is the last line of a paragraph that appears at the top of a page. An orphan is the first line of a paragraph that appears at the bottom of a page.

In Word, widows and orphans are automatically prevented from appearing in text. Word accomplishes this by adjusting the page breaks in a document. Because of this, the last line of text on various pages will not always occur at the same line measurement or count. If you wish to turn off the widow and orphan control, display the Paragraph dialog box with the Line and Page Breaks tab selected, and then click Widow/Orphan control. This removes the check mark from the option.

Keeping a Paragraph of Text Together

Even with widow/orphan control on, Word may insert a page break in a document between text in a paragraph or several paragraphs that should stay together as a unit. The Paragraph dialog box with the Line and Page Breaks tab selected contains options to keep a paragraph, a group of paragraphs, or a group of lines together.

To keep a paragraph together, you can instruct Word not to insert a page break within a paragraph. This format instruction is stored in the paragraph mark, so as the paragraph is moved within the document, the format instruction moves with it. To tell Word not to insert a page break within a paragraph, display the Paragraph dialog box with the Line and Page Breaks tab selected, and then click Keep lines together. The same steps can be used to keep a group of consecutive paragraphs together. To do this, select the paragraphs first, and then click Keep lines together.

With the Keep with next option at the Paragraph dialog box, you can tell Word to keep the paragraph where the insertion point is located together with the next paragraph. If there is not enough room for the paragraph and the next paragraph, Word moves both paragraphs to the next page.

Use the Page break before option if you want a particular paragraph to print at the top of a page. Position the insertion point in the paragraph that you want to begin a new page, display the Paragraph dialog box with the Line and Page Breaks tab selected, and then click Page break before.

exercise 8

Keeping Text Together

(Note: Due to slight differences in how printers interpret line height, a page break may not display in the report after the heading **Creating the Content**. *Before completing this exercise, check with your instructor to see if you need to make any minor changes to margins or font size for text and headings.)*

1. Open Report 01 as a read-only document.
2. Make the following changes to the document:
   a. Change the left and right margins to 1 inch.

b. Select the entire document and then change the font to 12-point Century Schoolbook.
c. Select the title, *DESKTOP PUBLISHING*, and then change the font to 14-point Arial bold.
d. Select the heading, *Defining Desktop Publishing*, and then change the font to 14-point Arial bold.
e. Use Format Painter to apply 14-point Arial bold to the remaining headings: *Initiating the Desktop Publishing Process*, *Planning the Publication*, and *Creating the Content*.

3. Tell Word to keep the heading *Creating the Content* and the paragraph that follows it together on the same page by completing the following steps:
   a. Position the insertion point on any character in the heading *Creating the Content*.
   b. Click Format, then Paragraph.
   c. At the Paragraph dialog box, click the Line and Page Breaks tab.
   d. Click Keep with next.
   e. Click OK or press Enter.
4. Save the document with Save As and name it Ch 12, Ex 08.
5. Print and then close Ch 12, Ex 08.

Inserting Hard Page Breaks

Word's default settings break each page after Line 9.8" (approximately). Word automatically inserts page breaks in a document as you edit it. Since Word does this automatically, you may find that page breaks sometimes occur in undesirable locations. To remedy this, you can insert your own page break.

In the Normal viewing mode, the Word page break, called a *soft* page break, displays as a row of dots across the screen. In the Page Layout viewing mode the page break displays as a gray bar between two pages. If you do not like where the soft page break is inserted in a document, you can insert your own page break. A page break that you insert in a document is called a *hard* page break. To insert a hard page break in a document, position the insertion point where you want the break to occur, click Insert, then Break. At the Break dialog box, make sure Page break is selected, and then click OK or press Enter. You can also insert a hard page break by positioning the insertion point where you want the break to occur in the document and then pressing Ctrl + Enter.

A hard page break displays in the Normal viewing mode as a line of dots with the words *Page Break* in the middle of the line. A hard page break displays in the same manner as a soft page break in the Page Layout viewing mode.

Soft page breaks automatically adjust if text is added to or deleted from a document. A hard page break does not adjust and is therefore less flexible than a soft page break. If you add or delete text from a document with a hard page break, check the break to determine whether it is still in a desirable location.

A hard page break can be deleted from a document. To delete a hard page break, position the insertion point on the page break, and then press the Delete key.

exercise 9

Inserting Hard Page Breaks

1. Open Report 01 as a read-only document.
2. Make the following changes to the document:
   a. Select the title, *DESKTOP PUBLISHING*, and then change the font to 14-point Univers bold. (If your printer does not support Univers, choose a similar sans serif typeface, such as Arial.)
   b. Select the heading, *Defining Desktop Publishing*, and then change the font to 14-point Univers bold.
   c. Use the Format Painter to apply 14-point Univers bold to the remaining headings: *Initiating the Desktop Publishing Process*, *Planning the Publication*, and *Creating the Content*.
   d. Change the left and right margins to 1.5 inches.
3. Insert a hard page break at the beginning of the last paragraph on the first page by completing the following steps:
   a. Position the insertion point at the beginning of the last paragraph on the first page that begins *In traditional publishing, several people....*
   b. Click Insert, then Break.
   c. At the Break dialog box, make sure Page break is selected, and then click OK or press Enter.
4. Insert a hard page break at the beginning of the last paragraph on the third page by completing the following steps:
   a. Position the insertion point at the beginning of the last paragraph on the third page that begins *Collect examples of effective designs*.
   b. Press Ctrl + Enter.
5. Save the document with Save As and name it Ch 12, Ex 09.
6. Print and then close Ch 12, Ex 09.

Changing Paper Size

Word assumes that you are printing on standard stationery—8.5 inches wide by 11 inches long. If you need to print text on stationery of a different size, change the paper size at the Page Setup dialog box with the Paper Size tab selected as shown in figure 12.6. To display this dialog box, click File, then Page Setup. At the Page Setup dialog box, click the Paper Size tab.

12.6

Page Setup Dialog Box with Paper Size Tab Selected

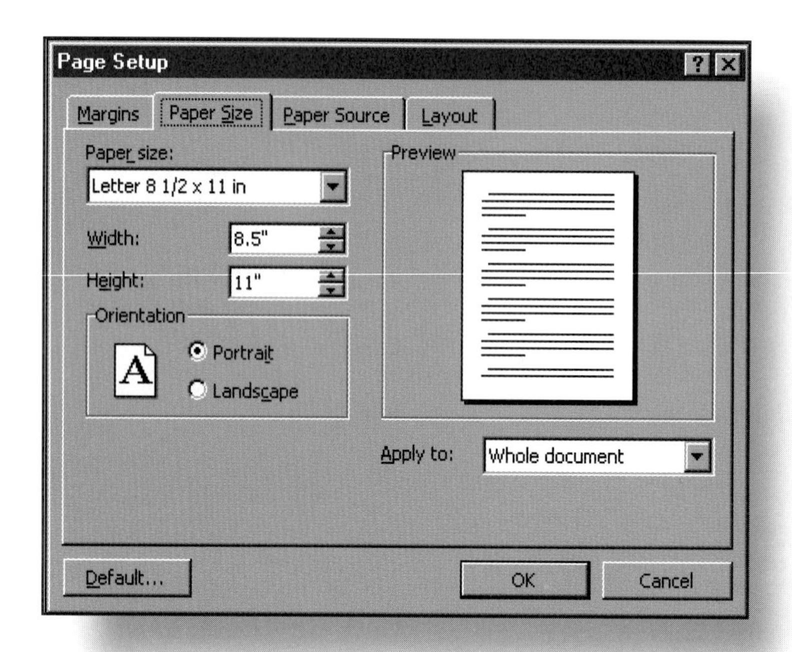

Word provides several predefined paper sizes. The number and type of paper sizes will vary depending on the selected printer. Use the predefined paper sizes if they are the necessary sizes. If the predefined sizes do not include what you need, create your own paper size with the Custom size option. If you choose the Custom size option under Paper size at the Page Setup dialog box, you can enter the desired measurements for the width and height of the paper size.

Word provides two orientations for paper sizes—Portrait and Landscape. Figure 12.7 illustrates how text appears on the page in portrait and landscape orientations.

12.7

Portrait and Landscape Orientations

By default, the change in paper size will affect the entire document. At the Page Setup dialog box, the Apply to option has a default setting of *Whole document*. This can be changed to *This point forward*. At this setting, the paper size change will affect text from the current position of the insertion point to the end of the document.

exercise 10

Changing Paper Size

1. Open Para 03 as a read-only document.
2. Change the paper size to 5.5 inches by 8.5 inches by completing the following steps:
   a. Click File, then Page Setup.
   b. At the Page Setup dialog box, click the Paper Size tab. (Skip this step if the Paper Size tab is already selected.)
   c. Click the down-pointing triangle to the right of the Width text box until 5.5" displays in the Width text box.
   d. Click the down-pointing triangle to the right of the Height text box until 8.5" displays in the Height text box.
   e. Click OK or press Enter.
3. Select the entire document and then change the font to 10-point Arial.
4. Save the document with Save As and name it Ch 12, Ex 10.
5. Print and then close Ch 12, Ex 10.

exercise 11

Changing to a Predesigned Paper Size

(Note: Check with your instructor before completing this exercise. Your printer may not be capable of printing on legal-sized stationery.)

1. Open Report 03 as a read-only document.
2. Insert a hard page break at the beginning of the line containing the title, *MODULE 2: PLANNING A NEWSLETTER*.
3. Change the paper size to Legal by completing the following steps:
   a. Click File, then Page Setup.
   b. At the Page Setup dialog box click the Paper Size tab. (Skip this step if the Paper Size tab is already selected.)
   c. Click the down-pointing triangle at the right of the Paper size option and then click *Legal 8.5 x 14 in* at the drop-down list. (This paper size may be listed as *Legal 8 1/2 x 14 in* or *US Legal*.)
   d. Click OK or press Enter.
4. Check the page breaks in the document and, if necessary, make changes to the page breaks.
5. Save the document with Save As and name it Ch 12, Ex 11.
6. Print and then close Ch 12, Ex 11. (Check with your instructor before printing to see if your printer is capable of printing legal-sized documents.)

Centering Text on the Page

Text in a Word document is aligned at the top of the page by default. You can change this alignment with the Vertical alignment option at the Page Setup dialog box with the Layout tab selected as shown in figure 12.8.

figure 12.8 **Page Setup Dialog Box with Layout Tab Selected**

The Vertical alignment option from the Page Setup dialog box contains three choices—Top, Center, and Justified. The default setting is Top, which aligns text at the top of the page. Choose Center if you want text centered vertically on the page. The Justified option will align text between the top and the bottom margins. The Center option positions text in the middle of the page vertically, while the Justified option adds space between paragraphs of text (not within) to fill the page from the top to bottom margins. If you center or justify text, the text does not display centered or justified on the screen in the Normal viewing mode but it does display centered or justified in the Page Layout viewing mode.

exercise 12

Vertically Centering Text

1. Open Notice 02.
2. Save the document with Save As and name it Ch 12, Ex 12.
3. Select the text in the document and then change the font to

24-point Goudy Old Style. (If this typeface is not available, choose a similar decorative typeface such as Bookman Old Style.)

4. Center the text between the top and bottom margins by completing the following steps:
   a. Delete the blank lines at the bottom of the document.
   b. Click File, then Page Setup.
   c. At the Page Setup dialog box, click the Layout tab. (Skip this step if the Layout tab is already selected.)
   d. Click the down-pointing triangle at the right of the Vertical alignment text box and then click *Center* at the drop-down list.
   e. Click OK or press Enter.
5. Save the document again with the same name (Ch 12, Ex 12).
6. Print and then close Ch 12, Ex 12.

exercise 13

Changing Paper Size and Justifying Text Between Top and Bottom Margins

1. Open Para 02 as a read-only document.
2. Change the paper size to 5.5 inches by 8.5 inches.
3. Justify the text between the top and bottom margins by completing the following steps:
   a. Click File, then Page Setup.
   b. At the Page Setup dialog box, make sure the Layout tab is selected.
   c. Click the down-pointing triangle at the right of the Vertical alignment text box and then click *Justified* at the drop-down list.
   d. Click OK or press Enter.
4. Save the document and name it Ch 12, Ex 13.
5. Print and then close Ch 12, Ex 13.

Previewing a Document

Before printing a document, viewing the document may be useful. Word's Print Preview feature displays the document in the screen as it will appear when printed. With this feature, you can view a partial page, single page, multiple pages, or zoom in on a particular area of a page.

Print Preview

To view a document, click File, then Print Preview; or click the Print Preview button on the Standard toolbar. (The Print Preview button is the fifth button from the left on the Standard toolbar.) When Print Preview is displayed, the page where the insertion point is located is displayed in the screen. Figure 12.9 shows a document in Print Preview.

12.9

Document in Print Preview

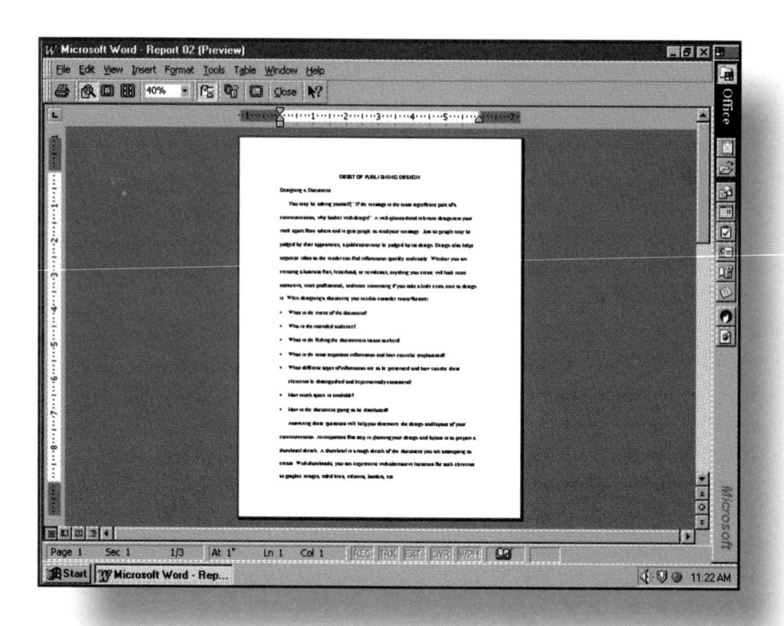

The toolbar along the top of the screen in Print Preview is the Print Preview toolbar. With buttons on this toolbar, you can change the display of the document, send a document to the printer, and turn the display of the Ruler on or off. Figure 12.10 shows each button from the Print Preview toolbar and identifies what each button will perform.

figure 12.10

Print Preview Toolbar Buttons

Click this button...	Named...	To do this...
	Print	Send the current document to the printer.
	Magnifier	Toggle the mouse pointer between a magnifying glass, which is used to view the document, and the normal mouse pointer, which is used to edit the document.
	One Page	Display individual pages in the document.
	Multiple Pages	Display multiple pages in the document (up to 18 pages).
40%	Zoom	Change viewing by percentage option or to Page Width, Whole Page, or Two Pages.

	View Ruler	Turn the display of the Ruler on or off.
	Shrink to Fit	Try to "shrink" the contents of the last page in the document onto the previous page if there is only a small amount of text on the last page.
	Full Screen	Toggle the screen display between the normal display and full screen display, which removes everything from the Print Preview screen except the document and the Print Preview toolbar.
Close	Close	Close Print Preview and return to document screen.
	Context Sensitive Help	Display context-sensitive help.

Earlier in this chapter, you learned that you can change the viewing mode by clicking the Normal View button on the horizontal scroll bar or the Page Layout View button. These buttons are also available in Print Preview. Clicking either of these buttons causes the document to display in the viewing mode you choose and also closes Print Preview.

While in Print Preview, you can move through a document using the insertion point movement keys, the horizontal and vertical scroll bars, and/or the Page Up and Page Down keys.

exercise 14

Viewing a Document with Print Preview

1. Open Report 04.
2. View the document by completing the following steps:
   a. Click the Print Preview button on the Standard toolbar.
   b. Click the Multiple Pages button on the Print Preview toolbar. (This causes a grid to appear immediately below the button.)
   c. Position the arrow pointer in the upper left portion of the grid, hold down the left mouse button, drag the mouse down and to the right until the message at the bottom of the grid displays as *2 x 2 Pages*, and then release the mouse button.
   d. Click the Full Screen button on the Print Preview toolbar. This displays only the pages in the document and the Print Preview toolbar.
   e. Click the Full Screen button again to restore the screen display.
   f. Click the One Page button on the Print Preview toolbar.
   g. Click the down-pointing triangle at the right of the Zoom button. From the drop-down list that displays, click *50%*.

h. Click the down-pointing triangle at the right of the Zoom button. From the drop-down list that displays, click *75%*.
i. Click the One Page button on the Print Preview toolbar.
j. Click the Close button on the Print Preview toolbar.

3. Close Report 04.

Editing in Print Preview

Print Preview is used to view a document before printing, but it can also be used to edit a document. To edit a document in Print Preview, you would complete the following steps:

1. Open the document containing text to be edited.
2. Display Print Preview by clicking File, then Print Preview; or clicking the Print Preview button on the Standard toolbar.
3. Make sure the Magnifier button on the Print Preview toolbar is active. (If the Magnifier button is active, it displays with a lighter gray background than the other buttons. By default, the Magnifier button is active when you first display Print Preview.)
4. Position the mouse pointer (displays as a magnifying glass) in the part of the document you want to edit and then click the left button. This changes the display to 100% magnification.
5. Click the Magnifier button to turn it off. This returns the mouse pointer to normal.
6. Edit the document in the normal manner.
7. Click the Magnifier button and then click the document. This returns the display of the document to the previous magnification.

Magnifier

In Print Preview you can change the top, bottom, left, and right margins using the rulers. In Print Preview, a horizontal ruler displays above the document and a vertical ruler displays at the left side of the document. If these rulers are not visible, clicking the View Ruler button on the Print Preview toolbar will display them.

View Ruler

Use the horizontal and vertical ruler to change margins in the same manner as you used the horizontal and vertical rulers in the normal document screen. The horizontal ruler contains a left and right margin boundary and the vertical ruler contains a top and bottom margin boundary. To change a margin, position the mouse pointer on the margin boundary until it turns into a double-headed arrow, and then drag the margin boundary to the desired position.

exercise 15

Editing a Document in Print Preview

1. Open Notice 01.
2. Save the document with Save As and name it Ch 12, Ex 15.
3. Display Print Preview and make changes to the document by completing the following steps:
   a. Click the Print Preview button on the Standard toolbar.
   b. Position the mouse pointer (displays as a magnifying glass) in the first paragraph of text in the document and then click the left button. This changes the display to 100% magnification.
   c. Click the Magnifier button to turn it off. This returns the mouse pointer to normal.
   d. Make the following edits to text in the first paragraph of the document:
      1) Change *6:00* to *6:30*.
      2) Change *9:30* to *10:00*.
      3) Change *Mike Shelton* to *Maggie Hayes*.
   e. Make the following edits to the text in the third paragraph of the document:
      1) Add *hamburgers,* after the words *Hot dogs,*.
      2) Change *9:00* to *9:30*.
   f. Click the Magnifier button and then click the document. This returns the display of the document to the previous magnification.
   g. Make sure the rulers are displayed. (If they are not displayed, click the View Ruler button on the Print Preview toolbar.)
   h. Make the following changes to the left, right, and top margins:
      1) Drag the left margin boundary to the right on the horizontal ruler until the 2-inch mark displays in the gray area.
      2) Drag the right margin boundary to the left on the horizontal ruler to the 4.5-inch mark in the white area.
      3) Drag the top margin boundary down on the vertical ruler until the 3-inch mark displays in the gray area.
   i. Click Close to close Print Preview.
4. Save the document again with the same name (Ch 12, Ex 15).
5. Print and then close Ch 12, Ex 15.

Changing the Document Zoom

In the previous section of this chapter you learned about the Zoom button on the Print Preview toolbar. With this button, you can change the percentage of display in Print Preview or change the display to Page Width, Whole Page, or Two Pages. The Zoom button changes the display of the document in Print Preview. You can also change the display of text at the document screen (not Print Preview) with the Zoom button on the Standard toolbar or with the Zoom option from the View drop-down menu. If you click the Zoom button on the Standard toolbar, the drop-down list shown in figure 12.11 displays.

12.11

Zoom Drop-Down List

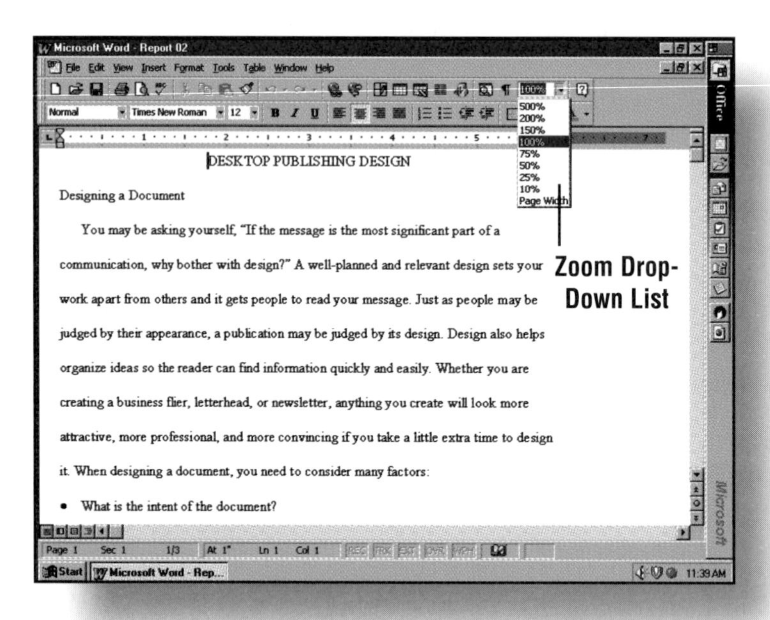

Click one of the percentage options to change the display to that percentage. Click the Page Width option and the screen display will change so that you can view text from the left to the right margins. When you make a change at the Zoom drop-down list, that change stays in effect for the document until you change to another option.

You can change the display of text at the document screen with options from the Zoom drop-down list and also at the Zoom dialog box shown in figure 12.12. To display the Zoom dialog box, click View, then Zoom.

figure 12.12 *Zoom Dialog Box*

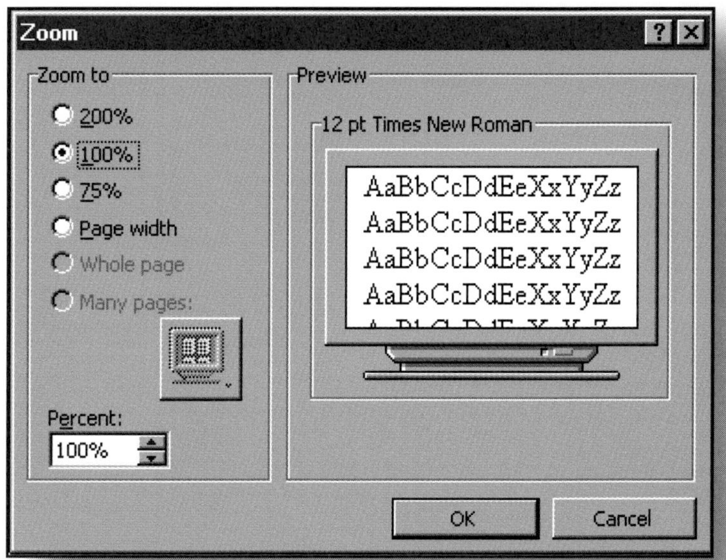

At the Zoom dialog box you can change the display to 200%, 100%, or 75%. You can also change the display to Page width. The Whole page and Many pages options are dimmed if the viewing mode is Normal. If the viewing mode is changed to Page Layout, the Whole page and Many pages options are available. To specify a percentage measurement, use the Percent option. Changes made at the Zoom dialog box stay in effect for the document until another change is made.

exercise 16

Changing the Display of Text Using Zoom

1. Open Report 03.
2. Change the display by completing the following steps:
   a. Click the Zoom button on the Standard toolbar and then click *50%* at the drop-down list.
   b. Click the Zoom button on the Standard toolbar and then click *Page Width* at the drop-down list.
   c. Click View, then Zoom.
   d. At the Zoom dialog box, click 200%.
   e. Click OK or press Enter.
   f. Click View, then Page Layout.
   g. Click View, then Zoom.
   h. At the Zoom dialog box, click Whole page.
   i. Click OK or press Enter.
   j. Click the Zoom button on the Standard toolbar and then click *100%* at the drop-down lsit.
3. Close Report 03.

chapter summary

- By default, a Word document contains 1.25-inch left and right margins and 1-inch top and bottom margins.
- Word inserts a page break at approximately 10 inches from the top of each page. With the default 1-inch top and bottom margins, this allows a total of 9 inches to be printed on a standard page. The page break displays as a row of dots in Normal viewing mode and as an actual break in the page in Page Layout.
- Margin settings can be changed visually with the Ruler; however, you must be in the Page Layout viewing mode to do this.
- Mirror margins can be created at the Page Setup dialog box. With this option, the measurements for left and right margins are applied to odd-numbered pages and reversed for even-numbered pages.
- For left-bound material to properly display on the page, change the gutter margins at the Page Setup dialog box from the default 0 inches to approximately 0.5 inch and also select the Mirror margins option.
- Formatting is generally applied to an entire document or to selected text. A document can also be divided into sections to which separate formatting can be applied.
- In Word, widows and orphans are automatically prevented from appearing in text. Turn off this feature at the Paragraph dialog box with the Line and Page Breaks tab selected.
- The Paragraph dialog box with the Line and Page Breaks tab selected contains options to keep a paragraph, a group of paragraphs, or a group of lines together.
- The page break that Word inserts automatically is a soft page break. A page break that you insert is a hard page break.
- To print text on a paper size that is different from the default of 8.5 by 11 inches, display the Page Setup dialog box with the Paper Size tab selected.
- The Vertical alignment option at the Page Setup dialog box contains three choices—Top, Center, and Justified.
- With Word's Print Preview feature, you can view a partial page, single page, multiple pages, or zoom in on a particular area of a page. With buttons on the Print Preview toolbar at the top of the Print Preview screen, you can change the display of the document, send a document to the printer, and turn the display of the rulers on or off.
- In addition to viewing how a document will look when printed, you can edit a document while in Print Preview. You can also change the margins while in Print Preview by using the rulers.
- The Zoom button changes the display of the document in Print Preview. You can also change the display of text at the document screen with the Zoom button on the Standard toolbar or with the Zoom option from the View drop-down menu.

commands review

	Mouse	Keyboard
Page Layout viewing mode	View, Page Layout; or click [icon] at left side of horizontal scroll bar	View, Page Layout
Normal viewing mode (default)	View, Normal; or click [icon] at left side of horizontal scroll bar	View, Normal
Page Setup dialog box	File, Page Setup	File, Page Setup
Display Ruler (or turn off display)	View, Ruler	View, Ruler
Insert continuous section break	Insert, Break, Continuous	Insert, Break, Continuous
Insert section break and begin new page	Insert, Break, Next page	Insert, Break, Next page
Paragraph dialog box	Format, Paragraph	Format, Paragraph
Insert hard page break	Insert, Break, Page break	CTRL + ENTER
Print Preview	File, Print Preview; or click [icon] on the Standard toolbar	File, Print Preview

check your understanding

Matching: In the space provided at the left, indicate the correct letter that matches each description. Some choices may be used more than once.

- A 1 inch
- B 8.5 inches
- C 9 inches
- D 11.5 inches
- E 1.25 inches
- F 10 inches
- G 11 inches
- H 9.5 inches
- I 0 inches
- J 1.5 inches

_______ **1.** Length of a standard piece of paper.
_______ **2.** Default top margin.
_______ **3.** Approximate number of vertical inches of text on a page.
_______ **4.** Width of a standard piece of paper.
_______ **5.** Default left margin.
_______ **6.** Default right margin.
_______ **7.** Default bottom margin.

_____ **8.** Default gutter margin.

_____ **9.** Approximate number of inches from the top of the page at which an automatic page break occurs on a page.

Completion: In the space provided at the right, indicate the correct term, symbol, or command.

1. A page break displays as a row of dots at this viewing mode. _____
2. Change margins in a document at this dialog box. _____
3. To move a margin boundary to a precise measurement, hold down this key while dragging the boundary. _____
4. Turn on/off the widow/orphan control at the Paragraph dialog box with this tab selected. _____
5. Press these keys on the keyboard to insert a hard page break in a document. _____
6. Word provides two orientations for paper sizes—Portrait and this. _____
7. The Vertical alignment option at the Page Setup dialog box contains three choices—Top, Center, and this. _____
8. Click this button on the Standard toolbar to preview a document. _____
9. Click this button on the Standard toolbar to change the percentage of display. _____

skill assessments

Note: Before completing the skill assessments, display the Open dialog box, and then select and delete documents created in chapter 10 that begin Ch 10. You may want to check with your instructor before deleting these documents.

Assessment 1

1. Open Report 02.
2. Save the document with Save As and name it Ch 12, SA 01.
3. Make the following changes to the document:
   a. Select the entire document and then change the font to 13-point Century Schoolbook. (To change the size to 13 points, you will need to select the current size in the Size text box and then key **13**.)
   b. Select the title, *DESKTOP PUBLISHING DESIGN*, and then change the font to 16-point Century Schoolbook bold.
   c. Use Format Painter to apply 16-point Century Schoolbook bold to the headings *Designing a Document* and *Creating Focus*.

d. Select the last two bulleted paragraphs in the first list of bulleted items. (These last two bulleted paragraphs should display at the bottom of the first page and the top of the second page.)
e. Display the Paragraph dialog box with the Line and Page Breaks tab selected, click Keep with next, and then close the dialog box.

4. Check page breaks and, if necessary, make adjustments to page breaks.
5. Save the document again with the same name (Ch 12, SA 01).
6. Print and then close Ch 12, SA 01.

Assessment 2

1. Open Report 02.
2. Save the document with Save As and name it Ch 12, SA 02.
3. Make the following changes to the document:
   a. Change the left margin to 2 inches and the right margin to 1 inch.
   b. Display the Page Setup dialog box with the Margins tab selected, click the Mirror margins option, and then close the dialog box.
   c. Select the entire document and then change the font to 12-point Garamond (or a similar serif typeface).
   d. Select the title, *DESKTOP PUBLISHING DESIGN*, and then change the font to 16-point Univers bold. (If your printer does not support Univers, choose a similar sans serif typeface.)
   e. Change the font to 16-point Univers bold for the headings *Designing a Document* and *Creating Focus*.
   f. Check the page breaks in the document and make changes, if needed.
4. Save the document again with the same name (Ch 12, SA 02).
5. Print and then close Ch 12, SA 02.

Assessment 3

1. Open Para 04 as a read-only document.
2. Make the following changes to the document:
   a. Change the paper size to 5.5 inches by 8.5 inches.
   b. Change the top and bottom margins to 1.5 inches and the left and right margins to 1 inch.
   c. Select the entire document then change the font to 10-point Arial.
   d. Change the vertical alignment of the text in the document to Justified.
3. Preview the document before printing.
4. Save the document with Save As and name it Ch 12, SA 03.
5. Print and then close Ch 12, SA 03.

Assessment 4

1. At a clear document screen, key the text shown in figure 12.13. Center and bold the text as indicated. Press the Enter key the number of times indicated in the brackets. (Do not key the information in brackets.)
2. Center the text vertically on the page.
3. Preview the document before printing.
4. Save the document and name it Ch 12, SA 04.
5. Print and then close Ch 12, SA 04.

Figure 12.13 • Assessment 4

SUPERVISORY TECHNIQUES
[press Enter 15 times]

by Charlie Fields
[press Enter 15 times]

BUS 210
November 8, 1999

chapter THIRTEEN

13 Manipulating Text Within and Between Documents

PERFORMANCE OBJECTIVES

Upon successful completion of chapter 13, you will be able to:

- **Delete, move, copy, and paste selected text.**
- **Save selected text as a separate document.**
- **Insert a document into another document.**
- **Open and close multiple documents.**
- **Split a window.**
- **Arrange windows.**
- **Size and move windows.**
- **Cut and paste or cut and copy text between documents.**

Some documents may need to be heavily revised, and these revisions may include deleting, moving, or copying blocks of text. This kind of editing is generally referred to as *cut and paste*. Cutting and pasting can be done within the same document, or text can be selected and then moved or copied to another document. Also, a document can be inserted into another document. This might be useful in a situation where you want to create a personalized document with standard text. You can open multiple documents and then cut and paste or copy and paste text between documents.

Working with Blocks of Text

When cutting and pasting, you work with blocks of text. A block of text is a portion of text that you have selected. (Chapter 2 explained the various methods for selecting text.) A block of text can be as small as one character or as large as an entire page or document. Once a block of text has been selected, it can be deleted, moved to a new location, or copied and placed in a certain location within a document. The last two operations involve using Word's Cut, Copy, and Paste features.

Deleting a Block of Text

Word offers different methods for deleting text from a document. To delete a single character, you can use either the Delete key or the Backspace key. To delete more than a single character, select the portion of text to be deleted, and then choose one of the following options:

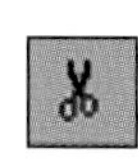

Cut

- Press Delete.
- Click the Cut button on the Standard toolbar.
- Choose Edit, then Cut.

Undo

Redo

If you press the Delete key, the text is deleted permanently. (You can restore deleted text with the Undo Clear option from the Edit menu or with the Undo or Redo buttons on the Standard toolbar.) The Cut button on the Standard toolbar and the Cut option from the Edit drop-down menu will delete the selected text and insert it to the *Clipboard*. Word's Clipboard is a temporary area of memory. The Clipboard holds text while it is being moved or copied to a new location in the document or to a different document. Text inserted in the Clipboard stays there until other text is inserted.

Delete selected text with the Delete key if you do not need it again. Use the other methods if you might want to insert deleted text in the current document or a different document.

exercise 1

Deleting Selected Text

1. Open Report 01.
2. Save the document with Save As and name it Ch 13, Ex 01.
3. Select and bold the title, *DESKTOP PUBLISHING*, and the headings, *Defining Desktop Publishing, Initiating the Desktop Publishing Process, Planning the Publication,* and *Creating the Content.*
4. Delete the following text in the report:
   a. Delete the last sentence in the second paragraph in the *Defining Desktop Publishing* section (the sentence that begins *Desktop Publishing involves using desktop publishing software...*) by completing the following steps:
      1) Select the sentence.
      2) Press the Delete key.
   b. Delete the last sentence in the third paragraph in the *Defining Desktop Publishing* section (the sentence that begins *Everything from a flyer to a newsletter...*) by completing the following steps:
      1) Select the sentence.
      2) Click the Cut button on the Standard toolbar.
   c. Delete the second paragraph in the *Planning the Publication* section of the report.
5. Check page breaks in the document and, if necessary, adjust the page breaks.
6. Save the document again with the same name (Ch 13, Ex 01).
7. Print and then close Ch 13, Ex 01.

Moving Blocks of Text

Word offers a variety of methods for moving text. After you have selected a block of text, move text with buttons on the Standard toolbar or options from the Edit drop-down menu.

To move a block of selected text from one location to another using buttons on the Standard toolbar, you would complete the following steps:

1. Select the text.
2. Click the Cut button on the Standard toolbar.
3. Position the insertion point at the location where the selected text is to be inserted.
4. Click the Paste button on the Standard toolbar.

Paste

To move a block of selected text from one location to another using options from the Edit menu, you would complete the following steps:

1. Select the text.
2. Choose Edit, then Cut.
3. Position the insertion point at the location where the selected text is to be inserted.
4. Choose Edit, then Paste.

In addition to the methods just described, a block of selected text can also be moved with the mouse. There are two methods for moving text with the mouse. You can use the mouse to drag selected text to a new location or use a shortcut menu.

To drag selected text to a new location, you would complete the following steps:

1. Select the text to be moved with the mouse.
2. Move the I-beam pointer inside the selected text until it becomes an arrow pointer.
3. Hold down the left mouse button, drag the arrow pointer (displays with a gray box attached) to the location where you want the selected text inserted, and then release the button.
4. Deselect the text.

When you hold down the left mouse button and drag the mouse, the arrow pointer displays with a small gray box attached. In addition, the insertion point displays as a grayed vertical bar. When the insertion point (grayed vertical bar) is located in the desired position, release the mouse button. The selected text is removed from its original position and inserted in the new location.

To move selected text with a shortcut menu, you would complete the following steps:

1. Select the text to be moved with the mouse.
2. Move the I-beam pointer inside the selected text until it becomes an arrow pointer.
3. Click the *right* mouse button.
4. At the shortcut menu that displays, click Cut.
5. Position the insertion point where the text is to be inserted.
6. Click the *right* mouse button to display the shortcut menu and then click Paste.

When selected text is cut from a document and inserted in the Clipboard, it stays in the Clipboard until other text is inserted in the Clipboard. For this reason, you can paste text from the Clipboard more than just once. For example, if you cut text to the Clipboard, you can paste this text in different locations within the document or other documents as many times as desired.

exercise 2

Moving Selected Text

1. Open Para 03.
2. Save the document with Save As and name it Ch 13, Ex 02.
3. Move the following text in the document:
   a. Move the second paragraph above the first paragraph by completing the following steps:
      1) Select the second paragraph including the blank line below the paragraph.
      2) Click the Cut button on the Standard toolbar.
      3) Position the insertion point at the beginning of the first paragraph.
      4) Click the Paste button on the Standard toolbar.
   b. Move the third paragraph above the second paragraph by completing the following steps:
      1) Select the third paragraph including the blank line below the paragraph.
      2) Click Edit, then Cut.
      3) Position the insertion point at the beginning of the second paragraph.
      4) Click Edit, then Paste.
   c. Move the first paragraph to the end of the document using the mouse by completing the following steps:
      1) Using the mouse, select the first paragraph including the blank line below the paragraph.
      2) Move the I-beam pointer inside the selected text until it becomes an arrow pointer.
      3) Hold down the left mouse button, drag the arrow pointer (displays with a small gray box attached) a double space below the last paragraph (make sure the insertion point, which displays as a grayed vertical bar, is positioned a double space below the last paragraph), and then release the mouse button.
      4) Deselect the text and then move the insertion point to the beginning of the third paragraph and press Enter.
4. Save the document again with the same name (Ch 13, Ex 02).
5. Print and then close Ch 13, Ex 02.

Copying a Block of Text

Copying selected text can be useful in documents that contain repetitive portions of text. You can use this function to insert duplicate portions of text in a document instead of rekeying the text. After you have selected a block of text, copy the text with buttons on the Standard toolbar or options from the Edit drop-down menu.

To copy text with the buttons on the Standard toolbar, you would complete the following steps:

1. Select the text to be copied.
2. Click the Copy button on the Standard toolbar.
3. Move the insertion point to the location where the copied text is to be inserted.
4. Click the Paste button on the Standard toolbar.

Copy

To copy text with options from the Edit drop-down menu, you would complete the following steps:

1. Select the text to be copied.
2. Click Edit, then Copy.
3. Move the insertion point to the location where the copied text is to be inserted.
4. Click Edit, then Paste.

Copying Selected Text with Buttons on the Standard Toolbar

1. Open Block 01.
2. Save the document with Save As and name it Ch 13, Ex 03.
3. Select the entire document, then change the font to 14-point Braggadocio. (If this typeface is not available, choose a fancy or decorative typeface.)
4. Copy the text in the document to the end of the document by completing the following steps:
   a. Select the text in the document and include the two blank lines below the text.
   b. Click the Copy button on the Standard toolbar.
   c. Move the insertion point to the end of the document.
   d. Click the Paste button on the Standard toolbar.
5. Copy the text again to the end of the document. To do this, position the insertion point at the end of the document, then click the Paste button on the Standard toolbar. (This inserts a copy of the text from the Clipboard.)
6. Save the document with the same name (Ch 13, Ex 03).
7. Print and then close Ch 13, Ex 03.

The mouse can also be used to copy a block of text in a document and insert the copy in a new location. To do this, complete the following steps:

1. Select the text with the mouse.
2. Move the I-beam pointer inside the selected text until it becomes an arrow pointer.
3. Hold down the Ctrl key and then the left mouse button. Drag the arrow pointer (displays with a small gray box and a box containing a plus symbol) to the location where you want the copied text inserted (make sure the insertion point, which displays as a grayed vertical bar, is positioned in the desired location), and then release the mouse button and then the Ctrl key.
4. Deselect the text.

If you select a block of text and then decide you selected the wrong text or you do not want to do anything with the block, you can deselect it. If you are using the mouse, click the left mouse button outside the selected text. If you are using the keyboard, press an arrow key to deselect text. If you selected with the Extend mode (F8), press Esc and then press an arrow key to deselect text.

exercise 4

Copying Selected Text Using the Mouse

1. Open Block 02.
2. Save the document with Save As and name it Ch 13, Ex 04.
3. Copy the text in the document using the mouse by completing the following steps:
   a. Select the text with the mouse. Include the two blank lines below the text.
   b. Move the I-beam pointer inside the selected text until it becomes an arrow pointer.
   c. Hold down the Ctrl key and then the left mouse button. Drag the arrow pointer (displays with a small gray box and a box with a plus symbol inside) to the end of the document immediately above the end-of-document marker (make sure the insertion point, which displays as a grayed vertical bar, is positioned immediately above the end-of-document marker), and then release the mouse button and then the Ctrl key.
   d. Deselect the text.
4. Select the entire document and then copy it to the end of the document.
5. Select one form and then copy it at the end of the document. (You should have a total of five forms. Make sure all forms fit on one page. If the form does not fit on one page, consider deleting any extra blank lines between forms.)
6. Save the document again with the same name (Ch 13, Ex 04).
7. Print and then close Ch 13, Ex 04.

Working with Documents

Some documents may contain standard information—information that remains the same. For example, a legal document, such as a will, may contain text that is standard and appears in all wills. Repetitive text can be saved as a separate document and then inserted into an existing document whenever needed.

There are two methods that can be used for saving text into a separate document. The first is to save a document just as you have been doing. The other method is to select standard text within a document and save it as a separate document.

Saving Standard Text

If you know in advance what information or text is standard and will be used again, you can save it as a separate document. You should determine how to break down the information based on how it will be used. After deciding how to break down the information, key the text at a clear document screen, and then save it in the normal manner.

Saving Selected Text

When you create a document and then realize that a portion of the text in the document will be needed for future documents, you can save it as a separate document. To do this, you would copy the text, paste it into a new document screen, and then save it in the normal manner.

Inserting a Document

A document containing standard text can be inserted into an existing document with the Fi<u>l</u>e option from the <u>I</u>nsert drop-down menu. To insert a standard document into an existing document, position the insertion point in the current document at the location where the standard text is to be inserted, and then click <u>I</u>nsert, then Fi<u>l</u>e. At the Insert File dialog box shown in figure 13.1, double-click the document name to be inserted.

13.1

Insert File Dialog Box

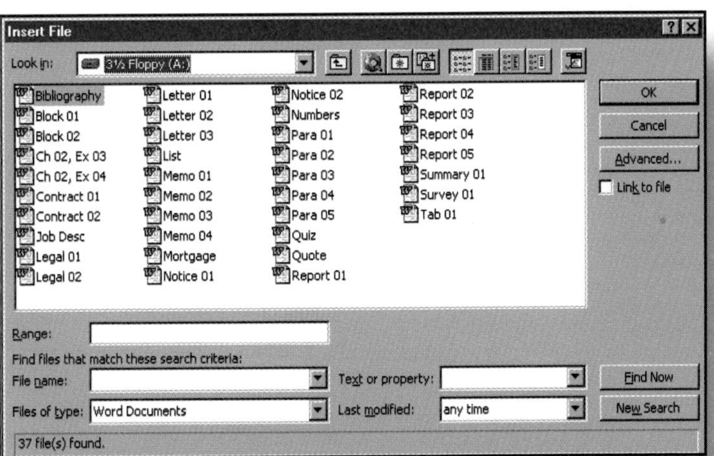

exercise 5

Saving Selected Text as a Separate Document

1. Open Memo 02.
2. Select the paragraphs containing book titles (the second paragraph through the fifth paragraph) and then save them as a separate document named *Textbooks* by completing the following steps:
   a. Select the second paragraph through the fifth paragraph (the paragraphs containing book titles).
   b. Click the Copy button on the Standard toolbar.
   c. Click the New button on the Standard toolbar.
   d. At the clear document screen, click the Paste button on the Standard toolbar.
   e. Save the document and name it *Textbooks*.
   f. Close the *Textbooks* document.
3. Close Memo 02 without saving any changes.
4. At a clear document screen, key the memo headings and the first paragraph of the text shown in figure 13.2. Use an appropriate memo format. After keying the first paragraph, press Enter twice, and then insert the *Textbooks* document by completing the following steps:
   a. Click Insert, then File.
   b. At the Insert File dialog box, double-click *Textbooks*.
5. Move the insertion point a double space below the last paragraph and then key the last paragraph shown in figure 13.2. Include your initials and the document name a double space below the last line of the paragraph.
6. Select the second through the fifth paragraphs (the paragraphs containing book titles) and then insert bullets before the paragraphs. (Use the Bullets button on the Formatting toolbar.)
7. Save the memo and name it Ch 13, Ex 05.
8. Print and then close Ch 13, Ex 05.

New

Exercise 5

DATE: December 2, 1999; TO: All OT Staff; FROM: Christy Edmonds; SUBJECT: BUSINESS COMMUNICATIONS BOOKS

The library has recently purchased several reference books on business communications. These books are now available at the library. The books that are available include:

[Insert *Textbooks* document here.]

You may want to use these reference books for your business communications classes. Students may also want to use them for preparing documents or writing reports.

XX:Ch 13, Ex 05

Working with Windows

Word 97 operates within the Windows environment created by the Windows program. However, when working in Word, a *window* refers to the document screen. The Windows program creates an environment in which various software programs are used with menu bars, scroll bars, and icons to represent programs and files. With the Windows program, you can open several different software programs and move between them quickly. Similarly, using windows in Word, you can open several different documents and move between them quickly.

Opening Multiple Windows

With multiple documents open, you can move the insertion point between them. You can move or copy information between documents or compare the contents of several documents. The maximum number of documents (windows) that you can have open at one time depends on the memory of your computer system and the amount of text in each document. When you open a new window, it is placed on top of the original window. Once multiple windows are opened, you can resize the windows to see all or a portion of them on the screen.

A document can be opened at the Open dialog box or a blank document can be opened by clicking the New button on the Standard toolbar. (The New button is the first button from the left on the Standard toolbar.) You can also open multiple documents at the same time at the Open dialog box. To do this, display the Open dialog box, click the first document to be opened, and then hold down the Ctrl key while clicking the remaining desired document names. Release the Ctrl key and then click the Open button.

When you are working in a document, the document fills the entire document screen. If you open another document without closing the first, the newly opened document will fill the document screen. The first document is still open, but it is covered by the new one. To see what documents are currently open, click Window on the Menu bar. When you click Window, the Window menu shown in figure 13.3 displays. (The number of documents and document names displayed at the bottom of the menu will vary.)

figure 13.3 *Window Menu*

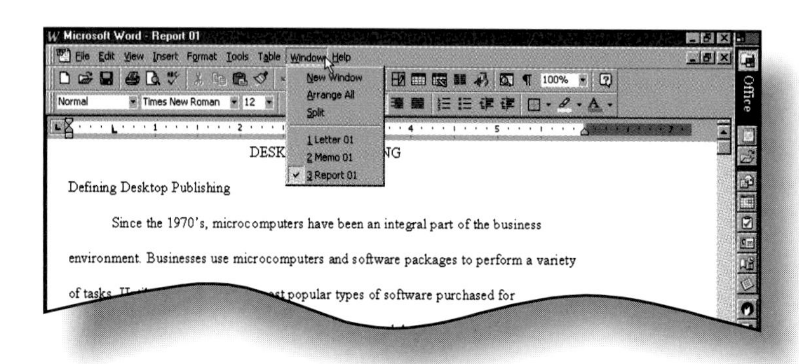

The open document names are displayed at the bottom of the menu. The document name with the check mark in front of it is the *active* document. The active document is the document containing the insertion point.

To make one of the other documents active, click the document name. If you are using the keyboard, key the number shown in front of the desired document. When you change the active document, the Window menu is removed and the new active document is displayed.

(Note: Some virus protection software will let you open only one document at a time.)

Closing Multiple Windows

All open documents can be closed at the same time. To do this, hold down the Shift key, and then click File on the Menu bar. This causes the File drop-down menu to display with the Close All option (instead of the Close option). Click the Close All option and all open documents will be closed.

exercise 6

Opening and Closing Multiple Windows

(Note: If you are using Word on a network system that contains a virus checker, you may not be able to open multiple documents at once.)

1. Open several documents at the same time by completing the following steps:
   a. Display the Open dialog box.

b. Click the document named *Block 01*.
c. Hold down the Ctrl key and then click *Letter 01* and then *Memo 01*.
d. Release the Ctrl key and then click the Open button.
2. Make *Letter 01* the active document by clicking Window and then 2.
3. Make *Block 01* the active document by clicking Window and then 1.
4. Close all open documents by completing the following steps:
   a. Hold down the Shift key.
   b. Click File on the Menu bar.
   c. Click Close All.

Splitting a Window

With the Split command from the Window drop-down menu you can divide a window into two *panes*. This is helpful if you want to view different parts of the same document at one time. You may want to display an outline for a report in one pane, for example, and the portion of the report that you are editing in the other. The original window is split into two panes that extend horizontally across the screen.

A window can be split with the Split option from the Window drop-down menu or with the split bar. To split the current document window using the Split option, click Window, then Split. This causes a wide gray line to display in the middle of the screen and the mouse pointer to display as a double-headed arrow pointing up and down with a small double line between. Move this double-headed arrow pointer up or down, if desired, by dragging the mouse or by pressing the up and/or down arrow keys on the keyboard. When the double-headed arrow is positioned at the desired location in the document, click the left mouse button or press the Enter key.

You can also split the window with the split bar. The split bar is the small gray horizontal bar above the up scroll triangle on the vertical scroll bar as identified in figure 13.4.

13.4

Split Bar

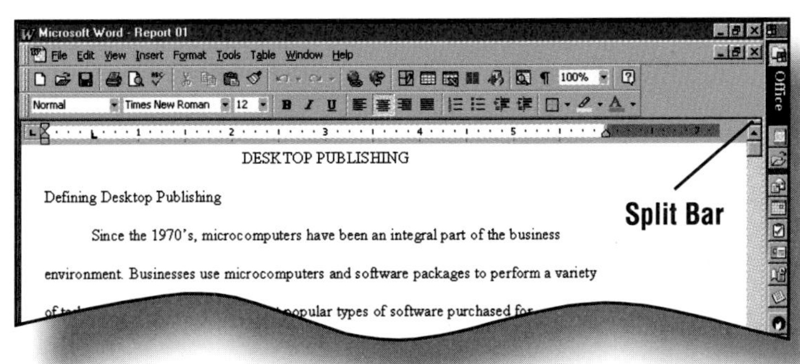

To split the window with the split bar, position the arrow pointer on the split bar until it turns into a short double line with an up- and down-pointing arrow. Hold down the left mouse button, drag the double-headed arrow into the document screen to the location where you want the window split, and then release the mouse button.

When a window is split, the insertion point is positioned in the bottom pane. To move the insertion point to the other pane with the mouse, position the I-beam pointer in the other pane, and then click the left mouse button. If you are using the keyboard, press F6 to move to the next pane. (You can also press Shift + F6, which is the Previous Pane command.) Figure 13.5 displays a document split into two windows.

figure 13.5 ***Split Window***

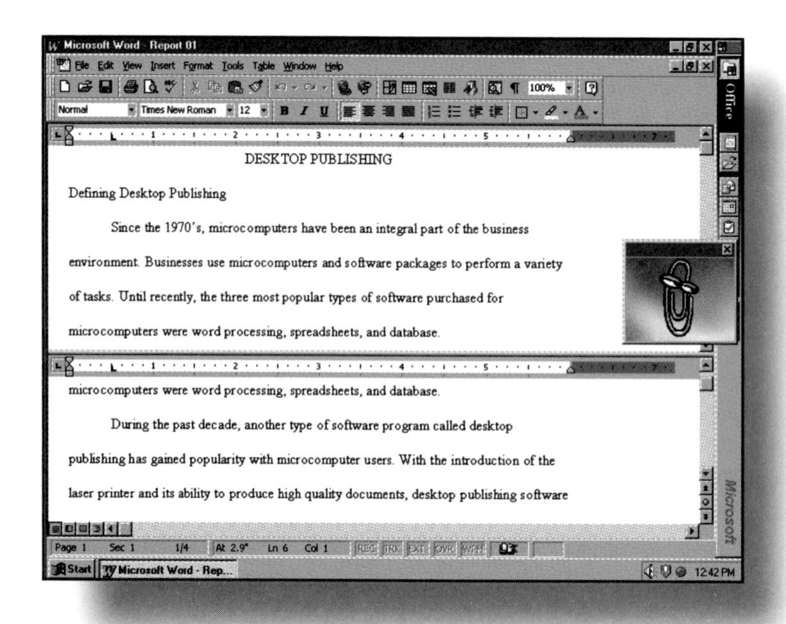

To remove the split line from the document, click Window, then Remove Split. You can also remove the split with the mouse. To do this, position the arrow pointer on the split line until it turns into a short double line with an up- and down-pointing arrow. Hold down the left mouse button, drag the split line up to the top of the screen or down to the bottom of the screen, and then release the mouse button.

exercise 7

Moving Selected Text Between Split Windows

1. Open Report 03.
2. Save the document with Save As and name it Ch 13, Ex 07.
3. Split the window by completing the following steps:
   a. Choose Window, then Split.
   b. With the split line displayed in the middle of the document screen, click the left mouse button.
   c. With the insertion point positioned in the bottom pane, move the *MODULE 1: DEFINING NEWSLETTER ELEMENTS* section below the *MODULE 2: PLANNING A NEWSLETTER* by completing the following steps:
      1) Select the *MODULE 1: DEFINING NEWSLETTER ELEMENTS* section from the title to right above *MODULE 2: PLANNING A NEWSLETTER*.
      2) Click the Cut button on the Standard toolbar.
      3) Position the arrow pointer at the end of the document in the top window pane, and then click the left mouse button.
      4) Click the Paste button on the Standard toolbar.
      5) Change the number in the two titles to *MODULE 1: PLANNING A NEWSLETTER* and *MODULE 2: DEFINING NEWSLETTER ELEMENTS*.
4. Insert a section break that begins a new page above *MODULE 2: DEFINING NEWSLETTER ELEMENTS* by completing the following steps:
   a. Position the arrow pointer immediately left of the *M* in *MODULE 2: DEFINING NEWSLETTER ELEMENTS* in the bottom window pane and then click the left mouse button.
   b. Click Insert, then Break.
   c. At the Break dialog box, click Next page.
   d. Click OK or press Enter.
5. Remove the split from the window by clicking Window, then Remove Split.
6. Check page breaks in the document and, if necessary, make corrections to the page breaks.
7. Save the document again with the same name (Ch 13, Ex 07).
8. Print and then close Ch 13, Ex 07.

Arranging Windows

If you have more than one document open, you can use the Arrange All option from the Window drop-down menu to view a portion of all open documents. To do this, choose Window, then Arrange All. Figure 13.6 shows a document screen with three open documents that have been arranged.

13.6

Arranged Documents

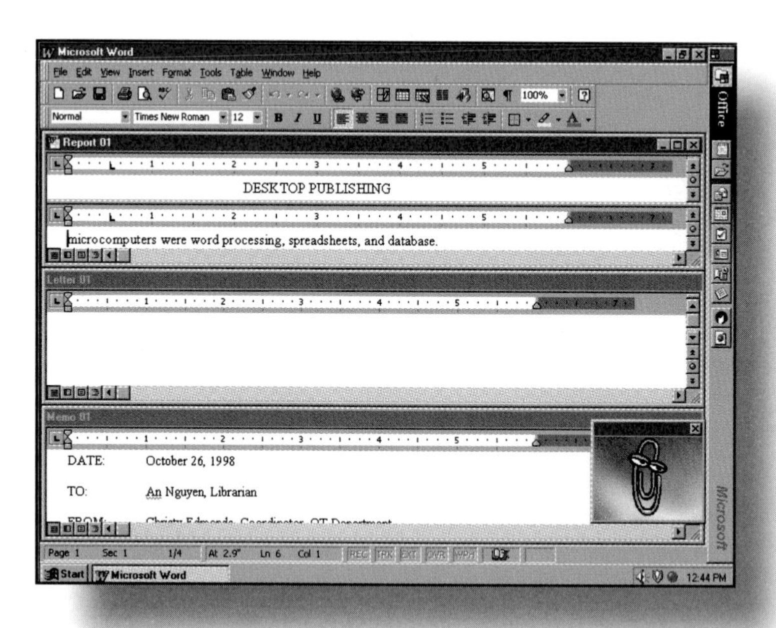

When open documents are arranged, a portion of each window is displayed on the screen. The title bar for each document is displayed along with the vertical and horizontal scroll bars.

exercise 8

Arranging Windows

1. Open the following documents: *Letter 02*, *Memo 02*, *Para 02*, and *Report 02*.
2. Arrange the windows by choosing Window, then Arrange All.
3. Make Letter 02 the active document by positioning the arrow pointer on the title bar for Letter 02 and then clicking the left mouse button.
4. Close Letter 02.
5. Make Para 02 active and then close it.
6. Closing the remaining documents.

Sizing and Moving Windows

Maximize

Minimize

Close

Restore

The Maximize and Minimize buttons in the upper right corner of the active document window can be used to change the size of the window. The Maximize button is the button in the upper right corner of the active document immediately left of the Close button. (The Close button is the button containing the X.) The Minimize button is located immediately left of the Maximize button.

If you arrange all open documents and then click the Maximize button in the active document, the active document expands to fill the document screen. In addition, the Maximize button changes to the Restore button. To return the active document back to its size before it was maximized, click the Restore button.

If you click the Minimize button in the active document, the document is reduced and positioned at the bottom left side of the screen. In addition, the Minimize button changes to the Restore button. To maximize a document that has been reduced, click the Maximize button in the title bar of the minimized document. You can also maximize a minimized document by double-clicking the title bar. Figure 13.7 shows an example of the document named *Memo 01* that has been minimized.

figure 13.7 *Minimized Document*

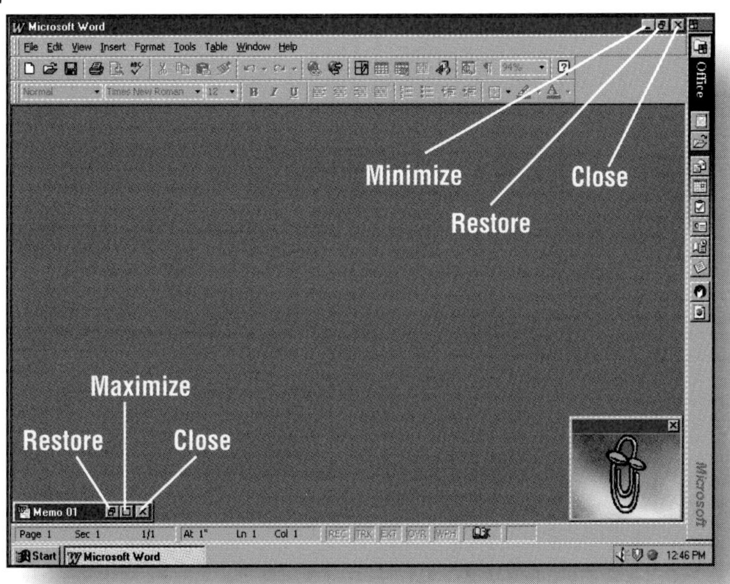

In addition to using the Minimize, Maximize, and Close buttons for a minimized document, you can also use a shortcut menu. To display the shortcut menu for a minimized document, position the arrow pointer on the title bar of the minimized document, and then click the left mouse button. This causes a shortcut menu to display with the options Restore, Move, Size, Minimize, Maximize, and Close. At this menu, click the desired option.

exercise 9

Minimizing, Maximizing, and Restoring Documents

1. Open Tab 01.
2. Maximize Tab 01 by clicking the Maximize button at the right side of the Title bar. (The Maximize button is the button at the right side of the Title bar, immediately left of the Close button.)
3. Open Memo 03.
4. Open Report 03.
5. Arrange the windows.
6. Make Memo 03 the active window.
7. Minimize Memo 03 using the mouse by clicking the Minimize button in the upper right corner of the active window.
8. Make Tab 01 the active document and then minimize Tab 01.
9. Restore the size of Tab 01 using a shortcut menu by completing the following steps:
   a. Position the arrow pointer on the Tab 01 Title bar and then click the left mouse button.
   b. Click Restore.
10. Restore the size of Memo 03 by clicking the Memo 03 Title bar and then clicking the Restore button at the right side of the Memo 03 Title bar.
11. Make Report 03 the active document and then close it.
12. Close Memo 03.
13. Maximize Tab 01 by clicking the Maximize button at the right side of the Tab 01 Title bar.
14. Close Tab 01.

The size of documents that have been arranged can be increased or decreased using the mouse. To increase or decrease the size of the active document window vertically, move the mouse pointer to the double line border at the right or left side of the window until it turns into a left- and right-pointing arrow. Hold down the left mouse button and then drag the border to the right or left. When the window is the desired size, release the mouse button.

To increase or decrease the size of the active window horizontally, move the mouse pointer to the double line border at the top or bottom of the window until it turns into an up- and down-pointing arrow. Hold down the left mouse button and then drag the border up or down to increase or decrease the size. When the window is the desired size, release the mouse button.

Documents that have been arranged can also be moved. To move an arranged document, make sure it is the active document, position the arrow pointer on the Title bar, hold down the left mouse button, drag the outline of the document window to the desired location, and then release the mouse button.

exercise 10

Changing the Size of a Window Using the Mouse

1. Open Memo 04.
2. Open Report 01.
3. Arrange the windows.
4. Change the size of the Report 01 document window by completing the following steps:
   a. Position the mouse pointer on the double line border at the right side of the window until it turns into a left- and right-pointing arrow.
   b. Hold down the left mouse button, drag the border to the left approximately 1 inch, and then release the mouse button.
   c. Position the mouse pointer on the double line border at the left side of the window until it turns into a left- and right-pointing arrow.
   d. Hold down the left mouse button, drag the border to the right approximately 1 inch, and then release the mouse button.
5. Make the same changes to Memo 04.
6. Close Memo 04.
7. Maximize Report 01 by clicking the Maximize button at the upper right side of the Report 01 window.
8. Close Report 01.

Cutting and Pasting Text Between Windows

With several documents open, you can easily move, copy, and/or paste text from one document to another. To move, copy, and/or paste text between documents, use the cutting and pasting options you learned earlier in this chapter together with the information about windows in this chapter.

exercise 11

Copying Selected Text from One Open Document to Another

1. At a clear document screen, key the memo shown in figure 13.8 in an appropriate memo format. (Press the Enter key three times after keying the first paragraph and before you key the second paragraph.)
2. Save the memo and name it Ch 13, Ex 11.
3. With Ch 13, Ex 11 still open in the screen, open Memo 02.
4. With Memo 02 as the active document, copy the first three books listed in the memo by completing the following steps:

a. Select the three paragraphs containing the first three book titles.
b. Click the Copy button on the Standard toolbar.
c. Deselect the text.
d. Make Ch 13, Ex 11 the active document.
e. Position the insertion point a double space below the first paragraph and then click the Paste button on the Standard toolbar.

5. Save the memo again with the same name (Ch 13, Ex 11).
6. Print and then close Ch 13, Ex 11.
7. Close Memo 02.

figure 13.8 — Exercise 11

DATE: November 16, 1999; TO: An Nguyen, Librarian; FROM: Marlene St. Claire, Assistant Librarian; SUBJECT: BUSINESS COMMUNICATIONS BOOKS

I found $80.50 in the library reference fund and $27.00 in the emergency fund. With these combined amounts, I was able to purchase the following books:

With funds that will become available January 1, we should be able to purchase the remaining two books.

XX:Ch 13, Ex 11

chapter summary

- Deleting, moving, or copying blocks of text within a document is generally referred to as *cutting and pasting*. A block of text can be as small as one character or as large as an entire page or document.
- When deleting a block of text, use the Delete key if you do not need that text again; use the Cut button on the Standard toolbar or the Cut option from the Edit drop-down menu if you might want to insert the deleted text in the current or a different document.
- Selected text can be copied in a document or a different document using the Copy and Paste buttons on the Standard toolbar or the Copy and Paste options from the Edit drop-down menu.

- Text that will be repeatedly used in one or more documents can be saved as a separate document. This text can be keyed and the document saved as usual, or the text can be selected within a document and saved as a separate document. This separate document can then be inserted into an existing document with the File option from the Insert drop-down menu.
- When working in Word 97, a window refers to the document screen.
- You can open multiple documents and copy or move text between documents or compare the contents of several documents.
- A new (empty) window can be opened in several ways.
- Each document that is opened will fill the entire editing window. Move among the open documents by clicking Window on the Menu bar and then clicking the left mouse button on the desired document name or keying the number in front of that document name. The active document is the document containing the insertion point.
- With the Split command from the Window drop-down menu, you can divide a window into two panes. This enables you to view different parts of the same document at one time.
- Use the Arrange All option from the Window drop-down menu to view a portion of all open documents.
- Use the Maximize, Minimize, and Restore buttons in the upper right corner of the window to reduce or increase the size of the active window.
- The size of documents that have been arranged can be changed using the mouse. A document that has been arranged can also be moved using the mouse.
- With several documents open, you can easily move, copy, and/or paste text from one document to another.

commands review

	Mouse	Keyboard
Delete one character		Press DEL or BACKSPACE
Delete selected text permanently		Press DEL
Delete selected text and insert it in the Clipboard	Edit, Cut; or click [Cut button] on Standard toolbar; or with I-beam pointer inside text block, click *right* mouse button, click Cut	Edit, Cut
Insert text from Clipboard to new location	Edit, Paste; or click [Paste button] on Standard toolbar; or click *right* mouse button, click Paste	Edit, Paste

Copy selected text	Edit, Copy, move insertion point to new location, then Edit, Paste; or click [Copy button] on Standard toolbar, then click [Paste button] at new location	Edit, Copy, move insertion point to new location, then Edit, Paste
Deselect text	Click left mouse button outside selected text	Press any ↑ ← → ↓
Save selected paragraph as separate document	Edit, Copy, or click [Copy button] on Standard toolbar; click [New button] on Standard toolbar; then click Edit, Paste, or click [Paste button] on Standard toolbar; then save in the normal manner	Edit, Copy; choose File, New, Enter; choose Edit, Paste, then save document in the normal manner
Insert document into another	With insertion point at the desired location for the standard text, click Insert, then File; double-click the desired document	With insertion point at the desired location for the standard text, choose Insert, then File; key document name; then press Enter
Split a window	Window, Split; or position arrow pointer on split box until it becomes an up- and down-pointing arrow, then hold down left mouse button, drag arrow down into document screen to desired location, then release mouse button	Window, Split
Remove split window	Window, Remove Split	Window, Remove Split
Move insertion point to other window	Position I-beam pointer in pane, click left mouse button	F6
Arrange all open documents	Window, Arrange All	Window, Arrange All
Minimize a document	Click [Minimize button] at right side of Menu bar	
Maximize a document	Click [Maximize button] at right side of Menu bar	
Size an arranged document using the mouse	With arrow pointer on double line border at right/left or top/bottom, hold down left mouse button, drag border to increase or decrease window size, then release mouse button	
Move an arranged document	Position arrow pointer in Title bar, hold down left mouse button, drag outline to desired position, then release mouse button	

check your understanding

Completion: In the space provided, indicate the correct term, command, or number.

1. Press this button on the keyboard if you want to permanently delete selected text. ________________
2. Click this button on the Standard toolbar to insert text currently located in the Clipboard at the location of the insertion point. ________________
3. To copy selected text with the mouse, hold down this key while dragging selected text. ________________
4. To deselect text with the mouse, do this. ________________
5. To insert a document into another document, click File from this drop-down menu. ________________
6. To close all open documents at the same time, hold down this key and then click File, then Close All. ________________
7. To remove a split line from a document, click Remove Split from this drop-down menu. ________________
8. Click this option from the Window drop-down menu to arrange all open documents. ________________
9. Expand the active document to fill the document screen by clicking this button located in the upper right corner of the active document. ________________
10. Click this button to shrink a document. ________________

skill assessments

Note: Before completing the skill assessments, display the Open dialog box, and then select and delete documents created in chapter 11 that begin Ch 11. You may want to check with your instructor before deleting these documents.

Assessment 1

1. Open Report 04.
2. Save the document with Save As and name it Ch 13, SA 01.
3. Make the following changes to the report:
   a. Select and then delete the last sentence in the first paragraph of the *Applying Desktop Publishing Guidelines* section.
   b. Select and then delete the last paragraph in the *Applying Desktop Publishing* section of the report (the paragraph that begins *If you decide to use color...*).
   c. Move the section titled *Creating Margins for Newsletters* above the section titled *Choosing Paper Size and Type*.

d. Select the entire document and then change to a serif font other than Times New Roman (you determine the font).
e. Check page breaks in the document and, if necessary, adjust the page breaks.
4. Save the document again with the same name (Ch 13, SA 01).
5. Print and then close Ch 13, SA 01.

Assessment 2

1. At a clear document screen, create the document shown in figure 13.9. Double space between lines and triple space after the last line in the document.
2. Make the following changes to the document:
   a. Change the font for the entire document to 14-point Goudy Old Style bold. (If this typeface is not available, choose a fancy or decorative typeface.)
   b. Select and then copy the text a triple space below the original text.
   c. Paste the text two more times. (There should be a total of four forms when you are done and they should fit on one page.)
3. Save the document and name it Ch 13, SA 02.
4. Print and then close Ch 13, SA 02.

Figure 13.9 • Assessment 2

NEWS FLASH!!

EMERALD HEIGHTS ELEMENTARY SCHOOL

No School, Friday, November 5, 1999

Elementary Teacher Work Day!

Assessment 3

1. Open Bibliography, Letter 01, Notice 01, and Quiz.
2. Make Notice 01 the active document.
3. Make Bibliography the active document.
4. Arrange all the windows.
5. Make Quiz the active document and then minimize it.
6. Minimize the remaining documents.
7. Make Bibliography active and then restore it.
8. Restore Letter 01.
9. Restore Notice 01.
10. Restore Quiz.
11. Close Quiz.

12. Close Notice 01.
13. Close Letter 01.
14. Maximize Bibliography.
15. Close Bibliography.

Assessment 4

1. At a clear editing window, key the letter shown in figure 13.10 in an appropriate letter format through the first paragraph (to the location where the bolded message is displayed).
2. Save the letter and name it Ch 13, SA 04.
3. With Ch 13, SA 04 still open, open Contract 01.
4. Arrange the windows.
5. With Contract 01 the active document, copy the first paragraph a double space below the first paragraph in the letter in Ch 13, SA 04.
6. Key the third paragraph in the letter as shown in figure 13.10.
7. Make Contract 01 the active document and then copy the sixth paragraph a double space below the third paragraph in the letter in Ch 13, SA 04.
8. Make Contract 01 the active document and then close it.
9. Maximize Ch 13, SA 04.
10. Key the remaining text in the letter.
11. Save the letter again with the same name (Ch 13, SA 04).
12. Print and then close Ch 13, SA 04.

Figure 13.10 • Assessment 4

April 21, 1999

Mr. Dennis Wong, President
Industrial Workers Union
795 South 63rd Street
Oklahoma City, OK 76554

Dear Mr. Wong:

I received the draft of the purpose and scope for the agreement between the Coleman Development Corporation and the Industrial Workers Union. In the first section of the agreement, I recommend adding the following paragraph between the third and fourth paragraphs:

[Insert the first paragraph from Contract 01 here.]

Additionally, I recommend adding the following paragraph between the fifth and sixth paragraphs:

[Insert the sixth paragraph from Contract 01 here.]

The preliminary agreement looks good. I feel confident that we can complete these contract negotiations by the end of the month.

Sincerely,

Julian Carr
Attorney at Law

XX:Ch 13, SA 04

chapter FOURTEEN

Creating Headers and Footers in a Document

PERFORMANCE OBJECTIVES

Upon successful completion of chapter 14, you will be able to:

- **Create a header and footer in a document.**
- **Format, edit, and delete a header or footer.**
- **Reposition a header or footer.**
- **Create a different header or footer on the first page of a document.**
- **Create a header or footer for odd pages and another for even pages.**
- **Create a header or footer for different sections in a document.**
- **Insert page numbering in a document.**

In a Word document, text can be created that prints at the top of every page and/or the bottom of every page. In addition, page numbering can be added to Word documents.

Working with Headers and Footers

Text that appears at the top of every page is called a *header* and text that appears at the bottom of every page is referred to as a *footer*. Headers and footers are common in manuscripts, textbooks, reports, and other publications.

Creating a Header or Footer

With the Header and Footer option from View, you can create a header or a footer. When you click View, then Header and Footer, Word automatically changes the viewing mode to Page Layout, dims the text in the document, inserts a pane where the header or footer is entered, and also inserts the Header and Footer toolbar. Figure 14.1 shows a document with a header pane and the Header and Footer toolbar displayed.

14.1 *Header Pane and Header and Footer Toolbar*

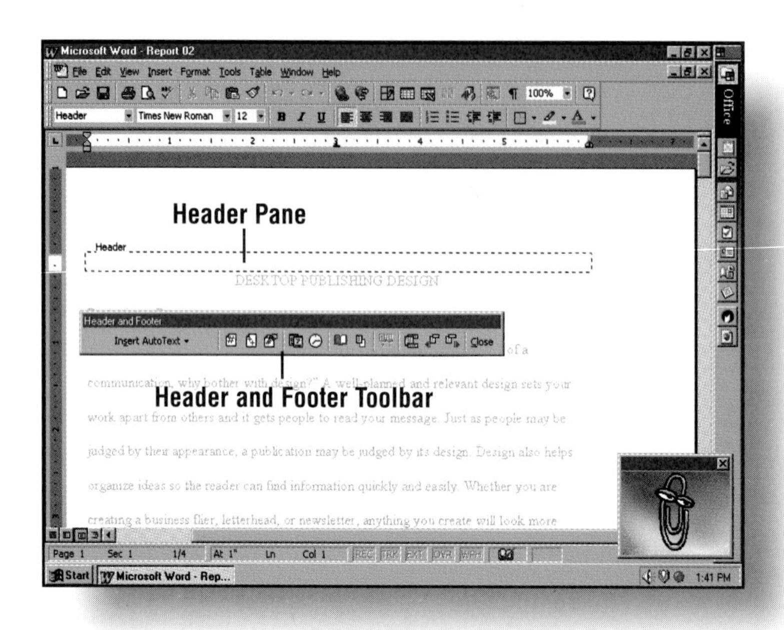

Switch Between Header and Footer

By default, the insertion point is positioned in the header pane. Key the header text in the header pane. If you are creating a footer, click the Switch Between Header and Footer button on the Header and Footer toolbar. This displays a footer pane where footer text is keyed.

Header and footer text can be formatted in the same manner as text in the document. For example, the font of header or footer text can be changed, character formatting such as bolding, italicizing, and underlining can be added, margins can be changed, and much more.

After keying the header or footer text, click the Close button on the Header and Footer toolbar. Clicking Close returns you to the previous view. If the Normal viewing mode was selected before a header was created, you are returned to the Normal viewing mode. If the Page Layout view was selected before a header was created, you are returned to that viewing mode. In the Normal viewing mode a header or footer does not display on the screen. A header or footer will display dimmed in the Page Layout viewing mode. If you want to view how a header and/or footer will print, click the Print Preview button on the Standard toolbar.

By default, a header and/or footer prints on every page in the document. Later in this chapter you will learn how to create headers/footers for specific sections of a document.

exercise 1

Creating a Header

1. Open Report 01.
2. Save the document with Save As and name it Ch 14, Ex 01.
3. Bold the title, *DESKTOP PUBLISHING*, and the four headings: *Defining Desktop Publishing*, *Initiating the Desktop Publishing Process*, *Planning the Publication*, and *Creating the Content*.
4. Create the header *Desktop Publishing* that is bolded and prints at the left margin on every page by completing the following steps:
   a. Click View, then Header and Footer.
   b. At the header pane, turn on bold, and then key **Desktop Publishing**. (If the Header and Footer toolbar is in the way, position the arrow pointer on any gray area on the toolbar or on the Title bar, hold down the left mouse button, drag the outline of the toolbar to a more desirable location, and then release the mouse button.)
   c. Click the Close button on the Header and Footer toolbar.
5. Display Print Preview to see how the header will appear on each page when printed. (Press the Page Down key to view the second and then third page of the report.) After previewing the document, close Print Preview.
6. Check page breaks in the document and, if necessary, adjust the page breaks.
7. Save the document again with the same name (Ch 14, Ex 01).
8. Print and then close Ch 14, Ex 01.

(Note: Most printers cannot print to the edge of the page. If your header does not print in exercise 1, you may need to increase the distance from the edge of the page to the header. To increase this measurement, display the Page Setup dialog box by clicking File, then Page Setup. At the Page Setup dialog box, make sure the Margins tab is selected, and then increase the number for the Header option as well as the Footer option in the From edge section of the dialog box. The amount of increase depends on your printer.)

Creating a footer is similar to creating a header. To create a footer you must switch to the footer pane. To do this, click the Switch Between Header and Footer button on the Header and Footer toolbar. Figure 14.2 displays the buttons on the Header and Footer toolbar, the name of the button, and what each button will perform.

14.2 ***Header and Footer Toolbar Buttons***

Click this button...	Named...	To do this...
Insert AutoText	Insert AutoText	Insert AutoText into header/footer.
	Insert Page Number	Insert page number in header/footer.
	Insert Number of Pages	Print the total number of pages in the active document.
	Format Page Number	Format the page numbers in the current section.
	Insert Date	Insert date in header/footer.
	Insert Time	Insert time in header/footer.
	Page Setup	Display Page Setup dialog box.
	Show/Hide Document Text	Turn on/off the display of document text.
	Same as Previous	Link/Unlink header/footer to or from previous section.
	Switch Between Header and Footer	Switch between the header pane and the footer pane.
	Show Previous	Show previous section's header/footer.
	Show Next	Show next section's header/footer.
Close	Close Header and Footer	Close header/footer pane.

Show/Hide Document Text

When creating a header or footer, the main document text is displayed but dimmed. This dimmed text can be hidden while creating a header or footer by clicking the Show/Hide Document Text button on the Header and Footer toolbar. To redisplay the dimmed document text, click the button again.

Formatting a Header or Footer

Header or footer text does not take on the character formatting of the document. For example, if you change the font for the document text, header or footer text remains at the default font. However, margin changes made to the document text do affect header or footer text.

If you want header or footer text character formatting to be the same as the document text, you must format header or footer text in the header or footer pane in the normal manner.

A header or footer contains three alignment settings. (These settings are designed to work with the default left and right margins of 1.25 inches. If changes are made to the margins, these settings may not operate as described.) If you want text aligned at the left margin, make sure the insertion point is positioned at the left side of the header or footer pane, and then key the text. To center text in the header or footer pane, press the Tab key. This moves the insertion point to a preset tab stop. From the left margin, pressing the Tab key twice will move the insertion point to the right margin of the header or footer pane. Text keyed at this tab stop will be right aligned.

Insert Page Number

With buttons on the Header and Footer toolbar, you can insert page numbering and the date and/or time in a header or footer. To insert page numbering in a header or footer, display the header or footer pane and then click the Insert Page Number button on the Header and Footer toolbar. This inserts the page number of the page where the insertion point is currently located. The correct page number will also appear on all other pages in the document. Click the Insert Date button on the Header and Footer toolbar to insert the current date in a header or footer, and click the Insert Time button to insert the current time in a header or footer.

Insert Date

Insert Time

exercise 2

Creating and Formatting a Footer

1. Open Report 02.
2. Save the document with Save As and name it Ch 14, Ex 02.
3. Select the entire document and then change the font to 12-point Century Schoolbook.
4. Bold the title, *DESKTOP PUBLISHING DESIGN*, and the two headings: *Designing a Document*, and *Creating Focus*.
5. Create the footer *Desktop Publishing Design* in 12-point Century Schoolbook bold that prints at the left margin of every page and *Page #* (where # represents the page number) in 12-point Century Schoolbook bold that prints at the right margin of every page by completing the following steps:
   a. Click View, then Header and Footer.
   b. Click the Switch Between Header and Footer button on the Header and Footer toolbar. (This displays the footer pane.)
   c. Change the font to 12-point Century Schoolbook bold.
   d. Key **Desktop Publishing Design**.
   e. Press the Tab key twice.
   f. Key **Page** and then press the space bar once.
   g. Click the Insert Page Number button on the Header and Footer toolbar.
   h. Select the page number and then change the font to 12-point Century Schoolbook bold.
   i. Click the Close button on the Header and Footer toolbar.
6. View the document in Print Preview.
7. Check page breaks in the document and, if necessary, adjust the page breaks.
8. Save the document again with the same name (Ch 14, Ex 02).
9. Print and then close Ch 14, Ex 02.

Editing a Header or Footer

Changes can be made to a header or footer in a document. There are two methods you can use to display a header or footer for editing. You can display a header or footer for editing in the Page Layout viewing mode. To do this, open the document containing the header or footer to be edited, click View, then Page Layout; or click the Page Layout View button at the left side of the horizontal scroll bar. Double-click the dimmed header or footer you want to edit. Edit the header or footer as needed and then double-click the dimmed document text to make it active.

Show Next

Show Previous

You can also display a header or footer for editing by clicking View, then Header and Footer. Click the Switch Between Header and Footer button (if you want to edit a footer), click the Show Next button or the Show Previous, if necessary, to display the header or footer you want to edit. When the proper header or footer pane is displayed, edit the header or footer as needed, and then click the Close button on the Header and Footer toolbar.

exercise 3

Editing a Footer

1. Open Ch 14, Ex 02.
2. Save the document with Save As and name it Ch 14, Ex 03.
3. Change the top margin for the report to 1.5 inches and the left and right margins to 1 inch.
4. Edit the footer by completing the following steps:
   a. Click View, then Header and Footer.
   b. Click the Switch Between Header and Footer button on the Header and Footer toolbar. (This will display the footer pane containing the footer created in exercise 2.)
   c. Delete *Desktop Publishing Design* from the footer pane. (Leave *Page #*, which is located toward the right margin.)
   d. Key **Designing Documents** at the left margin in the footer pane.
   e. Click the Close button on the Header and Footer toolbar.
5. View the document in Print Preview.
6. Check page breaks in the document and, if necessary, adjust the page breaks.
7. Save the document again with the same name (Ch 14, Ex 03).
8. Print and then close Ch 14, Ex 03.

Deleting a Header or Footer

A header or footer can be deleted from a document by deleting it from the header or footer pane. To delete a header or footer, change to the Page Layout viewing mode. Double-click the header or footer to be deleted. With the header or footer displayed in the header or footer pane, select the header or footer text and then press the Delete key. Click the Close button on the

Header and Footer toolbar to close the header or footer pane. (You can also close the header or footer pane by double-clicking the dimmed document text.)

A header or footer pane can also be displayed by clicking View, then Header and Footer. At the header pane, click the Switch Between Header and Footer, the Show Next, or the Show Previous buttons until the desired header or footer is displayed.

exercise 4

Deleting a Header and Creating a Footer

1. Open Ch 14, Ex 01.
2. Save the document with Save As and name it Ch 14, Ex 04.
3. Select the entire document and then change the font to 12-point Century Schoolbook.
4. Delete the header *Desktop Publishing* by completing the following steps:
   a. Change to the Page Layout view.
   b. Double-click the dimmed header.
   c. With the header displayed in the header pane, select the header text, and then press the Delete key.
   d. Close the header pane by double-clicking the dimmed document text.
5. Create the footer *Page* - # that prints centered and is set in 12-point Century Schoolbook bold. (Press the Tab key once to move the insertion point to the preset tab stop at the center of the footer. Click the Insert Page Number button on the Header and Footer toolbar to insert page numbering. Be sure to select the page number before changing the font to 12-point Century Schoolbook.)
6. Change the viewing mode back to Normal.
7. Check page breaks in the document and, if necessary, adjust the page breaks.
8. Save the document again with the same name (Ch 14, Ex 04).
9. Print and then close Ch 14, Ex 04. (You may want to preview the document before printing.)

Positioning a Header or Footer

Word inserts a header or footer 0.5 inch from the edge of the page. You can change this default position at the Page Setup dialog box. To change the distance from the edge of the paper, click View, then Header and Footer. Make sure the header you want to reposition is displayed. If not, click Show Next or Show Previous until it is visible. Click the Page Setup button on the Header and Footer toolbar. At the Page Setup dialog box, click the Margins tab to select it. Click the up- or down-pointing triangle after Header (located in the From edge section) until the desired measurement displays in the text box, and then click OK or press Enter. Click the Close button on the Header and Footer toolbar to close the header pane.

Page Setup

A header or footer can be positioned closer to the edge of the page by decreasing the number in the Header or Footer text box at the Page Setup dialog box. A header or footer can be positioned further from the edge of the page by increasing the number in the Header or Footer text box. If you increase the number, make sure the document top or bottom margin can accommodate the header or footer.

exercise 5

Positioning a Footer

1. Open Ch 14, Ex 04.
2. Save the document with Save As and name it Ch 14, Ex 05.
3. Change the top and bottom margins to 1.5 inches.
4. Change the position of the footer to 1 inch by completing the following steps:
   a. Click View, then Header and Footer.
   b. Click the Switch Between Header and Footer button to display the footer pane containing the footer *Page - #*.
   c. Click the Page Setup button on the Header and Footer toolbar.
   d. At the Page Setup dialog box, click the Margins tab.
   e. Select the *1"* measurement in the Footer text box (located in the From edge section) and then key **0.75**.
   f. Click OK or press Enter.
   g. Click the Close button on the Header and Footer toolbar.
5. Check page breaks in the document and, if necessary, make adjustments to the page breaks.
6. Save the document again with the same name (Ch 14, Ex 05).
7. Print and then close Ch 14, Ex 05. (You may want to preview the document before printing.)

Creating Different Headers/Footers in a Document

By default, Word will insert a header or footer on every page in the document. You can create different headers or footers within one document. For example, you can do the following:

- create a unique header or footer on the first page;
- omit a header or footer on the first page;
- create different headers or footers for odd and even pages; or
- create different headers or footers for sections in a document.

Creating a First Page Header/Footer

A different header or footer can be created on the first page of a document. To do this, position the insertion point anywhere in the first page, and then click View, then Header and Footer. (If you are creating a footer, click the

Switch Between Header and Footer button.) Click the Page Setup button on the Header and Footer toolbar. At the Page Setup dialog box, make sure the Layout tab is selected, click Different first page, and then click OK or press Enter. Key the desired text for the first page header or footer text. Click the Show Next button on the Header and Footer toolbar. (This opens another header or footer pane.) Key the text for the other header or footer that will print on all but the first page and then click Close at the Header and Footer toolbar. After creating the headers or footers, preview the document to see how the headers or footers will display when printed.

You can follow similar steps to omit a header or footer on the first page. For example, to omit a header or footer on the first page, complete the same steps as listed above except do not key text when the first header or footer pane is opened.

exercise 6

Creating a Header that Prints on All Pages Except the First Page

1. Open Report 02.
2. Save the document with Save As and name it Ch 14, Ex 06.
3. Bold the title and headings in the document.
4. Create the header *Desktop Publishing Design* that is bolded and prints at the right margin on all pages except the first page by completing the following steps:
   a. Position the insertion point anywhere in the first page.
   b. Click View, then Header and Footer.
   c. Click the Page Setup button on the Header and Footer toolbar.
   d. At the Page Setup dialog box, make sure the Layout tab is selected, and then click Different first page. (This inserts a check mark in the check box.)
   e. Click OK or press Enter.
   f. With the header pane displayed, click the Show Next button on the Header and Footer toolbar. (This opens another header pane.)
   g. Press the Tab key twice, turn on bold, and then key **Desktop Publishing Design**.
   h. Click the Close button on the Header and Footer toolbar.
5. Save the document again with the same name (Ch 14, Ex 06).
6. Print and then close Ch 14, Ex 06. (You may want to preview the document before printing.)

Creating a Header/Footer for Odd/Even Pages

Printing one header or footer on even pages and another header or footer on odd pages may be useful. You may want to do this in a document that will be bound after printing. To create a header or footer that prints on odd pages and another that prints on even pages, click View, then Header and Footer. (If you are creating a footer, click the Switch Between Header and Footer button.) Click the Page Setup button. At the Page Setup dialog box, make sure the Layout tab is selected, click Different odd and even, and then click OK or press Enter. (Make sure there is no check mark in the Different first page option.) At the odd header or footer pane, key the desired text. Click the Show Next button on the Header and Footer toolbar. At the even header or footer pane, key the desired text, and then click the Close button on the Header and Footer toolbar.

exercise 7

Creating a Footer for Odd Pages and Another for Even Pages

1. Open Report 02.
2. Save the document with Save As and name it Ch 14, Ex 07.
3. Change the font for the entire document to 12-point Century Schoolbook.
4. Create a footer that prints on all odd pages and another that prints on all even pages by completing the following steps:
   a. Click View, then Header and Footer.
   b. Click the Switch Between Header and Footer button. (This displays the footer pane.)
   c. Click the Page Setup button.
   d. At the Page Setup dialog box, make sure the Layout tab is selected, and then click Different odd and even. (Make sure there is no check mark in the Different first page option.)
   e. Click OK or press Enter.
   f. At the odd footer pane press the Tab key twice and then key **Desktop Publishing Design**.
   g. Select the footer text, *Desktop Publishing Design*, and then change the font to 12-point Century Schoolbook bold.
   h. Click the Show Next button on the Header and Footer toolbar.
   i. At the even footer pane key **Designing Documents**.
   j. Select the footer text, *Designing Documents*, and then change the font to 12-point Century Schoolbook bold.
   k. Click the Close button on the Header and Footer toolbar.
5. Save the document again with the same name (Ch 14, Ex 07).
6. Print and then close Ch 14, Ex 07. (You may want to preview the document before printing.)

Creating a Header/Footer for Different Sections

In chapter 12, you learned how to create different sections in a document. A section can be created that begins a new page or a continuous section can be created. If you want different headers and/or footers for pages in a document, divide the document into sections.

For example, if a document contains several chapters, you can create a section for each chapter, and then create a different header or footer for each section. When dividing a document into sections by chapter, insert a section break that also begins a new page.

When a header or footer is created for a specific section in a document, the header or footer can be created for all previous and next sections or just for next sections. If you want a header or footer to print on only those pages in a section and not the previous or next sections, you must deactivate the Same as Previous button. This tells Word not to print the header or footer on previous sections. Word will, however, print the header or footer on following sections. If you do not want the header or footer to print on following sections, create a blank header or footer at the next section. When creating a header or footer for a specific section in a document, preview the document to determine if the header or footer appears on the correct pages.

Same as Previous

exercise 8

Creating Footers for Different Sections

1. Open Report 03 as a read-only document.
2. Change the top margin to 1.5 inches.
3. Insert a section break that begins a new page at the line containing the module title, *MODULE 2: PLANNING A NEWSLETTER*. (Be sure to insert a section break and not a page break.)
4. Create module and page numbering footers for the two modules by completing the following steps:
   a. Position the insertion point at the beginning of the document.
   b. Click View, then Header and Footer.
   c. Click the Switch Between Header and Footer button.
   d. At the footer pane, turn on bold, key **Module 1**, and then press the Tab key twice. (This moves the insertion point to the right margin.) Key **Page**, press the space bar, key a hyphen (-), press the space bar again, and then click the Insert Page Number button on the Header and Footer toolbar.
   e. Select and then bold the page number.
   f. Click the Show Next button.
   g. Click the Same as Previous button to deactivate it.
   h. Change *Module 1* to *Module 2* in the footer.
   i. Click the Close button on the Header and Footer toolbar.
5. Check page breaks in the document and, if necessary, adjust the page breaks.
6. Save the document with Save As and name it Ch 14, Ex 08.
7. Print and then close Ch 14, Ex 08. (You may want to preview the document before printing.)

Inserting Page Numbering in a Document

Word, by default, does not print page numbers on a page. For documents such as memos and letters, this is appropriate. For longer documents, however, page numbers may be needed. Page numbers can be added to documents with options from the Page Numbers dialog box or in a header or footer. Earlier in this chapter, you learned about the Insert Page Number button on the Header and Footer toolbar. Clicking this button inserts page numbering in a header or footer.

In addition to a header or footer, page numbering can be added to a document with options from the Page Numbers dialog box shown in figure 14.3. To display this dialog box, click Insert, then Page Numbers.

figure 14.3 *Page Numbers Dialog Box*

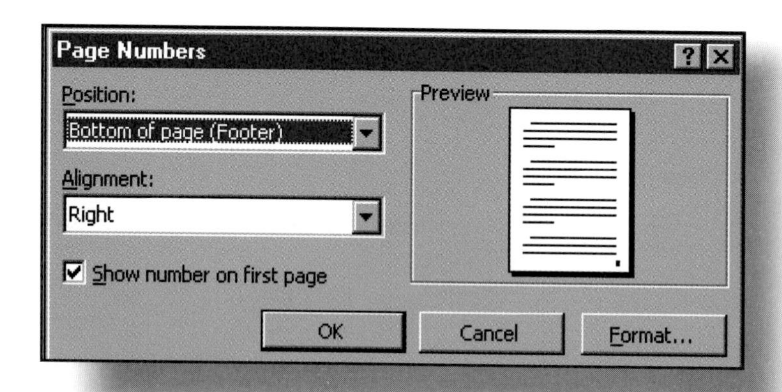

The Position option at the Page Numbers dialog box contains two choices—Top of page (Header) and Bottom of page (Footer). With choices from the Alignment option, you can insert page numbering at the left margin, center of the page, right margin, at the inside margin (the margin closest to the binding in bound material), and at the outside margin (the margin furthest from the binding in bound material).

If you turn on page numbering in a document, the page number will appear on all pages in the document including the first page. If you do not want page numbering to appear on the first page, remove the check mark from the Show number on first page option at the Page Numbers dialog box.

exercise 9

Numbering Pages at the Bottom Right Margin

1. Open Report 02.
2. Save the document with Save As and name it Ch 14, Ex 09.
3. Change the top margin to 1.5 inches and the left and right margins to 1 inch.
4. Number pages at the bottom right margin of the page by completing the following steps:

a. Click Insert, then Page Numbers.
b. At the Page Numbers dialog box, make sure the Position option displays as Bottom of page (Footer). (If not, click the down-pointing triangle after the option, and then click *Bottom of page (Footer)*.)
c. Make sure the Alignment option displays as *Right*. (If not, click the down-pointing triangle at the right of the Alignment text box, and then click *Right* at the drop-down list.)
d. Click OK or press Enter.

5. Check page breaks in the document and, if necessary, adjust the page breaks.
6. Save the document again with the same name (Ch 14, Ex 09).
7. Print and then close Ch 14, Ex 09. (You may want to preview the document before printing.)

Deleting Page Numbering

Page numbering in a document can be deleted in the same manner as deleting a header or footer. To delete page numbering in a document, click View, then Header and Footer. Display the header or footer pane containing the page numbering, select the page numbering, and then press the Delete key. Click the Close button on the Header and Footer toolbar.

Changing Page Numbering Format

At the Page Number Format dialog box shown in figure 14.4, you can change the numbering format, add chapter numbering, and specify where you want page numbering to begin and in what sections you want page numbering to appear. To display the Page Number Format dialog box, click the Format button at the Page Numbers dialog box.

14.4 **Page Number Format Dialog Box**

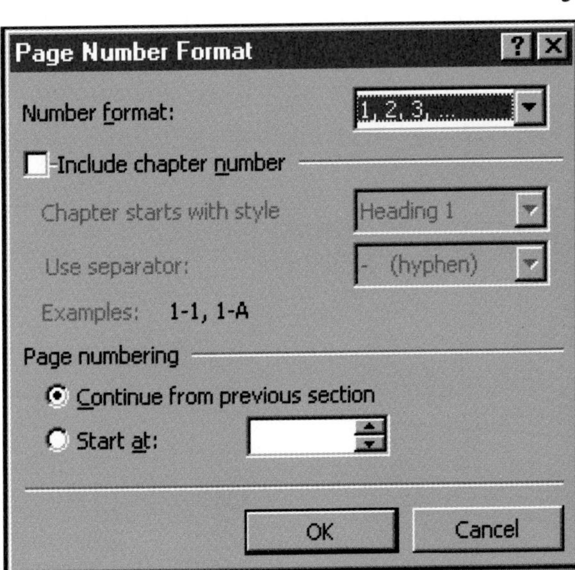

Click the Number format option from the Page Number Format dialog box to change the numbering from Arabic numbers (1, 2, 3, etc.), to lowercase letters (a, b, c, etc.), uppercase letters (A, B, C, etc.), lowercase Roman numerals (i, ii, iii, etc.), or uppercase Roman numerals (I, II, III, etc.).

Chapter numbering can be included in a document. Word will number chapters in a document if the chapter heading is formatted with a heading style. You will learn about heading styles in a later chapter.

By default, page numbering begins with 1 and continues sequentially from 1 through all pages and sections in a document. You can change the beginning page number with the Start at option at the Page Number Format dialog box. You can change the beginning page number at the beginning of the document or change the page number at the beginning of a section.

exercise 10

Numbering Pages with Roman Numerals at the Outside Margins

1. Open Report 03.
2. Save the document with Save As and name it Ch 14, Ex 10.
3. Turn on page numbering, change the page numbering to outside margins, use lowercase Roman numerals, and change the beginning number to 3 by completing the following steps:
   a. Click Insert, then Page Numbers.
   b. At the Page Numbers dialog box, change the Alignment to *Outside.*
   c. Click the Format button.
   d. At the Page Number Format dialog box, click the down-pointing triangle at the right of the Number format text box and then click *i, ii, iii, ...* at the drop-down list.
   e. Click Start at and then key **3**.
   f. Click OK or press Enter.
   g. Click OK or press Enter to close the Page Numbers dialog box.
4. Check page breaks in the document and, if necessary, adjust the page breaks.
5. Save the document again with the same name (Ch 14, Ex 10).
6. Print and then close Ch 14, Ex 10. (You may want to preview the document before printing.)

chapter summary

- Text that appears at the top of every page is called a header; text that appears at the bottom of every page is called a footer.
- When you click View, then Header and Footer, Word automatically changes the viewing mode to Page Layout, dims the text in the document, inserts a pane where the header or footer is entered, and also inserts the Header and Footer toolbar.
- To create a footer, switch to the footer pane by clicking the Switch Between Header and Footer button on the Header and Footer toolbar.
- A header or footer does not display in the Normal viewing mode but will display dimmed in the Page Layout viewing mode. To see how the header or footer will print, display Print Preview.
- Header or footer text does not take on any character formatting applied to the document. If you want header or footer text character formatting to be the same as the document text, format that text in the header or footer pane in the normal manner.
- A header or footer contains three alignment settings: left, center, and right. Press the Tab key to move the insertion point to the center alignment setting and then press the Tab key again to move the insertion point to the right alignment setting.
- With buttons on the Header and Footer toolbar, you can insert page numbering and the date and/or time in a header or footer.
- You can edit a header or footer in the Page Layout viewing mode or in the header or footer pane.
- A header or footer can be deleted at the header or footer pane. In the Page Layout viewing mode, double-click the header or footer. With the header or footer pane displayed, select the text, and then press the Delete key.
- Word inserts a header or footer 0.5 inch from the edge of the page. A header or footer can be repositioned at the Page Setup dialog box.
- You can create more than one header or footer in a document.
- Insert page numbering in a document with options from the Page Numbers dialog box or in a header or footer.

commands review

	Mouse	Keyboard
Create a Header or Footer	View, Header and Footer	View, Header and Footer
Print Preview	File, Print Preview; or click [Print Preview button] on the Standard toolbar	File, Print Preview
Page Numbers dialog box	Insert, Page Numbers	Insert, Page Numbers

check your understanding

Completion: In the space provided, indicate the correct term, command, or number needed to complete the sentence.

1. After clicking View, then Header and Footer, the insertion point is automatically positioned in the __________ pane.
2. To create a footer, click the __________ button on the Header and Footer toolbar.
3. Headers/footers can be created for different pages in a document, and they can also be created for different __________ in a document.
4. If the header you wish to edit is not visible in the header/footer pane, click the __________ button or the __________ button on the Header and Footer toolbar.
5. Click the __________ button on the Standard toolbar to see how headers/footers will look on the page when printed.
6. Create footers on odd and even pages at the __________ dialog box.
7. Page numbers do not display in the __________ viewing mode.
8. Delete page numbers in a document by first displaying the __________.
9. Display the Page Number Format dialog box by clicking __________ and then Page Numbers.
10. Change the beginning page number with the __________ option at the Page Number Format dialog box.

skill assessments

Note: Before completing the skill assessments, display the Open dialog box, and then select and delete documents created in chapter 12 that begin Ch 12. You may want to check with your instructor before deleting these documents.

Assessment 1

1. Open Report 02 as a read-only document.
2. Make the following changes to the document:
   a. Select the entire document and then change the font to 13-point Garamond.
   b. Select the title, *DESKTOP PUBLISHING DESIGN*, and then change the font to 14-point Arial bold.
   c. Select the heading *Designing a Document* and then change the font to 12-point Arial bold.
   d. Use the Format Painter to change the font to 12-point Arial bold for the heading *Creating Focus*.

e. Create the footer *Desktop Publishing Design* that is set in 12-point Arial bold and prints at the center of the footer pane.

3. Check page breaks in the document and, if necessary, adjust the page breaks.
4. Save the document with Save As and name it Ch 14, SA 01.
5. Print and then close Ch 14, SA 01. (You may want to preview the document before printing.)

Assessment 2

1. Open Ch 14, SA 01.
2. Save the document with Save As and name it Ch 14, SA 02.
3. Make the following changes to the document:
   a. Delete the footer in the document.
   b. Create the footer *Page #* (where the correct page number is inserted at the #) that is set in 12-point Arial bold and prints at the right margin on all odd pages.
   c. Create the footer *Desktop Publishing* that is set in 12-point Arial bold and prints at the left margin on all even pages.
4. Save the document again with the same name (Ch 14, SA 02).
5. Print and then close Ch 14, SA 02. (You may want to preview the document before printing.)

Assessment 3

1. Open Report 04 as a read-only document.
2. Make the following changes to the document:
   a. Select the entire document and then change the font to 12-point Century Schoolbook.
   b. Select the title, *MODULE 3: DESIGNING A NEWSLETTER*, and then change the font to 12-point Arial bold.
   c. Change the font to 12-point Arial bold for the following title and headings:
      Applying Desktop Publishing Guidelines
      MODULE 4: CREATING NEWSLETTER LAYOUT
      Choosing Paper Size and Type
      Choosing Paper Weight
      Creating Margins for Newsletters
   d. Insert a section break that begins a new page at the beginning of the line containing the title, *MODULE 4: CREATING NEWSLETTER LAYOUT*. (Be sure to insert a section break and not a page break.)
   e. Create the footer *Module 3: Designing a Newsletter*, that is set in 12-point Arial bold, is centered, and prints in the first section (the module 3 section).
   f. Create the footer *Module 4: Creating Newsletter Layout*, that is set in 12-point Arial bold, is centered, and prints in the second section (the module 4 section).
3. Check page breaks in the document and, if necessary, adjust the page breaks.
4. Save the document with Save As and name it Ch 14, SA 03.
5. Print and then close Ch 14, SA 03. (You may want to preview the document before printing.)

chapter FIFTEEN

Creating Footnotes and Endnotes

PERFORMANCE OBJECTIVES

Upon successful completion of chapter 15, you will be able to:

- **Create footnotes and endnotes.**
- **View and edit footnotes and endnotes.**
- **Move, copy, and delete footnotes and endnotes.**
- **Customize footnote and endnote settings.**
- **Convert footnotes to endnotes and endnotes to footnotes.**

A research paper or report contains information from a variety of sources. To give credit to those sources, a footnote can be inserted in the document. A *footnote* is an explanatory note or reference that is printed at the bottom of the page where it is referenced. An *endnote* is also an explanatory note or reference, but it prints at the end of the document.

Two steps are involved when creating a footnote or endnote. First, the note reference number is inserted in the document at the location where the note is referred to. The second step for creating a footnote or endnote is to key the note entry text.

Creating Footnotes and Endnotes

Footnotes and endnotes are created in a similar manner. To create a footnote in a document, you would complete the following steps:

1. Position the insertion point at the location in the document where the reference number is to appear.
2. Click Insert, then Footnote.
3. At the Footnote and Endnote dialog box shown in figure 15.1, make sure Footnote is selected, and then click OK or press Enter.
4. At the footnote pane shown in figure 15.2, key the footnote entry text.
5. Click the Close button or press Alt + Shift + C to close the footnote pane.

15.1

Footnote and Endnote Dialog Box

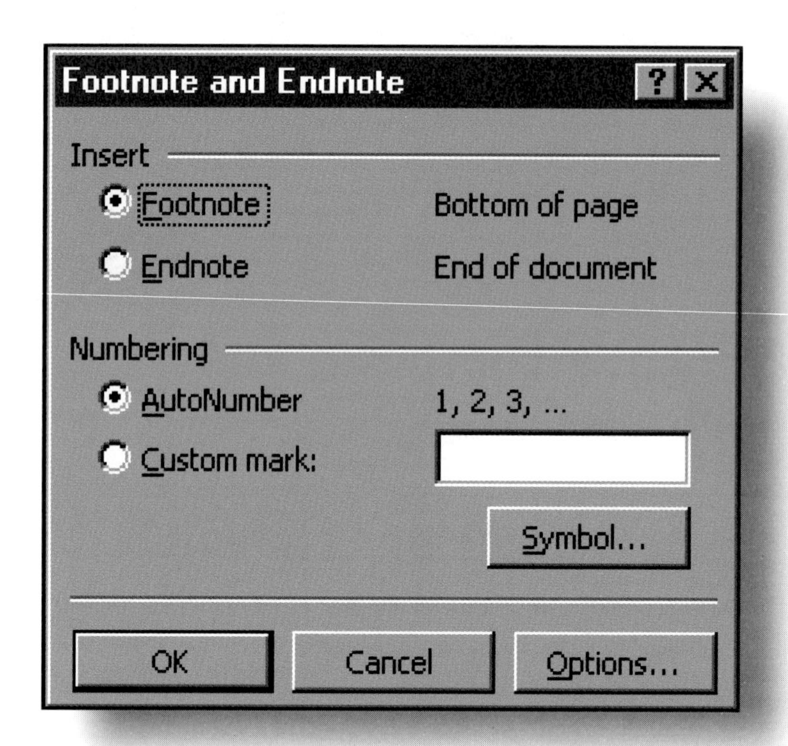

figure 15.2

Footnote Pane

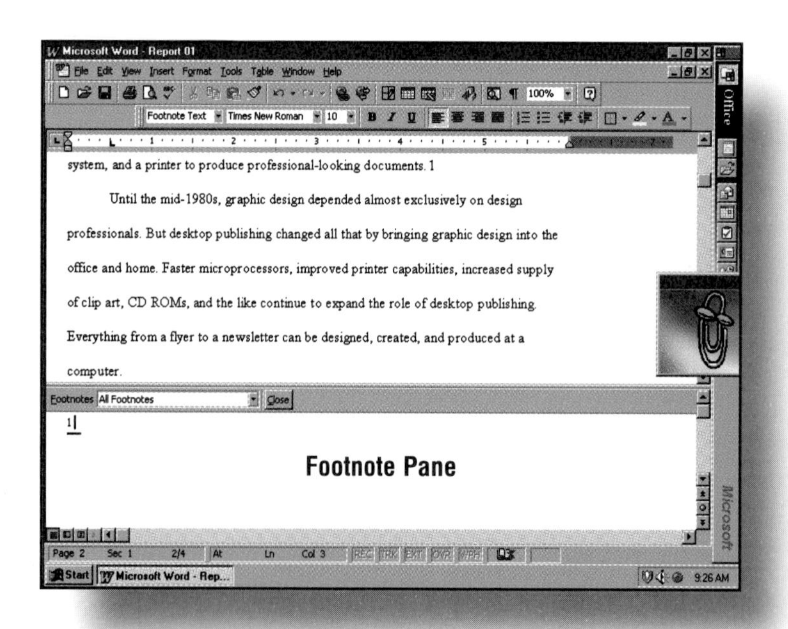

You can also create a footnote by pressing Alt + Ctrl + F. This displays the footnote pane. Key the footnote text and then click Close or press Alt + Shift + C to close the footnote pane. When creating footnotes, Word numbers footnotes with Arabic numbers (1, 2, 3, etc.).

If you press the Enter key after keying the footnote entry text, footnotes will be separated by a blank line (double space). If you do not want footnote text separated by a blank line, do not press the Enter key after keying the footnote entry text.

exercise 1

Creating Footnotes

1. Open Report 01.
2. Save the document with Save As and name it Ch 15, Ex 01.
3. Make the following changes to the document:
   a. Select the title, *DESKTOP PUBLISHING*, and then change the font to 14-point Arial bold. (If your printer does not support Arial bold, choose a similar sans serif typeface.)
   b. Select the heading, *Defining Desktop Publishing*, and then change the font to 14-point Arial bold.
   c. Use Format Painter to apply 14-point Arial bold to the remaining headings: *Initiating the Desktop Publishing Process*, *Planning the Publication*, and *Creating the Content*.
4. Create the first footnote shown in figure 15.3 at the end of the second paragraph in the *Defining Desktop Publishing* section by completing the following steps:
   a. Position the insertion point at the end of the second paragraph in the *Defining Desktop Publishing* section.
   b. Click Insert, then Footnote.
   c. At the Footnote and Endnote dialog box, make sure Footnote is selected, and then click OK or press Enter.
   d. At the footnote pane, key the first footnote shown in figure 15.3. Press the Enter key once after keying the footnote text (this will separate the first footnote from the second footnote by a blank line).
   e. Click the Close button to close the footnote pane.
5. Move the insertion point to the end of the fourth paragraph in the *Defining Desktop Publishing* section and then create the second footnote shown in figure 15.3 by completing steps similar to those in 4.
6. Move the insertion point to the end of the only paragraph in the *Initiating the Desktop Publishing Process* section and then create the third footnote shown in figure 15.3 by completing steps similar to those in 4.
7. Move the insertion point to the end of the last paragraph in the *Planning the Publication* section and then create the fourth footnote shown in figure 15.3.

8. Move the insertion point to the end of the last paragraph in the *Creating the Content* section (the last paragraph in the document) and then create the fifth footnote shown in figure 15.3.
9. Check page breaks in the document and, if necessary, adjust the page breaks.
10. Save the document again with the same name (Ch 15, Ex 01).
11. Print and then close Ch 15, Ex 01.

15.3 *Exercise 1*

Androtti, Yvonne, *Desktop Publishing Design*, Home Town Publishing, 1997, pages 102-112.

Bolle, Lynette and Jonathon Steadman, "Designing with Style," *Design Technologies*, January/February 1998, pages 22-24.

Doucette, Wayne, "Beginning the DTP Process," *Desktop Designs*, November 1997, pages 31-34.

Elstrom, Lisa, *Desktop Publishing Technologies*, Lilly-Harris Publishers, 1996, pages 88-94.

Busching, Wallace, "Designing a Newsletter," *Business Computing*, April 1997, pages 15-22.

Create an endnote in a similar manner as a footnote. At the Footnote and Endnote dialog box, click Endnote, and then click OK or press Enter. At the endnote pane, key the endnote entry text, and then click the Close button or press Alt + Shift + C.

You can also create an endnote by pressing Alt + Ctrl + E. This displays the endnote pane. Key the endnote text and then click the Close button or press Alt + Shift + C to close the endnote pane. When creating endnotes, Word numbers endnotes with lowercase Roman numerals (i, ii, iii, etc.) or Arabic numbers. The endnote numbering method will display after AutoNumber at the Footnote and Endnote dialog box. Later in this chapter, you will learn how to change the numbering method. Press the Enter key after keying the endnote entry text if you want the endnote separated from the next endnote by a blank line (double space).

Footnotes and endnotes can be formatted in the normal manner. The note reference number and the note entry number print in the default font at 8-point size. The note entry text prints in the default font size. The note reference and the note entry text can be formatted, if desired, to match the formatting of the document text.

Printing Footnotes and Endnotes

When a document containing footnotes is printed, Word automatically reduces the number of text lines on a page by the number of lines in the footnote plus two lines for spacing between the text and the footnote. If there is not enough room on the page, the footnote number and footnote entry text are taken to the next page. Word separates the footnotes from the text with a 2-inch separator line that begins at the left margin.

When endnotes are created in a document, Word prints all endnote references at the end of the document separated from the text by a 2-inch separator line.

exercise 2

Creating Endnotes

1. Open Report 02.
2. Save the document with Save As and name it Ch 15, Ex 02.
3. Make the following changes to the document:
   a. Select the entire document, then change the font to 12-point Century Schoolbook.
   b. Select the title, *DESKTOP PUBLISHING DESIGN*, and then change the font to 14-point Century Schoolbook bold.
   c. Apply 14-point Century Schoolbook bold to the headings, *Designing a Document* and *Creating Focus*.
4. Create the first endnote shown in figure 15.4 at the end of the last paragraph in the *Designing a Document* section by completing the following steps:
   a. Position the insertion point at the end of the last paragraph in the *Designing a Document* section.
   b. Click Insert, then Footnote.
   c. At the Footnote and Endnote dialog box, click Endnote.
   d. Click OK or press Enter.
   e. At the endnote pane, key the first endnote shown in figure 15.4. Press the Enter key once after keying the endnote text.
   f. Click the Close button to close the endnote pane.
5. Move the insertion point to the end of the first paragraph below the two bulleted paragraphs in the *Creating Focus* section and then create the second endnote shown in figure 15.4 by completing steps similar to those in 4.
6. Move the insertion point to the last paragraph in the document and then create the third endnote shown in figure 15.4 by completing steps similar to those in 4.
7. Check page breaks in the document and, if necessary, adjust the page breaks.
8. Save the document with the same name (Ch 15, Ex 02).
9. Print and then close Ch 15, Ex 02. (You may want to preview the document before printing.)

15.4

Exercise 2

Voller, Anthony, *Desktop Publishing Theory and Design*, Robison Publishing House, 1998, pages 82-91.

Rubiano, Lee and Eleanor Bolton, "Choosing the Right Typeface," *Designing Publications*, December 1997, pages 20-23.

Klein, Leland, "Focusing in on Your Document," *System Technologies*, March/April 1997, pages 9-12.

Viewing and Editing Footnotes and Endnotes

To edit existing footnote or endnote entry text, display the footnote or endnote text or the pane. There are several methods you can use for displaying the footnote or endnote text or pane.

In the Normal viewing mode, the footnote or endnote text does not display. To display footnotes or endnotes, change the viewing mode to Page Layout. Footnotes will display at the bottom of the page where they are referenced and endnotes will display at the end of the document. Footnotes or endnotes can be edited in the normal manner in the Page Layout viewing mode.

Display a footnote or endnote pane by choosing View, then Footnotes. (The Footnotes option is dimmed unless an open document contains footnotes or endnotes.) If the document contains footnotes, the footnote pane is opened. If the document contains endnotes, the endnote pane is opened. If the document contains both footnotes and endnotes, you can switch between the panes by choosing All Footnotes or All Endnotes from the view text box at the top of the footnote or endnote pane. To do this, click the down-pointing triangle at the right side of the view text box at the top of the pane, and then click *All Footnotes* or *All Endnotes*.

You can display a footnote or endnote pane in the Normal viewing mode with the split bar. The split bar is the small gray bar located immediately above the up-pointing triangle at the top of the vertical scroll bar. To view a footnote or endnote pane, position the arrow pointer on the split bar until it turns into a double line with an up- and down-pointing arrow. Hold down the Shift key and the left mouse button, drag the split bar down to somewhere in the middle of the document screen, and then release the mouse button and then the Shift key. The document displays in the upper portion of the split window and the footnote or endnote displays in the lower portion of the split window.

To close a footnote or endnote pane, you can click the Close button, drag the split bar back up to the top of the screen, or double-click the split bar.

Another method for opening a footnote or endnote pane is to double-click the footnote or endnote reference number in the document text. You can close a footnote or endnote pane by double-clicking the number before the footnote or endnote entry text in the pane.

With the footnote or endnote pane visible, you can move the insertion point between the pane and the document. To do this with the mouse, position the arrow pointer in the document text, click the left mouse button or position the arrow pointer in the footnote or endnote pane, and then click the left mouse button. If you are using the keyboard, press F6 to move the insertion point to the next pane. You can also press Shift + F6, which moves the insertion point to the previous pane.

exercise 3

Editing Footnotes

1. Open Ch 15, Ex 01.
2. Save the document with Save As and name it Ch 15, Ex 03.
3. Edit the footnotes by completing the following steps:
   a. Change the viewing mode to Page Layout.
   b. Move the insertion point to the bottom of the second page until the second footnote is visible.
   c. Make the following changes to the second footnote:
      1) Change *January/February* to *May/June*.
      2) Change *22-24* to *31-33*.
   d. Move the insertion point to the bottom of the third page until the fourth footnote is visible, then make the following changes to the fourth footnote:
      1) Change *Lilly-Harris Publishers* to *Gray Mountain Press*.
      2) Change *1996* to *1997*.
   e. Change the viewing mode back to Normal.
4. Save the document again with the same name (Ch 15, Ex 03).
5. Print and then close Ch 15, Ex 03.

exercise 4

Editing Endnotes

1. Open Ch 15, Ex 02.
2. Save the document with Save As and name it Ch 15, Ex 04.
3. Display the endnote pane and then change the font of the endnotes by completing the following steps:
   a. Click View, then Footnotes.
   b. At the endnote pane, select all endnote entry text and endnote numbers, and then change the font to 12-point Century Schoolbook.

c. Click the Close button to close the endnote pane.
4. Save the document again with the same name (Ch 15, Ex 04).
5. Print and then close Ch 15, Ex 04. (You may want to preview the document before printing.)

Finding Footnotes or Endnotes

In a document containing footnotes or endnotes, you can move the insertion point to a particular footnote or endnote at the Find and Replace dialog box with the Go To tab selected. To display this dialog box, click Edit, then Go To, or press Ctrl + G. You can also display the Find and Replace dialog box with the Go To tab selected by double-clicking the numbers on the Status bar that display the current page where the insertion point is positioned, a forward slash (/), and then the total number of pages in the document.

At the Find and Replace dialog box with the Go To tab selected, click *Footnote* in the Go to what list box. Click in the Enter footnote number text box, key the desired footnote number, and then click the Go To button. When the insertion point is positioned on the desired footnote or endnote reference number, click the Close button in the Find and Replace dialog box.

In the Page Layout viewing mode, you can move the insertion point to a particular footnote or endnote reference number in the document text or to an entry number in a footnote or endnote pane. To move the insertion point to a specific entry number in a footnote pane, position the insertion point on the reference number in the document text and then double-click the left mouse button. To move the insertion point to a specific reference number in the text document, double-click the entry text number in the footnote or endnote pane.

exercise 5

Displaying and Editing a Footnote

1. Open Ch 15, Ex 01.
2. Save the document with Save As and name it Ch 15, Ex 05.
3. Go to footnote number 3 and then edit the footnote by completing the following steps:
   a. Double-click the numbers *1/4* toward the left side of the Status bar.
   b. At the Find and Replace dialog box with the Go To tab selected, click *Footnote* in the Go to what list box.
   c. Click inside the Enter footnote number text box and then key **3**.
   d. Click the Go To button.
   e. When the insertion point is positioned on the footnote reference number 3, click the Close button to close the Find and Replace dialog box.

f. With the insertion point still positioned on the footnote reference number, double-click the mouse button. (This displays the footnote pane.)
g. Make the following changes to the third footnote:
   1) Change the name from *Doucette, Wayne* to *Matheson, Felicia*.
   2) Change the page numbers from *31-34* to *47-50*.
h. Click the Close button to close the footnote pane.

4. Save the document again with the same name (Ch 15, Ex 05).
5. Print only the page where footnote 3 is located.
6. Close Ch 15, Ex 05.

Moving, Copying, or Deleting Footnotes or Endnotes

Footnote or endnote reference numbers can be moved, copied, or deleted in a document. If a footnote or endnote reference number is moved, copied, or deleted, all footnotes or endnotes remaining in the document are automatically renumbered. To move a footnote or endnote in a document, select the reference mark of the footnote or endnote that you want moved, and then click Edit, then Cut; or click the Cut button on the Standard toolbar. Position the insertion point at the location where you want the footnote or endnote reference inserted and then click Edit, then Paste; or click the Paste button on the Standard toolbar. You can also move a reference number to a different location in the document by selecting the reference number and then dragging it to the desired location.

To copy a reference number, you would complete similar steps as used for moving except you would click Edit, then Copy; or click the Copy button on the Standard toolbar. A reference number can also be copied to a different location in the document by selecting the reference number, holding down the Ctrl key, dragging the reference number to the desired location, and then releasing the mouse key and then the Ctrl key.

To delete a footnote or endnote from a document, select the reference number, and then press the Delete key or the Backspace key. When the reference number is deleted, the entry text is also deleted.

exercise 6

Editing and Deleting Footnotes

1. Open Ch 15, Ex 01.
2. Save the document with Save As and name it Ch 15, Ex 06.
3. Select the entire document and then change the font to 12-point Century Schoolbook.
4. Display the footnote pane and then change the font to 12-point Century Schoolbook by completing the following steps:
   a. Click View, then Footnotes.

b. At the footnote pane, select all footnote entry text and footnote numbers, and then change the font to 12-point Century Schoolbook.
c. Click the Close button to close the footnote pane.
5. Delete the fourth footnote by completing the following steps:
a. Move the insertion point to the fourth footnote reference number in the document text.
b. Select the fourth footnote reference number and then press the Delete key or the Backspace key.
6. Move the third footnote reference number from the end of the only paragraph in *Initiating the Desktop Publishing Process* section to the end of the second paragraph in the *Planning the Publication* section by completing the following steps:
a. Move the insertion point to the third footnote reference number.
b. Select the third footnote reference number.
c. Click the Cut button on the Standard toolbar.
d. Position the insertion point at the end of the second paragraph in the *Planning the Publication* section.
e. Click the Paste button on the Standard toolbar.
7. Check page breaks in the document and, if necessary, adjust the page breaks.
8. Save the document again with the same name (Ch 15, Ex 06).
9. Print and then close Ch 15, Ex 06.

Customizing Footnote or Endnote Settings

Footnotes or endnotes contain default settings. These default settings can be changed with options from the footnote or endnote pane or with options from the Note Options dialog box. When a footnote or endnote pane is visible, a view text box displays at the upper left corner of the pane. If you click the down-pointing triangle at the right side of this text box, a drop-down menu displays as shown in figure 15.5. (The options will change depending on whether a footnote or endnote pane is open.)

15.5 **Footnote Pane Text Box Drop-Down Menu**

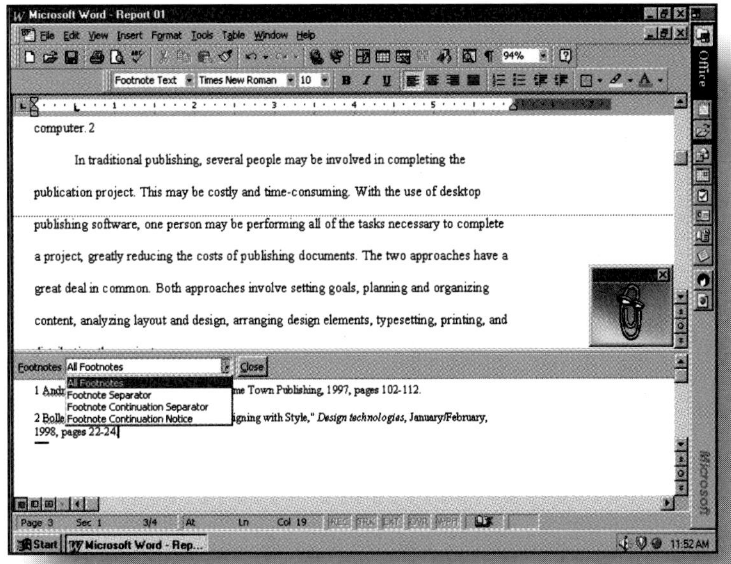

By default, Word inserts a 2-inch separator line that begins at the left margin and separates footnotes or endnotes from document text. Choose the *Footnote Separator* option to customize this line. When you click *Footnote Separator*, the pane display changes and shows the default separator line. Edit this line as desired. For example, you can delete it, change the position of the line, or lengthen or shorten the line. After customizing the line, click the Close button. Click the Reset button if you want to reset the separator line back to the default. Complete similar steps to customize the endnote separator line.

If a footnote or endnote continues onto more than one page, Word inserts a continuation separator line between the note and the document text. This continuation separator line prints from the left to the right margin. Choose the *Footnote Continuation Separator* option if you want to customize the footnote continuation separator line. After customizing the line, click the Close button to close the pane. Complete similar steps to customize a continuation separator line for endnotes.

If a footnote or endnote is continued on the next page, you can add text indicating that the note is continued on the next page. To do this, click the *Footnote Continuation Notice* option at the drop-down list, key the text you want to indicate that the note is continued, and then click the Close button. Complete similar steps to add continuation text to endnotes.

With options from the Note Options dialog box with the All Footnotes tab selected, shown in figure 15.6, you can further customize footnotes. To display this dialog box, click Insert, then Footnote. At the Footnote and Endnote dialog box, click the Options button. The Note Options dialog box will display in a similar manner if the All Endnotes tab is selected.

Note Options Dialog Box with All Footnotes Tab Selected

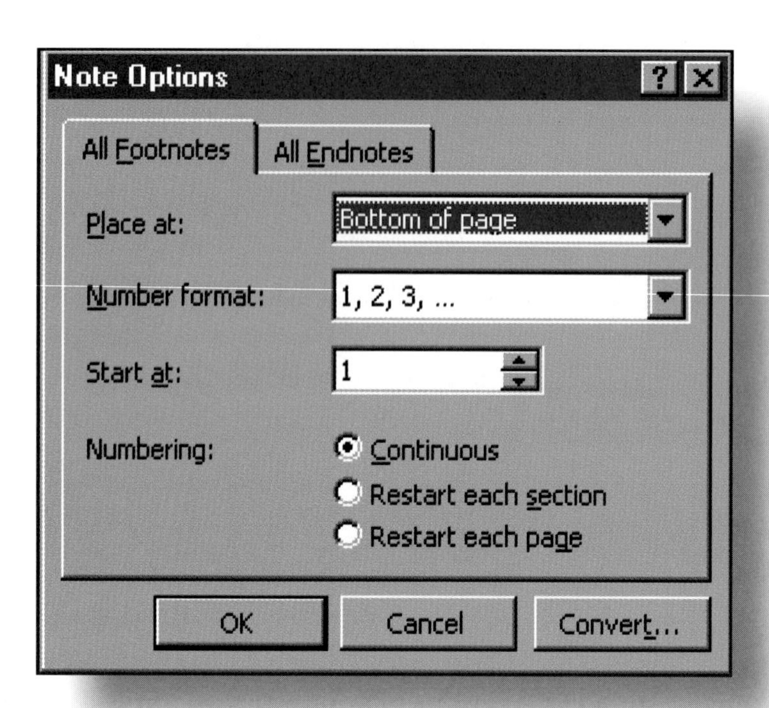

With the Place at option you can specify whether footnotes are printed at the bottom of the page or beneath text. By default, Word prints footnotes at the bottom of the page even if the text does not fill the entire page. Choose the *Beneath text* option from Place at if you want the footnote to print below the last line of text on the page.

The Place at option at the Note Options dialog box with the All Endnotes tab selected contains the choices *End of document* or *End of section*. At the default setting of *End of document*, endnotes print at the end of the document. Change this to *End of section* if you want endnotes to print at the end of the section in the document.

Word numbers footnotes with Arabic numbers and endnotes with lowercase Roman numerals. Change this default numbering with the Number format option at the Note Options dialog box. You can choose Arabic numbers, lowercase letters, uppercase letters, lowercase Roman numerals, uppercase Roman numerals, or special symbols.

Footnotes or endnotes are numbered sequentially beginning with 1. Use the Start at option from the Note Options dialog box if you want to change the beginning footnote or endnote number.

Word numbers footnotes or endnotes sequentially from the beginning to the end of a document. With options from the Numbering section of the Note Options dialog box you can change this to Restart each section, which restarts numbering at the beginning of each section, or Restart each page, which restarts numbering at the beginning of each page. (The Restart each page option is not available if the All Endnotes tab is selected.)

Footnotes or endnotes can be numbered with a symbol. To do this, click the Custom mark option at the Footnote and Endnote dialog box. (To display the Footnote and Endnote dialog box, click Insert, then Footnote.) To specify a symbol, click the Symbol button. This displays the Symbol dialog box. At the Symbol dialog box, click the desired symbol, and then click OK or press Enter. This inserts the selected symbol in the Custom mark text box. Continue creating the footnote or endnote in the normal manner.

exercise 7

Customizing Footnotes

1. Open Ch 15, Ex 06.
2. Save the document with Save As and name it Ch 15, Ex 07.
3. Customize the footnotes by completing the following steps:
   a. Click View, then Footnotes.
   b. At the footnote pane, click the down-pointing triangle to the right of the view text box, and then click *Footnote Separator*.
   c. At the footnote separator pane, click the Center button on the Standard toolbar. (This centers the separator line between the left and right margins.)
   d. Click the Close button to close the separator pane.
   e. Click Insert, then Footnote.
   f. At the Footnote and Endnote dialog box, click the Options button.
   g. At the Note Options dialog box, make sure the All Footnotes tab is selected.
   h. Click the down-pointing triangle at the right of the Place at text box and then click *Beneath text* at the drop-down list.
   i. Click the up-pointing triangle after the Start at option until *5* displays in the text box.
   j. Click OK or press Enter to close the Note Options dialog box.
   k. Click the Close button to close the Footnote and Endnote dialog box.
4. Check page breaks in the document and, if necessary, adjust the page breaks.
5. Save the document again with the same name (Ch 15, Ex 07).
6. Print and then close Ch 15, Ex 07.

Converting Footnotes and Endnotes

Word provides an option at the Note Options dialog box that lets you convert footnotes to endnotes or endnotes to footnotes. To use this option, display the Note Options dialog box, and then click the Convert button. At the Convert Notes dialog box shown in figure 15.7, specify whether you want to convert footnotes to endnotes or endnotes to footnotes, and then click OK. Close the Note Options dialog box and then the Footnote and Endnote dialog box.

15.7

Convert Notes Dialog Box

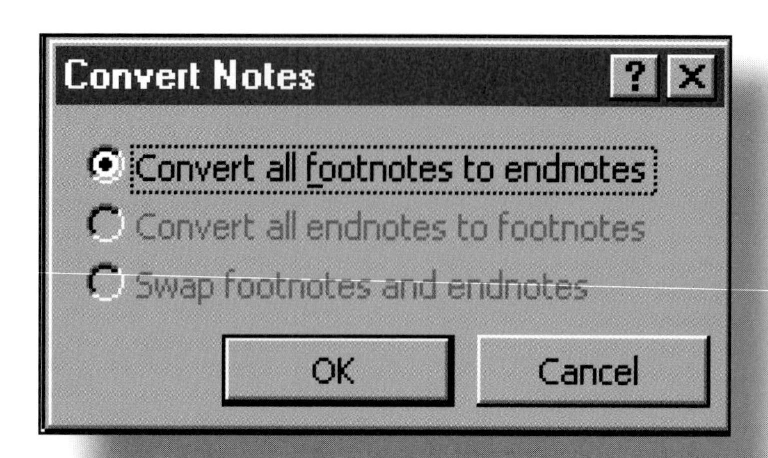

All footnotes and endnotes or individual footnotes or endnotes can be converted. To convert an individual endnote or footnote, click View, then Footnotes. Select the footnote or endnote to be converted. Position the insertion point in the footnote or endnote pane, and then click the *right* mouse button. At the shortcut menu that displays, click Convert to Footnote or Convert to Endnote. Click the Close button to close the footnote or endnote pane.

exercise 8

Converting Footnotes to Endnotes

1. Open Ch 15, Ex 06.
2. Save the document with Save As and name it Ch 15, Ex 08.
3. Convert the footnotes to endnotes by completing the following steps:
   a. Click Insert, then Footnote.
   b. At the Footnote and Endnote dialog box, click the Options button.
   c. At the Note Options dialog box, click the Convert button.
   d. At the Convert Notes dialog box, the Convert all footnotes to endnotes option is already selected so click OK or press Enter to close the Convert Notes dialog box.
   e. Click OK or press Enter to close the Note Options dialog box.
   f. Click the Close button to close the Footnote and Endnote dialog box.
4. Check page breaks in the document and, if necessary, adjust the page breaks.
5. Save the document again with the same name (Ch 15, Ex 08).
6. Print and then close Ch 15, Ex 08.

chapter summary

- Footnotes and endnotes are explanatory notes or references. Footnotes are printed at the bottom of the page; endnotes, at the end of the document.
- The first step in creating a footnote/endnote is to insert the note reference number at the location in the document where the note is referred to. The second step is to key the note entry text.
- The footnote/endnote text is keyed at the footnote or endnote pane.
- By default, footnotes are numbered with Arabic numbers; endnotes are numbered with lowercase Roman numerals.
- The note reference number and the note entry text can be formatted to match the formatting of the document text.
- When printing a document containing footnotes, Word reduces the number of text lines on a page by the number of lines in the footnote plus two lines. Word separates footnotes and endnotes from the text with a 2-inch separator line.
- Footnotes and endnotes can be viewed and edited in the Page Layout viewing mode. Several methods can be used to edit at the footnote/endnote pane.
- You can use the Find and Replace dialog box with the Go To tab selected to move the insertion point to a particular footnote or endnote.
- Several methods can be used to move or copy a reference number within a document. If a footnote or endnote reference number is moved, copied, or deleted, all other footnotes/endnotes are automatically renumbered.
- To delete a footnote or endnote, select the reference number, and then press the Delete key or the Backspace key.
- The footnote or endnote default settings can be changed with options from the footnote or endnote pane or from the Note Options dialog box. Customizing changes can be made to the separator line, the footnote location, and the reference numbers.
- Footnotes can be converted to endnotes, or endnotes converted to footnotes, at the Convert Notes dialog box.

commands review

	Mouse	Keyboard
Footnote and Endnote dialog box	Insert, Footnote	Insert, Footnote
Create a footnote at the footnote pane	Insert, Footnote, Footnote	ALT + CTRL + F
Create an endnote at the endnote pane	Insert, Footnote, Endnote	ALT + CTRL + E
Close footnote or endnote pane	Close	ALT + SHIFT + C

Edit the footnote	View, Footnotes; or with arrow pointer on split bar, hold Shift key and left mouse button, drag to middle of screen, release; or double-click reference number	ALT + CTRL + F
Edit the endnote	View, Footnotes; or with arrow pointer on split bar, hold Shift key and left mouse button, drag to middle of screen, release; or double-click reference number	ALT + CTRL + E
Note Options dialog box	At the Footnote and Endnote dialog box, click Options	At the Footnote and Endnote dialog box, choose Options
Convert Notes dialog box	At the Footnote and Endnote dialog box, click Options, then click Convert	At the Footnote and Endnote dialog box, choose Options, then choose Convert

check your understanding

Completion: In the space provided, indicate the correct term, command, or number.

1. To display the Footnote and Endnote dialog box, first click this option on the Menu bar. ____________
2. The footnote entry text is keyed here. ____________
3. By default, each footnote is separated by this number of blank lines. ____________
4. This is the keyboard command to access the footnote pane. ____________
5. Word numbers footnotes with this type of number. ____________
6. Display the Find and Replace dialog box with this tab selected to locate a specific footnote or endnote. ____________
7. One way to begin moving a reference number to another location is by selecting the reference mark and then clicking this option on the Menu bar. ____________
8. One way to copy a reference number to a different location is to select the number, hold down this key, and then drag the number to the desired location. ____________
9. If you want footnotes to begin with a number other than 1, display this dialog box. ____________

10. Footnotes or endnotes can be easily edited in this viewing mode. ____________

11. By default, Word separates footnotes from text in the document by this. ____________

12. Convert footnotes to endnotes with an option at this dialog box. ____________

skill assessments

Note: Before completing the skill assessments, display the Open dialog box, and then select and delete documents created in chapter 13 that begin Ch 13. You may want to check with your instructor before deleting these documents.

Assessment 1

1. Open Report 04.
2. Save the document with Save As and name it Ch 15, SA 01.
3. Make the following changes to the report:
   a. Insert a section break that begins a new page at the line containing the title, *MODULE 4: CREATING A NEWSLETTER LAYOUT.*
   b. Number each page except the first page at the upper right corner of the page.
   c. Create the first footnote shown in figure 15.8 at the end of the first paragraph in the *Applying Desktop Publishing Guidelines* section of the report.
   d. Create the second footnote shown in figure 15.8 at the end of the third paragraph in the *Applying Desktop Publishing Guidelines* section of the report.
   e. Create the third footnote shown in figure 15.8 at the end of the last paragraph in the *Applying Desktop Publishing Guidelines* section of the report (middle of the second page).
   f. Create the fourth footnote shown in figure 15.8 at the end of the only paragraph in the *Choosing Paper Size and Type* section of the report.
   g. Create the fifth footnote shown in figure 15.8 at the end of the only paragraph in the *Choosing Paper Weight* section of the report.
4. Check page breaks in the document and, if necessary, adjust the page breaks.
5. Save the document again with the same name (Ch 15, SA 01).
6. Print and then close Ch 15, SA 01.

Figure 15.8 • Assessment 1

Habermann, James, "Designing a Newsletter," *Desktop Designs*, January/February 1997, pages 23-29.

Pilante, Shirley G., "Adding Pizzazz to Your Newsletter," *Desktop Publisher*, September 1998, pages 32-39.

Maddock, Arlita G., "Guidelines for a Better Newsletter," *Business Computing*, June 1998, pages 9-14.

Alverso, Monica, "Paper Styles for Newsletters," *Design Technologies*, March 14, 1997, pages 45-51.

Alverso, Monica, "Paper Styles for Newsletters," *Design Technologies*, March 14, 1997, pages 52-53.

Assessment 2

1. Open Ch 15, SA 01.
2. Save the document with Save As and name it Ch 15, SA 02.
3. Make the following changes to the report:
   a. Select the entire document and then change the font to 12-point Century Schoolbook.
   b. Display the footnote pane, select all the footnotes, and then change the font to 12-point Century Schoolbook.
   c. Move the first footnote (the one after the first paragraph in the *Applying Desktop Publishing Guidelines* section) to the end of the fourth paragraph in the *Applying Desktop Publishing Guidelines* section.
   d. Delete the third footnote.
   e. Center the footnote separator line between the left and right margins.
4. Check page breaks in the document and, if necessary, adjust the page breaks.
5. Save the document again with the same name (Ch 15, SA 02).
6. Print and then close Ch 15, SA 02.

Assessment 3

1. Open Ch 15, SA 01.
2. Save the document with Save As and name it Ch 15, SA 03.
3. Make the following changes to the report:
   a. Change the font to 13-point Garamond for the document text and the footnotes.
   b. Convert the footnotes to endnotes.
   c. Make sure the endnotes are numbered with Arabic numbers. If they are not, change the numbering format to Arabic numbers.
4. Check page breaks in the document and, if necessary, adjust the page breaks.
5. Save the document again with the same name (Ch 15, SA 03).
6. Print and then close Ch 15, SA 03.

chapter SIXTEEN

Completing a Find and Replace

PERFORMANCE OBJECTIVES

Upon successful completion of chapter 16, you will be able to:

- **Find specific text or formatting in a document.**
- **Find specific text or formatting in a document and replace it with other text or formatting.**

With Word's Find and Replace feature, you can look for a specific word(s) or formatting within a document. This is helpful in locating the specific name of a person or company, a particular phrase, or a format. Once Word finds the text or formatting, you can delete it or edit the text as needed. You can also use the Find and Replace feature to find specific text or formatting and replace it with other text or formatting.

Finding Text

If you compose many documents at the keyboard, the Find and Replace feature can be helpful in locating words or phrases that are overused within a document. For example, if you overuse the phrase *I feel that...* in a document, you can find every occurrence of the phrase, and then decide to leave it in the document or edit it. The Find and Replace feature can also be used to move quickly to a specific location in a document. This is particularly useful in long documents if you want to position the insertion point at a specific location within a page.

To find specific text or formatting in a document, click Edit, and then Find. This displays the Find and Replace dialog box with the Find tab selected as shown in figure 16.1. Enter the characters for which you are searching in the Find what text box. You can enter up to 256 characters in this text box. Click the Find Next button and Word searches for and selects the first occurrence of the text in the document. Make corrections to the text if needed and then search for the next occurrence by clicking the Find Next button again. Click the Cancel button to close the Find and Replace dialog box.

16.1 *Find and Replace Dialog Box with Find Tab Selected*

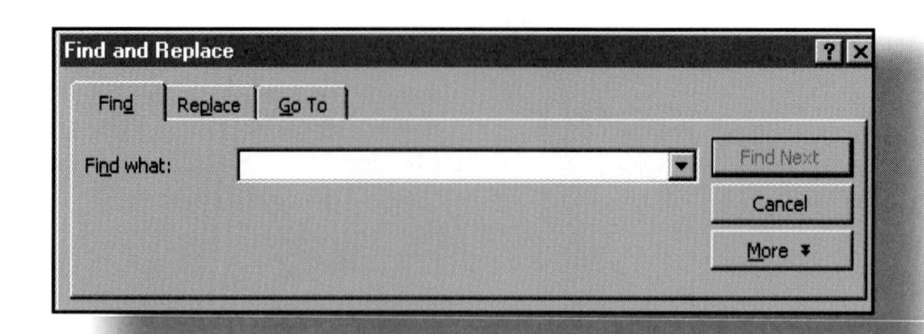

exercise 1

Finding Words

1. Open Report 01.
2. Find every occurrence of *desktop publishing* in the document by completing the following steps:
   a. With the insertion point positioned at the beginning of the document, click Edit, and then Find.
   b. At the Find and Replace dialog box with the Find tab selected, key **desktop publishing** in the Find what text box.
   c. Click the Find Next button.
   d. Word searches for and selects the first occurrence of *desktop publishing.*
   e. Search for the next occurrence of *desktop publishing* by clicking the Find Next button again.
   f. Continue clicking the Find Next button until the Office Assistant displays the message *Word has finished searching the document.*
   g. Click the Cancel button to close the Find and Replace dialog box (and remove the Office Assistant message).
3. Close Report 01.

The next time you open the Find and Replace dialog box, you can display a list of text for which you have searched by clicking the down-pointing triangle after the Find what text box. For example, if you searched for *type size* and then performed another search for *type style,* the third time you open the Find and Replace dialog box, clicking the down-pointing triangle after the Find what text box will display a drop-down list with *type style* and *type size.* Click text from this drop-down list if you want to perform a search on that text.

Choosing Find Check Box Options

The Find and Replace dialog box contains a variety of check boxes with options you can choose for completing a search. To display these options, click the More button located in the bottom right corner of the dialog box. This causes the Find and Replace dialog box to expand as shown in figure 16.2. Each option and what will occur if it is selected is described in figure 16.3.

16.2 ***Expanded Find and Replace Dialog Box***

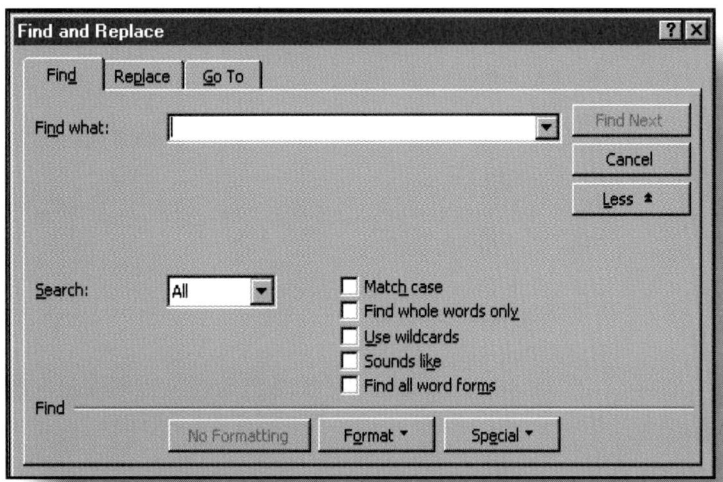

16.3 ***Options at the Find and Replace Dialog Box with the Find Tab Selected***

Choose this option	To
Match case	Exactly match the case of the search text. For example, if you search for *Book* and select the Match case option, Word will stop at *Book* but not *book* or *BOOK*.
Find whole words only	Find a whole word, not a part of a word. For example, if you search for *her* and did not select Find whole words only, Word would stop at t*here*, *here*, *her*s, etc.
Use wildcards	Search for wildcards, special characters, or special search operators.
Sounds like	Match words that sound alike but are spelled differently such as *know* and *no*.
Find all word forms	Find all forms of the word entered in the Find what text box. For example, if you enter *hold*, Word will stop at *held* and *holding*.

To remove the display of options toward the bottom of the Find and Replace dialog box, click the Less button. (The Less button was previously the More button.)

Choosing a Find Direction

The Search option at the Find and Replace dialog box has a default setting of All. At this setting, Word will search the entire document. This can be changed to Up or Down. Choose *Up* and Word will search the document from the insertion point to the beginning of the document. Choose *Down* and Word will search the document from the insertion point to the end of the document.

exercise 2

Finding Whole Words and Word Forms

1. Open Para 05.
2. Find every occurrence of the word *publishing* that exactly matches the case by completing the following steps:
   a. Make sure the insertion point is positioned at the beginning of the document.
   b. Click Edit, and then Find.
   c. At the Find and Replace dialog box with the Find tab selected, key **publishing** in the Find what text box.
   d. Click the More button located in the bottom right corner of the dialog box.
   e. Click the Match case option. (This inserts a check mark in the check box.)
   f. Click the Find whole words only option. (This inserts a check mark in the check box.)
   g. Click the Find Next button.
   h. Word searches for and selects the first occurrence of *publishing* (that exactly matches the case).
   i. Search for the next occurrence of *publishing* by clicking the Find Next button.
   j. Continue clicking the Find Next button until the Office Assistant displays the message *Word has finished searching the document.*
   k. Click the Cancel button to close the Find and Replace dialog box.
3. Find every occurrence of the word *produce* and all its word forms by completing the following steps:
   a. Make sure the insertion point is positioned at the beginning of the document.
   b. Click Edit, and then Find.
   c. At the Find and Replace dialog box with the Find tab selected, key **produce** in the Find what text box.

d. Click the Find all word forms option. (If this option if not visible, click the More button.)
e. Click the Find Next button.
f. Word searches for and selects the first occurrence of *produce* (or a word form of *produce*).
g. Search for the next occurrence of *produce* (or a word form of *produce*) by clicking the Find Next button.
h. Continue clicking the Find Next button until the Office Assistant displays the message *Word has finished searching the document.*
i. Remove the check mark from the Find all word forms option.
j. Click the Less button to turn off the display of the options toward the bottom of the dialog box.
k. Click the Cancel button to close the Find and Replace dialog box.

4. Close Para 05.

Finding Formatting

You can search a document for some character and paragraph formatting. For example, you can search for bold characters, characters set in a specific font, as well as some paragraph formatting such as indents and spacing. To search for specific formatting, display the Find and Replace dialog box with the Find tab selected, and then click the Format button. (If this button is not visible, click the More button.) At the pop-up list that displays, click the type of formatting for which you are searching (such as *Font* or *Paragraph*). At the specific formatting dialog box that displays, identify the formatting, and then close the dialog box. The formatting for which you are searching displays below the Find what text box.

The text and/or formatting that you searched for previously remains in the Find what text box. The next time you perform a search, the text you key in the Find what text box will replace the existing text. This does not, however, remove formatting. To remove previous formatting, click the No Formatting button that displays at the bottom of the expanded Find and Replace dialog box.

exercise 3

Finding Formatting

1. Open Survey 01.
2. Find all text set in bold by completing the following steps:
   a. Make sure the insertion point is positioned at the beginning of the document and then click Edit, and then Find.
   b. With the insertion point positioned in the Find what text box, press the Delete key. (This deletes any text that displays in the text box.)

c. Click the More button. (This expands the dialog box and displays additional options.)
d. Click the Format button.
e. At the pop-up list that displays, click *Font*.
f. At the Find Font dialog box, click *Bold* in the Font style list box.
g. Click OK or press Enter to close the Find Font dialog box.
h. At the Find and Replace dialog box, click the Find Next button.
i. Continue clicking the Find Next button until the Office Assistant displays the message *Word has finished searching the document.*
j. Click the Less button to turn off the display of the additional options.
k. Click the Cancel button to close the Find and Replace dialog box.

3. Close Survey 01.

Finding and Replacing Text

With Word's Find and Replace feature, you can look for specific characters or formatting and replace with other characters or formatting. With the Find and Replace feature, you can:

- Use abbreviations for common phrases when entering text and then replace the abbreviations with the actual text later.
- Set up standard documents with generic names and replace them with other names to make personalized documents.
- Find and replace formatting.

To use Find and Replace, click Edit, and then Replace. This displays the Find and Replace dialog box with the Replace tab selected as shown in figure 16.4.

16.4 *Find and Replace Dialog Box with the Replace Tab Selected*

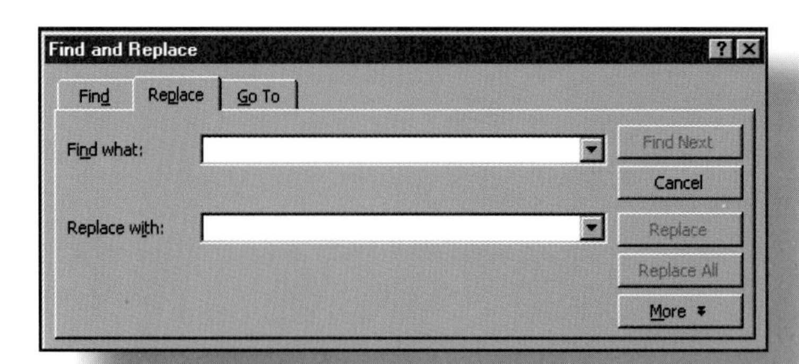

Enter the characters and/or formatting for which you are searching in the Find what text box. Press the Tab key to move the insertion point to the Replace with text box and then key the replacement text or insert the replacement formatting. You can also move the insertion point to the Replace with text box by clicking inside the text box.

The Find and Replace dialog box contains several command buttons at the right side. Click the Find Next button to tell Word to find the next occurrence of the characters and/or formatting. Click the Replace button to replace the characters or formatting and find the next occurrence. If you know that you want all occurrences of the characters or formatting in the Find what text box replaced with the characters or formatting in the Replace with text box, click the Replace All button. This replaces every occurrence from the location of the insertion point to the beginning or end of the document (depending on the search direction). Click the Cancel button to close the Find and Replace dialog box.

exercise 4

Finding and Replacing Text

1. Open Legal 01.
2. Save the document with Save As and name it Ch 16, Ex 04.
3. Find all occurrences of NAME1 and replace with ROSLYN C. KERR by completing the following steps:
   a. With the insertion point positioned at the beginning of the document, click Edit, and then Replace.
   b. At the Find and Replace dialog box with the Replace tab selected, click the More button.
   c. At the expanded dialog box, click the No Formatting button. (This removes the bold formatting from exercise 3.)
   d. With the insertion point positioned inside the Find what text box, key **NAME1**.
   e. Press the Tab key to move the insertion point to the Replace with text box.
   f. Key **ROSLYN C. KERR**.
   g. Click the Replace All button.
   h. When all replacements are made, the Office Assistant displays the message *Word has completed its search of the document and has made 5 replacements.* (Do not close the Find and Replace dialog box.)
4. With the Find and Replace dialog box still open, complete steps similar to those in 3d through 3g to find all occurrences of NAME2 and replace with JULIA C. RAINEY.
5. With the Find and Replace dialog box still open, complete steps similar to those in 3d through 3g to find the one occurrence of NUMBER and replace with C-9811.
6. Click the Less button at the Find and Replace dialog box to turn off the display of the additional options.

7. Close the Find and Replace dialog box.
8. Save the document again with the same name (Ch 16, Ex 04).
9. Print and then close Ch 16, Ex 04.

In exercise 4, Word made all replacements without getting confirmation from you. If you want to confirm each replacement before it is made, click the Find Next button to move to the first occurrence of the word. To replace the word, click the Replace button. To leave the word as written, click the Find Next button.

The next time you open the Find and Replace dialog box, you can display a list of text you have entered in the Replace with text box. To do this, click the down-pointing triangle after the Replace with text box, and then click the desired text at the drop-down list. This inserts it in the Replace with text box.

exercise 5

Finding and Replacing Specific Text

1. Open Report 04.
2. Make the following changes to the document:
   a. Select all the text in module 4, including the title.
   b. Copy and then paste the text to a new document screen.
   c. Save the new document as Ch 16, Ex 05.
   d. Make Report 04 the active window and then close the document.
3. With Ch 16, Ex 05 open, find some of the occurrences of *paper* and replace with *stationery* by completing the following steps:
   a. With the insertion point positioned at the beginning of the document, click Edit, and then Replace.
   b. At the Find and Replace dialog box, key **paper** in the Find what text box.
   c. Press the Tab key (this moves the insertion point to the Replace with text box) and then key **stationery**.
   d. Click the More button. (This expands the dialog box.)
   e. Click the Find whole words only option. (This inserts a check mark in the check box.)
   f. Click the Find Next button. (To see the first occurrence of *paper* you may need to drag down the Find and Replace dialog box. To do this, position the arrow pointer anywhere on the Find and Replace dialog box title bar, hold down the left mouse button, drag the outline of the dialog box down the screen, and then release the mouse button.) When Word stops at the first occurrence of *paper*, click the Replace button.
   g. Continue clicking the Replace button when Word stops at an occurrence of *paper*, except when *paper* falls after *8.5-by-11-inch*. At these occurrences, click the Find Next button.

h. When the find and replace is completed, click the Find whole words only option to remove the check mark from the check box.
i. Click the Less button.
j. Click the Close button to close the Find and Replace dialog box.
4. Save the document again with the same name (Ch 16, Ex 05).
5. Print and then close Ch 16, Ex 05.

Choosing Replace Check Box Options

If you click the More button at the Find and Replace dialog box with the Replace tab selected, the same options display as those in the Find and Replace dialog box with the Find tab selected. Refer to figure 16.3 for an explanation of the options. If you click the Find all word forms option, you can find all forms of a word and replace it with the correct form. For example, in exercise 6 you will search for all word forms of *produce* and replace with *create*. This means that Word will replace *produce* with *create*, *producing* with *creating*, and *produced* with *created*.

exercise 6

Finding and Replacing Word Forms

1. Open Para 05.
2. Save the document with Save As and name it Ch 16, Ex 06.
3. Find all forms of the word *produce* and replace it with forms of *create* by completing the following steps:
   a. Make sure the insertion point is positioned at the beginning of the document.
   b. Click Edit, and then Replace.
   c. At the Find and Replace dialog box with the Replace tab selected, key **produce** in the Find what text box.
   d. Press the Tab key and then key **create** in the Replace with text box.
   e. Click the More button.
   f. Click the Find all word forms option. (This inserts a check mark in the check box.)
   g. Click the Replace All button.
   h. At the Office Assistant message, *Replace All is not recommended with Find All Word Forms. Continue with Replace All?*, click OK.
   i. When the find and replace is completed, click the Find all word forms option to remove the check mark.
   j. Click the Less button.
   k. Click the Close button to close the Find and Replace dialog box.
4. Save the document again with the same name (Ch 16, Ex 06).
5. Print and then close Ch 16, Ex 06.

Finding and Replacing Formatting

With Word's Find and Replace feature, you can search for specific formatting or characters containing specific formatting and replace it with other characters or formatting. For example, you can search for the text *Type Style* set in 14-point Arial and replace it with the text *Type Style* set in 18-point Times New Roman. You can also search for specific formatting and delete it. For example, you can search for bold formatting and replace it with nothing. This will remove bold formatting from the document while leaving the text.

exercise 7

Finding and Replacing Formatting

1. Open Survey 01.
2. Save the document with Save As and name it Ch 16, Ex 07.
3. Search for all bolded text and replace with italics by completing the following steps:
   a. Click Edit, and then Replace.
   b. Delete any characters in the Find what text box. (If there is any formatting displayed below the Find what text box, click the More button and then click the No Formatting button.)
   c. Make sure the insertion point is positioned in the Find what text box and then click once on the Bold button on the Formatting toolbar.
   d. Press the Tab key. (This moves the insertion point to the Replace with text box.)
   e. Delete any characters in the Replace with text box. (If there is any formatting displayed below the Replace with text box, click the No Formatting button.)
   f. With the insertion point positioned in the Replace with text box, click once on the Bold button on the Formatting toolbar.
   g. Click once on the Italic button on the Formatting toolbar.
   h. Click once again on the Bold button on the Formatting toolbar.
   i. Click the Replace All button.
   j. When the find and replace is completed, click the More button to expand the dialog box. (Skip this step if the dialog box is already expanded.)
   k. With the insertion point positioned inside the Find what text box, click the No Formatting button that is located at the bottom of the dialog box.
   l. Click inside the Replace with text box and then click the No Formatting button that is located at the bottom of the dialog box.
   m. Click the Less button.
   n. Click the Close button to close the Find and Replace dialog box.
4. Save the document again with the same name (Ch 16, Ex 07).
5. Print and then close Ch 16, Ex 07.

exercise 8

Finding and Replacing Fonts

1. Open Survey 01.
2. Save the document with Save As and name it Ch 16, Ex 08.
3. Make the following changes to the document:
   a. Change the top and bottom margins to 0.75 inch and the left and right margins to 1 inch.
   b. Change the font for the entire document to 12-point Century Schoolbook.
   c. Select the title, *TEACHER DEVELOPMENT TOPICS*, and the subtitle, *Activities within Your Classroom*, and then change the font to 16-point Arial bold.
   d. Select *Directions:* (be sure to include the colon) in the first paragraph and then change the font to 14-point Arial bold. Use Format Painter to change the font to 14-point Arial bold for the following:

      Classroom Presentations:
      Expertise in Your Discipline:
      Information Technology:
      Thinking Skills:
      Active Listening:
4. Save the document again with the same name (Ch 16, Ex 08).
5. Print Ch 16, Ex 08.
6. With Ch 16, Ex 08 still open, find text set in 16-point Arial bold and replace it with text set in 14-point Century Schoolbook by completing the following steps:
   a. Move the insertion point to the beginning of the document and then display the Find and Replace dialog box.
   b. At the Find and Replace dialog box, click the More button.
   c. With the insertion point positioned in the Find what text box (make sure there is no text in the text box), click the Format button located at the bottom of the dialog box and then click *Font* at the pop-up list.
   d. At the Find Font dialog box, click *Arial* in the Font list box, click *Bold* in the Font style list box, and then click *16* in the Size list box
   e. Click OK or press Enter to close the Find Font dialog box.
   f. At the Find and Replace dialog box, click inside the Replace with text box. (Make sure there is no text in the text box.)
   g. Click the Format button located at the bottom of the dialog box and then click *Font* at the pop-up list.

h. At the Find Font dialog box, click *Century Schoolbook* in the Font list box, click *Bold* in the Font style list box, and then click *14* in the Size list box.
i. Click OK or press Enter to close the Find Font dialog box.
j. At the Find and Replace dialog box, click the Replace All button.

7. With the Find and Replace dialog box still open, find all text set in 14-point Arial bold and replace it with text set in 12-point Century Schoolbook bold by completing the following steps:
   a. Click inside the Find what text box at the Find and Replace dialog box.
   b. Click the No Formatting button located at the bottom of the dialog box.
   c. With the insertion point still positioned in the Find what text box, click the Format button located at the bottom of the dialog box and then click *Font* at the pop-up list.
   d. At the Find Font dialog box, click *Arial* in the Font list box, click *Bold* in the Font style list box, and then click *14* in the Size list box.
   e. Click OK or press Enter to close the Find Font dialog box.
   f. At the Find and Replace dialog box, click inside the Replace with text box.
   g. Click the No Formatting button located at the bottom of the dialog box.
   h. Click the Format button located at the bottom of the dialog box and then click *Font* at the pop-up list.
   i. At the Find Font dialog box, click *Century Schoolbook* in the Font list box, click *Bold* in the Font style list box, and then click *12* in the Size list box.
   j. Click OK or press Enter to close the dialog box.
   k. At the Find and Replace dialog box, click the Replace All button.
   l. When the find and replace is completed, click the Less button to turn off the display of the additional options.
   m. Close the Find and Replace dialog box.
8. Save the document again with the same name (Ch 16, Ex 08).
9. Print and then close Ch 16, Ex 08.

Finding Specific Documents

In this chapter you have learned to find specific text or formatting in a document. In chapter 5 you learned to use the Open dialog box to perform a variety of document maintenance functions. The concept of finding specific text can be applied to document maintenance. For example, you can search the list of files in the Open dialog box for documents containing a specific word or phrase. You can also search the list of files for specific document names.

To search for documents containing specific text, display the Open dialog box. At the Open dialog box, key the text for which you are searching in the Text or property text box, and then click the Find Now button. Word searches through the list of files and then displays only those documents containing the specified text.

You can use special operators to locate more than one word. For example, you can search for all documents that contain the last name *Nguyen* and the last name *Edmonds* by using the & operator. Figure 16.5 shows example operators that can be used and the results the search would return.

figure 16.5

Use this operator	and these documents will be found:
Nguyen&Edmonds	documents containing *Nguyen* and *Edmonds*
Nguyen|Edmonds	documents containing *Nguyen* or *Edmonds*
Christy..Edmonds	documents containing *Christy* followed by *Edmonds*
(desktop publishing guidelines)	documents containing all three words in any order
"desktop publishing guidelines"	documents containing three words in specific order

In addition to the operators in figure 16.5, you can use the asterisk (*) symbol to indicate a combination of letters or the question mark (?) to indicate one character. For example, you can enter **educa*** in the Text or property text box and Word will search documents for words that begin with *educa* and end with any combination such as *education*, *educating*, and *educated*. If you enter **probabl?** in the Text or property text box, Word will search documents for words that begin with *probabl* and end with any one character (such as *probable* and *probably*).

You can also search for documents with specific names. For example, suppose you wanted to display all documents created in chapter 15. To do this you would display the Open dialog box, key **Ch 15*** in the File name text box, and then click the Find Now button. The asterisk after *Ch 15* tells Word to find all documents with a name that begins with *Ch 15* and ends in any combination of letters.

exercise 9

Finding Documents Containing Specific Words

1. At a clear editing window, search for documents on your student data disk containing the names *Nguyen* and *Edmonds* by completing the following steps:
   a. Display the Open dialog box.
   b. If necessary, change the default folder to 3½ Floppy (A:).
   c. Click inside the Text or property text box and then key **Nguyen&Edmonds**.
   d. Click the Find Now button.
   e. When the search results display, write down the names of the documents that display in the list box.
   f. Close the Open dialog box.
2. Search for documents containing the names *Nguyen* or *Edmonds* by completing the following steps:
   a. Display the Open dialog box.
   b. If necessary, change the default folder to 3½ Floppy (A:).
   c. Click inside the Text or property text box and then key **Nguyen|Edmonds**.
   d. Click the Find Now button.
   e. When the search results display, write down the names of the documents that display in the list box.

f. Close the Open dialog box.
g. Compare the results of the first search with this search.

3. Search for documents containing the three words *desktop publishing guidelines* in any order by completing the following steps:
   a. Display the Open dialog box.
   b. If necessary, change the default folder to 3½ Floppy (A:).
   c. Click inside the Text or property text box and then key **(desktop publishing guidelines)**.
   d. Click the Find Now button.
   e. When the search results display, write down the names of the documents that display in the list box.
   f. Close the Open dialog box.
4. Search for documents containing the three words *desktop publishing guidelines* in that specific order by completing steps similar to those in step 3 except key **"desktop publishing guidelines"** in the Text or property text box. Compare the results of the previous search with this search.
5. Display documents with names that begin *Ch 16* by completing the following steps:
   a. Display the Open dialog box.
   b. If necessary, change the default folder to 3½ Floppy (A:).
   c. Key **Ch 16*** in the File name text box and then click the Find Now button.
   d. When the search results display, write down the names of the documents that display in the list box.
   e. Close the Open dialog box.

chapter summary

- Use the Find feature to quickly locate specific words, phrases, or formatting. Once located, these items can then be edited or deleted.
- A find begins at the location of the insertion point and searches from there to the beginning of the document (Up) or to the end (Down).
- When you open the Find and Replace dialog box, you can display a list of text for which you previously have searched by clicking the down-pointing triangle at the right of the Find what text box.
- The Find and Replace dialog box contains a variety of check boxes with options for completing a search, such as Match case, Find whole words only, Use wildcards, Sounds like, and Find all word forms.
- You can search a document for some character and paragraph formatting such as bold characters, specific fonts, indents, and spacing.
- With Word's Find and Replace feature, you can look for text or formatting and replace with other text or formatting.
- The Find and Replace dialog box contains buttons such as Find Next, Replace, Replace All, and Cancel. With these buttons you can choose to skip an occurrence of the search item, replace it, or replace all occurrences at once.
- The next time you open the Find and Replace dialog box, you can display a list of text you have entered in the Replace with text box.

commands review

	Mouse/Keyboard
Find and Replace dialog box with Find tab selected	Edit, Find
Find and Replace dialog box with Replace tab selected	Edit, Replace

check your understanding

Completion: In the space provided, indicate the correct term, command, or number.

1. Click this option from the Edit drop-down menu to display the Find and Replace dialog box with the Find tab selected. ______________
2. Click this option from the Edit drop-down menu to display the Find and Replace dialog box with the Replace tab selected. ______________
3. This is the total number of characters that can be entered in the Find what text box. ______________
4. If you want to replace every occurrence of what you are searching for in a document, click this button at the Find and Replace dialog box. ______________
5. Click this button at the Find and Replace dialog box if you do not want to replace an occurrence with the replace text. ______________
6. Click this button at the Find and Replace dialog box to display an expanded dialog box with additional options. ______________
7. Click this option at the Find and Replace dialog box if you are searching for only whole words. ______________
8. Click this option at the Find and Replace dialog box if you are searching for a word and all its forms. ______________

In the space provided below, write the steps you would complete to find all occurrences of the word *remove* and all its word forms and replace it with *delete* and all its word forms.

____

____

____

skill assessments

Note: Before completing the skill assessments, display the Open dialog box, and then select and delete documents created in chapter 14 that begin Ch 14. You may want to check with your instructor before deleting these documents.

Assessment 1

1. Open Contract 02.
2. Save the document with Save As and name it Ch 16, SA 01.
3. Make the following changes to the document:
   a. Find all occurrences of REINBERG MANUFACTURING and replace with COLEMAN CORPORATION.
   b. Find all occurrences of RM and replace with CC.
   c. Find all occurrences of LABOR WORKER'S UNION and replace with INDUSTRIAL WORKER'S UNION.
   d. Find all occurrences of LWU and replace with IWU.
4. Save the document again with the same name (Ch 16, SA 01).
5. Print and then close Ch 16, SA 01.

Assessment 2

1. Open Legal 02.
2. Save the document with Save As and name it Ch 16, SA 02.
3. Make the following changes to the document:
   a. Find all occurrences of NAME1 and replace with LEWIS N. HALL.
   b. Find the one occurrence of NUMBER and replace with C-9322
   c. Find all bold formatting and change to italic formatting, *except* the following:

      IN DISTRICT COURT NO. 4, KING COUNTY
      STATE OF WASHINGTON
      MARCIA DONOVAN
4. Save the document again with the same name (Ch 16, SA 02).
5. Print and then close Ch 16, SA 02.

Assessment 3

1. Open Ch 16, SA 01.
2. Save the document with Save As and name it Ch 16, SA 03.
3. Make the following changes to the document:
   a. Find bold formatting and remove it from the text in the document *except* the title.
   b. Change the top, left, and right margins to 1.5 inches.
   c. Create a footer that prints *AGREEMENT* bolded and centered at the bottom of the page.
4. Check the page break in the document and, if necessary, adjust the page break.
5. Save the document again with the same name (Ch 16, SA 03).
6. Print and then close Ch 16, SA 03.

Unit three

PERFORMANCE ASSESSMENTS

DEMONSTRATING YOUR SKILLS

Assessment one

1. At a clear document screen, make the following changes:
   a. Change the paper size to 5.5 inches by 8.5 inches.
   b. Change the left and right margins to 1 inch.
   c. Change the font to 13-point Garamond (or a similar typeface).
2. Key the memo shown in figure U3.1. You determine the tab stops for the text in columns.
3. Save the memo and name it Unit 3, PA 01.
4. Print and then close Unit 3, PA 01.

DATE: February 26, 1999

TO: Nicole Clark

FROM: Darryl Ellis

SUBJECT: TRAINING

Listed below are the dates that I attended cultural diversity training sessions. I have completed over 50 hours of training, which qualifies me as a cultural diversity specialist. Not listed are the hours I attended prior to my tenure as Trainer.

Date	Hrs
01/05/99	8
01/07/99	8
01/19/99	6
01/21/99	6
02/09/99	6
02/11/99	6
02/16/99	8
02/18/99	8

If you need further documentation, I can provide you with my training material.

XX:Unit 03, PA 01

Figure U3.1 • Assessment 1

Assessment two

1. Open Report 01.
2. Save the document with Save As and name it Unit 3, PA 02.
3. Make the following changes to the report:
   a. Select the entire document and then change the font to 12-point Century Schoolbook.
   b. Set the title and headings in 14-point Arial bold.
   c. Number the pages, except the first page, at the upper right margin.
   d. Create the footer DESKTOP PUBLISHING that prints centered at the bottom of every page and is set in 12-point Arial bold.
4. Check the page breaks in the document and, if necessary, adjust the page breaks.
5. Save the document again with the same name (Unit 3, PA 02).
6. Print and then close Unit 3, PA 02.

Assessment three

1. Open Report 04.
2. Save the document with Save As and name it Unit 3, PA 03.
3. Make the following changes to the document:
   a. Select the entire document and then change the font to 12-point Rockwell. (If Rockwell is not available, choose a similar serif typeface such as Century Schoolbook.)

b. Change the left and right margins to 1 inch.
c. Insert a section break that begins a new page at the line containing the title MODULE 4: CREATING NEWSLETTER LAYOUT. (Be sure to insert a section break and not a page break.)
d. Create the footer *Module 3: Designing a Newsletter* that prints at the left margin and *Page - #* that prints at the right margin on each page in the first section and is set in 12-point Rockwell bold.
e. Create the footer *Module 4: Creating Newsletter Layout* that prints at the left margin and *Page - #* that prints at the right margin on each page in the second section and is set in 12-point Rockwell bold.

4. Check the page breaks in the document and, if necessary, adjust the page breaks.
5. Save the report again with the same name (Unit 3, PA 03).
6. Print and then close Unit 3, PA 03.

Assessment four

1. Open Unit 3, PA 03.
2. Save the document with Save As and name it Unit 3, PA 04.
3. Make the following changes to the document:
   a. Delete the footer in the first section.
   b. Delete the footer in the second section.
   c. Create the header *Page - #* that prints at the top right margin on every page except the first page and is set in 12-point Rockwell bold.
   d. Create the first footnote shown in figure U3.2 at the end of the first paragraph in the *Applying Desktop Publishing Guidelines* section of the report.
   e. Create the second footnote shown in figure U3.2 at the end of the third paragraph in the *Applying Desktop Publishing Guidelines* section of the report.
   f. Create the third footnote shown in figure U3.2 at the end of the last paragraph in the *Applying Desktop Publishing Guidelines* section of the report.
   g. Create the fourth footnote shown in figure U3.2 at the end of the only paragraph in the *Choosing Paper Weight* section of the report.
   h. Display the footnote pane, select all the footnotes, and then change the font to 12-point Rockwell.
4. Check page breaks in the document and, if necessary, adjust the page breaks.
5. Save the document again with the same name (Unit 3, PA 04).
6. Print and then close Unit 3, PA 04.

Fellers, Laurie, *Desktop Publishing Design*, Cornwall & Lewis Publishing, 1997, pages 67-72.

Moriarity, Joel, "Adding Emphasis to Documents," *Desktop Publishing*, August 1998, pages 3-6.

Wong, Chun Man, *Desktop Publishing with Style*, Monroe-Ackerman Publishing, 1997, pages 87-93.

Jaquez, Andre, *Desktop Publishing Tips and Tricks*, Aurora Publishing House, 1998, pages 103-106.

Figure U3.2 • Assessment 4

Assessment five

1. Open Unit 3, PA 04.
2. Save the document with Save As and name it Unit 3, PA 05.
3. Make the following changes to the report:
   a. Convert the footnotes to endnotes.
   b. Make sure the endnotes numbering method is Arabic numbers.
   c. Edit endnote number 3 and change the publication year from *1997* to *1996* and change the pages from *87-93* to *61-68*.
4. Save the report again with the same name (Unit 3, PA 05).
5. Check the page breaks in the document and, if necessary, adjust the page breaks.
6. Print and then close Unit 3, PA 05.

Assessment six

1. Open Mortgage. This document is located on your student data disk.
2. Complete the following steps:
   a. Select the first paragraph, copy it to a new document, save it and name it Mort 01, and then close Mort 01.
   b. Select the second paragraph, copy it to a new document, save it and name it Mort 02, and then close Mort 02.
   c. Select the third paragraph, copy it to a new document, save it and name it Mort 03, and then close Mort 03.
   d. Select the fourth paragraph, copy it to a new document, save it and name it Mort 04, and then close Mort 04.
   e. Select the fifth paragraph, copy it to a new document, save it and name it Mort 05, and then close Mort 05.
   f. Select the sixth paragraph, copy it to a new document, save it and name it Mort 06, and then close Mort 06.

g. Select the seventh paragraph, copy it to a new document, save it and name it Mort 07, and then close Mort 07.

3. Close Mortgage.
4. At a clear document screen, create the document shown in figure U3.3. Insert the documents as indicated by the bracketed items.
5. Make the following changes to the document:
   a. Change the top and bottom margins to 1.5 inches.
   b. Number pages at the bottom center of the two pages.
6. Check the page break in the document and make sure it displays in a desirable position. (If not, insert your own page break.)
7. Save the document and name it Unit 3, PA 06.
8. Print and then close Unit 3, PA 06.

CONTRACT AND SECURITY AGREEMENT

BETWEEN

KEYSTONE MORTGAGE AND

DOUGLAS J. RICH AND PHYLLIS S. RICH

This contract is made this _____ day of ________________, 1999, between KEYSTONE MORTGAGE, Seller, and DOUGLAS J. RICH and PHYLLIS S. RICH, Buyers. Having been quoted a cash price and a credit price and having chosen to pay the credit price, the Buyers agree to buy and Seller agrees to sell, subject to all the terms of this contract, the land parcel located at 432 Royal Oaks Drive, Reno, NV 89334.

[Insert Mort 03 here.]

[Insert Mort 01 here.]

[Insert Mort 02 here.]

[Insert Mort 05 here.]

[Insert Mort 07 here.]

[Insert Mort 04 here.]

[Insert Mort 06 here.]

LEANNE S. TRENARY, President
KEYSTONE MORTGAGE

DOUGLAS J. RICH, Buyer

PHYLLIS S. RICH, Buyer

Figure U3.3 • Assessment 6

Assessment seven

1. Open Unit 3, PA 06.
2. Save the document with Save As and name it Unit 3, PA 07.
3. Make the following changes to the document:
    a. Double space the paragraphs within the body of the contract.
    b. Indent the first line of each paragraph.
    c. Delete the blank lines between paragraphs. (There should only be a double space between all text in the body of the contract.)
    d. Delete the page numbering.
    e. Create a footer that prints on every page, is bolded, and contains *CONTRACT* at the left margin and *Page* followed by the page number at the right margin.
    f. Complete the following find and replaces:
        1) Find DOUGLAS J. RICH and replace with JOHN T. SHEAHAN.
        2) Find PHYLLIS S. RICH and replace with KIRSTEN C. SHEAHAN.
4. Save the document again with the same name (Unit 3, PA 07).
5. Print and then close Unit 3, PA 07.

CREATING ORIGINAL DOCUMENTS

The following activities give you the opportunity to practice your writing skills along with demonstrating an understanding of some of the important Word features you have mastered in this unit. When composing the documents, use correct grammar, appropriate word choices, and clear sentence construction.

Assessment eight

Situation: You are responsible for formatting the report in the document named *Report 05* on your student data disk. This report will be left bound and should include page numbers and headers and/or footers. Change to a serif typeface (other than Times New Roman) for the body of the report and a sans serif typeface for the title and headings. Correct the spelling in the document. Save the formatted report and name it Unit 3, PA 08. Print and then close Unit 3, PA 08.

Assessment nine

Create an appropriate title page for the report formatted in assessment 8. Include your name as the author of the report. Save the title page and name it Unit 3, PA 09. Print and then close Unit 3, PA 09.

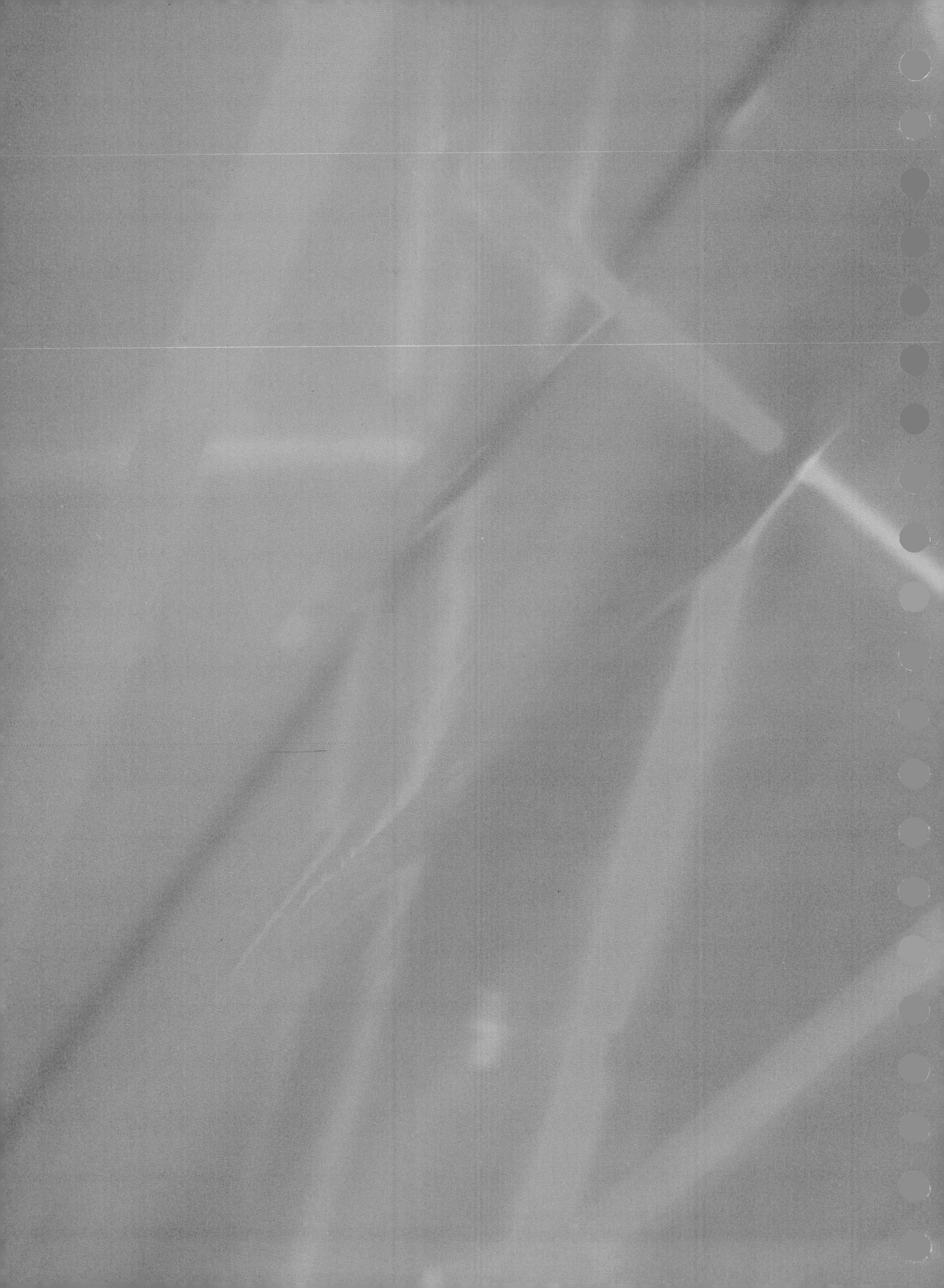

Unit four

ENHANCING THE VISUAL DISPLAY OF DOCUMENTS

In this unit, you will learn to add special features to documents and enhance the visual display of documents with borders, pictures, shapes, and WordArt text. You will also learn to browse the World Wide Web, locate specific sites on the Web, create a Web home page, and create hyperlinks.

scans

The Secretary's Commission on Achieving Necessary Skills

DECISION MAKING

TECHNOLOGY

PROBLEM SOLVING

COMMUNICATIONS

chapter SEVENTEEN

17 Enhancing and Manipulating Documents with Special Features

PERFORMANCE OBJECTIVES

Upon successful completion of chapter 17, you will be able to:

- **Hyphenate words in a document.**
- **Change the hyphenation options and hyphenation zones in a document.**
- **Add line numbering in a document.**
- **Add animation effects to text.**
- **Insert bookmarks in a document.**
- **Create, view, delete, and print comments.**
- **Record, run, pause, and delete macros.**
- **Assign a macro to a keyboard command and a toolbar.**

In this chapter, you will learn about Word features that will help you enhance the display of documents as well as manage and manipulate data within documents. The hyphenation feature hyphenates words at the end of lines, creating a less ragged margin. Add line numbering to documents such as legal documents and enhance the visual display of text on the screen by adding animation effects. Insert bookmarks in specific locations in a document to help you find those locations later and add comments to a document. Create macros that automate the formatting of a document.

Hyphenating Words

In some Word documents, especially documents with left and right margins wider than 1 inch, the right margin may appear quite ragged. If the paragraph alignment is changed to justified, the right margin will appear even, but there will be extra space added throughout the line. In these situations, hyphenating long words that fall at the end of the text line provides the document with a more balanced look.

Automatically Hyphenating Words

When using the hyphenation feature, you can tell Word to automatically hyphenate words in a document or you can manually insert hyphens. To automatically hyphenate words in a document, click Tools, point to Language, then click Hyphenation. At the Hyphenation dialog box shown in figure 17.1, click Automatically hyphenate document, and then click OK or press Enter.

figure 17.1

Hyphenation Dialog Box

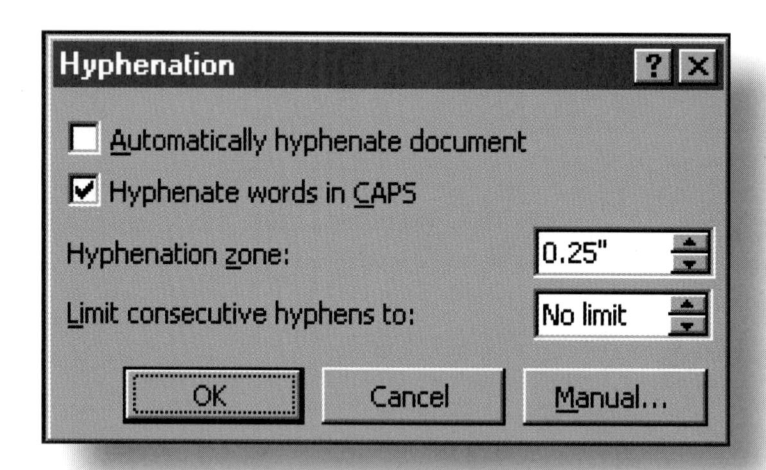

After hyphens are inserted automatically in the document, scroll through the document and check to see if hyphens display in appropriate locations within the words. If, after hyphenating words in a document, you want to remove all hyphens, immediately click the Undo button on the Standard toolbar. This must be done immediately after hyphenating since the Undo feature undoes only the last function.

Undo

Changing Hyphenation Options

By default, Word hyphenates words in all capital letters. If you do not want words in all capital letters hyphenated, remove the check mark from the Hyphenate words in CAPS option. With the Limit consecutive hyphens to option at the Hyphenation dialog box, you can limit the number of lines in a row that can end in hyphens. Generally, no more than two lines of text should display with a hyphen. To limit the hyphenation to two lines, click the up-pointing triangle at the right side of the Limit consecutive hyphens to option until *2* displays in the text box. You can also increase the number of lines by selecting the text that displays in the text box and then keying the desired number.

You can tell Word to ignore text in a paragraph or selected paragraphs when hyphenating. To do this, you would complete the following steps:

1. Position the insertion point in the paragraph or select the paragraphs where you do not want words hyphenated.

2. Click Format, then Paragraph.
3. At the Paragraph dialog box, click the Line and Page Breaks tab.
4. At the Paragraph dialog box with the Line and Page Breaks tab selected, click the Don't hyphenate option.
5. Click OK or press Enter.

Word will ignore the text in the paragraph or text in the selected paragraphs when hyphenating words in the document.

exercise 1

Automatically Hyphenating Words

1. Open Report 01.
2. Save the document with Save As and name it Ch 17, Ex 01.
3. Hyphenate words automatically in the report and limit consecutive hyphenations to 2 lines by completing the following steps:
   a. Click Tools, point to Language, and then click Hyphenation.
   b. At the Hyphenation dialog box, click the up-pointing triangle at the right of the Limit consecutive hyphens to text box until *2* displays in the text box.
   c. Click Automatically hyphenate document.
   d. Click OK or press Enter.
4. Save the document again with the same name (Ch 17, Ex 01).
5. Print and then close Ch 17, Ex 01.

The hyphen inserted during hyphenation is considered an *optional* hyphen. If the text is formatted and a hyphenated word no longer falls at the end of the text line, the optional hyphen is ignored. Later in this chapter, you will learn about the various types of hyphens.

Manually Hyphenating Words

If you want to control where a hyphen appears in a word during hyphenation, choose manual hyphenation. To do this, display the Hyphenation dialog box, and then click the Manual button. This displays the Manual Hyphenation: English (United States) dialog box as shown in figure 17.2. (The word in the Hyphenate at text box will vary.) At this dialog box, click Yes to hyphenate the word as indicated in the Hyphenate at text box; click No if you do not want the word hyphenated; or click Cancel to cancel hyphenation. Continue clicking Yes or No at the Manual Hyphenation: English (United States) dialog box. When the Office Assistant displays the message, *Hyphenation is complete.*, click in the document to remove the message. When hyphenating words, keep in mind the hyphenation guidelines shown in figure 17.3.

figure 17.2 *Manual Hyphenation: English (United States) Dialog Box*

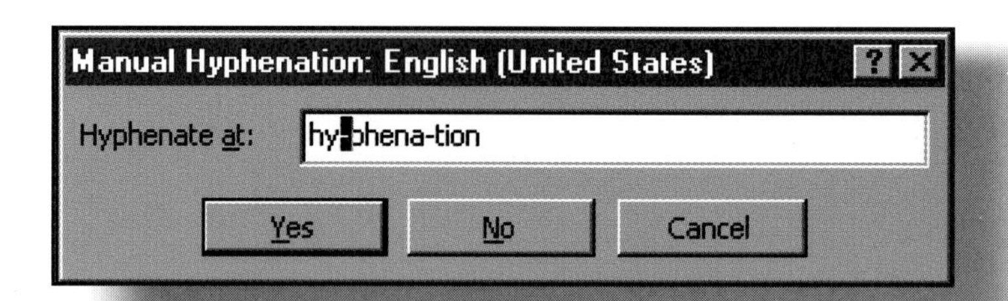

figure 17.3 *Hyphenation Guidelines*

Hyphenation Guidelines

Adapted from *The Paradigm Reference Manual* (Paradigm Publishing Inc., 1993)

One-Syllable Words: Do not divide one-syllable words such as length, served, or thoughts.

Multiple-Syllable Words: Divide multiple-syllable words between syllables, as in pub-lish.

Note: Some divisions between syllables can confuse a reader, particularly if one or both parts may be read as words by themselves. Examples include coin-sure, reed-ucate, and reap-portion. In such cases, break the word at a different place (co-insure, re-educate, and re-apportion).

Prefixes, Suffixes: Generally, divide after a prefix and before a suffix. If the root word ends in a double consonant, divide after the double consonant (example: bill-ing). If adding a suffix results in a double consonant, divide between the doubled letters, as in refer-ring.

Consecutive Line Ends: Avoid dividing words at the ends of more than two consecutive lines.

Abbreviations, Numbers, Contractions: Do not divide except for abbreviations already containing hyphens, as in CD-ROM.

Names of People: Avoid dividing a person's name. But if it becomes necessary, hyphenate the name according to the guidelines for common words.

Dash: Do not divide before a dash or between the hyphens if the dash consists of two hyphens.

At the Manual Hyphenation: English (United States) dialog box, you can reposition the hyphen in the Hyphenate at text box. Word displays the word with syllable breaks indicated by a hyphen. The position where the word will be hyphenated displays as a blinking black bar. If you want to hyphenate at a different location in the word, position the I-beam pointer at the desired location and then click the left mouse button. If you are using the keyboard, press the left or right arrow key until the hyphen is positioned in the desired location. After positioning the hyphen, click Yes.

exercise 2

Manually Hyphenating Words

1. Open Report 03.
2. Save the document with Save As and name it Ch 17, Ex 02.
3. Manually hyphenate words in the document by completing the following steps:
   a. Click Tools, point to Language, and then click Hyphenation.
   b. At the Hyphenation dialog box, select the text *No limit* that displays in the Limit consecutive hyphens to text box, and then key **2**.
   c. Click the Manual button.
   d. At the Manual Hyphenation: English (United States) dialog box, make one of the following choices:
      - Click Yes to hyphenate the word as indicated in the Hyphenate at text box.
      - Move the hyphen in the word to a more desirable location, and then click Yes.
      - Click No if you do not want the word hyphenated.
      - Click the Cancel button to cancel hyphenation.
   e. Continue clicking Yes, No, or Cancel at the Manual Hyphenation: English (United States) dialog box.
   f. When the Office Assistant displays the message, *Hyphenation is complete.*, click in the document to remove the message.
4. Save the document again with the same name (Ch 17, Ex 02).
5. Print and then close Ch 17, Ex 02.

If you want to remove all hyphens in a document, immediately click the Undo button on the Standard toolbar. To delete a few, but not all, of the optional hyphens inserted during hyphenation, use the Find and Replace dialog box. To do this, you would display the Find and Replace dialog box with the Replace tab selected, insert an optional hyphen symbol in the Find what text box, and make sure nothing displays in the Replace with text box. Complete the find and replace, clicking the Replace button to replace the hyphen with nothing or clicking the Find Next button to leave the hyphen in the document. The specific steps to do this are described in exercise 3.

exercise 3

Deleting Specific Optional Hyphens

1. Open Ch 17, Ex 02.
2. Save the document with Save As and name it Ch 17, Ex 03.
3. Delete the second, fourth, and sixth hyphens in the document by completing the following steps:
   a. Click Edit, then Replace.
   b. At the Find and Replace dialog box with the Replace tab selected, make sure there is no text in the Find what text box. If there is, press the Delete key. Make sure there is no formatting displayed below the Find what text box. If there is, click the More button and then click the No Formatting button.
   c. With the insertion point positioned in the Find what text box, make sure the dialog box is expanded (if not, click the More button), and then click the Special button.
   d. At the pop-up list of special characters that displays, click Optional Hyphen.
   e. Make sure there is no text in the Replace with text box and no formatting below the box.
   f. Click the Find Next button.
   g. When Word stops at the first occurrence of an optional hyphen (a hyphen inserted during hyphenation), click the Find Next button to leave the hyphen in the document and move to the next hyphen. (You may want to move down the Find and Replace dialog box so you can see some of the text in the document.)
   h. When Word stops at the second occurrence of an optional hyphen, click the Replace button.
   i. Continue clicking the Find Next button or Replace button until all hyphens have been found. (Replace the fourth and sixth optional hyphens. Leave the other hyphens in the document.)
   j. When the Office Assistant displays the message *Word has finished searching the document.*, click in the document to remove the message.
   k. Click the Close button to close the Find and Replace dialog box.
4. Save the document again with the same name (Ch 17, Ex 03).
5. Print and then close Ch 17, Ex 03.

Changing the Hyphenation Zone

Word uses a hyphenation zone of 0.25 inch from the right margin. If a word starts after the beginning of the hyphenation zone and continues beyond the end of the hyphenation zone, the word is wrapped to the next line. If a word starts at or before the beginning of the hyphenation zone and continues beyond the end of the hyphenation zone, it will be hyphenated during automatic hyphenation or presented for hyphenation during manual hyphenation.

If the hyphenation zone measurement is decreased, more words will be hyphenated. If the hyphenation zone measurement is increased, fewer words will be hyphenated. To change the hyphenation zone measurement, select the current measurement in the Hyphenation zone text box and then key the new measurement. You can also click the up-pointing triangle after the Hyphenation zone text box to increase the hyphenation zone, or click the down-pointing triangle to decrease the hyphenation zone. After changing the hyphenation zone measurement, continue hyphenation by completing steps similar to those presented earlier.

exercise 4

Changing the Hyphenation Zone, Then Hyphenating Words in a Document

1. Open Para 02.
2. Save the document with Save As and name it Ch 17, Ex 04.
3. Change the left and right margins to 1.5 inches.
4. Change the hyphenation zone, then hyphenate the text in the document automatically by completing the following steps:
   a. Click Tools, point to Language, and then click Hyphenation.
   b. At the Hyphenation dialog box, click the up-pointing triangle at the right of the Hyphenation zone text box until *0.4"* displays in the text box.
   c. Click Automatically hyphenate document.
   d. Click OK or press Enter.
5. Save the document again with the same name (Ch 17, Ex 04).
6. Print and then close Ch 17, Ex 04.

Inserting Hyphens

There are several ways that a hyphen is inserted in a document. The type of hyphen in a word like *co-worker* is called a *regular* hyphen. This hyphen is inserted by keying the minus sign on the keyboard. During hyphenation, Word will break hyphenated words, if necessary, at the hyphen.

A hyphen that you or Word inserts during hyphenation is considered an *optional* hyphen. An optional hyphen appears in the document screen and prints only if the word falls at the end of the text line. If text is adjusted and the word no longer falls at the end of the line, the optional hyphen is removed from the document screen and will not print. An optional hyphen can be inserted in a word by pressing Ctrl + -. If a word containing an optional hyphen falls at the end of the line, Word automatically breaks the word at the optional hyphen.

In some text, such as telephone numbers and Social Security numbers, you may want to insert a *nonbreaking* hyphen rather than a regular hyphen. A nonbreaking hyphen tells Word that the text is to be considered a unit and not to break it between lines. A nonbreaking hyphen is inserted in text by pressing Ctrl + Shift + -.

exercise 5

Keying a Memo with Nonbreaking Hyphens

1. At a clear document screen, key the memo shown in figure 17.4. Insert a nonbreaking hyphen between the numbers in the Social Security numbers and the telephone numbers. (Insert a nonbreaking hyphen by pressing Ctrl + Shift + -.)
2. Save the document and name it Ch 17, Ex 05.
3. Print and then close Ch 17, Ex 05.

figure 17.4

Exercise 5

DATE: February 24, 1999

TO: Lonnie Davidson

FROM: Dana Knowles

SUBJECT: NEW EMPLOYEE VERIFICATION

A New Employee Verification form has been received for Laurie Shipman, Alexander Yi, David Whitehouse, and Naomi Roth. Please confirm the numbers—Laurie Shipman, 326-22-7842; Alexander Yi, 193-61-9849; David Whitehouse, 355-90-6743; and Naomi Roth, 564-63-2417.

Many employees have asked for a toll-free number they can call from home to check on benefits. As a response to these requests, a toll-free number has been added which is 1-800-555-7800. Please provide the new employees with this number.

XX:Ch 17, Ex 05

Turning On Line Numbering

Lines in a document can be numbered with options from the Line Numbers dialog box. This has practical applications for certain legal papers or for reference purposes. To number lines in a document, click File, then Page Setup. At the Page Setup dialog box, click the Layout tab. At the Page Setup dialog box with the Layout tab selected, click the Line Numbers button. This displays the Line Numbers dialog box as shown in figure 17.5. At this dialog box, click Add line numbering, and then click OK to close the Line Numbers dialog box. Click OK to close the Page Setup dialog box.

17.5 *Line Numbers Dialog Box*

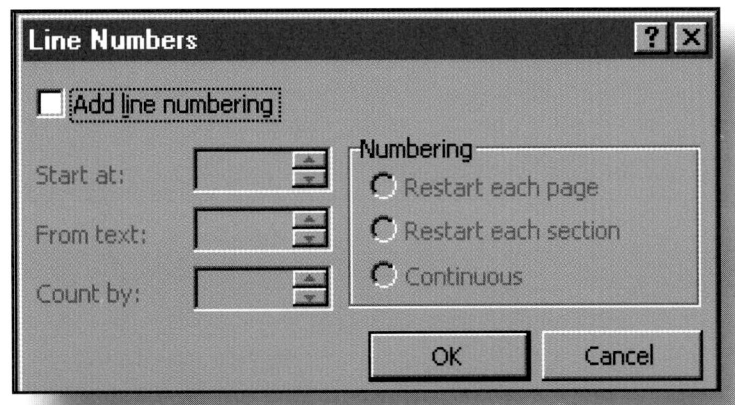

When you click Add line numbering at the Line Numbers dialog box, a variety of options become available. By default, Word begins line numbering with number 1. With the Start at option, you can change to a different beginning number. To change the beginning number, select the current number in the Start at text box and then key the new number. You can also click the up-pointing or down-pointing triangle at the right side of the Start at text box.

The From text option at the Line Numbers dialog box has a default setting of *Auto*. At this setting, line numbers are printed 0.25 inch from the text in the document. This measurement can be increased or decreased with the From text option.

With the Count by option at the Line Numbers dialog box, you can specify the interval between printed line numbers. For example, if you want every second line numbered, you would key **2** in the Count by text box.

Word starts numbering over at the beginning of each page. This is because the Restart each page option is selected. If you want line numbering to start over at the beginning of each section, click Restart each section. If you want lines numbered consecutively in a document, click Continuous.

When line numbering is turned on, line numbers will display in the Page Layout viewing mode or in Print Preview. At the Page Layout viewing mode, you may need to scroll the text in the document screen to the right to see the line numbers.

exercise 6

Numbering Lines in a Legal Document

1. Open Legal 01.
2. Save the document with Save As and name it Ch 17, Ex 06.
3. Complete the following find and replaces:
   a. Find NAME1 and replace with TRICIA C. WALKER.
   b. Find NAME2 and replace with STUART G. PERRY.
   c. Find NUMBER and replace with C-6801.
4. Fix the right parentheses after the name.
5. Turn on line numbering by completing the following steps:
   a. Click File, then Page Setup.
   b. At the Page Setup dialog box, click the Layout tab.
   c. Click the Line Numbers button.
   d. At the Line Numbers dialog box, click Add line numbering.
   e. Click OK or press Enter.
   f. At the Page Setup dialog box, click OK or press Enter.
6. View the document in Print Preview to see where the line number will print and then close Print Preview.
7. Save the document again with the same name (Ch 17, Ex 06).
8. Print and then close Ch 17, Ex 06.

Animating Text

Animation effects can be added to text at the Font dialog box with the Animation tab selected. To display this dialog box, shown in figure 17.6, click Format, then Font. At the Font dialog box click the Animation tab.

figure 17.6 ***Font Dialog Box with Animation Tab Selected***

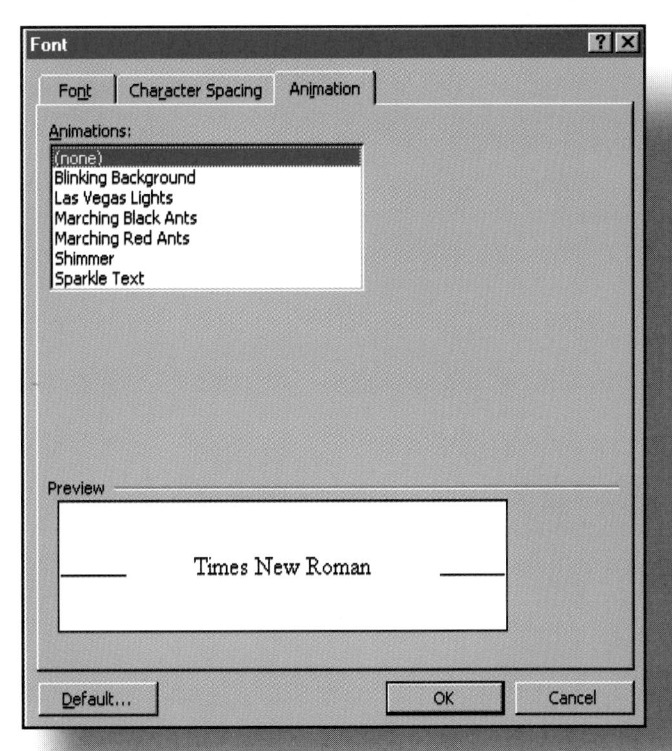

Animation effects can be added to text, such as a blinking background, a shimmer or sparkle. To add an animation effect, select the text, display the Font dialog box with the Animation tab selected, click the desired effect, and then close the Font dialog box. Animation effects added to text display in the screen but do not print.

exercise 7

Adding Animation Effects to Text

1. Open Notice 01.
2. Save the document with Save As and name it Ch 17, Ex 07.
3. Add sparkle to the title of the document by completing the following steps:
   a. Select the title *EMERALD HEIGHTS ELEMENTARY SCHOOL CARNIVAL*.
   b. Click Format, then Font.
   c. At the Font dialog box, click the Animation tab.
   d. Click the *Sparkle Text* option in the list box.
   e. Click OK to close the dialog box.
4. Save the document again with the same name (Ch 17, Ex 07).
5. Close Ch 17, Ex 07. (Printing is optional—the sparkle effect will not print.)

Using Bookmarks

In long documents, you may find it useful to mark a location in the document so you can quickly move the insertion point to the location. Create bookmarks for locations in a document at the Bookmark dialog box. When you create bookmarks, you can insert as many as needed in a document. To create a bookmark, position the insertion point at the location in the document where the bookmark is to appear, and then click Insert, then Bookmark. At the Bookmark dialog box shown in figure 17.7, key a name for the bookmark in the Bookmark name text box, and then click the Add button. Repeat these steps as many times as needed in a document to insert bookmarks.

figure 17.7 ***Bookmark Dialog Box***

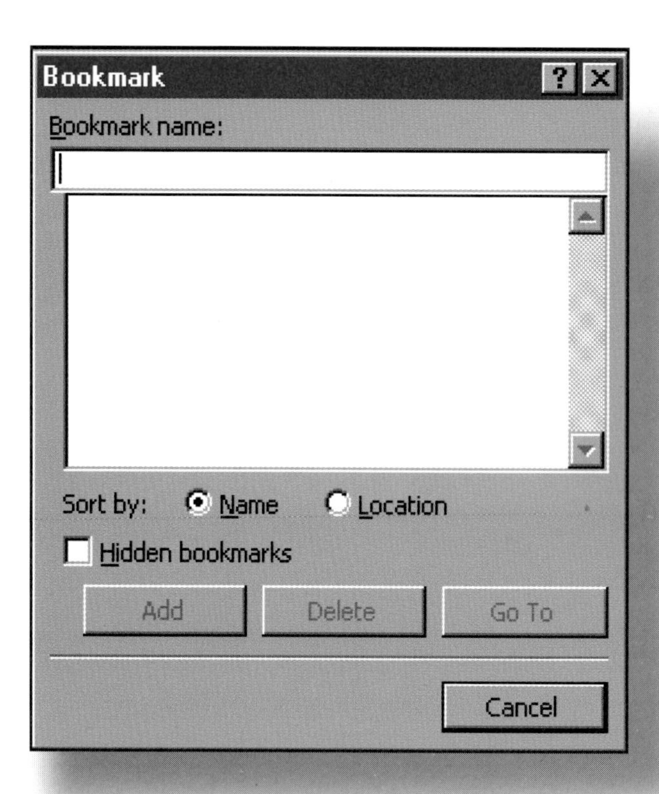

Make sure you give each bookmark a unique name. A bookmark name can contain a maximum of 40 characters and can include letters, numbers, and the underscore character (_). You cannot use spaces in a bookmark name. When you insert a bookmark in a document, by default the bookmark is not visible. To make a bookmark visible, click Tools, then Options. At the Options dialog box, click the View tab. At the Options dialog box with the View tab selected, click Bookmarks in the Show section of the dialog box. (This inserts a check mark in the Bookmarks check box.) Complete similar steps to turn off the display of bookmarks. A bookmark displays as an I-beam marker.

You can also create a bookmark for selected text. To do this, select the text first and then complete the steps to create a bookmark. When you create a bookmark for selected text, a left bracket ([) indicates the beginning of the selected text and a right bracket (]) indicates the end of the selected text.

After bookmarks have been inserted in a document, you can move the insertion point to a specific bookmark. To do this, click Insert, then Bookmark. At the Bookmark dialog box, double-click the bookmark name in the list box. You can also click once on the bookmark name and then click the Go To button. When Word stops at the location of the bookmark, click the Close button to close the Bookmark dialog box. If you move the insertion point to a bookmark created with selected text, Word moves the insertion to the bookmark and selects the text.

Bookmarks in a document are deleted at the Bookmark dialog box (not the document). To delete a bookmark, display the Bookmark dialog box, select the bookmark to be deleted in the list box, and then click the Delete button.

exercise 8

Inserting Bookmarks in a Document

1. Open Report 01.
2. Turn on the display of bookmarks by completing the following steps:
   a. Click Tools, then Options.
   b. At the Options dialog box, click the View tab.
   c. Click Bookmarks in the Show section. (This inserts a check mark in the Bookmarks check box.)
   d. Click OK or press Enter.
3. Insert a bookmark at the beginning of the heading *Defining Desktop Publishing* by completing the following steps:
   a. Position the insertion point at the beginning of the line containing the heading *Defining Desktop Publishing*.
   b. Click Insert, then Bookmark.
   c. At the Bookmark dialog box, key **Define** in the Bookmark name text box.
   d. Click the Add button.
4. Insert a bookmark at the beginning of the following headings with the names listed by following steps similar to those in 3.

Initiating the Desktop Publishing Process	=	Initiate
Planning the Publication	=	Plan
Creating the Content	=	Create

5. Position the insertion point at the *Define* bookmark by completing the following steps:
   a. Click Insert, then Bookmark.
   b. At the Bookmark dialog box, double-click *Define* in the list box.

c. When Word stops at the heading *Defining Desktop Publishing*, click the Close button to close the Bookmark dialog box.

6. Complete steps similar to those in 5 to move the insertion point to the *Initiate*, *Plan*, and *Create* bookmarks.
7. Turn off the display of bookmarks by completing steps similar to those in 2.
8. Close the report without saving the changes.

Inserting Comments

If you want to make comments in a document you are creating, or if a reviewer wants to make comments in a document written by someone else, insert a comment. A comment includes the initials of the person whose name was entered as the user information and a number. (In a school setting, this may not be your name.) For example, if *Linda Chambers* was the user's name, the first comment in a document would be named **LC1**. To determine what name is entered as the user, click Tools, then Options. At the Options dialog box, click the User Info tab. The name and initials of the user are displayed at this dialog box.

Creating a Comment

A comment is similar to a footnote or endnote in that a reference mark is inserted in a document and comment text is keyed at a comment pane. A comment mark will not display in the document screen by default. To show comment marks, turn on the display of nonprinting characters. You can also display comment marks by clicking Tools, then Options. At the Options dialog box, click the View tab. At the Options dialog box with the View tab selected, click Hidden text, and then click OK or press Enter. When inserting a comment mark in a document, position the insertion point where you want the mark to appear, or select text, and then create the comment.

To create a comment, select the text or item on which you want to comment or position the insertion point at the end of the text and then click Insert, then Comment. This changes the selected text to highlighted text (yellow background) and opens the comment pane shown in figure 17.8. At the comment pane, key comment text, and then click the Close button. You can also insert a comment in a document by clicking the Insert Comment button on the Reviewing toolbar. To display this toolbar, *right-click* on the Standard toolbar or the Formatting toolbar and then click *Reviewing* at the drop-down list that displays.

If you do not select text before creating a comment, Word will select the closest word to the insertion point.

17.8

Comment Pane

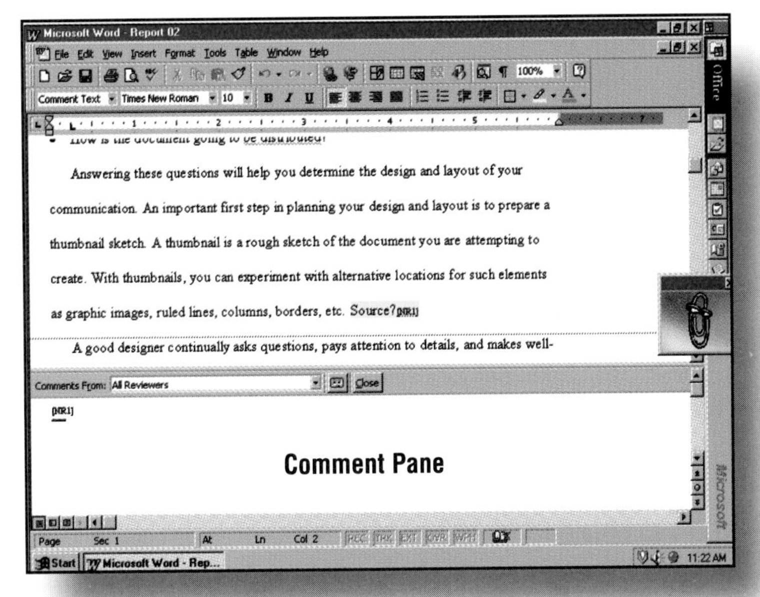

Viewing Comment Text

If you turn on the display of nonprinting characters or hidden text, the comment mark is visible but not the comment text entered in the comment pane. To view the comment text, click View, then Comments. This displays the comment pane with the comment text. After viewing the comment text, click Close to close the comment pane. You can also display the comment pane by *right-clicking* the comment mark and then clicking Edit Comment at the pop-up menu. Another method for displaying the comment pane is to click the Edit Comment button on the Reviewing toolbar. Word will locate the next comment in the document and then display that text in the comment pane.

Edit Comment

Deleting a Comment

Delete a comment in the same manner as a footnote or endnote is deleted. To delete a comment, select the comment mark and then press the Delete key. When the mark is deleted, the corresponding comment text is also deleted. You can also delete a comment mark and its corresponding text by positioning the insertion point on the comment mark and then clicking the Delete Comment button on the Reviewing toolbar. Another method is to position the I-beam pointer on a comment mark, click the *right* mouse button, and then click Delete Comment at the drop-down list.

Delete Comment

Printing a Comment

A document containing comments can be printed with the comments, or you can choose to print just the comments and not the document. To print a document and comments, display the Print dialog box, and then click the

Options button. This displays the Print dialog box with the Print tab selected. At this dialog box click Comments (this inserts a check mark in the check box). Click OK or press Enter to close the Print dialog box with the Print tab selected. Click OK or press Enter to close the Print dialog box and send the document to the printer.

To print only comments in a document, display the Print dialog box. At the Print dialog box, click the down-pointing triangle at the right side of the Print what option and then click *Comments* at the drop-down list. Click OK or press Enter to close the Print dialog box and send the comments to the printer.

Comments are printed on a separate page from the document. The page number where the comment occurs in the document is printed along with the comment mark and the comment text.

exercise 9

Creating Comments in a Document

1. Open Report 02.
2. Save the document with Save As and name it Ch 17, Ex 09.
3. Turn on the display of comment marks by completing the following steps:
   a. Click Tools, then Options.
   b. At the Options dialog box, click the View tab.
   c. At the Options dialog box with the View tab selected, click Hidden text in the Nonprinting characters section.
   d. Click OK or press Enter.
4. Create a comment at the end of the first paragraph below the bulleted items on the first page in the report by completing the following steps:
   a. Position the insertion point at the end of the first paragraph below the bulleted items on the first page in the report.
   b. Key **Source?**.
   c. Select *Source?*.
   d. Click Insert, then Comment.
   e. At the Comment pane, key **Please add the source for the information in this paragraph.**
   f. Click the Close button.
5. Move the insertion point to the end of the last paragraph in the *Designing a Document* section of the report. Key **Examples?** and then select *Examples?*. Create a comment with the text *Include several examples of flyers containing graphic elements and color.* Do this by completing similar steps to those in 4.
6. Move the insertion point to the end of the last paragraph in the report. Key **Illustrations** and then select *Illustrations*. Create a comment with the text, *Add several illustrations of focal points in a document.*, by completing steps similar to those in 4.
7. Save the document again with the same name (Ch 17, Ex 09).

8. Print the document and the comments by completing the following steps:
   a. Display the Print dialog box.
   b. At the Print dialog box, click the Options button.
   c. At the Print dialog box with the Print tab selected, click Comments. (This inserts a check mark in the Comments check box and the Hidden text check box.)
   d. Click OK or press Enter.
   e. At the Print dialog box, click OK or press Enter.
9. Turn off the display of comment marks by completing steps similar to those in 3.
10. Turn off the printing of comments by completing the following steps:
   a. Display the Print dialog box.
   b. At the Print dialog box, click the Options button.
   c. At the Print dialog box with the Print tab selected, click Comments, and then click Hidden text.
   d. Click OK or press Enter.
   e. Click the Close button to close the Print dialog box.
11. Close Ch 17, Ex 09.

Creating Macros

In chapter 8, you learned about the AutoText feature that simplifies inserting commonly used words, names, or phrases in a document. Word includes another time-saving feature called *macros*. With macros, you can automate the formatting of a document. The word *macro* was coined by computer programmers for a collection of commands used to make a large programming job easier and save time. A Word macro is a document containing recorded commands that can accomplish a task automatically and save time.

In Word, creating a macro is referred to as *recording*. As a macro is being recorded, all the keys pressed and the menus and dialog boxes displayed are recorded and become part of the macro. For example, you can record a macro to change the left or right margins or insert page numbering in a document.

There are two steps involved in working with macros: recording a macro and running a macro. Word's macro feature can also be used to write macros. For more information on writing macros, please refer to Microsoft Word documentation.

Recording a Macro

Recording a macro involves turning on the macro recorder, performing the steps to be recorded, and then turning off the recorder. To record a macro, click Tools, point to Macro, then click Record New Macro. You can also double-click the REC button that displays on the Status bar. This displays the Record Macro dialog box shown in figure 17.9. At this dialog box, key a name for the macro in the Macro name text box. A macro name must begin with a letter and can contain only letters and numbers. You can also key a description for the macro in the Description text box located at the bottom of the dialog box. A macro description can contain a maximum of 255 characters and may include spaces. After keying a description for the macro, click OK or press Enter. This displays the document screen with the Macro Record toolbar displayed as shown in figure 17.10. At this screen, perform the actions to be recorded. After all steps to be recorded have been performed, stop the recording of the macro by clicking the Stop Recording button on the Macro Record toolbar, or by double-clicking the REC button on the Status bar.

figure 17.9 *Record Macro Dialog Box*

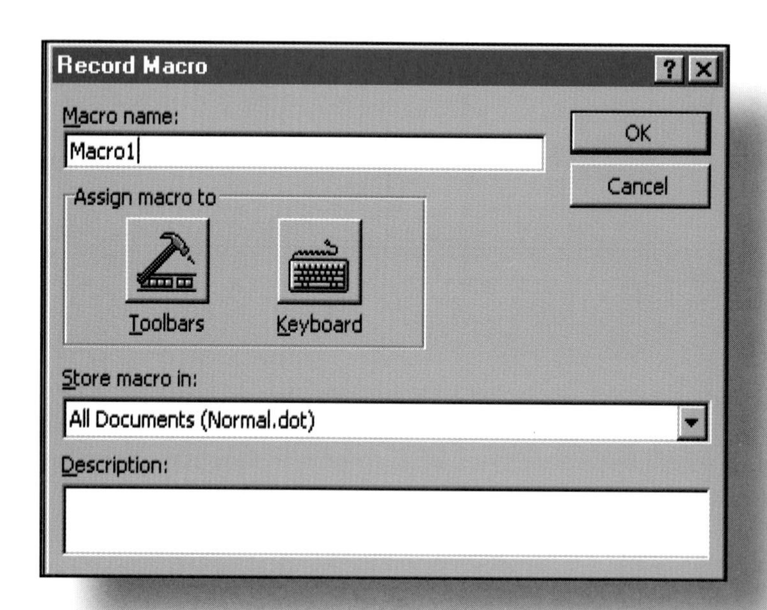

figure 17.10 *Macro Record Toolbar*

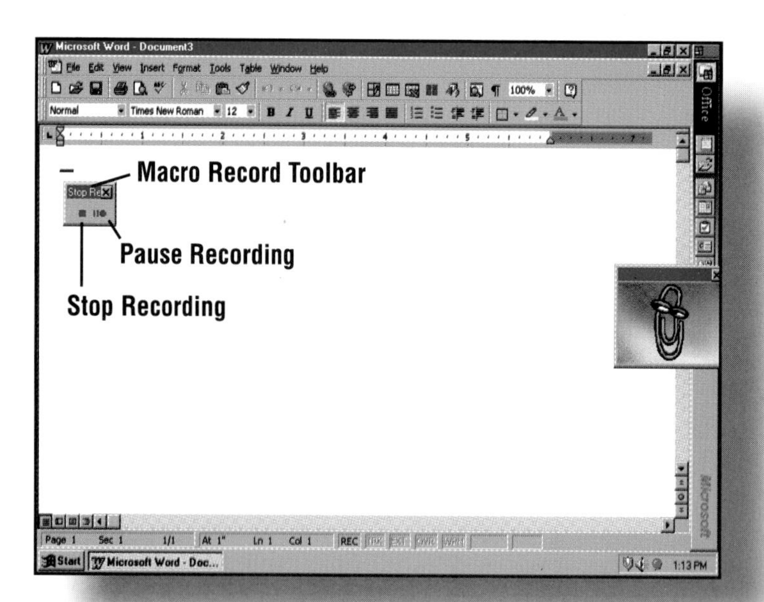

exercise 10

Recording Macros

1. Record a macro named *Ind01* that indents text in a paragraph 0.5 inch and hang indents second and subsequent lines of the paragraph by completing the following steps:
   a. At a clear document screen, double-click the REC button on the Status bar.
   b. At the Record Macro dialog box, key **Ind01** in the Macro name text box.
   c. Click inside the Description text box and then key **Indent and hang text in paragraph**. (If there is any text located in the Description text box, select the text first, and then key **Indent and hang text in paragraph**.)
   d. Click OK.
   e. At the document screen with the Macro Record toolbar displayed, complete the following steps:
      1) Click Format, then Paragraph.
      2) At the Paragraph dialog box, click the up-pointing triangle at the right side of the Left option until *0.5"* displays in the Left text box.
      3) Click the down-pointing triangle at the right side of the Special text box and then click *Hanging* at the drop-down list.
      4) Click OK or press Enter.
   f. Double-click the REC button on the Status bar.
2. Complete steps similar to those in 1 to create a macro named *Ind02* that indents text in a paragraph 1 inch and hang indents second and subsequent lines of the paragraph.
3. Record a macro named *Format01* that changes the top margin to 1.5 inches and the left and right margins to 1 inch by completing the following steps:
   a. At a clear document screen, click Tools, point to Macro, and then click Record New Macro.
   b. At the Record Macro dialog box, key **Format01** in the Macro name text box.
   c. Click in the Description text box (or select existing text in the Description text box) and then key **Change top, left, and right margins**.
   d. Click OK.
   e. At the document screen with the Macro Record toolbar displayed, change the top margin to 1.5 inches and the left and right margins to 1 inch.
   f. Click the Stop Recording button on the Macro Record toolbar.
4. Close the document without saving it.

Running a Macro

After a macro has been recorded, it can be run in a document. To run a macro, click Tools, point to Macro, and then click Macros. At the Macros dialog box, click the desired macro name in the list box, and then click the Run button. You can also just double-click the desired macro name in the list box.

exercise 11

Running Macros

1. Open Survey 01.
2. Save the document with Save As and name it Ch 17, Ex 11.
3. Run the *Format01* macro by completing the following steps:
   a. Click Tools, point to Macro, and then click Macros.
   b. At the Macros dialog box, click *Format01* in the Macro name list box, and then click the Run button.
4. Run the *Ind01* macro for the first numbered paragraph by completing the following steps:
   a. Position the insertion point anywhere in the paragraph that begins with 1.
   b. Click Tools, point to Macro, and then click Macros.
   c. At the Macros dialog box, double-click *Ind01* in the list box.
5. Complete steps similar to those in 4 to run the macro for each of the numbered paragraphs (just the numbered paragraphs, not the lettered paragraphs).
6. Run the *Ind02* macro for the lettered paragraph (a through d) after the first numbered paragraph by completing the following steps:
   a. Select paragraphs a through d below the first numbered paragraph.
   b. Click Tools, point to Macro, then click Macros.
   c. At the Macros dialog box, double-click *Ind02* in the list box.
7. Complete steps similar to those in 6a through 6c to run the macro for the lettered paragraphs below each of the numbered paragraphs.
8. Save the document again with the same name (Ch 17, Ex 11).
9. Print and then close Ch 17, Ex 11.

Pausing and Then Resuming a Macro

Pause Recording

When recording a macro, you can temporarily suspend the recording, perform actions that are not recorded, and then resume recording the macro. To pause the recording of a macro, click the Pause Recording button on the Macro Record toolbar. To resume recording the macro, click the Resume Recorder button (previously the Pause Recording button).

Deleting a Macro

If you no longer need a macro that has been recorded, it can be deleted. To delete a macro, click Tools, point to Macro, and then click Macros. At the Macros dialog box, click the macro name in the list box and then click the Delete button. At the Office Assistant message asking if you want to delete the macro, click Yes. Click the Close button to close the Macros dialog box.

exercise 12

Deleting Macros

1. At a clear document screen, delete the *Format01* macro by completing the following steps:
   a. Click Tools, point to Macro, and then click Macros.
   b. At the Macros dialog box, click *Format01* in the list box.
   c. Click the Delete button.
   d. At the Office Assistant message asking if you want to delete *Format01*, click Yes.
   e. Click the Close button to close the Macros dialog box.
2. Close the document.

Assigning a Macro a Keyboard Command

If you use a macro on a regular basis, you may want to assign it a keyboard command. To run a macro that has been assigned a keyboard command, all you do is press the keys assigned to the macro. A macro can be assigned a keyboard command with a letter plus Alt + Ctrl, Ctrl + Shift, or Alt + Shift. Word has already used many combinations for Word functions. For example, pressing Ctrl + Shift + A changes selected text to all capital letters.

With the Alt + Ctrl combination, the following letters are available for assigning to a macro: A, B, D, G, H, J, Q, W, and X. With the Ctrl + Shift combination, the following letters are available for assigning to a macro: G, J, O, R, X, and Y. The following letters are available with the Alt + Shift combination: B, G, H, J, Q, S, V, W, Y, and Z.

Assign a keyboard command to a macro at the Record Macro dialog box. In exercise 13 you will record a macro and then assign the macro to a keyboard command. If you delete the macro, the keyboard command is also deleted. This allows you to use the key combination again.

exercise 13

Recording and Assigning a Keyboard Command to a Macro

1. Record a macro named *Ltrhd01* that contains the letterhead text shown in figure 17.11 and assign it the keyboard command Alt + Shift + S by completing the following steps:
   a. At a clear document screen, double-click the REC button on the Status bar.
   b. At the Record Macro dialog box, key **Ltrhd01** in the Macro name text box.
   c. Click in the Description text box (or select existing text in the Description text box) and then key **St. Francis Letterhead**.
   d. Click the Keyboard button.
   e. At the Customize Keyboard dialog box with the insertion point positioned in the Press new shortcut key text box, press Alt + Shift + S.
   f. Click the Assign button.
   g. Click the Close button.
   h. At the document screen with the Macro Record toolbar displayed, create the letterhead shown in figure 17.11 by completing the following steps:
      1) Press Ctrl + E.
      2) Key **ST. FRANCIS MEDICAL CENTER**.
      3) Press Enter and then key **300 Blue Ridge Boulevard**.
      4) Press Enter and then key **Kansas City, MO 63009**.
      5) Press Enter and then key **(816) 555-2000**.
      6) Press Enter.
      7) Press Ctrl + L to return the paragraph alignment to left.
      8) Press Enter.
      9) Select (using the keyboard) the hospital name, address, and telephone number, then change the font to 18-point Goudy Old Style bold (or a similar serif typeface).
      10) Deselect the text (using the keyboard).
   i. Click the Stop Recording button on the Macro Record toolbar.
2. Close the document without saving changes.
3. At a clear document screen, run the *Ltrhd01* macro by pressing Alt + Shift + S.
4. With the insertion point a double space below the letterhead, turn off the automatic numbering feature. (To do this, click Tools, then AutoCorrect. At the AutoCorrect dialog box, click the AutoFormat As You Type tab. Remove the check mark from the Automatic numbered lists option and then click OK to close the dialog box.)
5. Key the letter shown in figure 17.12. (Press the Tab key after keying the numbers *1.* and *2.* and the letters *a.* and *b.*)

6. After keying the letter, make the following changes:
   a. Change the top and bottom margins to 0.75 inch and the left and right margins to 1 inch.
   b. Run the *Ind01* macro for the numbered paragraphs and the *Ind02* macro for the lettered paragraphs.
7. If necessary, turn on the automatic numbering option. (For help, refer to step 4.)
8. Save the letter and name it Ch 17, Ex 13.
9. Print and then close Ch 17, Ex 13.

17.11 *Exercise 13*

ST. FRANCIS MEDICAL CENTER
300 Blue Ridge Boulevard
Kansas City, MO 63009
(816) 555-2000

17.12 *Exercise 13*

May 12, 1999

Mr. Victor Durham
Good Samaritan Hospital
1201 James Street
St. Louis, MO 62033

Dear Victor:

Congratulations on obtaining eight new nursing positions at your hospital. The attached registered nurse job description is generic. Depending on the specialty, additional responsibilities are added such as:

1. Uses the nursing process to prescribe, coordinate, and delegate patient care from admission through discharge.
a. Analyzes the patient's condition and reports changes to the appropriate health care provider.
b. Observes patient for signs and symptoms, collects data on patient; reports and documents results.
2. Teaches patient, family, staff, and students.
a. Assumes responsibility for patient and family teaching and discharge planning.
b. Participates in orientation of new staff and/or acts as preceptor.

I am interested in hearing about your recruitment plan. We are hiring additional medical personnel in the fall at St. Francis so I need to begin formulating a recruitment plan.

Sincerely,

Mariah Jackson

XX:Ch 17, Ex 13

Attachment

Assigning a Macro to the Toolbar

A macro that you use on a very regular basis can be added to a toolbar. To run a macro from a toolbar, just click the button. In exercise 14, you will assign a macro to the Standard toolbar. A macro can be assigned to any toolbar that is displayed. For example, a macro can be assigned to the Formatting toolbar if that toolbar is displayed in the document screen.

An existing macro can also be assigned to a toolbar. To do this, display the Customize dialog box. At the Customize dialog box, click *Macros* in the Categories list box. Position the arrow pointer on the desired macro in the Macros list box, hold down the left mouse button, drag the outline of the button to the desired location on the desired toolbar, and then release the mouse button. Click the Close button to close the Customize dialog box.

A macro button can be removed from a toolbar with the Customize dialog box open. To do this, display the Customize dialog box with the Toolbars tab selected. Position the arrow pointer on the button to be removed, hold down the left mouse button, drag the outline of the button off the toolbar, and then release the mouse button. Click Close to close the Customize dialog box. When a macro button is removed from a toolbar, the macro is not deleted. Delete the macro at the Macros dialog box.

exercise 14

Assigning a Macro to the Standard Toolbar

1. At a clear document screen, create a macro named *Tab01* and assign it to the Standard toolbar by completing the following steps:
   a. Double-click the REC button on the Status bar.
   b. At the Macro Record dialog box, key **Tab01** in the Macro name text box.
   c. Click inside the Description text box (or select text) and then key **Set left tabs at 0.5 and 1.0 and right tab with leaders at 5.5**.
   d. Click the Toolbars button.
   e. At the Customize dialog box shown in figure 17.13, position the arrow pointer on the *Tab01* macro in the Commands list box. (This macro name may display as *Normal.NewMacros.Tab01*.) Hold down the left mouse button, drag the large I-beam pointer representing the macro between the Spelling and Grammar button and the Cut button on the Standard toolbar, and then release the mouse button.
   f. Shorten the name of the macro by completing the following steps:
      1) With the Customize dialog box still displayed, position the arrow pointer on the Tab01 button on the Standard toolbar, and then click the *right* mouse button.
      2) At the drop-down list that displays, click Name. (This moves the insertion point inside the text box containing the full macro name.)
      3) Delete the existing name, key **T01** in the Name text box, and then press Enter.
   g. Click the Close button to close the Customize dialog box.
   h. At the document screen with the Macro Record toolbar displayed, complete the necessary steps to set left tabs at the 0.5-inch mark and the 1-inch mark and a right tab with preceding leaders at 5.5-inch mark. (You must do this at the Tabs dialog box, not on the Ruler.)
   i. After setting the tabs, click the Stop Recording button on the Macro Record toolbar.

2. Close the document without saving it.
3. At a clear document screen create the document shown in figure 17.14 by completing the following steps:
   a. Click the *T01* button on the Standard toolbar.
   b. Key the text as shown in figure 17.14. (Key the first column of text at the first tab stop, not the left margin.)
4. Save the document and name it Ch 17, Ex 14.
5. Print and then close Ch 17, Ex 14.
6. Remove the *T01* button from the Standard toolbar by completing the following steps:
   a. At a clear document screen, click Tools, then Customize.
   b. At the Customize dialog box, make sure the Toolbars tab is selected.
   c. Position the arrow pointer on the *T01* button on the Standard toolbar, hold down the left mouse button, drag the outline of the button off the toolbar, and then release the mouse button.
   d. Click the Close button to close the Customize dialog box.

figure 17.13 ***Customize Dialog Box***

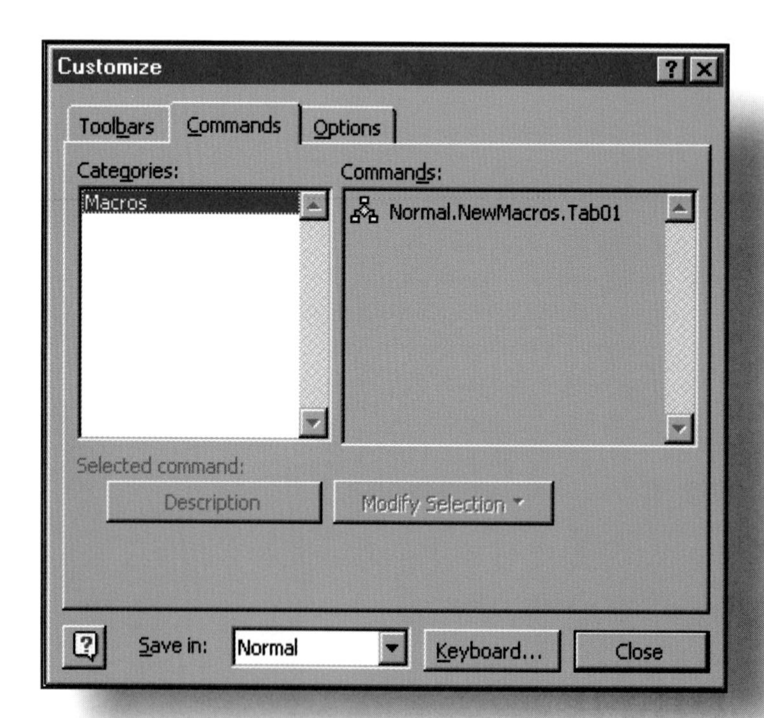

17.14 *Exercise 14*

COLEMAN DEVELOPMENT CORPORATION

Mandy Armstead ....Chief Executive Officer

Stephanie Branson ....President

Brandon Kent ....Vice President

Conrad Wheeler ....Vice President

Selene Resnick ....Vice President

Aurora Madsen ....Vice President

Paul O'Shea ....Development Manager

chapter summary

- Word's hyphenation feature can help achieve a more balanced look when the right margin of a left-justified document is particularly ragged, or when the lines in justified paragraphs include large spaces.
- In addition to automatic or manual hyphenation, these options are also available at the Hyphenation dialog box: choose to hyphenate words that are in all capital letters, limit the number of consecutive lines that can end in hyphens, or tell Word to ignore text in selected text when hyphenating.
- To remove all manual or automatic hyphenations immediately after hyphenating, use the Undo feature. Delete specific hyphens at the Find and Replace dialog box with the Replace tab selected.
- The default hyphenation zone is 0.25 inch from the right margin. If the hyphenation zone is decreased at the Hyphenation dialog box, more words will be hyphenated. If the zone is increased, fewer words will be hyphenated.
- Keying a minus sign in a document inserts a *regular* hyphen. A hyphen inserted during the hyphenation process is called an *optional* hyphen. Insert a *nonbreaking* hyphen in words or groups of numbers that should be kept together on one line.

- Lines in a document can be numbered with options from the Line Numbers dialog box.
- Animate text in the screen with options at the Font dialog box with the Animation tab selected.
- Create bookmarks to mark a location in the document so you can later move the insertion point quickly to that location. Create or delete bookmarks at the Bookmark dialog box.
- Comments can be inserted in a document. The comment mark and/or the comment text can be hidden or displayed.
- Word's Macro feature is primarily used for executing a series of commands or applying formatting.
- Recording a macro involves turning on the macro recorder, performing the steps to be recorded, and then turning off the recorder.
- You can temporarily suspend the recording of a macro by clicking the Pause Recording button on the Macro Record toolbar.
- Run, delete, or rename a macro from the Macros dialog box.
- Assign a keyboard command to a macro at the Record Macro dialog box.
- A macro that you use quite often can be added to a toolbar.

commands review

	Mouse	Keyboard
Hyphenation dialog box	Tools, Language, Hyphenation	Tools, Language, Hyphenation
Remove all manual or automatic hyphens	Click [Undo button] on the Standard toolbar	Edit, Undo Hyphenation
Find and Replace dialog box with Replace tab selected	Edit, Replace	Edit, Replace
Insert an optional hyphen		CTRL + -
Insert a nonbreaking hyphen		CTRL + SHIFT + -
Line Numbering dialog box	File, Page Setup, click Layout tab, then Line Numbers	File, Page Setup, choose Layout tab, then Line Numbers
Font dialog box	Format, Font	Format, Font
Create a bookmark	Edit, Bookmark, key unique name for the bookmark, click Add	Edit, Bookmark, key unique name for the bookmark, choose Add
Move insertion point to a bookmark	Edit, Bookmark, double-click bookmark name, click Close	Edit, Bookmark, key or select name, choose Go To, choose Close

Insert comment	Insert, Comment, key remarks, click Close; or click [button] on Reviewing toolbar, key remarks, click Close	Insert, Comment, key remarks, choose Close
Macros dialog box	Tools, Macro, Macros	Tools, Macro, Macros
Record Macro dialog box	Double-click REC button on Status bar; or click Tools, Macro, then Record New Macro	Tools, Macro, Record New Macro

check your understanding

Completion: In the space provided at the right, indicate the correct term, command, or number.

1. This is the keyboard command to insert an optional hyphen when hyphenation is off. ________
2. This is the default measurement for the hyphenation zone. ________
3. Press this key to insert a regular hyphen. ________
4. This is the name of the feature that will delete all hyphens immediately after hyphenation. ________
5. Do this to the hyphenation zone if you want to hyphenate more words in a document. ________
6. Add animation effects to selected text at the Font dialog box with this tab selected. ________
7. Click the New Comment button on this toolbar to insert a comment in a document. ________
8. To print comments with a document, insert a check mark in this check box at the Print dialog box with the Print tab selected. ________
9. Double-click this button on the Status bar to display the Record Macro dialog box. ________
10. Click Tools, point to this option, and then click Hyphenation to display the Hyphenation dialog box. ________
11. A macro can be assigned a keyboard command or it can be assigned to this. ________

In the space provided below, list the steps needed to record a macro that changes the font to 18-point Arial bold. Name the macro *Font18*.

___

___

___

___

In the space provided below, list the steps needed to run the *Font18* macro.

___

___

___

skill assessments

Note: Before completing the skill assessments, display the Open dialog box, and then select and delete documents created in chapter 15 that begin Ch 15. You may want to check with your instructor before deleting these documents.

Assessment 1

1. Open Para 04.
2. Save the document with Save As and name it Ch 17, SA 01.
3. Make the following changes to the document:
   a. Select the entire document and then change the font to 12-point Arial.
   b. Change the left and right margins for the document to 2 inches.
   c. Change the hyphenation zone to 0.5 inch and then hyphenate the text in the document automatically.
4. Save the document again with the same name (Ch 17, SA 01).
5. Print and then close Ch 17, SA 01.

Assessment 2

1. Open Report 01.
2. Save the document with Save As and name it Ch 17, SA 02.
3. Make the following changes to the report:
   a. Select the entire document and then change the font to 13-point Garamond.
   b. Set the title and the headings in 14-point Arial bold.
   c. Select the text in the body of the report (everything except the title) and then make the following changes:
      1) Change the line spacing to single.
      2) Change the spacing before and after paragraphs to 6 points.

        3) Change the paragraph alignment to justified.
    d. Hyphenate the document manually.
    e. Create a comment at the end of the second paragraph in the *Defining Desktop Publishing* section of the report. Key the words **Color printers?**, select the words, and then create the comment with the following text: *Include information on color printers.*
    f. Create a comment at the end of the last paragraph in the *Planning the Publication* section of the report. Key the word **Examples**, select the word, and then create the comment with the following text: *Include examples of effective designs.*
4. Save the document again with the same name (Ch 17, SA 02).
5. Print the document and the comments. (After printing the document and the comments, be sure to remove the check marks in the Comments and Hidden text check boxes at the Print dialog box with the Print tab selected.)
6. Close Ch 17, SA 02.

Assessment 3

1. Open Legal 02.
2. Save the document with Save As and name it Ch 17, SA 03.
3. Make the following changes to the document:
    a. Select the entire document and then change the font to 12-point Arial.
    b. Complete the following find and replaces:
        1) Find NAME1 and replace with KRISTEN LONG.
        2) Find NUMBER and replace with C-9903.
    c. Automatically hyphenate the text in the document.
    d. Turn on line numbering in the document.
    e. If necessary, realign any right parentheses in the heading that may have moved.
    f. Change the left and right margins to 1 inch. (Make sure the document fits on one page. If not, shorten the top and bottom margins to 0.75 inch.)
4. Save the document again with the same name (Ch 17, SA 03).
5. Print and then close Ch 17, SA 03.

Assessment 4

1. Open Notice 02.
2. Save the document with Save As and name it Ch 17, SA 04.
3. Make the following changes to the document:
    a. Select the entire document.
    b. Set the selected text in a decorative typeface and type size of your choosing.
    c. Add an animation effect to all the text or just the first line of text.
4. Save the document again with the same name (Ch 17, SA 04).
5. Print and then close Ch 17, SA 04. (The animation effect will not print.)

Assessment 5

1. At a clear document screen, record a macro named *Ltrhd02* that contains the letterhead text shown in figure 17.15 and assign it the keyboard command, Alt + Ctrl + G. (The text in figure 17.15 is set in 18-point Goudy Old Style bold.)
2. Close the document without saving it.

3. At a clear document screen, run the *Ltrhd02* macro.
4. With the insertion point a double space below the letterhead, key the letter shown in figure 17.16. Use the Bullets button on the Formatting toolbar to insert the bullets as shown in the document. (Make sure the letter fits on one page. If not, change the top and bottom margins to 0.75 inch and the left and right margins to 1 inch.)
5. Save the letter and name it Ch 17, SA 05.
6. Print and then close Ch 17, SA 05.

Figure 17.15 • Assessment 5

GOOD SAMARITAN HOSPITAL
1201 James Street
St. Louis, MO 62033
(816) 555-1201

Figure 17.16 • Assessment 5

May 18, 1999

Ms. Mariah Jackson
St. Francis Medical Center
300 Blue Ridge Boulevard
Kansas City, MO 63009

Dear Mariah:

The registered nurse job description was very timely. I was able to use the basic outline to create a job description for the hospital. For one of the positions, the following information was included:

- Functions with the awareness of safety needs and implements appropriate safety measure.

    - Demonstrates adherence to all unit hospital safety standards.
    - Follows established standards in emergency situations.
- Recognizes, communicates, delegates, and coordinates management of emergent situations.
- Demonstrates awareness of legal issues on all aspects of patient care and unit function and takes action to limit or reduce risks.
    - Completes unusual occurrence form for all patient incidents.
    - Adheres to organizational standards in the area of patient confidentiality.

The information was provided by our legal department. Safety and legal issues are an integral part of medical services.

Very truly yours,

Victor Durham

XX:Ch 17, SA 05

Assessment 6

1. At a clear document screen, run the *Tab01* macro and then create the document shown in figure 17.17. (Key the text in the first column at the first tab stop, not the left margin.)
2. After creating the document, save it and name it Ch 17, SA 06.
3. Print and then close Ch 17, SA 06.
4. Delete all macros displayed in the Macros dialog box.

Figure 17.17 • Assessment 6

COLEMAN DEVELOPMENT CORPORATION

Human Resources Department, Extension Numbers

Nicole Clark 129

Jack Takagawa 143

Darryl Ellis 317

Lynette Lagasi 211

Jolene Sinclair 339

Matthew Franklin 122

chapter EIGHTEEN

18 Adding Borders and Inserting Clip Art

PERFORMANCE OBJECTIVES

Upon successful completion of chapter 18, you will be able to:

- **Add borders to paragraphs of text with options from the Borders button on the Formatting toolbar.**
- **Add borders and shading to paragraphs of text with options at the Borders and Shading dialog box.**
- **Add a border line to a footer.**
- **Insert, size, move, and format clip art images in a document.**
- **Insert pictures in a document.**
- **Create and format a text box.**

Microsoft Word 97 contains a variety of features that help you enhance the visual appeal of a document. In this chapter, you will learn to add a border to a paragraph or selected paragraphs in a document, and add color and shading to a border. You will also learn to enhance a document by inserting a clip art image, picture, or text box.

Adding Borders with the Borders Button

Every paragraph you create in Word contains an invisible frame. A border that appears around this frame can be added to a paragraph. A border can be added to specific sides of the paragraph or to all sides. The type of border line and thickness of the line can be customized. In addition, you can add shading and fill to the border.

When a border is added to a paragraph of text, the border expands and contracts as text is inserted or deleted from the paragraph. You can create a border around a single paragraph or a border around selected paragraphs.

Creating a Border

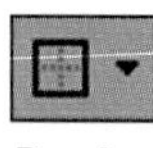
Border

One method for creating a border is to use options from the Border button on the Formatting toolbar. The name of the button changes depending on the border choice that was previously selected at the button drop-down palette. When Word is first opened, the button name displays as Outside Border. Position the arrow pointer on the down-pointing triangle at the right side of the Border button and then click the left mouse button. This causes a list of border choices to display as shown in figure 18.1.

figure 18.1 *Border Options*

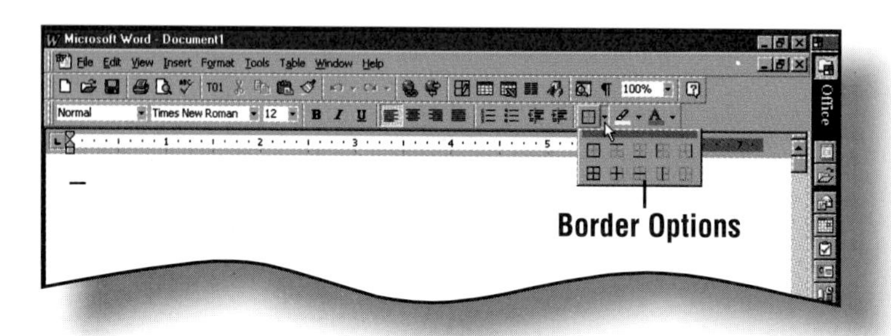

Click the option that will insert the desired border. For example, to insert a border at the bottom of the paragraph, click the middle option in the top row. Clicking an option will add the border to the paragraph where the insertion point is located. To add a border to more than one paragraph, select the paragraphs first and then click the desired option.

exercise 1

Adding Borders to Paragraphs of Text

1. Open Para 02.
2. Save the document with Save As and name it Ch 18, Ex 01.
3. Create a border around the first paragraph by completing the following steps:
   a. Position the insertion point anywhere in the first paragraph.
   b. Position the arrow pointer on the Border button on the Formatting toolbar and wait for the ScreenTip to display. Make sure the ScreenTip displays as Outside Border and then click the button. (If this is not the name for the button, click the down-pointing triangle at the right side of the button and then click the first option in the first row at the drop-down list of options.)
4. Complete steps similar to those in 3 to add a border to the second paragraph.
5. Complete steps similar to those in 3 to add a border to the third paragraph.
6. Save the document again with the same name (Ch 18, Ex 01).

7. Print Ch 18, Ex 01.
8. With the document still open, remove the borders by completing the following steps:
   a. Select the three paragraphs in the document. (You do not have to select all the text in the first and last paragraphs, just a portion.)
   b. Click the down-pointing triangle at the right side of the Border button on the Formatting toolbar and then click the last option in the bottom row. (This removes the borders from the three paragraphs.)
   c. Deselect the text.
9. Add a border around and between the paragraphs by completing the following steps:
   a. Select from the middle of the first paragraph to somewhere in the middle of the third paragraph.
   b. Click the down-pointing triangle at the right side of the Border button and then click the first option in the second row.
   c. Deselect the text.
10. Save the document again with the same name (Ch 18, Ex 01).
11. Print and then close Ch 18, Ex 01.

Adding Borders and Shading

As you learned in the previous section, borders can be added to a paragraph or selected paragraphs with options from the Border button on the Formatting toolbar. If you want to customize the line creating the border or add shading, use options from the Borders and Shading dialog box. To display this dialog box, shown in figure 18.2, click Format, then Borders and Shading.

figure 18.2 **Borders and Shading Dialog Box with the Borders Tab Selected**

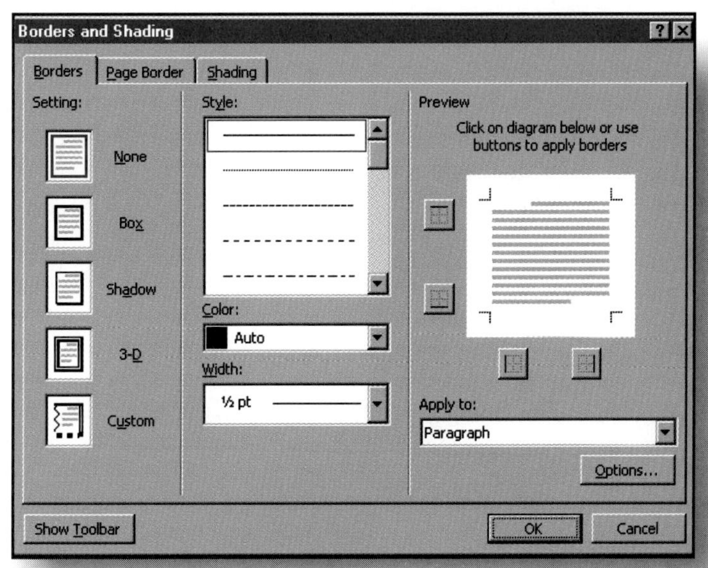

The buttons in the Setting section of the dialog box contain a visual display of line options. For example, click the Box button to insert a border around the paragraph (or selected paragraphs). Click the 3-D button to insert a border with a shadow, creating a three-dimensional look.

With the options in the Style list box, you can change the line style. To change the line style, click the desired style in the list box. If the desired style is not visible, scroll through the list box to display the desired style.

The default line color is black. This can be changed to a different color. To do this, click the down-pointing triangle at the right side of the Color text box and then click the desired color at the drop-down list. If the desired color is not visible, scroll down the list.

The default line width is ½ point. The line width can be changed by clicking the down-pointing triangle at the right side of the Width text box and then clicking the desired width at the pop-up iist.

The diagram in the Preview section offers another method for inserting border lines. Specify where you want a border line to appear by clicking the desired location on the diagram. For example, if you want to insert a border at the bottom of the paragraph (or selected paragraphs), click the bottom portion of the diagram in the Preview section. This adds a border line to the diagram. You can also click a button in the Preview section that displays the desired border. For example, to add a border at the right side of the paragraph (or selected paragraphs), click the button that displays at the bottom of the diagram at the right side.

The Apply to option has a setting of *Paragraph*. This specifies to what the border and shading will apply. Click the Options button and options display for setting the desired distance between the edge of the border and the text.

exercise 2

Adding a Customized Border to a Document

1. Open Notice 02.
2. Save the document with Save As and name it Ch 18, Ex 02.
3. Make the following changes to the document:
   a. With the insertion point at the beginning of the document, press the Enter key twice.
   b. Select the entire document and then change the font to 18-point Mistral bold and the text color to Dark Red. (If Mistral is not available, choose a fancy, decorative typeface.)
   c. With the entire document still selected, add a dark blue shadow border by completing the following steps:
      1) Click Format, then Borders and Shading.
      2) At the Borders and Shading dialog box with the Borders tab selected, click the Shadow button.
      3) Click the down-pointing triangle at the right side of the Width text box and then click the *6 pt* line at the pop-up list.

4) Click the down-pointing triangle at the right side of the Color text box and then click *Dark Blue* at the drop-down list. (You will need to scroll down the list to display Dark Blue.)
5) Click OK or press Enter.

4. Deselect the text and then save the document again with the same name (Ch 18, Ex 02).
5. Print and then close Ch 18, Ex 02.

Adding Shading

With choices from the Borders and Shading dialog box with the Shading tab selected, shown in figure 18.3, you can add shading to the border around text. Fill color choices display in the upper left corner of the dialog box. To add a fill, click the desired color in this section. If you want to add a pattern, click the down-pointing triangle at the right side of the Style text box and then click the desired pattern at the drop-down list. If a pattern is added inside a border, the color of the pattern can be changed with the Color option. Click the down-pointing triangle at the right side of the Color text box and then click the desired color at the drop-down list.

The Preview area of the Borders and Shading dialog box with the Shading tab selected displays how the border shading and/or pattern will display.

18.3 ***Borders and Shading Dialog Box with Shading Tab Selected***

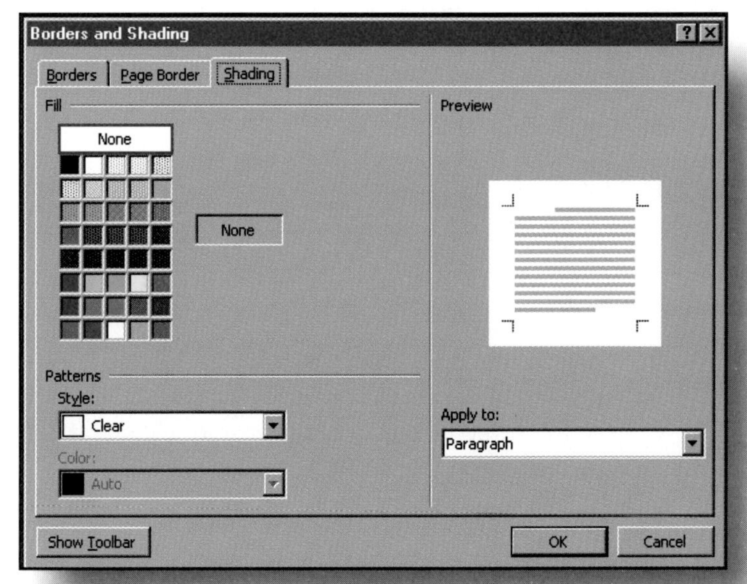

exercise 3

Adding Borders and Shading to Paragraphs of Text

1. Open Para 03.
2. Save the document with Save As and name it Ch 18, Ex 03.
3. Create a border around all the paragraphs in the document that is 3 points thick and contains 25 percent shading by completing the following steps:
   a. Select all paragraphs in the document.
   b. Click Format, then Borders and Shading.
   c. At the Borders and Shading dialog box with the Borders tab selected, click the Box button located at the left side of the dialog box.
   d. Click the down-pointing triangle at the right side of the Width text box and then click *3 pt* at the pop-up list.
   e. Make sure that *Auto* is selected in the Color text box. If not, click the down-pointing triangle at the right side of the Color text box and then click *Auto* at the drop-down list. (This option is located at the beginning of the list.)
   f. Click the Shading tab.
   g. Click the light turquoise color in the Fill section of the dialog box.
   h. Click the down-pointing triangle at the right side of the Style list box and then click *5%* at the drop-down list.
   i. Click OK to close the dialog box.
4. Deselect the text and then save the document again with the same name (Ch 18, Ex 03).
5. Print and then close Ch 18, Ex 03.

exercise 4

Adding a Border and Shading to a Document

1. Open Notice 03.
2. Save the document with Save As and name it Ch 18, Ex 04.
3. Make the following changes to the document:
   a. With the insertion point positioned at the beginning of the document, press the Enter key twice.
   b. Select the entire document and then change the paragraph alignment to centered.
   c. With the entire document still selected, add a border and shading by completing the following steps:
      1) Click Format, then Borders and Shading.

2) At the Borders and Shading dialog box with the Borders tab selected, click the Box button located at the left side of the dialog box.
3) Click the down-pointing triangle at the right side of the Width text box and then click *2 ¼ pt* at the pop-up list.
4) Click the bottom line of the diagram in the Preview section. (This removes the line.)
5) Click the top line of the diagram in the Preview section. (This removes the line.)
6) Click the Shading tab.
7) At the Borders and Shading dialog box with the Shading tab selected, click the first color in the last row in the Fill section (this is a bright pink color).
8) Click OK to close the dialog box.

4. Deselect the text and then save the document again with the same name (Ch 18, Ex 04).
5. Print and then close Ch 18, Ex 04.

Word's border feature can be used to add lines in headers and/or footers. For example, you can add a line below text in a header or add a line above text in a footer. This line acts as a graphics element that adds visual appeal to a document.

exercise 5

Adding a Footer and Border Line to a Document

1. Open Report 02.
2. Save the document with Save As and name it Ch 18, Ex 05.
3. Create a footer that prints on every page of the document and contains a border line by completing the following steps:
   a. Click View, then Header and Footer.
   b. At the header pane, click the Switch Between Header and Footer button on the Header and Footer toolbar.
   c. At the footer pane, turn on bold, and then key **Desktop Publishing** at the left margin.
   d. Press the Tab key twice.
   e. Key **Page** and then press the space bar.
   f. Click the Insert Page Number button on the Header and Footer toolbar.
   g. Select the number 1 and then turn on bold.
   h. Click Format, then Borders and Shading.
   i. At the Borders and Shading dialog box with the Borders tab selected, click the down-pointing triangle at the right side of the Style list box until the first thick/thin double line displays and then click the thick/thin double line.

j. Check the diagram in the Preview section of the dialog box. If there are any lines displayed in this diagram, click each line to remove it.
k. Click the top portion of the diagram to insert a thick/thin line at the top.
l. Click OK to close the dialog box.
m. Click the Close button to close the Header and Footer toolbar.

4. Check the page breaks in the report and, if necessary, adjust the page breaks.
5. Save the document again with the same name (Ch 18, Ex 05).
6. Print and then close Ch 18, Ex 05.

Adding Page Borders

The borders you have created have been included in a paragraph of text or selected paragraphs. Word also includes a page border feature that will insert a border around an entire page rather than just a paragraph. To insert a page border in a document, click Format, then Borders and Shading. At the Borders and Shading dialog box, click the Page Border tab. This displays the dialog box as shown in figure 18.4.

18.4 **Borders and Shading Dialog Box with Page Border Tab Selected**

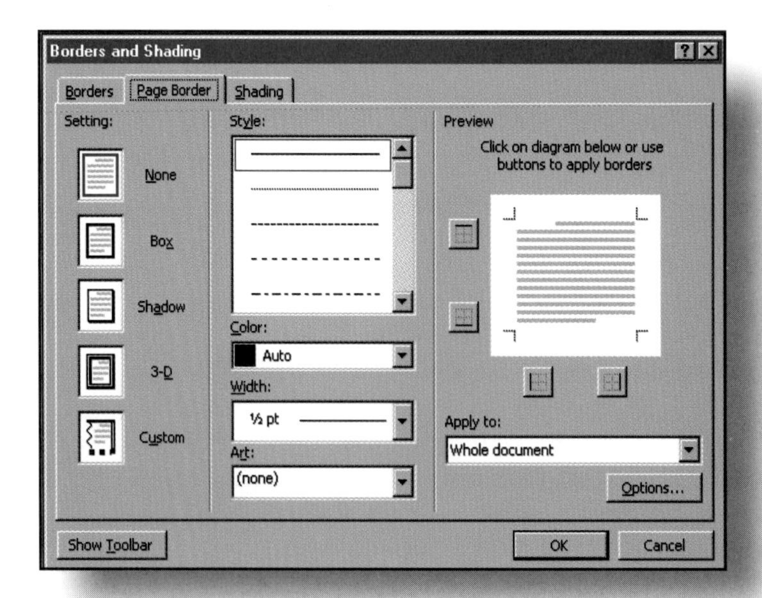

The options at the Borders and Shading dialog box with the Page Border tab selected are basically the same as those for paragraph borders. The difference is that the border is inserted around the page rather than the paragraph of text.

exercise 6

Inserting a Page Border in a Document

1. Open Report 02.
2. Save the document with Save As and name it Ch 18, Ex 06.
3. Make the following changes to the document:
   a. Select the entire document and then change the font to 12-point Garamond (or a similar serif typeface).
   b. Bold the following title and headings in the document:
      DESKTOP PUBLISHING DESIGN
      Designing a Document
      Creating Focus
4. Add a border to each page in the document by completing the following steps:
   a. With the insertion point positioned at the beginning of the document, click Format, then Borders and Shading.
   b. At the Borders and Shading dialog box, click the Page Border tab.
   c. Click the Box button in the Setting section.
   d. Scroll down the list of line styles in the Style list box until the end of the list displays and then click the third line from the end.
   e. Click OK to close the dialog box.
5. Save the document again with the same name (Ch 18, Ex 06).
6. Print and then close Ch 18, Ex 06.

The Borders and Shading dialog box with the Page Border tab selected offers an option for inserting on the page a border containing an image. To display the images available, click the down-pointing triangle at the right side of the Art text box and then scroll down the list. Click the desired image; this image is used to create the border around the page.

exercise 7

Inserting a Page Border Containing Balloons

1. Open Notice 01.
2. Save the document with Save As and name it Ch 18, Ex 07.
3. Make the following changes to the document:

a. Select the entire document and then change to a decorative font of your choosing.
b. Center the text vertically on the page by completing the following steps:
    1) Click File, then Page Setup.
    2) At the Page Setup dialog box, click the Layout tab.
    3) At the Page Setup dialog box with the Layout tab selected, click the down-pointing triangle at the right side of the Vertical alignment text box, and then click *Center* at the drop-down list.
    4) Click OK to close the Page Setup dialog box.

4. Add a decorative border to the document by completing the following steps:
    a. Click Format, then Borders and Shading.
    b. At the Borders and Shading dialog box, click the Page Border tab.
    c. Click the Box button in the Setting section.
    d. Click the down-pointing triangle at the right side of the Art text box.
    e. At the drop-down list that displays, scroll down the list until balloons display and then click the balloons.
    f. Click OK to close the dialog box.
5. Save the document again with the same name (Ch 18, Ex 07).
6. Print and then close Ch 18, Ex 07.

Adding Clip Art to Documents

Word 97 includes a gallery of clip art images that can be inserted in a document. To insert a clip art image, click Insert, point to Picture, and then click Clip Art. This displays the Microsoft Clip Gallery 3.0 dialog box with the Clip Art tab selected as shown in figure 18.5. (You may receive a message on the screen telling you that additional clips are available on the Microsoft Office 97 CD-ROM. At this message, click OK.)

Another method for displaying the Microsoft Clip Gallery 3.0 is to click Insert, then Object. At the Object dialog box with the Create New tab selected, double-click *Microsoft Clip Gallery* in the list box.

18.5 **Microsoft Clip Gallery 3.0 Dialog Box with Clip Art Tab Selected**

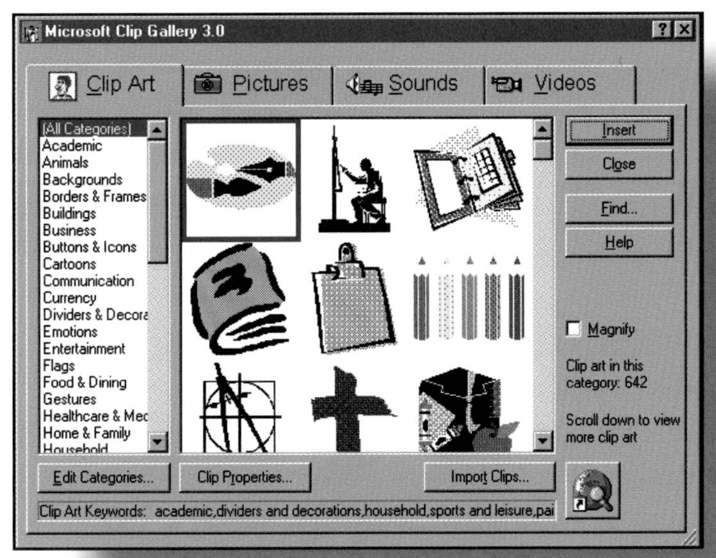

At the Microsoft Clip Gallery 3.0 dialog box with the Clip Art tab selected, the clip art images display in the middle of the dialog box. For easier viewing, clip art images can be displayed by category. To do this, click the desired category in the list box that displays at the left side of the dialog box. For example, if you click *Business* in the list box, images display in the middle of the dialog box that pertain to business. To insert an image into a document, double-click the desired clip art image, or click the image once, and then click the Insert button. When a clip art image is inserted in a document, Word automatically changes to the Page Layout viewing mode.

(Note: The availability of clip art images will vary depending on the type of installation and the amount of space available for the images. In some exercises requiring you to insert a clip art image, the image will display at the margin next to the instruction and general information about the image will be provided. An alternative image may also be included in the margin. If you do not have the requested image, look for the alternative. If the alternative image is also not available, substitute a similar image.)

Sizing a Clip Art Image

Once a clip art image is inserted in a document, it can be sized and/or moved. Click once on a clip art image and white sizing handles display around the edges of the image. To change the size of an image, position the arrow pointer on a sizing handle until it turns into a double-headed arrow, hold down the left mouse button, drag the sizing handle in or out to decrease or increase the size of the image, and then release the mouse button.

Use the middle sizing handles at the left or right side of the image to make the image wider or thinner. Use the middle sizing handles at the top or bottom of the image to make the image taller or shorter. Use the sizing handles at the corners of the image to change both the width and height at the same time.

As mentioned earlier, when a clip art image is inserted in a document, Word automatically changes to the Page Layout viewing mode. In Page Layout viewing mode, a horizontal ruler displays toward the top of the screen and a vertical ruler displays along the left side of the screen. You can use these rulers to help you size the image to a particular measurement.

Moving a Clip Art Image

Move a clip art image by dragging the image. To do this, click once on the image to select it. Position the arrow pointer on the image, hold down the left mouse button, drag the outline of the image to the desired position, and then release the mouse button. To deselect an image, click anywhere in the document outside the image.

exercise 8

Inserting, Sizing, and Moving a Clip Art Image in a Word Document

1. At a clear document screen, insert and then size a clip art image by completing the following steps:
   a. Click Insert, point to Picture, and then click Clip Art. (If a message box displays telling you that additional clips are available on the Microsoft Office 97 CD-ROM, click OK.)
   b. At the Microsoft Clip Gallery 3.0 dialog box (see figure 18.5), scroll through the list of images that displays in the middle of the dialog box.
   c. After viewing some of the clip art images, double-click an image of your choosing. (This inserts the image in the document screen and changes the viewing mode to Page Layout.)
   d. Change the size of the image by completing the following steps:
      1) If necessary, click the down scroll triangle on the vertical scroll bar until the bottom sizing handles are displayed.
      2) Drag the middle sizing handle at the bottom of the clip art image to approximately the 2½-inch mark on the vertical ruler (located at the left side of the screen).
      3) Drag the middle sizing handle at the right side of the clip art image to approximately the 2½-inch mark on the horizontal ruler (located toward the top of the screen).
   e. Move the clip art image by completing the following steps:
      1) Click the down-pointing arrow at the right side of the Zoom button on the Standard toolbar and then click *Whole Page* at the drop-down list.
      2) With the clip art image still selected, position the arrow pointer inside the image. (The arrow pointer displays with a four-headed arrow attached.)

3) Hold down the left mouse button, drag the image to the middle of the page, and then release the mouse button.
4) Click the down-pointing triangle at the right side of the Zoom button on the Standard toolbar and then click *100%* at the drop-down list.

f. Click outside the image to deselect it.

2. Save the document and name it Ch 18, Ex 08.
3. Print and then close Ch 18, Ex 08.

Zoom

Formatting Clip Art Images with Buttons on the Picture Toolbar

Clip art images inserted in a document can be formatted in a variety of ways. Formatting might include adding fill color and border lines, increasing or decreasing the brightness or contrast, choosing a wrapping style, and cropping the image. A variety of methods are available for changing the formatting of a clip art image. You can format an image with buttons on the Picture toolbar or options at the Format Picture dialog box.

To display the Picture toolbar, position the arrow pointer on a clip art image, click the *right* mouse button, and then click Show Picture Toolbar. This displays the Picture toolbar shown in figure 18.6. The buttons on the Picture toolbar are described in figure 18.7.

18.6 Picture Toolbar

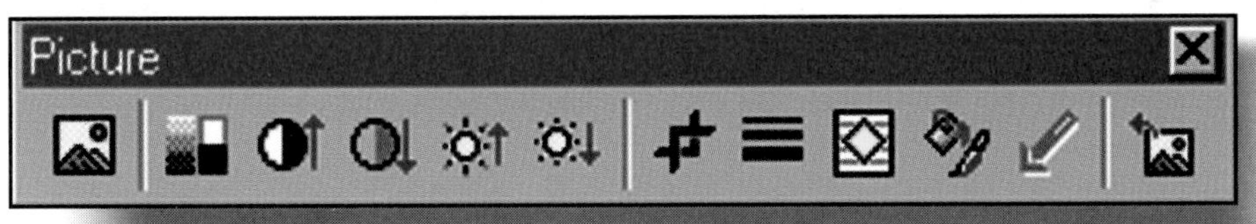

18.7 Picture Toolbar Buttons

Click this button...	Named...	To do this...
	Insert Picture	Display the Insert Picture dialog box with a list of subfolders containing additional images.
	Image Control	Display a drop-down list with options for controlling how the image displays. Options include Automatic, Grayscale, Black & White, and Watermark.

	More Contrast	Increase contrast of the image.
	Less Contrast	Decrease contrast of the image.
	More Brightness	Increase brightness of the image.
	Less Brightness	Decrease brightness of the image.
	Crop	Crop image so only a specific portion of the image is visible.
	Line Style	Insert a border around the image and specify the border line style.
	Text Wrapping	Specify how text will wrap around or through the image. Choices include Square, Tight, Through, None, Top and Bottom, and Edit Wrap Points.
	Format Picture	Display Format Picture dialog box with options for formatting the image. Tabs in the dialog box include Colors and Lines, Size, Position, Wrapping, and Picture.
	Set Transparent Color	This button is not active.
	Reset Picture	Reset image to its original size, position, and color.

exercise 9

Inserting, Sizing, and Customizing a Clip Art Image

1. At a clear document screen, create the letterhead shown in figure 18.8 by completing the following steps:
   a. Insert, size, and customize the image by completing the following steps:
      1) Click Insert, point to Picture, and then click Clip Art.
      2) At the Microsoft Clip Gallery 3.0 dialog box, click *Entertainment* in the list box located at the left side of the dialog box. Scroll through the list of images displayed in the middle of the dialog box until the image at the margin displays. When this image displays, double-click it. (If this image is not available, double-click an image of your choosing.)

      3) Scroll down the screen until the bottom right corner sizing handle displays. Using this sizing handle, decrease the size of the image to approximately 1.5 inches (height and width). (Use the horizontal and vertical rulers to help you size the image.)

4) With the image still selected, display the Picture toolbar. To do this, position the arrow pointer in the image, click the *right* mouse button, and then click Show Picture Toolbar.
5) Add a double line border around the image. To do this, click the Line Style button on the Picture toolbar and then click the *3 pt* double line that displays toward the bottom of the drop-down list.
6) Increase the brightness of the image by clicking five times on the More Brightness button on the Picture toolbar.
7) Change the wrapping style by clicking the Text Wrapping button on the Picture toolbar and then clicking Square at the drop-down list.
8) Click outside the image to deselect the image (and remove the Picture toolbar).

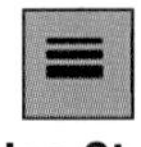
Line Style

More Brightness

Text Wrapping

b. Key the text in the document in figure 18.8 by completing the following steps:
1) Change the font to 24-point Copperplate Gothic Bold. (If this typeface is not available, choose a similar decorative typeface.)
2) Change the paragraph alignment to Right.
3) Key **Magic by Merlin** and then press Enter. (The Copperplate Gothic Bold typeface uses small caps for lowercase letters.)
4) Change the point size to 16 points.
5) Key **1204 Ridgeway Avenue** and then press Enter.
6) Key **Richmond, VA 24365** and then press Enter.
7) Key **(804) 555-8880** and then press Enter.
8) Key **www.merlinmagic.com**.

2. Save the document and name it Ch 18, Ex 09.
3. Print and then close Ch 18, Ex 09.

18.8 — Exercise 9

MAGIC BY MERLIN
1204 RIDGEWAY AVENUE
RICHMOND, VA 24365
(804) 555-8880
WWW.MERLINMAGIC.COM

exercise 10

Cropping and Adding a Border to a Clip Art Image

1. At a clear document screen, insert a clip art image in a document, add a border to the image, crop the image, and then move the image by completing the following steps:
   a. Click Insert, point to Picture, and then click Clip Art.
   b. At the Microsoft Clip Gallery 3.0 dialog box, click *Cartoons* in the list box located at the left side of the dialog box. Scroll through the list of images displayed in the middle of the dialog box until the image at the margin displays. When this image displays, double-click it. (If this image is not available, look for another image that contains a flag.)

   c. Scroll down the screen until the bottom right corner of the image is visible. Position the arrow pointer (turns into a double-headed arrow pointing diagonally) on the bottom right sizing handle, hold down the left mouse button, and then decrease the size of the image. Decrease the width of the image to approximately 2 inches and the height to approximately 3 inches. (Use the horizontal and vertical rulers as a guide.)
   d. Make sure the Picture toolbar is displayed. (If it is not, position the arrow pointer in the image, click the *right* mouse button, and then click Show Picture Toolbar.)
   e. Crop the image so that only the flag and a portion of the flag pole displays by completing the following steps:
      1) Click the Crop button on the Picture toolbar.

Crop

      2) Position the arrow pointer on a sizing handle (the arrow pointer turns into a crop tool, which is a black square with overlapping lines), hold down the left mouse button, and then drag into the image to isolate just the flag and a portion of the flag pole.
      3) Continue dragging sizing handles (make sure the arrow pointer turns into the crop tool) until only the flag and flag pole appear in the image border. (This may take some practice. If you are not satisfied with the result, click the Reset Picture button on the Picture toolbar and then try again.)

Reset Picture

      4) With the flag and flag pole isolated, click the Crop tool on the Picture toolbar to turn it off.
      5) With the image still selected, add a border line by clicking the Line Style button on the Picture toolbar and then clicking the *1 ½ pt* option at the drop-down list.
   f. Drag the image to the middle of the screen and then deselect the image.
2. Save the image and name it Ch 18, Ex 10.
3. Print and then close Ch 18, Ex 10.

Formatting Clip Art Images at the Format Picture Dialog Box

With buttons on the Picture toolbar you can customize a clip art image. The same options on the Picture toolbar are also available at the Format Picture dialog box, along with additional options. To display the Format Picture dialog box, select a clip art image, and then click Format, then Picture. You can also display the Format Picture dialog box by selecting a clip art image, displaying the Picture toolbar, and then clicking the Format Picture button on the Picture toolbar.

Format Picture

The Format Picture dialog box displays with a variety of tabs. When you first display the Format Picture, more than likely, the Picture tab will be selected as shown in figure 18.9. With options from this dialog box, you can use specific measurements to crop an image and change the color, brightness, and contrast of an image. These same options were available with buttons on the Picture toolbar.

18.9 ***Format Picture Dialog Box with Picture Tab Selected***

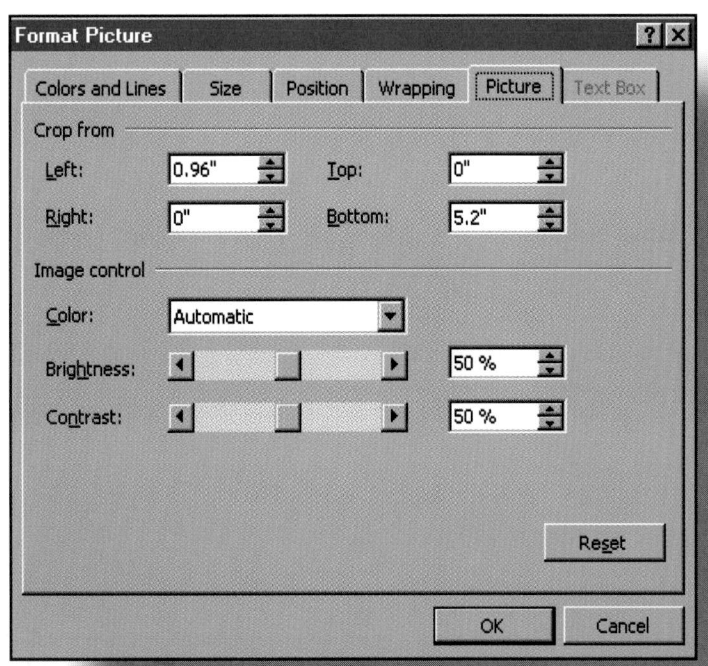

If you click the Colors and Lines tab on the Format Picture dialog box, the dialog box displays as shown in figure 18.10. A clip art image is inserted inside a border. This border is not visible by default. A fill can be added inside the border of the clip art image with the Color option in the Fill section. A border line can be added to the image with choices from the Color options in the Line section. When you choose a border line color, the Dashed, Style, and Weight options become available. Use these options to further customize the border line.

figure 18.10 ***Format Picture Dialog Box with Colors and Lines Tab Selected***

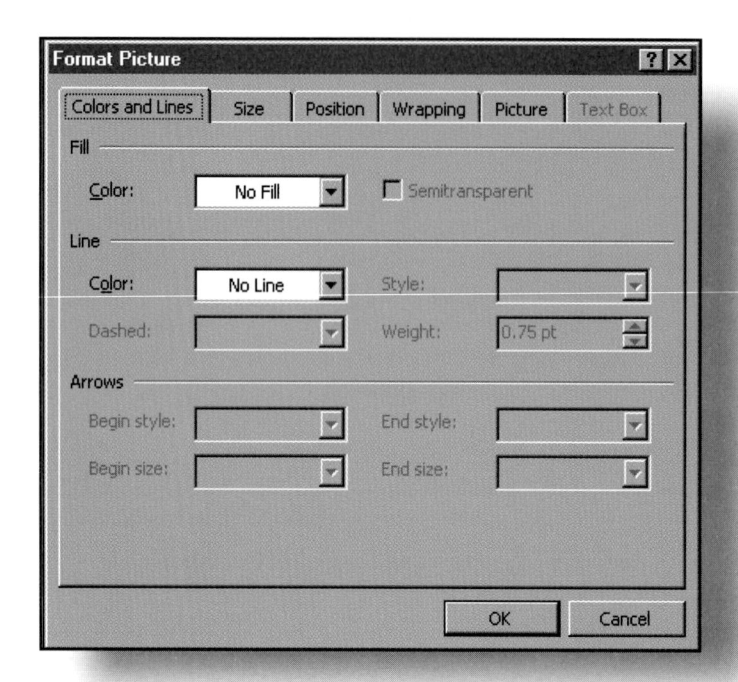

Click the Size tab at the Format Picture dialog box and the dialog box displays as shown in figure 18.11. At this dialog box, you can specify the height and width of the image as well as specify a percentage of scale for the height and width of the image.

18.11 ***Format Picture Dialog Box with Size Tab Selected***

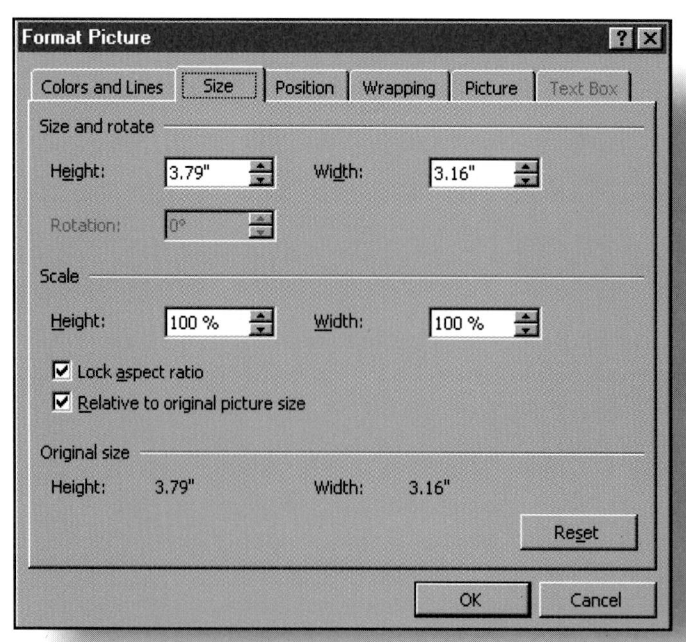

You can move a selected image to a specific location on the page by dragging it with the mouse. You can also position the image on the page with options at the Format Picture dialog box with the Position tab selected. This dialog box is shown in figure 18.12.

18.12 ***Format Picture Dialog Box with Position Tab Selected***

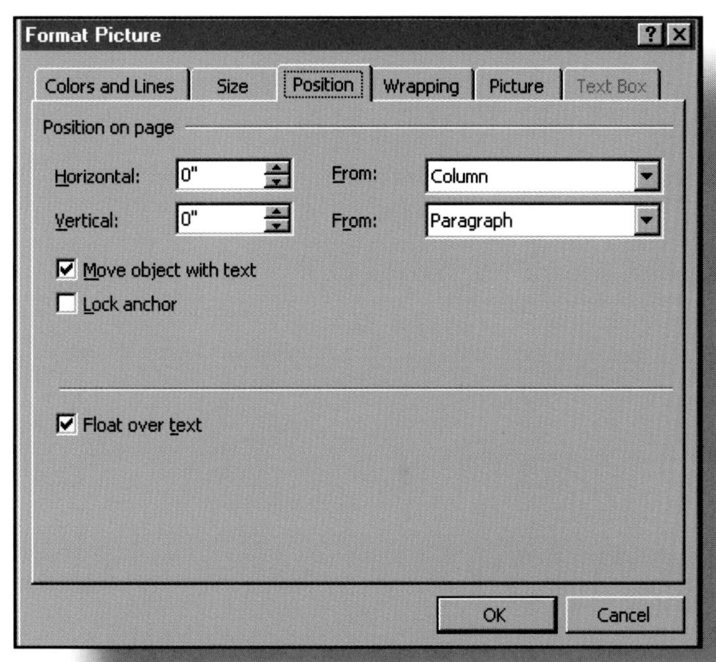

The options at the Format Picture dialog box with the Wrapping tab are similar to those from the button on the Picture toolbar. At this dialog box, shown in figure 18.13, click the option that represents how you want text to wrap around the image. Use the measurement along the bottom of the dialog box to specify the distance the text is from the image.

18.13 Format Picture Dialog Box with Wrapping Tab Selected

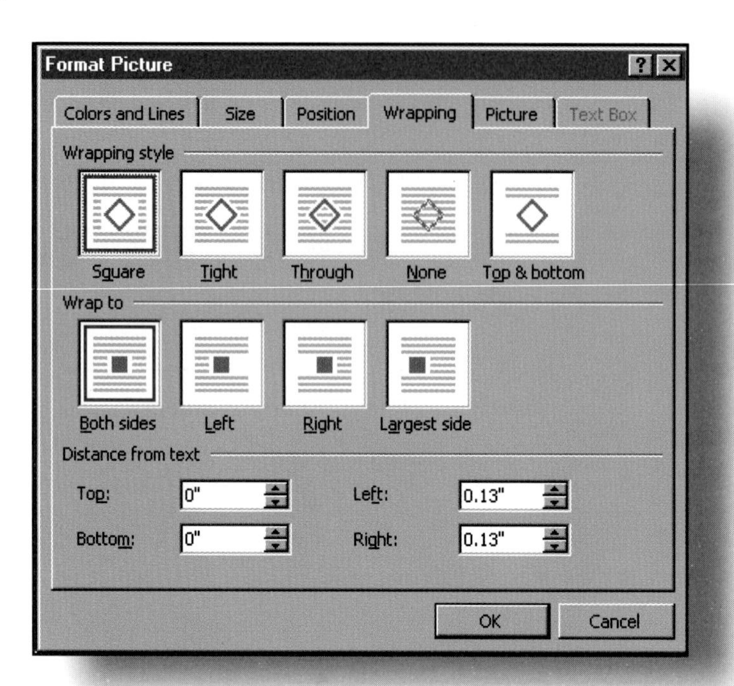

exercise 11

Formatting a Clip Art Image at the Format Picture Dialog Box

1. Open Para 04.
2. Save the document with Save As and name it Ch 18, Ex 11.
3. Select the entire document and then change the font to 13-point Garamond. (If this typeface is not available, choose a similar serif typeface such as Century Schoolbook.)
4. Deselect the text and then move the insertion point to the beginning of the document.
5. Insert a clip art image of a computer in the document by completing the following steps:
   a. Click Insert, point to Picture, and then click Clip Art.
   b. At the Microsoft Clip Gallery 3.0 dialog box, click *Business* in the list box located at the left side of the dialog box. Look for the image of a computer in this category and then double-click the image. If there is no computer image available in this category, click the *(All Categories)* option, scroll through the list until a computer image displays, and then double-click the image.

c. Add a border, change the size, position the image, and change the text wrap by completing the following steps:
   1) With the image still selected, click Format, then Picture.
   2) At the Format Picture dialog box, click the Colors and Lines tab.
   3) Click the down-pointing triangle at the right side of the Color text box in the Line section and then click the Black color option (first option in the first row).
   4) Click the up-pointing triangle at the right side of the Weight text box until *1 pt* displays in the text box.
   5) Click the Size tab located at the top of the dialog box.
   6) Select the current measurement in the Width text box located in the Size and rotate section of the dialog box and then key **2**.
   7) Click the Position tab located at the top of the dialog box.
   8) Click the down-pointing triangle at the right side of the From text box (located to the right of the Horizontal text box) and then click *Margin* at the drop-down list.
   9) Select the current measurement in the Horizontal text box and then key **2**.
   10) Select the current measurement in the Vertical text box and then key **1**.
   11) Click the Wrapping tab located at the top of the dialog box.
   12) Click the Square option in the Wrapping style section of the dialog box.
   13) Click the Both sides option in the Wrap to section of the dialog box.
   14) Click OK to close the Format Picture dialog box.

6. At the document screen, click outside the image to deselect it. (Make sure the computer image is displayed in the middle of the document. If the image appears to be out of alignment, select the image, and then drag it to a more desirable location.)
7. Save the document again with the same name (Ch 18, Ex 11).
8. Print and then close Ch 18, Ex 11.

Inserting Pictures

In the previous section of this chapter, you learned how to insert clip art images in a document. Actual pictures can also be inserted in a document. Depending on the installation of Word 97, some pictures may or may not be available. To display what pictures are available for inserting in a document, click Insert, point to Picture, and then click Clip Art. At the Microsoft Clip Gallery 3.0 dialog box, click the Pictures tab. Any installed pictures will display in the middle of the dialog box in the list box. Double-click the picture you want inserted in the document. A picture is formatted in the same way as a clip art image. The same buttons on the Picture toolbar are available as well as the Format Picture dialog box.

exercise 12

Inserting and Formatting a Picture

1. Open Para 04.
2. Save the document with Save As and name it Ch 18, Ex 12.
3. Insert a picture in the document by completing the following steps:
   a. Click Insert, point to Picture, and then click Clip Art.
   b. At the Microsoft Clip Gallery 3.0 dialog box, click the Pictures tab.
   c. Click the *(All Categories)* option in the list box at the left side of the dialog box.
   d. With all of the installed pictures displayed, scroll through the list until you see a picture of a keyboard or a picture of a computer, and then double-click the picture.
   e. Change the size of the picture, position the picture, and change the text wrap by completing the following steps:
      1) With the picture still selected, click Format, then Picture.
      2) At the Format Picture dialog box, click the Size tab located at the top of the dialog box.
      3) Select the current measurement in the Width text box located in the Size and rotate section of the dialog box and then key **2**.
      4) Click the Position tab located at the top of the dialog box.
      5) Click the down-pointing triangle at the right side of the From text box (located to the right of the Horizontal text box) and then click *Margin* at the drop-down list.
      6) Select the current measurement in the Horizontal text box and then key **2**.
      7) Select the current measurement in the Vertical text box and then key **1**.
      8) Click the Wrapping tab located at the top of the dialog box.
      9) Click the Square option in the Wrapping style section of the dialog box.
      10) Click the Both sides option in the Wrap to section of the dialog box.
      11) Click OK to close the Format Picture dialog box.
4. At the document screen, click outside the picture to deselect it. (Make sure the picture is displayed in the middle of the document. If the picture appears to be out of alignment, select the picture, and then drag it to a more desirable location.
5. Save the document again with the same name (Ch 18, Ex 12).
6. Print and then close Ch 18, Ex 12.

Inserting a Text Box

A text box can be drawn in a document and then text can be keyed in the box. To insert a text box in a document, click Insert, then Text Box. This changes the I-beam pointer to cross hairs. Position the cross hairs in the document, hold down the left mouse button, drag the cross hairs until the box is the desired size, and then release the mouse button. The insertion point is positioned inside the text box. Key the desired text and then click outside the text box to deselect it.

A text box can be sized and moved in the same manner as a clip art image or a picture. You can also format a text box in the same manner as a clip art image or picture. To format a text box, select the box and then click Format, then Text Box. This displays the Format Text Box dialog box that contains the same tabs and options as the Format Picture dialog box.

exercise 13

Inserting and Formatting a Text Box

1. Open Para 03.
2. Save the document with Save As and name it Ch 18, Ex 13.
3. Make the following changes to the document:
   a. Join all the paragraphs so there is only one paragraph in the document.
   b. Select the entire document and then change the font to 13-point Goudy Old Style. (If this typeface is not available, choose a similar typeface.)
   c. Deselect the text.
4. Insert a text box in the middle of the paragraph by completing the following steps:
   a. Click Insert, then Text Box.
   b. Using the horizontal and vertical rulers, draw a text box with these specifications:
      1) The box should span from the 1.5-inch mark on the horizontal ruler to the 4.5-inch mark on the horizontal ruler.
      2) The box should begin at approximately the 1-inch mark on the vertical ruler and extend down approximately two-thirds of an inch.
   c. With the insertion point positioned inside the text box, make the following changes:
      1) Click the Center button on the Formatting toolbar.
      2) Change the font to 14-point Arial bold.
      3) Key **Flyers are one of the least expensive forms of advertising.**
   d. With the text box still selected, wrap the text around the box by completing the following steps:
      1) Click Format, then Text Box.
      2) At the Format Text Box dialog box, click the Wrapping tab.

3) Click the Tight option in the Wrapping style section.
4) Click the Both sides option in the Wrap to section.
5) Click OK to close the dialog box.

e. Check to see if the text box is positioned approximately in the middle of the paragraph. If it is not, drag the box to a more desirable location.

f. Deselect the text box.

5. Save the document again with the same name (Ch 18, Ex 13).
6. Print and then close Ch 18, Ex 13.

chapter summary

- Every paragraph created in Word contains in invisible frame. A border that appears around this frame can be added to a paragraph.
- Options from the Border button on the Formatting toolbar can be used to insert borders around a paragraph or selected paragraphs.
- Use options at the Borders and Shading dialog box with the Borders tab selected to add a customized border to a paragraph or selected paragraphs.
- Use options at the Borders and Shading dialog box with the Shading tab selected to add shading or a pattern to a paragraph of text or selected paragraphs.
- Add a page border to a document at the Borders and Shading dialog box with the Page Border tab selected.
- Clip art images are available at the Microsoft Clip Gallery 3.0 dialog box. The images available will depend on the type of installation and the amount of space available for the images.
- Clip art images in the Microsoft Clip Gallery 3.0 dialog box are grouped into categories. These categories are listed at the left side of the dialog box.
- Use the sizing handles around a selected clip art image to size the image.
- A selected clip art image can be dragged to a different location in the document using the mouse.
- The Picture toolbar contains buttons for formatting a clip art image.
- The same formatting options plus additional options are available at the Format Picture dialog box.
- Display any installed pictures at the Microsoft Clip Gallery 3.0 dialog box with the Pictures tab selected. The formatting options available for a clip art image are also available for a picture.
- With the Text Box option from the Insert drop-down menu, a text box can be drawn in a document. The formatting options available for a clip art image are also available for a text box.

commands review

	Mouse/Keyboard
Borders and Shading dialog box	Format, Borders and Shading
Microsoft Clip Gallery 3.0 dialog box	Insert, Picture, Clip Art; or Insert, Object, double-click *Microsoft Clip Gallery*

check your understanding

Completion: In the space provided at the right, indicate the correct term, command, or number.

1. The Border button is located on this toolbar. ____________
2. Click this option on the Menu bar and then click Borders and Shading to display the Borders and Shading dialog box. ____________
3. Click this button, located in the Setting section of the Borders and Shading dialog box, to add a border to paragraphs that has a three-dimensional look. ____________
4. A diagram displays in this section of the Borders and Shading dialog box that displays how the border will appear in the document. ____________
5. Click this tab at the Borders and Shading dialog box to display options for adding a page border to a document. ____________
6. This is the default border line width in point size. ____________
7. When a clip art image is inserted in a document, Word automatically changes to this viewing mode. ____________
8. Use the sizing handles located at this location in a selected clip art image to change both the width and height at the same time. ____________
9. Use buttons on this toolbar to customize a clip art image. ____________
10. Specify the width and height of a clip art image at the Format Picture dialog box with this tab selected. ____________
11. To insert a text box in a document, click this option on the Menu bar and then click Text Box. ____________

In the space provided below, write the steps you would complete to insert a clip art image of a computer disk into a document.

____

____

____

skill assessments

Note: Before completing the skill assessments, display the Open dialog box, and then select and delete documents created in chapter 16 that begin Ch 16. You may want to check with your instructor before deleting these documents.

Assessment 1

1. Open Report 03.
2. Save the document with Save As and name it Ch 18, SA 01.
3. Make the following changes to the document:
   a. Select the entire document and then set it in a serif typeface of your choosing (other than Times New Roman).
   b. Set the title and headings in the report in a bold sans serif typeface of your choosing.
   c. Create a header with these specifications:
      1) Create a header that prints on all pages *except* the first page.
      2) Include the text **Newsletter Elements** that prints at the left margin and **Page #** (where the proper page number is inserted) that prints at the right margin.
      3) Insert a border of your choosing at the bottom of the header text.
4. Save the document again with the same name (Ch 18, SA 01).
5. Print and then close Ch 18, SA 01.

Assessment 2

1. Open Survey 01.
2. Save the document with Save As and name it Ch 18, SA 02.
3. Make the following changes to the document:
   a. Change the left and right margins to 1 inch.
   b. Select the title and the subtitle and then change the font to 14-point Times New Roman bold.
   c. Select the first numbered paragraph and the four lettered paragraphs below it. Display the Borders and Shading dialog box, click the Box button at the left side of the dialog box, change the Width option to *¾ pt*, and then close the dialog box. (A border will display around the paragraphs and between the numbered paragraph and the lettered paragraphs.)
   d. Select the second numbered paragraph and the four lettered paragraphs below it and add the same border line as that in step 3c.
   e. Select the third numbered paragraph and the four lettered paragraphs below it and add the same border line as that in step 3c.
   f. Select the fourth numbered paragraph and the four lettered paragraphs below it and add the same border line as that in step 3c.
   g. Select the fifth numbered paragraph and the four lettered paragraphs below it and add the same border line as that in step 3c.
   h. Make sure the document fits on one page. (If not, decrease the top and/or bottom margins until the text fits on one page.)
4. Save the document again with the same name (Ch 18, SA 02).
5. Print and then close Ch 18, SA 02.

Assessment 3

1. Open Notice 02.
2. Save the document with Save As and name it Ch 18, SA 03.
3. Make the following changes to the document:
   a. Set the text in the document in a decorative font of your choosing. (You also determine the font size and font color.)
   b. Center the text vertically on the page.
   c. Insert a page border using one of the images available in the Art drop-down list.
4. Save the document again with the same name (Ch 18, SA 03).
5. Print and then close Ch 18, SA 03.

Assessment 4

1. At a clear document screen, create the letterhead shown in figure 18.14 with the following specifications:
   a. Insert the clip art image shown in the figure. (Look for this clip art in the *Science & Technology* category. If you do not find it in that category, display all categories and then scroll through the list. If this image is not available, choose a different image.)
   b. Decrease the size of the image until it is approximately 1.5 inches wide and 1.5 inches high.
   c. Display the Picture toolbar for this image, click the Text Wrapping button, and then click Square at the drop-down list.
   d. Change the font to 18-point Goudy Old Style and then key the text shown in the figure, aligned at the right margin.
2. Save the document and name it Ch 18, SA 04.
3. Print and then close Ch 18, SA 04.

Figure 18.14 • Assessment 4

BERGMAN & GALLOWAY
Attorneys at Law
2500 Madison Street
Seattle, WA 98300
(206) 555-4455

Assessment 5

1. At a clear document screen, create an announcement that contains the following information:
   a. Include the following text:

      SULLIVAN TRAVELS
      782 North 23rd Street
      Portland, Maine 01232
      Open House
      Thursday, April 8, 1999
      9:00 a.m. - 8:30 p.m.
      Stop by and check out our new offices!
      Sign up for a drawing for a free cruise!

   b. Set the above text in a decorative typeface and type size of your choosing. Add any additional text you desire.
   c. Include a decorative page border.
   d. Insert at least one clip art image or picture (related to travel) and position it in an appealing location on the page.
2. Save the document and name it Ch 18, SA 05.
3. Print and then close Ch 18, SA 05.

19 Using Microsoft Draw

PERFORMANCE OBJECTIVES

Upon completion of chapter 19, you will be able to:

- **Draw shapes using buttons on the Drawing toolbar.**
- **Create autoshapes using a button on the Drawing toolbar.**
- **Create a text box with a button on the Drawing toolbar.**
- **Select, delete, move, copy, and size drawn objects.**
- **Customize a drawn object by adding fill color and shading, changing the line color and style, and adding shadow and 3-D effects.**
- **Create a watermark.**
- **Flip an object.**
- **Add callouts.**

Microsoft Word 97 includes a drawing feature with tools for drawing and customizing objects. Word's drawing feature provides many of the features of a stand-alone draw program. With the drawing feature you can draw free hand, draw shapes and objects, and create text boxes and watermarks. In this chapter, you will learn the basic functions of the drawing feature. For more sophisticated and varying ideas on how to use the drawing feature, please refer to the Word help guide.

Drawing Shapes and Lines

You can use the drawing feature to draw a variety of shapes such as circles, squares, rectangles, ovals, and to draw straight lines, free form lines, lines with arrows, and much more. To use the drawing feature, the Drawing toolbar must be displayed. To display this toolbar, shown in figure 19.1, position the arrow pointer on the Standard or Formatting toolbar, click the *right* mouse button, and then click *Drawing* at the drop-down list. A description of each button is provided in figure 19.2. As soon as you click a button on the Drawing toolbar, Word switches to the Page Layout viewing mode.

Drawing Toolbar

figure 19.2 **Drawing Toolbar Buttons**

Click this button...	Named...	To do this...
	Draw	Display a pop-up menu with options for grouping and positioning drawings.
	Select Objects	Select text or objects.
	Free Rotate	Rotate selected object to any degree by dragging a corner of the object in the desired direction.
	AutoShapes	Display a palette of shapes that can be drawn in a document. (To draw a shape circumscribed within a perfect square, hold down the Shift key while drawing the shape.)
	Line	Draw a line in a document.
	Arrow	Insert a line with an arrowhead. (To draw at 15-degree angles, hold down the Shift key.)
	Rectangle	Draw a rectangle in a document. (To draw a perfect square, hold down the Shift key while drawing the shape.)
	Oval	Draw an oval in a document. (To draw a perfect circle, hold down the Shift key while drawing the shape.)
	Text Box	Create text in a text box. (To add text that does not wrap, click the button, click in the document, then key the text. To add text that does wrap, click the button, drag to create a box, then key the text.)
	Insert WordArt	Insert a Microsoft Office drawing object.
	Fill Color	Fill selected object with a color, pattern, texture, or shaded fill.
	Line Color	Change color of selected line.
	Font Color	Format selected text with a color.
	Line Style	Change thickness of selected line or change it to a compound line.
	Dash Style	Change style of selected line, arc, or border to dashed.

	Arrow Style	Add arrowheads to a selected line, arc, or open freeform.
	Shadow	Add or remove an object shadow.
	3-D	Add or remove a 3-D effect.

With some of the buttons on the Drawing toolbar, you can draw a shape. If you draw a shape with the Line button or the Arrow button, the shape you draw is considered a *line drawing*. If you draw a shape with the Rectangle or Oval button, the shape you draw is considered an *enclosed object*. Later in this chapter you will learn how to add fill color to an enclosed object.

Line

Arrow

If you want to draw the same shape more than once, double-click the shape button on the Drawing toolbar. After drawing the shapes, click the button again to deactivate it.

Rectangle

Oval

Drawing a Circle and Square

1. At a clear document screen, draw a circle and a square by completing the following steps:
   a. Display the Drawing toolbar by positioning the arrow pointer on the Standard or Formatting toolbar, clicking the *right* mouse button, and then clicking *Drawing* at the drop-down list. (Skip this step if the Drawing toolbar is already displayed.)
   b. Click the Oval button on the Drawing toolbar.
   c. Position the cross hairs in the document screen toward the left side.
   d. Hold down the Shift key and the left mouse button, drag the mouse down and to the right until the outline image displays as approximately a 2-inch circle, release the mouse button, and then the Shift key.
   e. Click the Rectangle button on the Drawing toolbar.
   f. Position the cross hairs in the document screen toward the right side.
   g. Hold down the Shift key and the left mouse button, drag the mouse down and to the right until the outline image displays as approximately a 2-inch square, release the mouse button, and then the Shift key.
2. Save the document and name it Ch 19, Ex 01.
3. Print and then close Ch 19, Ex 01.

With the Line button, you can draw a line in the document screen. To do this, click the Line button on the Drawing toolbar, position the cross hairs where you want to begin the line, hold down the left mouse button, drag the line to the location where you want the line to end, and then release the mouse button.

You can add as many lines as desired in the document screen by repeating the steps above. For example, you can draw a triangle by drawing three lines. If you want to draw more than one line, double-click the Line button. This makes the button active. After drawing all the necessary lines, click the Line button again to deactivate it.

exercise 2

Creating a Line with the Arrow Button

1. At a clear document screen, create the document shown in figure 19.3 by completing the following steps:
   a. Make sure the Drawing toolbar is displayed.
   b. Change the font to 24-point Copperplate Gothic Bold (or a similar decorative typeface).
   c. Click the Center button on the Formatting toolbar.
   d. Key **Mainline Manufacturing**. (The Copperplate Gothic Bold typeface uses small caps for lowercase letters.)
   e. Press the Enter key.
   f. Click the Arrow button on the Drawing toolbar.
   g. Draw the line as shown in figure 19.3. (The line will display with an arrow on one end. This will be changed in the next step.)
   h. With the line still selected (a white sizing handle displays at each end), click the Arrow Style button on the Drawing toolbar.

Arrow Style

   i. At the pop-up list that displays, click the second option from the bottom of the list.
2. Save the completed document and name it Ch 19, Ex 02.
3. Print and then close Ch 19, Ex 02.

figure 19.3 *Exercise 2*

MAINLINE MANUFACTURING

Creating AutoShapes

With options from the AutoShapes button, you can choose from a variety of predesigned shapes. Click the AutoShapes button and a pop-up menu displays. Point to the desired menu option and a side menu displays. This side menu will offer autoshape choices for the selected option. For example, if you point to the Basic Shapes option, a number of shapes such as a circle, square, triangle, box, stop sign, etc., display at the right side of the pop-up menu. Click the desired shape and the arrow pointer turns into cross hairs. Position the cross hairs in the document screen, hold down the left mouse button, drag to create the shape, and then release the button.

AutoShapes ▾

AutoShapes

exercise 3

Writing Your Name

1. At a clear document screen, write your first name by completing the following steps:
   a. Make sure the Drawing toolbar is displayed.
   b. Click the AutoShapes button on the Drawing toolbar, point to Lines, and then click the Scribble button. (The Scribble button is the last button in the bottom row. Position the arrow pointer on this button and *Scribble* displays in a yellow box after one second.)
   c. Position the mouse pointer in the document screen, hold down the left mouse button, and then move the mouse pointer (a pencil) in the necessary directions to draw your first name. When you release the mouse button, white sizing handles display around your name. If you need to continue drawing your name (for example, to cross a "T"), select the Scribble button again. (If you are not satisfied with the results, make sure white sizing handles display around your name and then press the Delete key. Draw your name again.)
2. Save the document with Save As and name it Ch 19, Ex 03.
3. Print and then close Ch 19, Ex 03.

exercise 4

Creating Stars

1. At a clear document screen, create a variety of stars by completing the following steps:
   a. Make sure the Drawing toolbar is displayed.
   b. Click the AutoShapes button on the Drawing toolbar, point to Stars and Banners, and then click the 8-Point Star button (first button from the left in the second row from the top).

c. Position the cross hairs in the document screen, hold down the left mouse button, drag the cross hairs to create the star, and then release the mouse button.
d. The star displays with a small yellow box inside. This box is referred to as an *adjustment handle*. Position the arrow pointer on the adjustment handle, hold down the left mouse button, drag about halfway into the star, and then release the mouse button. (This causes the points of the star to drag into the star.)
e. Click the AutoShapes button on the Drawing toolbar, point to Stars and Banners, and then click 16-point Star (second button from the left in the second row from the top).
f. Position the cross hairs in the document screen, hold down the left mouse button, drag the cross hairs to create the star, and then release the mouse button.
g. Use the adjustment handle to drag the points of the star into the star.
h. Experiment with a few other star and/or banner buttons.

2. Save the document and name it Ch 19, Ex 04.
3. Print and then close Ch 19, Ex 04.

Creating a Text Box

Text Box

With the Text Box button on the Drawing toolbar, you can create a box and then insert text inside the box. Text inside a box can be formatted in the normal manner. For example, you can change the font, alignment, or indent of the text.

To create a text box, click the Text Box button, position the cross hairs in the document screen where you want the text to appear, hold down the left mouse button, drag to create the box, and then release the mouse button. This causes a box to appear in the drawing area as shown in figure 19.4. Key the text in the box. If the text you key fills more than the first line in the box, the text wraps to the next line. (The box, however, will not increase in size. If you need more room in the text box, select the box, and then use the sizing handles to make it bigger.)

19.4

Text Box

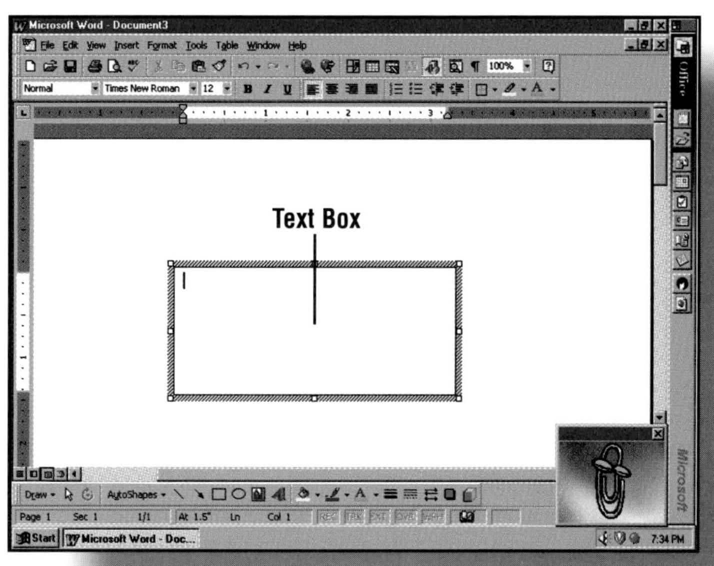

exercise 5

Creating an Oval and Then Keying Text Inside

1. At a clear document screen, create an oval shape, and then create a text box inside the oval with the words *Linda Shing* and *Superintendent* by completing the following steps:
   a. Make sure the Drawing toolbar is displayed and then click the Oval button.
   b. Position the cross hairs in the document screen (approximately below the 1.5-inch mark on the horizontal ruler), hold down the left mouse button, drag the mouse down and to the right until you have drawn an oval that is approximately 3 inches wide and 2 inches tall, and then release the mouse button.
   c. Click the Text Box button.
   d. Draw a text box inside the oval shape from the left side to the right side that is approximately 1 inch tall.
   e. Click the Center button on the Formatting toolbar and then press the Enter key once.
   f. Key **Linda Shing** in the text box and then press Enter.
   g. Key **Superintendent**. (The name and title should be centered in the oval. If not, insert or delete hard returns until the text appears centered.)
2. Save the document and name it Ch 19, Ex 05.
3. Print and then close Ch 19, Ex 05.

Changing Objects

Shapes drawn using tools on the Drawing toolbar are referred to as objects. An object can be customized in a variety of ways. For example, an object can be selected and then moved, copied, or deleted; or the size of the object can be changed.

Selecting an Object

After an object has been created in a document, you may decide to make changes or delete the object. To do this, the object must be selected. To select an enclosed object, position the I-beam anywhere inside the object (the arrow pointer displays with a four-headed arrow attached) and then click the left mouse button. To select a line, position the I-beam on the line until the I-beam pointer turns into an arrow with a four-headed arrow attached, and then click the left mouse button. When an object is selected, it displays surrounded by white sizing handles. Once an object is selected, it can be edited, such as changing the fill and the line, it can be moved, or it can be deleted.

Select Objects

If a document screen contains more than one object, you can select several objects at once using the Select Objects button on the Drawing toolbar. This is the button containing the arrow. To do this, click the Select Objects button, position the cross hairs in the upper left corner of the area containing the objects, hold down the left mouse button, drag the outline to the lower right corner of the area containing the objects, and then release the mouse button. You can also select more than one object by holding down the Shift key as you click each object.

Each object in the selected area displays surrounded by white sizing handles. Objects in the selected area are connected. For example, if you move one of the objects in the selected area, the other objects move relatively.

Deleting an Object

An object you have drawn can be deleted from the document screen. To do this, select the object, and then press the Delete key.

Moving an Object

An object can be moved to a different location in this document. To do this with an enclosed object, position the insertion point inside the object (arrow pointer displays with a four-headed arrow attached), hold down the left mouse button, drag the outline of the object to the new location, and then release the mouse button. If you selected more than one object, moving one of the objects will also move the other objects. To move a line, select the line, and then position the I-beam pointer on the line until it turns into an arrow pointer with a four-headed arrow attached. Hold down the left mouse button, drag the outline of the line to the desired location, and then release the mouse button.

You can move a selected object with the keyboard by pressing one of the arrow keys. For example, to move an object down the screen, select the object, and then press the down arrow key.

Copying an Object

Moving an object removes the object from its original position and inserts it into a new location. If you want the object to stay in its original location and an exact copy to be inserted in a new location, use the Ctrl key while dragging the object.

exercise 6

Creating an Organizational Chart in Draw

1. At a clear document screen, create the organizational chart shown in figure 19.5 by completing the following steps:
   a. With the Drawing toolbar displayed, click the Text Box button.
   b. Draw a text box from approximately the 2-inch mark on the horizontal ruler to the 4-inch mark on the horizontal ruler. Make the box about an inch in height.
   c. Press Enter to move the insertion point down one line inside the text box.
   d. Click the Center button on the Formatting toolbar.
   e. Key **Blaine Dowler**.
   f. Press Enter and then key **Principal**.
   g. Position the I-beam pointer at the bottom of the text box until it turns into an arrow with a four-headed arrow attached.
   h. Hold down the Ctrl key and the left mouse button (this causes the four-headed arrow to change to a plus symbol), drag the outline of the text box down and to the left as shown in figure 19.5, and then release the left mouse button. (Do not release the Ctrl key.)
   i. With the Ctrl key still down, and the arrow pointer displayed with the plus symbol attached, hold down the left mouse button, drag the outline of the text box to the right as shown in figure 19.5, release the mouse button, and then release the Ctrl key.
   j. After copying the text box, key the names and titles shown in figure 19.5 in the second and third text boxes over the name *Blaine Dowler* and title *Principal*.
2. Save the document and name it Ch 19, Ex 06.
3. Print and then close Ch 19, Ex 06.

figure 19.5

Exercise 6

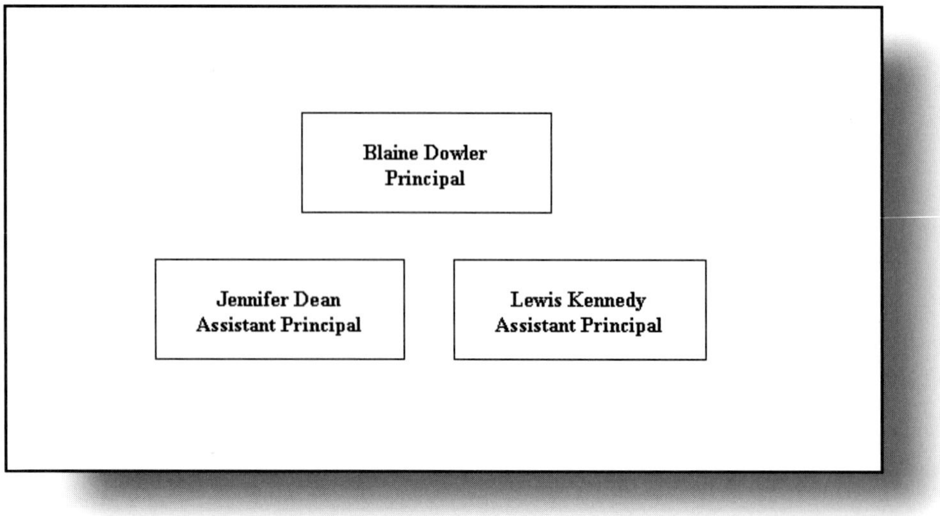

Blaine Dowler
Principal

Jennifer Dean
Assistant Principal

Lewis Kennedy
Assistant Principal

Sizing an Object

With the sizing handles that appear around an object when it is selected, the size of the object can be changed. To change the size of the object, select it, and then position the I-beam pointer or the arrow pointer on a sizing handle until it turns into a double-headed arrow. Hold down the left mouse button, drag the outline of the shape toward or away from the center of the object until it is the desired size, and then release the mouse button.

exercise 7

Creating and Sizing a Text Box

1. At a clear document screen, create a text box, key text in the box, and then size the box by completing the following steps:
   a. With the Drawing toolbar displayed, click the Text Box button, and then draw a text box in the document screen that is approximately 2 inches wide and 2.5 inches tall.
   b. With the insertion point inside the text box, change the font to 14-point Arial bold.
   c. Click the Center button on the Formatting toolbar.
   d. Key **COLEMAN DEVELOPMENT CORPORATION** (this will wrap).
   e. Press the Enter key.
   f. Key **3451 Classen Boulevard** (this will also wrap).

g. Press Enter.
h. Key **Oklahoma City, OK 76341**.
i. Press Enter.
j. Key **(801) 555-4500**.
k. With the text box selected, use the white sizing handles around the text box to make the box wider until the company name displays on one line and you can see all the text. Make the text box narrower so there is little space between the text and the bottom line of the box.
l. Drag the text box to the middle of the document screen.

2. Save the document and name it Ch 19, Ex 07.
3. Print and then close Ch 19, Ex 07.

Customizing Objects

With buttons on the Drawing toolbar, you can add fill color or pattern to an enclosed object, change thickness and color of the line that draws the object, and change the position of the object.

Adding Fill Shading or Color

Fill Color

With the Fill Color button on the Drawing toolbar, shading or color can be added to an enclosed object such as a shape or a text box. To add shading or color to an enclosed object, select the object to which you want shading or color added, and then click the Fill Color button. This will fill the object with the fill color displayed on the Fill Color button. If you want to choose a different color, select the object, and then click the down-pointing triangle at the right side of the Fill Color button. This causes a palette of color choices to display. At this palette click the desired fill color.

The Fill Color palette also includes two options—More Fill Colors and Fill Effects. Click the More Fill Colors option and the Colors dialog box shown in figure 19.6 displays. At this dialog box, click the desired color in the Colors section, and then click OK.

Click the other option at the Fill Color palette, Fill Effects, and the Fill Effects dialog box shown in figure 19.7 displays. At this dialog box, you can specify the number of colors, a shading style, and a shading variant. Make the desired choices at this dialog box and then click OK.

figure 19.6

Colors Dialog Box

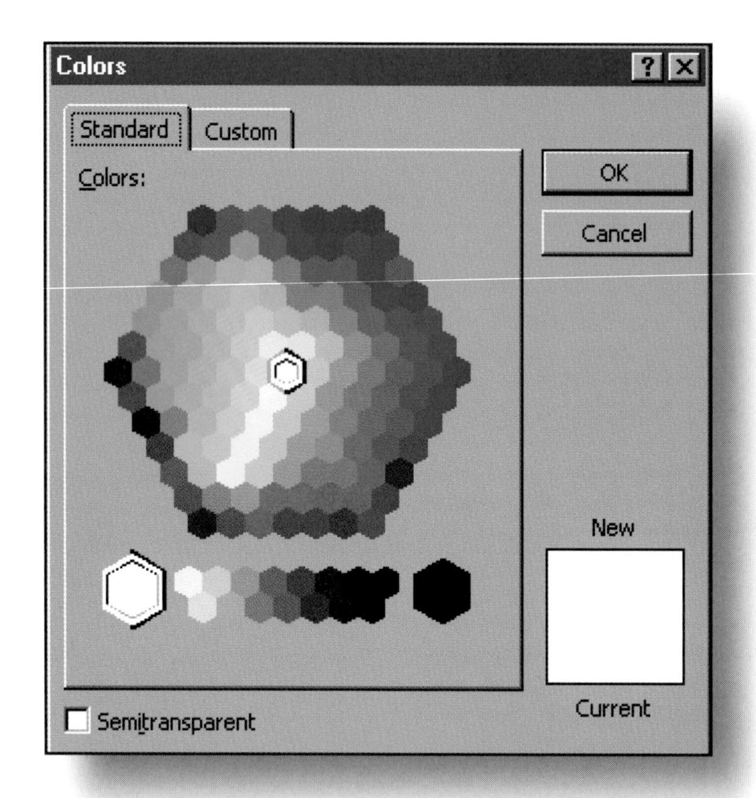

figure 19.7

Fill Effects Dialog Box

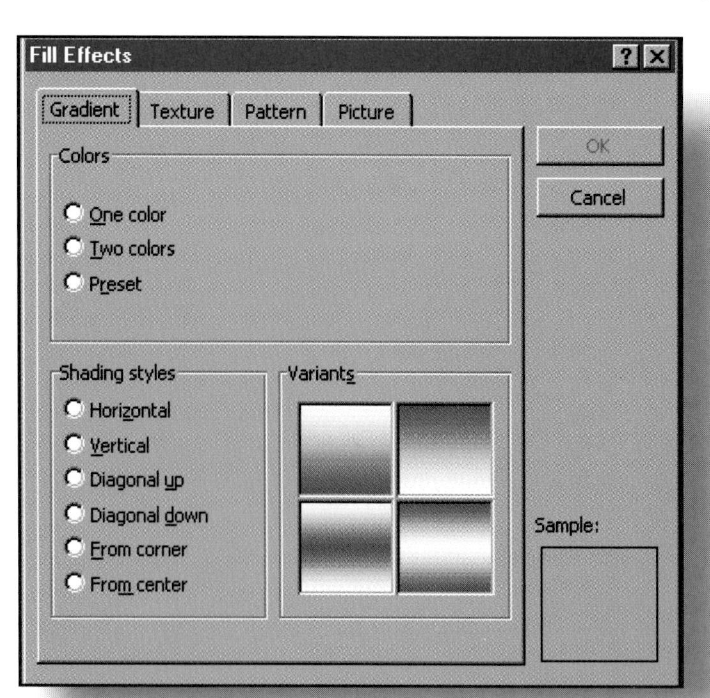

Changing Line Color

A line, shape, or text box is drawn with a black line. The color of this line can be changed with the Line Color button on the Drawing toolbar. Select an object and then click the Line Color button and the line color of the selected object changes to the color displayed on the button. If you want to choose a different color, select the object and then click the down-pointing triangle at the right side of the Line Color button. This causes a palette of color choices to display. At this palette, click the desired color.

Line Color

The Line Color palette also includes two options—More Line Colors and Patterned Lines. Click the More Line Colors option and the Colors dialog box shown in figure 19.6 displays. Click the Patterned Lines option and the Patterned Lines dialog box shown in figure 19.8 displays. Choose a pattern and a foreground and/or background color for the object at this dialog box.

figure 19.8 *Patterned Lines Dialog Box*

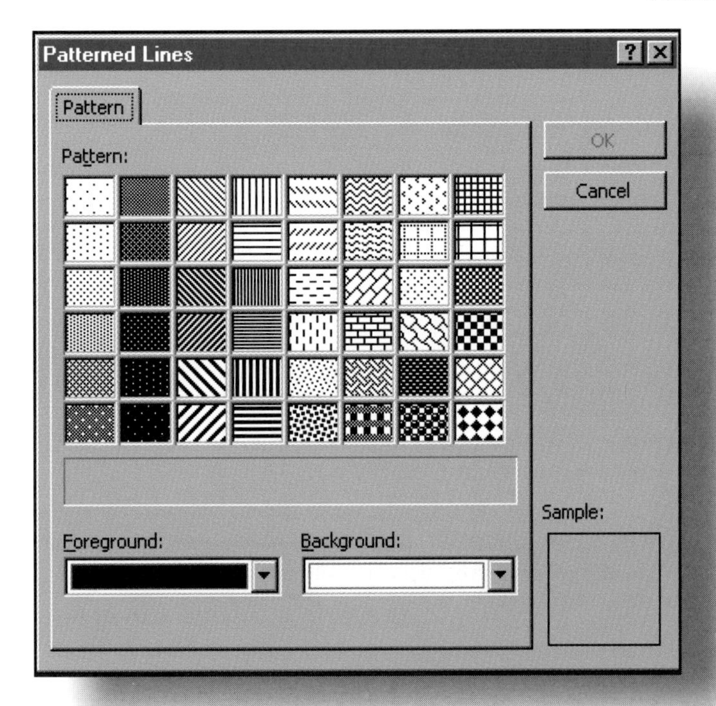

In some situations, you may want to remove the line around an object. For example, you may want to remove the lines of a text box after text has been added to it. To remove lines, select the object, click the down-pointing triangle at the right side of the Line Color button, and then click *No Line* at the pop-up menu.

exercise 8

Changing Fill Color

1. Open Ch 19, Ex 05.
2. Save the document with Save As and name it Ch 19, Ex 08.
3. Change the fill color of the oval shape by completing the following steps:
   a. Select the oval shape by positioning the I-beam pointer on the line that forms the oval until it turns into an arrow with a four-headed arrow attached, then clicking the left mouse button.
   b. Click the down-pointing triangle at the right side of the Fill Color button on the Drawing toolbar.
   c. At the palette that displays, click the blue button (the sixth color from the left in the second row).
   d. Select the text box.
   e. Click the down-pointing triangle at the right side of the Fill Color button on the Drawing toolbar.
   f. At the palette that displays, click the light blue button (the sixth color from the left in the last row).
   g. Deselect the text box.
4. Save the document again with the same name (Ch 19, Ex 08).
5. Print and then close Ch 19, Ex 08.

Changing Line Style

Line Style

By default, Word draws shapes and text boxes with a thin black line. This line can be changed to a thicker line, a broken line, or a line with an arrow pointer. To change the line style, click the down-pointing triangle at the right side of the Line Style button, then click the desired line style at the pop-up menu that displays. Click the More Lines option at the pop-up menu and the Format AutoShape dialog box displays with the Colors and Lines tab selected. This dialog box contains the same options as the Format Picture dialog box.

Dash Style

Click the Dash Style button if you want to draw an object with a dashed line. Clicking this button causes a pop-up list to display containing dashed line options.

exercise 9

Changing Line Style and Color

1. Open Ch 19, Ex 06.
2. Save the document with Save As and name it Ch 19, Ex 09.
3. Change the line style and color of the top box by completing the following steps:

a. Position the I-beam pointer on one of the lines of the text box containing the name *Blaine Dowler* until it turns into an arrow with a four-headed arrow attached and then double-click the left mouse button. (This displays the Format Text Box dialog box.)
b. At the Format Text Box dialog box, click the Colors and Lines tab.
c. Click the down-pointing triangle to the right of the Color option in the Fill section and then click the red color (first color from the left in the third row).
d. Select the current point size measurement in the Weight text box and then key **4**.
e. Click OK or press Enter to close the Format Text Box dialog box.

4. Complete steps similar to those in 3 to change the line style and color for the text box at the left (containing the name *Jennifer Dean*).
5. Complete steps similar to those in 3 to change the line style and color for the text box at the right (containing the name *Lewis Kennedy*).
6. Save the document again with the same name (Ch 19, Ex 09).
7. Print and then close Ch 19, Ex 09.

Adding Shadow and 3-D Effects

Shadow

Click the Shadow button on the Drawing toolbar and a palette of shadow options displays. Click the desired option or click the Shadow Settings option and a Shadow Settings toolbar displays. This toolbar contains buttons for turning shadows off or on and buttons for nudging the shadow up, down, left, or right.

3-D

If you want to add a three-dimensional look to an object, select the object, and then click the 3-D button on the Drawing toolbar. This displays a palette of three-dimensional choices as well as a 3-D Settings option. Click this option and the 3-D Settings toolbar displays. This toolbar contains buttons for turning 3-D on or off and changing the tilt, depth, direction, and light source.

exercise 10

Adding Shadow and 3-D Effects to an Object

1. At a clear document screen, create a shape and add shadow and then 3-D effects to the shape by completing the following steps:
   a. With the Drawing toolbar displayed, click the Rectangle button.

b. Draw a rectangle in the document (you determine the size).
c. With the rectangle selected, add a fill color of your choosing.
d. With the rectangle still selected, click the Shadow button on the Drawing toolbar, and then click a shadow option. (You determine the shadow).
e. Experiment with a few other shadow options. Click the Shadow Settings option and then experiment with buttons on the Shadow Settings toolbar. When done using the toolbar, click the Close button located in the upper right corner of the toolbar to turn it off.
f. Save the document and name it Ch 19, Ex 10.
g. Print Ch 19, Ex 10.
h. Remove the Shadow effect from the rectangle. To do this, select the rectangle, click the Shadow button, and then click *No Shadow*.
i. With the rectangle still selected, add a 3-D effect to the rectangle by clicking the 3-D button on the Drawing toolbar, and then clicking a 3-D option (you determine the option).
j. Experiment with a few other 3-D options. Click the 3-D Settings option and then experiment with buttons on the 3-D Settings toolbar. When done using the toolbar, click the Close button located in the upper right corner of the toolbar to turn it off.

2. Save the document again with the same name (Ch 19, Ex 10).
3. Print and then close Ch 19, Ex 10.

exercise 11

Creating a Logo with a Three-Dimensional Effect

1. At a clear document screen, create the logo shown in figure 19.9 by completing the following steps:
   a. With the Drawing toolbar displayed, click the Rectangle button.
   b. Draw a rectangle in the document screen that is approximately 3 inches wide and 1.5 inches high.
   c. Size and position the rectangle, add fill color, and add a 3-D effect by completing the following steps:
      1) With the rectangle selected, position the arrow pointer inside the rectangle (displays with a four-headed arrow attached) and then double-click the left mouse button. (This displays the Format AutoShape dialog box.)
      2) At the Format AutoShape dialog box, click the Size tab.
      3) Select the current measurement in the Height text box in the Size and rotate section of the dialog box and then key **1.5**.

4) Select the current measurement in the Width text box in the Size and rotate section of the dialog box and then key **3**.
5) Click the Position tab at the top of the dialog box.
6) Click the down-pointing triangle at the right of the From text box and then click *Margin* at the drop-down list.
7) Select the current measurement in the Horizontal text box in the Position on page section of the dialog box and then key **1.6**.
8) Select the current measurement in the Vertical text box in the Position on page section of the dialog box and then key **0.2**.
9) Click the Colors and Lines tab at the top of the dialog box.
10) Click the down-pointing triangle at the right side of the Color option in the Fill section and then click the turquoise color (fifth color from the left in the fourth row).
11) Click OK to close the Format AutoShape dialog box.
12) With the rectangle still selected, click the 3-D button on the Drawing toolbar and then click the first 3-D option in the first row.
13) Deselect the rectangle.

d. Draw a text box inside the rectangle that is approximately 2 inches wide and 1 inch high.
e. Key the text inside the box as shown in figure 19.9 by completing the following steps:
   1) Change the font to 18-point Arial bold.
   2) Click the Center button on the Formatting toolbar.
   3) Key **3-D** and then press Enter.
   4) Key **Construction**.
f. Size and position the text box, add fill color, and add a 3-D effect by completing the following steps:
   1) With the text box selected, position the arrow pointer on one of the lines of the text box until it displays with a four-headed arrow attached and then double-click the left mouse button. (This displays the Format Text Box dialog box.)
   2) At the Format Text Box dialog box, click the Size tab.
   3) Select the current measurement in the Height text box in the Size and rotate section of the dialog box and then key **0.7**.
   4) Select the current measurement in the Width text box in the Size and rotate section of the dialog box and then key **2**.
   5) Click the Position tab at the top of the dialog box.
   6) Click the down-pointing triangle at the right of the From text box and then click *Margin* at the drop-down list.

7) Select the current measurement in the Horizontal text box in the Position on page section of the dialog box and then key **2**.
8) Select the current measurement in the Vertical text box in the Position on page section of the dialog box and then key **0.6**.
9) Click the Colors and Lines tab at the top of the dialog box.
10) Click the down-pointing triangle at the right side of the Color option in the Fill section and then click the turquoise color (fifth color from the left in the fourth row).
11) Click OK to close the Format Text Box dialog box.
12) With the text box still selected, click the 3-D button on the Drawing toolbar and then click the first 3-D option in the first row.
13) Deselect the text box.

2. Save the document and name it Ch 19, Ex 11.
3. Print and then close Ch 19, Ex 11.

figure 19.9 *Exercise 11*

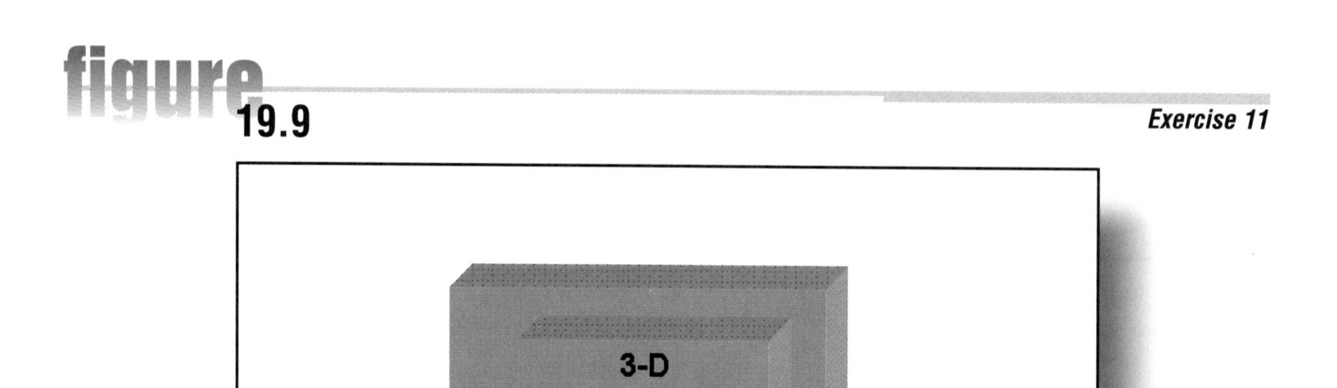

Creating a Watermark

An interesting effect can be created in a document with a watermark. A *watermark* is a lightened image that displays in a document. Text can be inserted in front of the watermark, creating a document with a foreground and a background. The foreground is the text and the background is the watermark image. Figure 19.10 shows an example of a watermark. The scales image is the watermark and creates the background, while the text of the letter displays in front of the watermark and creates the foreground.

figure 19.10 ***Watermark Example***

May 12, 1998

Ms. Anna M. Omura
4320 Loredo Avenue
Bellevue, WA 98001

Dear Ms. Omura:

Re: OMURA v. JOSTEN
Case No. C430-2

The attorney, Michael Clark, of MORIARTY & CLARK, is representing the defendant, Nelson Josten, in our case number C430-2. A response to our complaint has been filed with the court. A copy of the complaint is attached.

I am preparing interrogatories which will be presented to Nelson Josten during a deposition. The deposition should be scheduled within the next two weeks. I would like to schedule the deposition for either Wednesday, May 27, or Thursday, May 28. Please let me know which day is convenient for you.

Sincerely,

SPERRY, BRAND & FULTON

Everett Fulton
Attorney at Law

XX:Letter 02

Attachment

A Word document contains three levels: the text layer, a layer above the text, and a layer behind. The text layer is the one in which you generally work in a document. An object created with buttons on the Drawing toolbar can be drawn in a document containing text. By default, the object will display above the text layer, covering the text. If you want the object and the text in the document to display, move the object behind the text. You can do this with options from the Draw button on the Drawing toolbar.

Draw ▾

Draw

Creating a watermark involves using the Image Control button on the Picture toolbar (described in chapter 18) along with an option at the Draw button pop-up menu. Click the Draw button on the Drawing toolbar and a pop-up menu displays. At this menu, point to Order and another side menu displays as shown in figure 19.11. Use options at this side menu to bring a selected object in front of another object, move it behind another object, or move the selected object in front of or behind text. In exercise 13, you will be creating a watermark using a clip art image and then moving it behind the text in the document.

figure 19.11

Order Side Menu

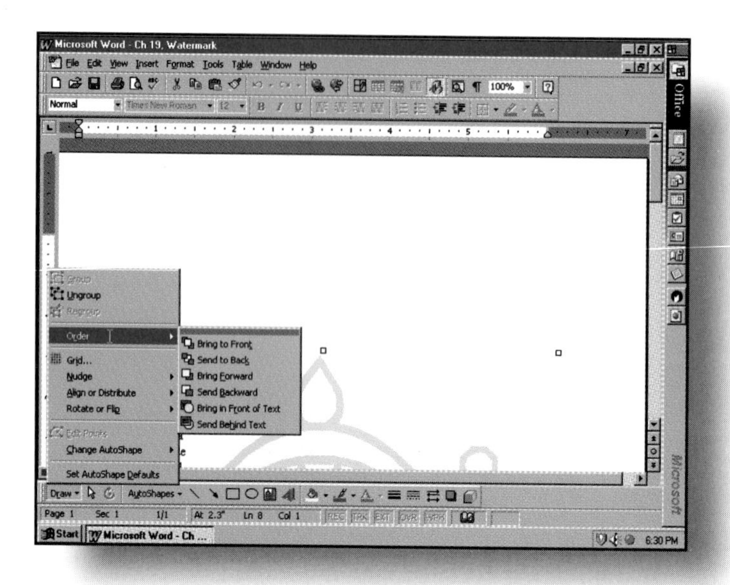

exercise 12

Creating a Watermark in a Document

1. Open Notice 02.
2. Save the document with Save As and name it Ch 19, Ex 12.
3. Make the following changes to the document:
   a. Select the entire document and then change the font to 18-point Goudy Old Style bold (or a similar decorative typeface).
   b. Deselect the text.
   c. Move the insertion point to the beginning of the document.
   d. Display the Microsoft Clip Gallery 3.0 dialog box, and look for the image displayed in the margin by clicking *Seasons* in the list box that displays at the left side of the dialog box. Scroll through the list until the image displays and then double-click the image. (If the image is not available, look for any image of a flower or flowers, and then double-click the image.)

   e. Increase the size of the image by dragging the middle sizing handle at the right side to approximately the 4-inch mark on the horizontal ruler. Drag the middle sizing handle at the bottom to approximately the 4-inch mark on the vertical ruler. (You may want to scroll down the document to display the 4-inch mark on the vertical ruler before dragging down the sizing handle.)
   f. Display the Picture toolbar by positioning the arrow pointer on the image, clicking the *right* mouse button, and then

clicking Show Picture Toolbar. (Skip this step if the Picture toolbar is already displayed.)

g. Click the Image Control button on the Picture toolbar and then click Watermark at the drop-down list that displays.

h. Click the Text Wrapping button on the Picture toolbar and then click None at the drop-down list that displays.

i. With the watermark image still selected, drag it to the right so it is better centered over the text.

j. Send the image behind the text by completing the following steps:

   1) With the Drawing toolbar displayed, click the Draw button that displays at the left side of the Drawing toolbar.

   2) At the pop-up menu that displays, point to Order, and then click Send Behind Text.

k. Click outside the image to deselect it.

4. Save the document again with the same name (Ch 19, Ex 12).
5. Print and then close Ch 19, Ex 12.

Objects created in Draw can overlap. If you want to move an object behind another, select the object, click the Draw button, point to Order, and then click Send to Back. You can also click the Send Backward option. The Send to Back option places the selected object behind other overlapping objects while the Send Backward option moves the selected object one step closer to the bottom of a stack of objects.

To bring the selected object to the front, click Draw, point to Order, and then click Bring to Front. You can also click Bring Forward. The Bring to Front option places the selected object in front of other overlapping objects while the Bring Forward option moves the selected object one step closer to the top of a stack of objects.

Flipping and Rotating an Object

A selected object can be rotated and flipped horizontally or vertically. To rotate or flip an object, select the object, click the Draw button on the Drawing toolbar, point to Rotate or Flip, and then click the desired rotation or flip option at the side menu that displays. A drawn object can be rotated, but a text box cannot.

exercise 13

Creating a Letterhead and Rotating an Arrow

1. At a clear document screen, create the letterhead shown in figure 19.12 by completing the following steps:

   a. Press Enter four times.

   b. Click the Center button on the Formatting toolbar.

c. Change the font to 36-point Impact. (If Impact is not available, choose a similar typeface.)
d. Key **Quick Time Printing**.
e. Create the yellow arrow at the left side of the text by completing the following steps:
   1) Click the AutoShapes button on the Drawing toolbar.
   2) Point to Block Arrows. (This displays a side menu.)
   3) Click the first arrow from the left in the third row (the Bent Arrow).
   4) Draw the arrow at the left side of the text as shown in figure 19.12. If you are not satisfied with the location of the arrow, drag it to the desired location. If you are not satisfied with the size of the arrow, use the sizing handles to increase or decrease the size.
   5) With the arrow still selected, add yellow fill. To do this, click the down-pointing triangle at the right side of the Fill Color button on the Drawing toolbar. At the palette of color choices that displays, click the yellow color (third color from the left in the fourth row).
f. With the yellow arrow still selected, copy it to the right side of the text. To do this, hold down the Ctrl key and then the left mouse button. Drag the arrow to the right side of the text and then release the mouse button and then the Ctrl key.
g. Flip the arrow horizontally by completing the following steps:
   1) With the arrow at the right side of the text still selected, click the Draw button on the Drawing toolbar.
   2) At the pop-up menu that displays, point to Rotate or Flip.
   3) At the side menu that displays, click Flip Horizontal.
h. If necessary, reposition the arrow so it displays as shown in figure 19.12.

2. Save the document and name it Ch 19, Ex 13.
3. Print and then close Ch 19, Ex 13.

figure 19.12 *Exercise 13*

Adding Callouts

Callouts are a useful tool for identifying parts of an illustration or picture. Many figures in this textbook include callouts identifying Word features. For example, figure 19.4 includes a callout identifying the text box.

To create a callout, click the AutoShapes button, point to Callouts, and then click the desired callout design at the side menu that displays. Position the cross hairs at the location where you want the callout to point, hold down the left mouse button, drag to the location where callout text is to display, and then release the mouse button. (This inserts a text box in the document screen.) Key the callout text in the text box. Text in the text box can be formatted in the normal manner.

The line that connects to the callout text box can be changed. For example, if you want the line to point in a slightly different direction, position the arrow pointer (with the four-headed arrow attached) on the callout line and then click the left mouse button. This causes yellow adjustment handles to display at each end of the line. Position the arrow pointer on one of the adjustment handles, hold down the left mouse button, drag the line in the desired direction, and then release the mouse button.

exercise 14

Adding Callouts to a Clip Art Image

1. At a clear document screen, create the document shown in figure 19.13 by completing the following steps:
   a. Display the Microsoft Clip Gallery 3.0 dialog box, look for the computer image shown in figure 19.13 in the *Science & Technology* category, and then double-click the image. (If this computer image is not available, click *(All Categories)*, scroll through the list until you find an image of a computer, and then double-click the image.)
   b. Decrease the size of the image by dragging the bottom right sizing handle to approximately the 3-inch mark on the horizontal ruler and then the 2.5-inch mark on the vertical ruler.
   c. With the computer image still selected, drag the image to the middle of the screen.
   d. Add the callout for the monitor by completing the following steps:
      1) Click the AutoShapes button on the Drawing toolbar.
      2) At the pop-up menu that displays, point to Callouts.
      3) Click the second callout option from the left in the fourth row. (Position the arrow pointer on this option and after one second a ToolTip displays with the name *Line Callout 2 (No Border)*.)
      4) Position the cross hairs close to the monitor, hold down the left mouse button, drag to the right (try to keep the line even), and then release the mouse button.

5) With the insertion point inside the text box, change the font to 14-point Arial bold, and then key **Monitor**.
6) Click outside the text box to deselect it.

e. Complete steps similar to those in 1d to create the remaining callouts (*Mouse*, *Keyboard*, and *CPU*). If the text *Keyboard* wraps within the callout text box, use a sizing handle to increase the size of the callout text box. You may want to decrease the size of the callout text for the box containing *CPU*.

2. Save the document and name it Ch 19, Ex 14.
3. Print and then close Ch 19, Ex 14.

figure 19.13

Exercise 14

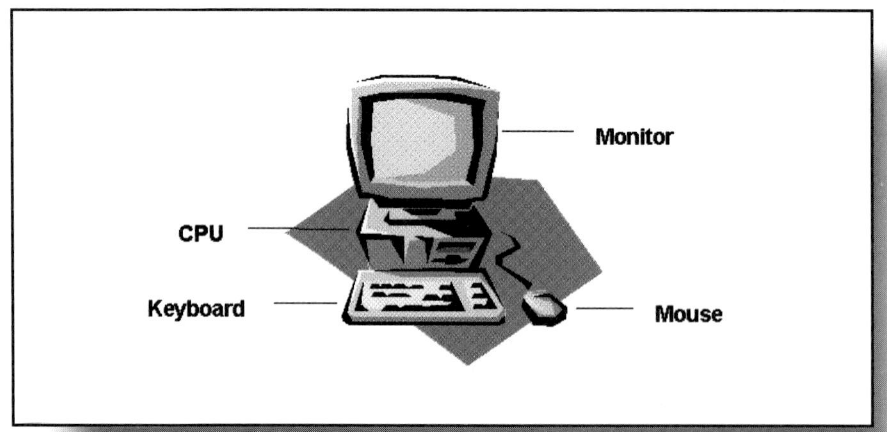

chapter summary

- Create your own shapes and images with buttons on the Drawing toolbar.
- Display the Drawing toolbar by positioning the arrow pointer on the Standard or Formatting toolbar, clicking the *right* mouse button, and then clicking *Drawing* at the drop-down list.
- A shape drawn with the Line or Arrow buttons is considered a line drawing. A shape drawn with the Rectangle or Oval buttons is considered an enclosed object. Fill color can be added to enclosed objects.
- Click the Line button to draw a line in the document screen. To draw more than one line, double-click the Line button.
- A variety of predesigned shapes is available from the AutoShapes button on the Drawing toolbar.

- Create a text box by clicking the Text Box button on the Drawing toolbar and then drawing the box in the document screen.
- A text box can be drawn inside of a drawn shape.
- To select an enclosed object, position the I-beam anywhere inside the object and then click the left mouse button. To select a line, position the I-beam pointer on the line until the I-beam pointer turns into an arrow with a four-headed arrow attached, and then click the left mouse button.
- To select several objects at once, click the Select Objects button, position the cross hairs in the upper left corner of the area containing the objects, hold down the left mouse button, drag the outline to the lower right corner of the area containing the objects, and then release the mouse button. You can also select more than one object by holding down the Shift key and then clicking each object.
- To delete an object, select it, and then press the Delete key.
- To move an object, select it, and then drag it to the desired location.
- To copy an object, select it, and then hold down the Ctrl key. Drag the outline of the object to the desired location and then release the mouse button and then the Ctrl key.
- Use the white sizing handles that display around a selected object to increase or decrease the size of the object.
- Add fill color to an enclosed object with the Fill Color button on the Drawing toolbar.
- Change the line color with the Line Color button on the Drawing toolbar.
- Change the line style with the Line Style, Dash Style, or Arrow Style buttons on the Drawing toolbar.
- Add a shadow effect to an object with options from the Shadow button on the Drawing toolbar.
- Add a three-dimensional effect to an object with options from the 3-D button on the Drawing toolbar.
- A watermark is a lightened image that displays in a document, generally behind text. Move a watermark image behind text with options from the Draw button on the Drawing toolbar.
- An object (but not a text box) can be flipped and rotated with options from the Draw button on the Drawing toolbar.
- Add a callout to an image with options from the AutoShapes button on the Drawing toolbar.

commands review

	Mouse/Keyboard
Display Drawing toolbar	Position arrow pointer on Standard or Formatting toolbar, click the *right* mouse button, and then click *Drawing* at the drop-down list.
Colors dialog box	Click down-pointing triangle at right side of [button] and then click More Fill Colors.
Fill Effects dialog box	Click down-pointing triangle at right side of [button] and then click Fill Effects.
Patterned Lines dialog box	Click down-pointing triangle at right side of [button] and then click Patterned Lines.
Format Text Box dialog box	Double-click text box.
Shadow Settings toolbar	Click [button] and then click Shadow Settings.
3-D Settings toolbar	Click [button] and then click 3-D Settings.
Format AutoShape dialog box	Double-click a shape.

check your understanding

Completion: In the space provided at the right, indicate the correct term, command, or number.

1. Choose a variety of predesigned shapes by first clicking this button on the Drawing toolbar. ____________
2. If the viewing mode is set at Normal, clicking any button on the Drawing toolbar causes Word to change to this viewing mode. ____________
3. To create a box and then insert text inside the box, begin by clicking this button on the Drawing toolbar. ____________
4. To select one object, position the I-beam pointer on the object until the pointer displays with this attached. ____________
5. To change the width and height of an object at the same time, use one of these sizing handles. ____________
6. To draw a perfect circle, click the Oval button on the Drawing toolbar, hold down this key, and then draw the circle. ____________
7. If you want to draw the same shape more than once, do this on the shape button on the Drawing toolbar. ____________
8. This is a useful tool for identifying parts of an illustration or picture. ____________

9. Click this button on the Drawing toolbar to display a variety of three-dimensional effects. ________________

10. To select more than one object, hold down this key on the keyboard, and then click each object. ________________

11. To copy a selected object, hold down this key on the keyboard while dragging the object. ________________

12. This term refers to a lightened image that displays in a document. ________________

13. A drawn object can be rotated or flipped, but not this type of box. ________________

14. To display a list of callouts, click this button on the Drawing toolbar, and then point to Callouts. ________________

In the space provided below, write the steps you would complete to draw a perfect square and then fill that square with red color. (Assume the Drawing toolbar is already displayed.)

____

____

____

skill assessments

Note: Before completing the skill assessments, display the Open dialog box, and then select and delete documents created in chapter 17 that begin Ch 17. You may want to check with your instructor before deleting these documents.

Assessment 1

1. At a clear document screen, draw the square, circle, and rectangle shown in figure 19.14. After drawing the shapes, make the following changes:
   a. Select each shape, click the Line Style button on the Drawing toolbar, and then click the *2¼ pt* option. (This makes the line thicker.)
   b. Add red fill to the circle, yellow fill to the square, and blue fill to the rectangle.
2. Save the document and name it Ch 19, SA 01.
3. Print and then close Ch 19, SA 01.

Figure 19.14 • Assessment 1

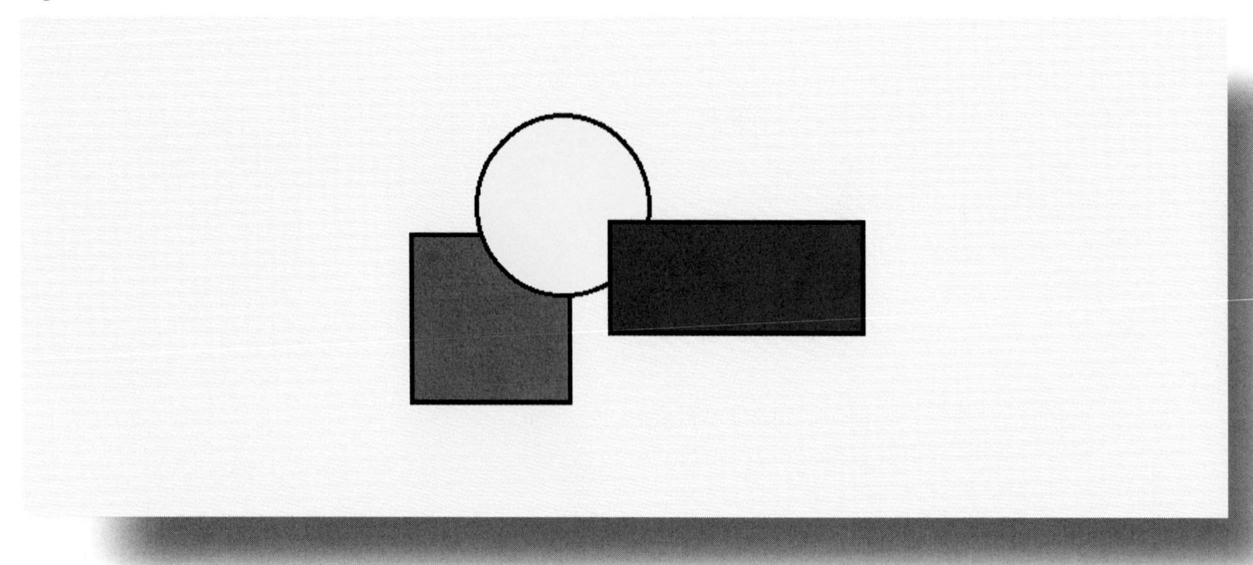

Assessment 2

1. At a clear document screen, create the organizational chart shown in figure 19.15 with the following specifications:
   a. Key the title bolded and centered as shown in the figure.
   b. Press the Enter key three times and then create the first text box with the following specifications:
      1) Change the font to 12-point Arial bold.
      2) Key the text in the first box as shown in figure 19.15.
      3) Add pale blue fill to the text box.
   c. After creating the first text box, copy the text box the number of times needed for the document. Change the title inside the boxes as shown in figure 19.15.
   d. Use the Line button on the Drawing toolbar to create the lines connecting the rectangles.
   e. Select the title, *DEPARTMENT OF TRAINING AND EDUCATION*, and then change the font to 14-point Arial bold.
2. Save the document and name it Ch 19, SA 02.
3. Print and then close Ch 19, SA 02.

Figure 19.15 • Assessment 2

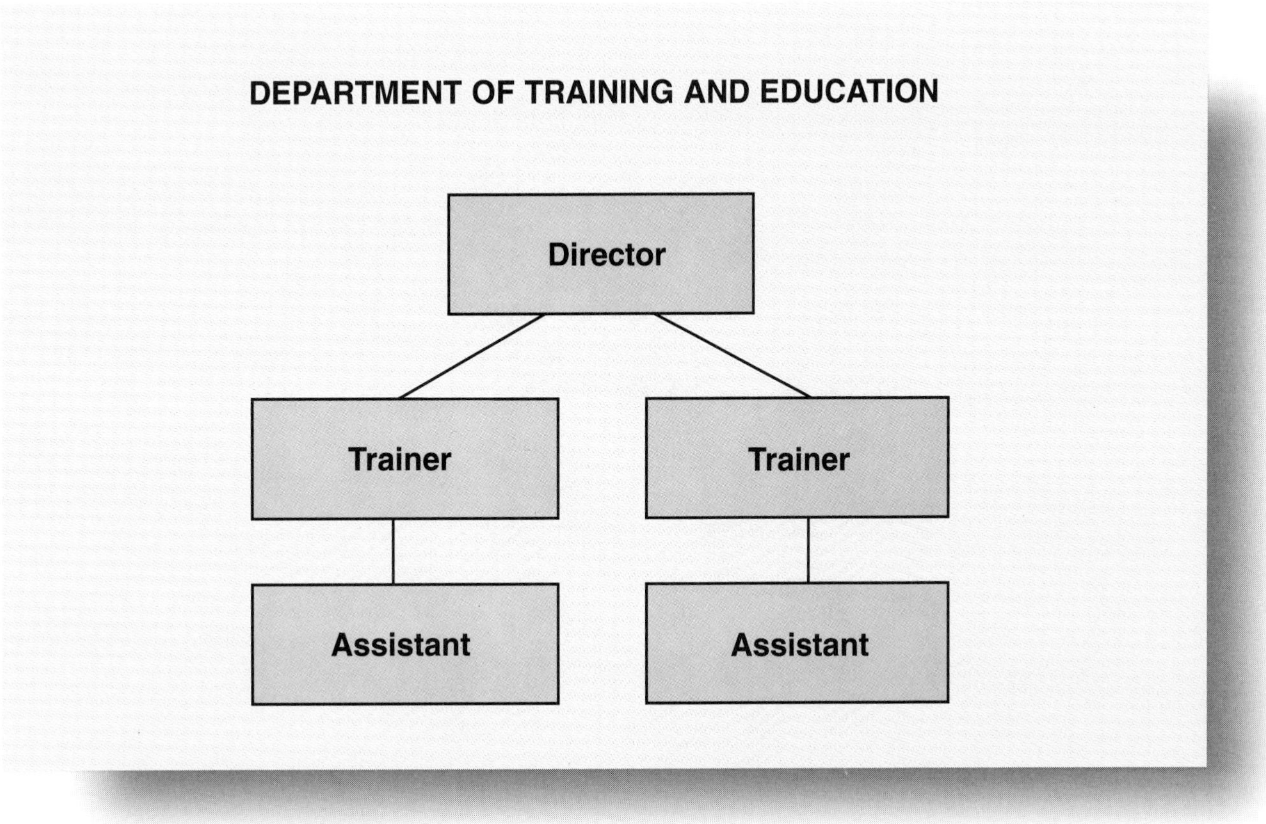

DEPARTMENT OF TRAINING AND EDUCATION

Director

Trainer

Trainer

Assistant

Assistant

Assessment 3

1. At a clear document screen, create the object shown in figure 19.16 with the following specifications:
   a. Create the star with the 16-Point Star autoshape. Make the star approximately 5.5 inches wide and 4.5 inches tall. (Use the adjustment handle to drag in the points slightly.)
   b. Add light yellow fill to the star.
   c. Draw a text box inside the star.
   d. Key the text shown inside the star in figure 19.16. Set the name *Taylor Ewing* in 28-point Impact bold. (If Impact is not available, choose a similar typeface.) Set the remaining text in 18-point Impact bold.
   e. With the text box selected, remove the black line, and then add light yellow fill. (To remove the black line from the text box, click the down-pointing triangle at the right side of the Line Color button on the Drawing toolbar, and then click *No Line* at the palette of color choices.)
2. Save the document and name it Ch 19, SA 03.
3. Print and then close Ch 19, SA 03.

Figure 19.16 • Assessment 3

Assessment 4

1. Open Notice 03.
2. Save the document with Save As and name it Ch 19, SA 04.
3. Make the following changes to the document:
   a. Change the font for all text in the document to a serif typeface and type size of your choosing.
   b. Center all the text in the document.
   c. Insert a clip art image in the document that fits the text in the document.
   d. Format the clip art image so it displays as a watermark behind the text in the document.
4. Save the document again with the same name (Ch 19, SA 04).
5. Print and then close Ch 19, SA 04.

Assessment 5

1. At a clear document screen, create the document shown in figure 19.17 with the following specifications:
   a. Create the first triangle with an autoshape from the Basic Shapes option.
   b. Copy the triangle to create a total of five triangles.
   c. Select and then flip vertically two of the triangles.
   d. Move the triangles so they are positioned as shown in figure 19.17.
   e. Add fill color to the triangles as shown in the figure.
2. Save the document and name it Ch 19, SA 05.
3. Print and then close Ch 19, SA 05.

Figure 19.17 • Assessment 5

Assessment 6

1. At a clear document screen, create the document shown in figure 19.18 with the following specifications:
   a. Insert the clip art images as shown in the figure. (These clip art images are located in the *Buildings* category. If these clip art images are not available, insert other images of your choosing and then add appropriate callouts.)
   b. Add the callouts shown in figure 19.18.
2. Save the document and name it Ch 19, SA 06.
3. Print and then close Ch 19, SA 06.

Figure 19.18 • Assessment 6

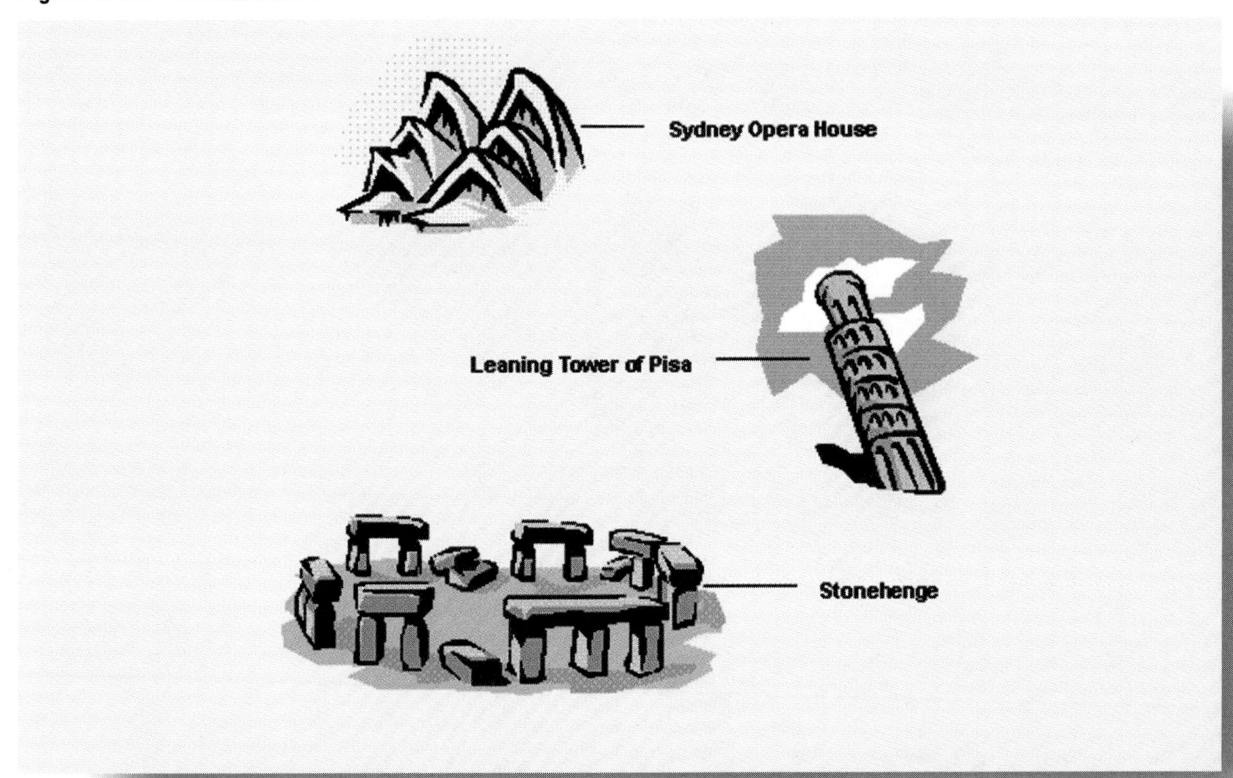

chapter TWENTY

Using WordArt and Equation Editor

PERFORMANCE OBJECTIVES

Upon completion of chapter 20, you will be able to:

- **Modify text with WordArt.**
- **Size and move a WordArt text box.**
- **Change the font and font size of WordArt text.**
- **Customize WordArt text with buttons on the WordArt toolbar.**
- **Customize WordArt text with buttons on the Drawing toolbar.**
- **Create and edit an equation with the Microsoft Equation 3.0 equation editor.**

Word provides a supplementary application named WordArt that you can use to modify and conform text to a variety of shapes. This application uses object linking and embedding (OLE) to create and add objects to a Word document. You can also use the WordArt application to create text in a variety of shapes and alignments, and to add 3-D effects. With the Microsoft Equation 3.0 equation editor application, you can create mathematical equations with proper formatting.

Using WordArt

With the WordArt application, you can distort or modify text to conform to a variety of shapes. This is useful for creating company logos and headings. With WordArt, you can change the font, style, and alignment of text. You can also use different fill patterns and colors, customize border lines, and add shadow and three-dimensional effects.

To enter WordArt, click Insert, point to Picture, and then click WordArt. This displays the WordArt Gallery shown in figure 20.1. Another method for displaying the WordArt Gallery is to click View, point to Toolbars, and then click WordArt, or position the arrow pointer on a toolbar, click the *right* mouse button, and then click WordArt at the drop-down menu. This displays the WordArt toolbar shown in figure 20.2. Click the Insert WordArt button on the WordArt toolbar and the WordArt Gallery displays.

Insert WordArt

figure 20.1

WordArt Gallery

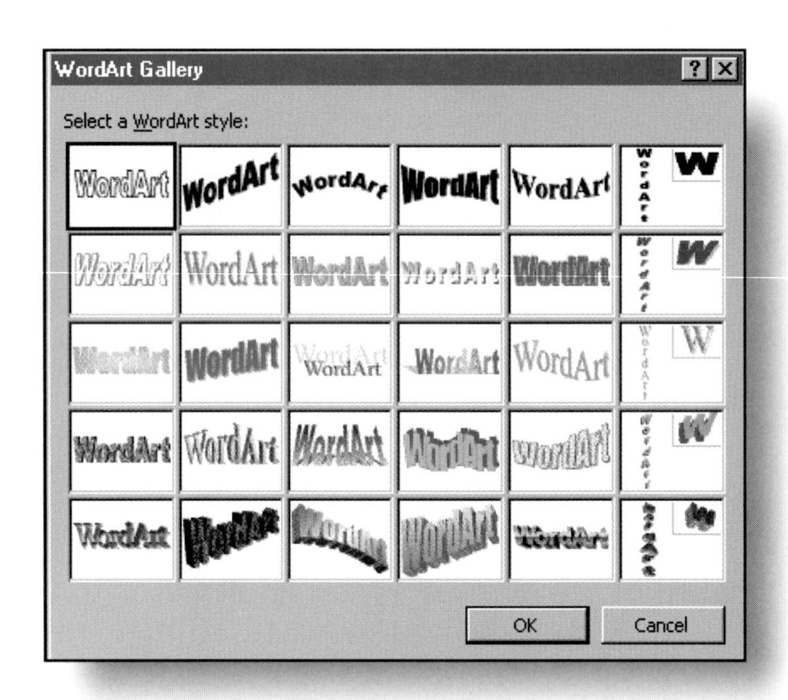

figure 20.2

WordArt Toolbar

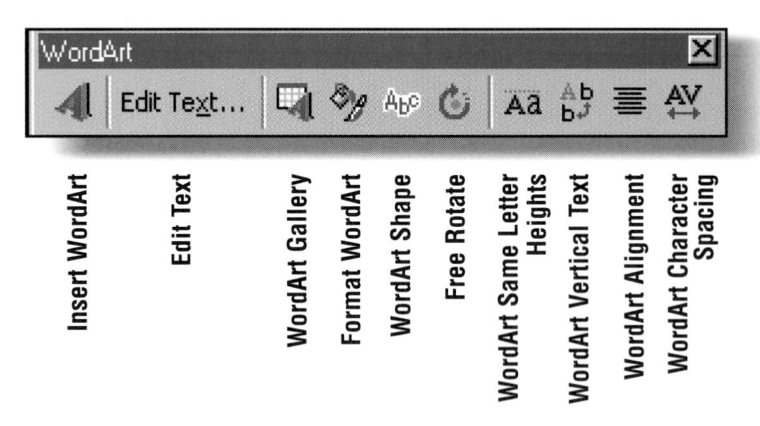

Entering Text

Double-click a WordArt choice at the WordArt Gallery and the Edit WordArt Text dialog box displays as shown in figure 20.3. At the Edit WordArt Text dialog box, the words *Your Text Here* are automatically selected in the Text box. Key the text in the text box and the original words are removed. Press the Enter key if you want to move the insertion point to the next line. After keying the desired text, click the OK button.

20.3

Edit WordArt Text Dialog Box

Sizing and Moving WordArt

When you click the OK button, the WordArt text is displayed in the document with the formatting you selected at the WordArt Gallery. The WordArt text is surrounded by white sizing handles and the WordArt toolbar displays near the text.

Use the white sizing handles to change the height and width of the WordArt text. Use the yellow diamond located at the bottom of the WordArt text to change the slant of the WordArt text. To do this, position the arrow pointer on the yellow diamond, hold down the left mouse button, drag to the left or right, and then release the mouse button. This moves the yellow diamond along the bottom of the WordArt and changes the slant of the WordArt text.

To move WordArt text, position the arrow pointer on any letter of the WordArt text until the arrow pointer displays with a four-headed arrow attached. Hold down the left mouse button, drag the outline of the WordArt text box to the desired position, and then release the mouse button.

When all changes have been made to the WordArt text, click outside the WordArt text box. This removes from the screen the white sizing handles, the yellow diamond, and the WordArt toolbar.

Changing the Font and Font Size

The font for WordArt text will vary depending on the choice you make at the WordArt Gallery. You can change the font at the Edit WordArt Text dialog box with the Font option. To do this, click the down-pointing triangle at the right side of the Font text box. This causes a drop-down menu of font choices to display. Scroll through the list until the desired font is visible and then click the desired font.

The font size can be changed by clicking the down-pointing triangle at the right side of the Size text box. This causes a drop-down menu of size options to display. Scroll through the list of sizes until the desired size is visible and then click the size.

Bold

Italic

The Edit WordArt Text dialog box contains Bold and Italic buttons. Click the Bold button to apply bold formatting to the WordArt text and click the Italic button to apply italic formatting.

exercise 1

Creating a Letterhead with WordArt

1. At a clear document screen, create the letterhead shown in figure 20.4 using WordArt by completing the following steps:
   a. At a clear document screen, press Enter eight times, and then move the insertion point back up to the first line.
   b. Click Insert, point to Picture, and then click WordArt.
   c. At the WordArt Gallery, double-click the first option from the left in the last row.
   d. At the Edit WordArt Text dialog box, make the following changes:
      1) Change the font to Arial and the size to 32 by completing the following steps:
         a) Click the down-pointing triangle at the right side of the Font text box.
         b) At the drop-down menu that displays, scroll up the list until *Arial* is visible, and then click Arial.
         c) Click the down-pointing triangle at the right side of the Size text box.
         d) At the drop-down menu that displays, click *32*.
      2) Select the text *Your Text Here* in the Text box.
      3) Key **Mountain**, press Enter, and then key **Community College**.
      4) Click the OK button.
   e. Change the size of the WordArt box by completing the following steps:
      1) Position the arrow pointer on the middle white sizing handle located at the bottom of the WordArt text.
      2) Hold down the left mouse button, drag up approximately one-quarter inch, and then release the mouse button. (Use the vertical ruler along the left side of the screen as a guide.)
   f. Change the location of the WordArt by completing the following steps:
      1) Position the arrow pointer on any letter of the WordArt text until the arrow pointer displays with a four-headed arrow attached.
      2) Hold down the left mouse button and then drag the outline of the WordArt box to the left until the top is positioned at approximately the 0-inch mark on the vertical ruler and the left side of the WordArt box is located at approximately the 0-inch mark on the horizontal ruler.
      3) When the outline of the WordArt box is located in the desired position, release the mouse button.

g. Position the I-beam pointer below the WordArt text and then click the left mouse button. (This removes the white sizing handles, the yellow diamond, and the WordArt toolbar.)
h. Create the border line shown in figure 20.4 by completing the following steps:
    1) Make sure the insertion point is positioned immediately below the text *Community College*.
    2) Click Format, then Borders and Shading.
    3) At the Borders and Shading dialog box with the Borders tab selected, scroll down the Style list box until the line shown in figure 20.4 displays (this is a thin/thick/thin line) and then click the line.
    4) At the Preview diagram at the right side of the dialog box, click the top, left, and right borders (this leaves the bottom border).
    5) Click OK to close the dialog box.
i. Move the insertion point below the border line and then click the Align Right button on the Formatting toolbar.
j. Key **A great place to learn!**
k. Select the text *A great place to learn!* and then change the font to 12-point Arial bold.

2. Save the document and name it Ch 20, Ex 01.
3. Print and then close Ch 20, Ex 01.

20.4 *Exercise 1*

Mountain
Community College

A great place to learn!

Customizing WordArt

Insert WordArt

WordArt Gallery

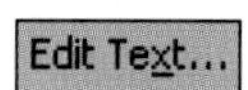

Edit Text

The WordArt toolbar contains buttons for customizing the WordArt text. Figure 20.2 displays the WordArt toolbar with the buttons identified. Click the Insert WordArt button and the WordArt Gallery shown in figure 20.1 displays. You can also display this gallery by clicking the WordArt Gallery button on the WordArt toolbar. Click the Edit Text button and the Edit WordArt Text dialog box displays.

Customizing WordArt with Options at the Format WordArt Dialog Box

Format WordArt

WordArt text can be customized at the Format WordArt dialog box shown in figure 20.5. To display this dialog box, click the Format WordArt button on the WordArt toolbar.

figure 20.5 *Format WordArt Dialog Box with the Colors and Lines Tab Selected*

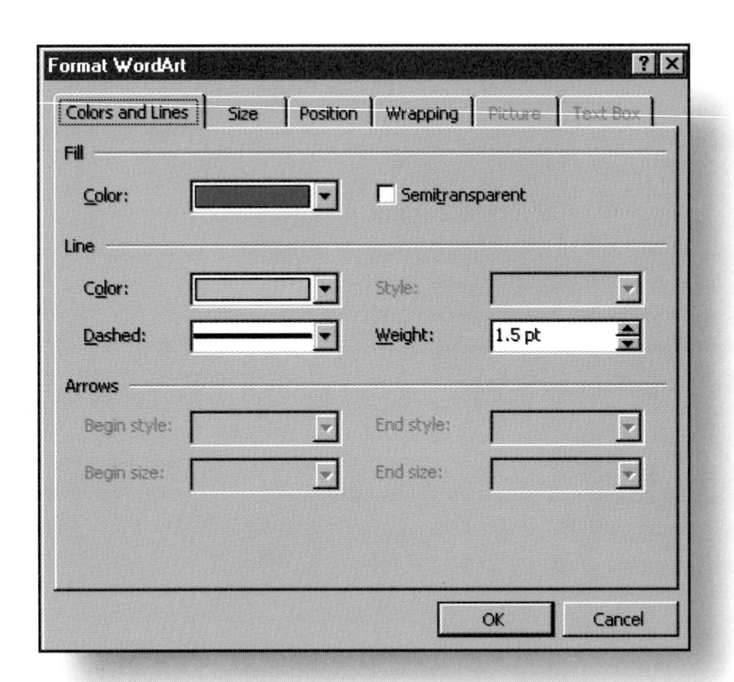

Change the color of the WordArt text and the line creating the text at the Format WordArt dialog box with the Colors and Lines tab selected. Click the Size tab and the dialog box displays options for changing the size and rotation of the WordArt text as well as the scale of the text. To change the position of WordArt text, click the Position tab. At the Format WordArt dialog box with the Position tab selected, you can specify the horizontal and vertical position of the WordArt text. If you want to specify how text will wrap around WordArt text, click the Wrapping tab at the Format WordArt dialog box. This displays the dialog box with options for wrapping text such as Square, Tight, Through, None, and Top & bottom.

When all changes have been made to the Format WordArt dialog box, click the OK button. This removes the dialog box and applies the formatting to the WordArt text.

Changing Shapes

WordArt Shape

The WordArt Gallery contains a variety of predesigned WordArt options. Formatting is already applied to these gallery choices. You can, however, customize the gallery choices with buttons on the WordArt toolbar. Use options from the WordArt Shape button to customize the shape of WordArt text. Click the WordArt Shape button on the WordArt toolbar and a palette of shape choices displays as shown in figure 20.6.

20.6 **WordArt Shape Palette**

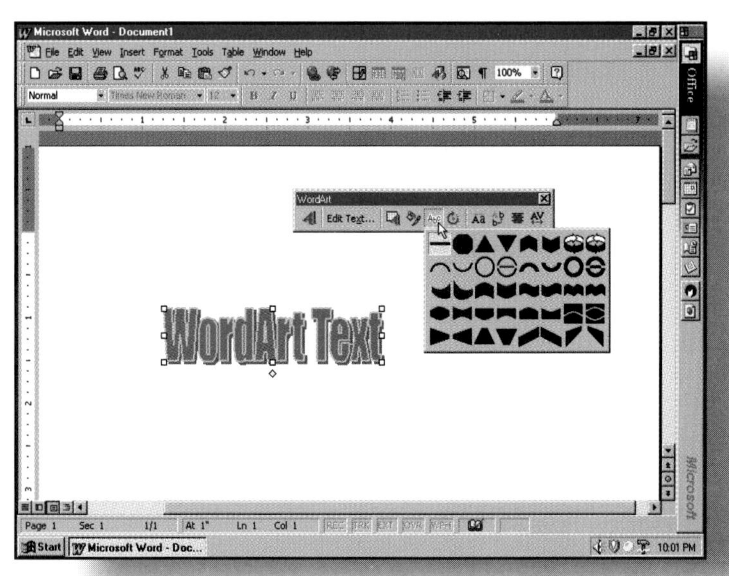

With the choices at the WordArt Shape palette, you can conform text to a variety of shapes. To select a shape, click the desired shape, and the WordArt text will conform to the selected shape. If you want to return text to the default shape, click the first shape in the first row.

exercise 2

Creating, Shaping, and Sizing WordArt Text

1. At a clear document screen, create WordArt text, and then shape and size the text by completing the following steps:
   a. Click Insert, point to Picture, then click WordArt.
   b. At the WordArt Gallery, double-click the fifth option from the left in the first row.
   c. At the Edit WordArt Text dialog box, key **Emerald Heights Elementary School**. (Press the space bar once after keying *School*.)
   d. Click the OK button.
   e. Change the shape of the WordArt text by completing the following steps:
      1) Click the WordArt Shape button.
      2) At the palette of shape choices, click the third shape from the left in the second row (Circle [Curve]).
   f. Change the size and color of the WordArt text by completing the following steps:
      1) Click the Format WordArt button on the WordArt toolbar.
      2) At the Format WordArt dialog box with the Colors and

Lines tab selected, click the down-pointing triangle to the right of the Color box in the Fill section.

3) At the color palette that displays, click the sea green color (fourth color option from the left in the third row).
4) Click the Size tab.
5) At the Format WordArt dialog box with the Size tab selected, select the current measurement in the Height text box, and then key **6**.
6) Select the current measurement in the Width text box and then key **6**.
7) Click the OK button to close the dialog box.

g. Click outside the WordArt text (this deselects the WordArt text box).

2. Save the document and name it Ch 20, Ex 02.
3. Print and then close Ch 20, Ex 02.

Rotating WordArt Text

Free Rotate

Click the Free Rotate button on the WordArt toolbar and small green circles display in each corner of the WordArt box. Use these rotation handles to rotate the WordArt text. To do this, position the arrow pointer on one of the small green circles until a circled arrow displays and the arrow pointer disappears. Hold down the left mouse button and the circled arrow changes to four arrows in a circle. With the left mouse button held down, drag the outline of the WordArt box to the desired rotation, and then release the mouse button.

Changing Letter Height

WordArt Same Letter Heights

By default, the height of WordArt uppercase letters will be greater than the height of lowercase letters. If you want all letters to have the same height, click the WordArt Same Letter Heights button on the WordArt toolbar.

Changing Vertical Alignment

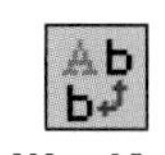

WordArt Vertical Text

WordArt text is displayed in a horizontal orientation. This can be changed to a vertical orientation by clicking the WordArt Vertical Text button on the WordArt toolbar.

Changing Text Alignment

WordArt Alignment

Text in a WordArt text box is center aligned by default. With options from the WordArt Alignment button on the WordArt toolbar, this alignment can be changed. When you click the WordArt Alignment button, a drop-down menu displays with the following options: Left Align, Center, Right Align, Word Justify, Letter Justify, and Stretch Justify.

Click the Left Align option if you want text aligned at the left side of the WordArt text box. Click Right Align to align text at the right side of the text box. Choose the Word Justify to space the words to fit in the WordArt box. Use the Letter Justify option to space out the letters to fit in the WordArt box. Click the last option, Stretch Justify, to stretch letters to fit in the WordArt box.

Changing Character Spacing

Click the WordArt Character Spacing button on the WordArt toolbar and a drop-down menu displays with options for determining character spacing. By default, the Normal option is selected at the WordArt Character Spacing drop-down menu. Choose one of the other options to either tighten up or loosen the spacing between characters. These options include Very Tight, Tight, Loose, Very Loose, and Custom.

WordArt Character Spacing

Kerning is a term that refers to the decrease of space between specific letter pairs. By default the Kern Character Pairs option is selected. If you do not want letter pairs kerned, remove the check mark from this option.

exercise 3

Creating and Then Customizing WordArt Text

1. At a clear document screen, create WordArt text, and then change the font, shape, and size of the text by completing the following steps:
   a. Click Insert, point to Picture, and then click WordArt.
   b. At the WordArt Gallery, double-click the second option from the left in the second row.
   c. At the Edit WordArt Text dialog box, make the following changes:
      1) Change the font to Braggadocio.
      2) Select the text *Your Text Here* and then key **Now is the time**.
      3) Press Enter and then key **to get out and**.
      4) Press Enter and then key **vote!**.
      5) Click OK to close the Edit WordArt Text dialog box.
   d. Change the alignment, size, and position of the WordArt text by completing the following steps:
      1) Click the WordArt Alignment button on the WordArt toolbar and then click Letter Justify at the drop-down menu.
      2) Change the size and position of the WordArt by completing the following steps:
         a) Click the Format WordArt button on the WordArt toolbar.
         b) At the Format WordArt dialog box, click the Size tab.
         c) At the Format WordArt dialog box with the Size tab selected, select the current measurement in the Height text box, and then key **2.5**.
         d) Select the current measurement in the Width text box and then key **6**.
         e) Click the Position tab.
         f) At the Format WordArt dialog box with the Position tab selected, select the current measurement in the Horizontal text box, and then key **0**. (Be sure to key a zero and not a capital O.)

g) Click OK to close the Format WordArt dialog box.

e. Click outside the WordArt text to deselect the WordArt box.

2. Save the document and name it Ch 20, Ex 03.
3. Print and then close Ch 20, Ex 03.

Customizing WordArt with Buttons on the Drawing Toolbar

In the previous chapter, you learned about the buttons on the Drawing toolbar. Buttons on this toolbar can also be used to customize WordArt text. For example, with buttons on the Drawing toolbar, you can change the letter color, line color, and line style, add a shadow, and add a three-dimensional effect.

To display the Drawing toolbar shown in figure 20.7, click View, point to Toolbars, and then click Drawing. You can also position the arrow pointer on any visible toolbar, click the *right* mouse button, and then click Drawing at the drop-down menu. Figure 20.7 identifies several buttons on the Drawing toolbar that can be used to create and then customize WordArt text. The Drawing toolbar contains the Insert WordArt button. Click this button and the WordArt Gallery shown in figure 20.1 displays.

Insert WordArt

figure 20.7

Drawing Toolbar

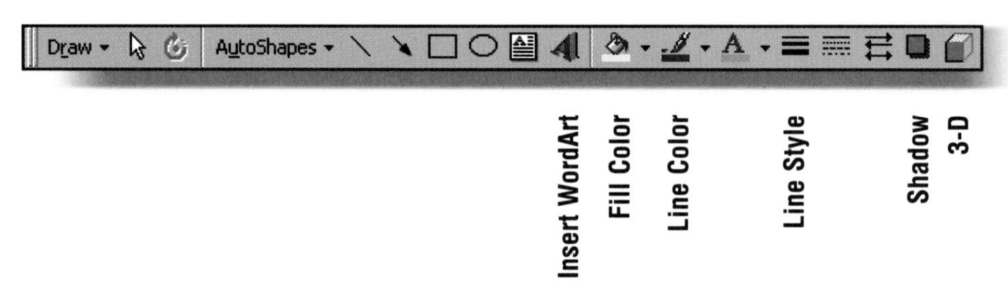

Adding Fill Shading or Color

Fill Color

With the Fill Color button on the Drawing toolbar, shading or color can be added to WordArt text. Click the Fill Color button and the WordArt text will be filled with the fill color displayed on the button. If you want to choose a different color, click the down-pointing triangle at the right side of the Fill Color button. This causes a palette of color choices to display. At this palette, click the desired fill color.

The Fill Color palette also includes two options—More Fill Colors and Fill Effects. Click the More Fill Colors option and the Colors dialog box with the Standard tab selected displays as shown in figure 20.8. At this dialog box, click the desired color in the Colors section, and then click OK. Create customized colors by clicking the Custom tab at the Colors dialog box.

20.8

Color Dialog Box with Standard Tab Selected

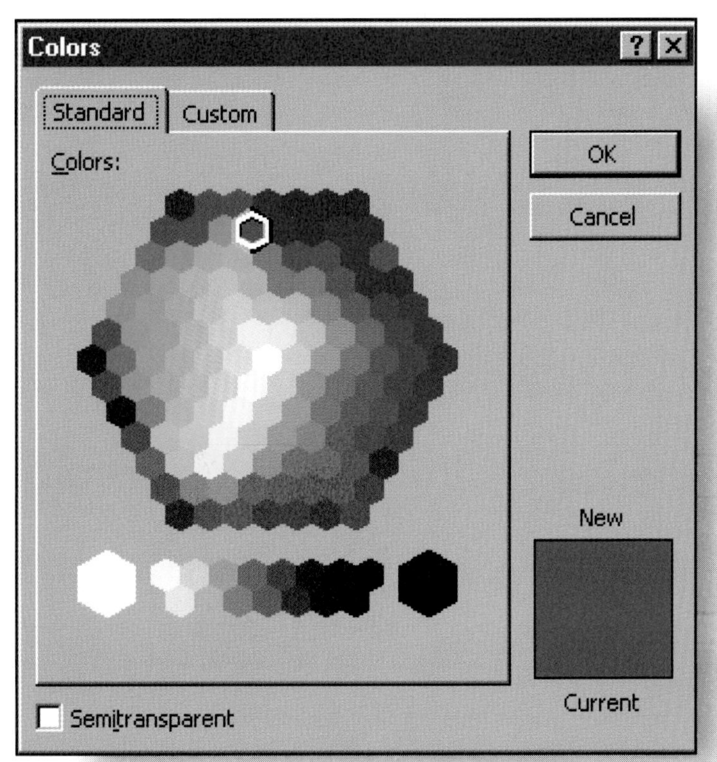

Click the other option at the Fill Color palette, Fill Effects, and the Fill Effects dialog box with the Gradient tab selected displays as shown in figure 20.9. At the dialog box with the Gradient tab selected, you can specify how many colors you want used in the gradient. You can also specify the style of gradient such as horizontal, vertical, diagonal, from the corner, or from the center.

Click the Texture tab to choose a texture to be applied to the WordArt text. If you want to add a pattern to the WordArt text, click the Pattern tab. After making the desired choices at the dialog box, click OK.

figure 20.9 *Fill Effects Dialog Box with the Gradient Tab Selected*

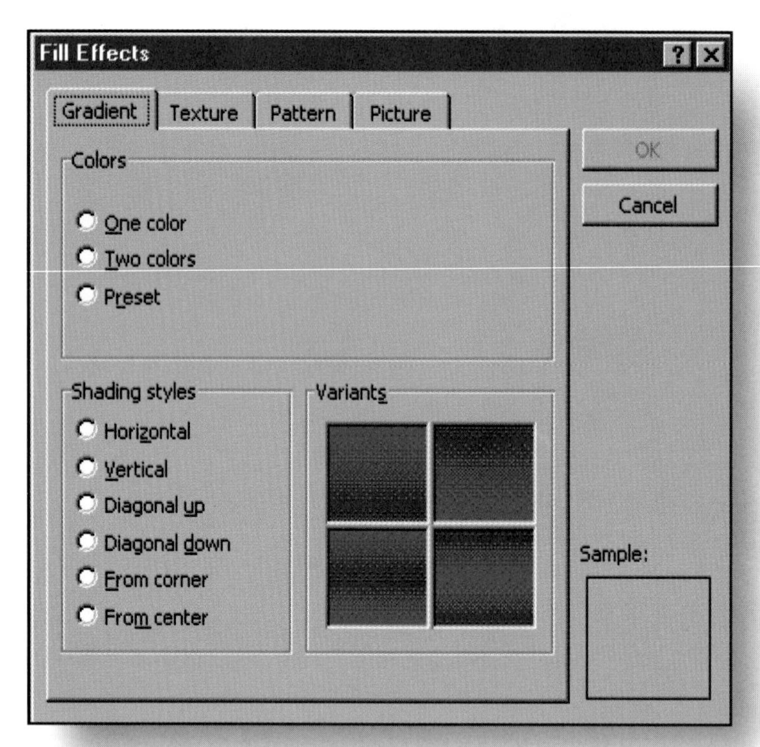

exercise 4

Creating and Then Changing the Gradient, Color, and Shading of WordArt Text

1. At a clear document screen, create the letterhead shown in figure 20.10 using WordArt by completing the following steps:
   a. Press the Enter key eight times and then move the insertion point back to the beginning of the document.
   b. At a clear document screen, display the Drawing toolbar by clicking View, pointing to Toolbars, and then clicking Drawing.
   c. Click the Insert WordArt button on the Drawing toolbar.
   d. At the WordArt Gallery, double-click the third option from the left in the first row.
   e. At the Edit WordArt Text dialog box, key **Kentwood School District**, and then click OK to close the dialog box.
   f. Click the WordArt Shape button on the WordArt toolbar.
   g. Click the fifth shape from the left in the first row (Chevron Up).
   h. Change the size and position of the WordArt by completing the following steps:

1) Click the Format WordArt button on the WordArt toolbar.
2) At the Format WordArt dialog box, click the Size tab.
3) At the Format WordArt dialog box with the Size tab selected, select the current measurement in the Height text box, and then key **1**.
4) Select the current measurement in the Width text box and then key **2.5**.
5) Click the Position tab.
6) At the Format WordArt dialog box with the Position tab selected, select the current measurement in the Horizontal text box, and then key **0**. (Be sure to key a zero and not a capital O.)
7) Click OK to close the Format WordArt dialog box.

i. Add a gradient and change colors by completing the following steps:
1) Click the down-pointing triangle at the right side of the Fill Color button on the Drawing toolbar.
2) At the palette of color choices that displays, click Fill Effects located at the bottom of the palette.
3) At the Fill Effects dialog box with the Gradient tab selected, make the following changes:
   a) Click in the circle preceding Two colors.
   b) Click the down-pointing triangle at the right side of the Color 1 box and then click the plum color at the color palette (seventh color from the left in the fourth row).
   c) Click the down-pointing triangle at the right side of the Color 2 box and then click the lavender color at the color palette (seventh color from the left in the fifth row).
4) Click OK to close the Fill Effects dialog box.

j. Click outside the WordArt text to deselect the WordArt box.

k. Make sure the insertion point is positioned immediately below *Kentwood School District* and then create the border line by completing the following steps:
1) Click Format, then Borders and Shading.
2) At the Borders and Shading dialog box with the Borders tab selected, click the line style shown in figure 20.10 in the Style list box.
3) Click the down-pointing triangle at the right side of the Color box.
4) At the drop-down list, scroll through the list until *Violet* is visible and then click *Violet*.
5) Click the top, left, and right side of the diagram in the Preview section of the dialog box.
6) Click OK to close the dialog box.

2. Save the document and name it Ch 20, Ex 04.
3. Print and then close Ch 20, Ex 04.

20.10

Exercise 4

Changing Line Color

Line Color

WordArt text is surrounded by a border line. The color of this line can be changed with the Line Color button on the Drawing toolbar. Click the Line Color button and the line color of the WordArt text changes to the color displayed on the button. If you want to choose a different color, click the down-pointing triangle at the right side of the Line Color button. This causes a palette of color choices to display. At this palette, click the desired color.

The Line Color palette also includes two options—More Line Colors and Patterned Lines. Click the More Line Colors option and the Colors dialog box shown in figure 20.8 displays. Click the Patterned Lines option and the Patterned Lines dialog box shown in figure 20.11 displays. Choose a pattern and a foreground and/or or background color for the object at this dialog box.

figure 20.11

Patterned Lines Dialog Box

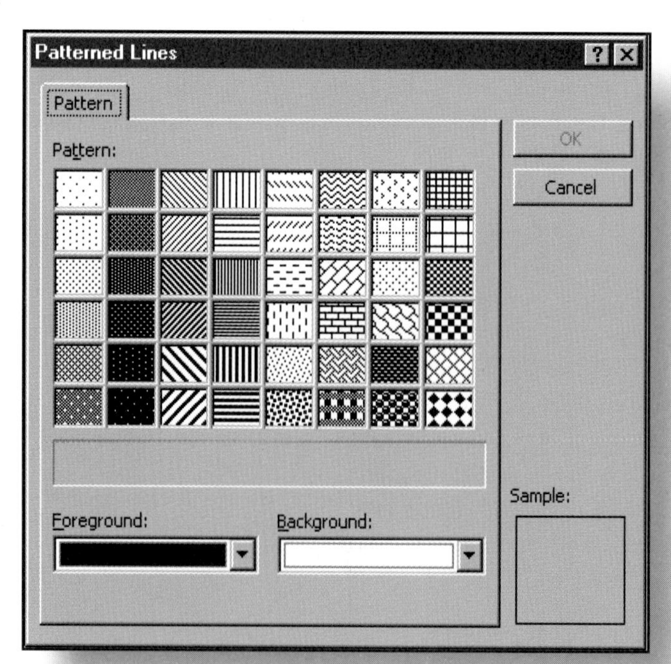

In some situations, you may want to remove the line around WordArt text. To do this, click the down-pointing triangle at the right side of the Line Color button, and then click *No Line* at the pop-up menu.

Changing Line Style

Line Style

The WordArt text line can be changed with options from the Line Style button on the Drawing toolbar. To change the line style, click the Line Style button, and then click the desired line style at the pop-up menu that displays.

Adding Shadow and 3-D Effects

Shadow

Click the Shadow button on the Drawing toolbar and a palette of shadow options displays. Click the desired option or click the Shadow Settings option and a Shadow Settings toolbar displays. This toolbar contains buttons for turning shadows off or on and buttons for nudging the shadow up, down, left, or right.

3-D

If you want to add a three-dimensional look to an object, select the object, and then click the 3-D button on the Drawing toolbar. This displays a palette of three-dimensional choices as well as a 3-D Settings option. Click this option and the 3-D Settings toolbar displays. This toolbar contains buttons for turning 3-D on or off and changing the tilt, depth, direction, and light source.

exercise 5

Creating and Then Changing the Pattern, Color, and Shading of WordArt Text

1. Create the WordArt text shown in figure 20.12 by completing the following steps:
   a. At a clear document screen, make sure the Drawing toolbar is displayed. (If not, click View, point to Toolbars, and then click Drawing.)
   b. Click the Insert WordArt button on the Drawing toolbar.
   c. At the WordArt Gallery, double-click the third option from the left in the first row.
   d. At the Edit WordArt Text dialog box, key **Surfing the Internet**, and then click OK to close the dialog box.
   e. Click the WordArt Shape button on the WordArt toolbar.
   f. Click the second shape from the left in the fourth row (Deflate).
   g. Change the size and position of the WordArt by completing the following steps:
      1) Click the Format WordArt button on the WordArt toolbar.
      2) At the Format WordArt dialog box, click the Size tab.
      3) At the Format WordArt dialog box with the Size tab selected, select the current measurement in the Height text box, and then key **2**.
      4) Select the current measurement in the Width text box and then key **6**.

5) Click the Position tab.
6) At the Format WordArt dialog box with the Position tab selected, select the current measurement in the Horizontal text box, and then key **0**. (Be sure to key a zero and not a capital O.)
7) Click OK to close the Format WordArt dialog box.

h. Add a pattern and change colors by completing the following steps:
1) Click the down-pointing triangle at the right side of the Fill Color button on the Drawing toolbar.
2) At the palette of color choices that displays, click Fill Effects located at the bottom of the palette.
3) At the Fill Effects dialog box, click the Pattern tab.
4) At the Fill Effects dialog box with the Pattern tab selected, make the following changes:
   a) Click the fourth pattern option from the left in the second row.
   b) Click the down-pointing triangle at the right side of the Foreground box.
   c) At the color palette that displays, click the turquoise color (fifth color from the left in the fourth row).
   d) Click the down-pointing triangle at the right side of the Background box.
   e) At the color palette that displays, click the pink color (first color from the left in the fourth row).
5) Click OK to close the Fill Effects dialog box.

i. Add a shadow to the text by clicking the Shadow button on the Drawing toolbar and then clicking the second shadow option from the left in the fourth row (Shadow Style 14).

j. Click outside the WordArt text to deselect the WordArt box.

2. Save the document and name it Ch 20, Ex 05.
3. Print and then close Ch 20, Ex 05.

figure 20.12 ***Exercise 5***

exercise 6

Changing the Color and Border Line of WordArt Text

1. Open Ch 20, Ex 04.
2. Save the document with Save As and name it Ch 20, Ex 06.
3. Customize the WordArt text by completing the following steps:
   a. Position the arrow pointer on any letter of the WordArt text *Kentwood School District* until the arrow pointer displays with a four-headed arrow attached, and then click the left mouse button. (This selects the WordArt and also displays the WordArt toolbar.)
   b. Change the size of the WordArt by completing the following steps:
      1) Click the Format WordArt button on the WordArt toolbar.
      2) At the Format WordArt dialog box, click the Size tab.
      3) At the Format WordArt dialog box with the Size tab selected, select the current measurement in the Width text box and then key **6**.
      4) Click OK to close the Format WordArt dialog box.
   c. Change the WordArt text color to yellow by clicking the down-pointing triangle at the right side of the Fill Color button on the Drawing toolbar and then clicking yellow at the color palette (third color from the left in the fourth row).
   d. Change the thickness of the text border line by clicking the Line Style button on the Drawing toolbar and then clicking *1½ pt* at the pop-up menu.
   e. Change the text border line color to plum by clicking the down-pointing triangle at the right side of the Line Color button on the Drawing toolbar and then clicking plum at the color palette (seventh color from the left in the fourth row).
   f. Add a shadow to the WordArt text by clicking the Shadow button on the Drawing toolbar and then clicking the second shadow option from the left in the first row (Shadow Style 2).
   g. Click outside the WordArt text box to deselect it.
4. Save the document again with the same name (Ch 20, Ex 06).
5. Print and then close Ch 20, Ex 06.

Using the Equation Editor

With Word's equation editor application called Microsoft Equation 3.0, you can create mathematical equations with proper formatting. The equation editor does the formatting for you, such as reducing the font size of exponents, applying italics to variables, and adjusting the spacing between equation elements.

Creating an Equation

To create an equation, you must access the equation editor application, Microsoft Equation 3.0. To do this, click Insert, then Object. At the Object dialog box with the Create New tab selected, double-click *Microsoft Equation 3.0* in the Object type list box. When you enter the equation editor, the screen displays as shown in figure 20.13.

figure 20.13 **Equation Editor Screen**

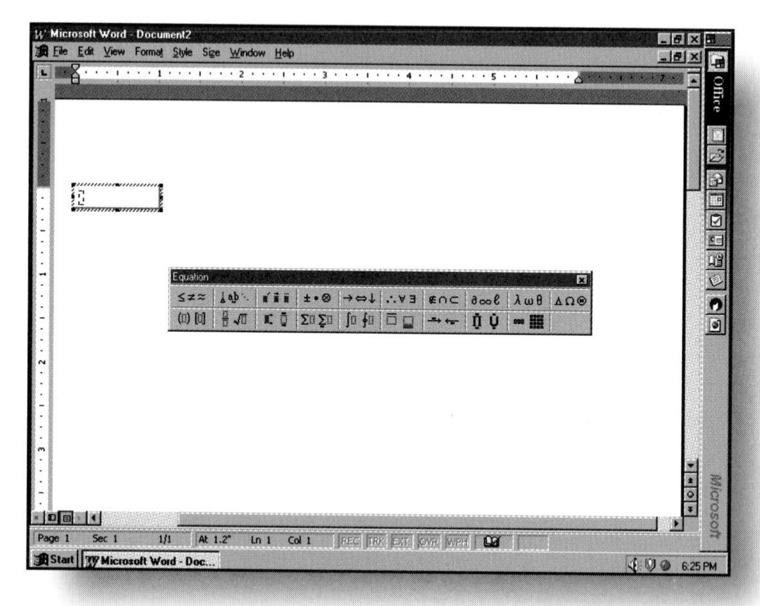

A text box displays in the upper left corner of the document screen. Key text for the equation in this box, or insert symbols and templates from the Equation Editor toolbar. The514 Equation Editor toolbar contains options for creating an equation. The top row on the toolbar contains symbols such as Greek characters that are used to write an equation. The bottom row of the toolbar contains templates. These templates contain such things as fractions and radicals, integrals, overbars and underbars, and arrows. Figure 20.14 identifies the name of each button on the Equation Editor toolbar.

figure 20.14 Equation Editor Toolbar Buttons

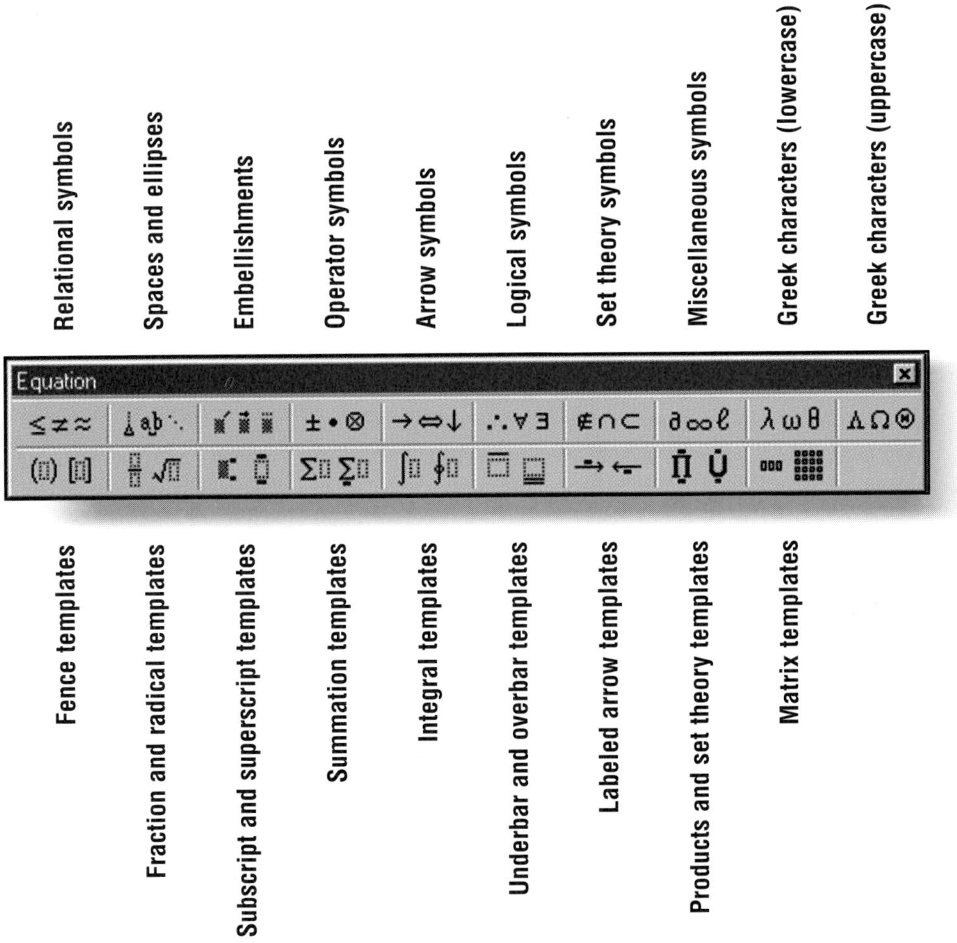

Relational symbols
Spaces and ellipses
Embellishments
Operator symbols
Arrow symbols
Logical symbols
Set theory symbols
Miscellaneous symbols
Greek characters (lowercase)
Greek characters (uppercase)

Equation

Fence templates
Fraction and radical templates
Subscript and superscript templates
Summation templates
Integral templates
Underbar and overbar templates
Labeled arrow templates
Products and set theory templates
Matrix templates

When you first open the equation editor, a text box is inserted in the upper left corner of the screen and the insertion point is positioned inside this box in a *slot* (a small box with a dashed border). The Equation Editor toolbar displays below this text box. With the insertion point inside the text box in the slot, key text or add symbols or templates with buttons on the Equation Editor toolbar.

As you enter text or insert symbols in the slot inside the text box, the slot expands. Some options from an Equation Editor toolbar button insert a slot such as the subscript and superscript options. To add an item from the Equation Editor toolbar, click the desired button on the toolbar. This causes a palette to display with a variety of options. Click one of the options on the palette and the symbol or character is inserted in the text box in the slot where the insertion point is located. When creating a symbol with the equation editor, you do not add spacing or formatting—the equation editor does that for you.

The steps to create equations in the exercises in this chapter are provided. For more information on writing extensive equations, please refer to the Microsoft Word reference guide.

exercise 7

Creating an Equation

Fence templates

Fraction and radical templates

Subscript and superscript templates

1. At a clear document screen, create the equation shown in figure 20.15 by completing the following steps:
   a. At a clear document screen, click Insert, then Object.
   b. At the Object dialog box with the Create New tab selected, double-click *Microsoft Equation 3.0*.
   c. With the insertion point positioned in the slot inside the text box, key **A=P**. (Do not press the space bar. The equation editor will determine the spacing.)
   d. Click the Fence templates button on the Equation Editor toolbar (the first button from the left in the bottom row).
   e. At the palette that displays, click the first option from the left in the top row.
   f. Key **1+**.
   g. Click the Fraction and radical templates button on the Equation Editor toolbar (the second button from the left in the bottom row).
   h. At the palette that displays, click the first option from the left in the top row.
   i. With the insertion point inside the top slot, key **1**.
   j. Position the tip of the arrow pointer inside the bottom slot and then click the left mouse button.
   k. Key **m**.
   l. Position the tip of the arrow pointer to the right of the right parenthesis and then click the left mouse button. (This moves the insertion point outside of the parentheses.)
   m. Click the Subscript and superscript templates button on the Equation Editor (the third button from the left in the bottom row).
   n. At the palette that displays, click the first option from the left in the first row.
   o. Key **nm**.
   p. Click in the document screen outside the text box and the Equation Editor toolbar. (This closes the equation editor and deselects the text box containing the equation.)
2. Save the document and name it Ch 20, Ex 07.
3. Print and then close Ch 20, Ex 07.

figure 20.15 *Exercise 7*

$$A = P\left(1+\frac{1}{m}\right)^{nm}$$

Editing an Equation

An equation created with the equation editor can be edited. To do this, position the arrow pointer on the equation, then double-click the left mouse button. This displays the equation in a text box and inserts the Equation Editor toolbar.

Click an equation once and white sizing handles display around the equation. Use these sizing handles to increase or decrease the size of the equation. To move an equation, position the arrow pointer on a selected equation. When the arrow pointer displays with a four-headed arrow attached, hold down the left mouse button, drag the equation to the desired location, and then release the mouse button.

exercise 8

Creating, Sizing, and Moving Equations

1. At a clear document screen, create the document shown in figure 20.16 by completing the following steps:
   a. Key the title and subtitle centered and bolded as shown in figure 20.16.
   b. After keying the subtitle, turn off bold, press Enter three times, and then return the alignment back to Left.
   c. Create the first equation shown in figure 20.16 by completing the following steps:
      1) Click Insert, then Object.
      2) At the Object dialog box with the Create New tab selected, double-click *Microsoft Equation 3.0*.
      3) With the insertion point positioned in the slot inside the text box, key **P=R**. (Do not press the space bar. The equation editor will determine the spacing.)
      4) Click the Fence templates button on the Equation Editor toolbar (the first button from the left in the bottom row).
      5) At the palette that displays, click the second option from the left in the top row.
      6) Click the Fraction and radical templates button on the Equation Editor toolbar (the second button from the left in the bottom row).
      7) At the palette that displays, click the first option from the left in the top row.
      8) With the insertion point inside the top slot, key **1-**.
      9) Click the Fence templates button on the Equation Editor toolbar (the first button from the left in the bottom row).
      10) At the palette that displays, click the first button from the left in the top row.
      11) Key **1+i**.
      12) Position the tip of the arrow pointer immediately to the right of the right parenthesis but left of the right bracket and then click the left mouse button. (The blinking vertical bar should be only the length of the top row.)

13) Click the Subscript and superscript templates button on the Equation Editor toolbar (the third button from the left in the bottom row).
14) From the palette that displays, click the first button from the left in the top row.
15) Key **-n**.
16) Position the tip of the arrow pointer in the bottom slot and then click the left mouse button.
17) Key **i**.
18) Click in the document screen outside the text box and the Equation Editor toolbar.

d. After creating the first equation, press the Enter key four or five times to separate the first equation from the second equation.
e. Save the document and name it Ch 20, Ex 08.
f. Complete the following steps to create the second formula in the figure:
   1) Click Insert, then Object.
   2) At the Object dialog box with the Create New tab selected, double-click *Microsoft Equation 3.0*.
   3) With the insertion point positioned in the slot inside the text box, key **S=R**. (Do not press the space bar. The equation editor will determine the spacing.)
   4) Click the Fence templates button on the Equation Editor toolbar (the first button from the left in the bottom row).
   5) At the palette that displays, click the second option from the left in the top row.
   6) Click the Fraction and radical templates button on the Equation Editor toolbar (the second button from the left in the bottom row).
   7) At the palette that displays, click the option at the left in the first row.
   8) Click the Fence templates button on the Equation Editor toolbar (the first button from the left in the bottom row).
   9) At the palette that displays, click the first button from the left in the top row.
   10) With the insertion point inside the top slot, key **1+i**.
   11) Position the tip of the arrow pointer immediately to the right of the right parenthesis but left of the right bracket and then click the left mouse button. (The blinking vertical bar should be only the length of the top row.)
   12) Click the Subscript and superscript templates button on the Equation Editor toolbar (the third button from the left in the bottom row).
   13) From the palette that displays, click the first button from the left in the top row.
   14) Key **n**.
   15) Position the tip of the arrow pointer immediately to the right of the superscript number but left of the right bracket and then click the left mouse button.

16) Key **-1**.

17) Position the tip of the arrow pointer in the bottom slot and then click the left mouse button.

18) Key **i**.

19) Click in the document screen outside the text box and the Equation Editor toolbar.

g. Select the first equation, increase the width of the equation text box approximately one-half an inch, and then drag the equation to the right to approximately the middle of the screen.

h. Select the second equation, increase the width of the equation text box approximately one-half an inch, and then drag the equation to the right until it displays below the first equation.

2. Save the document with the same name (Ch 20, Ex 08).
3. Print and then close Ch 20, Ex 08.

figure 20.16

Exercise 8

MATH 145

Formulas for Mathematics of Finance

$$P = R\left[\frac{1-(1+i)^{-n}}{i}\right]$$

$$S = R\left[\frac{(1+i)^{n}-1}{i}\right]$$

chapter summary

- With the WordArt application, you can distort or modify text to conform to a variety of shapes. With WordArt, you can change the font, size, and alignment of text. You can also add fill color, line color, change the line style, and add shadow and three-dimensional effects.
- Display the WordArt Gallery by clicking Insert, pointing to Picture, and then clicking WordArt. Another method for displaying the WordArt Gallery is to position the arrow pointer on a toolbar, click the *right* mouse button, and then click WordArt.

- Select an option at the WordArt Gallery by double-clicking the desired option.
- After choosing an option at the WordArt Gallery, the Edit WordArt Text dialog box displays. At this dialog box, key the WordArt text, and specify a font and font size.
- Use the white sizing handles around WordArt text to change the size.
- Move WordArt text by positioning the arrow pointer on any letter until it displays with a four-headed arrow, hold down the left mouse button, move the outline of the WordArt box to the desired position, then release the mouse button.
- Customize WordArt text with buttons on the WordArt toolbar. The WordArt toolbar contains the following buttons:

Insert WordArt	Free Rotate
Edit Text	WordArt Same Letter Heights
WordArt Gallery	WordArt Vertical Text
Format WordArt	WordArt Alignment
WordArt Shape	WordArt Character Spacing

- The following buttons on the Drawing toolbar can be used to create and customize WordArt:

Insert WordArt	Line Style
Fill Color	Shadow
Line Color	3-D

- With Word's equation editor application called Microsoft Equation 3.0, you can create mathematical equations with proper formatting.
- To edit an equation created with the equation editor, position the arrow pointer on the equation, and then double-click the left mouse button.

commands review

	Mouse/Keyboard
WordArt Gallery	Click Insert, point to Picture, click WordArt; position arrow pointer on toolbar, click *right* mouse button, then click WordArt; or click Insert WordArt button on Drawing toolbar
Format WordArt dialog box	Click [button] on WordArt toolbar
WordArt shape palette	Click [button] on WordArt toolbar
Drawing toolbar	Click View, point to Toolbars, click Drawing; or position arrow pointer on toolbar, click *right* mouse button, then click Drawing
Colors dialog box	Click down-pointing triangle at right side of [button] on Drawing toolbar and then click More Fill Colors
Fill Effects dialog box	Click down-pointing triangle at right side of [button] on Drawing toolbar and then click Fill Effects

Patterned Lines dialog box	Click down-pointing triangle at right side of [icon] on Drawing toolbar and then click Patterned Lines
Microsoft Equation 3.0	Click Insert, Object, then double-click *Microsoft Equation 3.0*

check your understanding

Completion: In the space provided at the right, indicate the correct term, command, or number.

1. Click Insert, point to Picture, and then click WordArt and this displays on the screen. ________
2. Key WordArt text at this dialog box. ________
3. Click this button on the WordArt toolbar to display a palette of shape options. ________
4. Click this button on the WordArt toolbar to display the WordArt Gallery. ________
5. Click this button on the WordArt toolbar to make each letter of the WordArt text the same height. ________
6. Click this button on the Drawing toolbar to change the color of WordArt text. ________
7. To add a three-dimensional look to WordArt text, click this button on the Drawing toolbar. ________
8. Display the equation editor screen by double-clicking this option at the Object dialog box with the Create New tab selected. ________
9. The bottom row of the Equation editor toolbar contains these. ________
10. When the equation editor is opened, a text box is inserted in the document and the insertion point is positioned inside a box called this. ________

skill assessments

Note: Before completing the skill assessments, display the Open dialog box, and then select and delete documents created in chapter 18 that begin Ch 18. You may want to check with your instructor before deleting these documents.

Assessment 1

1. At a clear document screen, create the WordArt text and border line shown in figure 20.17 by completing the following steps:
   a. Press the Enter key eight times and then move the insertion point up to the first line.

b. Display the WordArt Gallery.
c. Double-click the third option from the left in the first row.
d. Key **Mountain**, press Enter, and then key **High School**.
e. Change the shape of the text to a triangle. (*Hint: Click the WordArt Shape button on the WordArt toolbar.*)
f. Display the Format WordArt dialog box with the Size tab selected and then change the height to *1.2* and the width to *2*.
g. Display the Format WordArt dialog box with the Position tab selected and then change the horizontal position to 0 (zero).
h. Deselect the WordArt text.
i. Insert a thick/thin border below the high school name as shown in figure 20.17. (Do this at the Borders and Shading dialog box.)

2. Save the document and name it Ch 20, SA 01.
3. Print and then close Ch 20, SA 01.

Figure 20.17 • Assessment 1

Assessment 2

1. At a clear document screen, create the WordArt text shown in figure 20.18 with the following specifications (your text will appear much larger than what you see in figure 20.18):
   a. Display the WordArt Gallery.
   b. Double-click the fifth option from the left in the first row.
   c. Key the following at the Edit WordArt Text dialog box:
      1) Key **Coleman Development Corporation** and then press Enter.
      2) Key **Forest Renovation** and then press Enter.
      3) Key **and Revitalization Project**.
      4) Click OK to close the dialog box.
   d. Change the shape of the text to a Button (Curve). (*Hint: Click the WordArt Shape button on the WordArt toolbar and then click the fourth option from the left in the second row.*)
   e. Display the Format WordArt dialog box with the Size tab selected and then change the height to *6* and the width to *6*.

f. Display the Format WordArt dialog box with the Position tab selected and then change the horizontal position to 0 (zero).
g. Change the WordArt text color to green.
h. Add a shadow to the WordArt text.
i. Deselect the WordArt text box.

2. Save the document and name it Ch 20, SA 02.
3. Print and then close Ch 20, SA 02.

Figure 20.18 • Assessment 2

Assessment 3

1. At a clear document screen, create the text *Madison Creek Elementary School* as WordArt text. You determine the formatting of the text and include at least the following:
   a. Change the shape of the WordArt text.
   b. Add a gradient to the WordArt text.
   c. Change the color of the WordArt text.
   d. Add a shadow to the WordArt text.
2. Save the document and name it Ch 20, SA 03.
3. Print and then close Ch 20, SA 03.

Assessment 4

1. At a clear document screen, create the document shown in figure 20.19 (center and bold the title and subtitle as shown). Create the equation by completing the following steps:
   a. Open Microsoft Equation 3.0.
   b. With the insertion point positioned in the slot inside the text box, key **r=1-**.
   c. Click the Fraction and radical templates button on the Equation Editor toolbar (the second button from the left in the bottom row).
   d. At the palette that displays, click the first option from the left in the first row.
   e. With the insertion point inside the top slot, key **6**.
   f. Click the Greek characters (uppercase) button (the last button in the top row).

g. From the palette that displays, click the second option from the left in the fifth row.
h. Key **d**.
i. Click the Subscript and superscript templates button on the Equation Editor toolbar (the third button from the left in the bottom row).
j. From the palette that displays, click the first option from the left in the first row.
k. Key **2**.
l. Position the tip of the arrow pointer in the bottom slot and then click the left mouse button.
m. Key **n**.
n. Click the Fence templates button on the Equation Editor toolbar (the first button from the left in the bottom row).
o. At the palette that displays, click the first option from the left in the top row.
p. Key **n**.
q. Click the Subscript and superscript templates button on the Equation Editor toolbar (the third button from the left in the bottom row).
r. From the palette that displays, click the first option from the left in the first row.
s. Key **2**.
t. Position the tip of the arrow pointer outside the superscript slot but before the right parenthesis and then click the left mouse button.
u. Key **-1**.
v. Click in the document screen outside the text box and the Equation Editor toolbar.
w. Click the equation to select it and then increase the width and height approximately 1 inch.
x. Move the equation to the middle of the screen.

2. Save the document and name it Ch 20, SA 04.
3. Print and then close Ch 20, SA 04.

Figure 20.19 • Assessment 4

STATISTICS FORMULAS FOR CORRELATION ANALYSIS

Rank-Order Correlation

$$r=1-\frac{6\Sigma d^2}{n(n^2-1)}$$

chapter TWENTY-ONE

21 Exploring the Internet

PERFORMANCE OBJECTIVES

Upon successful completion of chapter 21, you will be able to:

- **Browse the World Wide Web from within Word.**
- **Locate specific sites on the Web.**
- **Search for specific information on the Internet.**
- **Create a Web home page.**
- **Create hyperlinks.**

Increasingly, businesses are accessing the Internet to conduct research, publish product or catalog information, communicate, and market products globally. In Microsoft Word 97, you can jump to the Internet and browse the World Wide Web. You can also create a document in Word and then convert it to a Web document with HyperText Markup Language (HTML) codes. HTML "tags" attached to information in a Web document enable the links and jumps between documents and data resources to operate. Information provided by the tags also instructs the browser software how to display text, images, animations, or sounds.

Understanding the Internet

The *Internet* is a network of computers connected around the world. In 1969, the U.S. Defense Department created a network to allow researchers at different sites to exchange information. The first network consisted of only four computers. Since then, the number of networks that have connected has grown exponentially, and it is no longer just a vehicle of information for researchers, but can be used by anyone with a modem. An *intranet* is an internet that is secure and used exclusively by one corporation and its employees.

Users access the Internet for several purposes: to communicate using e-mail, to subscribe to news groups, to transfer files, to socialize with other users around the globe in "chat" rooms, and largely to access virtually any kind of information imaginable.

To use the Internet, you generally need three things—an Internet Service Provider (ISP), a program to browse the Web (called a Web browser), and a search engine (used to locate specific data on the Internet).

A variety of Internet Service Providers are available. Local ISPs are available as well as commercial ISPs such as Microsoft Network®, America Online®, AT&T WorldNet Service®, and CompuServe®. To complete the exercises in this chapter, you will need access to the Internet through an ISP. Check with your instructor to determine the ISP used by your school to connect to the Internet.

Once you are connected to the Internet, you can access the *World Wide Web*. The World Wide Web is the most commonly used application on the Internet. The World Wide Web is a set of standards and protocols used to access information available on the Internet. The Internet is the physical network utilized to carry the data. To access the Web and maneuver within the Web, you need a software program called a *Web browser*. A Web browser allows you to move around the Internet by pointing and clicking with the mouse. A popular Web browser designed by Microsoft is the Microsoft Internet Explorer. The exercises in this chapter are created with the assumption that you will have Microsoft Internet Explorer available. If you will be using a different Web browser, some of the steps in the exercises may vary.

A phenomenal amount of information is available on the Internet. Searching through all that information to find the specific information you need can be an overwhelming task. Software programs, called *search engines*, have been created to help you search more quickly and easily for the desired information. There are many search engines available on the Internet, each offering the opportunity to search for specific information. As you use different search engines, you may find you prefer one over the others.

Browsing the World Wide Web

In this chapter, you will be completing several exercises and assessments that require you to search for locations and information on the World Wide Web. To do this, you will need the following:

1. A modem or network connection to a server with Internet access.
2. Browser software installed and configured. (This chapter will explore the World Wide Web using Microsoft Internet Explorer.)
3. An Internet Service Provider account.

A *modem* is a hardware device that allows data to be carried over telephone lines. The word "modem" is derived from MODulator/DEModulator. The modem attached to your computer converts digital data into an analog signal that can be transferred over telephone lines. At the other end of the connection is another modem that converts the analog signal back to digital data for the receiving computer. There are internal and external modems available in a variety of speeds. Modem speed is measured in terms of the number of bits per second data is transferred. If you are using a computer connected to a network, the network server will route the data through its modem, or to another server with a modem.

An Internet Service Provider (ISP) sells access to the Internet. In order to provide this access, the ISP must have in place the hardware and software necessary to support access to the Internet, phone lines to accept the modem connections, and support staff to assist their customers. The ISP is responsible for configuring their computers, routers, and software to enable connectivity to every other individual and computer that make up the Internet.

Locating URLs on the Internet

We all know that we can dial a telephone number of a friend or relative in any country around the world and establish a connection within seconds. The global telephone system is an amazing network that functions because of a common set of protocols and standards that are agreed upon by each country. The Internet operates on the same principle. Computer protocols known as TCP/IP (Transmission Control Protocol/Internet Protocol) form the base of the Internet. Protocols are simply agreements on how various hardware and software should communicate with each other. The Internet Service Provider becomes the Domain Name Service (DNS), *the route to the Internet*. The DNS and IP determine how to route your computer to another location/computer on the Internet. Every computer directly linked to the Internet has a unique IP address.

This explanation has been overly simplified. The technical details on how computer A can "talk" to computer B do not directly involve a computer user any more than does picking up a phone in Vancouver, British Columbia, and dialing a number in San Diego, California.

Uniform Resource Locators, referred to as URLs, are the method used to identify locations on the Internet. The format of a URL is *http://server-name.path*. The first part of the URL, *http://*, identifies the protocol. The letters *http* stand for HyperText Transfer Protocol, which is the protocol or language used to transfer data within the World Wide Web. The colon and slashes separate the protocol from the server name. The server name is the second component of the URL. For example, in the URL *http://home.netscape.com*, the server name is identified as *home.netscape*. The last part of the URL specifies the domain to which the server belongs. For example, *.com* refers to "commercial" and establishes that the URL is a commercial company. Other examples of domains include *.edu* for "educational," *.gov* for "government," and *.mil* for "military." Some examples of URLs are displayed in figure 21.1.

21.1 ***Sample URLs***

URL	*Connects to...*
http://www.microsoft.com	Microsoft Corporation home page
http://www.emcp.com	EMC/Paradigm Publishing home page
http://lcweb.loc.gov	Library of Congress home page
http://pbs.org	Public Broadcasting Service home page
http://www.xerox.com	Xerox home page
http://www.kodak.com	Eastman Kodak home page
http://www.alaska-air.com	Alaska Airlines home page

Web Toolbar

If you know the URL for a specific Web site and would like to visit that site, key the URL in the Address section of the Web toolbar. To display the Web toolbar as shown in figure 21.2, click the Web Toolbar button located on the Standard toolbar. Before keying a URL in the Address text box on the Web toolbar, make sure you are connected to the Internet through your Internet Service Provider. When keying a URL, you must key the address exactly as written, including any colons (:) or slashes (/).

When you are connected to a URL, the home page for the specific URL (Web site) displays. The home page is the starting point for viewing the Web site. At the home page, you can choose to "branch off" the home page to other pages within the Web site or jump to other Web sites. You do this with hyperlinks that are embedded in the home page. You will learn more about hyperlinks in the next section of this chapter. In exercise 1, you will be visiting some Web site home pages using URLs.

figure 21.2 *Web Toolbar*

exercise 1

Visiting Web Site Home Pages

1. Make sure you are connected to the Internet through an Internet Service Provider.
2. Explore several locations on the World Wide Web from within Word by completing the following steps:
   a. Display the Web toolbar by clicking the Web Toolbar button located on the Standard toolbar.
   b. Click in the Address text box located on the Web toolbar. (This will select the current document name in the text box.)
   c. Display the home page for Microsoft Web site by keying **http://www.microsoft.com** and then pressing Enter.
   d. In a few moments, the Microsoft Web site home page will display. The home page will display similar to the one shown in figure 21.3. Home pages are updated frequently, so the Microsoft home page you are viewing will vary slightly from what you see in figure 21.3. Scroll down the home page, reading the information about Microsoft.
   e. After reading about Microsoft, view the Web site home page for *The New York Times* newspaper. To do this, click the current address located in the Address text box, key **http://www.nytimes.com** and then press Enter. Read the information that displays about the newspaper.
3. After reading the information displayed on *The New York Times* home page, return to the Word screen by clicking File, then Close.

Using the Internet Explorer Program

In exercise 1, you visited the first Web site by keying the URL in the Address text box in the Web toolbar. This opened the Internet Explorer program window and also displayed the home page for the Web site. The Internet Explorer program window contains many features similar to the Word window. These features are shown in figure 21.3 and described in figure 21.4. Figure 21.3 displays the Internet Explorer program window with the Microsoft Corporation Web site home page displayed.

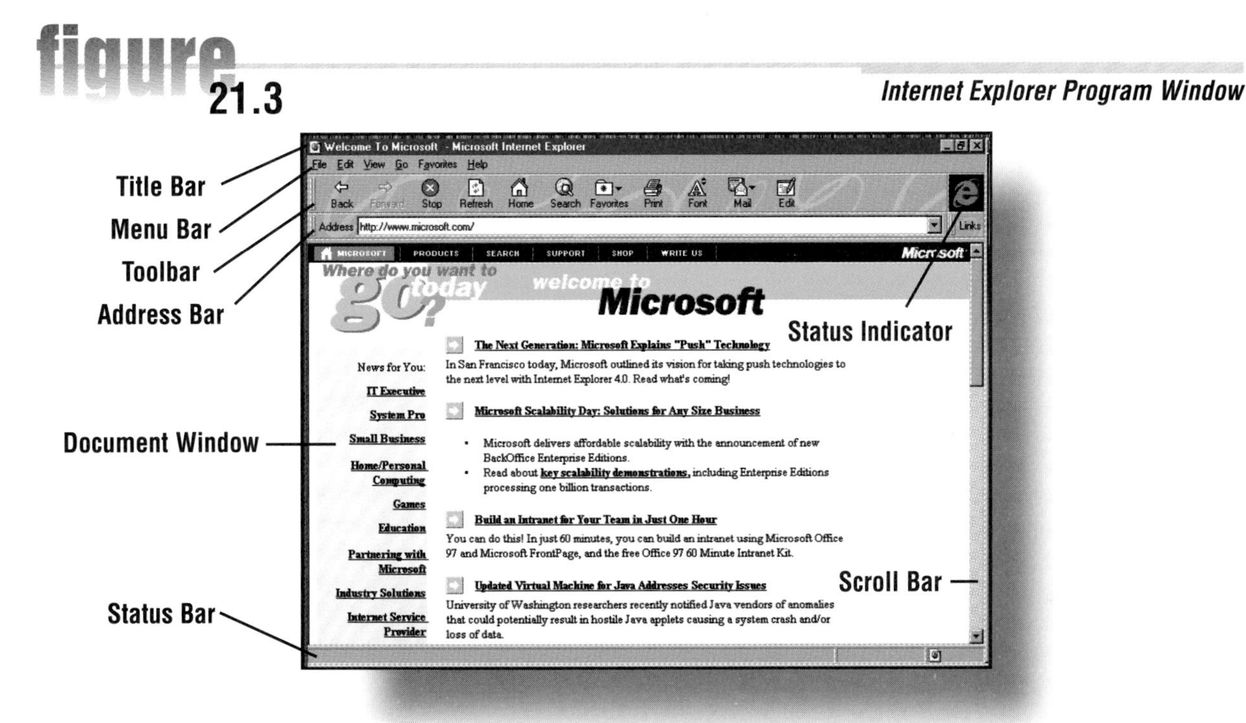

Internet Explorer Program Window

The various features of the Internet Explorer window are identified in figure 21.3. These features are described in figure 21.4.

Internet Explorer Program Window Features

Internet Explorer Feature	Description
Title bar	Displays the name of the Web page followed by the name of the program—Microsoft Internet Explorer
Menu bar	Contains a list of options for using and customizing Internet Explorer

Toolbar	Contains buttons for commonly used features such as navigating, searching, printing, and formatting
Address bar	Displays the address of the current Web site home page
Status indicator	Status indicator is the Internet Explorer logo; animates (moves) when a Web site is being loaded
Document window	Displays the contents of the current Web site
Scroll bar	Use the scroll bar to display information in the current Web page
Status bar	Displays information about connection progress and the percentage of information that has been transferred

The Internet Explorer toolbar contains buttons for accessing a variety of commands. The buttons and a description of each button are included in figure 21.5.

figure 21.5 ***Internet Explorer Toolbar Buttons***

Click this...	To do this...
Back	Display previous Web page.
Forward	Display next Web page.
Stop	Stop loading a page.
Refresh	Refresh (update) contents of current page.
Home	Display the default home page.
Search	Display the Search page.
Favorites	Display the Favorites list.
Print	Print the current Web page.
Font	Increase or decrease font size of selected text.
Mail	Display Mail and News options.
Edit	Display current Web page in a Word document screen for editing.

Opening the History Folder

As you visit different Web sites, Internet Explorer keeps track of the sites with such information as the name and address of the site, the date visited, and when the site was last updated. This information is inserted in the history folder. The Internet Explorer will keep a list of sites visited for the past 20 days. This information can be useful for remembering Internet addresses previously visited and for monitoring Internet use.

To display this list, click Go on the Internet Explorer Menu bar and then click Open History Folder at the drop-down list. This displays the History dialog box like the one shown in figure 21.6. The site title displays in alphabetical order at the left side of the dialog box, followed by the Internet address. Additional information includes the date the site was last visited and the last date the site was updated. After viewing the History dialog box, close the dialog box by clicking the Close button located at the right side of the dialog box Title bar.

Internet Explorer History Dialog Box

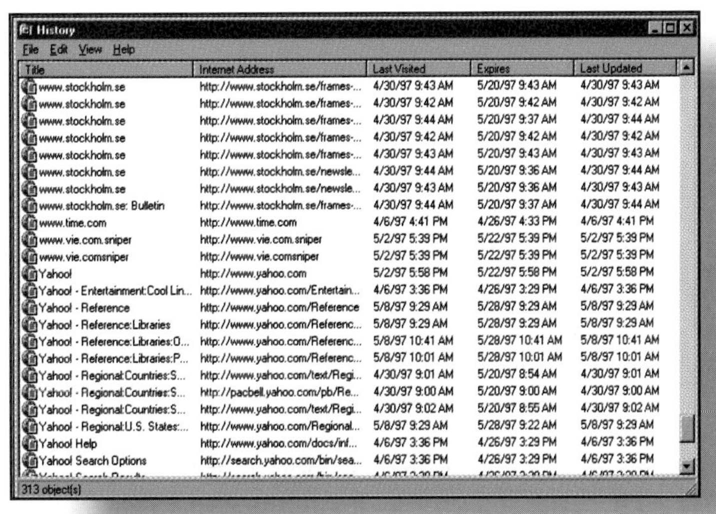

Adding Favorite Sites to the Favorites List

If you find a site that you would like to visit on a regular basis, that site can be added to a Favorites list. To do this, display the site, and then click the Favorites button on the Internet Explorer toolbar. At the drop-down menu that displays, click Add To Favorites. An Add to Favorites dialog box displays with a suggested name for the favorite site in the Name text box. You can key a different name for the favorite site or leave it as written. Click OK to add the site to the Favorites list. After a site has been added to the Favorites list, you can jump quickly to that site by clicking the Favorites button on the Internet Explorer toolbar and then clicking the site name at the drop-down list.

Favorites

Using Hyperlinks

As you were viewing the Web site home pages for Microsoft and *The New York Times*, did you notice text that displayed in a different color and was also underlined? Text displayed in a different color and underlined indicates text that has been identified as a *hyperlink*. A hyperlink allows you to link or connect to another item. A hyperlink can display in a variety of ways. It can display as text in a different color and underlined or as headings or buttons. Move the mouse pointer to a hyperlink and the mouse pointer turns into a hand. This is one method for determining if an item is a hyperlink.

To use a hyperlink, position the mouse pointer on the desired hyperlink until the pointer turns into a hand, and then click the left mouse button. For example, when you displayed *The New York Times* home page, you could have clicked the hyperlink *Tour the Site* to display information on what is available on the Web site. At the Microsoft Corporation home page, you could have clicked the hyperlink *PRODUCT* located at the top of the page to display information about Microsoft products. Most pages contain a variety of hyperlinks. Using these links, you can zero in on the exact information for which you are searching.

Back

Forward

The Internet Explorer program window contains a toolbar as described in figure 21.5. If you click a hyperlink, clicking the Back button on the toolbar will display the previous page or location. If you clicked the Back button and then would like to go back to the hyperlink, click the Forward button. By clicking the Back button, you can back your way out of any hyperlinks and return to the default Web home page.

In exercise 2, you will be using Internet Explorer to access the World Wide Web, locate specific Web site home pages, use hyperlinks to display specific information, add a URL to the Favorites list, and display the History folder.

exercise 2

Exploring the Web and Using Hyperlinks

1. Explore several locations on the World Wide Web from within Word using Internet Explorer and hyperlinks by completing the following steps:
   a. Make sure you are connected to the Internet through an Internet Service Provider.
   b. Turn on the display of the Web toolbar by clicking the Web Toolbar button on the Standard toolbar. (Skip this step if the Web toolbar is already displayed.)
   c. Click the current document name in the Address text box on the Web toolbar.
   d. Display the Web site home page for the Smithsonian Institution by keying **http://www.si.edu/** and then pressing Enter.
   e. Add the Smithsonian Institution Web site home page to the Favorites list by completing the following steps:

1) Click the Favorites button located on the Internet Explorer toolbar.
2) At the drop-down menu that displays, click Add To Favorites.
3) At the Add to Favorites dialog box, key **Smithsonian** in the Name text box, and then click OK.

f. Jump to other pages linked to the Smithsonian Institution Web site home page using hyperlinks by completing the following steps:
1) Click the hyperlink *RESOURCES, TOURS* that displays in a picture in the upper right corner of the Web page.
2) In a few moments, a Resources and Tours page will display. Scroll down this page until *Resources of the Smithsonian* is visible.
3) In the Resources of the Smithsonian section, a list box should be visible with the option *Encyclopedia Smithsonian*. Click this option to select it and then click the *Go to Resource* button located immediately above the list box.
4) At the next Web page containing categories of frequently asked questions, click a category that interests you.
5) Continue to click hyperlinks to discover information about a particular topic.
6) After making several hyperlinks, click the Back button until the Smithsonian Institution Web site home page displays.

g. Search for United Airlines flight departure times from Buffalo, New York, to Miami, Florida, by completing the following steps:
1) Click in the Address text box to select the current URL, key **http://www.ual.com**, and then press Enter.
2) At the United Airlines Web site home page, click the *FLIGHT INFO/RESERVATIONS* hyperlink that displays by the spinning globe.
3) At the next page, scroll down the page until the hyperlink text *Flight Search* is visible and then click it.
4) At the next page, change the date to tomorrow's date. (To do this, click the down-pointing triangle at the right side of the Day text box, and then click tomorrow's day in the list box. If tomorrow is the beginning of the next month, change the month in the Month text box.)
5) Leave the time at *6:00 AM* and the passengers at *1*.
6) Scroll through the Boarding City list box until *Buffalo,NY - BUF* displays and then click it.
7) Scroll through the Arrival City list box until *Miami,FL - MIA* displays and then click it.
8) Scroll down the page until the hyperlink *RETRIEVE FLIGHTS* displays and then click this hyperlink.

Print

9) After a few moments, information on flights displays. Print this information by completing the following steps:
   a) Click the Print button on the Internet Explorer toolbar.
   b) At the Print dialog box, make sure the correct printer is selected, and then click OK.

h. Jump to the home page for the Smithsonian Institution by completing the following steps:
   1) Click the Favorites button on the Internet Explorer toolbar.
   2) At the drop-down list that displays, click *Smithsonian*.

i. Display the History dialog box showing the sites visited in the past 20 days by completing the following steps:
   1) Click Go on the Internet Explorer Menu bar.
   2) Click Open History Folder at the drop-down menu.
   3) At the History dialog box, scroll through the list of sites visited within the last 20 days (the site titles are alphabetized).
   4) After viewing the list, click the Close button located at the right side of the History dialog box Title bar.

2. Close the Internet Explorer by clicking File, then Close.
3. If the Windows 95 desktop displays, click the Microsoft Word button that displays on the taskbar. (This will display the Word document screen.)

Finding Information Using Search Engines

In the previous exercises, you jumped around the Web by keying URLs, which is a fast way to move from site to site. Often, however, you will access the Web to search for information and you will not know the URL that you want to visit.

Search engines are valuable tools to assist a user in locating information on a topic by simply keying a few words or a short phrase. There are many search engines available on the Internet such as Yahoo, InfoSeek, Excite, and AltaVista. Each offers the opportunity to search for specific information. As you use different search engines, you may find you prefer one over the others. To search for information using a search engine you would follow these basic steps:

1. Make sure you are connected to the Internet.
2. Click the Search the Web button on the Web toolbar.
3. At the Internet Explorer Search page, like the one shown in figure 21.7, click the desired search engine.
4. Key a word or phrase in the Search text box and then click the button that begins the search.
5. The search engine will display a list of Web sites (called "hits") that contain the key word or phrase. Scroll through the list of hits and read the short descriptions. You can jump to any of the sites by clicking the hyperlink. Use the Back button to return to the list and select another site.

21.7 ***Internet Explorer Search Page***

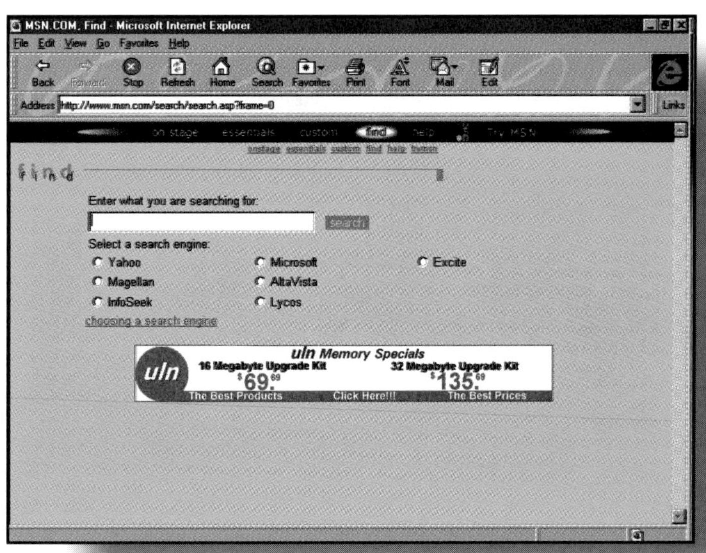

As you gain experience searching the Web, you will develop methods to refine your search techniques and tools to limit the time spent browsing. Before you begin a research project, jot down your key words or phrases and think about ways to limit the sites that will be selected by being as specific as possible without restricting the search. As you will see in the next exercise, you can become overwhelmed with the number of sites that will be selected.

exercise 3

Using Search Engines to Locate Information on the Web

Note: Web pages and search indexes are changing constantly. If the instructions in this exercise do not match what you are viewing, you may need to substitute different articles than the ones instructed here.

1. Jump to the World Wide Web from within Word and search for information on Franklin D. Roosevelt using the Yahoo search engine by completing these steps:
   a. In Word, click the Search the Web button on the Web toolbar.
   b. At the Internet Explorer Search page, like the one shown in figure 21.7, complete the following steps: (If the Internet Explorer program window does not display similar to the one shown in figure 21.7, you can go to this site by clicking the current address in the Address text box, keying **http://www.msn.com/search/search.asp?frame=0**, and then pressing Enter.)

1) Key **Franklin D. Roosevelt** in the *Enter what you are searching for* text box.
2) Click in the white circle immediately in front of *Yahoo*.
3) Click the *search* button that displays at the right side of the text box (not the Search button on the Internet Explorer toolbar).

c. In a few moments, the Yahoo search engine will return with a list of sites that meet your search criteria. Scroll down the page to see some of the sites that have been selected. (The number of sites selected will vary. The Internet changes on a daily basis with new information being added constantly.)
d. Scroll through the list until a hyperlink displays that mentions *Franklin D. Roosevelt Library* in the title and then click the link.
e. Print the page that displays. To do this, click the Print button on the Internet Explorer toolbar. At the Print dialog box, make sure the correct printer is selected, and then click OK.
f. After printing the information, click the Back button.
g. Click the Back button again to return to the Internet Explorer Search page.

2. Search for information on the South African white shark using the InfoSeek search engine by completing the following steps:
   a. At the Internet Explorer Search page, key **South African white shark** in the *Enter what you are searching for* text box.
   b. Click in the white circle immediately in front of *InfoSeek*.
   c. Click the *search* button that displays at the right side of the text box (not the Search button on the Internet Explorer toolbar).
   d. In a few moments, the InfoSeek search engine will return with a list of sites that meet your search criteria. Scroll down the page to see the sites that have been selected. (The number of sites selected will vary. The Internet changes on a daily basis with new information being added constantly.)
   e. Choose a site that will present information on the South African White Shark Research Institution and then click the hyperlink.
   f. Print the page by clicking the Print button on the Internet Explorer toolbar, then clicking OK at the Print dialog box.
   g. After printing the information, click the Back button.
   h. Click the Back button again to return to the Internet Explorer Search page.
3. Click File, then Close to close the Internet Explorer.

Completing Advanced Searches

The Internet contains a phenomenal amount of information. Some searches can result in millions of "hits" (sites). Wading through all these sites can be time consuming and counterproductive. Narrowing a search to very specific criteria can greatly reduce the number of hits for a search. For example, if you search for *physician-assisted suicide* using the Excite search engine, more than 600,000 documents may be found.

To reduce the number of documents found and to find only those documents containing very specific information, use *search operators*. Search operators may vary between search engines. Some operators may work within many engines, while others are specific to certain search engines. Some common search operators include symbols such as a quotation mark ("), a plus symbol (+), and a minus symbol (-). Figure 21.8 describes the operators and an explanation of each.

figure 21.8 ***Search Operators***

Operator	Explanation
Plus (+)	Key a plus symbol directly in front of a word and only those documents containing the word will be found. Do not space after the symbol or before the next word or symbol (if there is one). If you are including more than one word, space between the first word and the next symbol or word. **Example:** Key **+baseball +rules** and only those documents containing both *baseball* and *rules* will be found
Minus (-)	Key a minus symbol directly in front of a word that you do not want included in the search. This symbol is helpful in situations where you want to find a specific topic but want to narrow it by excluding certain parts of the topic. **Example:** Key **+whales -blue -killer** and the search engine will find those documents containing *whales* but not *blue* or *killer*.
Quotation Marks(")	If you enter terms for a search such as *national institute of mental health*, a search engine will find documents containing any or all of the four words in any order. If you want only those documents found containing *national institute of mental health* in this specific order, enclose the words in quotation marks. **Example:** Key **"national institute of mental health"** and the search engine will find those documents containing the four words in the order specified between the quotation marks.

In addition to search operators, some search engines recognize Boolean operators when conducting a search. (Boolean operators are based on Boolean algebra [named after George Boole, an English mathematician], which is a mathematical system originally devised for the analysis of symbolic logic.) Boolean operators include AND, AND NOT, OR, and parentheses. Boolean operators must be keyed in all capital letters with a space on either side. Boolean operators are explained in figure 21.9.

figure 21.9 ***Boolean Operators***

Operator	Function
AND	Find documents with words joined by AND. **Example:** Key **Disneyland AND California** and the search engine will find those documents containing both *Disneyland* and *California*.
OR	Find documents that contain at least one of the words joined by OR. **Example:** Key **volcanoes OR lahars** and the search engine will find those documents containing either *volcanoes* or *lahars*.
AND NOT	Find documents that contain the word before AND NOT but not the word after. **Example:** Key **bicycling AND NOT racing** and the search engine will find those documents containing the word *bicycling* but not the word *racing*.

Not all search engines use Boolean operators to limit searches. Each search engine should contain a Web page that explains how to conduct what is considered an advanced search. In exercise 4, you will be using two different search engines to find information and also print information on how to perform an advanced search with each of the two search engines.

exercise 4

Using Search Operators to Search for Specific Information on the Web

1. Jump to the World Wide Web from within Word and search for information on the *Department of Social and Health Services* using the InfoSeek search engine by completing these steps:
   a. In Word, click the Search the Web button on the Web toolbar.
   b. At the Internet Explorer Search page, like the one shown in figure 21.7, complete the following steps: (If the Internet Explorer program window does not display similar to the one shown in figure 21.7, you can go to this site by clicking

the current address in the Address text box, keying **http://www.msn.com/search/search.asp?frame=0**, and then pressing Enter.)

1) Key **Department of Social and Health Services** in the *Enter what you are searching for* text box.
2) Click in the white circle immediately in front of *InfoSeek*.
3) Click the *search* button that displays at the right side of the text box.

c. In a few moments, the InfoSeek search engine will return with a list of sites that meet your search criteria. Scroll down the page to see some of the sites that have been selected. Write down the total number of sites found by InfoSeek. (This information displays toward the top of the page.)

d. Learn about InfoSeek search operators you can use to narrow the search by completing the following steps:

1) Scroll to the end of the InfoSeek page containing the first ten hits on *Department of Social and Health Services*.
2) At the end of the list, look for the hyperlink *Tips* and then click it.
3) At the next Web page, click the hyperlink *Search Examples*. (You will need to scroll down the page to display this link.)
4) At the next Web page, read the information on searches and search examples and then print the page. (To do this, click the Print button on the Internet Explorer toolbar, and then click OK at the Print dialog box.)
5) Click the Back button on the Internet Explorer toolbar to return to the previous Web page.
6) Click the Back button again to return to the previous Web page. (This should be the page containing the first hits on *Department of Social and Health Services*.)
7) The bottom of the Web page containing the first hits on *Department of Social and Health Services* should display. At the bottom of this page, look for the empty text box that displays to the left of the *Tips* hyperlink and the *seek* button. Click inside this text box and then key **"Department of Social and Health Services"**.
8) Click the *seek* button located at the right side of the text box. (This tells InfoSeek to search for documents that contain *Department of Social and Health Services* in that sequence. This will narrow the search.)
9) In a few moments, the InfoSeek search engine will return with a list of sites that meet the criteria. Write down the total number of sites found by InfoSeek. Compare this number to the previous number. The number found with the search containing the quotation marks around *Department of Social and Health Services*

should be considerably lower than the search without the quotation marks.

   e. Click the Back button twice to return to the Internet Explorer Search page.

2. Find information on white sharks using the Excite search engine, and then find information on white sharks but not South African white sharks by completing the following steps:
   a. At the Internet Explorer Search page, key **white sharks** in the *Enter what you are searching for* text box.
   b. Click in the white circle immediately in front of *Excite*.
   c. Click the *search* button that displays at the right side of the text box.
   d. In a few moments, the Excite search engine will return with a list of sites that meet the criteria. Write down the total number of sites found by Excite.
   e. Display information on advanced searches in Excite by clicking the *Search Tips* hyperlink that displays toward the beginning of the page. (This hyperlink may be quite small.)
   f. At the next Web page, click the *Advanced search* hyperlink in the *How to Use Excite Search* section.
   g. At the next Web page, read the information on advanced searches and then print the page. (To do this, click the Print button on the Internet Explorer toolbar, and then click OK at the Print dialog box.)
   h. Click the Back button twice to return to the Excite Search Results page.
   i. Narrow the search to documents containing *white sharks* but not *South African*. To do this, complete the following steps:
      1) At the beginning of the Excite Search Results page, select the text *white sharks* currently displayed in the white text box in front of the gray *Search* button and then key **+white +sharks -South -African**.
      2) Click the *Search* button.
      3) In a few moments, the Excite search engine will return with a list of sites that meet the criteria. Write down the total number of sites found by Excite. Compare this number to the previous number. The number found with the search containing the plus and minus symbols should be considerably lower than the search without the symbols.
   j. Click the Back button until the Internet Explorer Search page displays.

3. Click File, then Close to close the Internet Explorer.

Each search engine Web site should contain information on how to narrow a search or conduct an advanced search. You may want to experiment with some of the other search engines to see if you can find information on how to conduct advanced searches within each.

Creating a Web Home Page

Now that you have been "surfing the net," you have visited several Web site home pages and have an idea how a home page displays. These home pages were designed using a language called HyperText Markup Language (HTML). This is a language that Web browsers use to read hypertext documents. In the past, a person needed knowledge of HTML to design a home page. Now a home page can be created in Word with the Web Page Wizard, or a Word document can be converted to HTML.

Before creating a home page, consider the information you want contained in the home page. Carefully plan the layout of the information and where to position hyperlinks. Good page design is a key element to a successful home page. Often a company will hire a professional Web page designer to do their home page. Before designing a home page, you may want to visit a variety of home pages and consider some of the following questions: What elements are included on the home page? How are the elements distributed on the page? Is the information organized logically and is it easy to read? Is the home page visually appealing? Evaluating home pages on the Web will help you when designing your own.

Word provides two methods for creating a home page. With one method you use a Web page template or the Web Page Wizard. The other method is to create the home page at a Word screen and then convert it to HTML.

Creating a Home Page Using the Web Page Wizard

Word provides a wizard that will help you prepare a Web home page. Using the wizard, you can choose a Web page type and a visual style. Choose the Web Page Wizard at the New dialog box with the Web Pages tab selected, as shown in figure 21.10. To use the Web Page Wizard, double-click the Web Page Wizard icon. At the first Web Page Wizard dialog box, choose a Web page type and then click the Next > button. At the second Web Page Wizard dialog box, choose a visual style and then click the Finish button. With the Web home page displayed, key the desired information.

21.10 *New Dialog Box with Web Pages Tab Selected*

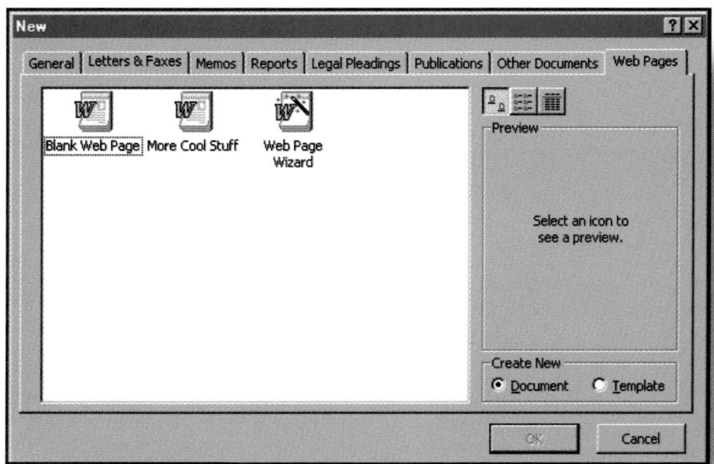

exercise 5

Creating a Web Home Page Using the Web Page Wizard

1. Create a Web home page using the Web Page Wizard by completing the following steps:
   a. At a blank Word screen, click File, then New.
   b. At the New dialog box, click the Web Pages tab.
   c. At the New dialog box with the Web Pages tab selected, double-click the Web Page Wizard icon.
   d. If a message box displays with the question *Would you like to access the Internet to check for a new version of Web page authoring tools?*, click the No button.
   e. At the first Web Page Wizard dialog box, make sure *Simple Layout* is selected in the list box (if not, click *Simple Layout*), and then click the Next > button that displays toward the bottom of the dialog box.
   f. At the second Web Page Wizard dialog box, click *Jazzy* in the list box, and then click the Finish button that displays toward the bottom of the dialog box.
   g. At the Web page document, key the text shown in figure 21.11 by completing the following steps:
      1) Select the text *Insert Heading Here* and then key **Sandford Computers**.
      2) Select the text *Replace the sample text with your own text, graphics, and multimedia files. To provide a link to another page, select text, and click Hyperlink on the Insert menu.*, and then key the text shown in the first paragraph below the heading *Sandford Computers* in figure 21.11.
      3) Select and then delete the text *Type some text.* that displays above the first bullet.
      4) Select the text *Add a list item.* that displays after the first bullet and then key **Pentium microprocessors**.
      5) Select the text *Add a list item.* that displays after the second bullet and then key **Monitors (14 inches up to 24 inches)**.
      6) Select the text *Add a list item.* that displays after the third bullet and then key **Input devices (keyboards, mice, etc.)**.
      7) Press the Enter key (this moves the insertion point down to the next line) and then click the Bullets button on the Formatting toolbar. (This inserts a bullet in the Web page.)
      8) Key **Printers (inkjet and laser)**.
      9) Continue to key the remaining bulleted items shown in figure 21.11.
      10) Select the text *Type some text.* that displays below the last bullet and then key the text shown below the last bullet in figure 21.11.

11) Select and then delete the text in blue that displays below the horizontal line (toward the end of the document). This is the text *Related Page 1* | *Related Page 2* | *Related Page 3*.

2. Save the completed Web home page on your student data disk in the normal manner and name it Sandford Home Page. (This document is saved as an HTML document.)
3. Print and then close Sandford Home Page.

21.11

Exercise 5

Sandford Computers

Sandford Computers is your source for low-cost hardware. Ordering the latest in computer hardware and peripherals couldn't be easier! Just log on to our Web site, identify the hardware or peripheral you want to order, and specify a payment method. We will get your hardware to you within 10 working days! We offer the following in hardware and peripherals:

- Pentium microprocessors
- Monitors (14 inches up to 24 inches)
- Input devices (keyboards, mice, etc.)
- Printers (inkjet and laser)
- CD-ROM drives
- High-speed modems
- RAM upgrade kits
- Sound cards
- Speakers

We purchase hardware directly from the manufacturer at incredibly low prices and then pass those savings on to you. We order directly from the following companies:

Dell

Hewlett Packard

Micron Technology, Inc.

NEC

In this chapter, you will be saving your Web home page on your student data disk. For a home page to be available on the Web, you must have access to a Web server. Large businesses usually have their own server, and you would have to contact the Information Systems department of the company to arrange for space on the server to store your HTML documents (home pages). The other option is to rent space from an Internet Service Provider (ISP). The ISP you use to access the Web will also arrange to store your Web page. Check out all of the fees involved, as there are many different fee structures in existence.

Creating Hyperlinks

Insert Hyperlink

The business Web sites you have visited, such as Microsoft and United Airlines, have included hyperlinks to connect you to other pages or Web sites. You can create your own hyperlinks in your home page. To do this, select the text you want specified as the hyperlink, and then click the Insert Hyperlink button on the Standard toolbar. At the Insert Hyperlink dialog box shown in figure 21.12, key the Web site URL in the Link to file or URL text box, and then click OK.

figure 21.12 *Insert Hyperlink Dialog Box*

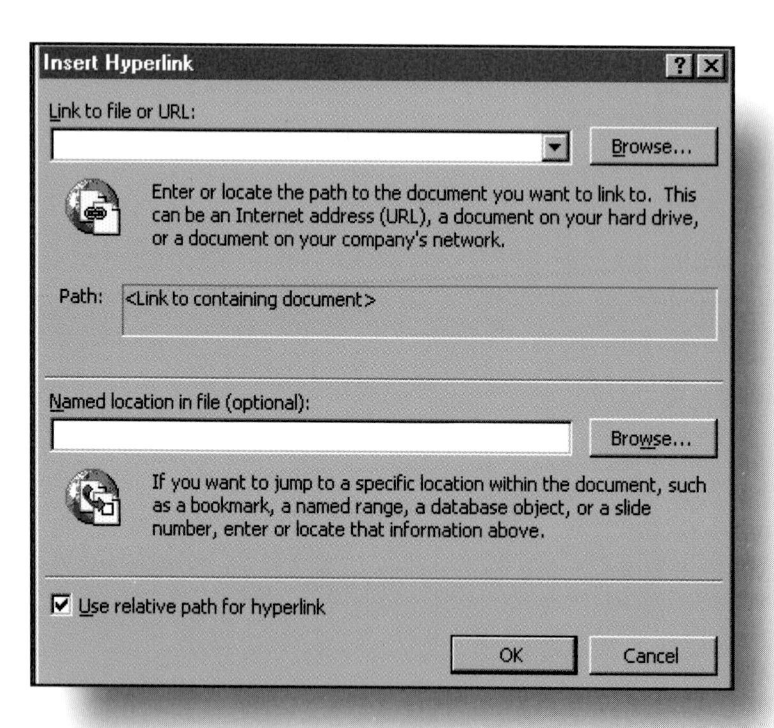

Another method for creating a hyperlink is to key the URL in a Word document. When you key the complete URL, Word automatically converts the URL to a hyperlink and changes the color of the URL. In exercise 6, you will be establishing hyperlinks from the Sandford Computers home page to computer companies listed in the home page.

exercise 6

Creating Hyperlinks

1. Open Sandford Home Page.
2. Create a hyperlink so that clicking *Dell* will display the Dell home page by completing the following steps:
   a. Select the text *Dell* that displays toward the bottom of the page.
   b. Click the Insert Hyperlink button on the Standard toolbar.
   c. At the Insert Hyperlink dialog box, key **http://www.dell.com** in the Link to file or URL text box, then click OK. (This changes *Dell* text to blue and adds underlining.)
3. Complete steps similar to those in step 2 to create a hyperlink from Hewlett Packard to the URL *http://www.hp.com*.
4. Complete steps similar to those in step 2 to create a hyperlink from Micron Technology, Inc. to the URL *http://www.micron.com*.
5. Complete steps similar to those in step 2 to create a hyperlink from NEC to the URL *http://www.nec.com*.
6. Click the Save button on the Standard toolbar to save the Web page with the hyperlinks added.
7. Jump to the hyperlink sites by completing the following steps:
   a. Click the hyperlink *Dell* that displays after the first bullet. (This text displays in blue.)
   b. When the Web home page displays for Dell, scroll through the home page clicking on any hyperlinks that interest you.
   c. When you are done viewing the Dell home page, click the Back button on the Internet Explorer toolbar until the Sandford Computers home page displays.
   d. Click each of the other hyperlinks (*Hewlett Packard*, *Micron Technology, Inc.*, and *NEC*) to display the Web home page for each of these companies.
8. After viewing the home pages for each company, close the Sandford Computers home page.

Converting a Word Document to a Web Page

In exercise 6, you created a Web home page using the Web Page Wizard. A Web home page can also be created as a Word document and then converted to a Web page. When you save a Word document as a Web page, the document closes and then reopens in the HTML format. The Web page displays similar to the way it will appear in a Web browser. Formatting that is not supported by HTML is removed from the document. To convert a Word document to HTML format, open the Word document, click File, and then Save as HTML. The document is saved with the same name but with a different extension.

Applying Formatting to a Web Page

When you open a Web page document in Word, you can apply formatting to the document with Menu bar options as well as buttons on the toolbars. For example, click the Format option on the Menu bar, and a drop-down menu displays with options for changing the font; adding bullets or numbering; changing text color, case, and style; and adding a background. With options from the Insert drop-down menu, you can add a horizontal line to the document; add a picture, video, or background sound; and add scrolling text. In exercise 7, you will be converting a Word document to the HTML format and then adding formatting to the document.

Previewing a Web Page

Web Page Preview

After creating a Web page or converting a Word document to a Web page, you may want to preview the document. To do this, make sure you have saved the document and then click the Web Page Preview button on the Standard toolbar. This will display the Web page in the Internet Explorer program window. If you want to return to the Web page document in Word, click File, then Close.

exercise 7

Converting a Word Document to HTML and Applying Formatting

1. Open Gardening Home Page. (This document is located on your student data disk.)
2. Convert the document to a Web page by completing the following steps:
   a. Click File, then Save as HTML.
   b. At the Save As HTML dialog box, key **Gardening Web Page** and then press Enter or click the Save button.
3. When the document redisplays as an HTML document, format the document by completing the following steps:
   a. Add a light green background to the document by completing the following steps:
      1) Click Format, then Background.
      2) At the palette of background color choices, click the light green color that displays fourth from the left in the last row.
   b. Apply formatting to the company name and address by completing the following steps:
      1) Select the company name and Web address.
      2) Click twice the Increase Font Size button on the Formatting toolbar.
      3) Click the Bold button on the Formatting toolbar.
      4) Deselect the text.

Increase Font Size

c. Add a horizontal line below the Web address by completing the following steps:
   1) Position the insertion point on the blank line below the Web address.
   2) Click Insert, then Horizontal Line.
   3) At the Horizontal Line dialog box, double-click the seventh horizontal line option from the top. (This is a series of dots in various sizes.)
   4) If necessary, close the gap between the Web address and the line.

d. Change the bullets by completing the following steps:
   1) Select the three bulleted paragraphs.
   2) Click the Bullets button on the Formatting toolbar. (This removes the bullets.)
   3) With the paragraphs still selected, click Format, then Bullets and Numbering.
   4) At the Bullets and Numbering dialog box, double-click the square, green bullet that displays third from the left in the second row.
   5) Deselect the text.

e. Add scrolling text to the Web page by completing the following steps:
   1) Move the insertion point to the end of the document (below the last line of text).
   2) Click Insert, then Scrolling Text.
   3) At the Scrolling Text dialog box, make the following changes:
      a) Click the down-pointing triangle at the right of the Background Color text box (displays with the word *Auto*).
      b) At the drop-down list of colors, click the Yellow color.
      c) Select the words *Sample Text* that display in the Type the Scrolling Text Here text box, then key **Contact our site regularly for up-to-date information on gardening sites on the Web.**
      d) Click the OK button to close the dialog box.
      e) Deselect the scrolling text box.

4. Save the formatting changes to the Web page document by clicking the Save button on the Standard toolbar.
5. Preview the Web page by clicking the Web Page Preview button on the Standard toolbar.
6. Click File, then Close to return to the document in Word.
7. Close Gardening Web Page.

chapter summary

- The Internet is a network of computers connected around the world, allowing exchange of information.
- Word provides the ability to jump to the Internet from the Word document screen.
- The World Wide Web is the most commonly used application on the Internet and is a set of standards and protocols used to access information available on the Internet.
- A software program used to access the Web is referred to as a Web browser.
- To locate information on the World Wide Web you need a modem, browser software, and an Internet Service Provider account. An Internet Service Provider sells access to the Internet.
- A modem is a hardware device that carries data over telephone lines.
- Uniform Resource Locators (URLs) are the method used to identify locations on the Web.
- A Web page can contain hyperlinks. Click a link to connect to another site, location, or page.
- Use a search engine such as Yahoo, InfoSeek, or Excite to locate information on the Internet on a specific topic by keying a few words or a short phrase.
- Home pages are Web documents that describe a company, school, government, or individual and are created using a language called HyperText Markup Language (HTML).
- A home page can be created in Word and then converted to an HTML document, or you can create a Web home page using the Web Page Wizard.
- Preview a Web page document by clicking the Web Page Preview button on the Standard toolbar.
- One method for creating a hyperlink is to select the text and then click the Insert Hyperlink button on the Standard toolbar. At the Insert Hyperlink dialog box, key the URL and then click OK.
- Save a Word document as a Web page by clicking File, then Save as HTML. At the Save As HTML dialog box, key a name for the Web page document and then click Save.
- Format a Web page with Menu bar options as well as buttons on toolbars.

commands review

	Mouse
Display the Web toolbar	Click [button] on Standard toolbar; or right-click any toolbar, then click *Web* at the drop-down menu
Display Internet Explorer Search page	Click [button] on the Web toolbar
Display History dialog box	Click Go on Internet Explorer Menu bar, then click Open History Folder at drop-down list

Save Word document in HTML format	File, Save as HTML
Preview a Web page	Click [icon] on Standard toolbar
Display Horizontal Line dialog box	With Web page document open, click Insert, Horizontal Line
Display Bullets and Numbering dialog box	With Web page document open, click Format, Bullets and Numbering
Display Scroll Text dialog box	With Web page document open, click Insert, Scrolling Text

check your understanding

Completion: In the space provided at the right, indicate the correct term or command.

1. List three reasons why users access the Internet. ____________ ____________ ____________
2. The word "modem" is derived from this. ____________
3. The letters ISP stand for this. ____________
4. This is the method used to identify locations on the Internet. ____________
5. Click this in a home page to link to another page or location. ____________
6. Click this button in the Internet Explorer program window to display the previous page or location. ____________
7. List at least three search engines that can be used to search for specific information on the Internet. ____________ ____________ ____________
8. A home page on the Web is created using this language. ____________
9. A home page can be created in Word and then converted to HTML or created with this feature. ____________
10. Click this button on the Standard toolbar to add a hyperlink to selected text. ____________
11. Click this button on the Standard toolbar to view the Web page document in the Internet Explorer program window. ____________
12. Save a Word document in HTML formatting by clicking this option from the File drop-down menu. ____________
13. Apply background shading to a Web document by clicking Background at this drop-down menu. ____________

In the space provided, list the text and operators you would use to complete the following searches using either the InfoSeek or Excite search engine.

1. Search for documents containing the words *Better Business Bureau* in that sequence. ____________________

2. Search for documents containing *travel* but not *international*. ____________________

3. Search for documents containing *dolphins* or *porpoises*. ____________________

skill assessments

Note: Before completing the skill assessments, display the Open dialog box, and then select and delete documents created in chapter 19 that begin Ch 19. You may want to check with your instructor before deleting these documents.

Assessment 1

1. Make sure you are connected to the Internet and then jump to the following sites:
   a. At a clear Word document screen, jump to the Microsoft home page at the URL *http://www.microsoft.com*. At the Microsoft home page, display a page containing a list of Microsoft products and then print this page.
   b. Jump to the Smithsonian Institution Web site at *http://www.si.edu/*. (If this Web site is still in the Favorites list, you can jump to the site by clicking the Favorites button and then clicking *Smithsonian* at the drop-down list.) At the Smithsonian Institution home page, click the RESOURCES TOURS hyperlink. At the next page, scroll down the page. Click an option in the *Go to a Perspective* list box that interests you, and then click the Go to a Perspective button. Continue clicking hyperlinks to find a site that interests you and then print the information in the site.
   c. Jump to the Northwest Airlines Web site at *http://www.nwa.com*. At the site, find flights available for tomorrow from Seattle, Washington, to Chicago, Illinois.
   d. When the page displays with flight information, print the page.
2. Close the Internet Explorer.

Assessment 2

1. Make sure you are connected to the Internet.
2. In Word, click the Search the Web button on the Web toolbar. (If the Internet Explorer program window does not display, you can go to this site by clicking the current address in the Address text box, keying

   http://www.msn.com/search/search.asp?frame=0

   and then pressing Enter.)
3. At the Internet Explorer Search page, complete the following searches:
   a. Use the Yahoo search engine to find information on cross-country skiing.

b. At the Yahoo page displaying some of the documents found, scroll through the list to find a cross-country skiing site that interests you. Display the Web site and then print the page.
c. Click the Back button until the Internet Explorer Search page displays.
d. Use the AltaVista search engine to find information on Yellowstone Park.
e. At the AltaVista page displaying documents on Yellowstone Park, scroll through the list, find a document that interests you, display the home page, and then print the page.
f. Click the Back button until the Internet Explorer Search page displays.
g. Use the InfoSeek search engine to find documents on fly fishing in New Zealand. (To limit the search, key "fly fishing in New Zealand" at the Internet Explorer Search page.)
h. When InfoSeek displays a list of documents, find a document that interests you, display the site, and then print the page.
i. Click the Back button until the Internet Explorer Search page displays.

4. Close the Internet Explorer.

Assessment 3

1. Use the Web Page Wizard to create a Web home page for the Peninsula Mountain Biking Club containing a calendar of events with the following specifications:
   a. At the first Web Page Wizard dialog box, choose *Calendar* in the list box.
   b. At the second Web Page Wizard dialog box, choose *Outdoors* in the list box.
   c. At the calendar Web page, make the following changes:
      1) Select the text *Insert Heading Here* and then key **Peninsula Mountain Biking Club**.
      2) Select the text *Month and Year* and then key **June 1999**.
      3) Select the text *Type some text.* and then key **Calendar of Events**.
      4) Click in the first cell below *Saturday* and then key **June 5: 20k Ride, Mill Creek**.
      5) Click in the second cell below *Wednesday* and then key **June 9: Club Meeting, Hansen Park**.
      6) Click in the fourth cell below *Wednesday* and then key **June 23: Club Meeting, Hansen Park**.
      7) Click in the third cell below *Tuesday* and then key **June 15: Safety Program, Elm Elementary**.
      8) Click in the fourth cell below *Saturday* and then key **June 26: White Water Canyon Ride**.
      9) Select and then delete the text *Type some text.* that displays below the calendar.
      10) Select and then delete the text that displays at the bottom of the page. (This is the text *Related Page 1* | *Related Page 2* | *Related Page 3*.)
2. Save the Web page and name it PMB Home Page.
3. Print and then close PMB Home Page.

Assessment 4

1. Open the Travel Home Page document. (This document is located on your student data disk.)
2. Make the following changes to the document:
   a. Save the document in HTML format with the name ITC Home Page.
   b. Make the following formatting changes to the document:
      1) Increase the font size for the club name and Web site. (You determine the size.)
      2) Add a horizontal line of your choosing somewhere toward the beginning of the document and toward the end of the document. (You determine the horizontal line style and the location.)
      3) Add the scrolling text *Space is limited so sign up now for our summer tour of Scandinavia!* somewhere in the document.
      4) Select *Danish Tourist Board* and then create a hyperlink to *http://www.visitdenmark.com*.
      5) Select *Danops Denmark* and then create a hyperlink to *http://www.danops.dk/*.
      6) Select *Travel in Finland* and then create a hyperlink to *http://www.travel.fi/int/*.
      7) Select *Welcome to Finland* and then create a hyperlink to *http://www.publiscan.fi/*.
      8) Select *Guide to Sweden* and then create a hyperlink to *http://www.swedenguide.com*.
      9) Select *The Swedish Touring Group* and then create a hyperlink to *http://www.stfturist.se/*.
      10) Select *Travel Norway* and then create a hyperlink to *http://www.travel-norway.com*.
      11) Select *Norwegian Travel Information Network* and then create a hyperlink to *http://www.oslonett.no/NTIN/NTIN.html*.
      12) Make sure the text for the home page fits on one page. (If it does not, delete some blank lines.)
3. Save the document again with the same name (ITC Home Page).
4. Print and then close ITC Home Page.

Unit four

PERFORMANCE ASSESSMENTS

DEMONSTRATING YOUR SKILLS

Assessment one

1. At a clear document screen, create a macro named *Formhead* that is assigned the shortcut command, Alt + Ctrl + H, which selects text and changes the font to 14-point Arial bold. (*Hint: At a clear document screen, key* ***This is a heading***. This gives you text to select when recording the macro.)
2. Close the document without saving it.
3. At a clear document screen, open Report 01.
4. Save the document with Save As and name it Unit 4, PA 01.
5. Make the following changes to the report:
   a. Select the entire document, then change the font to 12-point Century Schoolbook (or a similar serif typeface).
   b. Select the text in the document except the title, change the line spacing to single, and then change the paragraph spacing before and after to 6 points.
   c. Run the Alt + Ctrl + H macro for the title and the four headings.
   d. Hyphenate words in the document manually.
6. Save the document again with the same name (Unit 4, PA 01).
7. Print and then close Unit 4, PA 01.

Assessment two

1. Open Notice 03.
2. Save the document with Save As and name it Unit 4, PA 02.
3. Make the following changes to the document:
   a. Horizontally and vertically center the text on the page.
   b. Select the text and then change to a decorative typeface in a larger point size and a different color.

c. Insert a page border using one of the art images.
4. Save the document again with the same name (Unit 4, PA 02).
5. Print and then close Unit 4, PA 02.

Assessment three

1. At a clear document screen, create the document shown in figure U4.1 by completing the following steps:
   a. Insert the clip art image shown in the figure. (If this clip art image is not available, choose a similar image.)
   b. Format the picture so that the height is 2 inches and the width is 2.8 inches.
   c. Change the wrapping style to Square.
   d. Change the font to 14-point Arial bold.
   e. Change the paragraph to center alignment.
   f. Key the text shown in figure U4.1.
2. After creating the document, save it and name it Unit 4, PA 03.
3. Print and then close Unit 4, PA 03.

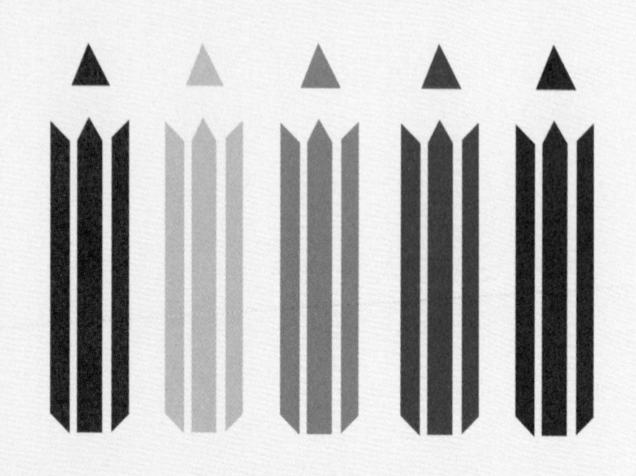

Explore Your Writing Talents!
Young Writers' Workshop
July 12 - 15, 1999
9:00 - 11:30 a.m.
Fall Valley Elementary School

Figure U4.1 • Assessment 3

Assessment four

1. Open Unit 4, PA 03.
2. Save the document with Save As and name it Unit 4, PA 04.
3. Change the clip art image to a watermark that displays behind the text in the document.
4. Save the document again with the same name (Unit 4, PA 04).
5. Print and then close Unit 4, PA 04.

Assessment five

1. At a clear document screen, create the letterhead shown in figure U4.2 with the following specifications:
   a. Key the text right aligned as shown in figure U4.2.
   b. Select the title and then change the font to 18-point Tahoma bold and change the text color to Dark Blue.
   c. Select the address and telephone number and then change the font to 16-point Tahoma bold. (Keep the text color set at Dark Blue.)
   d. Create the shapes shown using buttons on the Drawing toolbar. (Be sure to add the fill as shown in the shapes in figure U4.2.)
2. Save the document and name it Unit 4, PA 05.
3. Print and then close Unit 4, PA 05.

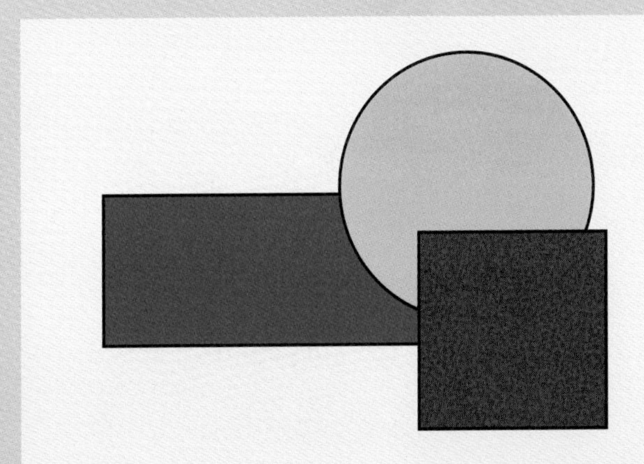

MODERN DESIGNS
2002 Hughes Road
Tucson, AZ 89322
(801) 555-2002

Figure U4.2 • Assessment 5

Assessment six

1. At a clear document screen, create the document shown in figure U4.3 with the following specifications:
   a. Press the Enter key six times and then change the font to 16-point Bookman Old Style and the text color to Red.
   b. Key the text centered as shown in figure U4.3.
   c. Display the Drawing toolbar.
   d. Click the AutoShapes button, point to Basic Shapes, and then click the heart shape.
   e. Draw a heart shape as shown in figure U4.3. Add red fill to the heart.
   f. Copy the heart as many times as needed to create the heart border around the text.
2. Save the document and name it Unit 4, PA 06.
3. Print and then close Unit 4, PA 06.

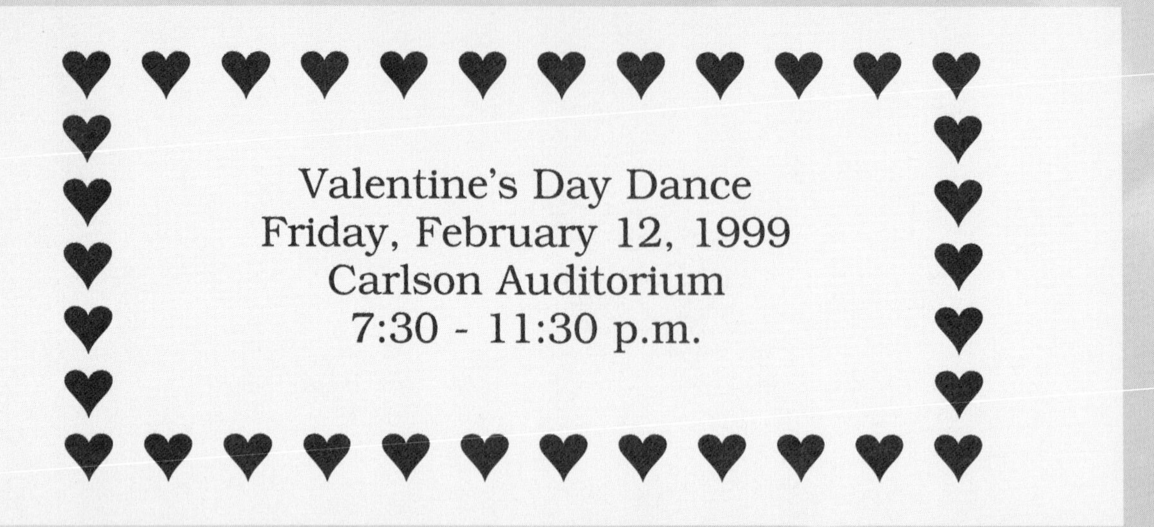

Valentine's Day Dance
Friday, February 12, 1999
Carlson Auditorium
7:30 - 11:30 p.m.

Figure U4.3 • Assessment 6

Assessment Seven

1. At a clear document screen, use WordArt to create the letterhead shown in figure U4.4 by completing the following steps:
   a. Press the Enter key nine times and then move the insertion point back to the beginning of the document.
   b. Display the WordArt Gallery and then double-click the third option from the left in the first row.
   c. Key **THE DUPONT DAILY** at the Edit WordArt Text dialog box.
   d. Display the Format WordArt dialog box with the Size tab selected and then change the height and width to 2 inches.
   e. Display the Format WordArt dialog box with the Position tab selected and then change the horizontal position to 0.15 inches.
   f. Click outside the WordArt text to deselect the WordArt box.
   g. Insert the border line shown in figure U4.4. *(Hint: Do this at the Borders and Shading dialog box.)*
2. Save the document and name it Unit 4, PA 07.
3. Print and then close Unit 4, PA 07.

Figure U4.4 • Assessment 7

Assessment eight

1. At a clear document screen, create the organizational diagram shown in figure U4.5 by completing the following steps:
   a. Display the Drawing toolbar.
   b. Use the Text Box button to draw the first box. Key the text shown in the first box and then add the light yellow fill.
   c. Copy the text box to create the other boxes. Change the text inside the boxes as shown in figure U4.5.
   d. Draw the lines connecting the boxes as shown in the figure.
2. Save the document and name it Unit 4, PA 08.
3. Print and then close Unit 4, PA 08.

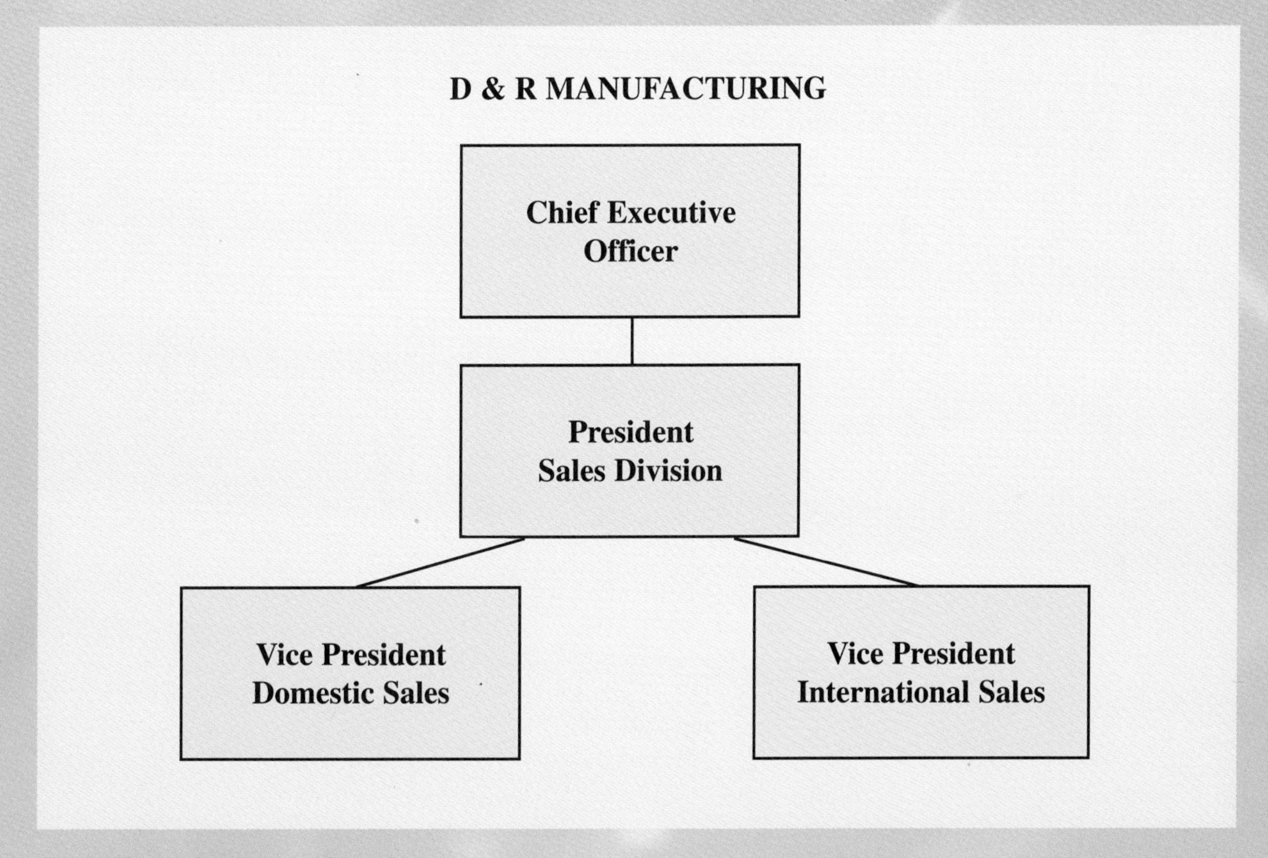

Figure U4.5 • Assessment 8

Assessment nine

1. Make sure you are connected to the Internet.
2. Display the Web toolbar and then click the Search the Web button.
3. At the Internet Explorer program window, search for information on *mountain climbing* specifically on *Mt. Everest*. (Use the Excite search engine and key **mountain climbing AND Mt. Everest** as the search text.)
4. Scroll through the list of responses and jump to a site that interests you. Read the information on the home page and then print the home page. After printing the home page, jump to any other hyperlinks that interest you.
5. Explore other sites related to this topic.
6. Click the Back button until the Internet Explorer Search page displays.
7. Search for information on job opportunities specifically in the technology field. (You determine the search engine and the search text.)
8. Scroll through the list of responses and jump to a site that interests you.
9. Print the site's home page.
10. Explore any other technology employment sites that interest you.
11. Close Internet Explorer.

Assessment ten

1. Make sure you are connected to the Internet.
2. Jump to the SAS Airlines home page at *http://sas.se*.
3. Find information on flight availability from Seattle, Washington, to Copenhagen, Denmark, for two weeks from today. *(Hint: At the SAS home page, look for a hyperlink to* Travel Service. *At the next page, look for a hyperlink to* Worldwide Timetable.*)*
4. When the timetable page displays, specify the city of departure (Seattle) and the city of arrival (Copenhagen) and the day and month of travel. When the information on departing flights displays, print the page.
5. Scroll to the bottom of the page on flights to Copenhagen and then enter information for the return. Set the return day from Copenhagen to Seattle for two weeks from the day of departure.
6. When the information on return flights displays, print the page.
7. Close Internet Explorer.

Assessment eleven

1. Using the Web Page Wizard, create a Web site home page for Video Online with the following information:

a. Include the following at the top of the Web page:
Video Online
www.videos.com
1-800-555-0998

b. Include the following information in the Web page:

Video Online owns the largest inventory of videos in the world! Order your favorite video today! We offer all videos at a 5% discount. Each month, special videos are offered at additional discounts of up to 50%. To order your videos, let us know what videos you want to purchase and provide us with billing information on our secured order form. Your videos will arrive at your home within 5 business days. Click a category below that interests you and then discover the incredible number of videos available.

- Action
- Drama
- Suspense
- Comedy
- Romance
- Science Fiction
- Classics
- Music

c. Add any additional information to further describe the business and the services.

2. Save the completed Web page and name it Video Online Web Page.
3. Print and then close Video Online Web Page.

CREATING ORIGINAL DOCUMENTS

The following activities give you the opportunity to practice your writing skills along with demonstrating an understanding of some of the important Word features you have mastered in this unit. When composing the documents, use correct grammar, appropriate word choices, and clear sentence constructions.

Assessment twelve

Situation: You work for Video Express, a video rental store. You have been asked to design a letterhead for the store. When designing the letterhead, include an appropriate clip art image and a border along with the following information:

Video Express
3340 Walden Circle
Memphis, TN 74633
(615) 555-9005

Save the letterhead and name it Unit 4, PA 12. Print and then close Unit 4, PA 12.

Assessment thirteen

Situation: You are Tina Singleton, manager of Video Express. Your store has seen a steady increase in customers and you need to increase the number of copies of videos to meet the needs of your customers. Write a letter to World Wide Distributors (use the letterhead created in Assessment 12) asking them to increase the number of copies of videos they send to your store. In the same letter, ask them to send you any free promotional materials they have available. Also, the last order of videos received from World Wide Distributors included several damaged videos. Explain in your letter that you are sending these videos back and would like replacements.

Save the letter and name it Unit 4, PA 13. Print and then close Unit 4, PA 13.

Assessment fourteen

Create an announcement for Video Express telling customers that they will receive a liter of soda and a large bag of popcorn when they rent three or more videos at one time. This offer is good for the month of March. Include an appropriate clip art image in the announcement. Also, consider using WordArt on some of the text in the announcement.

Save the announcement and name it Unit 4, PA 14. Print and then close Unit 4, PA 14.

Unit five

ENHANCING THE PRESENTATION OF TEXT

In this unit, you will learn to enhance the presentation of text by formatting text into tables, charts, or columns. You will also learn to automate the formatting of text using styles.

scans

The Secretary's Commission on Achieving Necessary Skills

DECISION MAKING

TECHNOLOGY

PROBLEM SOLVING

COMMUNICATIONS

chapter TWENTY-TWO

22 Creating and Formatting Tables

PERFORMANCE OBJECTIVES

Upon successful completion of chapter 22, you will be able to:

- **Create a table.**
- **Enter and edit text within cells in a table.**
- **Delete a table.**
- **Format a table by adding borders and shading, changing column width, aligning text within cells, inserting and deleting columns and rows, and merging and splitting cells.**
- **Apply formatting to a table with one of Word's predesigned AutoFormats.**
- **Create and format a table using buttons on the Tables and Borders toolbar.**
- **Perform calculations on values in a table.**
- **Convert text to a table and table text to normal text.**

Word provides a variety of features that help you organize data. With Word's Tables feature, you can create data in columns and rows. This data can consist of text, values, and formulas. The Tables feature can create columns of data in a manner similar to a spreadsheet. Many basic spreadsheet functions, such as inserting values, totaling numbers, and inserting formulas, can be performed in a Word table. In this chapter, you will learn how to create a table and use basic spreadsheet features.

With a Word table, a form can be created that contains boxes of information called *cells*. A cell is the intersection between a row and a column. A cell can contain text, characters, numbers, data, graphics, or formulas. Data within a cell can be formatted to display left, right, or center aligned, and can include character formatting such as bold, italics, and underlining. The formatting choices available with the Tables feature are quite extensive and allow flexibility in creating a variety of tables.

Creating a Table

Insert Table

A table can be created with the Insert Table button on the Standard toolbar or the Table option from the Menu bar. The Insert Table button is located toward the right side of the Standard toolbar. To create a table with the Insert Table button, position the arrow pointer on the Insert Table button on the Standard toolbar, and then hold down the left mouse button. This causes a grid to appear as shown in figure 22.1. Move the arrow pointer down and to the right until the correct number of rows and columns displays below the grid and then release the mouse button. As you move the arrow pointer in the grid, selected columns and rows are highlighted, and the number of rows and columns displays below the grid.

figure 22.1 Table Grid

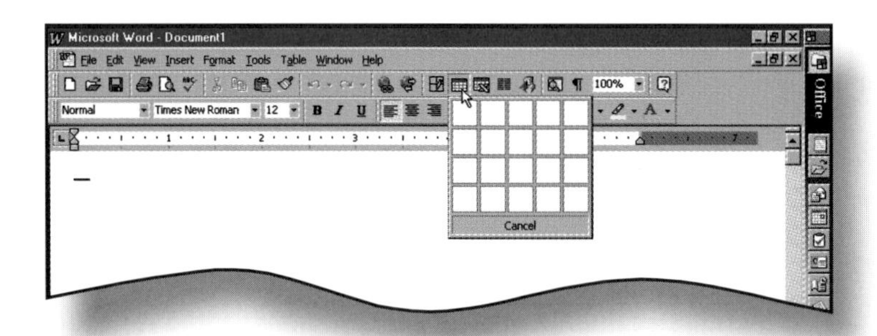

A table can also be created with options at the Insert Table dialog box shown in figure 22.2. Display the Insert Table dialog box by clicking Table, then Insert Table. At the Insert Table dialog box, key the desired number of columns in the Number of columns text box. Click Number of rows, key the desired number of rows, and then click OK or press Enter. You can also key the desired number of columns in the Number of columns text box, press the Tab key, key the desired number of rows in the Number of rows text box, and then click OK or press Enter. A table is inserted in the document at the location of the insertion point.

figure 22.2 Insert Table Dialog Box

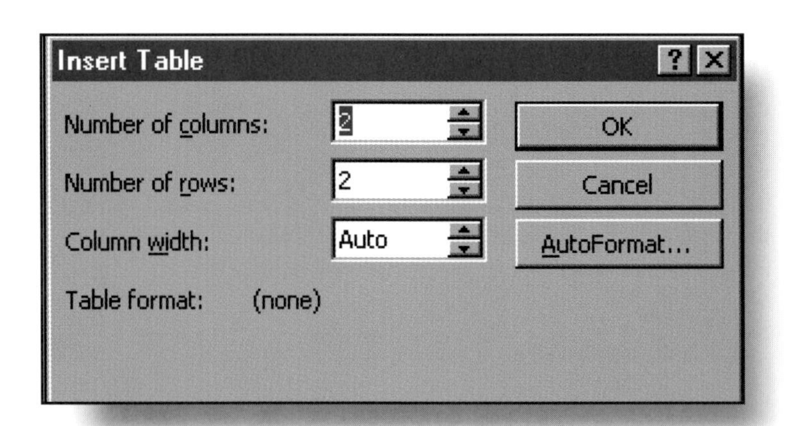

Figure 22.3 shows an example of a table with five columns and three rows. Various parts of the table are identified in figure 22.3, such as the gridlines, move table column marker, end-of-cell marker, and the end-of-row marker. In a table, nonprinting characters identify the end of a cell and the end of a row. To view these characters, click the Show/Hide ¶ button on the Standard toolbar. The end-of-cell marker displays inside each cell and the end-of-row marker displays at the end of a row of cells. These markers are identified in figure 22.3.

figure 22.3 *Table*

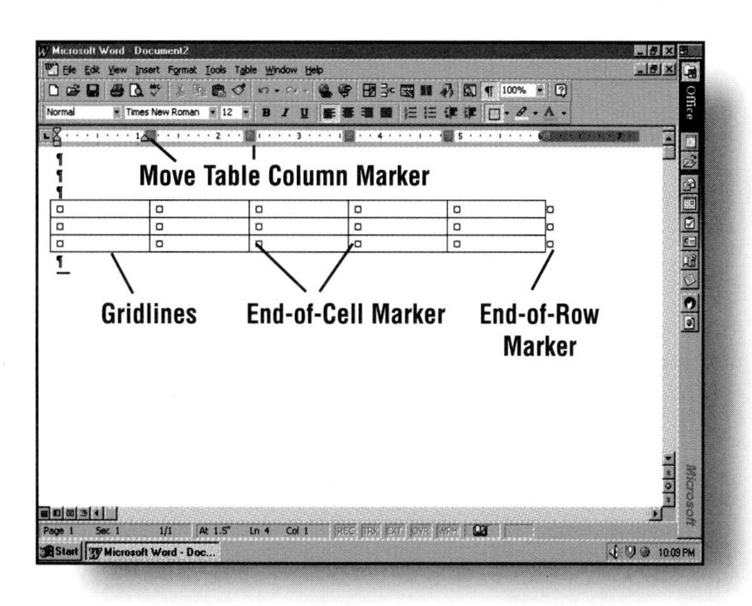

When a table is created, the insertion point is located in the cell in the upper left corner of the table. Cells in a table contain a cell designation. Columns in a table are lettered from left to right, beginning with A. The cell in the upper left corner of the table is cell A1. The cell to the right of A1 is B1, the cell to the right of B1 is C1, and so on. Rows are numbered beginning with 1. The cells below A1 are A2, A3, A4, and so on. Some cell designations are shown in figure 22.4.

figure 22.4 *Cell Designations*

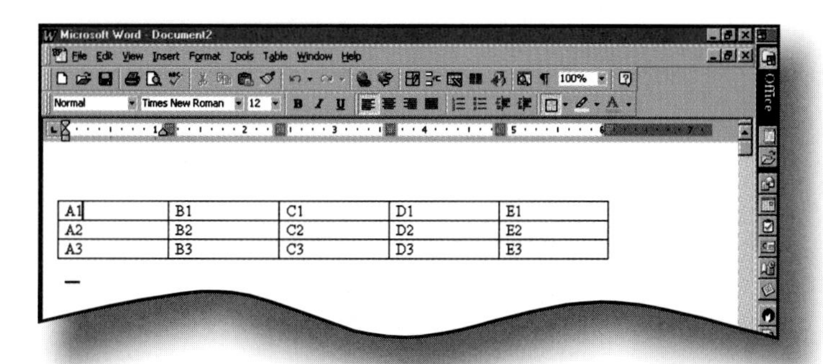

If the Ruler is displayed at the top of the document screen, move table column markers display on the Ruler. These markers represent the end of a column and are useful in changing the width of columns. Figure 22.3 identifies a move table column marker.

Entering Text in Cells

With the insertion point positioned in a cell, key or edit text. Move the insertion point to other cells with the mouse by positioning the I-beam pointer in the desired cell and then clicking the left mouse button. If you are using the keyboard, press Tab to move the insertion point to the next cell or press Shift + Tab to move the insertion point to the previous cell.

If the text you key does not fit on one line, it wraps to the next line within the same cell. Or, if you press Enter within a cell, the insertion point is moved to the next line within the same cell. The cell vertically lengthens to accommodate the text, and all cells in that row also lengthen. Pressing the Tab key in a table causes the insertion point to move to the next cell in the table. If you want to move the insertion point to a tab stop within a cell, press Ctrl + Tab.

If the insertion point is located in the last cell of the table and you press the Tab key, Word adds another row to the table. To avoid this situation, make sure you do not press the Tab key after entering text in the last cell, or immediately click the Undo button on the Standard toolbar. You can insert a page break within a table by pressing Ctrl + Enter. The page break is inserted between rows, not within.

When all information has been entered in the cells, move the insertion point below the table and, if necessary, continue keying the document, or save the document in the normal manner.

Moving the Insertion Point Within a Table

To move the insertion point to different cells within the table using the mouse, position the I-beam pointer in the desired cell, and then click the left button. To move the insertion point to different cells within the table using the keyboard, refer to the information shown in figure 22.5.

figure 22.5 *Insertion Point Movement within a Table*

To move the insertion point	Press these keys
to next cell	TAB
to preceding cell	SHIFT + TAB
forward one character	→
backward one character	←
to previous row	↑
to next row	↓
to first cell in the row	ALT + HOME (or ALT + 7 on numeric keypad*)
to last cell in the row	ALT + END (or ALT + 1 on numeric keypad*)
to top cell in the column	ALT + PG UP (or ALT + 9 on numeric keypad*)
to bottom cell in the column	ALT + PG DN (or ALT + 3 on numeric keypad*)
	**Num Lock must be off.*

exercise 1

Creating a Table with the Insert Table Button

1. At a clear document screen, create the document shown in figure 22.6 by completing the following steps:
   a. Change the paragraph alignment to center and turn on bold.
   b. Key **COLEMAN DEVELOPMENT CORPORATION**.
   c. Press Enter twice.
   d. Key **Human Resources Department**.
   e. Press Enter three times.
   f. Turn off bold and then change the paragraph alignment to left.
   g. Create the table by completing the following steps:
      1) Position the arrow pointer on the Insert Table button on the Standard toolbar.
      2) Hold down the left mouse button. This causes a grid to appear.
      3) Move the arrow pointer down and to the right until the number below the grid displays as *6 x 2* and then release the mouse button.
   h. Key the text in the cells as indicated in figure 22.6. Press the Tab key to move to the next cell or press Shift + Tab to move to the preceding cell. (If you accidentally press the Enter key within a cell, immediately press the Backspace key. Do not press Tab after keying the text in the last cell. If you do, another row is inserted in the table. If this happens, immediately click the Undo button on the Standard toolbar.)
2. Save the table and name it Ch 22, Ex 01.
3. Print and then close Ch 22, Ex 01.

figure 22.6 *Exercise 1*

COLEMAN DEVELOPMENT CORPORATION

Human Resources Department

Stephanie Branson	President
Brandon Kent	Vice President
Nicole Clark	Director
Jack Takagawa	Assistant Director
Darryl Ellis	Trainer
Lynette Lagasi	Trainer

exercise 2

Creating a Table at the Insert Table Dialog Box

1. At a clear document screen, create the table shown in figure 22.7 by completing the following steps:
   a. Change the paragraph alignment to center and turn on bold.
   b. Key **COLEMAN DEVELOPMENT CORPORATION**.
   c. Press Enter twice.
   d. Key **Executive Officers**.
   e. Press Enter three times.
   f. Turn off bold and change the paragraph alignment to left.
   g. Create the table by completing the following steps:
      1) Click Table, then Insert Table.
      2) At the Insert Table dialog box, key **3** in the Number of columns text box. (The insertion point is automatically positioned in this text box.)
      3) Press Tab (this moves the insertion point to the Number of rows option) and then key **5**.
      4) Click OK or press Enter.
   h. Key the text in the cells as indicated in figure 22.7. Press the Tab key to move to the next cell or press Shift + Tab to move to the preceding cell. To create the text in the third column, press Ctrl + Tab, and then key the text. (This moves the insertion point to a tab stop within the cell.)
2. Save the table and name it Ch 22, Ex 02.
3. Print and then close Ch 22, Ex 02.

figure 22.7

Exercise 2

COLEMAN DEVELOPMENT CORPORATION

Executive Officers

Chief Executive Officer	Mandy Armstead	#1034
President	Stephanie Branson	#1046
Vice President	Conrad Wheeler	#3092
Vice President	Selene Resnick	#3441
Vice President	Aurora Madsen	#2190

Selecting Cells

A table can be formatted in special ways. For example, the alignment of text in cells or rows can be changed or character formatting can be added. To identify the cells that are to be affected by the formatting, the specific cells need to be selected.

Selecting in a Table with the Mouse

The arrow pointer can be used to select a cell, row, column, or an entire table. The left edge of each cell, between the left column border and the end-of-cell marker or first character in the cell, is called the *cell selection bar*. When the arrow pointer is positioned in the cell selection bar, it turns into an arrow pointing up and to the right (instead of the left). To select a particular cell, position the arrow pointer in the cell selection bar at the left edge of the cell until it turns into an arrow pointing up and to the right, as shown in figure 22.8, and then click the left mouse button.

22.8

Cell Selection Bar

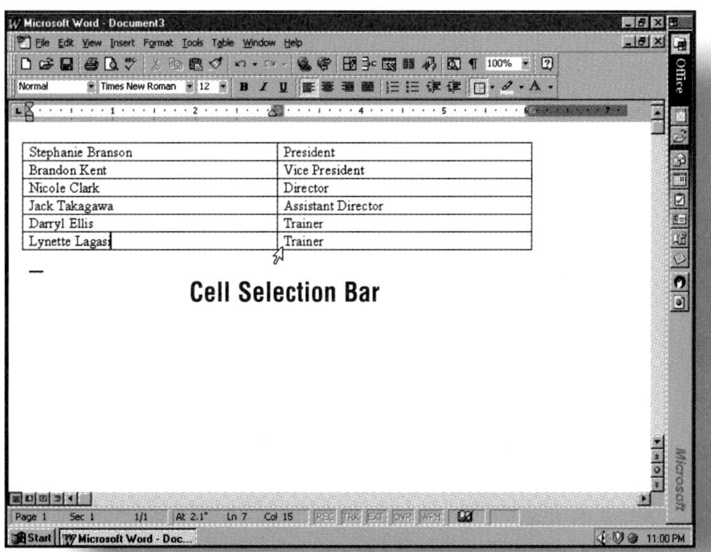

Each row in a table contains a row selection bar, which is the space just to the left of the left edge of the table. Figure 22.9 shows the arrow pointer in the row selection bar. When the arrow pointer is positioned in the row selection bar, the arrow pointer turns into an arrow pointing up and to the right.

To select a row, position the arrow pointer in the row selection bar at the left edge of the table until it turns into an arrow pointing up and to the right, and then click the left mouse button. You can also select a row by positioning the arrow pointer in the cell selection bar of any cell in the row and then double-clicking the left mouse button.

22.9 **Row Selection Bar**

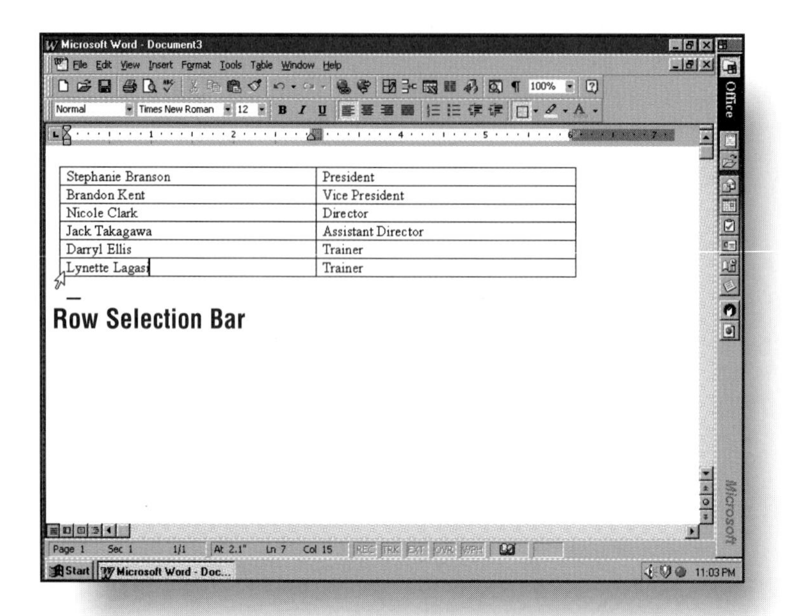

To select a column, position the arrow pointer on the uppermost horizontal gridline of the table in the appropriate column until it turns into a short, downward-pointing arrow. Click the left mouse button to select the column.

Once you have selected a particular cell, row, or column, hold down the Shift key; position the I-beam pointer in another cell, row, or column; then click the left mouse button. This selects all cells in the table from the location of the first selected cell, row, or column, to the location of the I-beam pointer.

Cells in a table can also be selected by positioning the I-beam pointer in the first cell to be selected, holding down the left mouse button, dragging the I-beam pointer to the last cell to be selected, and then releasing the mouse button.

To select all cells within a table using the mouse, position the I-beam pointer in any cell in the table, hold down the Alt key, and then double-click the left mouse button. You can also position the arrow pointer in the row selection bar at the left edge of the table until it turns into an arrow pointing up and to the right, hold down the left mouse button, drag down to select all rows in the table, and then release the left mouse button.

If you want to select only a portion of text within a cell (rather than the entire cell), position the I-beam pointer at the beginning of the text, and then hold down the left mouse button as you drag the mouse across the text. When a cell is selected, the entire cell is changed to black. When text within cells is selected, only those lines containing text are selected.

exercise 3

Selecting and Formatting Cells in a Table

1. Open Ch 22, Ex 01.
2. Save the document with Save As and name it Ch 22, Ex 03.
3. Select and then bold the text in the cells in the first column using the mouse by completing the following steps:
   a. Position the arrow pointer on the uppermost horizontal gridline of the first column in the table until it turns into a short, downward-pointing arrow.
   b. Click the left mouse button.
   c. Click the Bold button on the Standard toolbar.
4. Select and then italicize the text in the cells in the second column by completing steps similar to those in 3a through 3c.
5. Save the document again with the same name (Ch 22, Ex 03).
6. Print and then close Ch 22, Ex 03.

Selecting in a Table with the Keyboard

The keyboard can be used to select specific cells within a table. Figure 22.10 displays the commands for selecting specific amounts of a table.

figure 22.10 *Selecting in a Table with the Keyboard*

To select	Press...
the next cell's contents	TAB
the preceding cell's contents	SHIFT + TAB
the entire table	ALT + 5 (on numeric keypad with Num Lock off)
adjacent cells	Hold SHIFT, then press an arrow key repeatedly
a column	Position insertion point in top cell of column, hold down SHIFT, then press ↓ until column is selected

If you want to select only text within cells, rather than the entire cell, press F8 to turn on the Extend mode, and then move the insertion point with an arrow key. When a cell is selected, the entire cell is changed to black. When text within a cell is selected, only those lines containing text are selected.

Selecting Cells with the Table Drop-Down Menu

A row or column of cells or all cells in a table can be selected with options from the Table drop-down menu. For example, to select a row of cells in a table, position the insertion point in any cell in the row, click Table, then Select Row.

To select cells in a column, position the insertion point in any cell in the column, click Table, then Select Column. To select all cells in the table, position the insertion point in any cell in the table, click Table, then Select Table.

exercise 4

Selecting and Formatting Cells Using the Keyboard and the Table Drop-Down Menu

1. Open Ch 22, Ex 02.
2. Save the document with Save As and name it Ch 22, Ex 04.
3. Select and then bold the text in the cells in the first column using the keyboard by completing the following steps:
   a. Position the insertion point in the first cell of the first column (cell A1).
   b. Hold down the Shift key and then press the down arrow key four times. (This should select all cells in the first column.)
   c. Press Ctrl + B.
4. Select and then bold the text in the cells in the second column using the Table drop-down menu by completing the following steps:
   a. Position the insertion point in any cell in the second column.
   b. Click Table, then Select Column.
   c. Click the Bold button on the Standard toolbar.
5. Select and then italicize the text in the cells in the third column by completing steps similar to those in 3a through 3c or 4a through 4c.
6. Save the document again with the same name (Ch 22, Ex 04).
7. Print and then close Ch 22, Ex 04.

Deleting a Table

All text in cells within a table can be deleted, leaving the table gridlines, or all text and the gridlines can be deleted. To delete the text, leaving the gridlines, select the table, and then press the Delete key. If just the table is selected, the text in each cell is deleted, leaving the gridlines. To delete the text in cells and the gridlines, select the table, click Table, and then click Delete Rows.

exercise 5

Copying and Deleting a Table

1. Open Ch 22, Ex 02.
2. Save the document with Save As and name it Ch 22, Ex 05.
3. Make the following changes to the document:
   a. Select and then delete the title, *COLEMAN DEVELOPMENT CORPORATION*, and the subtitle, *Executive Officers*.
   b. Move the insertion point below the table and then press the Enter key three times.
   c. Select the table by completing the following steps:
      1) Position the insertion point in any cell in the table.
      2) Click Table, then Select Table.
   d. With the table selected, click the Copy button on the Standard toolbar.
   e. Move the insertion point to the end of the document and then click the Paste button on the Standard toolbar. (This inserts a copy of the table at the end of the document.)
   f. Select and then delete the first table in the document by completing the following steps:
      1) Select the entire table. To do this, position the insertion point in any cell in the table and then click Table, then Select Table.
      2) Click Table, then Delete Rows.
4. Save the document again with the same name (Ch 22, Ex 05).
5. Print and then close Ch 22, Ex 05.

Formatting a Table

A table that has been created with Word's Tables feature can be formatted in a variety of ways. For example, borders and shading can be added to cells; rows and columns can be inserted or deleted; cells can be split or merged; and the alignment of the table can be changed.

Adding Borders

The gridlines creating a table can be customized with border options. Borders can be added to a selected cell(s) or an entire table with options at the Borders and Shading dialog box shown in figure 22.11. To display this dialog box, select a cell(s) or the entire table, click Format, and then click Borders and Shading.

figure 22.11 ***Borders and Shading Dialog Box with Borders Tab Selected***

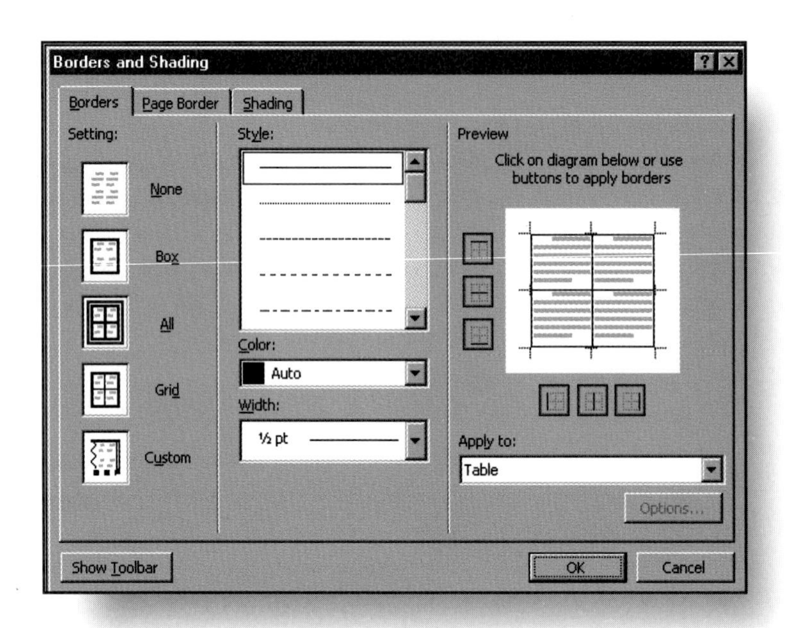

If you want a border option to apply to a specific cell, select the cell first, and then display the Borders and Shading dialog box. The Borders and Shading Apply to option will display with *Cell* in the text box. If the insertion point is positioned in a table (with no cell selected) or if the entire table is selected, changes made at the Borders and Shading dialog box will affect the entire table and the Apply to option will display with *Table*. Figure 22.12 describes the options available at the Borders and Shading dialog box.

figure 22.12 ***Options at the Borders and Shading Dialog Box with Borders Tab Selected***

Choose this option	To do this
None	Remove all borders from selected cell(s) or table
Box	Insert a box border around the selected cell(s) or table
All	Insert a box border around and between selected cell(s) or table and apply preset shadow formatting to border
Grid	Insert a box border around selected cell(s) or table and apply preset 3-D border formatting making the border look like a "window"
Custom	Create a custom border using options in the Preview diagram

Style	Choose a border style
Color	Choose a border color
Width	Specify the width of the border
Preview diagram	Click the sides of the Preview diagram to add or remove the currently selected settings
Apply to	Specify to what the border and shading should be applied
Options	Set additional margin and position settings (only available when Apply to is set at *Paragraph* or when Page Border tab is selected)

exercise 6

Creating a Table with Border Lines Around and Between Cells

1. At a clear document screen, create the document shown in figure 22.13 by completing the following steps:
   a. Change the paragraph alignment to center and turn on bold.
   b. Key **COLEMAN DEVELOPMENT CORPORATION**.
   c. Press Enter twice and then key **Department Directors**.
   d. Press Enter once, turn off bold, and then change the paragraph alignment to left.
   e. Press Enter twice and then create a table with 2 columns and 8 rows (8 x 2).
   f. Key the text in the first cell (cell A1) by completing the following steps:
      1) Click the Center button on the Formatting toolbar.
      2) Click the Bold button on the Formatting toolbar.
      3) Key **Name**.
   g. Press the Tab key to move the insertion point to the next cell (cell B1). Complete steps similar to those in step 1f to center and bold the column heading *Department*.
   h. Key the text in the remaining cells as indicated in figure 22.13. Press the Tab key to move to the next cell or press Shift + Tab to move to the preceding cell. Press Ctrl + Tab before keying each entry in cells A2 through B8.
   i. Add thick teal lines around the table and a thin teal line between columns by completing the following steps:
      1) Position the insertion point in any cell in the table. (Make sure no text or cell is selected.)
      2) Click Format, then Borders and Shading.

3) At the Borders and Shading dialog box with the Borders tab selected, click the None option in the Setting section. (This removes all borders from the Preview diagram.)
4) Click the Custom option.
5) Scroll to the end of the line styles in the Style list box until the last line option is displayed and then click the last line option.
6) Change the line color to teal by clicking the down-pointing triangle at the right side of the Color option, and then clicking *Teal* at the drop-down list. (You will need to scroll down the list of colors to display Teal.)
7) Apply the border to the outside of the table by completing the following steps:
    a) Click the top button at the left side of the Preview diagram. (This inserts a teal shadow border at the top of the Preview diagram.)
    b) Click the bottom button at the left side of the Preview diagram. (This inserts a teal shadow border at the bottom of the table.)
    c) Click the first button from the left at the bottom of the Preview diagram. (This inserts a teal shadow border at the left side of the table.)
    d) Click the last button at the bottom of the Preview diagram. (This inserts a teal shadow border at the right side of the table.)
8) Add a single teal line between columns by completing the following steps:
    a) Scroll to the beginning of the line styles in the Style list box and then click the first line style (a single line).
    b) Change the line color to teal. (To do this, click the down-pointing triangle at the right of the Color option, and then click *Teal* at the drop-down list. You will need to scroll down the list of colors to display Teal.)
    c) Click the middle button at the bottom of the Preview diagram. (This inserts a single teal line between columns.)
9) Click OK to close the Borders and Shading dialog box.

2. Save the document and name it Ch 22, Ex 06.
3. Print and then close Ch 22, Ex 06.

22.13 *Exercise 6*

COLEMAN DEVELOPMENT CORPORATION

Department Directors

Name	Department
Paul O'Shea	Development
Nicole Clark	Human Resources
Timothy Watson	Administrative Services
Erica Torres	Research
Andrea Okamato	Financial Planning
Leigh Marcus	Support Services
Troy Severson	Sales

Adding Shading

To add visual appeal to a table, shading can be added to cells. Shading can be added to cells or selected cells with options at the Borders and Shading dialog box with the Shading tab selected as shown in figure 22.14. Figure 22.15 describes the options available at the Borders and Shading dialog box.

22.14 *Borders and Shading Dialog Box with Shading Tab Selected*

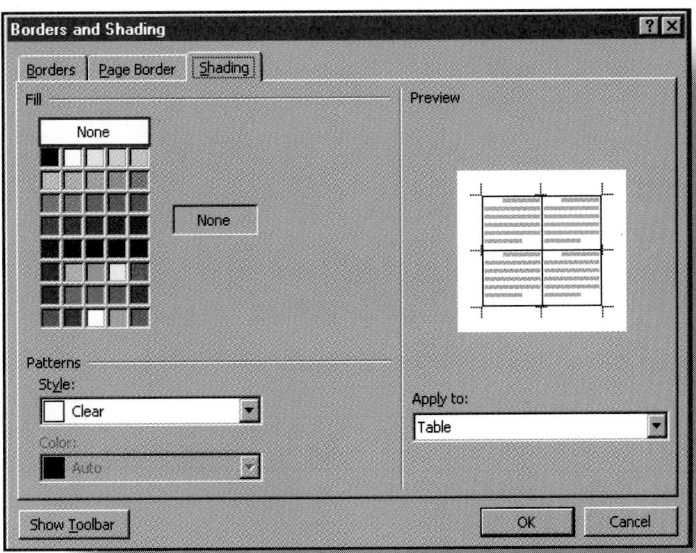

figure 22.15 *Options at the Borders and Shading Dialog Box with Shading Tab Selected*

Choose this option	To do this
Fill	Choose a fill color for selected cell(s) or entire table
Style	Choose a shading style to apply "over" fill color
Color	Choose a color for the lines and dots in the selected shading pattern
Preview diagram	Click the sides of the Preview diagram to add or remove the currently selected fill, style, and color
Apply to	Specify to what the border and shading should be applied

exercise 7

Adding a Border and Shading to a Table

1. Open Ch 22, Ex 02.
2. Save the document with Save As and name it Ch 22, Ex 07.
3. Add a border and shading to the table by completing the following steps:
   a. Move the insertion point to a cell within the table.
   b. Click Format, then Borders and Shading.
   c. At the Borders and Shading dialog box, make sure the Borders tab is selected.
   d. Change the Color option to Dark Blue. (You will need to scroll down the Color drop-down list to display Dark Blue.)
   e. Choose a double-line style in the Style list box.
   f. Click the Box option.
   g. Click the Shading tab.
   h. At the Borders and Shading dialog box with the Shading tab selected, click the turquoise color in the Fill section. (The turquoise color is the second color from the left in the third row from the bottom.)
   i. Click OK to close the dialog box.
4. Add a fill to the second column of cells by completing the following steps:
   a. Select cells B1 through B5.
   b. Click Format, then Borders and Shading.
   c. At the Borders and Shading dialog box, make sure the Shading tab is selected.

d. At the Borders and Shading dialog box with the Shading tab selected, click the down-pointing triangle at the right side of the Style option, and then click *5%* at the drop-down list.
e. Click OK to close the Borders and Shading dialog box.
f. Deselect the cells.

5. Save the document again with the same name (Ch 22, Ex 07).
6. Print and then close Ch 22, Ex 07.

Changing Column Width

When a table is created, the columns are the same width. The width of the columns depends on the number of columns as well as the document margins. In some tables, you may want to change the width of certain columns to accommodate more or less text. You can change the width of columns using the mouse on the Ruler, in a table, or with options from the Cell Height and Width dialog box.

Changing Column Width Using the Ruler

When the insertion point is positioned in a table, the column widths are displayed on the Ruler. These move table column markers are identified in figure 22.3. To change the column width using move table column markers on the Ruler, you would position the arrow pointer on the move table column marker to be moved until it turns into a left- and right-pointing arrow, hold down the left mouse button, and then drag the marker to make the column wider or narrower. (As you drag the marker, any move table column markers to the right are also moved.) When the move table column marker is in the desired position, release the mouse button.

If you want to see the column measurements as you move a move table column marker, hold down the Alt key while you drag the marker. You can also view the column measurements by positioning the arrow pointer on a move table column marker, holding down the Alt key, and then holding down the left mouse button.

If you only want to move the move table column marker where the arrow pointer is positioned, hold down the Shift key, and then drag the marker on the Ruler. This does not change the overall size of the table. To change the column width of the column where the insertion point is positioned and all columns to the right, hold down the Ctrl key and the Shift key while you drag the move table column marker.

The first line indent marker, the left indent marker, the right indent marker, and the hanging indent marker display on the Ruler for the column where the insertion point is positioned. These markers can be used to adjust the left or right column margins, indent the first line in a cell, or create a hanging indent. Changes made to the column margins affect only the column where the insertion point is positioned.

exercise 8

Creating a Table and Then Changing Column Width Using the Ruler

1. At a clear document screen, create the document shown in figure 22.16 by completing the following steps:
   a. Key the heading and first paragraph of the memo shown in figure 22.16.
   b. Create the table below the first paragraph by completing the following steps:
      1) Create a table with 3 columns and 7 rows (7 x 3).
      2) Change the width of the first column using the mouse by completing the following steps:
         a) Make sure the Ruler is displayed.
         b) Position the arrow pointer on the move table column marker between the 1-inch mark and the 3-inch mark on the Ruler until it turns into an arrow pointing left and right.
         c) Hold down the Shift key and the Ctrl key, and then the left mouse button.
         d) Drag the marker to the 3-inch mark, then release the Shift key and the Ctrl key, and then the mouse button.
      3) Key the text in the cells. Bold and center the text as shown. Press Ctrl + Tab before keying the text in cells A2 through A7.
      4) Add a double-line border around the table by completing the following steps:
         a) With the insertion point positioned in any cell in the table, click Format, then Borders and Shading.
         b) At the Borders and Shading dialog box, make sure the Borders tab is selected.
         c) Scroll down the Style list box until the first double-line option is displayed and then click the first double-line option.
         d) Click the button that displays before the Grid option.
         e) Click OK to close the dialog box.
      5) Add 10 percent fill to cells A1, B1, and C1 by completing the following steps:
         a) Select cells A1, B1, and C1.
         b) Click Format, then Borders and Shading.
         c) At the Borders and Shading dialog box, click the Shading tab.
         d) At the Borders and Shading dialog box with the Shading tab selected, click the down-pointing triangle at the right side of the Style option, and then click *10%* at the drop-down list.

e) Click OK to close the Borders and Shading dialog box.

c. Position the insertion point below the table and then key the remaining text shown in figure 22.16.

2. Save the document and name it Ch 22, Ex 08.
3. Print and then close Ch 22, Ex 08.

figure 22.16

Exercise 8

DATE: April 5, 1999

TO: Renée Williams

FROM: Kyle McCleary

SUBJECT: DESKTOP PUBLISHING TRAINING

The deadline for signing up for the desktop publishing training was March 31. A total of six employees are registered for the training. The list of employees, employee number, and department is displayed in the table below.

Name	Employee #	Department
Gwenn Peterson	312-304-0098	Human Resources
Stanley Matias	123-293-5847	Human Resources
Deanne Merante	326-499-4834	Financial Planning
Karen Collier	654-300-6224	Sales
Michael Salas	231-392-8663	Sales
Anthony Bartels	654-332-3483	Support Services

Room 200 has been reserved for the training. Please let me know what special equipment you will need. There will be seven computers available in the room.

XX:Ch 22, Ex 08

Changing Column Width Using the Mouse

You can use the gridlines to change column widths within the table. To change column widths using the gridlines, position the arrow pointer on the gridline separating columns until the insertion point turns into a left- and right-pointing arrow with a vertical double line between. Hold down the left mouse button, drag the gridline to the desired location, and then release the mouse button. Only the gridline where the insertion point is positioned is moved. If you want to change column widths for all columns to the right and increase the width of the table, hold down the Shift key while dragging the gridline. Hold down the Shift key and Ctrl key while dragging the gridline if you want to change the width of all columns to the right without changing the size of the table.

In a table containing text or other features, you can adjust the width of one column to accommodate the longest line of text in the column. To do this, position the I-beam pointer on the right column gridline until it turns into a left- and right-pointing arrow with a vertical double line, and then double-click the left mouse button. To automatically size more than one column, select the columns first, and then double-click on a gridline.

Changing Column Width Using the Cell Height and Width Dialog Box

If you know the exact measurement for columns in a table, you can change column widths using the Cell Height and Width dialog box with the Column tab selected as shown in figure 22.17. For example, to change the column width of a column, position the insertion point in any cell in the column, click Table, then Cell Height and Width. At the Cell Height and Width dialog box with the Column tab selected, click Width of column *x* (where *x* represents the number of the column where the insertion point is positioned), and then key the desired width measurement. Click OK or press Enter to close the dialog box.

figure 22.17 *Cell Height and Width Dialog Box with Column Tab Selected*

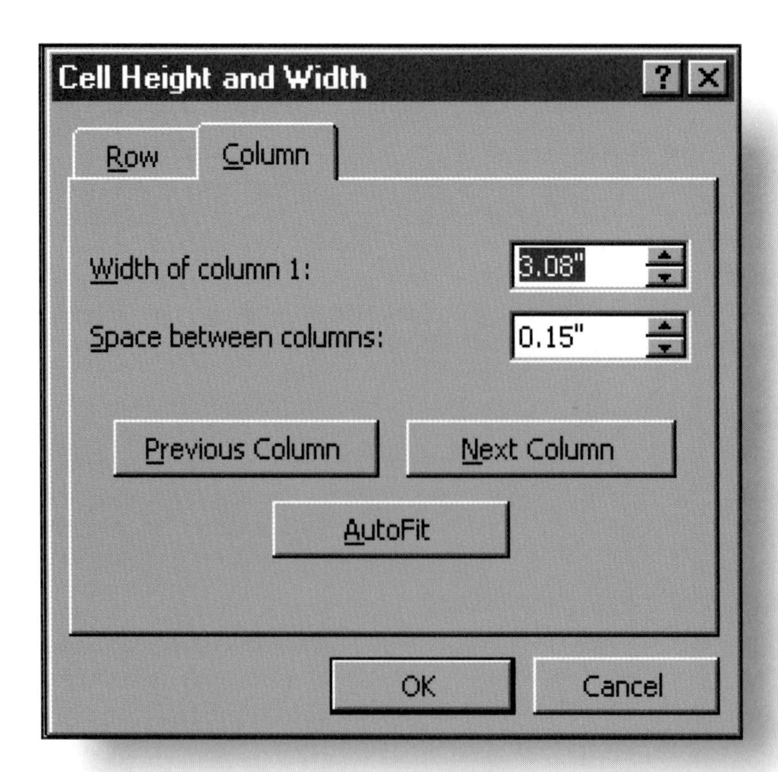

exercise 9

Changing Column Width in a Table Using Gridlines

1. Open Ch 22, Ex 02.
2. Save the document with Save As and name it Ch 22, Ex 09.
3. Change the width of the columns and add border lines and shading by completing the following steps:
   a. Position the arrow pointer on the gridline separating the first and second columns until it turns into a left- and right-pointing arrow with a vertical double line between.
   b. Hold down the left mouse button, drag the gridline to the left approximately one-quarter of an inch, and then release the mouse button. (Make sure the text in the first column does not wrap.)
   c. Position the arrow pointer on the gridline separating the second and third columns until it turns into a left- and right-pointing arrow with a vertical double line between.
   d. Hold down the left mouse button, drag the gridline to the left approximately three-quarters of an inch, and then release the mouse button. (Make sure the text in the second column does not wrap.)
   e. Position the insertion point in any cell in the third column.
   f. Click Table, then Cell Height and Width.
   g. At the Cell Height and Width dialog box, click the Column tab. (Skip this step if the Column tab is already selected.)
   h. Click the down-pointing triangle to the right of the Width of column 3 text box until *1.6"* displays in the text box.
   i. Click OK or press Enter.
   j. Add the following to the table:
      1) Add a thick/thin double-line border around the table.
      2) Add a single line between the columns.
      3) Add a light color fill to all cells in the table (you determine the color).
4. Save the document again with the same name (Ch 22, Ex 09).
5. Print and then close Ch 22, Ex 09. (The table will not be centered between the margins.)

Changing Cell Alignment

By default, text in cells aligns at the left side of the cell. Like normal text, this alignment can be changed to center, right, or justified. To change the alignment of text in cells, select the cells, and then click the desired alignment button on the Formatting toolbar. You can also change the alignment of text in selected cells with the Alignment option at the Paragraph dialog box with the Indents and Spacing tab selected or with a shortcut command. For example, to change the alignment of text to center in all cells in the second column of a table, you would select all cells in the second column, and then click the Center button on the Formatting toolbar.

exercise 10

Changing Cell Alignment in a Table

1. Open Ch 22, Ex 08.
2. Save the document with Save As and name it Ch 22, Ex 10.
3. Change the alignment of text in cells B2 through C7 to center by completing the following steps:
   a. Position the insertion point in cell B2 (the cell containing the number *312-304-0098*).
   b. Hold down the Shift key, press the down arrow key five times, and then the right arrow key once. (This selects cells B2 through C7.)
   c. Click the Center button on the Formatting toolbar.
   d. Deselect the cells.
4. Save the document again with the same name (Ch 22, Ex 10).
5. Print and then close Ch 22, Ex 10.

Aligning the Table

At the Cell Height and Width dialog box with the Row tab selected, the horizontal placement of rows or an entire table can be specified. By default, a table and the rows in a table are aligned at the left margin. This can be changed to center or right. For example, to center an entire table horizontally between margins in the document, you would position the insertion point in any cell in the table, click Table, then Cell Height and Width. (Make sure the Row tab is selected.) At the Cell Height and Width dialog box with the Row tab selected, click Center in the Alignment section of the dialog box, and then click OK or press Enter.

To align a table or selected rows at the right margin, you would click Right at the Cell Height and Width dialog box.

exercise 11

Horizontally Aligning a Table

1. Open Ch 22, Ex 09.
2. Save the document with Save As and name it Ch 22, Ex 11.
3. Center the table horizontally by completing the following steps:
   a. Position the insertion point in any cell in the table.
   b. Click Table, then Cell Height and Width.
   c. At the Cell Height and Width dialog box, click the Row tab. (Skip this step if the Row tab is already selected.)
   d. Click Center in the Alignment section of the dialog box.
   e. Click OK or press Enter.
4. Save the document again with the same name (Ch 22, Ex 11).
5. Print and then close Ch 22, Ex 11.

Inserting Rows

After a table has been created, rows can be added (inserted) to the table. There are several methods you can use to insert rows. The Insert Rows option from the Table drop-down menu can be used to insert a row in a table. By default, a row is inserted above the row where the insertion point is positioned. To insert a row in a table, position the insertion point in the row below where the row is to be inserted, click Table, then Insert Rows. If you want to insert more than one row, select the number of rows in the table that you want inserted, and then click Table, then Insert Rows.

You can also insert rows by selecting a row or several rows and then clicking the Insert Rows button on the Standard toolbar. The Insert Table button becomes the Insert Rows button on the Standard toolbar when a row or several rows are selected in a table.

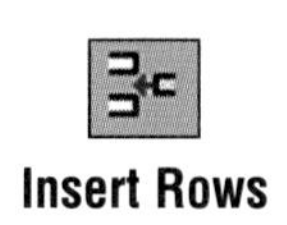
Insert Rows

Another method for inserting a row or several rows is to position the I-beam inside the table, click the *right* mouse button, and then click Insert Rows. Also, a row can be inserted at the end of the table by positioning the insertion point in the last cell in the table and then pressing the Tab key.

exercise 12

Inserting Rows in a Table

1. Open Ch 22, Ex 08.
2. Save the document with Save As and name it Ch 22, Ex 12.
3. Add two rows to the table by completing the following steps:
   a. Select the fourth and fifth row in the table.
   b. Click Table, then Insert Rows.
   c. Deselect the rows.
   d. Position the insertion point in cell A4 (below *Stanley Matias*), press Ctrl + Tab, and then key **Richard Paige**.
   e. Key the following text in the specified cell:
      B4 = 412-335-2255
      C4 = Human Resources
      A5 = Cynthia Kohler
      B5 = 566-345-2408
      C5 = Financial Planning
4. Change the word *six* in the first paragraph to *eight*. Change the word *seven* in the last paragraph to *nine*.
5. Save the document again with the same name (Ch 22, Ex 12).
6. Print and then close Ch 22, Ex 12.

Inserting Columns

Columns can be inserted in a table in much the same way as rows. To insert a column, select a column or group of columns, and then click Table, then Insert Columns. You can also insert a column (or columns) by selecting the column and then clicking the Insert Columns button on the Standard toolbar.

Insert Columns

The Insert Table button on the Standard toolbar becomes the Insert Columns button when a column or columns are selected. You can also insert a column or a group of columns by selecting the column(s), clicking the *right* mouse button, and then clicking Insert Columns at the drop-down menu. Word inserts a column or columns to the left of the selected column or columns. A table can contain a maximum of 31 columns. If you want to add a column to the right side of the table, select all the end-of-row markers, and then click the Insert Columns button on the Standard toolbar.

exercise 13

Inserting a Column in a Table

1. Open Ch 22, Ex 01.
2. Save the document with Save As and name it Ch 22, Ex 13.
3. Make the following changes to the table:
   a. Add a row to the table by completing the following steps:
      1) Position the insertion point in any cell in the first row.
      2) Click Table, then Insert Rows.
      3) Position the insertion point in cell A1 (the first cell in the first row), change the alignment to center, turn on bold, and then key **Name**.
      4) Press the Tab key to move the insertion point to the next cell (cell B1), change the alignment to center, turn on bold, and then key **Title**.
   b. Add a column to the right side of the table by completing the following steps:
      1) Click the Show/Hide ¶ button on the Standard toolbar to turn on the display of nonprinting characters.
      2) Position the I-beam pointer on the first end-of-row marker toward the top of the row at the far right side of the table until it turns into a small downward-pointing arrow.
      3) Click the left mouse button. (This will select all of the end-of-row markers at the right side of the table.)
      4) Click Table, then Insert Columns.
      5) Deselect the column.
   c. Change the width of the first column to 1.5 inches by completing the following steps:
      1) Position the insertion point in any cell in the first column.
      2) Click Table, then Cell Height and Width.
      3) At the Cell Height and Width dialog box, click the Column tab. (Skip this step if the Column tab is already selected.)
      4) Click the up- or down-pointing triangle to the right of the Width of column 1 text box until *1.5*" displays in the text box.
      5) Click OK or press Enter.
   d. Change the width of the second column to 1.5 inches and

the width of the third column to 1 inch by completing steps similar to those in step 3c.

e. Select the cells in the last column (cells C1 through C6) and then change the alignment to center.

f. Key the following text in the specified cells:

C1	=	**Ext.**
C2	=	1029
C3	=	2311
C4	=	3290
C5	=	2100
C6	=	1392
C7	=	2596

g. Click the Show/Hide ¶ button to turn off the display of nonprinting characters.

h. Center the table horizontally by completing the following steps:
   1) Position the insertion point in any cell in the table.
   2) Click Table, then Cell Height and Width.
   3) At the Cell Height and Width dialog box, click the Row tab. (Skip this step if the Row tab is already selected.)
   4) Click Center in the Alignment section of the dialog box.
   5) Click OK or press Enter.

4. Save the document again with the same name (Ch 22, Ex 13).
5. Print and then close Ch 22, Ex 13.

Deleting Cells, Rows, or Columns

Specific cells, rows, or columns in a table can be deleted. To delete a specific cell in a table, you would select the cell to be deleted, click Table, then Delete Cells. At the Delete Cells dialog box shown in figure 22.18, click OK or press Enter.

figure 22.18 *Delete Cells Dialog Box*

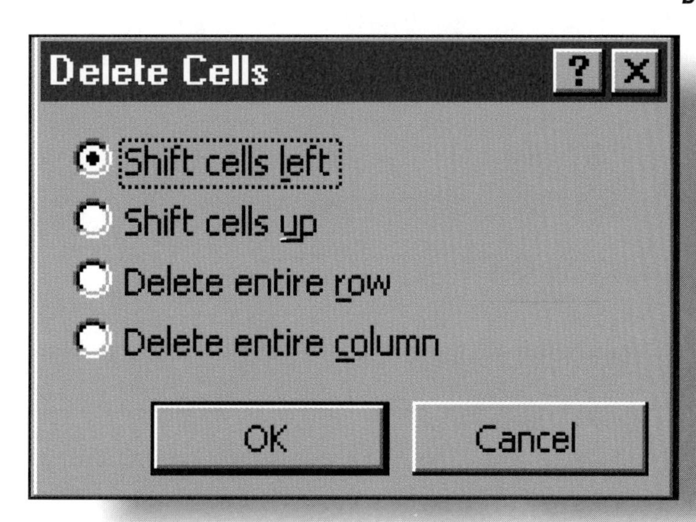

At the Delete Cells dialog box, the Shift cells left option is selected by default. At this option, cells will shift left after the selected cell (or cells) is deleted. Click the Shift cells up option if you want cells moved up after the selected cell (or cells) is deleted. Click Delete entire row to delete the row where the insertion point is positioned, or click Delete entire column to delete the column where the insertion point is positioned.

The Delete Cells dialog box can also be displayed by positioning the I-beam pointer at the table, clicking the *right* mouse button, then clicking Delete Cells in the drop-down menu.

A row can be deleted at the Delete Cells dialog box by choosing the Delete entire row option. A row or selected rows can also be deleted with the Delete Rows option from the Table drop-down menu. For example, to delete selected rows, select the rows in the table to be deleted, click Table, then Delete Rows.

A column can be deleted at the Delete Cells dialog box by choosing the Delete entire column option. A column or selected columns can also be deleted with the Delete Columns option from the Table drop-down menu. For example, to delete selected columns, you would select the columns in the table to be deleted, click Table, then Delete Columns.

exercise 14

Deleting Rows and Columns in a Table

1. Open Ch 22, Ex 12.
2. Save the document with Save As and name it Ch 22, Ex 14.
3. Make the following changes to the table:
   a. Delete the last row in the table by completing the following steps:
      1) Select the last row.
      2) Click Table, then Delete Rows.
   b. Delete the middle column by completing the following steps:
      1) Select the middle column.
      2) Click Table, then Delete Columns.
   c. Center the table horizontally.
   d. Change the word *eight* in the first paragraph to *seven*. Change the word *nine* in the last paragraph to *eight*.
4. Save the document again with the same name (Ch 22, Ex 14).
5. Print and then close Ch 22, Ex 14.

Merging Cells

Cells can be merged with the Merge Cells option from the Table drop-down menu. Before merging cells, the cells to be merged must be selected.

Splitting Cells

With the Split Cells option from the Table drop-down menu, you can split a cell or a row or column of cells. To split a cell, position the insertion point in the cell to be split, click Table, then Split Cells. At the Split Cells dialog box shown in figure 22.19, make sure the desired number of columns displays in the Number of columns text box, and then click OK or press Enter. To split an entire column or row of cells, select the column or row first, click Table, then Split Cells.

figure 22.19 *Split Cells Dialog Box*

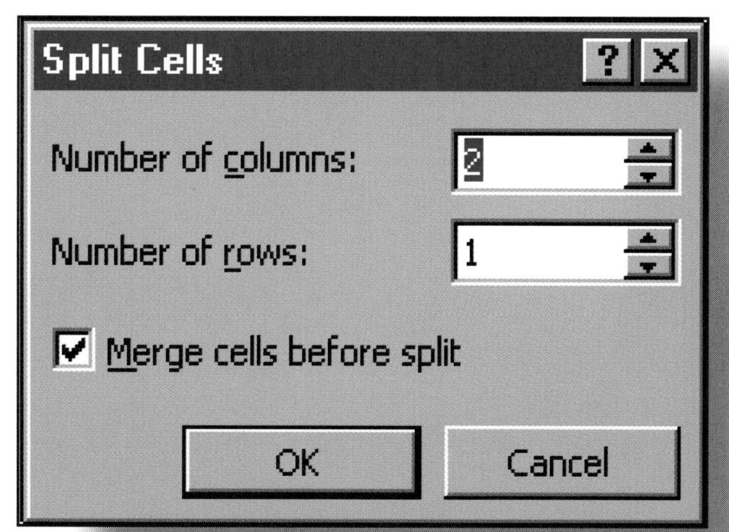

exercise 15

Creating a Table with Merged Cells

1. At a clear document screen, create the table shown in figure 22.20 by completing the following steps:
   a. Create a table with 3 columns and 10 rows (10 x 3).
   b. Change the width of the first column to 3 inches, the width of the second column to 2 inches, and the width of the third column to 1 inch.
   c. Merge the cells in the first row by completing the following steps:
      1) Select the first row.
      2) Click Table, then Merge Cells.
   d. Merge the cells in the second row by completing steps similar to those in step 1c.

e. Select the entire table and then change the font to 12-point Arial bold.

f. Key the text in the cells as shown. Center align the text as indicated.

g. Add a double-line border around the outside of the table and a single-line border on the inside of the table by completing the following steps:

1) Position the insertion point in any cell in the table.
2) Click Format, then Borders and Shading.
3) At the Borders and Shading dialog box, make sure the Borders tab is selected.
4) Make sure the first line style (a single line) is selected in the Style list box.
5) Click the Grid option.
6) Scroll down the line styles in the Style list box until the first double line displays, and then click it.
7) Click OK or press Enter to close the Borders and Shading dialog box.

h. Select the third row and then add 20 percent fill.

2. Save the document and name it Ch 22, Ex 15.
3. Print and then close Ch 22, Ex 15.

figure 22.20 *Exercise 15*

TRAINING AND EDUCATION DEPARTMENT		
Desktop Publishing Training		
Name	Department	Emp #

Formatting with AutoFormat

Formatting a table, such as adding borders or shading, aligning text in cells, changing fonts, etc., can take some time. Word has provided predesigned table formats that can quickly format your table for you. Table formats are contained in the Table AutoFormat dialog box shown in figure 22.21. To display this dialog box, position the insertion point in any cell in a table, click Table, then Table AutoFormat.

figure 22.21 *Table AutoFormat Dialog Box*

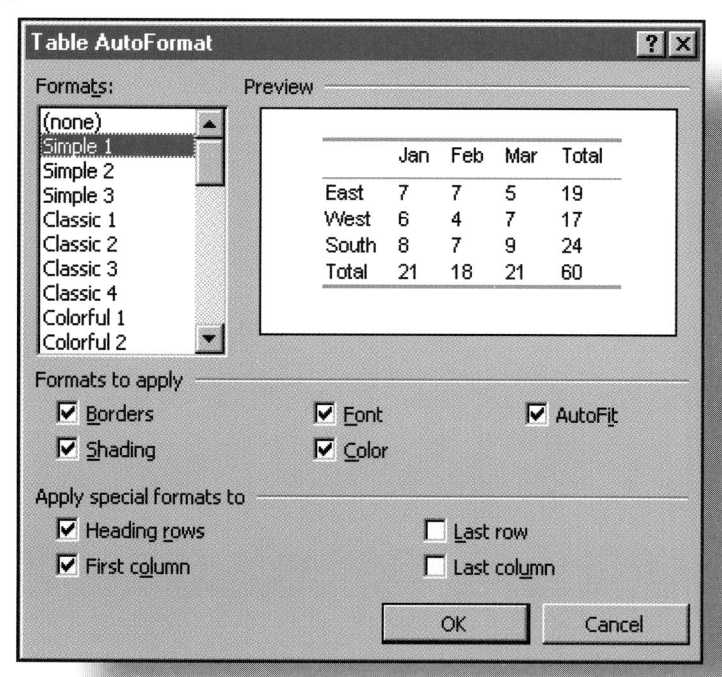

Predesigned table formats are displayed in the Formats list box. Select a table format in the Formats list box and preview the appearance of the table in the Preview diagram. When previewing predesigned table formats, you can make some changes to the predesigned format by removing check marks from the options in the Formats to apply section of the dialog box. For example, if you like a predesigned format created by Word except for the shading, select the format in the Formats list box in the dialog box, and then click the Shading check box. This removes the check mark from the Shading check box and also removes the shading from the table shown in the Preview diagram.

If you want to apply the special formatting only to specific parts of the table, select the parts of the table you want the formatting applied to in the Apply special formats to section of the dialog box. For example, if you want the table formatting only applied to the first column in the table, insert a check mark in the First column option and remove the check marks from the other options.

exercise 16

Formatting a Table Using the Table AutoFormat Dialog Box

1. Open Ch 22, Ex 01.
2. Save the document with Save As and name it Ch 22, Ex 16.
3. Make the following changes to the table:
   a. Select the first row and then insert a row.
   b. Key **Name** in the first cell in the first column (cell A1), centered and bolded.
   c. Key **Title** in the first cell in the second column (cell B1), centered and bolded.
   d. Automatically format the table by completing the following steps:
      1) Position the insertion point in any cell in the table.
      2) Click Table, then Table AutoFormat.
      3) At the Table AutoFormat dialog box, click the down-pointing triangle to the right of the Formats list box until *Colorful 3* is visible, and then click *Colorful 3*.
      4) Click OK or press Enter.
   e. Center the table horizontally.
4. Save the document again with the same name (Ch 22, Ex 16).
5. Print and then close Ch 22, Ex 16.

Creating a Table Using the Tables and Borders Toolbar

Word includes a Tables and Borders toolbar with options you can use to create a more free-form table. With buttons on the Tables and Borders toolbar, shown in figure 22.22, you can draw a table with specific borders and then customize the table as well as the text inside the table. For example, you can change the style, weight, and color of the table border and add shading and fill color to the table. Use buttons on the toolbar to change the alignment of text inside the table, sort the text in ascending or descending order, and also change the direction of text in the cell. Click the Change Text Direction button on the Tables and Borders toolbar and text inside a cell or selected cells is rotated 90 degrees. To display this toolbar, click the Tables and Borders button on the Standard toolbar. Figure 22.23 identifies the buttons on the toolbar and the purpose of each.

Tables and Borders

figure 22.22 *Tables and Borders Toolbar*

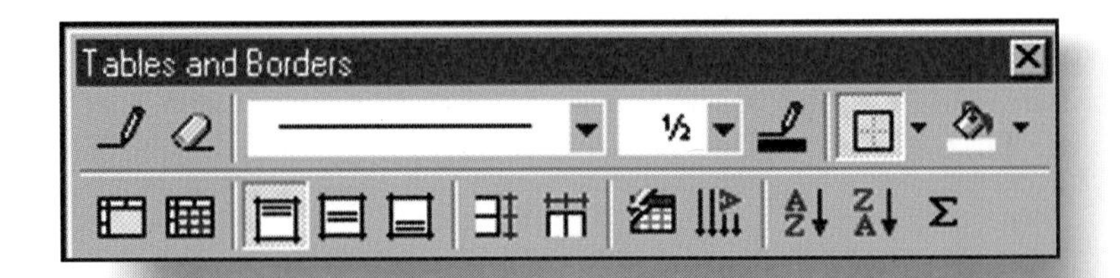

figure 22.23 *Buttons on the Tables and Borders Toolbar*

Click this button...	Named...	To do this...
	Draw Table	Insert a table where you drag in the document
	Eraser	Erase border and/or cell lines
	Line Style	Specify the border line style
½	Line Weight	Specify the thickness of the border line
	Border Color	Specify the border line color
	Outside Border	Add or remove border around selected text, paragraph, cells, or other object
	Shading Color	Add, modify, or remove fill color from selected object
	Merge Cells	Combine contents of selected adjacent cells into one cell
	Split Cells	Split selected cells in number of rows and columns specified
	Align Top	Align horizontally oriented text at top of cell
	Center Vertically	Center horizontally oriented text between top and bottom of cell
	Align Bottom	Align horizontally oriented text at bottom of cell
	Distribute Rows Evenly	Change selected rows or cells to equal row height
	Distribute Columns Evenly	Change selected columns or cells to equal column width
	Table AutoFormat	Apply predesigned formats to table or selected cells
	Change Text Direction	Orient selected text in a cell horizontally left or right
	Sort Ascending	Sort selected items alphabetically or numerically in ascending order
	Sort Descending	Sort selected items alphabetically or numerically in descending order
Σ	AutoSum	Insert total of a column or row in cell

To create a table using buttons on the Tables and Borders toolbar, you would complete the following steps:

1. Turn on the display of the Tables and Borders toolbar by clicking the Tables and Borders button on the Standard toolbar. (The viewing mode is automatically changed to Page Layout.)
2. Position the mouse pointer (displays as a pencil) in the area of the editing window where you want the upper left corner of the table to display.
3. Hold down the left mouse button, drag the pencil pointer down and to the right until the outline displays the desired size of the table, and then release the mouse button. (This creates the border of the table.)
4. Use the pencil pointer to draw the row and column lines.
5. Click inside the cell where you want to key text.
6. Key the desired text. (When you key text, the pencil pointer turns into the normal mouse pointer.)

Shading Color

Many of the buttons on the Tables and Borders toolbar can be used to customize the table. For example, you can change the line style with Line Style options and then draw the desired portion of the table. Or, you can change the line style and then redraw lines in an existing table. Use options from the Shading Color button to add color to a cell or selected cells in a table.

exercise 17

Drawing a Table Using the Tables and Borders Toolbar

Eraser

Draw Table

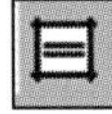

Center Vertically

Distribute Rows Evenly

1. At a clear document screen, draw the table shown in figure 22.24 by completing the following steps:
   a. Key the title centered and bolded as shown in figure 22.24.
   b. Press the Enter key three times after keying the title and then return the paragraph alignment to left.
   c. Turn on the display of the Tables and Borders toolbar by clicking the Tables and Borders button on the Standard toolbar.
   d. Position the mouse pointer (displays as a pencil) in the editing window and draw the table, row, and column lines as shown in figure 22.24. (To draw the lines, position the pencil in the desired location, hold down the left mouse button, draw the line, and then release the button. If you want to erase a line, click the Eraser button on the Tables and Borders toolbar and then drag across the line. To continue drawing the table, click the Draw Table button.)
   e. Select all cells in the table and then click the Center Vertically button on the Tables and Borders toolbar.
   f. With all cells in the table still selected, click the Distribute Rows Evenly button on the Tables and Borders toolbar.

g. Select all cells in the second and third columns and then click the Center button on the Formatting toolbar. (This button is located on the Formatting toolbar—not the Tables and Borders toolbar.)
h. Click in the first cell.
i. Key the text in the cells as shown in figure 22.24. (If text wraps in a cell, widen the column.)

2. Turn off the display of the Tables and Borders toolbar by clicking the Tables and Borders button on the Standard toolbar.
3. Save the document and name it Ch 22, Ex 17.
4. Print and then close Ch 22, Ex 17.

22.24

Exercise 17

PROJECTED DEPARTMENT EXPENSES

Department	1998	1999
Support Services	$10,200	$11,355
Human Resources	$11,545	$12,800
Finance and Resource Management	$15,355	$16,433
Administration	$21,435	$24,700
Manufacturing and Production	$75,455	$81,600

exercise 18

Customizing a Table with the Tables and Borders Toolbar

1. Open Ch 22, Ex 17.
2. Save the document with Save As and name it Ch 22, Ex 18.
3. Customize the table by completing the following steps:
   a. Turn on the display of the Tables and Borders toolbar by

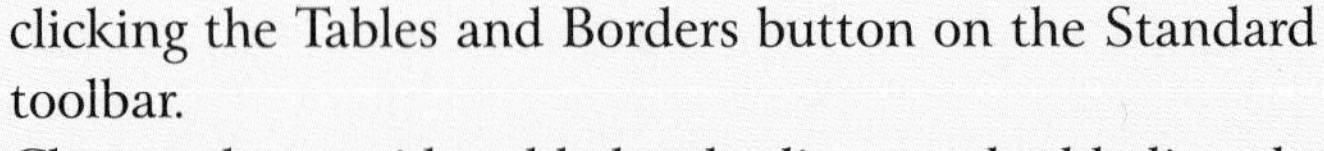

clicking the Tables and Borders button on the Standard toolbar.

b. Change the outside table border lines to double lines by completing the following steps:
   1) Click the down-pointing triangle at the right side of the Line Style button.

Line Style

   2) At the drop-down list that displays, click the first double-line style.
   3) Position the pencil pointer in the upper left corner of the table, hold down the left mouse button, drag the pencil down the left side of the table until it reaches the bottom, and then release the mouse button. (This changes the single line to a double line.)
   4) Change the bottom border of the table to a double line by dragging the pencil across the bottom border. (Be sure to hold down the left mouse button as you drag.)
   5) Change the right border of the table to a double line by dragging the pencil along the right border.
   6) Change the top border of the table to a double line by dragging the pencil along the top border.

c. Click the Draw Table button to deselect it.

d. Add gray shading to cells by completing the following steps:
   1) Select cells A2 through C6.
   2) Click the down-pointing triangle at the right side of the Shading Color button on the Tables and Borders toolbar.
   3) At the palette of color choices that displays, click the Gray-25% color (this is the third option from the left in the second row).

e. Add light turquoise shading to cells by completing the following steps:
   1) Select cells A1, B1, and C1.
   2) Click the down-pointing arrow at the right side of the Shading Color button on the Tables and Borders toolbar.
   3) At the palette of color choices, click the light turquoise color (second color from the left in the sixth row).

f. Sort the text in cells A2 through A6 alphabetically in descending order by completing the following steps:
   1) Select cells A2 through A6.
   2) Click the Sort Descending button on the Tables and Borders toolbar.

Sort Descending

g. Redraw the lines that were changed when text in cells was sorted.

4. Save the document again with the same name (Ch 22, Ex 18).
5. Print and then close Ch 22, Ex 18.

Performing Calculations

Numbers in a table can be calculated. Numbers can be added, subtracted, multiplied, and divided. In addition, you can calculate averages, percentages, and minimum and maximum values. Calculations can be performed in a Word table; however, for complex calculations, use a Microsoft Excel worksheet.

To perform a calculation in a table, position the insertion point in the cell where you want the result of the calculation to display. This cell should be empty. By default, Word assumes that you want to calculate the sum of cells immediately above or to the left of the cell where the insertion point is positioned. This default calculation can be changed.

As an example of how to calculate sums, you would complete the following steps to calculate the sum of cells in C2 through C5 and insert the result of the calculation in cell C6:

1. Position the insertion point in cell C6.
2. Click Table, then Formula.
3. At the Formula dialog box, the calculation *=SUM(ABOVE)* will display in the Formula text box. This is the desired formula to calculate the sum.
4. Click OK or press Enter.

Word adds the numbers in cells C2 through C5 and then inserts the result of this calculation in cell C6. To perform other types of calculations such as subtraction, multiplication, and division, the formula displayed in the Formula text box at the Formula dialog box must be changed. You can use an arithmetic sign to write a formula. For example, the formula A2-A3 (A2 minus A3) can be inserted in cell A4, which tells Word to insert the difference of A2 and A3 in cell A4. If changes are made to the numbers in cells A2 and A3, the value in A4 can be recalculated.

Four basic operators can be used when writing formulas: the plus sign (+) for addition, the minus sign (hyphen) for subtraction, the asterisk (*) for multiplication, and the forward slash (/) for division. If there are two or more operators in a calculation, Word calculates from left to right. If you want to change the order of calculation, use parentheses around the part of the calculation to be performed first.

In the default formula, the SUM part of the formula is called a function. Word provides other functions you can use to write a formula. These functions are available with the Paste function option at the Formula dialog box. For example, you can use the AVERAGE function to average numbers in cells. Examples of how formulas can be written are shown in figure 22.25.

The numbering format can be specified at the Formula dialog box. For example, if you are calculating money amounts, you can specify that the calculated numbers display with two numbers following the decimal point. To specify the numbering format, display the Formula dialog box, and then click the down-pointing triangle to the right of the Number format option. Click the desired formatting at the drop-down list that displays.

22.25 *Example Formulas*

Cell E4 is the total price of items.
Cell B4 contains the quantity of items, and cell D4 contains the unit price. The formula for cell E4 is **=B4*D4**. (This formula multiplies the quantity of items in cell B4 by the unit price in cell D4.)

Cell D3 is the percentage of increase of sales from the previous year.
Cell B3 contains the amount of sales for the previous year, and cell C3 contains the amount of sales for the current year. The formula for cell D3 is **=C3-B3/C3*100**. (This formula subtracts the amount of sales last year from the amount of sales this year. The remaining amount is divided by the amount of sales this year and then multiplied by 100 to display the product as a percentage.)

Cell E1 is the average of test scores.
Cells A1 through D1 contain test scores. The formula to calculate the average score is **=(A1+B1+C1+D1)/4**. (This formula adds the scores from cells A1 through D1 and then divides that sum by 4.) You can also enter the formula as = **AVERAGE(LEFT)**. The AVERAGE function tells Word to average all entries left of cell E1.

19

Calculating Net Profit

1. At a clear document screen, create the document shown in figure 22.26 by completing the following steps:
   a. Press the Enter key once.
   b. Create a table with 4 columns and 6 rows (6 x 4).
   c. Select the first row and then merge the cells.
   d. Position the insertion point in the first row, press the Enter key once, change the alignment to center, turn on bold, key **COLEMAN CORPORATION**, and then press Enter once.
   e. Select the second row in the table and then click the Bold and the Center buttons on the Formatting toolbar.
   f. Select cells A3 through A6 and then change the alignment to center.
   g. Select cells B3 through D6 and then change the alignment to right.
   h. Key the text in the cells as shown in figure 22.26.

i. Add border lines and shading to the table as shown in figure 22.26.
j. Insert a formula in cell D3 by completing the following steps:
   1) Position the insertion point in cell D3 (the cell below *Net Profit*).
   2) Click Table, then Formula.
   3) At the Formula dialog box, delete the formula in the Formula text box.
   4) Key **=B3-C3** in the Formula text box.
   5) Click the down-pointing triangle at the right side of the Number format text box and then click the third option from the top of the drop-down list.
   6) Click OK or press Enter.
k. Insert the formula **=B4-C4** in cell D4 by completing steps similar to those in step 1j.
l. Insert the formula **=B5-C5** in cell D5 by completing steps similar to those in step 1j.
m. Insert the formula **=B6-C6** in cell D6 by completing steps similar to those in step 1j.

2. Save the document and name it Ch 22, Ex 19.
3. Print and then close Ch 22, Ex 19.

22.26

Exercise 19

COLEMAN CORPORATION			
Year	**Income**	**Expenses**	**Net Profit**
1995	$4,390,130.20	$3,104,530.45	
1996	4,560,439.86	3,239,478.10	
1997	4,687,390.33	3,669,092.20	
1998	5,001,058.75	3,945,230.68	

exercise 20

Averaging Test Scores

1. Open Table 01.
2. Save the document with Save As and name it Ch 22, Ex 20.
3. Insert a formula in cell F3 to average test scores by completing the following steps:
   a. Position the insertion point in cell F3 (the cell below *Ave.*).
   b. Click Table, then Formula.
   c. Delete the formula in the Formula text box *except* the equals sign.
   d. With the insertion point positioned immediately after the equals sign, click the down-pointing triangle to the right of the Paste function text box.
   e. At the drop-down list that displays, click *AVERAGE*.
   f. With the insertion point positioned between the left and right parentheses, key **left**.
   g. Click the down-pointing triangle to the right of the Number format text box and then click the fifth option from the top (0%) at the drop-down list.
   h. Click OK or press Enter.
4. Position the insertion point in cell F4 and then complete steps similar to those in step 3 to insert a formula to average test scores.
5. Position the insertion point in cell F5 and then complete steps similar to those in step 3 to insert a formula to average test scores.
6. Position the insertion point in cell F6 and then complete steps similar to those in step 3 to insert a formula to average test scores.
7. Position the insertion point in cell F7 and then complete steps similar to those in step 3 to insert a formula to average test scores.
8. Position the insertion point in cell F8 and then complete steps similar to those in step 3 to insert a formula to average test scores.
9. Save the document again with the same name (Ch 22, Ex 20).
10. Print and then close Ch 22, Ex 20.

If changes are made to numbers in cells that are part of a formula, select the result of the calculation, and then press the F9 function key. This recalculates the formula and inserts the new result of the calculation in the cell. You can also recalculate by completing the following steps:

1. Select the number in the cell containing the formula.
2. Click Table, then Formula.
3. At the Formula dialog box, click OK or press Enter.

exercise 21

Recalculating Test Scores

1. Open Ch 22, Ex 20.
2. Save the document with Save As and name it Ch 22, Ex 21.
3. Make the following changes to the table:
   a. Change the number in cell C3 from 81 to 85.
   b. Change the number in cell D5 from 90 to 96.
   c. Change the number in cell D8 from 87 to 95.
   d. Position the I-beam pointer in cell F3, click the left mouse button (this inserts a gray background around the numbers in the cell), and then press F9. (Pressing F9 recalculates the average.)
   e. Click the number in cell F5 and then press F9.
   f. Click the number in cell F8 and then press F9.
4. Save the document again with the same name (Ch 22, Ex 21).
5. Print and then close Ch 22, Ex 21.

Converting Text to/from a Table

Text in a document separated by paragraph marks, commas, or tabs can be converted to a table. Text in a table can also be converted to ordinary text.

Converting Text to a Table

To convert text to a table, the text must be separated by paragraph marks, commas, or tabs. To convert text to a table, you would select the text, and then click the Insert Table button on the Standard toolbar.

If you want control over how the text is converted to a table, convert the text with the Convert Text to Table option from the Table drop-down menu. To do this, you would select the text to be converted, and then click Table, then Convert Text to Table. At the Convert Text to Table dialog box, shown in figure 22.27, make any necessary changes, and then click OK or press Enter.

Convert Text to Table Dialog Box

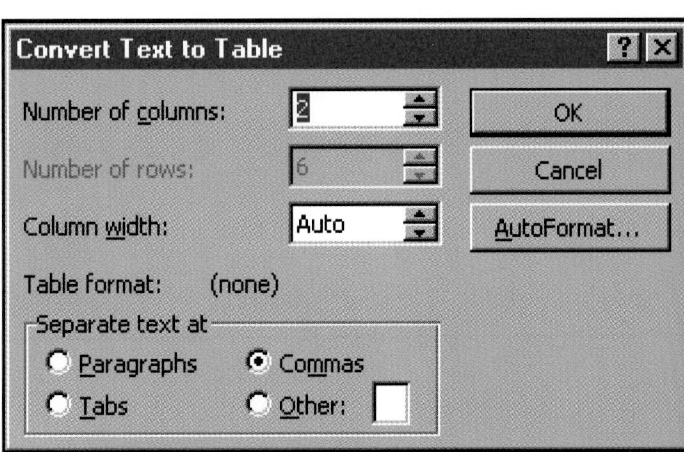

At the Convert Text to Table dialog box, you can specify the number of columns desired in the table. Word will automatically insert a number in the Number of columns text box based on the text and separators in the document. By default, Word will automatically determine column widths. To specify column widths, click Column width, and then enter the desired column measurement.

Word will determine what is used to separate text into columns. This is specified in the Separate text at section of the Convert Text to Table dialog box. Choose a different option in this section if you want to change what Word uses to separate text into columns.

exercise 22

Converting Text to a Table

1. At a clear document screen, create the document shown in figure 22.28 by completing the following steps:
   a. Key **KENTWOOD SCHOOL DISTRICT** centered and bolded.
   b. Press the Enter key twice and then change the alignment back to left.
   c. Key the text shown in figure 22.28 exactly as shown (do not space after the comma).
   d. Convert the text to a table by completing the following steps:
      1) Select the text (except the title and the blank line below the title).
      2) Click Table, then Convert Text to Table.
      3) At the Convert Text to Table dialog box, make sure Commas is selected in the Separate text at section of the dialog box, and then click OK or press Enter.
   e. With the insertion point positioned in any cell within the table, automatically format the table with the *Colorful 1* option at the Table AutoFormat dialog box.
   f. Center the table horizontally.
2. Save the document and name it Ch 22, Ex 22.
3. Print and then close Ch 22, Ex 22.

22.28

Exercise 22

KENTWOOD SCHOOL DISTRICT

Title,Name
Superintendent,Linda Shing
Assistant Superintendent,Rodney Valenzuela
Curriculum Specialist,Sarah Brennan
Support Specialist,Gabriel Goodrow
Information Specialist,Janet Griffin-Leon

Converting a Table to Text

Text in a table can be converted to ordinary text. You can specify whether text is to be separated by paragraph marks, tabs, commas, or other symbols. To convert text in a table to ordinary text, you would select the table, click Table, then Convert Table to Text. At the Convert Table to Text dialog box, shown in figure 22.29, specify whether you want text to be separated by paragraph marks, tabs, commas, or other symbol, and then click OK or press Enter.

22.29

Convert Table to Text Dialog Box

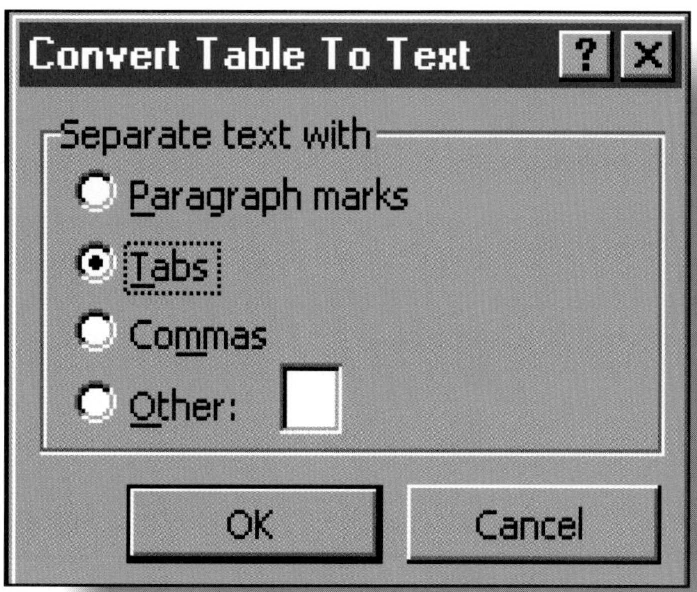

exercise 23

Converting a Table to Text

1. Open Ch 22, Ex 01.
2. Save the document with Save As and name it Ch 22, Ex 23.
3. Convert the table to text by completing the following steps:
   a. Select the table.
   b. Click Table, then Convert Table to Text.
   c. At the Convert Table to Text dialog box, make sure Tabs is selected, and then click OK or press Enter.
   d. Deselect the text.
4. Save the document again with the same name (Ch 22, Ex 23).
5. Print and then close Ch 22, Ex 23.

chapter summary

- Word's Tables feature can be used to create columns and rows of information. A cell is the intersection between a row and a column.
- A table can contain text, characters, numbers, data, graphics, or formulas. It can be extensively formatted and can include calculations.
- A table can be created with the Insert Table button on the Standard toolbar or by clicking the Table option from the Menu bar.
- Columns in a table are lettered from left to right beginning with A. Rows are numbered from top to bottom beginning with 1.
- The lines that form the cells of the table are called gridlines.
- With the insertion point positioned in a cell, key or edit text as you would normal text.
- To move the insertion point to different cells within the table using the mouse, position the I-beam pointer in the desired cell, and then click the left mouse button.
- To move the insertion point to different cells within the table using the keyboard, refer to the information shown in figure 22.5 in this chapter.
- Position the arrow pointer on the cell selection bar, the row selection bar, or the top gridline of a column to select a cell, row, or column. Or, position the I-beam pointer and use the mouse to select a portion of the table.
- To use the keyboard to select specific cells within a table, refer to the information shown in figure 22.10 in this chapter.
- A row or column of cells or all cells in a table can be selected with options from the Table drop-down menu.

- All text in cells within a table can be deleted, leaving the table gridlines, or all text and the gridlines can be deleted.
- Borders and shading can be added to cells, rows and columns can be inserted or deleted, cells can be split or merged, and the alignment of the table can be changed.
- Column width can be changed using the mouse on the Ruler, in a table, or at the Cell Height and Width dialog box.
- After a table has been created, various methods can be used to add rows and/or columns.
- Specific cells in a table or rows or columns in a table can be deleted.
- Word has provided predesigned table formats in the Table AutoFormat dialog box that can quickly format your table.
- Use buttons on the Tables and Borders toolbar to create and customize a table. Click the Tables and Borders button on the Standard toolbar to turn on the display of the Tables and Borders toolbar.
- Numbers in a table can be calculated by inserting a formula in a cell at the Formula dialog box.
- Text in a document separated by paragraph marks, commas, or tabs can be converted to a table using the Insert Table button on the Standard toolbar or at the Convert Text to Table dialog box. Text in a table can be converted to ordinary text at the Convert Table to Text dialog box.

commands review

	Mouse /Keyboard
Create table with Standard toolbar	With arrow pointer on [Insert Table button] on Standard toolbar, hold down left mouse button, move arrow pointer down and right until desired table size displays, then release button
Display Insert Table dialog box	Table, Insert Table
Move insertion point to next cell	TAB
Move insertion point to previous cell	SHIFT + TAB
Insert tab within a cell	CTRL + TAB
Insert page break within a table	CTRL + ENTER
Select a row, column, or all cells with Table drop-down menu	Position insertion point, click Table, then Select Row (or Select Column or Select Table)
Delete text only from table	Select table, press Delete
Delete text and gridlines	Select table, then click Table, Delete Rows
Display Cell Height and Width dialog box	Table, Cell Height and Width

Delete cells, rows, or columns	Select cell(s), click Table, Delete Cells, then Delete Entire Row or Delete Entire Column
Display Table AutoFormat dialog box	With insertion point in a cell, click Table, Table AutoFormat
Turn on/off display of Tables and Borders toolbar	Click [button] on Standard toolbar
Display Formula dialog box	Table, Formula
Display Convert Text to Table dialog box	Table, Convert Text to Table
Display Convert Table to Text dialog box	Table, Convert Table to Text

check your understanding

Completion: In the space provided at the right, indicate the correct term, command, or number.

1. Use this button to create a table the quickest way possible. ____________
2. This is another name for the lines that form the cells of the table. ____________
3. The end-of-row marker displays only when this button is active on the Standard toolbar. ____________
4. The move table column markers display here. ____________
5. Use this keyboard command to move the insertion point to the previous cell. ____________
6. Use this keyboard command to insert a tab within a cell. ____________
7. This is the name given to the space just to the left of the left edge of a table. ____________
8. To select all cells within a table using the mouse, position the I-beam pointer in any cell, click Table, and then click this at the drop-down menu. ____________
9. Use this keyboard command to select all cells within a table. ____________
10. To add shading to a cell or selected cells, display this dialog box. ____________
11. Change the width of columns using the mouse, the Cell Height and Width dialog box, or this. ____________
12. Text in cells aligns at this side of the cell by default. ____________

13. One method for inserting rows in a table is to position the I-beam pointer inside the table, click the right mouse button, and then click this. ____________

14. A column or group of columns that is added to a table will be inserted on this side of the selected column(s). ____________

15. Choose this option at the Delete Cells dialog box if you want cells moved up after selected cells are deleted. ____________

16. To merge cells A1 and B1, select A1 and B1, and then click this at the Table drop-down menu. ____________

17. To divide one cell into two columns, click this at the Table drop-down menu. ____________

18. Choose predesigned table formats at this dialog box. ____________

19. Click this button on the Tables and Borders toolbar to add, modify, or remove fill color from selected objects. ____________

20. Click this button on the Tables and Borders toolbar to change the border line style. ____________

21. This is the operator for multiplication that is used when writing formulas in a table. ____________

22. This is the formula to add cells D2, D3, and D4, and then divide the total by 5. ____________

23. This is the formula to multiply A1 by B1. ____________

24. This calculation will display in the Formula text box in the Formula dialog box by default. ____________

skill assessments

Note: Before completing the skill assessments, display the Open dialog box, and then select and delete documents created in chapter 20 that begin Ch 20. You may want to check with your instructor before deleting these documents.

Assessment 1

1. At a clear document screen, create the table shown in figure 22.30. Bold and center the text as shown.
2. Save the document and name it Ch 22, SA 01.
3. Print and then close Ch 22, SA 01.

Figure 22.30 • Assessment 1

Name	Title	Department
Stanley McPherson	Vice President	Administrative Services
Chad Lowell	Director	Resource Management
Katherine Lewandowski	Director	Marketing and Sales
Anna Keibler	Assistant Director	Marketing and Sales
Kim Millerton	Administrative Assistant	Resource Management

Assessment 2

1. At a clear document screen, create the memo shown in figure 22.31 by completing the following steps:
   a. Key the headings and the first paragraph of the memo.
   b. With the insertion point a double space below the memo, create a table with 3 columns and 5 rows (5 x 3).
   c. Change the width of the first column to 2.25 inches, the width of the middle column to 1.5 inches, and the width of the third column to 2.25 inches.
   d. Select the cells in the second column and then change the alignment to center.
   e. Select the cells in the third column and then change the alignment to right.
   f. Key the text in the cells as shown in figure 22.31.
   g. After completing the table, position the insertion point a double space below the table, and then key the rest of the memo.
2. Save the document and name it Ch 22, SA 02.
3. Print and then close Ch 22, SA 02.

Figure 22.31 • Assessment 2

DATE: September 21, 1999

TO: Shawn O'Connell

FROM: David Olmsted

SUBJECT: SEPTEMBER NEWSLETTER

The following information needs to be included in the October newsletter under the heading, *Newsletter Resources.*

Superintendent	Linda Shing	Administrative Services
Assistant Superintendent	Rodney Valenzuela	Administrative Services
Curriculum Specialist	Sarah Brennan	District Headquarters
Newsletter Editor	David Olmsted	Shoreline Junior High School
Newsletter Assistant Editor	Christine Long	Oak Ridge Elementary School

Please include how employees can submit articles or items of interest to be published in the newsletter.

XX:Ch 22, SA 02

Assessment 3

1. At a clear document screen, create the table shown in figure 22.32 with the following specifications:
   a. Press the Enter key once and then create a table with 3 columns and 10 rows (10 x 3).
   b. Change the width of the first column to 2 inches, the width of the second column to 3 inches, and the width of the third column to 1 inch.
   c. Merge the cells in the first row (cells A1, B1 and C1).
   d. Key the text in the cells as indicated. Bold and center text as shown. Before keying the text in the first cell, press the Enter key once. After keying the text in the cell centered and bolded, press the Enter key once.
   e. Add border lines and shading to the table as shown in figure 22.32.
2. Save the document and name it Ch 22, SA 03.
3. Print and then close Ch 22, SA 03.

Figure 22.32 • Assessment 3

KENTWOOD SCHOOL DISTRICT		
Name	**School**	**Phone**
Devon Holleman	Kentwood High School	555-4555
Tina Pascual-Anderson	Mountain View Junior High School	555-1322
Mitchell Langford	Shoreline Junior High School	555-8770
Blaine Dowler	Emerald Heights Elementary School	555-4435
Tara Sandifer	Oak Ridge Elementary School	555-6644
Keith Gunter	Madison Creek Elementary School	555-5360
Corey Merritt	Bell Valley Elementary School	555-2287
Alfredo Marcoe	South Bend Elementary School	555-5667

Assessment 4

1. At a clear document screen, create the table shown in figure 22.33 with the following specifications:
   a. Create a table with 4 columns and 11 rows (11 x 4).
   b. With the insertion point positioned in the table, drag the move table column marker on the Ruler between the 1-inch mark and the 2-inch mark to the 4-inch mark on the Ruler.
   c. Merge the cells in the first row.
   d. Merge the cells in the second row.
   e. Select the first two rows in the table and then change the alignment to center.
   f. Select cells B3 through D11 and then change the alignment to center.
   g. Select the first two rows in the table and then change the font to 14-point Times New Roman bold.
   h. Select the cells in third row and then change the font to 12-point Times New Roman bold.
   i. Select the remaining cells in the table and then change the font to 10-point Times New Roman and insert a left tab stop at the 0.25-inch mark on the Ruler.
   j. Key the text in the cells as indicated in the figure 22.33. Press Ctrl + Tab after the numbers to indent the insertion point.
   k. Add border lines as indicated in figure 22.33.
2. Save the document and name it Ch 22, SA 04.
3. Print and then close Ch 22, SA 04.

Figure 22.33 • Assessment 4

KENTWOOD SCHOOL DISTRICT			
Technology Study Question #6			
How will technology change your work environment?	**H.S.**	**J.H.S.**	**E.S.**
1. Improved access to centralized database.	1	2	2
2. Telephone lines for voice and data use in classroom.	3	2	1
3. Increased student access to information.	4	3	2
4. Better communication among peers.	4	4	3
5. Develop and implement a technology classroom model.	5	2	4
6. Technology to meet individual learning styles.	4	4	3
7. Elimination of textbook as primary delivery system.	5	2	3
8. Developing buildings as community learning/resource centers.	6	4	5

Assessment 5

1. At a clear document screen, create the document shown in figure 22.34 by completing the following steps:
   a. Key the headings and the first paragraph of the memo shown in figure 22.34.
   b. With the insertion point a double space below the first paragraph of the memo, create a table with 4 columns and 5 rows.
   c. Select the cells in the first row and then change the alignment to center.
   d. Select cells B2 through D5 and then change the alignment to right.
   e. Key the text in the cells as indicated. (Do not apply any special formatting to the text. This will be done with Table AutoFormat.)
   f. Position the insertion point in any cell in the table and then apply the *List 8* formatting at the Table AutoFormat dialog box.
   g. Center the table horizontally.
   h. Position the insertion point in cell D2 and then insert the formula **=C2-B2** and change the numbering format to two numbers after the decimal.
   i. Position the insertion point in cell D3 and then insert the formula **=C3-B3** and change the numbering format to two numbers after the decimal.
   j. Position the insertion point in cell D4 and then insert the formula **=C4-B4** and change the numbering format to two numbers after the decimal.
   k. Position the insertion point in cell D5 and then insert the formula **=C5-B5** and change the numbering format to two numbers after the decimal.
2. After completing the table, move the insertion point a double space below the table and then key the rest of the memo.
3. Save the document and name it Ch 22, SA 05.
4. Print and then close Ch 22, SA 05.

Figure 22.34 • Assessment 5

DATE: June 2, 1999

TO: Corey Merritt, Principal

FROM: Ted Klein, PTO Treasurer

SUBJECT: FUND-RAISING EVENTS FOR 1998-99

During the 1998-1999 school year, four major fund-raising events were sponsored by the Bell Valley Elementary School PTO. These fund-raising events were very successful due to the time donated by parents, teachers, staff, and children of Bell Valley Elementary School. The following table shows the costs and profits for each event.

Event	Costs	Revenue	Net Profit
Walk-a-thon	$2,130.50	$7,340.35	
Fall Carnival	1,459.18	2,004.50	
T-Shirt Sales	2,340.00	3,120.80	
Rummage Sale	250.30	695.00	

As you can see from the table, the walk-a-thon generated the most profit. This was the fourth year we have sponsored a walk-a-thon and each year the profits nearly double. The rummage sale raised the least amount of money and seemed to require the most time from PTO members and volunteers. At our next PTO meeting, we will discuss whether or not to sponsor a rummage sale next year.

XX:Ch 22, SA 05

Assessment 6

1. At a clear document screen, create the table shown in figure 22.35 by completing the following steps:
   a. Press the Enter key and then create a table with 4 columns and 8 rows (8 x 4).
   b. Drag the move table column marker between the 1-inch mark and the 2-inch mark to the 2-inch mark on the Ruler.
   c. Merge the cells in the first row.
   d. Select the first two rows, then change the alignment to center and change the font to 14-point Century Gothic bold.
   e. Select cells B3 through D8 and then change the alignment to right.
   f. Select cells A3 through D8 and then change the font to 12-point Century Gothic.
   g. Key the text in the cells as shown in figure 22.35. (Press Ctrl + Tab before keying the states in the first column.)
   h. Insert the formula **=C3-B3** in cell D3 and change the number format to two decimals. Insert the appropriate formula in cells D4, D5, D6, D7, and D8 to subtract Last Year numbers from This Year numbers. (Be sure to change the number format to two decimals.)
   i. Insert border lines and shading as shown in figure 22.35.
2. Save the document and name it Ch 22, SA 06.
3. Print and then close Ch 22, SA 06.

Figure 22.35 • Assessment 6

MARIN CORPORATION Sales in Selected States			
State	**Last Year**	**This Year**	**Difference**
Washington	$1,304,293.90	$1,540,394.23	
Oregon	1,450,340.24	1,550,345.98	
Idaho	990,435.33	998,320.45	
California	3,340,288.45	3,445,230.50	
Nevada	1,032,483.78	1,224,889.34	
Texas	2,553,294.50	2,654,340.08	

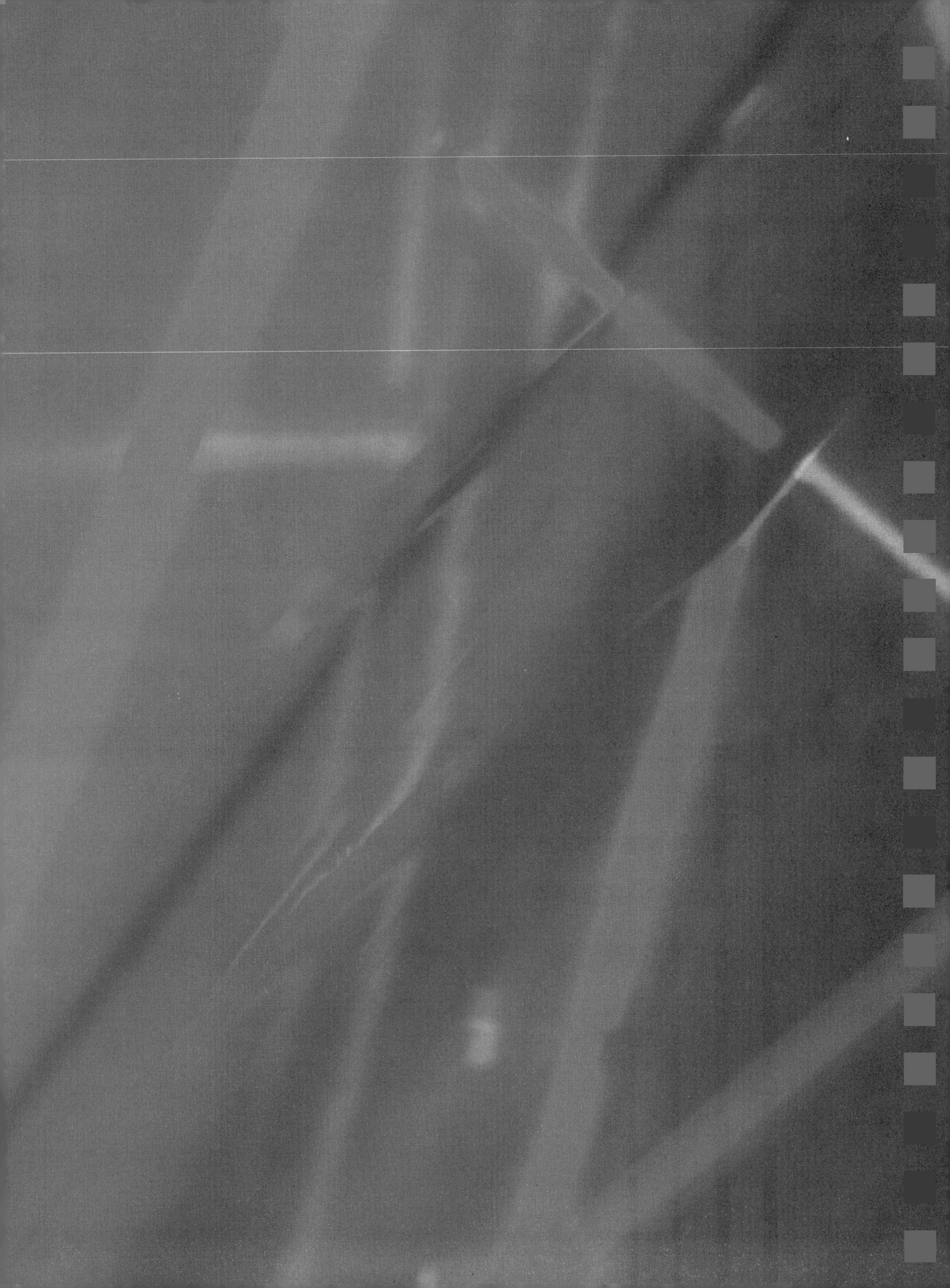

chapter TWENTY-THREE

Creating Charts in Word

PERFORMANCE OBJECTIVES

Upon successful completion of chapter 23, you will be able to:

- **Create a chart with data in a Word table.**
- **Size and move a chart.**
- **Change the type of chart and choose a custom chart type.**
- **Change data in a chart.**
- **Add, delete, and customize chart elements.**

In chapter 22 you learned to create data in tables. While this does an adequate job of representing data, a chart can be created from data in a table to provide a more visual presentation of the data. A chart is sometimes referred to as a *graph* and is a picture of numeric data. A chart can be created with data in a table or data in a spreadsheet created in other programs such as Microsoft Excel. Charts are created with the Microsoft Graph 97 Chart application. With Microsoft Graph, you can create a variety of charts including bar and column charts, pie charts, area charts, and much more.

Creating a Chart

A chart can be created in Word by entering data in a datasheet provided by Microsoft Graph, or a chart can be created from data in a table or worksheet. In this chapter, you will learn how to create a chart using data from a table. To create a chart in Word using data in a table, you would select the table, then click Insert, then Object. This displays the Object dialog box with the Create New tab selected, as shown in figure 23.1. At this dialog box, double-click *Microsoft Graph 97 Chart* in the Object type list box. (You may need to scroll down the list to make *Microsoft Graph 97 Chart* visible.) Microsoft Graph takes the data from the table and creates a chart. For example, suppose you wanted to chart the data shown in the table in figure 23.2. To do this with Microsoft Graph, you would complete the following steps:

1. Select the entire table.
2. Click Insert, then Object.
3. At the Object dialog box with the Create New tab selected, double-click *Microsoft Graph 97 Chart* in the Object type list box.
4. A datasheet is inserted in the document above the table and the chart created by Microsoft Graph is inserted below the table as shown in figure 23.3. Click outside the chart to close Graph and remove the datasheet.

figure 23.1 ***Object Dialog Box***

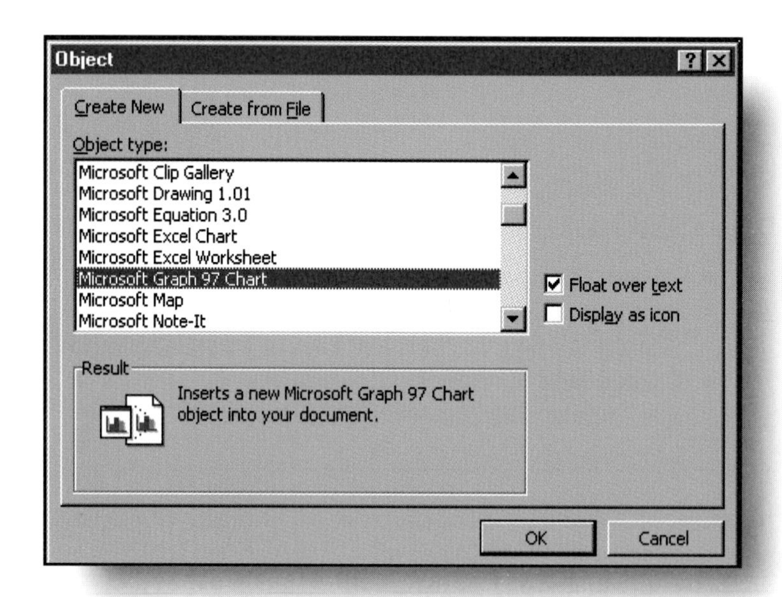

figure 23.2 ***Table***

Salesperson	April	May
A. Perez	20,405	19,340
J. White	28,966	29,485
L. Ching	41,309	25,340

figure 23.3 **Chart Based on Table**

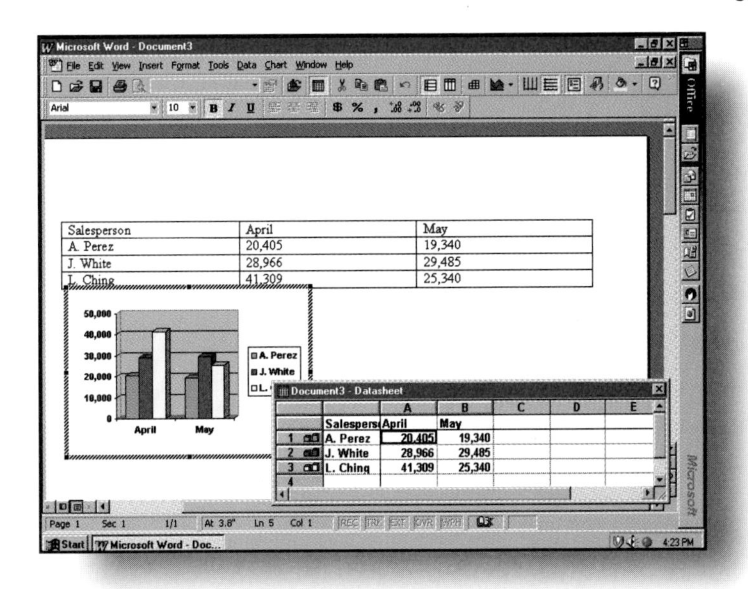

By default, Microsoft Graph charts the data in an orientation referred to as *data series in rows*. The text in the first row of the table is the category names. Text in the left column is the series names. Graph uses the series names as labels for the legend. For example, the names A. Perez, J. White, and L. Ching that display in the first column (except the first cell) are used for the legend. The legend is the box that labels the different colors used by each series of bars. The data in the first row, April and May (except the first cell), is used for the x-axis. The x-axis is the horizontal axis that runs along the bottom of the chart.

In a chart, such as in figure 23.3, the left side of the chart displays the values and is referred to as the z-axis. The z-axis is generally marked like a ruler and is broken into units by marks called *ticks*. Next to each tick mark is the amount of the value at that particular point on the axis. The values in the chart in figure 23.3 are broken into tick marks by ten thousands beginning with zero and continuing to 50,000. The values for the z-axis will vary depending on the data in the table.

exercise 1

Creating a Chart with Data in a Table

1. Open Table 02.
2. Save the document with Save As and name it Ch 23, Ex 01.
3. Create a chart by completing the following steps:
   a. Position the insertion point in any cell in the table and then click Table, then Select Table.

   b. Click Insert, then Object.
   c. At the Object dialog box with the Create New tab selected, double-click *Microsoft Graph 97 Chart* in the Object type list box.
   d. When the datasheet and chart display, click outside the chart and the datasheet. (This closes Graph and removes the datasheet.)
4. Delete the table in the document by completing the following steps:
   a. Select the entire table (be sure to select the table and *not* the chart).
   b. With the table selected, click Table, then Delete Rows.
5. Save the document again with the same name (Ch 23, Ex 01).
6. Print and then close Ch 23, Ex 01.

Deleting a Chart

A chart created in Word can be deleted by clicking once in the chart to select it and then pressing the Delete key.

Moving and Sizing a Chart

The size of a chart can be increased or decreased. To change the size, click in the chart to select the chart. When the chart is selected, white sizing handles display around the chart. Change the size of the chart by dragging a sizing handle that displays around the chart.

To move a chart, click the chart to select it. With the chart selected, move the arrow pointer inside the chart (displays with a four-headed arrow attached), hold down the left mouse button, drag the chart to the desired location, then release the mouse button.

exercise 2

Sizing and Moving a Chart

1. Open Ch 23, Ex 01.
2. Save the document with Save As and name it Ch 23, Ex 02.
3. Size and move the chart by completing the following steps:
   a. Change the Zoom to Whole Page. To do this, click the down-pointing triangle at the right of the Zoom button on the Standard toolbar, then click *Whole Page* at the drop-down menu.
   b. Click in the chart to select it (white sizing handles display around the chart).
   c. Drag the middle sizing handle at the right side of the chart to the right approximately 3 inches (using the measurements displayed toward the top of the screen on the horizontal ruler).

d. Drag the middle sizing handle at the bottom of the chart down approximately 2 inches (using the measurements displayed at the left side of the screen on the vertical ruler).
e. With the chart still selected, position the arrow pointer (displays with a four-headed arrow attached) inside the chart, hold down the left mouse button, drag the outline of the chart to the middle of the page, then release the mouse button.
f. Click outside the chart to deselect it.
g. Change the Zoom back to 100%. To do this, click the down-pointing triangle at the right of the Zoom button, then click *100%* at the drop-down menu.

4. Save the document again with the same name (Ch 23, Ex 02).
5. Print and then close Ch 23, Ex 02.

Changing the Chart Type

In Graph, fourteen basic chart types are available along with built-in autoformats that can be applied to save time to get the desired look for the chart. Figure 23.4 shows an illustration and explanation of the fourteen chart types.

figure 23.4 *Types of Charts*

Type	Description
Area	An Area chart emphasizes the magnitude of change, rather than time and the rate of change. It also shows the relationship of parts to a whole by displaying the sum of the plotted values.
Bar	A Bar chart shows individual figures at a specific time, or shows variations between components but not in relationship to the whole.
Bubble	A Bubble chart compares sets of three values in a manner similar to a scatter chart with the third value displayed as the size of the bubble marker.
Column	A Column chart compares separate (noncontinuous) items as they vary over time.
Cone	A Cone chart displays columns with a conical shape.
Cylinder	A Cylinder chart displays columns with a cylindrical shape.
Doughnut	A Doughnut chart shows the relationship of parts to the whole.
Line	A Line chart shows trends and change over time at even intervals. It emphasizes the rate of change over time rather than the magnitude of change.

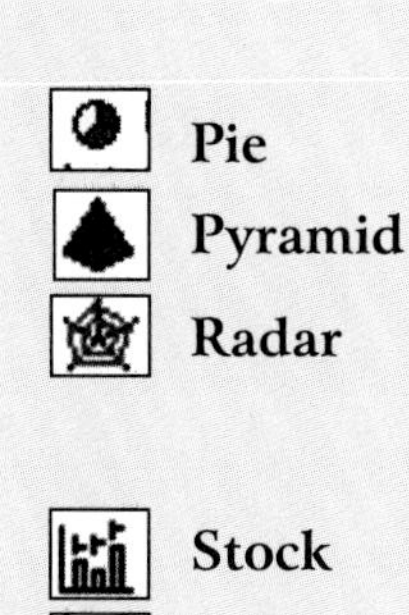

Pie	A Pie chart shows proportions and relationships of parts to the whole.
Pyramid	A Pyramid chart displays columns with a pyramid shape.
Radar	A Radar chart emphasizes differences and amounts of change over time and variations and trends. Each category has its own value axis radiating from the center point. Lines connect all values in the same series.
Stock	A Stock chart shows four values for a stock—open, high, low, and close.
Surface	A Surface chart shows trends in values across two dimensions in a continuous curve.
XY (Scatter)	A Scatter chart either shows the relationships among numeric values in several data series or plots the interception points between x and y values. It shows uneven intervals of data and is commonly used in scientific data.

Chart Type

The default chart type created by Graph is a Column chart. This default chart type can be changed with the Chart Type button on the Graph Standard toolbar or at the Chart Type dialog box. (The chart must be displayed in Microsoft Graph 97 for the Graph Standard toolbar to display. To display Microsoft Graph 97 for an existing chart, double-click the chart.) To change the chart type with the Chart Type button, click the down-pointing triangle at the right side of the button, then, at the drop-down list that displays, click the desired chart type. The drop-down list that displays contains a visual representation of chart types. Click the chart that represents the desired chart type.

A chart type can also be selected at the Chart Type dialog box with the Standard Types tab selected, as shown in figure 23.5. To display this dialog box, click Chart, then Chart Type.

23.5 *Chart Type Dialog Box with Standard Types Tab Selected*

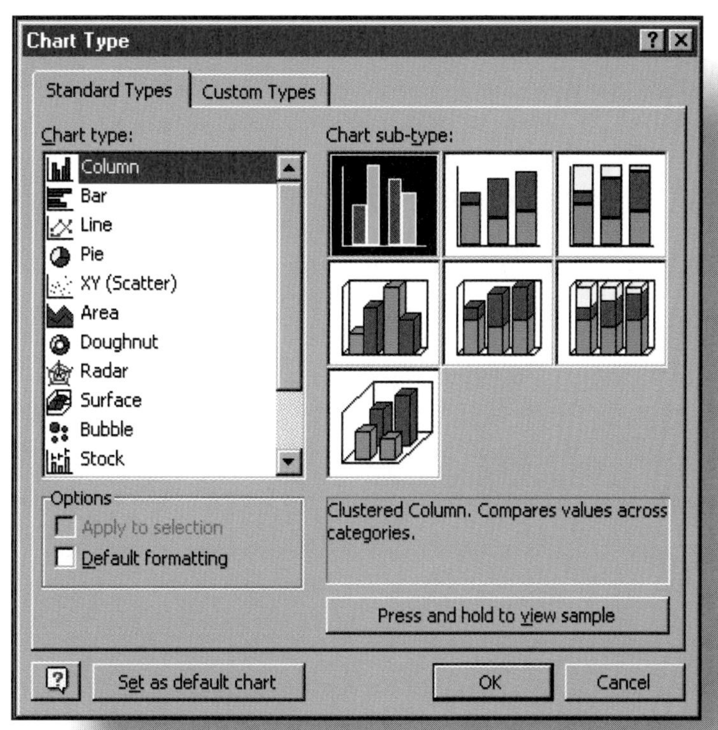

The various chart types display in the Chart type list box. A description of the selected chart type displays in the lower right corner of the dialog box (above the Press and hold to view sample button). Click a different chart type in the Chart type list box and the description changes. When you click a different chart type, the sample charts that display in the Chart sub-type list box change. Graph provides chart sub-types that contain different combinations of enhancements for each chart type. With these sub-types, you can choose a chart with different enhancements or formatting without having to customize the chart yourself.

If you would like to see a sample of a particular chart, click the desired chart type in the Chart type list box and then click the desired sub-type chart in the Chart sub-type list box. Position the arrow pointer on the Press and hold to view sample button and hold down the left mouse button. This causes a sample chart to display in the selected chart type and sub-type chosen.

The default chart type is a Column chart. This default can be changed by clicking the desired chart type in the Chart type list box and then clicking the Set as default chart button that displays toward the bottom of the dialog box.

exercise 3

Changing the Chart Type

1. Open Ch 23, Ex 01.
2. Save the document with Save As and name it Ch 23, Ex 03.
3. Change the chart type to Line by completing the following steps:
   a. Change the Zoom to Whole Page.
   b. Position the arrow pointer in the chart, then double-click the left mouse button.
   c. Close the datasheet. (To do this, click the View Datasheet button on the Graph Standard toolbar; or, click the Close button that displays in the upper right corner of the datasheet.)
   d. Click Chart, then Chart Type.
   e. At the Chart Type dialog box, click *Line* in the Chart type list box.
   f. Change the chart sub-type by clicking the first chart in the second row in the Chart sub-type list box. (Skip this step if the sub-type is already selected.)
   g. View a sample of how this sub-type chart will display by positioning the arrow pointer on the Press and hold to view sample button and then holding down the left mouse button. After viewing a sample of the selected Line chart, release the mouse button.
   h. Click OK to close the Chart Type dialog box.
   i. Click outside the chart to close Graph and deselect the chart.
   j. Click the chart once to select it.
   k. Increase the height and width of the chart approximately two inches.
   l. With the chart still selected, drag the chart to the middle of the page.
   m. Click outside the chart to deselect it.
4. Save the document again with the same name (Ch 23, Ex 03).
5. Print Ch 23, Ex 03.
6. With Ch 23, Ex 03 still open, complete the following steps:
   a. Double-click the chart.
   b. Click Chart, then Chart Type.
   c. At the Chart Type dialog box, click *Bar* in the Chart type list box.
   d. Click the first chart type in the second row in the Chart sub-type list box.
   e. View a sample of how this sub-type chart will display by positioning the arrow pointer on the Press and hold to view sample button and then holding down the left mouse button. After viewing a sample of the selected Bar chart, release the mouse button.

View Datasheet

f. Click OK to close the Chart Type dialog box.
g. Click outside the chart to close Graph and deselect the chart.
h. If the chart decreases in size, increase the height and width approximately two inches. (Skip this step if the chart remains the same size.)
i. Make sure the chart still displays in the middle of the page. If not, click the chart to select it, drag the chart to the middle of the page, then deselect the chart.
j. Change the Zoom to 100 percent.

7. Save the document again with the same name (Ch 23, Ex 03).
8. Print and then close Ch 23, Ex 03.

Choosing a Custom Chart Type

Graph offers a variety of preformatted custom charts. A custom chart can be chosen at the Chart Type dialog box with the Custom Types tab selected as shown in figure 23.6. To display this dialog box, double-click a chart to display the chart in Graph and then click Chart, then Chart Type.

23.6 *Chart Type Dialog Box with Custom Types Tab Selected*

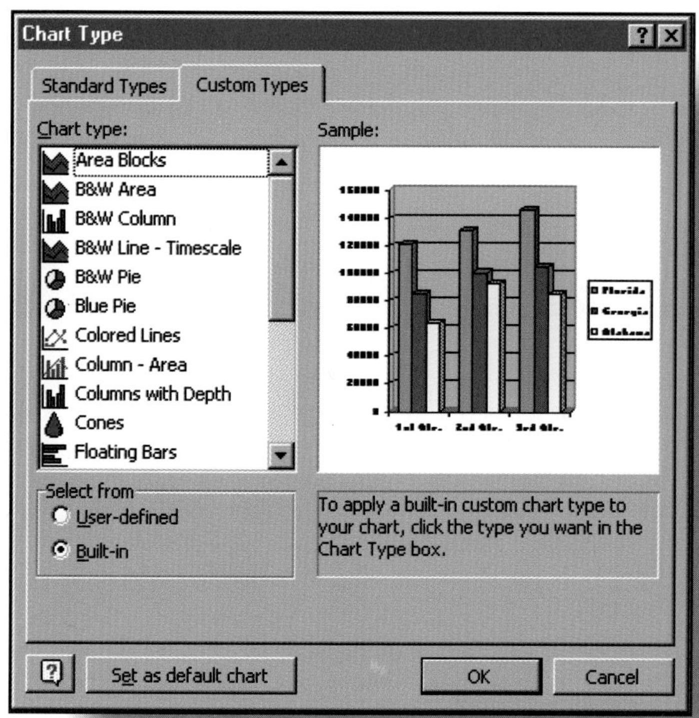

You can also choose a custom chart for an existing chart with a shortcut menu. To do this, position the arrow pointer in a white portion of the chart (inside the chart but outside any chart element), and then click the *right* mouse button. At the shortcut menu that displays, click *Chart Type*. At the Chart Type dialog box, click the Custom Types tab. Click the desired custom chart type in the Chart type list box.

exercise 4

Choosing a Custom Chart Type

1. Open Ch 23, Ex 01.
2. Save the document with Save As and name it Ch 23, Ex 04.
3. Choose a custom chart type by completing the following steps:
   a. Double-click the chart. (This displays the chart in Graph.)
   b. Close the datasheet.
   c. Click Chart, then Chart Type.
   d. At the Chart Type dialog box, click the Custom Types tab.
   e. At the Chart Type dialog box with the Custom Types tab selected, click *B&W Column* in the Chart type list box.
   f. Click OK to close the Chart Type dialog box.
4. Click outside the chart. (This closes Graph and deselects the chart.)
5. Size and move the chart by completing the following steps:
   a. Change the Zoom to Whole Page.
   b. Click once on the chart to select it. Increase the height and width of the chart (you determine the size) and then move the chart to the middle of the page.
   c. Click outside the chart to deselect it.
   d. Change the Zoom to 100 percent.
6. Save the document again with the same name (Ch 23, Ex 04).
7. Print and then close Ch 23, Ex 04.

Changing Data in Cells

Graph uses data in cells to create a chart. In a Word table, this data can be changed and the chart will reflect the changes. If you use a table to create a chart, the information from the table is automatically inserted in the chart datasheet. When a chart is created, the datasheet displays over the chart. Data in the datasheet can be changed in a manner similar to a table. You can move the insertion point to cells within the datasheet, select the cell contents, and then make changes. In a datasheet, the mouse pointer displays as a white plus sign. If the datasheet has been closed, you can display it by clicking the View Datasheet button on the Graph Standard toolbar.

To select a cell with the mouse, position the mouse pointer (white plus sign) in the desired cell, then click the left mouse button. To select multiple cells, drag the mouse pointer across the cells. To select a row or column, click the row or column header. To select all cells in the datasheet, click the gray rectangle at the top left corner where row and column headings intersect.

With a cell or cells selected, you can cut, copy, and/or paste data in cells using the Cut, Copy, or Paste buttons on the Graph Standard toolbar or options at the Edit drop-down menu.

exercise 5

Editing a Datasheet in a Chart

1. Open Ch 23, Ex 01.
2. Save the document with Save As and name it Ch 23, Ex 05.
3. Change the contents of certain cells in the datasheet by completing the following steps:
   a. Change the Zoom to Whole Page.
   b. Double-click the chart.
   c. Position the mouse pointer (displays as a white plus sign) in the datasheet in the cell containing the amount *84560*, click the left mouse button (this selects the cell contents), and then key **98650**.
   d. Position the insertion point in the cell containing the amount *100540*, click the left mouse button, then key **106540**.
   e. Position the insertion point in the cell containing the amount *104532*, click the left mouse button, then key **110245**.
4. Click outside the chart. (This removes the datasheet, updates the chart, and deselects the chart.)
5. Select the chart, increase the height and width of the chart (you determine the size), move the chart to the middle of the page, and then deselect the chart.
6. Change the Zoom to 100 percent.
7. Save the document again with the same name (Ch 23, Ex 05).
8. Print and then close Ch 23, Ex 05.

Changing the Data Series

When a chart is created, Graph uses the data in the first row (except the first cell) to create the x-axis (the information along the bottom of the chart) and uses the data in the first column (except the first cell) to create the legend. For example, in the chart in figure 23.3, the names (A. Perez, J. White, and L. Ching) were used for the legend and the months (April and May) were used for the x-axis (along the bottom of the chart).

When a chart is created, the By Row button on the Graph Standard toolbar is active by default. This indicates that Graph uses the data in the first row (except the first cell) to create the x-axis for the chart. This can be changed by clicking the By Column button on the Graph Standard toolbar. Click the By Column button and the data in the first column (except the first cell) is used to create the x-axis. The active button on the Graph Standard toolbar displays with a light gray background.

By Row

By Column

exercise 6

Changing the Data Series in a Chart

1. Open Ch 23, Ex 01.
2. Save the document with Save As and name it Ch 23, Ex 06.
3. Change the data series from rows to column by completing the following steps:
   a. Change the Zoom to Whole Page.
   b. Double-click the chart.
   c. Close the datasheet.
   d. Click the By Column button on the Graph Standard toolbar. (Notice that this changes the x-axis to the states—Florida, Georgia, Alabama.)
4. Click outside the chart.
5. Click the chart to select it, increase the height and width of the chart (you determine the size), move the chart to the middle of the page, and then deselect the chart.
6. Change the Zoom to 100 percent.
7. Save the document again with the same name (Ch 23, Ex 06).
8. Print and then close Ch 23, Ex 06.

Adding Chart Elements

When a chart is created by Graph, certain chart elements are automatically inserted, including a chart legend and labels for the axes. Other chart elements can be added, such as a chart title and data labels. These elements can be added to a chart with options at the Chart Options dialog box shown in figure 23.7. To display this dialog box, click Chart, then Chart Options. You can also display this dialog box by positioning the arrow pointer in a white portion of the chart (outside any chart elements), clicking the *right* mouse button, then clicking *Chart Options* at the shortcut menu that displays.

figure 23.7 ***Chart Options Dialog Box with Titles Tab Selected***

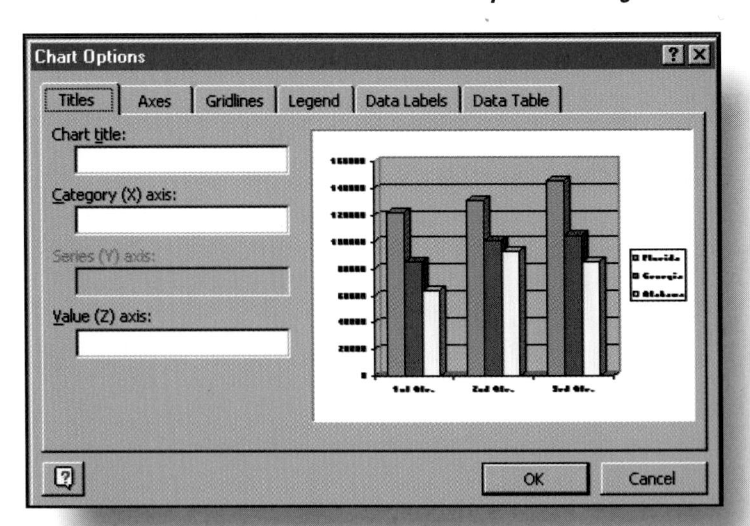

To add a chart element, click the desired tab at the Chart Options dialog box, and then choose the desired chart element. For example, to add a title to a chart, display the Chart Options dialog box, and then click the Titles tab. At the Chart Options dialog box with the Titles tab selected, click inside the Chart title text box, key the desired title, and then click the OK button to close the dialog box.

exercise 7

Creating a Pie Chart and Adding Chart Elements

1. Open Table 03.
2. Save the document with Save As and name it Ch 23, Ex 07.
3. Create a Pie chart with the data in the table by completing the following steps:
   a. Position the insertion point in any cell in the table, click Table, then Select Table.
   b. Click Insert, then Object.
   c. At the Object dialog box with the Create New tab selected, double-click *Microsoft Graph 97 Chart* in the Object type list box.
   d. When the datasheet and chart display, close the datasheet.
   e. Change to a Pie chart by completing the following steps:
      1) Click the down-pointing triangle at the right side of the Chart Type button.
      2) At the drop-down palette of chart type options, click the first pie chart option in the fifth row.
   f. Click the By Column button on the Graph Standard toolbar.
4. Add a title and data labels to the Pie chart and move the legend by completing the following steps:
   a. Click Chart, then Chart Options.
   b. At the Chart Options dialog box, click the Titles tab. (Skip this step if the Titles tab is already selected.)
   c. At the Chart Options dialog box with the Titles tab selected, click inside the Chart title text box, and then key **DEPARTMENT EXPENSES BY PERCENTAGE.**
   d. Click the Data Labels tab.
   e. At the Chart Options dialog box with the Data Labels tab selected, click Show percent.
   f. Click the Legend tab.
   g. At the Chart Options dialog box with the Legend tab selected, click Left.
   h. Click OK to close the Chart Options dialog box.
   i. Click outside the chart to close Graph.
5. Delete the table in the document by completing the following steps:

a. Select the entire table (be sure to select the table and not the chart).
b. With the table selected, click Table, then Delete Rows.

6. Size and move the chart by completing the following steps:
   a. Change the Zoom to Whole Page.
   b. Click in the chart to select it.
   c. Drag the middle sizing handle at the right side of the chart to the right approximately 3 inches (using the measurements displayed toward the top of the screen on the horizontal ruler).
   d. Drag the middle sizing handle at the bottom of the chart down approximately 2 inches (using the measurements displayed at the left side of the screen on the vertical ruler).
   e. With the chart selected, position the arrow pointer (displays with a four-headed arrow attached) inside the chart, hold down the left mouse button, drag the outline of the chart to the middle of the page, and then release the mouse button.
   f. Click outside the chart to deselect it.
   g. Change the Zoom back to 100 percent.
7. Save the document again with the same name (Ch 23, Ex 07).
8. Print and then close Ch 23, Ex 07.

Moving/Sizing Chart Elements

When additional elements are added to a chart, the chart can become quite full and elements may overlap. If elements in a chart overlap, an element can be selected and then moved. To select an element, position the arrow pointer on a portion of the element, and then click the left mouse button. This causes sizing handles to display around the element. Position the mouse pointer toward the edge of the selected element until it turns into an arrow pointer, hold down the left mouse button, drag the element to the desired location, and then release the mouse button. To change the size of an element, drag the sizing handles in the desired direction.

As you move the arrow pointer around a chart that is displayed in Graph, a yellow box will display when the arrow pointer is positioned on a chart or chart element. For example, if you position the arrow pointer on a chart legend, a yellow box displays next to the arrow pointer with the text *Legend*. This yellow box can help you position the arrow pointer correctly before selecting an element.

Deleting/Removing Chart Elements

Chart elements can be selected by clicking the desired element. Once an element is selected, it can be moved and it can also be deleted. To delete a selected element, press the Delete key. If you delete a chart element and then decide you want it redisplayed in the chart, immediately click the Undo button on the Graph Standard toolbar.

exercise 8

Moving and Sizing Chart Elements

1. Open Ch 23, Ex 07.
2. Save the document with Save As and name it Ch 23, Ex 08.
3. Move and size chart elements by completing the following steps:
   a. Change the Zoom to 50 percent.
   b. Double-click the chart.
   c. Close the datasheet.
   d. Move the legend to the right side of the chart by completing the following steps:
      1) Click the legend to select it. (Before clicking the legend, make sure a yellow box displays by the arrow pointer with the text *Legend*.)
      2) With the arrow pointer positioned in the legend, hold down the left mouse button, drag the outline of the legend to the right side of the chart, and then release the mouse button. (The legend will overlap the pie chart.)
   e. Move the pie to the left by completing the following steps:
      1) Select the pie. To do this, position the arrow pointer in a gray portion of the border that displays around the pie, and then click the left mouse button. (Before clicking the left mouse button, make sure a yellow box displays by the arrow pointer with the text *Plot Area*.) This should insert sizing handles around the square border around the pie. If not, try selecting the pie again.
      2) With the pie selected, position the arrow pointer inside the gray border surrounding the pie (not inside the pie), hold down the left mouse button, drag the outline of the pie to the left until it looks balanced with the legend, and then release the mouse button.
   f. With the pie still selected, increase the size of the pie by completing the following steps:
      1) Position the arrow pointer on the black sizing handle that displays in the bottom right corner of the selected pie until the pointer turns into a double-headed arrow pointing diagonally.
      2) Hold down the left mouse button, drag the pie border down and to the right to increase the size of the pie, and then release the mouse button. (You determine the size.)
      3) If the pie overlaps the legend, move the pie and/or move the legend.
   g. Click outside the chart to deselect it.
4. Save the document again with the same name (Ch 23, Ex 08).
5. Print and then close Ch 23, Ex 08.

Adding Gridlines

Gridlines can be added to a chart for the category, series, and value. Depending on the chart, some but not all of these options may be available. To add gridlines, display the Chart Options dialog box and then click the Gridlines tab. This displays the Chart Options dialog box with the Gridlines tab selected as shown in figure 23.8. At this dialog box, insert a check mark in those options for which you want gridlines.

figure 23.8 *Chart Options Dialog Box with Gridlines Tab Selected*

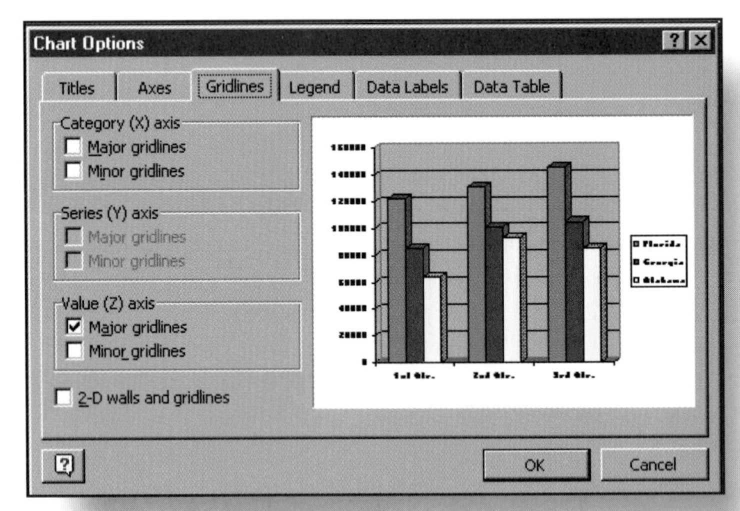

Category Axis Gridlines

Value Axis Gridlines

In addition to the options at the Gridlines dialog box, horizontal and/or vertical gridlines can be added to a chart with the Category Axis Gridlines button and the Value Axis Gridlines button on the Graph Standard toolbar.

exercise 9

Adding Gridlines to a Chart

1. Open Ch 23, Ex 01.
2. Save the chart with Save As and name it Ch 23, Ex 09.
3. Add gridlines to the chart by completing the following steps:
   a. Change the Zoom to Whole Page.
   b. Double-click the chart.
   c. Close the datasheet.
   d. Click Chart, then Chart Options.
   e. At the Chart Options dialog box, click the Gridlines tab.
   f. At the Chart Options dialog box with the Gridlines tab

selected, insert a check mark in the two options in the *Category (X) axis* section and also the two options in the *Value (Z) axis* section.

g. Click OK to close the Chart Options dialog box.
h. Click outside the chart to close Graph and deselect the chart.
i. Click the chart to select it, increase the size of the chart (you determine the size), move the chart to the middle of the page, and then deselect the chart.
j. Change the Zoom to 100 percent.

4. Save the document again with the same name (Ch 23, Ex 09).
5. Print and then close Ch 23, Ex 09.

Formatting a Chart and Chart Elements

A variety of formatting options are available for a chart or elements in a chart. Formatting can include adding a pattern, changing background and foreground colors of the selected element or chart, changing the font, and changing the element alignment or placement. If you double-click a chart element, a formatting dialog box displays. For example, if you double-click in a chart (outside any specific chart element) the Format Chart Area dialog box displays. Click the Font tab and the dialog box displays as shown in figure 23.9. At this dialog box, choose a font face, style, and size for the text in the chart as well as a font color and a background. You can also display the Format Chart Area dialog box by clicking once to select the chart area and then clicking Format, then Selected Chart Area.

figure 23.9 **Format Chart Area Dialog Box with Font Tab Selected**

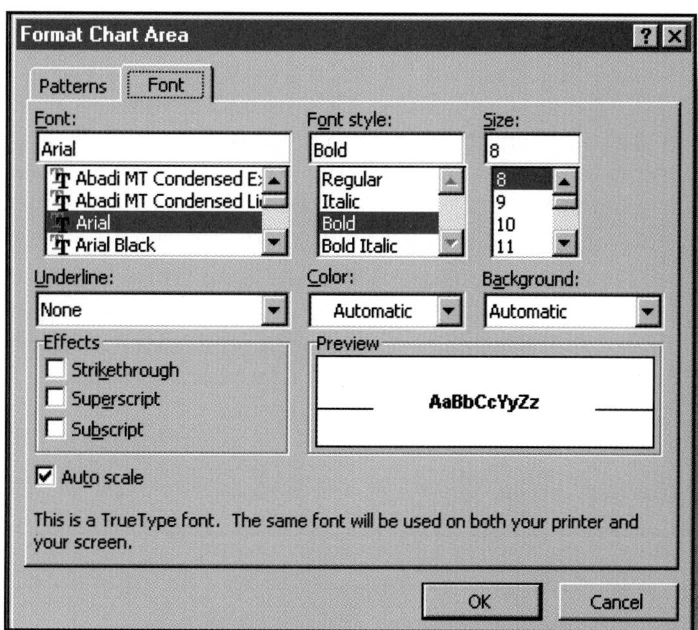

If you click the Patterns tab at the Format Chart Area dialog box, the dialog box displays as shown in figure 23.10. At this dialog box, you can add a border and/or pattern to the chart and change the border style.

23.10

Format Chart Area with Patterns Tab Selected

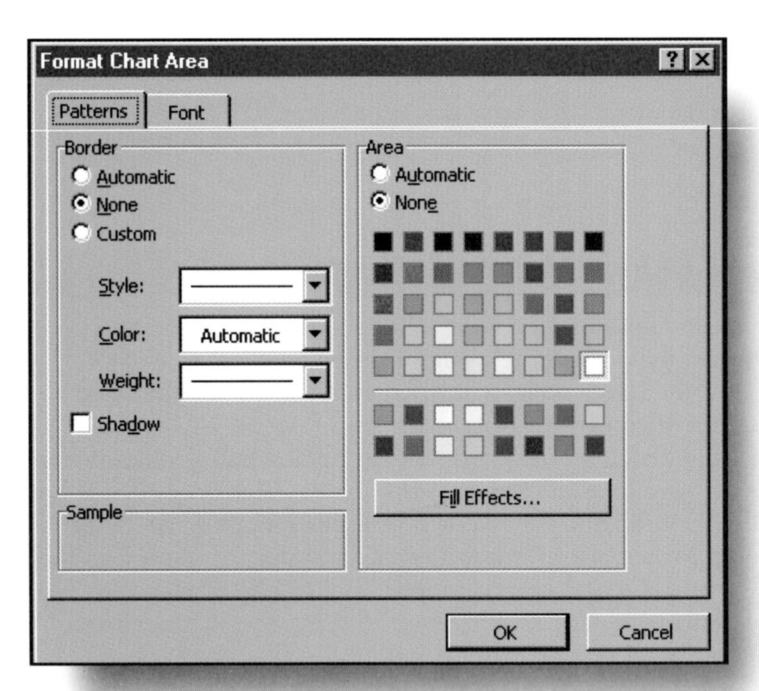

The font and pattern of chart elements can also be customized, along with additional formatting for specific elements. For example, if you double-click a chart title, the Format Chart Title dialog box displays. (You can also display this dialog box by clicking once on the title, then clicking Format, then Selected Chart Title.) This dialog box contains three tabs—Patterns, Font, and Alignment. Clicking the Patterns or the Font tab displays the same options as those available at the Format Chart Area dialog box. Click the Alignment tab and options for changing the text alignment (horizontal or vertical) display along with options for the title orientation.

Double-click a chart legend and the Format Legend dialog box displays with three tabs—Patterns, Font, and Placement. (You can also display this dialog box by clicking once on the legend, then clicking Format, then Selected Legend.) Clicking the Patterns or the Font tab displays the same options as those available at the Format Chart Area dialog box. Click the Placement tab to display options for specifying the location of the legend in relation to the chart.

Each chart element contains a formatting dialog box. To display this dialog box, double-click the desired chart element. For example, double-click text in either the x-axis or the z-axis and the Format Axis dialog box displays.

exercise 10

Customizing a Chart and Chart Elements

1. Open Ch 23, Ex 01.
2. Save the document with Save As and name it Ch 23, Ex 10.
3. Double-click the chart. (This displays the chart in Graph.)
4. Close the datasheet.
5. Customize the chart by completing the following steps:
   a. Double-click in the chart area outside any chart elements.
   b. At the Format Chart Area dialog box, make sure the Patterns tab is selected (if not, click the Patterns tab).
   c. At the Format Chart Area dialog box with the Patterns tab selected, click the light purple color (last color in the sixth row).
   d. Click the Font tab.
   e. At the Format Chart Area dialog box with the Font tab selected, click Garamond in the Font list box. (You will need to scroll down the Font list to display Garamond. If this typeface is not available, choose a similar serif typeface.)
   f. Click OK to close the Format Chart Area dialog box.
6. Customize the legend in the chart by completing the following steps:
   a. Double-click the legend. (This displays the Format Legend dialog box.)
   b. At the Format Legend dialog box click the Patterns tab. (Skip this step if the Patterns tab is already selected.)
   c. Click the light blue color (fifth color from the left in the fifth row).
   d. Click the Placement tab.
   e. At the Format Legend dialog box with the Placement tab selected, click Left.
   f. Click OK to close the Format Legend dialog box.
7. Click outside the chart to close Graph.
8. Change the Zoom to Whole Page.
9. Select the chart, increase the height and width of the chart (you determine the size), move the chart to the middle of the page, and then deselect the chart.
10. Change the Zoom to 100 percent.
11. Save the document again with the same name (Ch 23, Ex 10).
12. Print and then close Ch 23, Ex 10.

exercise 11

Customizing Elements in a Chart

1. At a clear document screen, key the headings and the first paragraph of the memo in figure 23.11. (To align the text after the memo headings *DATE:*, *TO:*, *FROM:*, and *SUBJECT:*, press the Tab key. You will need to press the Tab key twice after *DATE:* and *TO:* and once after *FROM:* and *SUBJECT:*.)
2. With the insertion point positioned a double space below the first paragraph in the memo, create the table as shown in figure 23.11. After creating the table, move the insertion point below the table, and then press Enter twice.
3. Create a Pie chart for the table, change the position of the legend, and add a title by completing the following steps:
   a. Select the entire table.
   b. Click Insert, then Object.
   c. At the Object dialog box with the Create New tab selected, double-click *Microsoft Graph 97 Chart* in the Object type list box.
   d. When the datasheet and chart display, close the datasheet.
   e. Change to a Pie chart by completing the following steps:
      1) Click the down-pointing triangle at the right side of the Chart Type button.
      2) At the drop-down palette of chart type options, click the first pie chart option in the fifth row.
   f. Click the By Column button on the Graph Standard toolbar.
4. Add a title and data labels to the Pie chart by completing the following steps:
   a. Click Chart, then Chart Options.
   b. At the Chart Options dialog box, click the Titles tab. (Skip this step if the Titles tab is already selected.)
   c. At the Chart Options dialog box with the Titles tab selected, click inside the Chart title text box, and then key **Software Training**.
   d. Click the Data Labels tab.
   e. At the Chart Options dialog box with the Data Labels tab selected, click Show percent.
   f. Click OK to close the Chart Options dialog box.
   g. Click outside the chart to close Graph.
5. Delete the table in the document by completing the following steps:
   a. Select the entire table (be sure to select the table and *not* the chart).
   b. With the table selected, click Table, then Delete Rows.

6. Click the chart to select it and then move it so it is centered between the left and right margins.
7. Change the font for the title and legend and add a border and shading by completing the following steps:
   a. Double-click the chart. (This displays the chart in Graph.)
   b. Double-click the title *Software Training*.
   c. At the Format Chart Title dialog box, click the Font tab, and then change the font to 10-point Times New Roman bold (or a similar serif typeface).
   d. Click the Patterns tab.
   e. Click the white circle before Custom in the Border section of the dialog box.
   f. Click the down-pointing triangle to the right of the Weight text box. From the drop-down menu that displays, click the third option.
   g. Click the check box before the Shadow option.
   h. Add a light yellow background color to the title by clicking the third color from the left in the fifth row.
   i. Click OK to close the Format Chart Title dialog box.
8. Format the legend in the chart with the same options as the title (except change the font to 6-point Times New Roman bold) by completing steps similar to those in step 7. (When changing the font, you will need to select the current number in the Size list box at the Format Legend dialog box with the Font tab selected and then key **6**.)
9. Select the gray border that displays behind the pie and then increase the size of the pie by dragging one of the corner sizing handles. Increase the size of the pie so it is easier to read, but still fits inside the chart area.
10. Click outside the chart window to close Graph and deselect the chart.
11. Press Ctrl + End to move the insertion point to the end of the document and then key the paragraph and the initials and document name displayed in figure 23.11 below the table.
12. Save the document and name it Ch 23, Ex 11.
13. Print and then close Ch 23, Ex 11.

figure 23.11

Exercise 11

DATE: (current date)

TO: Timothy Watson, Director

FROM: Dana Jordan, Administrative Assistant

SUBJECT: EMPLOYEE TRAINING SURVEY

All employee training surveys have been collected. I have analyzed the section of the survey dealing with training needs. The chart below shows the percentage of people requesting training on the specified software.

Software	Percentage
Word Processing	42
Spreadsheet	29
Product Assessment	18
Database	11

As you can see by the chart, word processing is the software most requested by employees for training. I will finish analyzing the rest of the survey by the end of next week.

XX:Ch 23, Ex 11

Changing Element Colors

Fill Color

A fill color can be added to a chart or a chart element with the Fill Color button on the Graph Standard toolbar. To add a fill color, select the chart or the chart element, and then click the down-pointing triangle at the right side of the Fill Color button on the Graph Standard toolbar. This displays a palette of color choices as shown in figure 23.12. Click the desired color on the palette.

23.12 *Fill Color Button Palette*

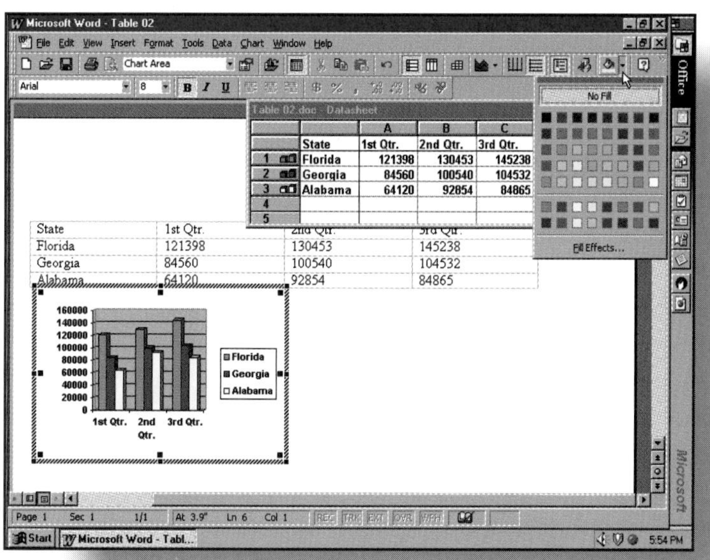

exercise 12

Changing Element Fill Colors in a Chart

1. Open Ch 23, Ex 01.
2. Save the document with Save As and name it Ch 23, Ex 12.
3. Change the colors of the bars in the chart by completing the following steps:
   a. Click the chart once to select it.
   b. Increase the width and height of the chart approximately 2 inches.
   c. Double-click the chart.
   d. Close the datasheet.
   e. Change the color of the blue bars (for Florida) to red by completing the following steps:
      1) Position the arrow pointer on any blue bar in the chart, then click the left mouse button. (This selects the three blue bars.)
      2) Click the down-pointing triangle at the right of the Fill Color button on the Graph Standard toolbar.
      3) At the color palette, click the red color (first color in the third row).
   f. Change the color of the maroon bars (for Georgia) to blue by completing steps similar to those in step 3e. (Choose the blue color in the second row, sixth from the left.)

g. Change the color of the light yellow bars (for Alabama) to green by completing steps similar to those in step 3e. (Choose the green color in the second row, fourth from the left.)
h. Add a background color to the chart by completing the following steps:
   1) Select the entire chart. (To do this, position the arrow pointer inside the chart window but outside the chart, and then click the left mouse button.)
   2) Click the down-pointing triangle at the right of the Fill Color button.
   3) From the color palette that displays, click the turquoise color in the fourth row, fifth from the left.
i. Click outside the chart window to close Graph and deselect the chart.

4. Save the document again with the same name (Ch 23, Ex 12).
5. Print and then close Ch 23, Ex 12.

chapter summary

- A chart can be created in Word with the Microsoft Graph 97 Chart application.
- One method for creating a chart in Word is to create and then select a table, display the Object dialog box, and then double-click *Microsoft Graph 97 Chart* in the Object type list box.
- In a chart the x-axis is the horizontal axis that runs along the bottom of the chart. The left side of the chart generally displays values and is referred to as the z-axis.
- Delete a chart by selecting the chart and then pressing the Delete key.
- To change the size of a chart, click the chart to select it, and then use the sizing handles that display around the chart to increase or decrease the size.
- To move a chart, click the chart to select it, and then drag the chart to the desired location.
- Fourteen basic chart types are available in Microsoft Graph 97 Chart along with built-in autoformats. The 14 chart types are Area, Bar, Bubble, Column, Cone, Cylinder, Doughnut, Line, Pie, Pyramid, Radar, Stock, Surface, and XY (Scatter).
- The default chart type created by Graph is a Column chart.
- A chart type can be selected at the Chart Type dialog box with the Standard Types tab selected.
- A custom chart can be selected at the Chart Type dialog box with the Custom Types tab selected.
- Change data in the datasheet and the chart will reflect the change.

- Add chart elements at the Chart Options dialog box.
- A selected chart or chart element can be moved, sized, or deleted.
- Add gridlines to a chart at the Chart Options dialog box with the Gridlines tab selected.
- Format a chart or a chart element by double-clicking the chart or the element. This displays a formatting dialog box for the chart or specific element.
- Add fill color to a chart or a chart element with the Fill Color button on the Graph Standard toolbar.

commands review

	Mouse/Keyboard
Create a chart in Word	Select the table, click Insert, then Object. At Object dialog box with the Create New tab selected, double-click *Microsoft Graph 97 Chart* in the Object type list box
Change chart type	Click [button] on the Graph Standard toolbar, then click desired chart at the drop-down list
Display Chart Type dialog box	In Graph, click Chart, then Chart Type
Choose a custom chart type	In Graph, click Chart, then Chart Type. At Chart Type dialog box, click the Custom Types tab, then click the desired custom chart type in the Chart type list box
Turn on/off display of datasheet	Click [button] on Graph Standard toolbar
Display Chart Options dialog box	In Graph, click Chart, then Chart Options
Display formatting dialog box for a chart or a chart element	In Graph, double-click the chart or chart element

check your understanding

Completion: In the space provided at the right, indicate the correct term, command, or number.

1. To create a chart, double-click *Microsoft Graph 97 Chart* at this dialog box. ____________
2. This is the horizontal axis that runs along the bottom of a chart. ____________
3. Click this button on the Graph Standard toolbar to turn off the display of the datasheet. ____________

4. Change the size of a selected chart by dragging these. ____________
5. Make changes to a chart created in Word by editing the data in this. ____________
6. If you double-click the title of a chart, this dialog box displays. ____________
7. If you double-click the legend of a chart, this dialog box displays. ____________
8. Use this type of chart to show proportions and relationships of parts to the whole. ____________
9. Use this type of chart to show variations between components but not in relationship to the whole. ____________

List the steps you would complete to create a default chart with data in a table.

____

____

____

skill assessments

Note: Before completing the skill assessments, display the Open dialog box, and then select and delete documents created in chapter 21 that begin Ch 21. You may want to check with your instructor before deleting these documents.

Assessment 1

1. Open Table 04.
2. Save the document with Save As and name it Ch 23, SA 01.
3. Select the table and then create a chart with the default settings.
4. After creating the chart, select the table, and then delete it.
5. Make the following changes to the chart:
   a. With the chart displayed in Graph, add the title *GROSS PRODUCT SALES*.
   b. Click outside the chart to close Graph.
   c. Change the Zoom to Whole Page.
   d. Select the chart, increase the width and height of the chart approximately two inches, move the chart to the middle of the page, and then deselect the chart.
   e. Change the Zoom to 100 percent.
6. Save the document again with the same name (Ch 23, SA 01).
7. Print and then close Ch 23, SA 01.

Assessment 2

1. Open Ch 23, SA 01.
2. Save the document with Save As and name it Ch 23, SA 02.
3. Change the Zoom to 50 percent.
4. Double-click the chart and then make the following changes to the chart:
   a. Change the color of each bar in the chart (you determine the colors).
   b. Add a light background color to the chart.
   c. Add a light background color (one that complements the chart background color) to the legend.
   d. Change the font for the title to a serif typeface of your choosing in a larger point size.
   e. Change the font for the legend to the same typeface (do not increase the size) as that used for the title.
5. Change the Zoom to 100 percent.
6. Save the document again with the same name (Ch 23, SA 02).
7. Print and then close Ch 23, SA 02.

Assessment 3

1. Open Table 05.
2. Save the document with Save As and name it Ch 23, SA 03.
3. Create a chart from the table with the following elements:
   a. Change the chart type to Line.
   b. Click the By Column button on the Graph Standard toolbar.
   c. Add the chart title *Population Growth - 1960 to 1990*.
   d. Add major and minor vertical lines to both axes.
   e. Click outside the chart window to close Graph.
   f. Change the Zoom to Whole Page.
   g. Select and then delete the table (*not* the chart).
   h. Select the chart, increase the size of the chart (you determine the size), move the chart to the middle of the page, and then deselect the chart.
   i. Change the Zoom to 100 percent.
4. Save the document again with the same name (Ch 23, SA 03).
5. Print and then close Ch 23, SA 03.

Assessment 4

1. At a clear document screen, key the headings and the first paragraph of the memo in figure 23.13.
2. With the insertion point a double space below the first paragraph, create the table as shown in figure 23.13. After creating the table, move the insertion point below the table, and then press Enter twice.
3. Create a pie chart for the table with the following elements:
   a. Change the chart type to Pie.
   b. Click the By Column button on the Graph Standard toolbar.
   c. Add the title *Investment Assets* to the chart.
   d. Add percentage data labels to the pie.
4. Click outside the chart to close Graph.
5. Select the entire table (*not* the chart) and then delete it.

6. Select the chart, move it so it is positioned between the left and right margins of the document, and then deselect the chart.
7. Double-click the chart and then make the following changes:
   a. Decrease the size of the legend.
   b. Increase the size of the pie.
   c. Make sure chart elements do not overlap.
8. Click outside the chart to close Graph.
9. Press Ctrl + End to move the insertion point to the end of the document and then key the paragraph and the initials and document name below the chart as shown in figure 23.13.
10. Save the document and name it Ch 23, SA 04.
11. Print and then close Ch 23, SA 04.

Figure 23.13 • Assessment 4

DATE: (current date)

TO: Lee Hunter, Editor

FROM: Paula Diaz, Investment Coordinator

SUBJECT: INVESTMENT ASSETS

The charts presented in last month's newsletter to investors looked great. Presenting data in a chart has much more visual impact on readers than displaying it in a table. I would like the following pie chart included in the investment section of the newsletter.

Invested Assets	Percentage
Mortgage Loans	34
Bonds	26
Business Loans	20
Real Estate	13
Other	7

I am currently gathering data on stock market investments. If you want this information for the next newsletter, please let me know.

XX:Ch 23, SA 04

chapter TWENTY-FOUR

Formatting Text into Columns

PERFORMANCE OBJECTIVES

Upon successful completion of chapter 24, you will be able to:

- **Format text in newspaper columns.**
- **Insert a column break in a document.**
- **Format text in side-by-side columns.**
- **Edit text in newspaper columns and side-by-side columns.**

When preparing a document containing text, an important point to consider is the readability of the document. Readability refers to the ease with which a person can read and understand groups of words. The line length of text in a document can enhance or detract from the readability of text. If the line length is too long, the reader may lose his or her place on the line and have a difficult time moving to the next line below. To improve the readability of some documents such as newsletters or reports, you may want to set the text in columns.

Text can be set in two different types of columns in Word. One type, called newspaper columns, is commonly used for text in newspapers, newsletters, and magazines. The other type, called side-by-side columns, is used for text that you want to keep aligned horizontally.

Newspaper columns contain text that flows up and down in the document. When the first column on the page is filled with text, the insertion point moves to the top of the next column on the same page. When the last column on the page is filled with text, the insertion point moves to the beginning of the first column on the next page.

Side-by-side columns contain text that is grouped across the page in rows. The next row begins a double space below the longest column entry of the previous row. In Word, the Tables feature is used to create side-by-side columns.

Creating Newspaper Columns

Newspaper columns contain text that flows up and down in the document, as shown in figure 24.1. When the first column on the page is filled with text, the insertion point moves to the top of the next column on the same page.

figure 24.1 *Newspaper Columns*

TEXT FLOWS FROM TOP TO BOTTOM IN THE FIRST COLUMN...
...THEN TO THE TOP OF THE NEXT COLUMN AND SO ON.

Columns

Newspaper columns can be created with the Columns button on the Standard toolbar or with options from the Columns dialog box. Columns of equal width are created with the Columns button on the Standard toolbar. To create columns of unequal width, use the Columns dialog box. The formatting for newspaper columns can be established before the text is keyed or it can be applied to existing text. Keying text first and then formatting it into newspaper columns is generally faster.

A document can include as many columns as there is room for on the page. Word determines how many columns can be included on the page based on the page width, the margin widths, and the size and spacing of the columns. Columns must be at least one-half inch in width.

Changes in columns affect the entire document or the section of the document in which the insertion point is positioned. If you want to create different numbers or styles of columns in a document, divide the document into sections.

There are three methods for inserting section breaks into a document. One method is to use the Break dialog box. (To display this dialog box, click Insert, then Break.) Another method is to use the Columns dialog box and specify that text is to be formatted into columns from the location of the insertion point forward in the document. The third method is to select the text first and then apply column formatting.

Creating Newspaper Columns with the Columns Button

To use the Columns button on the Standard toolbar, position the arrow pointer on the button, and then hold down the left mouse button. This causes a grid to display as shown in figure 24.2. Drag the mouse down and to the right until the desired number of columns displays with a blue background on the Columns grid and then release the mouse button.

figure 24.2 *Columns Grid*

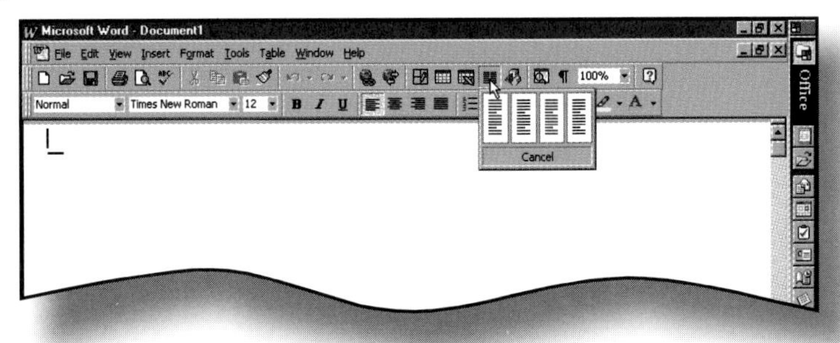

If a document contains a title and you want that title to span both columns, position the insertion point at the left margin where the first line of text that will begin the columns displays, click Insert, then Break. This displays the Break dialog box. At the Break dialog box, click Continuous, and then click OK or press Enter.

In addition to the method just described, you could also format the text in a document into columns and not the title by selecting the text in the document (excluding the title), and then using the Columns button on the Standard toolbar to create the columns. A third method is explained in the next section on creating columns with options from the Columns dialog box.

In the Normal viewing mode, text will display in a single column at the left side of the document screen. If you want to view columns as they will appear when printed, change to the Page Layout viewing mode.

exercise 1

Formatting Text into Newspaper Columns Using the Columns Button

1. Open Report 01.
2. Save the document with Save As and name it Ch 24, Ex 01.
3. Change to the Page Layout viewing mode.
4. Select the title and then change the font to 14-point Times New Roman bold.
5. Select each of the following headings individually and then turn on bold:

Defining Desktop Publishing
Initiating the Desktop Publishing Process
Planning the Publication
Creating the Content

6. Select the text in the document from the beginning of the heading, *Defining Desktop Publishing*, to the end of the document (this is all text except the title and the blank line below the title). With the text selected, make the following changes:
   a. Change the font to 11-point Times New Roman.
   b. Change the line spacing to single.
   c. Display the Tabs dialog box and then set a left tab at 0.25 inch.
   d. Format the text into two newspaper columns by positioning the arrow pointer on the Columns button on the Standard toolbar, holding down the left mouse button, dragging the mouse down and to the right until two columns display with a blue background on the Columns grid (and *2 Columns* displays below the grid), and then releasing the mouse button.
   e. Deselect the text.
   f. Insert 6 points of space below the heading *Defining Desktop Publishing.*
   g. Insert 6 points of space above and below the following headings:
      Initiating the Desktop Publishing Process
      Planning the Publication
      Creating the Content
7. Save the document again with the same name (Ch 24, Ex 01).
8. Print page 1 of the document.
9. Close Ch 24, Ex 01.

Creating Newspaper Columns with the Columns Dialog Box

The Columns dialog box can be used to create newspaper columns that are equal or unequal in width. To display the Columns dialog box shown in figure 24.3, click Format, then Columns.

figure 24.3 ***Columns Dialog Box***

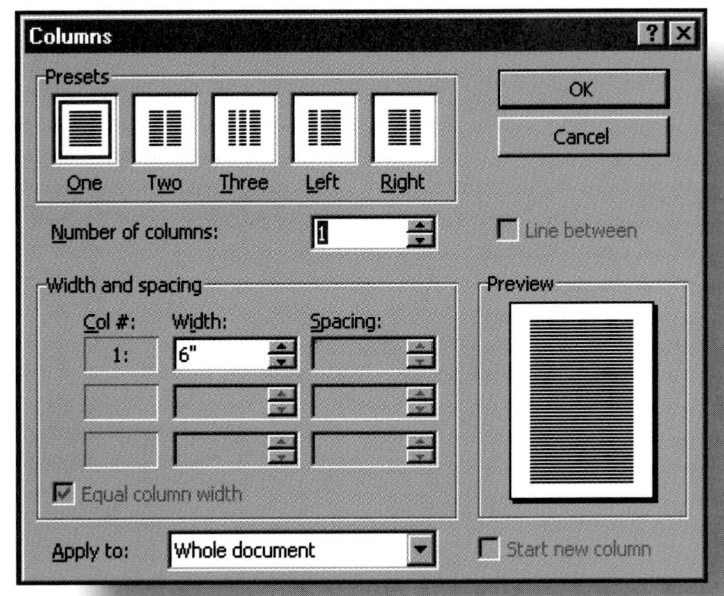

If you are creating columns of equal width, key the number of columns desired for the document in the Number of columns text box. You can also click the up-pointing triangle to the right of the Number of columns text box until the desired number displays.

You can also use options in the Presets section of the dialog box to specify the number of columns. By default, the One option is selected in the Presets section. Click the Two option if you want two columns of text in a document or click Three if you want three. If you click the Left option, the right column of text will be twice as wide as the left column of text. Click the Right option if you want the left column twice as wide. The options contain a Preview box showing what the columns will look like.

Word automatically determines column widths for the number of columns specified. By default, the Equal column width option contains a check mark. At this setting, column widths are the same. If you want to enter your own column widths or change the amount of space between columns, specify the number of columns desired, and then click Equal column width to remove the check mark from the check box. When the check mark is removed, column measurements display in black below the Col #, Width, and Spacing options. To change the measurements of the columns, click the up- or down-pointing triangles to the right of the width and spacing options until the desired measurements display in the text box. If you are using the keyboard, press the Tab key until the column or spacing measurement you want to change is selected, and then key the new measurement.

The dialog box only has room to display measurements for three columns. If you specify more than three columns, a vertical scroll bar displays to the left of the column numbers. To view other column measurements, click the down-pointing triangle at the bottom of the scroll bar.

By default, columns are separated by 0.5 inch of space. The amount of space between columns can be increased or decreased with the Spacing option. At this option, you can key a new measurement for the amount of spacing between columns or you can click the up- or down-pointing triangle after the text box to increase or decrease the measurement.

By default, column formatting is applied to the whole document. With the Apply to option at the bottom of the Columns dialog box, you can change this from *Whole document* to *This point forward*. At the *This point forward* option, a section break is inserted and the column formatting is applied to text from the location of the insertion point to the end of the document or until other column formatting is encountered.

exercise 2

Formatting Text into Newspaper Columns Using the Columns Dialog Box

1. Open Report 02.
2. Save the document with Save As and name it Ch 24, Ex 02.
3. Select the entire document and then make the following changes:
   a. Change the font to 10-point Times New Roman.
   b. Display the Tabs dialog box and then set a left tab at 0.2 inch.
   c. Deselect the text.
   d. Bold the title of the document as well as the two headings in the document.
4. Format the text (except the title) into three columns by completing the following steps:
   a. Position the insertion point at the left margin of the heading *Designing a Document*.
   b. Click Format, then Columns.
   c. At the Columns dialog box, click the Three option in the Presets section.
   d. Click the down-pointing triangle at the right side of the Apply to text box and then click *This point forward* at the drop-down list.
   e. Click OK or press Enter.
5. Save the document again with the same name (Ch 24, Ex 02).
6. Print and then close Ch 24, Ex 02.

A line can be inserted between columns that sets off the columns and adds visual separation of the columns. To insert a line between columns, click Line between at the Columns dialog box. The line between columns is the length of the longest column in the section. The line can be seen in the Page Layout viewing mode or in Print Preview. With the Start new column option, you can specify where to begin a new column of text. The Start new column option is dimmed until the Apply to option is set at *This point forward*. When you enter column settings in the Column dialog box, an example of how the columns will appear is shown in the Preview box in the lower right corner of the dialog box.

exercise 3

Formatting Text into Uneven Newspaper Columns with a Line Between

1. Open Report 03.
2. Copy a portion of the report into a new document and then save the new document by completing the following steps:
   a. Select the text in the *MODULE 1: DEFINING NEWSLETTER ELEMENTS* section of the report. (Select from the module 1 title to just before the title, *MODULE 2: PLANNING A NEWSLETTER*.)
   b. Click the Copy button on the Standard toolbar.
   c. Click the New button on the Standard toolbar.
   d. At the clear document screen, click the Paste button on the Standard toolbar.
   e. Save the document and name it Ch 24, Ex 03.
   f. Make Report 03 the active document and then close it. (This will display Ch 24, Ex 03 in the document screen.)
3. With Ch 24, Ex 03 open, make the following changes:
   a. Select the entire document and then change the font to 11-point Times New Roman.
   b. Set the title, *MODULE 1: DEFINING NEWSLETTER ELEMENTS*, in 14-point Arial bold.
   c. Set the two headings, *Designing a Newsletter* and *Defining Basic Newsletter Elements*, in 10-point Arial bold.
   d. Select the text from the beginning of the heading *Designing a Newsletter* to the end of the document and then change the line spacing to single.
   e. Insert 6 points of space below the heading *Designing a Newsletter*.
   f. Insert 6 points of space above and below the heading *Defining Basic Newsletter Elements*.
4. Format the text of the report into uneven columns with a line between by completing the following steps:
   a. Change to the Page Layout viewing mode.
   b. Position the insertion point at the left margin of the heading *Designing a Newsletter*.
   c. Click Format, then Columns.
   d. At the Columns dialog box, click the down-pointing triangle at the right side of the Apply to text box, and then click *This point forward* at the drop-down list.
   e. Click Left in the Presets section of the Columns dialog box.
   f. Click Line between.
   g. Click OK or press Enter.
5. Save the document again with the same name (Ch 24, Ex 03).
6. Print and then close Ch 24, Ex 03.

Inserting a Column and/or Page Break

When formatting text into columns, Word automatically breaks the columns to fit the page. At times, column breaks may appear in an undesirable location. For example, a heading may appear at the bottom of the column, while the text after the heading begins at the top of the next column. You can insert a column break into a document to control where columns end and begin on the page.

To insert a column break, position the insertion point where you want the new column to begin, and then press Ctrl + Shift + Enter. You can also insert a column break by positioning the insertion point at the location where the new column is to begin, and then clicking Insert, and then Break. At the Break dialog box, click Column break, and then click OK or press Enter.

If you insert a column break in the last column on a page, the column begins on the next page. If you want a column that is not the last column on the page to begin on the next page, insert a page break. To do this, press Ctrl + Enter. You can also insert a page break by positioning the insertion point at the location in the text where you want the new page to begin, and then clicking Insert, and then Break. At the Break dialog box, click Page Break, and then click OK or press Enter.

exercise 4

Formatting Text into Newspaper Columns and Inserting a Column Break

1. Open Ch 24, Ex 03.
2. Save the document with Save As and name it Ch 24, Ex 04.
3. Make the following changes to the report:
   a. Select the entire document and then change the font to 12-point Garamond.
   b. Change the columns to two even columns by completing the following steps:
      1) Position the insertion point immediately left of the *D* in *Designing a Newsletter*.
      2) Click Format, then Columns.
      3) At the Columns dialog box, click Two in the Presets section.
      4) Click OK or press Enter to close the dialog box.
   c. Insert a column break at the heading *Defining Basic Newsletter Elements* by completing the following steps:
      1) Position the insertion point immediately left of the *D* in *Defining*. (This heading is located at the bottom of the first column.)
      2) Click Insert, then Break.
      3) At the Break dialog box, click Column break.
      4) Click OK or press Enter.

d. Remove the 6 points of spacing above the heading *Defining Basic Newsletter Elements*.

4. Save the document again with the same name (Ch 24, Ex 04).
5. Print only the first page of Ch 24, Ex 04 and then close Ch 24, Ex 04.

Editing Text in Columns

To edit text formatted into columns, move the insertion point either within or between columns.

Moving the Insertion Point Within Columns

To move the insertion point in a document using the mouse, position the arrow pointer where desired, and then click the left button. If you are using the keyboard, the insertion point movement keys—up, down, left, and right arrows—cause the insertion point to move in the direction indicated. If you press the up or down arrow key, the insertion point moves up or down within the column. If the insertion point is located on the last line of a column on a page, pressing the down arrow key will cause the insertion point to move to the beginning in the same column on the next page. If the insertion point is located on the beginning of a line of text in columns, pressing the up arrow key will cause the insertion point to move to the end of the same column on the previous page.

The left and right arrow keys move the insertion point in the direction indicated within the column. When the insertion point gets to the end of the line within the column, it moves down to the beginning of the next line within the same column.

Moving the Insertion Point Between Columns

You can use the mouse or the keyboard to move the insertion point between columns. If you are using the mouse, position the I-beam pointer where desired, and then click the left button. If you are using the keyboard, press Alt + up arrow to move the insertion point to the top of the previous column, or press Alt + down arrow to move the insertion point to the top of the next column.

exercise 5

Editing Text in Newspaper Columns

1. Open Ch 24, Ex 01.
2. Save the document with Save As and name it Ch 24, Ex 05.
3. Make the following changes to the report:
   a. Select the entire document and then change the font to 11-point Arrus BT. (If Arrus BT is not available, choose a serif typeface such as Garamond or Century Schoolbook.)
   b. Select the title and then change the font to 16-point Univers bold. (If Univers is not available, choose a sans serif typeface such as Arial or Tahoma.)
   c. Select the heading, *Defining Desktop Publishing*, and then change the font to 12-point Univers bold.
   d. Use Format Painter to apply 12-point Univers bold to the following headings:
      Initiating the Desktop Publishing Process
      Planning the Publication
      Creating the Content
4. Save the document again with the same name (Ch 24, Ex 05).
5. Print only the first page of Ch 24, Ex 05.
6. Close Ch 24, Ex 05.

Removing Column Formatting

If a document contains text formatted into columns, the column formatting can be removed with the Columns button on the Standard toolbar or with the Columns dialog box. To remove column formatting using the Columns button, position the insertion point in the section containing columns, or select the text in columns. Click the Columns button on the Standard toolbar and then click the first column in the Columns grid.

To remove column formatting using the Columns dialog box, position the insertion point in the section containing columns, or select the text in columns, and then click Format, then Columns. At the Columns dialog box, click One in the Presets section, and then click OK or press Enter.

Changing Column Width and Spacing

The width of and spacing between text formatted into columns can be changed with the column marker on the horizontal ruler. The horizontal ruler is displayed when the viewing mode is changed to Page Layout. The horizontal ruler and the column marker are identified in figure 24.4.

figure 24.4

Column Marker on the Horizontal Ruler

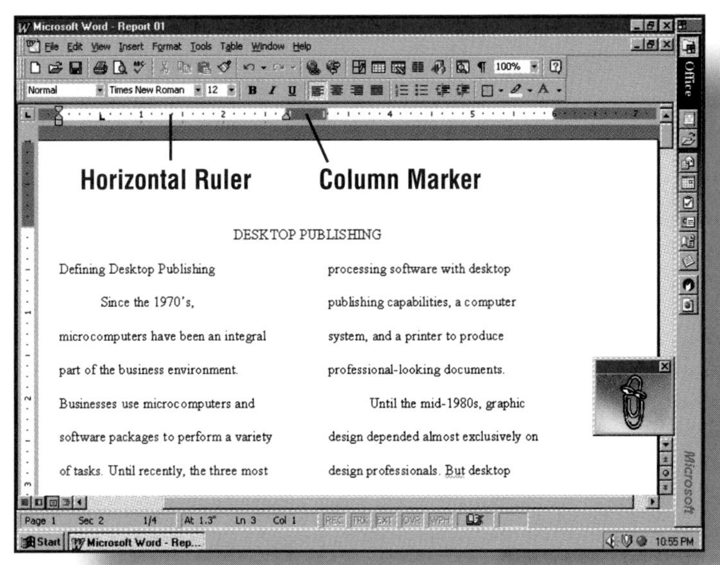

To change the width (and also the spacing) of columns of text in a document using the column marker on the horizontal ruler, position the arrow pointer on the left or right edge of the column marker on the horizontal ruler until it turns into a double-headed arrow pointing left and right. Hold down the left mouse button, drag the column marker to the left or right to make the column of text wider or thinner, and then release the mouse button. Hold down the Alt key while dragging the column marker and measurements display on the horizontal ruler. Measurements display for the columns as well as the space between columns.

If the columns are of equal width, changing the width of one column changes the width of all columns. If the columns are of unequal width, changing the width of a column only changes that column.

exercise 6

Changing Spacing between Newspaper Columns Using the Column Marker

1. Open Ch 24, Ex 05.
2. Save the document with Save As and name it Ch 24, Ex 06.
3. Make sure that the viewing mode is Page Layout. (If not, click View, then Page Layout.)
4. Position the insertion point anywhere in the heading, *Defining Desktop Publishing*, and then change the spacing between columns using the column marker on the horizontal ruler by completing the following steps:

a. Position the arrow pointer at the left side of the column marker on the horizontal ruler until it turns into a double-headed arrow pointing left and right.
b. Hold down the left mouse button and then the Alt key.
c. Drag the mouse to the right until the measurement inside the column marker displays as 0.25".
d. Release the mouse button and then the Alt key.

5. Save the document again with the same name (Ch 24, Ex 06).
6. Print only the first page of Ch 24, Ex 06.
7. Close Ch 24, Ex 06.

Balancing Columns on a Page

In a document containing text formatted into columns, Word automatically lines up (balances) the last line of text at the bottom of each column, except the last page. Text in the first column of the last page may flow to the end of the page, while the text in the second column may end far short of the end of the page. Columns can be balanced by inserting a section break at the end of the text. To do this, position the insertion point at the end of the text in the last column of the section you want to balance, and then click Insert, then Break. At the Break dialog box, click Continuous, and then click OK or press Enter. Figure 24.5 shows the last page of a document containing unbalanced columns and a page where the columns have been balanced.

24.5 *Unbalanced and Balanced Columns*

BALANCED COLUMNS

exercise 7

Changing the Width and Balancing Newspaper Columns

1. Open Ch 24, Ex 02.
2. Save the document with Save As and name it Ch 24, Ex 07.
3. Make the following changes to the report:
   a. Change the width of the spacing between columns by completing the following steps:
      1) Move the insertion point to the beginning of the heading *Designing a Document*.
      2) Position the arrow pointer at the left side of the first column marker from the left on the horizontal ruler until it turns into a double-headed arrow point left and right.
      3) Hold down the left mouse button and then the Alt key.
      4) Drag the mouse to the right until the measurement inside the column marker displays as approximately 0.28".
      5) Release the mouse button and then the Alt key.
   b. Position the insertion point immediately right of the period at the end of the report and then insert a continuous break to balance the columns on the third page by completing the following steps:
      1) Move the insertion point to the end of the document.
      2) Click Insert, then Break.
      3) At the Break dialog box, click Continuous.
      4) Click OK or press Enter.
4. Save the document again with the same name (Ch 24, Ex 07).
5. Print and then close Ch 24, Ex 07.

exercise 8

Creating a Newsletter Heading and Then Formatting Text into Newspaper Columns

1. At a clear document screen, create the heading for the newsletter shown in figure 24.6 by completing the following steps:
   a. Press the Enter key once and then move the insertion point back up to the first line.
   b. Change the font to 18-point Arial bold.
   c. Key **Kentwood School District**.
   d. With the insertion point positioned immediately to the right of *Kentwood School District*, insert the border line by completing the following steps:
      1) Click Format, then Borders and Shading.

2) At the Borders and Shading dialog box with the Borders tab selected, click a thick/thin border line style of your choosing in the Style list box.
3) Remove the lines around the diagram in the Preview section *except* the bottom line. To do this, click the line at the top of the diagram, click the line at the left side of the diagram, and then click the line at the right side of the diagram. (The only line remaining should display at the bottom of the diagram.)
4) Click OK or press Enter.

e. Press the down arrow key on the keyboard.
f. Click the Align Right button on the Formatting toolbar.
g. Change the font to 14-point Arial bold.
h. Key **September Newsletter** and then press Enter.
i. Key **David Olmsted, Editor** and then press Enter.
j. Click the Align Left button on the Formatting toolbar.
k. Press Ctrl + space bar to remove the font formatting.
l. Press the Enter key twice.

2. Insert the document named *News 01* into the current document. (Use the File option from the Insert drop-down menu to do this.)
3. Make the following changes to the document:
   a. Change the left and right margins to 1 inch.
   b. Change the font to 14-point Times New Roman bold for the following headings: *Welcome Back*, *Double Shifting*, and *Emergency Kits*. (*Hint: Use Format Painter.*)
   c. Position the insertion point at the beginning of *Welcome Back* and then format the text from *Welcome Back* to the end of the document into two newspaper columns. (*Hint: Change the Apply to option at the Columns dialog box to* This point forward.)

   d. Insert the clip art shown at the margin at the beginning of the paragraph that begins *"We hope your family had an opportunity to..."*, by completing the following steps:
      1) Position the insertion point at the beginning of the paragraph that begins *"We hope your family had an opportunity to...."*
      2) Click Insert, point to Picture, and then click Clip Art.
      3) At the Microsoft Clip Gallery 3.0 dialog box, click *Food & Dining* in the list box located at the left side of the dialog box. Scroll through the list of images displayed in the middle of the dialog box until the image at the margin displays. When this image displays, double-click it. (If this image is not available, double-click an image of your choosing.)
      4) Scroll down the screen until the bottom right corner sizing handle displays. Using this sizing handle, decrease

the size of the image to approximately 1.5 inches (height and width). (Use the horizontal and vertical rulers to help you size the image.)

5) With the image still selected, display the Picture toolbar. To do this, position the arrow pointer in the image, click the *right* mouse button, and then click Show Picture Toolbar.
6) Change the wrapping style by clicking the Text Wrapping button on the Picture toolbar and then clicking Square at the drop-down list.
7) Click outside the image to deselect the image (and remove the Picture toolbar).

4. Save the document and name it Ch 24, Ex 08.
5. Print and then close Ch 24, Ex 08.

24.6

Exercise 8

Kentwood School District

September Newsletter
David Olmsted, Editor

Creating Side-by-Side Columns

Side-by-side columns contain text in paragraphs that are horizontally aligned as shown in figure 24.7. Such text is read one paragraph at a time from left to right. With Word, you can format this type of column using the Tables feature. Side-by-side columns are often used in an agenda, itinerary, résumé, script, or address list.

figure 24.7 Side-by-Side Columns

Insert Table

Side-by-side columns are created by inserting a table into a document using either the Insert Table button on the Standard toolbar or the Insert Table dialog box. (Refer to chapter 22 for a review of creating and formatting tables.)

exercise 9

Creating a Résumé with Side-by-Side Columns (Table)

1. At a clear document screen, create the résumé shown in figure 24.8 by completing the following steps:
   a. Press Enter once and then press the up arrow key to move the insertion point back to the first line.
   b. Change the font to 18-point Arial bold and then key **MARIA CERVANTES**.
   c. With the insertion point positioned immediately to the right of *MARIA CERVANTES*, insert the border line shown in figure 24.8 with options at the Borders and Shading dialog box. (*Hint: Refer to exercise 8, step 1d.*)
   d. Press the down arrow key to move the insertion point below the border line.
   e. Change the paragraph alignment to right and the font to 14-point Arial bold.
   f. Key the address and telephone number as shown in figure 24.8. Press the Enter key to end the lines as shown in the figure.

g. After keying the telephone number, press the Enter key twice, and then change the paragraph alignment to left.
h. Create a table with 2 columns and 5 rows.
i. Change the width of the first column to 2 inches and the width of the second column to 4 inches.
j. Select the first column and then change the font to 12-point Arial bold.
k. Select the second column and then change the font to 12-point Times New Roman.
l. With the insertion point positioned inside the table, remove the gridlines by completing the following steps:
    1) Click Format, then Borders and Shading.
    2) At the Borders and Shading dialog box with the Borders tab selected, click the None box in the Setting section.
    3) Click OK to close the dialog box. (Light gray lines will display as the gridlines. These gray lines will not print.)
m. Key the text shown in figure 24.8. (Insert the em dash symbol (—) after the words *College* and *School* at the Symbol dialog box with the *(normal text)* font selected. It is the third symbol from the left in the eighth row.) When you have completed keying text in the second column, press the Enter key once. (This separates the rows by a blank line.) When keying the two columns of text in the SKILLS section, use Ctrl + Tab to move the insertion point to a tab setting within the same cell to create the text in the second column.
n. Change the top and bottom margins to 0.8 inch.

2. Save the résumé document and name it Ch 24, Ex 09.
3. Print and then close Ch 24, Ex 09.

24.8

Exercise 9

MARIA CERVANTES

1023 Westside Drive, Apt. 211
Little Rock, AR 84061
(413) 555-5007

OBJECTIVE

A position as a medical secretary in a company that provides opportunity for growth and advancement.

EDUCATION

Jefferson College—Associate of Arts and Sciences, Medical Secretary, June 1999

Bethel High School—Honor Graduate, 1997

SKILLS

Keyboarding (80+ wpm)	Desktop publishing
Medical terminology	Word processing
Medical procedures	Machine transcription
Accounting	10-key calculator
Database management	Spreadsheet
Employee training	Supervision

EMPLOYMENT

Medical Secretary, Little Rock Doctor's Clinic, 311 Fifth Street, Little Rock, AR 84021. Duties included answering the telephone, taking messages, scheduling appointments, filing manually and electronically, and transcribing and preparing medical documents.

Assistant Manager, Spearman's Sporting Goods, 331 Southcenter Drive, Little Rock, AR 84025. Duties included supervising employees, training new employees, taking inventory, helping customers, and operating a cash register.

Food Server, Rainbow Restaurant, 1200 Lexington Boulevard, Little Rock, AR 84021. Duties included waiting on customers, hosting birthday parties, cooking, operating cash register and drive-through window, and taking and filling customer orders.

ORGANIZATIONS

President, Student Government, Bethel High School, 1996-1997

Treasurer, Student Government, Bethel High School, 1995-1996

Member, Phi Beta Lambda, 1995-1997

chapter summary

- Setting text in columns may improve the readability of some documents such as newsletters or reports.
- The two types of columns available in Word are newspaper columns and side-by-side columns.
- Newspaper columns of equal width can be created with the Columns button on the Standard toolbar or with options from the Columns dialog box. To create columns of unequal width, use the Columns dialog box.
- Keying text first and then formatting it into newspaper columns is generally faster, but the formatting can be established before the text is keyed.
- By default, column formatting is applied to the whole document.
- In the Normal viewing mode, text will display in a single column at the left side of the document screen. Change to the Page Layout viewing mode to view columns as they will appear when printed.
- Options at the Columns dialog box let you change the spacing between columns, apply columns formatting from the point of the insertion point forward, insert a line between columns, or start a new column.
- To move the insertion point in a document with columns using the mouse, position the arrow pointer where desired, and then click the left button. To move the insertion point with the keyboard, use the arrow keys.
- Column formatting can be removed with the Columns button on the Standard toolbar or at the Columns dialog box.
- The width of and spacing between text formatted into columns can be changed with the column marker on the horizontal ruler.
- Word automatically lines up (balances) the last line of text at the bottom of each column. The last page of columns can be balanced by inserting a section break at the end of the text.
- Side-by-side columns contain text in paragraphs that are horizontally aligned.
- Create side-by-side columns by inserting a table into a document using either the Insert Table button on the Standard toolbar or the Insert Table dialog box.

commands review

	Mouse	Keyboard
Display Columns dialog box	Format, Columns	Format, Columns
Insert a column break	Insert, Break, Column break	CTRL + SHIFT + ENTER
Insert a page break	Insert, Break, Page break	CTRL + ENTER
Insert a section break	Insert, Break, Continuous	Insert, Break, Continuous
Move insertion point between columns	Position I-beam pointer where desired, click left button	ALT + ↑ (top of previous column) ALT + ↓ (top of next column)

check your understanding

Completion: In the space provided at the right, indicate the correct term, command, or number.

1. This type of column contains text that flows up and down in the document. __________
2. This is the minimum width for a column. __________
3. This type of column is used for an agenda or itinerary. __________
4. Change to this viewing mode to view columns as they will appear when printed. __________
5. The Columns button is located on this toolbar. __________
6. Click this option in the Presets section of the Columns dialog box to specify that the left column is to be twice as wide as the right column. __________
7. To create different styles of columns in a document, divide the document into these. __________
8. Create columns of unequal width here. __________
9. Columns are separated by this amount of space by default. __________
10. To insert a vertical line between columns, click this option at the Columns dialog box. __________
11. Insert this (or these) into a document to control where columns end and begin on the page. __________
12. Use this on the horizontal ruler to change the width of columns. __________
13. To balance all columns on the last page of text, insert this at the end of the text. __________

skill assessments

Note: Before completing the skill assessments, display the Open dialog box, and then select and delete documents created in chapter 22 that begin Ch 22. You may want to check with your instructor before deleting these documents.

Assessment 1

1. Open Report 02.
2. Save the document with Save As and name it Ch 24, SA 01.
3. Make the following changes to the report:
   a. Change the left and right margins to 1 inch.
   b. Select the text from the heading *Designing a Document* to the end of the document, display the Paragraph dialog box (with the Indents and Spacing tab selected), and then change the first line indent to 0.25 inch.
   c. Set the title, *DESKTOP PUBLISHING DESIGN*, and the headings *Designing a Document* and *Creating Focus* in 14-point Times New Roman bold.
   d. Format the text from the heading *Designing a Document* to the end of the document into two newspaper columns.
4. Save the document again with the same name (Ch 24, SA 01).
5. Print and then close Ch 24, SA 01.

Assessment 2

1. Open Report 04.
2. Make the following changes to the document:
   a. Select the text (including the title) in module 3.
   b. Copy the selected text to a new document.
   c. Save this new document as Ch 24, SA 02.
   d. Make Report 04 the active document and then close Report 04.
3. With Ch 24, SA 02 the active document, make the following changes:
   a. Select the text from the heading *Applying Desktop Publishing Guidelines* to the end of the document and then make the following changes:
      1) Change the line spacing to single.
      2) Format the selected text into two evenly spaced newspaper columns with a line between.
   b. Deselect the text.
   c. Add 6 points of space below the heading *Applying Desktop Publishing Guidelines*.
   d. Change to the Page Layout viewing mode.
   e. Select the title, *MODULE 3: DESIGNING A NEWSLETTER*, and then change the font to 14-point Arial bold.
   f. Select the heading, *Applying Desktop Publishing Guidelines*, and then change the font to 10-point Arial bold.
   g. Position the insertion point after the last period at the end of the document and then insert a continuous section break.
4. Save the document again with the same name (Ch 24, SA 02).
5. Print and then close Ch 24, SA 02.

Assessment 3

1. Open Ch 24, SA 02.
2. Save the document with Save As and name it Ch 24, SA 03.
3. Make the following changes to the document:
   a. Position the insertion point anywhere within the text formatted in columns, display the Columns dialog box, and then remove the check mark in the Line between option.
   b. Insert the clip art image shown at the margin with the following specifications:
      1) Change the width of the picture to 2.5 inches and the height to 1.4 inches.
      2) Display the Picture toolbar and then change the wrapping style to Square.
      3) Change the Zoom to Whole Page, drag the image so it is centered between the columns in the middle of the text, deselect the image, and then change the Zoom to 100 percent.
4. Save the document again with the same name (Ch 24, SA 03).
5. Print and then close Ch 24, SA 03.

Assessment 4

1. At a clear document screen, create the document shown in figure 24.9 with the following specifications:
   a. Change the font to 14-point Arial.
   b. Key **APRIL SPORTS ACTIVITIES** bolded and centered.
   c. Turn off bold and press Enter three times.
   d. Change the paragraph alignment back to left and change the font to 12-point Arial.
   e. Create a table with 3 columns and 8 rows. Make the following changes to the table:
      1) Change the width of the first column to 1 inch, the second column to 1.5 inches, and the third column to 3.5 inches.
      2) Select the first row and then change the alignment to center and turn on bold.
      3) Remove the gridlines from the table. (Light gray lines will display as the gridlines. These gray lines will not print.)
   f. Key the text in the cells as shown in figure 24.9. After keying the text in the last cell of each column, press the Enter key once. (This separates the rows by a blank line.)
2. After keying the text in the cells, save the document and name it Ch 24, SA 04.
3. Print and then close Ch 24, SA 04.

Figure 24.9 • Assessment 4

APRIL SPORTS ACTIVITIES

Day	Time	Activity
April 5	3:30 - 5:00 p.m.	Junior Varsity Tennis, Shoreline Junior High School vs. Lakeview Junior High School
April 7	6:30 - 8:30 p.m.	Ninth Grade Baseball Jamboree, Mountain View Junior High School
April 9	7:00 - 10:00 p.m.	Varsity Baseball Game, Kentwood High School vs. Bethel High School
April 12	3:30 - 5:30 p.m.	Varsity Tennis Tournament, Kentwood High School vs. Roosevelt High School
April 14	3:30 - 6:00 p.m.	Junior Varsity Baseball, Shoreline Junior High School vs. Lakeview Junior High School
April 16	7:00 - 10:00 p.m.	Varsity Football Game, Kentwood High School vs. Roosevelt High School
April 21	3:30 - 6:00 p.m.	Varsity Tennis Tournament, Kentwood High School vs. Bethel High School

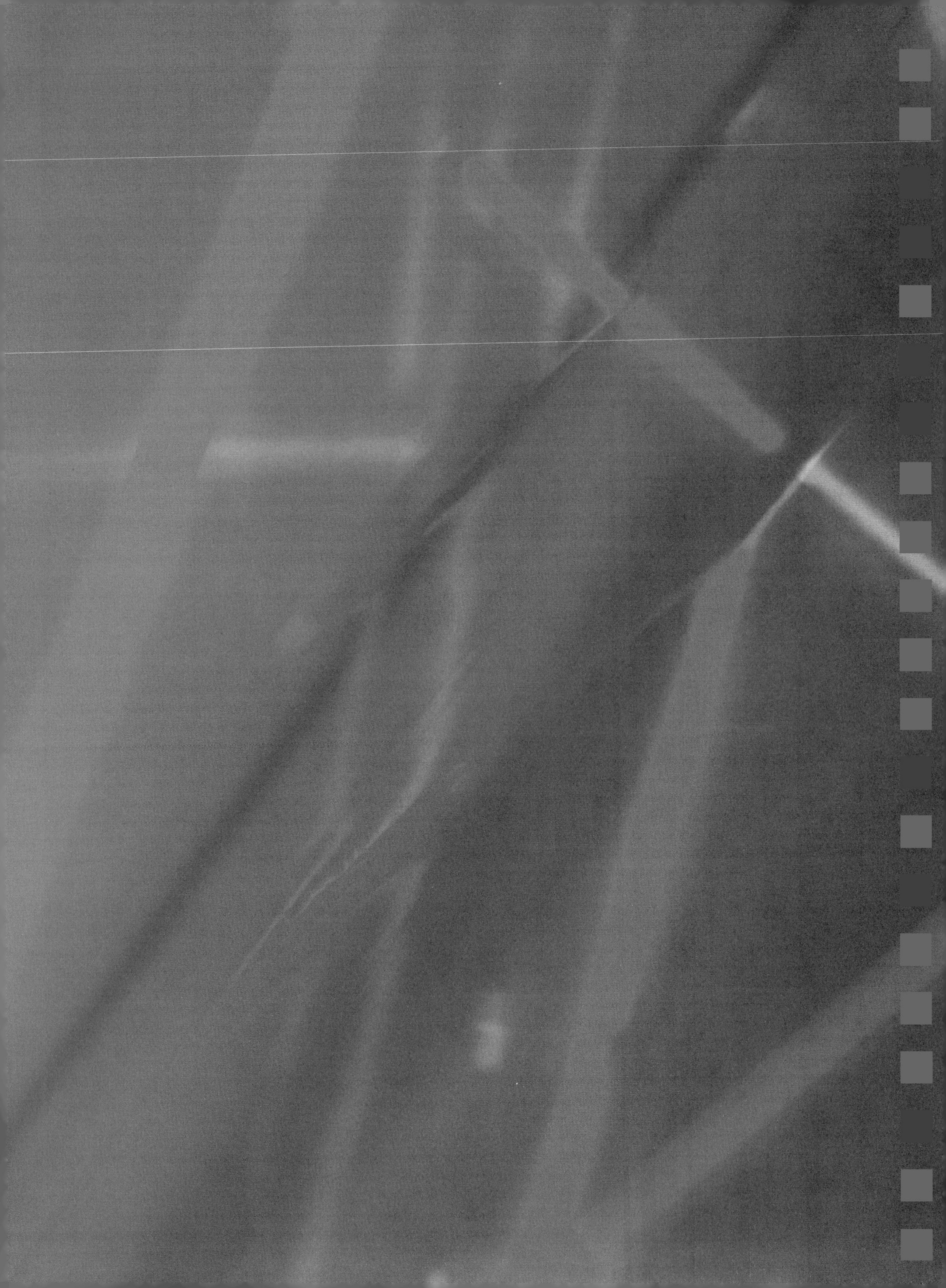

25 Formatting with Styles

PERFORMANCE OBJECTIVES

Upon successful completion of chapter 25, you will be able to:

- **Format text with a style.**
- **Apply a standard style.**
- **Create a style.**
- **Apply a style.**
- **Assign a shortcut key combination to a style.**
- **Modify, remove, rename, and delete a style.**

Some documents, such as company newsletters, reports, or brochures, may be created on a regular basis. These documents should maintain a consistency in formatting each time they are created. For example, a newsletter should maintain a consistency from issue to issue, and a company report should contain consistent formatting each time one is created.

Formatting that is applied to a variety of documents on a regular basis or that maintains a consistency within a publication can be applied to text using a *style*. In Word, a style is a set of formatting instructions saved with a specific name in order to use the formatting instructions over and over.

One benefit of styles is that when the formatting instructions contained within a style are changed, all the text to which the style has been applied is automatically updated. For example, suppose for subheadings in a newsletter you create a style that sets text in 18-point Arial bold. After applying the style to several subheadings in the document, you decide that the subheadings would look better if they are set in 14-point Times New Roman bold instead. To change all the subheadings at once in the document, you change the formatting instructions stored in the style. All subheadings with the style applied are automatically changed to 14-point Times New Roman bold.

Styles are created for a particular document and are saved with the document. Each time the document is opened, the styles are available.

Formatting Text with Styles

As you learned in an earlier chapter, a Word document, by default, is based on the Normal template document. Within a normal template document, a Normal style is applied to text by default. This Normal style sets text in the default font (this may vary depending on what you have selected or what printer you are using), uses left alignment and single spacing, and turns on the Widow/Orphan control. In addition to this Normal style, other predesigned styles are available in a document based on the Normal template document. These styles can be displayed by clicking the down-pointing triangle to the right of the Style button on the Formatting toolbar.

Normal

Style

Other template documents also contain predesigned styles. If you choose a different template document from the New dialog box, click the down-pointing triangle to the right of the Style button on the Formatting toolbar to display the names of styles available for that particular template document.

Styles can be changed and/or applied to text in three ways. The quickest way to apply styles to text in a document is with Word's AutoFormat feature. The advantage to using AutoFormat is that Word automatically applies the styles without you having to select them. The disadvantage is that you have less control over the styles that are applied.

Another method you can use to apply styles is to select a new template at the Style Gallery dialog box. The advantage to this is that you can preview your document as it will appear if formatted with various templates, and then apply the desired template. The disadvantage is that you have less control over the selection of styles.

A third method for applying styles to text is to make changes to those styles available in the template upon which your document is based. The advantage to this method is that you can format a document any way you want by creating and selecting styles. The disadvantage is that you have to create and/or select a style for each element in the document that you want formatted.

Formatting with AutoFormat

Word provides a variety of predesigned styles in the Normal template document that can be applied to text in a document. With this feature, called AutoFormat, Word goes through a document paragraph by paragraph and applies appropriate styles. For example, Word changes the font and size for heading text and adds bullets to listed items. The formatting is done automatically; all you do is sit back and watch Word do the work.

A document can be formatted by displaying the AutoFormat dialog box shown in figure 25.1. To display this dialog box, click Format, then AutoFormat. At the AutoFormat dialog box with the AutoFormat now option selected, click OK. This applies formatting to the open document. Figure 25.2 shows Report 01 with formatting applied to text with the AutoFormat feature.

figure 25.1

AutoFormat Dialog Box

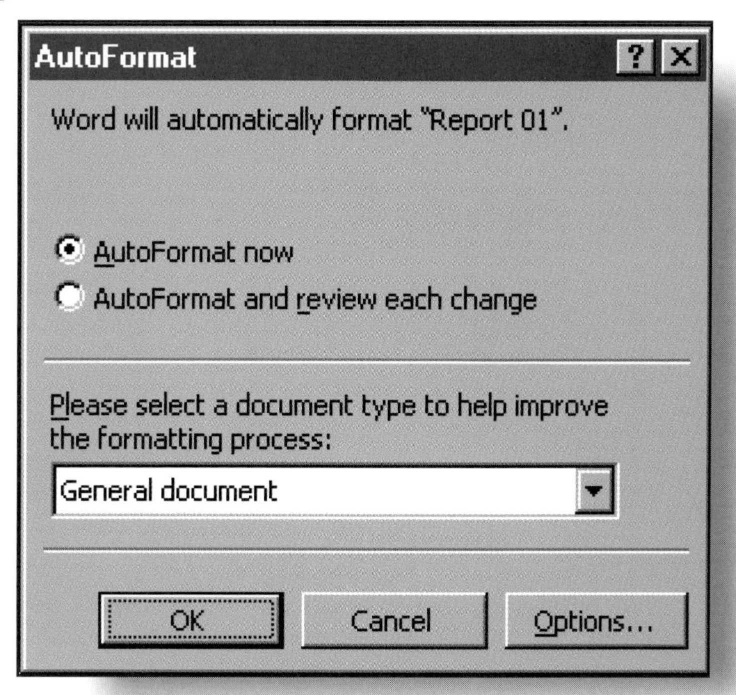

figure 25.2

Document Formatted with AutoFormat

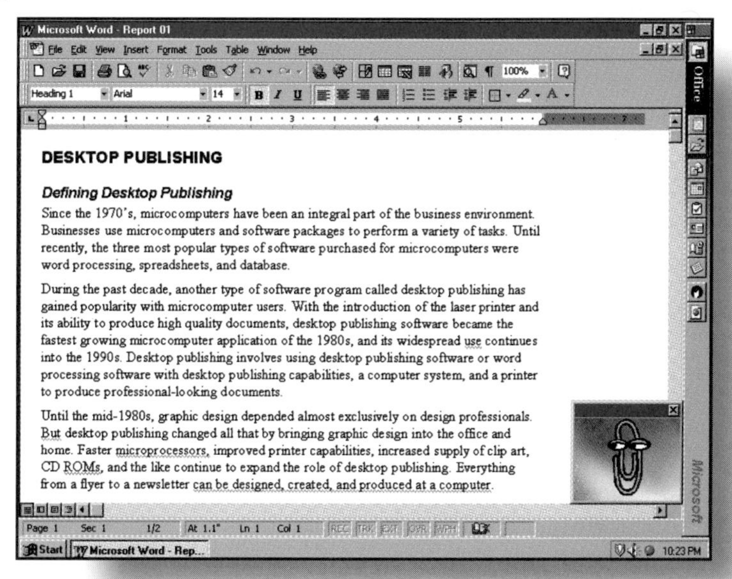

exercise 1

Formatting a Document with AutoFormat

1. Open Report 01.
2. Save the document with Save As and name it Ch 25, Ex 01.
3. Automatically format the document by completing the following steps:
   a. Click Format, then AutoFormat.
   b. At the AutoFormat dialog box, make sure the AutoFormat now option is selected (if not, click this option), and then click OK.
4. Save the document again with the same name (Ch 25, Ex 01).
5. Print and then close Ch 25, Ex 01.

When AutoFormat applies styles to a document, it also makes corrections as follows:

- Uses formatting rules to find and format headings, body text, lists, superscript, subscript, addresses, and letter closings.
- Replaces straight quotes and apostrophes with typesetting quotation marks.
- Deletes extra paragraph marks.
- Replaces horizontal spaces inserted with the space bar or the Tab key with indents.
- Replaces hyphens, asterisks, or other characters used to list items with a bullet (•).

If, after automatically formatting a document, you want to undo the changes, immediately click the Undo button on the Standard toolbar.

Reviewing/Rejecting Formatting Changes

At the AutoFormat dialog box, you can choose to review and then accept or reject changes made by AutoFormat. To do this, you would complete the following steps:

1. Open the document you want to automatically format, then click Format, then AutoFormat.
2. At the AutoFormat dialog box, click the AutoFormat and review each change option, and then click OK.
3. After Word automatically applies the styles, the AutoFormat dialog box displays with the message:
   Formatting completed. You can now:
   - *Accept or reject all changes.*
   - *Review and reject individual changes.*
   - *Choose a custom look with Style Gallery.*

   At this message, click the Review Changes button.

4. At the Review AutoFormat Changes dialog box, shown in figure 25.3, accept or reject the changes and then click the Cancel button.
5. At the next dialog box, click the Accept All button.

figure 25.3 *Review AutoFormat Changes Dialog Box*

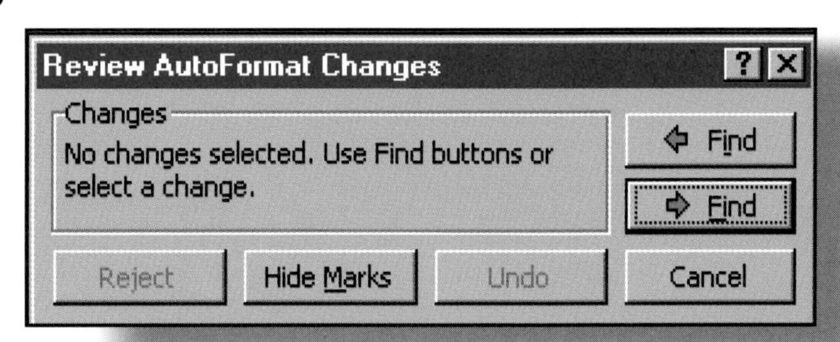

When Word displays the document for review, temporary revision marks are displayed. Revision marks are described in figure 25.4.

figure 25.4 *AutoFormat Revision Marks*

This revision mark...	Means...
Blue paragraph mark	a style was applied to the paragraph.
Red paragraph mark	the paragraph mark was deleted.
Strikethrough character (-)	text or spaces were deleted.
Underline (_)	the underline character (displays in blue) was added.
Vertical bar in left margin	text or formatting was changed in that line.

As you review changes in a document, Word selects text with formatting applied. If you want to reject the formatting, click the Reject button, and then click the ➜ Find button to find the next formatting. If you want to leave the formatting as displayed, click the ➜ Find button to find the next formatting. If you want to find the previous formatting, click the ← Find button. To hide the revision marks in a document, click the Hide Marks button.

If the Review AutoFormat Changes dialog box is in the way of text you want to see in the document, position the arrow pointer in the title bar of the dialog box, hold down the left mouse button, drag the outline of the dialog box to a new location, and then release the mouse button.

exercise 2

Formatting Specific Portions of a Document with AutoFormat

1. Open Contract 02.
2. Save the document with Save As and name it Ch 25, Ex 02.
3. Format the document with the AutoFormat feature and reject some formatting by completing the following steps:
   a. Click Format, then AutoFormat.
   b. At the AutoFormat dialog box, click the AutoFormat and review each change option, and then click OK.
   c. After Word automatically applies the styles, the AutoFormat dialog box displays with the message:
      Formatting completed. You can now:
      - *Accept or reject all changes.*
      - *Review and reject individual changes.*
      - *Choose a custom look with Style Gallery.*

      At this message, click the Review Changes button.
   d. At the Review AutoFormat Changes dialog box, click the → Find button once, and then click the Reject button. (This removes the formatting from the first line of the title.)
   e. Click the → Find button once and then click the Reject button. (This removes the formatting from the second line of the title.)
   f. Click the Cancel button to close the dialog box.
   g. At the AutoFormat dialog box, click the Accept All button.
4. Select the two lines of the title and then change the font size to 14 points.
5. Save the document again with the same name (Ch 25, Ex 02).
6. Print and then close Ch 25, Ex 02.

Changing AutoFormat Options

Word follows certain rules when formatting text with AutoFormat. You can make changes to these rules. To do this, click the Options button at the AutoFormat dialog box or click Tools, then AutoCorrect. At the AutoCorrect dialog box, click the AutoFormat tab. Either method displays the dialog box shown in figure 25.5.

At the AutoCorrect dialog box with the AutoFormat tab selected, remove the check mark from a check box if you do not want the option active, or insert a check mark if you do want the option active.

25.5 AutoCorrect Dialog Box with AutoFormat Tab Selected

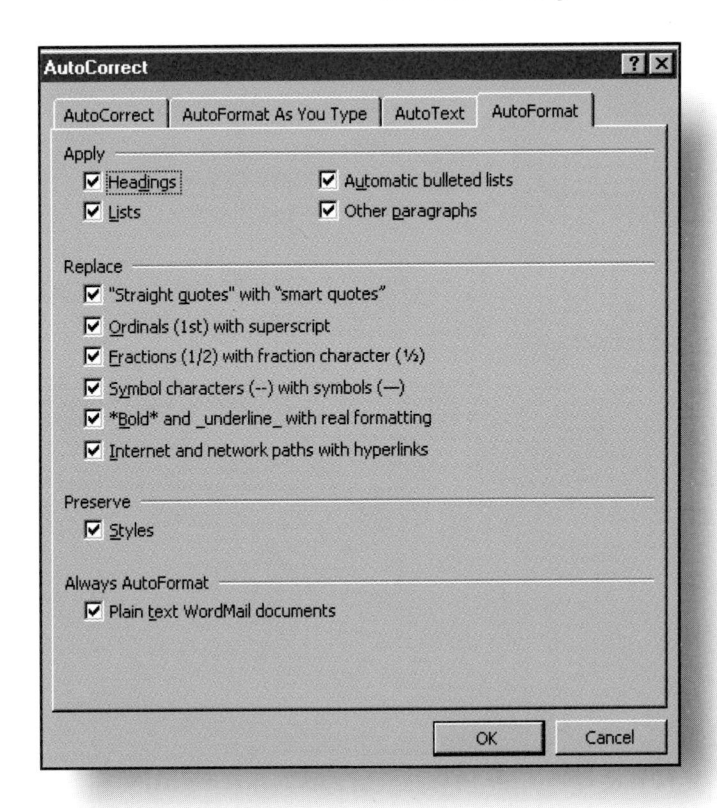

Formatting Text with the Style Gallery

As you learned in an earlier chapter, each document is based on a template, with the Normal template document the default. The styles applied to text with AutoFormat are the styles available with the Normal template document. Word also provides predesigned styles with other template documents. You can use the Style Gallery dialog box to apply styles from other templates to the current document. This provides you with a large number of predesigned styles for formatting text. To display the Style Gallery dialog box shown in figure 25.6, click Format, then Style Gallery.

At the Style Gallery dialog box, the template documents are displayed in the Template list box. The open document is displayed in the Preview of section of the dialog box. With this section, you can choose templates from the Template list box and see how the formatting is applied to the open document.

At the bottom of the Style Gallery dialog box, the Document option is selected in the Preview section. If you click Example, Word will insert a sample document in the Preview of section that displays the formatting applied to the document. Click Style samples and styles will display in the Preview of section of the dialog box rather than the document or sample document.

25.6

Style Gallery Dialog Box

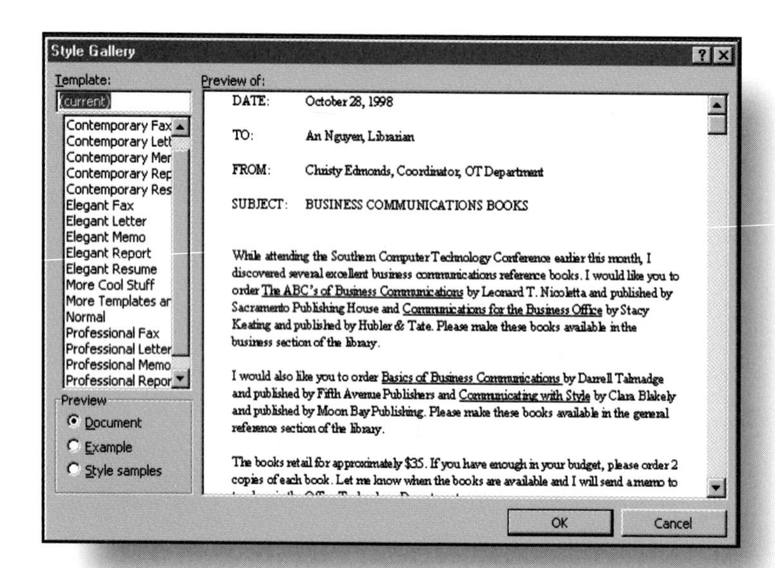

exercise 3

Formatting a Memo with Styles from a Memo Template

1. Open Memo 01.
2. Save the document with Save As and name it Ch 25, Ex 03.
3. Format the memo at the Style Gallery by completing the following steps:
   a. Click Format, then Style Gallery.
   b. At the Style Gallery dialog box, click *Elegant Memo* in the Template list box.
   c. Click OK or press Enter.
   d. At the memo, properly align the text after the FROM: heading by inserting a Tab between the heading and the text.
4. Save the document again with the same name (Ch 25, Ex 03).
5. Print and then close Ch 25, Ex 03.

exercise 4

Formatting a Document with Styles from a Report Template

1. Open Contract 02.
2. Save the document with Save As and name it Ch 25, Ex 04.
3. Format the contract at the Style Gallery by completing the following steps:
   a. Click Format, then Style Gallery.
   b. At the Style Gallery dialog box, click *Contemporary Report* in the Template list box.
   c. Click OK or press Enter.
4. Save the document again with the same name (Ch 25, Ex 04).
5. Print and then close Ch 25, Ex 04.

Applying Standard Styles

As you learned earlier in this chapter, Word provides predesigned or standard styles for each template document. You can apply these standard styles to text in a document. You can do this with the AutoFormat feature or you can apply styles individually with the Style button on the Formatting toolbar or at the Style dialog box.

To apply a style with the Style button on the Formatting toolbar, position the insertion point in the paragraph to which you want the style applied, or select the text, and then click the down-pointing triangle to the right of the Style button (the first button on the left). This causes a drop-down list to display as shown in figure 25.7. Click the desired style in the list to apply the style to the text in the document.

figure 25.7 **Style Drop-Down List**

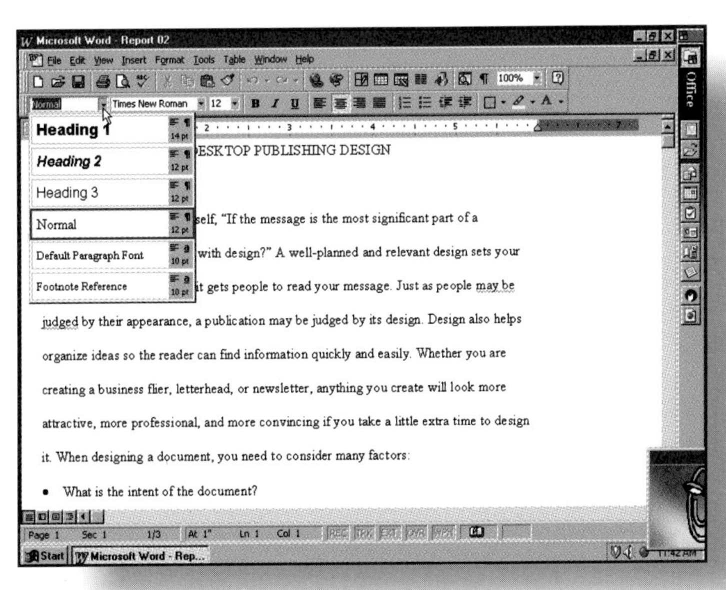

When you click a style in the drop-down list, the list is removed from the screen and the style is applied to the text. This formatting applied by the style will vary. For example, the *Heading 1* style applies the font 14-point Arial bold and the *Heading 2* style applies the font 12-point Arial bold italic. At the Style drop-down list, an icon with a brief visual presentation of the style displays at the right side of the drop-down list.

When a style is applied to text, the style name displays in the Style button on the Formatting toolbar. In addition, the font for the style displays in the Font button and the size for the style displays in the Font Size button. This helps you identify the formatting that is applied to text with the style.

The Style drop-down list displays only a few styles. Word provides many more predesigned styles than this that you can use to format text in a document. You can display the list of styles available with Word at the Style dialog box, shown in figure 25.8. To display the Style dialog box, click Format, then Style.

figure 25.8

Style Dialog Box

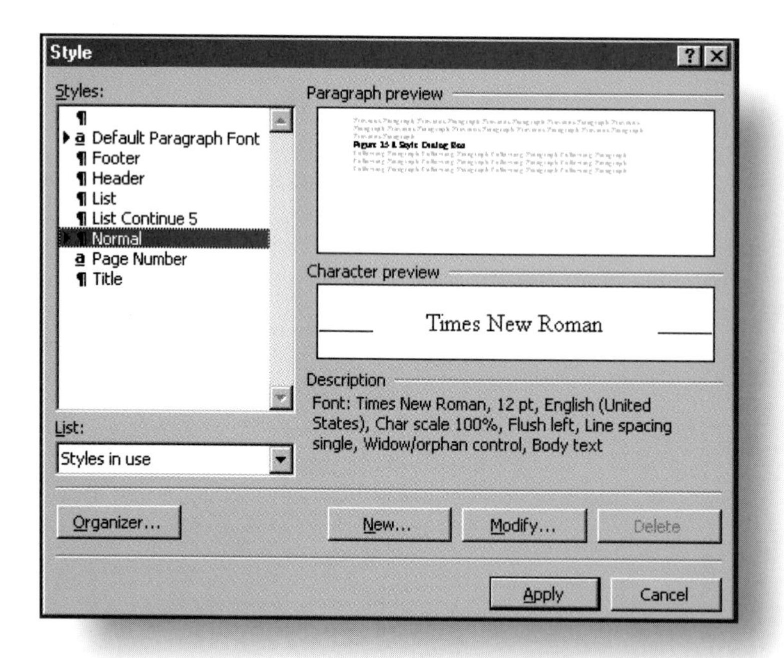

To display the entire list of styles provided by Word, click the down-pointing triangle at the right side of the List text box, and then click *All styles* at the drop-down list. When you click *All styles*, the list of styles in the Styles list box displays as shown in figure 25.9. The list is longer than the list box. In the Styles list box, paragraph styles are preceded by a paragraph mark (¶) and character styles are preceded by the symbol a.

figure 25.9 ***Style Dialog Box with All Styles Displayed***

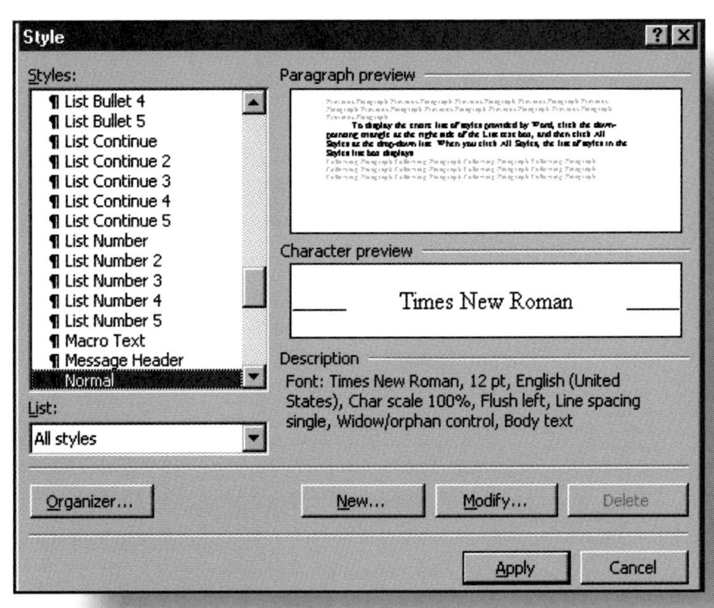

At the right side of the Style dialog box, the Paragraph preview box displays an example of how the selected style will format text. The Character preview box displays the font used to format text. A description of the style is displayed in the Description section of the dialog box.

To apply a style at the Style dialog box, position the insertion point within the paragraph of text to be formatted; or, if applying a character style, select the text, and then click Format, then Style. At the Style dialog box, click the down-pointing triangle at the right side of the List text box, and then click *All styles.* Click the desired style in the list and then click the Apply button.

exercise 5

Formatting a Document with Styles

1. Open Report 02.
2. Save the document with Save As and name it Ch 25, Ex 05.
3. Make the following changes to the report:
   a. Select the entire document and then change the line spacing to single.
   b. Position the insertion point at the beginning of the heading *Designing a Document* and then press the Enter key once.
   c. Position the insertion point at the beginning of the heading *Creating Focus* and then press the Enter key once.

4. Format the title and headings in the report using styles by completing the following steps:
    a. Position the insertion point anywhere within the title, *DESKTOP PUBLISHING DESIGN*, and then apply the *Title* style by completing the following steps:
        1) Click Format, then Style.
        2) At the Style dialog box, click the down-pointing triangle to the right of the List text box, and then click *All styles*.
        3) Scroll down the list of styles in the Styles list box until *Title* is visible and then click *Title*.
        4) Click the Apply button.
    b. Position the insertion point anywhere within the heading, *Designing a Document*, and then apply the *Subtitle* style by completing steps similar to those in 4a.
    c. Position the insertion point anywhere within the heading, *Creating Focus*, and then apply the *Subtitle* style by completing steps similar to those in 4a.
5. Save the document again with the same name (Ch 25, Ex 05).
6. Print and then close Ch 25, Ex 05.

Creating Styles

If all the styles predesigned by Word do not contain the formatting you desire, you can create your own style. A style can be created in two ways. You can either apply the desired formatting instructions to a paragraph and then save those instructions in a style, or you can specify the formatting instructions for a particular style without applying them to text. The first method is useful if you want to see how text appears when certain formatting instructions are applied to it. The second method is often used when you know the particular format that you want to use for certain paragraphs.

When you create your own style, you must give the style a name. When naming a style, avoid using the names already used by Word. The list of style names will display in the Styles list box at the Style dialog box if *All styles* is selected in the List text box. When naming a style, try to name it something that gives you an idea what the style will accomplish. Consider the following when naming a style:

- A style name can contain a maximum of 253 characters.
- A style name can contain spaces and commas.
- A style name is case-sensitive. Uppercase and lowercase letters can be used.
- Do not use the backslash (\), braces ({}) or a semicolon (;) when naming a style.

Creating a Style by Example

A style can be easily created by formatting text first and then using the Style button on the Formatting toolbar or the Style dialog box to create the style. To do this, position the insertion point in a paragraph of text containing the formatting you wish to include in the style, and then click the down-pointing triangle to the right of the Style button on the Formatting toolbar. Make sure the *Normal* style is selected in the drop-down list, key a unique name for the style, and then press Enter. This creates the style and also displays the style in the Style button. The new style will be visible in the Style drop-down list from the Formatting toolbar as well as the Style dialog box.

A style can also be created by example using the Style dialog box. To do this, position the insertion point in a paragraph of text containing the formatting you wish to include in the style, and then click Format, then Style. At the Style dialog box, click the New button. At the New Style dialog box, key a name for the style in the Name text box, and then click OK or press Enter. At the Style dialog box, click the Close button.

exercise 6

Creating Styles by Example

1. Open Style. (This document is located on your student data disk.)
2. Save the document with Save As and name it Sty 01.
3. Create a style by example named *Title 1* by completing the following steps:
   a. Position the insertion point anywhere in the title, *TITLE OF DOCUMENT*.
   b. Click the down-pointing triangle to the right of the Style button on the Formatting toolbar.
   c. Make sure the *Normal* style is selected in the drop-down menu. If not, select the *Normal* style.
   d. Key **Title 1** and then press Enter.
4. Create a style by example named *Subtitle 1* using the *Subtitle of Document* text by completing steps similar to those in 3.
5. Select all the text in the document and then delete it. (This removes the text but keeps the styles you created.)
6. Save the document again with the same name (Sty 01).
7. Close Sty 01.

Creating a Style Using the Style Dialog Box

A style can be created before you use it rather than creating it by example. To do this, use options from the Style dialog box shown in figure 25.8. The Style dialog box can be used to create a style by applying the desired formatting instructions to text or by entering the specific formats without applying them to text.

To create a style at the Style dialog box, you would display the Style dialog box, and then click the New button. At the New Style dialog box, key a name for the style in the Name text box, and specify whether you are creating a paragraph or character style at the Style type option. Click the Format button and then click the desired formatting options. These options are displayed in figure 25.10. When all formatting has been selected, click the Close button.

figure 25.10 ***Style Formatting Options***

Choose this...	To select this type of formatting...
Font	Font, style, size, color, superscript, subscript, and character spacing.
Paragraph	Paragraph alignment, indentations, spacing, and line spacing. (Not available for character styles.)
Tabs	Tab stop measurements, alignment, leaders, or clear tabs.
Border	Border location, color, style, and shading. (Not available for character styles.)
Language	Language that the spell checker, thesaurus, and grammar checker use for the current paragraph.
Frame	Horizontal and vertical positioning of object, size of object, and text wrapping style.
Numbering	Bulleted and numbered paragraphs in various styles. (Not available for character styles.)

exercise 7

Creating Styles at the Styles Dialog Box

1. Open Sty 01.
2. Create a style using the Style dialog box named *Indent 1* that indents text 0.5 inch and adds 12 points of space after the paragraph by completing the following steps:
   a. Click Format, then Style.
   b. At the Style dialog box, click the New button.
   c. At the New Style dialog box, key **Indent 1** in the Name text box.
   d. Click the Format button that displays toward the bottom of the dialog box and then click Paragraph at the pop-up list.
   e. At the Paragraph dialog box, click the up-pointing triangle to the right of the Left text box until *0.5"* displays in the text box.

f. Click the up-pointing triangle to the right of the After text box until *12 pt* displays in the text box.
g. Click OK to close the Paragraph dialog box.
h. Click OK to close the New Style dialog box.
i. Click Close to close the Style dialog box.

3. Create a style named *Font 1*, using the Style dialog box, that changes the font to Century Schoolbook by completing the following steps:
   a. Click Format, then Style.
   b. At the Style dialog box, click the New button.
   c. At the New Style dialog box, key **Font 1** in the Name text box.
   d. Click the down-pointing triangle at the right side of the Style type text box and then click *Character* at the drop-down list.
   e. Click the Format button that displays toward the bottom of the dialog box and then click Font at the pop-up list.
   f. At the Font dialog box, click *Century Schoolbook* in the Font list box, *Regular* in the Font style list box, and *12* in the Size list box.
   g. Click OK or press Enter to close the Font dialog box.
   h. Click OK or press Enter to close the New Style dialog box.
   i. Click Close to close the Style dialog box.
4. Save the document again with the same name (Sty 01).
5. Close Sty 01.

Applying a Style

A style can be applied to the paragraph where the insertion point is positioned. You can also select several paragraphs and then apply a paragraph style. If you are applying a style that contains character formatting, you must select the text first, and then apply the style. A style can be applied using the Style button on the Formatting toolbar or the Style dialog box.

To apply a style using the Style button, position the insertion point in the paragraph to which you want the style applied, or select the text, and then click the down-pointing triangle to the right of the Style button. At the drop-down list of styles, click the desired style.

To apply a style using the Style dialog box, position the insertion point in the paragraph to which you want the style applied, or select the text, and then click Format, then Style. At the Style dialog box, click the desired style in the Styles list box. (To view the entire list of styles offered by Word, click the down-pointing triangle at the right side of the List text box, and then click *All styles*.) With the desired style selected, click the Apply button.

exercise 8

Applying Styles in a Document Using the Style Button

1. Open Sty 01.
2. Save the document with Save As and name it Ch 25, Ex 08.
3. Insert the document named Survey 01 into the Ch 25, Ex 08 document. (*Hint: Use the File option from the Insert drop-down menu to do this.*)
4. Apply the *Title 1* style to the title *TEACHER DEVELOPMENT TOPICS* by completing the following steps:
   a. Position the insertion point anywhere in the title *TEACHER DEVELOPMENT TOPICS.*
   b. Click the down-pointing triangle to the right of the Style button.
   c. Click *Title 1* in the drop-down menu.
5. Apply the *Subtitle 1* style to the subtitle *Activities within your Classroom* by completing steps similar to those in 4.
6. Apply the *Font 1* style to text in the document (except the title and subtitle) by completing the following steps:
   a. Select the text in the document (except the title and subtitle).
   b. Click the down-pointing triangle to the right of the Style button.
   c. Click *Font 1* in the drop-down menu.
7. Save the document again with the same name (Ch 25, Ex 08).
8. Print and then close Ch 25, Ex 08.

exercise 9

Applying Styles in a Document Using the Style Button and the Style Dialog Box

1. Open Sty 01.
2. Save the document with Save As and name it Ch 25, Ex 09.
3. Insert the document named Quiz into the Ch 25, Ex 09 document. (*Hint: Use the File option from the Insert drop-down menu to do this.*)
4. Position the insertion point on any character in the title *CHAPTER QUIZ* and then apply the *Title 1* style.
5. Select the text in the document (except the title) and then apply the *Font 1* style.
6. Apply the *Indent 1* style to the text in the document (except the title) by completing the following steps:
   a. Select the text in the document (except the title).
   b. Click Format, then Style.

c. At the Style dialog box, click *Indent 1* in the Styles list box.
d. Click the Apply button.
7. Save the document again with the same name (Ch 25, Ex 09).
8. Print and then close Ch 25, Ex 09.

Assigning a Shortcut Key Combination to a Style

A style can be applied quickly in a document if a shortcut key has been assigned to the style. You can use the letters A through Z, numbers 0 through 9, the Delete and Insert keys, combined with the Ctrl, Alt, and Shift keys to create a shortcut key combination. Word has already assigned shortcut key combinations to many features. If you assign a shortcut key combination to a style that is already used by Word, the message *Currently assigned to (name of feature)* displays. When this happens, choose another shortcut key combination. To create a shortcut key combination for a style, you would complete the following steps:

1. Open the document containing the style to which you want to assign a shortcut key combination.
2. Click Format, then Style.
3. At the Style dialog box, click the style for which you want to assign a shortcut key combination in the Styles list box.
4. Click the Modify button
5. At the Modify Style dialog box, click the Shortcut Key button.
6. At the Customize Keyboard dialog box shown in figure 25.11, key the shortcut key combination in the Press new shortcut key text box.
7. Click the Assign button.
8. Click the Close button to close the Customize Keyboard dialog box.
9. At the Modify Style dialog box, click OK.
10. At the Style dialog box, click the Close button.

figure 25.11 **Customize Keyboard Dialog Box**

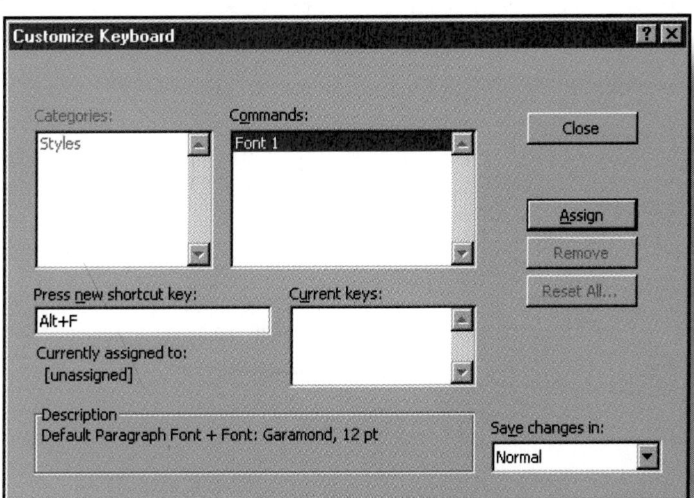

exercise 10

Assigning Shortcut Key Combinations to Styles

1. Open Sty 01.
2. Save the document with Save As and name it Sty 02.
3. Create the shortcut key combination, Alt + F, for the *Font 1* style by completing the following steps:
   a. Click Format, then Style.
   b. At the Style dialog box, click *Font 1* in the Styles list box. (You will need to scroll up the list box to display this style.)
   c. Click the Modify button.
   d. At the Modify Style dialog box, click the Shortcut Key button.
   e. At the Customize Keyboard dialog box, press Alt + F.
   f. Click the Assign button.
   g. Click the Close button to close the Customize Keyboard dialog box.
   h. Click OK to close the Modify Style dialog box.
   i. Click Close to close the Style dialog box.
4. Create the shortcut key combination, Alt + I, for the *Indent 1* style by completing steps similar to those in 3.
5. Create the shortcut key combination, Alt + S, for the *Subtitle 1* style by completing steps similar to those in 3.
6. Create the shortcut key combination, Alt + T, for the *Title 1* style by completing steps similar to those in 3.
7. Save the document again with the same name (Sty 02).
8. Close Sty 02.

exercise 11

Applying Styles in a Document with Shortcut Key Combinations

1. Open Sty 02.
2. Save the document with Save As and name it Ch 25, Ex 11.
3. Insert the document Report 01 into the Ch 25, Ex 11 document.
4. Select the entire document and then change line spacing to single.
5. Position the insertion point on any character in the title *DESKTOP PUBLISHING* and then apply the *Title 1* style by pressing Alt + T.
6. Position the insertion point on any character in the subtitle *Defining Desktop Publishing* and then apply the *Subtitle 1* style by pressing Alt + S.
7. Apply the *Subtitle 1* style to the following headings:

Initiating the Desktop Publishing Process
Planning the Publication
Creating the Content

8. Save the document again with the same name (Ch 25, Ex 11).
9. Print and then close Ch 25, Ex 11.

To remove a shortcut key combination from a style, display the Customize Keyboard dialog box for the specific style and then click the Remove button.

exercise 12

Removing a Shortcut Key Combination

1. Open Sty 02.
2. Save the document with Save As and name it Sty 03.
3. Remove the shortcut key combination, Alt + I, by completing the following steps:
   a. Click Format, then Style.
   b. At the Style dialog box, click *Indent 1* in the Styles list box. (You will need to scroll up the list to display this style.)
   c. Click the Modify button.
   d. At the Modify Style dialog box, click the Shortcut Key button.
   e. At the Customize Keyboard dialog box, click *Alt + I* in the Current keys list box.
   f. Click the Remove button.
   g. Click the Close button to close the Customize Keyboard dialog box.
   h. At the Modify Style dialog box, click OK.
   i. At the Style dialog box, click the Close button.
4. Save the document again with the same name (Sty 03).
5. Close Sty 03.

Modifying a Style

Once a style has been created, you can modify the style by changing the formatting instructions that it contains either with the Style button on the Formatting toolbar or the Style dialog box. When you modify a style by changing the formatting instructions, all text to which that style has been applied is changed accordingly. To modify a style using the Style button on the Formatting toolbar, you would complete the following steps:

1. Open the document containing a style you want to modify.
2. Reformat text with the formatting instructions you want changed in the style.

3. Select the text.
4. Click the down-pointing triangle to the right of the Style button on the Formatting toolbar.
5. At the drop-down list of styles, click the style name you want to modify.
6. When Word displays the Modify Style dialog box shown in figure 25.12, click the *Update the style to reflect recent changes?* option.
7. Click OK to close the dialog box.

figure 25.12 **Modify Style Dialog Box**

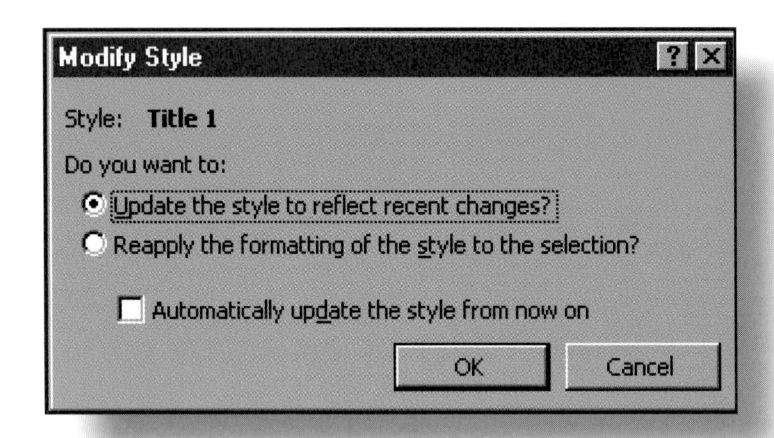

You can also modify a style at the Style dialog box. To modify a style at the Style dialog box, you would complete the following steps:

1. Open the document containing the style you want to modify.
2. Click Format, then Style.
3. At the Style dialog box, click the style name you want to modify in the Styles list box.
4. Click the Modify button.
5. At the Modify Style dialog box shown in figure 25.13, add or delete formatting options by clicking the Format button, and then changing the appropriate options.
6. When all changes have been made, click OK to close the Modify Style dialog box.
7. At the Style dialog box, click the Close button

figure 25.13 *Modify Style Dialog Box*

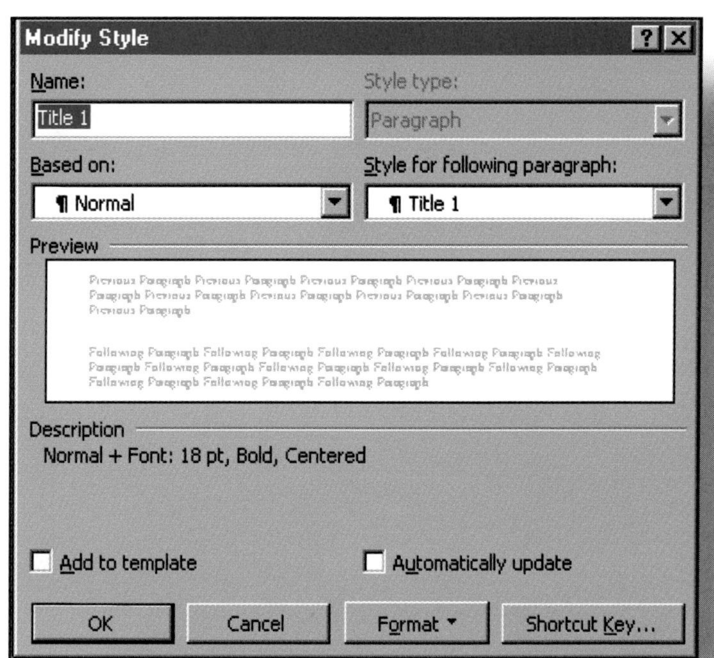

exercise 13

Modifying Styles

1. Open Ch 25, Ex 11.
2. Save the document with Save As and name it Ch 25, Ex 13.
3. Modify the *Title 1* style by completing the following steps:
   a. Select the title, *DESKTOP PUBLISHING*.
   b. Change the font to 18-point Arial bold.
   c. Display the Paragraph dialog box and then change the spacing after the paragraph to 6 points.
   d. With the text still selected, click the down-pointing triangle to the right of Style button.
   e. At the drop-down list of styles, click *Title 1*.
   f. At the Modify Style dialog box, click the *Update the style to reflect recent changes?* option.
   g. Click OK to close the Modify Style dialog box.
   h. Deselect the text.
4. Modify the *Subtitle 1* style by completing the following steps:
   a. Click Format, then Style.
   b. At the Style dialog box, click *Subtitle 1* in the Styles list box.
   c. Click the Modify button.

d. At the Modify Style dialog box, change the font to 14-point Arial bold by completing the following steps:
    1) Click the Format button located toward the bottom of the dialog box.
    2) At the pop-up list that displays, click *Font*.
    3) At the Font dialog box, click *Arial* in the Font list box, *Bold* in the Font style list box, and *14* in the Size list box.
    4) Click OK or press Enter to close the Font dialog box.

e. At the Modify Style dialog box, change the spacing before and after the paragraph to 6 points by completing the following steps:
    1) Click the Format button located toward the bottom of the dialog box.
    2) Click *Paragraph* at the pop-up list.
    3) At the Paragraph dialog box, click once on the up-pointing triangle to the right of the After text box. (This inserts *6 pt* in the text box.)
    4) Click once on the up-pointing triangle at the right of the Before text box. (This inserts *6 pt* in the text box.)
    5) Click OK or press Enter.

f. At the Modify Style dialog box, click OK.

g. Click the Close button to close the Style dialog box.

5. Check the page breaks in the document and, if necessary, adjust the page breaks.
6. Save the document again with the same name (Ch 25, Ex 13).
7. Print and then close Ch 25, Ex 13. (The title should print in 18-point Arial bold and the four headings should print in 14-point Arial bold.)

Removing a Style from Text

You may apply a style to text in a document and then change your mind and wish to remove the style. If you decide to remove the style immediately after applying it (before performing some other action), click the Undo button on the Standard toolbar. You can also click Edit, then Undo Style. When a style is removed, the style that was previously applied to the text is applied once again (usually this is the Normal style).

You can also remove a style from text by applying a new style. Only one style can be applied at a time to the same text. For example, if you applied the *Heading 1* style to text and then later decide you want to remove it, position the insertion point in the text containing the *Heading 1* style, then apply the *Normal* style.

Renaming a Style

As you create more and more styles in a particular document, you may find that you need to rename existing styles to avoid duplicating style names. When a style is renamed, the formatting instructions contained within the style remain the same. Any text to which the style has been applied reflects the new name. You can rename styles that you create as often as needed, but you cannot rename Word's standard styles. To rename a style, click the Modify button at the Style dialog box. At the Modify Style dialog box, key the new name for the style, and then click OK or press Enter to return to the Style dialog box. At the Style dialog box, click the Close button.

exercise 14

Modifying Styles

1. Open Sty 01.
2. Save the document with Save As and name it Sty 04.
3. Modify the *Title 1* style by completing the following steps:
   a. Click Format, then Style.
   b. At the Style dialog box, click *Title 1* in the Styles list box.
   c. Click the Modify button.
   d. At the Modify Style dialog box, change the font to 18-point Arial bold by completing the following steps:
      1) Click the Format button that displays toward the bottom of the dialog box.
      2) Click *Font* at the pop-up list.
      3) At the Font dialog box, click *Arial* in the Font list box, *Bold* in the Font style list box, and *18* in the Size list box.
      4) Click OK or press Enter to close the Font dialog box.
   e. Click the Format button located toward the bottom of the dialog box and then click *Paragraph* at the pop-up list.
   f. At the Paragraph dialog box, change the spacing after the paragraph to 12 points.
   g. Click OK or press Enter to close the Paragraph dialog box.
   h. At the Modify Style dialog box, click OK.
   i. Click the Close button to close the Style dialog box.
4. Modify the *Subtitle 1* style so the font is 14-point Arial bold and the space after the paragraph is 12 points by completing steps similar to those in 3.
5. Modify the *Font 1* style by completing the following steps:
   a. Key **This is sample text.**
   b. Select *This is sample text.*
   c. Apply the *Font 1* style to the text. (To do this, click the down-pointing triangle to the right of the Style button on the Formatting toolbar, and then click *Font 1*.)
   d. With the text still selected, change the font to 12-point Bookman Old Style. (If this typeface is not available, choose a similar serif typeface [other than Century Schoolbook and Times New Roman].)
   e. Click the down-pointing triangle to the right of the Style button on the Formatting toolbar.

f. At the drop-down list of styles, click *Font 1*.
g. At the Modify Style dialog box, click the *Update the style to reflect recent changes?* option, and then click OK or press Enter.
h. Deselect the text.
6. Select the text in the document and then press the Delete key.
7. Save the document again with the same name (Sty 04).
8. Close Sty 04.

Deleting a Style

A style can be deleted in a document and any style to which that style is applied is returned to the Normal style. To delete a style, display the Style dialog box, select the style name you want to delete in the Styles list box, and then click the Delete button. At the message asking if you want to delete the style, click Yes. Click the Close button to close the Style dialog box. You can delete styles that you create, but you cannot delete Word's standard styles.

You can delete several styles at once at the Organizer dialog box. To do this, you would complete the following steps:

1. Open the document containing the styles you want to delete.
2. Click Format, then Style.
3. At the Style dialog box, click the Organizer button.
4. At the Organizer dialog box, select the style names you want deleted in the In list box at the left side of the dialog box.
5. Click the Delete button.
6. At the question asking if you want to delete the first style, click Yes to All. (This tells Word to delete all selected styles.)
7. Click the Close button to close the Organizer dialog box.

exercise 15

Deleting Styles

1. Open Sty 04.
2. Insert the document named *Report 02* into the Sty 04 document.
3. Save the document with Save As and name it Ch 25, Ex 15.
4. Delete the *Indent 1* style by completing the following steps:
   a. Click Format, then Style.
   b. At the Style dialog box, click *Indent 1* in the Styles list box.
   c. Click the Delete button.
   d. At the message asking if you want to delete the style, click Yes.
   e. Click the Close button to close the Style dialog box.
5. Select the entire document and then apply the *Font 1* style.
6. Apply the *Title 1* style to the title, *DESKTOP PUBLISHING DESIGN*.

7. Apply the *Subtitle 1* style to the headings *Designing a Document* and *Creating Focus*.
8. Save the document again with the same name (Ch 25, Ex 15).
9. Print and then close Ch 25, Ex 15.

chapter summary

- Formatting that is applied to a variety of documents on a regular basis or that maintains a consistency within a publication can be applied to text using a *style*. A style is a set of formatting instructions saved with a specific name in order to use the formatting over and over.
- When the formatting instructions contained within a style are changed, all the text to which the style has been applied is automatically updated.
- Styles are created for a particular document and are saved with the document.
- In addition to the Normal style that is applied to text by default, other predesigned styles are available in a document based on the Normal template document. Other template documents also contain predesigned styles.
- Styles can be changed and/or applied to text in three ways: 1) use Word's AutoFormat feature; 2) select a new template at the Style Gallery dialog box; or 3) make changes to styles available in the template upon which your document is based.
- When formatting with the AutoFormat feature, you can review and then accept or reject changes.
- At the Style Gallery dialog box, you can see the effects of styles on the open document in the Preview section.
- To display the entire list of styles provided by Word, click the down-pointing triangle at the right of the List text box at the Style dialog box, and then click *All styles* at the drop-down list.
- A new style can be created in two ways: apply the desired formatting instructions to a paragraph and then save those instructions in a style; or, specify the formatting instructions for a style without applying the formatting to text.
- A style can be applied to the paragraph where the insertion point is positioned, or select several paragraphs and then apply a paragraph style.
- A style can be applied using the Style button on the Formatting toolbar or the Style dialog box.
- A style can be applied quickly in a document if a shortcut key combination has been assigned to the style.
- You can modify a style by changing the formatting instructions that it contains either with the Style button on the Formatting toolbar or the Style dialog box.
- You can delete a style from a document or rename a style at the Style dialog box.
- You can remove a style from text by applying a new style, since only one style can be applied at a time to the same text.

commands review

	Mouse/Keyboard
Format a document with AutoFormat	Click Format, AutoFormat, then click OK
Undo AutoFormat changes	Immediately click [Undo button] on the Standard toolbar
Display Style Gallery dialog box	Click Format, Style Gallery
Display Style dialog box	Click Format, Style

check your understanding

Completion: In the space provided at the right, indicate the correct term, command, or number.

1. This is a set of formatting instructions saved with a name in order to use the formatting repeatedly. ____________
2. By default, a Word document is based on this template document. ____________
3. The predesigned styles based on the default template document are displayed by clicking this button on the Formatting toolbar. ____________
4. The quickest way to apply styles in a document is with this feature. ____________
5. To display the AutoFormat dialog box, click this option on the menu bar, and then click AutoFormat. ____________
6. If, after automatically formatting a document, you want to remove the formatting, immediately click this button on the Standard toolbar. ____________
7. Use this dialog box to apply styles from other templates besides the default template to the current document. ____________
8. This is the maximum number of characters a style name can contain. ____________
9. Create a new style at this dialog box. ____________
10. Delete several styles at once at this dialog box. ____________

skill assessments

Note: Before completing the skill assessments, display the Open dialog box, and then select and delete documents created in chapter 23 that begin Ch 23. You may want to check with your instructor before deleting these documents.

Assessment 1

1. Open Report 03.
2. Save the document with Save As and name it Ch 25, SA 01.
3. Automatically format the document at the AutoFormat dialog box.
4. Save the document again with the same name (Ch 25, SA 01).
5. Print and then close Ch 25, SA 01.

Assessment 2

1. Open Notice 01.
2. Save the document with Save As and name it Ch 25, SA 02.
3. Format the document at the Style Gallery with the *Professional Report* template.
4. Save the document again with the same name (Ch 25, SA 02).
5. Print and then close Ch 25, SA 02.

Assessment 3

1. Open Sty 03.
2. Save the document with Save As and name it Ch 25, SA 03.
3. Make the following changes to the document:
   a. Change the alignment to center and then key **KENTWOOD SCHOOL DISTRICT**.
   b. Press the Enter key and then key **September Newsletter**.
   c. Press the Enter key and then key **David Olmsted, Editor**.
   d. Press the Enter key three times.
   e. Change the alignment to left.
4. Insert the document named News 01 into the Ch 25, SA 03 document.
5. Make the following changes to the document:
   a. Change the left and right margins to 1 inch.
   b. Delete the blank line below each of the following headings: *Welcome Back*, *Double Shifting*, and *Emergency Kits*.
   c. Apply the *Title 1* style to the following text:
      KENTWOOD SCHOOL DISTRICT
      September Newsletter
      David Olmsted, Editor
   d. Apply the *Subtitle 1* style to the following text:
      Welcome Back
      Double Shifting
      Emergency Kits
6. Save the document again with the same name (Ch 25, SA 03). (Make sure the document fits on one page. If not, consider decreasing slightly the left and right margins or the top and bottom margins.)
7. Print and then close Ch 25, SA 03.

Assessment 4

1. Open Ch 25, SA 03.
2. Save the document with Save As and name it Ch 25, SA 04.
3. Make the following changes to the document:
   a. Modify the *Title 1* style so the font is 16-point Arial bold.
   b. Modify the *Subtitle 1* style so the font is 14-point Arial bold and the space after the paragraph is 6 points.
   c. Position the insertion point at the beginning of the document and then insert the clip art image in the margin (if this image is not available, choose a similar image) with the following specifications:

      1) Format the picture so the width is 1.4 inches wide and the height is 1.2 inches.
      2) Change the wrapping style to Square.

   d. After inserting and formatting the clip art image, you may need to move down the heading *Welcome Back*. To do this, position the insertion point immediately left of the *W* in *Welcome*, and then press the Enter key.
4. Make sure the document fits on one page. If it does not, consider decreasing the top and bottom margins to approximately 0.75 inch.
5. Save the document again with the same name (Ch 25, SA 04).
6. Print and then close Ch 25, SA 04.

Unit five

PERFORMANCE ASSESSMENTS

DEMONSTRATING YOUR SKILLS

Assessment one

1. At a clear document screen, create the table shown in figure U5.1. Include the lines and shading as shown in the figure.
2. Save the document and name it Unit 5, PA 01.
3. Print and then close Unit 5, PA 01.

COLEMAN DEVELOPMENT CORPORATION		
Community Development Committee Members		
Name	Company	Address

Figure U5.1 • Assessment 1

Assessment two

1. At a clear document screen, create the table shown in figure U5.2. (The width of the first column is 2.6 inches and the width of the second and third columns is 1.7 inches. Include the lines and shading as shown in the figure.)
2. After creating the table, insert the formula *=SUM(ABOVE)* to calculate the amounts in the *First Half* column and the *Second Half* column.
3. Save the document and name it Unit 5, PA 02.
4. Print and then close Unit 5, PA 02.

COLEMAN DEVELOPMENT CORPORATION		
BALANCE SHEET		
Asset	**First Half**	**Second Half**
Bonds	$52,450,356.03	$53,340,559.00
Stocks	7,466,960.25	8,096,255.05
Mortgages	41,783,552.66	43,110,894.50
Real Estate	8,640,700.50	13,577,110.55
Long-Term Investments	1,155,220.24	1,098,452.85
Short-Term Investments	959,745.65	890,452.70
Other Assets	543,225.15	618,256.75
Total		

Figure U5.2 • Assessment 2

Assessment three

1. Open Table 06.
2. Save the document with Save As and name it Unit 5, PA 03.
3. Create a Column chart with the table with the following elements:
   a. Add the title, *REVENUE RESOURCES*, to the chart.
   b. Select and then delete the table.
   c. Change the Zoom to Whole Page.
   d. Increase the size of the chart. (You determine the size. Make sure it fits within the margins.)
   e. Move the chart to the middle of the page.
   f. Change the Zoom back to 100 percent.
4. Save the document again with the same name (Unit 5, PA 03).
5. Print and then close Unit 5, PA 03.

Assessment four

1. Open Table 07.
2. Save the document with Save As and name it Unit 5, PA 04.
3. Create a Pie chart for the table with the following elements:
   a. Change the chart type to a two-dimensional pie.
   b. Make sure the data is displayed properly in the Pie chart. (*Hint: You may need to click the* By Column *button on the Graph Standard toolbar.*)
   c. Add the title *SCHOOL EXPENDITURES*.
   d. Add percent data labels to the pieces of the pie in the chart.
   e. Select and then delete the table.
   f. Increase the size of the chart (you determine the size; make sure it fits within the margins).
   g. Change the Zoom to Whole Page.
   h. Move the chart to the middle of the page.
   i. Change the Zoom back to 100 percent.
4. Save the document again with the same name (Unit 5, PA 04).
5. Print and then close Unit 5, PA 04.

Assessment five

1. Open Report 03.
2. Save the document with Save As and name it Unit 5, PA 05.
3. Make the following changes to the report:
   a. Select the text from *MODULE 2: PLANNING A NEWSLETTER* to the end of the document, then delete it.
   b. Select the entire document and then make the following changes:
      1) Change the font to 11-point Times New Roman.
      2) Change the line spacing to single.
   c. Insert another hard return between the title *MODULE 1: DEFINING NEWSLETTER ELEMENTS* and the heading *Designing a Newsletter*.
   d. Insert a hard return above the heading *Defining Basic Newsletter Elements*.
   e. Format the text, except the title and the two blank lines below the title, into two evenly spaced columns with the spacing between changed to 0.4 inch and a line inserted between the columns.
   f. Set the title *MODULE 1: DEFINING NEWSLETTER ELEMENTS* in 14-point Arial bold.
   g. Set the two headings (*Designing a Newsletter* and *Defining Basic Newsletter Elements*) in 11-point Arial bold.
4. Save the document again with the same name (Unit 5, PA 05).
5. Print and then close Unit 5, PA 05.

Assessment six

1. At a clear document screen, create the following styles:
   a. Create a style named *Title Formatting* that changes text to a sans serif typeface (you determine the typeface) in 16-point size and bold type style.
   b. Create a style named *Heading Formatting* that changes text to a sans serif typeface (use the same typeface as the previous style) in 12-point size and bold type style.
2. Save the document and name it Unit 5, PA 06.
3. With Unit 5, PA 06 still open, insert the file named Report 05 into Unit 5, PA 06.
4. Make the following changes to the document:
   a. Select the entire document and then set a tab at 0.25 inch on the Ruler.
   b. Complete a spelling check on the document.
   c. Apply the *Title Formatting* style to the title *STRUCTURED PUBLICATIONS*.
   d. Apply the *Heading Formatting* style to the following headings:
      Cover
      Title Page
      Copyright Page
      Preface
      Table of Contents
      Body Text
      Appendix
      Bibliography
      Glossary
      Index
5. Check the page break and, if necessary, adjust the page break.
6. Save the document again with the same name (Unit 5, PA 06).
7. Print Unit 5, PA 06.
8. With Unit 5, PA 06 still open, save the document with Save As and name it Unit 5, PA 06 Second.
9. Make the following changes to the document:
   a. Edit the *Title Formatting* style so it changes text to a serif font (you choose the font) set in 16-point size and bold type style.
   b. Edit the *Heading Formatting* style so it changes text to a serif font (you choose the font) set in 14-point size and bold type style.
10. Save the document again with the same name (Unit 5, PA 06 Second).
11. Print and then close Unit 5, PA 06 Second.

CREATING ORIGINAL DOCUMENTS

Assessment seven

Situation: Check the career center at your school, the Employment Security Department in your city, or the local newspaper for a job announcement that interests you. Using the résumé you created for exercise 9 in chapter 24 as an example, design a résumé for yourself. Save the résumé and name it Unit 5, PA 07. Print and then close Unit 5, PA 07.

Assessment eight

Situation: You are an administrative assistant in the Financial Planning Department at Coleman Development Corporation. You have been asked by your supervisor to prepare a table showing equipment expenditures for each department as shown below:

COLEMAN DEVELOPMENT CORPORATION
Equipment Expenditures

Department	**Amount**
Human Resources	$20,459.34
Research	98,490.80
Financial Planning	14,439.50
Support Services	10,340.00
Sales	21,492.80
Public Relations	32,400.00
Total Amount	(Calculate total)

Create a table with the data and insert a formula to calculate the total. Save this document and name it Unit 5, PA 08. Print and then close Unit 5, PA 08.

Assessment nine

Situation: You work for Lifetime Annuity Association and you have been asked by your supervisor to create a document that shows customers' average household expenditures. Include the following information:

Average Household Expenditures

This pie chart shows how a typical two-paycheck household with an average after-tax income of $42,000 spends its annual income. How does your family's spending compare?

Include this information in the pie chart:

Expenditure	Percent of Income
Housing	29%
Transportation	17%
Food	15%
Insurance	12%
Health Care	4%
Other	15%

Besides the day-to-day living expenses shown in the chart, added unforeseen expenses may also arise. These could include outstanding medical bills, unpaid debts, and additional child care. How long will the proceeds from your current life insurance last once your family pays for these expenses and then begins to pay for the necessities of life?

When determining your family's life insurance needs, you will want to consider if your coverage will be adequate 5, 10, or even 15 years from now. Your family's financial needs may change over the years and inflation will gradually erode the value of your policy.

When creating the document, consider what typeface you will use, where you will place elements on the page, and how you will create the pie chart. Include a title for this document. Save the document and name it Unit 5, PA 09. Print and then close Unit 5, PA 09.

Unit Six

ORGANIZING TEXT IN DOCUMENTS

In this unit, you will learn to organize text in documents using the sorting and selecting features; format text into outlines; create fill-in business forms; and create tables of contents, indexes, and tables of authorities.

scans

The Secretary's Commission on Achieving Necessary Skills

D E C I S I O N   M A K I N G

T E C H N O L O G Y

P R O B L E M   S O L V I N G

C O M M U N I C A T I O N S

chapter TWENTY-SIX

26 Sorting and Selecting

PERFORMANCE OBJECTIVES

Upon successful completion of chapter 26, you will be able to:

- **Sort text in paragraphs, columns, tables, and data source documents.**
- **Sort on more than one field.**
- **Select specific information from a document.**

Word is primarily a word processing program, but it also includes some basic database functions. With a database program, you can alphabetize information or arrange numbers numerically and select specific records from a document.

In Word, you can sort text in paragraphs, text in rows in tables, or records in a data source. Sorting can be done alphabetically, numerically, or by date. You can also select specific records from a data source to be merged with a main document. Word can perform the three types of sorts shown in figure 26.1.

figure 26.1 *Types of Sorts*

Alphanumeric: In an alphanumeric sort, Word arranges the text in the following order: special symbols such as @ and # first, numbers second, and letters third. You can tell Word to sort text in all uppercase letters first, followed by words beginning with uppercase letters, and then words beginning with lowercase letters.

Numeric: In a numeric sort, Word arranges the text in numeric order and ignores any alphabetic text. Only the numbers 0 through 9 and symbols pertaining to numbers—such as $, %, -, ( ), a decimal point, and a comma—are recognized.

Date: In a date sort, Word sorts dates that are expressed in common date format, such as 05-15-99; 05/15/99; May 15, 1999; or 15 May 1999. Word does not sort dates that include abbreviated month names without periods. Dates expressed as a month, day, or year by themselves are also not sorted.

Sorting Text in Paragraphs

Text arranged in paragraphs can be sorted by the first character of the paragraph. This character can be a number, a symbol (such as $ or #), or a letter. The paragraphs to be sorted can be keyed at the left margin or indented with the Tab key. Unless you select paragraphs to be sorted, Word sorts the entire document.

Paragraphs can be sorted either alphanumerically, numerically, or by date. In an alphanumeric sort, punctuation marks or special symbols are sorted first, followed by numbers, and then text. If you sort paragraphs either alphanumerically or numerically, dates are treated as regular numbers.

To sort text in paragraphs, open the document containing the paragraphs to be sorted. (If the document contains text you do not want sorted with the paragraphs, select the paragraphs.) Click Table, then Sort, and the Sort Text dialog box displays as shown in figure 26.2. At this dialog box, make sure *Paragraphs* displays in the Sort by text box, Ascending is selected, and then click OK or press Enter.

26.2 ***Sort Text Dialog Box***

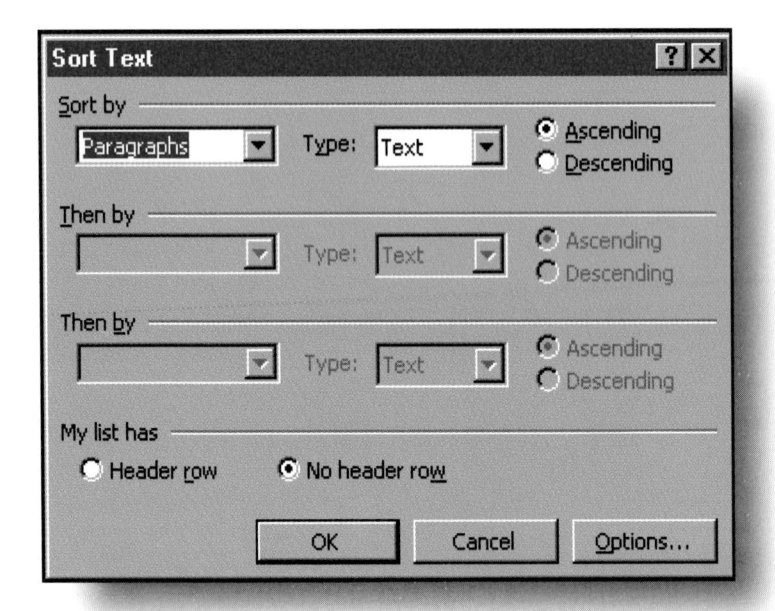

The Sort by option at the Sort Text dialog box has a default setting of *Paragraphs*. This default setting changes depending on the text in the document. For example, if you are sorting a table, the Sort by option has a default setting of *Column 1*. If you are sorting only the first word of each paragraph in the document, leave the Sort by option at the default of *Paragraphs*.

The Type option at the Sort Text dialog box has a default setting of *Text*. This can be changed to *Number* or *Date*. Figure 26.1 specifies how Word will sort numbers and dates.

When Word sorts paragraphs that are separated by two hard returns (two strokes of the Enter key), the hard returns are removed and inserted at the beginning of the document.

exercise 1

Sorting Paragraphs Alphabetically

1. Open Bibliography.
2. Save the document with Save As and name it Ch 26, Ex 01.
3. Sort the paragraphs alphabetically by the last name by completing the following steps:
   a. Click Table, then Sort.
   b. At the Sort Text dialog box, make sure *Paragraphs* displays in the Sort by text box and the Ascending option is selected.
   c. Click OK or press Enter.
   d. Deselect the text.
   e. Delete the hard returns at the beginning of the document.
   f. Add space below each paragraph by completing the following steps:
      1) Press Ctrl + A to select the entire document.
      2) Click Format, then Paragraph.
      3) At the Paragraph dialog box with the Indents and Spacing tab selected, click the up-pointing triangle at the right side of the After text box (in the Spacing section) until *12 pt* displays in the text box.
      4) Click OK to close the dialog box.
4. Save the document again with the same name (Ch 26, Ex 01).
5. Print and then close Ch 26, Ex 01.

Changing Sort Options

The Sort by options will also vary depending on options at the Sort Options dialog box shown in figure 26.3. To display the Sort Options dialog box, open a document containing text to be sorted, click Table, then Sort. At the Sort Text dialog box, click the Options button.

26.3

Sort Options Dialog Box

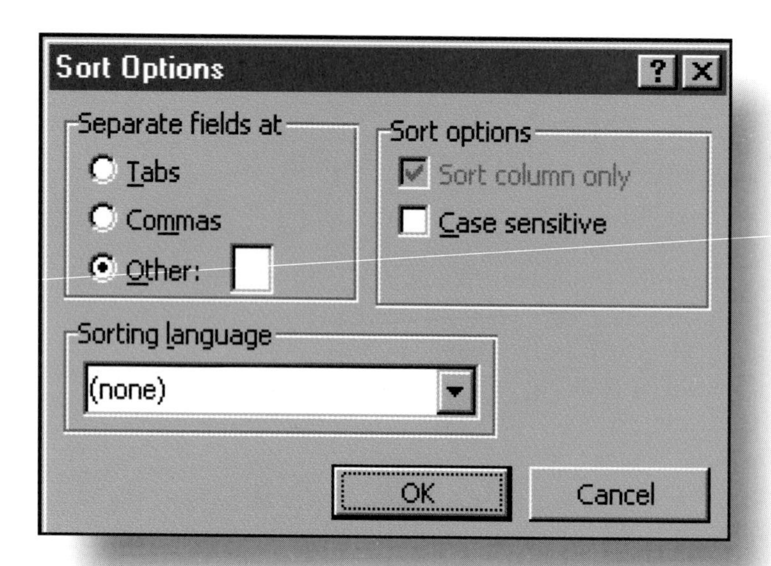

The Separate fields at section of the dialog box contains three options. The first option, Tabs, is selected by default. At this setting, Word assumes that text to be sorted is divided by tabs. This can be changed to Commas or Other. With the Other setting, you can specify the character that divides text to be sorted. For example, suppose a document contains first and last names in paragraphs separated by a space and you want to sort by the last name. To do this, you would click Other at the Sort Options dialog box, and then press the space bar. (This inserts a space, which is not visible, in the Other text box.) If names are separated by a comma, click Commas as the separator.

The Sort Options dialog box contains two choices in the Sort Options section. The first choice, Sort column only, sorts only the selected column. This choice is dimmed unless a column of text is selected. If a check mark appears in the Case sensitive check box, Word will sort text so that a word whose first letter is a capital letter is sorted before any word with the same first letter in lowercase. This option is available only if *Text* is selected in the Type text box at the Sort Text dialog box.

When you make changes at the Sort Options dialog box, the choices available with Sort by at the Sort Text dialog box will vary. For example, if you click Other at the Sort Options dialog box, and then press the space bar, the choices for Sort by at the Sort Text dialog box will include *Word 1, Word 2, Word 3,* etc.

exercise 2

Sorting Text Alphabetically by First and Last Name

1. At a clear document screen, key the text shown in figure 26.4. Begin each line of text at the left margin.
2. After keying the text, save the document and name it Ch 26, Ex 02.
3. With Ch 26, Ex 02 still open in the document screen, sort the text alphabetically by first name by completing the following steps:
   a. Click Table, then Sort.
   b. At the Sort Text dialog box, make sure *Paragraphs* displays in the Sort by text box and the Ascending option is selected.
   c. Click OK or press Enter.
   d. Deselect the text.
4. Save the document again with the same name (Ch 26, Ex 02).
5. Print Ch 26, Ex 02.
6. With Ch 26, Ex 02 still displayed in the document screen, sort the text by the last name (second word) by completing the following steps:
   a. Click Table, then Sort.
   b. At the Sort Text dialog box, click the Options button.
   c. At the Sort Options dialog box, click Other, and then press the space bar.
   d. Click OK or press Enter.
   e. At the Sort Text dialog box, click the down-pointing triangle at the right side of the Sort by option, and then click *Word 2* at the drop-down list.
   f. Make sure the Ascending option is selected.
   g. Click OK or press Enter.
   h. Deselect the text.
7. Save the document again with the same name (Ch 26, Ex 02).
8. Print and then close Ch 26, Ex 02.

figure 26.4 *Exercise 2*

Paul O'Shea, Development Manager
Nicole Clark, Director
Jack Takagawa, Assistant Director
Darryl Ellis, Trainer
Lynette Lagasi, Trainer
Timothy Watson, Director
Erica Torres, Director
Andrea Okamato, Director

Sorting Text in Columns

Text arranged in columns with tabs between the columns can be sorted alphabetically or numerically. Text in columns must be separated with tabs. When sorting text in columns, Word sorts by *fields*. Text keyed at the left margin is considered *Field 1*, text keyed at the first tab stop is considered *Field 2*, and so on. To sort text arranged in columns, display the Sort Text dialog box, and then click the Options button. At the Sort Options dialog box, make sure Tabs is selected in the Separate fields at section of the dialog box, and then click OK or press Enter. At the Sort Text dialog box, display the appropriate field number in the Sort by text box, and then click OK or press Enter.

When sorting text in columns, only one tab can be inserted between columns when keying the text. If you press the Tab key more than once between columns, Word recognizes each tab as a separate column. In this case, the field number you specify may correspond to an empty column rather than the desired column.

exercise 3

Sorting Text in Columns

1. At a clear document screen, create the document shown in figure 26.5 by completing the following steps:
   a. Set left tabs on the Ruler at the 0.5-inch mark, the 2.5-inch mark, and the 5-inch mark.
   b. Key the text in columns as shown in figure 26.5. Press the Tab key before keying each entry in the first column. (Be sure to press the Tab key before keying the first column.)
2. Save the document and name it Ch 26, Ex 03.
3. With Ch 26, Ex 03 still displayed in the document screen, sort the first column alphabetically by last name by completing the following steps:
   a. Select the text in all three columns *except* the headings.
   b. Click Table, then Sort.
   c. At the Sort Text dialog box, click the Options button.
   d. At the Sort Options dialog box, make sure Tabs is selected in the Separate fields at section of the dialog box. (If not, click Tabs.)
   e. Click OK or press Enter to close the Sort Options dialog box.
   f. At the Sort Text dialog box, click the down-pointing triangle at the right side of the Sort by text box, and then click *Field 2* at the drop-down list. (Field 2 is the first tab stop.)
   g. Make sure Ascending is selected.
   h. Click OK or press Enter.
   i. Deselect the text.
4. Save the document again with the same name (Ch 26, Ex 03).

5. Print Ch 26, Ex 03.
6. With Ch 26, Ex 03 still open in the document screen, sort the third column of text numerically by completing the following steps:
   a. Select the text in all three columns except the headings.
   b. Click Table, then Sort.
   c. At the Sort Text dialog box, click the Options button.
   d. At the Sort Options dialog box, make sure Tabs is selected in the Separate fields at section of the dialog box. (If not, click Tabs.)
   e. Click OK or press Enter to close the Sort Options dialog box.
   f. At the Sort Text dialog box, click the down-pointing triangle at the right side of the Sort by text box, and then click *Field 4* at the drop-down list. (Field 4 is the third tab stop.)
   g. Make sure *Number* displays in the Type text box. (If not, click the down-pointing triangle at the right side of the Type text box, and then click *Number* from the drop-down list.)
   h. Make sure Ascending is selected.
   i. Click OK or press Enter.
   j. Deselect the text.
7. Save the document again with the same name (Ch 26, Ex 03).
8. Print and then close Ch 26, Ex 03.

figure 26.5 *Exercise 3*

Employee	**Department**	**Ext.**
Clark, Nicole	Human Resources	3221
Takagawa, Jack	Human Resources	4120
Watson, Timothy	Administrative Services	1094
Torres, Erica	Research	5530
Baxter, Lisa	Administrative Services	2287
Marcus, Leigh	Support Services	5338
Gibson, Todd	Research	2988

exercise 4

Sorting Text by Date

1. At a clear document screen, create the document shown in figure 26.6. (Set left tabs for the columns, including the first column. You determine the tab settings. Be sure to press the Tab key before keying each entry in the first column.)
2. Save the document and name it Ch 26, Ex 04.
3. With Ch 26, Ex 04 still displayed in the document screen, sort the second column by date by completing the following steps:
   a. Select the text in all three columns *except* the title.
   b. Click Table, then Sort.
   c. At the Sort Text dialog box, click the Options button.
   d. At the Sort Options dialog box, make sure Tabs is selected in the Separate fields at section of the dialog box. (If not, click Tabs.)
   e. Click OK or press Enter to close the Sort Options dialog box.
   f. At the Sort Text dialog box, click the down-pointing triangle at the right side of the Sort by text box, and then click *Field 3* at the drop-down list. (Field 3 is the second tab stop.)
   g. Make sure *Date* appears in the Type text box and Ascending is selected.
   h. Click OK or press Enter.
   i. Deselect the text.
4. Save the document again with the same name (Ch 26, Ex 04).
5. Print and then close Ch 26, Ex 04.

26.6

Exercise 4

TRAINING SCHEDULE

Desktop Publishing	09/07/99	1:00 - 3:00 p.m.
Word Processing	10/04/99	9:00 - 11:00 a.m.
Database Management	08/25/99	1:30 - 3:30 p.m.
Spreadsheet	09/15/99	2:00 - 3:30 p.m.

Sorting on More than One Field

When sorting text, you can sort on more than one field. For example, in the text shown in the columns in figure 26.7, you can sort the text alphabetically by school name and then tell Word to sort the last names alphabetically within the school names. To do this, you would tell Word to sort on Field 3 (the second tab stop), and then sort on Field 2 (the first tab stop). Word sorts the second column of text (Field 3) alphabetically by school name and then sorts the names in the first column of text (Field 2) by last name. This results in the columns displaying as shown in figure 26.8.

figure 26.7 *Columns*

Employee	School	Ext.
Sandifer, Tara	Oakridge E. S.	6644
Dean, Jennifer	Emerald Heights E. S.	4435
Long, Christine	Oakridge E. S.	1203
Dowler, Blaine	Emerald Heights E. S.	3203
Anderson, Louise	Oakridge E. S.	6554

figure 26.8 *Sorted Columns*

Employee	School	Ext.
Dean, Jennifer	Emerald Heights E. S.	4435
Dowler, Blaine	Emerald Heights E. S.	3203
Anderson, Louise	Oakridge E. S.	6554
Long, Christine	Oakridge E. S.	1203
Sandifer, Tara	Oakridge E. S.	6644

Notice that the school names in the second column in figure 26.8 are alphabetized and that the last names *within* the school names are alphabetized. For example, *Anderson* is sorted before *Long* within *Oakridge E. S.*

exercise 5

Sorting on Two Fields

1. Open Ch 26, Ex 03.
2. Save the document with Save As and name it Ch 26, Ex 05.
3. Sort the text in columns alphabetically by department and then alphabetically by last name by completing the following steps:
   a. Select the text in all three columns *except* the headings.
   b. Click Table, then Sort.
   c. At the Sort Text dialog box, click the Options button.
   d. At the Sort Options dialog box, make sure Tabs is selected in the Separate fields at section of the dialog box. (If not, click Tabs.)
   e. Click OK or press Enter to close the Sort Options dialog box.
   f. At the Sort Text dialog box, click the down-pointing triangle at the right side of the Sort by text box, and then click *Field 3* at the drop-down list. (Field 3 is the second tab stop.)
   g. Click the down-pointing triangle at the right side of the Then by text box, and then click *Field 2* at the drop-down list.
   h. Make sure Ascending is selected.
   i. Click OK or press Enter.
   j. Deselect the text.
4. Save the document again with the same name (Ch 26, Ex 05).
5. Print and then close Ch 26, Ex 05.

Specifying a Header Row

The Sort Text dialog box contains the option, Header row, in the My list has section. If a document contains only columns of text with headings, you can use this option to tell Word to sort all text except for the headings of the columns.

exercise 6

Sorting Text in Columns with a Header Row

1. Open Ch 26, Ex 05.
2. Save the document with Save As and name it Ch 26, Ex 06.
3. Sort the third column of text numerically by the extension number by completing the following steps:
   a. With the columns displayed in the document screen, position the insertion point anywhere within the document.
   b. Click Table, then Sort.
   c. At the Sort Text dialog box, click Header row in the My list has section of the dialog box.

d. Click the Options button.
e. At the Sort Options dialog box, make sure Tabs is selected in the Separate fields at section of the dialog box. (If not, click Tabs.)
f. Click OK or press Enter to close the Sort Options dialog box.
g. At the Sort Text dialog box, click the down-pointing triangle at the right side of the Sort by text box, and then click *Ext.* at the drop-down list.
h. Make sure Ascending is selected.
i. If there is any text displayed in the Then by text box, click the down-pointing triangle to the right of the box, and then click *(none)* at the drop-down list.
j. Click OK or press Enter.
k. Deselect the text.

4. Save the document again with the same name (Ch 26, Ex 06).
5. Print and then close Ch 26, Ex 06.

Sorting Text in Tables

Sorting text in columns within tables is very similar to sorting columns of text separated by tabs. The same principles that apply to sorting columns of text also apply to sorting text within table columns. If a table contains a header row, you can tell Word not to include the header row when sorting by clicking Header row at the Sort dialog box. (The Sort Text dialog box becomes the Sort dialog box when sorting a table.) You can also select the cells in the table, except the header row, and then complete the sort.

If Header row is selected at the Sort dialog box, the information in the header row becomes the Sort by options. For example, in the table shown in figure 26.9, if Header row is selected, the Sort by options are *Salesperson, January Sales,* and *February Sales*.

26.9

Table

Salesperson	January Sales	February Sales
Tirado, Jessica	120,440.35	130,302.45
Stanton, Kenneth	149,895.05	155,784.25
Madison, Ramon	180,320.40	193,100.55
Fiscus, Marlana	200,345.10	210,450.25

exercise 7

Sorting Text Alphabetically in a Table

1. Open Table 03.
2. Save the document with Save As and name it Ch 26, Ex 07.
3. Sort the text alphabetically in the first column by completing the following steps:
   a. Position the insertion point anywhere within the table.
   b. Click Table, then Sort.
   c. At the Sort dialog box, click Header row in the My list has section of the dialog box.
   d. Make sure *Category* displays in the Sort by text box.
   e. Make sure Ascending is selected.
   f. Click OK or press Enter.
4. Save the document again with the same name (Ch 26, Ex 07).
5. Print and then close Ch 26, Ex 07.

In exercise 7, you selected Header row at the Sort dialog box. You can also sort text in a table by first selecting the cells you want sorted and then displaying the Sort dialog box.

exercise 8

Sorting Selected Text in a Table

1. Open Table 04.
2. Save the document with Save As and name it Ch 26, Ex 08.
3. Sort the numbers in the second column in descending order by completing the following steps:
   a. Select all the cells in the table except the cells in the first row.
   b. Click Table, then Sort.
   c. At the Sort dialog box, click the down-pointing triangle at the right side of the Sort by text box, and then click *Column 2* at the drop-down list.
   d. Click Descending.
   e. Click OK or press Enter.
4. With the insertion point positioned anywhere in the table, display the Table AutoFormat dialog box, and then apply the *Classic 2* format.
5. Save the document again with the same name (Ch 26, Ex 08).
6. Print and then close Ch 26, Ex 08.

Sorting Records in a Data Source

In an earlier chapter, you learned how to create a data source document. When a data source document is opened from a main document, the Database toolbar displays below the Formatting toolbar. You can also display the Database toolbar without opening the main document by clicking View, pointing to Toolbars, and then clicking Database. Another method is to right-click the Standard or Formatting toolbar and then click Database.

Sort Ascending

Sort Descending

Records in a data source can be sorted with the Sort Ascending and Sort Descending buttons on the Database toolbar. In addition to sorting with the buttons on the Database toolbar, you can sort a data source as you learned in the previous section of this chapter, "Sorting Text in Tables." This is because a data source is established in a table.

exercise 9

Sorting Text in a Data Source Using the Database Toolbar

1. Sort the records in the *Client list ds* document alphabetically by last name by completing the following steps:
   a. Open *Client list ds*.
   b. Save the document with Save As and name it Ch 26, Ex 09.
   c. Display the Database toolbar by right-clicking the Standard toolbar and then clicking Database at the drop-down list.
   d. Position the insertion point in any cell in the *LastName* column.
   e. Click the Sort Ascending button on the Database toolbar.
   f. Deselect the text.
   g. Turn off the display of the Database toolbar by right-clicking the Standard toolbar and then clicking Database at the drop-down list.
2. Save the document again with the same name (Ch 26, Ex 09).
3. Print and then close Ch 26, Ex 09.

Text in a data source document can also be sorted like text in a normal table. In exercise 10, you will sort the records numerically by Zip Code.

exercise 10

Sorting Text Numerically in a Data Source Document

1. Sort the records in the *Client list ds* document numerically by Zip Code by completing the following steps:
   a. Open *Client list ds*.
   b. Save the document with Save As and name it Ch 26, Ex 10.

c. Position the insertion point in any cell in the table.
d. Click Table, then Sort.
e. At the Sort dialog box, click Header row in the My list has section of the dialog box. (This option may already be selected.)
f. Click the down-pointing triangle at the right side of the Sort by text box and then click *PostalCode* at the drop-down list.
g. Make sure *Number* displays in the Type text box.
h. Make sure Ascending is selected. (If not, click Ascending.)
i. Click OK or press Enter.
j. Deselect the text.

2. Save the document again with the same name (Ch 26, Ex 10).
3. Print and then close Ch 26, Ex 10.

Sorting at the Query Options Dialog Box

Mail Merge

In addition to the two methods just described for sorting records in a data source, you can also sort records at the Query Options dialog box with the Sort Records tab selected. To display the Query Options dialog box shown in figure 26.10, open a main document, and then click the Mail Merge button on the Mail Merge toolbar. At the Mail Merge dialog box, click the Query Options button. At the Query Options dialog box, click the Sort Records tab.

figure 26.10 *Query Options Dialog Box with Sort Records Tab Selected*

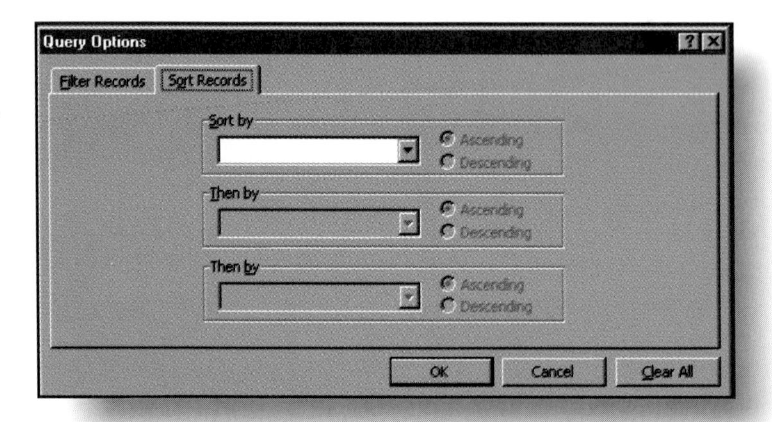

exercise 11

Sorting Text in a Data Source Document at the Query Options Dialog Box

1. Sort the records alphabetically by *City* in the *Client list ds* data source document attached to the *Open house md* main document by completing the following steps:

a. Open *Open house md*.
b. Click the Mail Merge button on the Mail Merge toolbar.
c. At the Merge dialog box, click the Query Options button.
d. At the Query Options dialog box, click the Sort Records tab.
e. At the Query Options dialog box with the Sort Records tab selected, click the down-pointing triangle at the right side of the Sort by text box, and then click *City* at the drop-down list.
f. Make sure Ascending is selected.
g. Click OK or press Enter.
h. At the Merge dialog box, click the Close button.
i. Click the Edit Data Source button on the Mail Merge toolbar.
j. At the Data Form dialog box, click the View Source button.

Edit Data Source

2. With the data source document displayed, click the Print button on the Standard toolbar.
3. Close *Client list ds* without saving the changes.
4. Close *Open house md* without saving the changes.

Selecting Records

If you have created a main document and a data source document to create personalized form letters, there may be situations that arise where you want to merge the main document with specific records in the data source. For example, you may want to send a letter to customers with a specific Zip Code or who live in a certain city.

With options from the Query Options dialog box with the Filter Records tab selected, shown in figure 26.11, you can select records for merging with the main document that meet certain criteria. For example, in exercise 12, you will select records of clients with a Zip Code higher than 10300.

figure 26.11 *Query Options Dialog Box with Filter Records Tab Selected*

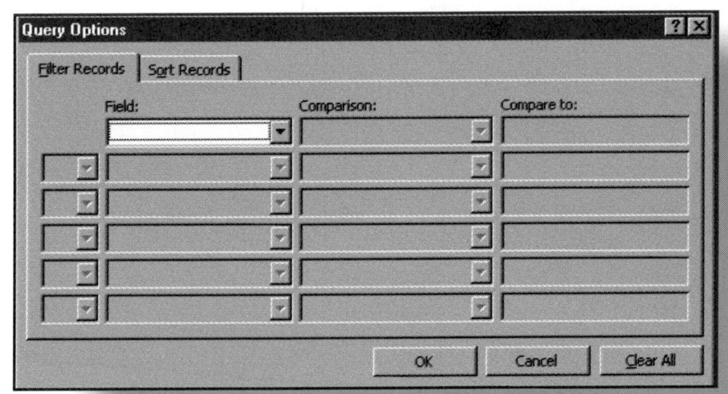

When you select a field from the Field drop-down list, Word automatically inserts *Equal to* in the Comparison text box. There are other comparisons you can make. Clicking the down-pointing triangle to the right of the Comparison text box causes a drop-down list to display with these additional options: *Not equal to, Less than, Greater than, Less than or equal, Greater than or equal, is blank*, and *is not blank*. Use one of these options to create a select equation. For example, select all customers with a Zip Code higher than 90543 by clicking *PostalCode* at the Field drop-down list. Click the down-pointing triangle at the right of the Comparison text box and then click *Greater than*. Key **90543** in the Compare to text box.

exercise 12

Selecting Records with Specific Zip Codes

1. Select the records with a Zip Code higher than 10300 in the *Client list ds* data source document attached to the *Open house md* main document, and then merge the records to a new document by completing the following steps:
   a. Open *Open house md*.
   b. Click the Mail Merge button on the Mail Merge toolbar.
   c. At the Merge dialog box, click the Query Options button.
   d. At the Query Options dialog box, make sure the Filter Records tab is selected.
   e. Click the down-pointing triangle at the right of the Field text box, click the down-pointing triangle at the bottom of the vertical scroll bar until *PostalCode* is displayed, and then click *PostalCode*. (When *PostalCode* is inserted in the Field text box, Word inserts *Equal to* in the Comparison text box and positions the insertion point in the Compare to text box.)
   f. With the insertion point positioned in the Compare to text box, key **10300**.
   g. Click the down-pointing triangle at the right of the Comparison text box, and then click *Greater than* at the drop-down list.
   h. Click OK or press Enter.
   i. At the Merge dialog box, make sure *New document* displays in the Merge to text box, and then click the Merge button.
2. Save the merged document and name it Ch 26, Ex 12.
3. Print and then close Ch 26, Ex 12.
4. Close *Open house md* without saving the changes.

When a field is selected from the field drop-down list, Word automatically inserts *And* in the first box at the left side of the dialog box. This can be changed, if needed, to *Or*. With the *And* and *Or* options, you can specify more than one condition for selecting records. For example, in exercise 13, you will select all records of clients living in the cities of *Hopkinton* or *Bow*. If the *Client list ds* document contained another field such as a specific financial plan for each customer, you could select all customers in a specific city that subscribe to a specific financial plan. For this situation, you would use the *And* option.

If you want to clear the current options at the Query Options dialog box with the Filter Records tab selected, click the Clear All button. This clears any text from text boxes and leaves the dialog box on the screen. Click Cancel if you want to close the Query Options dialog box without specifying any records.

exercise 13

Selecting Records Containing Specific Cities

1. Select the records in the *Client list ds* data source document attached to the *Open house md* main document that contain the city Hopkinton or Bow by completing the following steps:
   a. Open *Open house md*.
   b. Click the Mail Merge button on the Mail Merge toolbar.
   c. At the Merge dialog box, click the Query Options button.
   d. At the Query Options dialog box, make sure the Filter Records tab is selected.
   e. Click the down-pointing triangle to the right of the Field text box, click the down-pointing triangle at the bottom of the vertical scroll bar until *City* is displayed, and then click *City*.
   f. With the insertion point positioned in the Compare to text box, key **Hopkinton**.
   g. Click the down-pointing triangle to the right of the text box containing the word *And* (at the left side of the dialog box) and then click *Or* at the drop-down list.
   h. Click the down-pointing triangle to the right of the second Field text box, click the down-pointing triangle at the bottom of the vertical scroll bar until *City* is displayed, and then click *City*.
   i. With the insertion point positioned in the second Compare to text box (the one below the box containing *Hopkinton*), key **Bow**.
   j. Click OK or press Enter.
   k. At the Merge dialog box, make sure *New document* displays in the Merge to text box, and then click the Merge button.
2. Save the merged document and name it Ch 26, Ex 13.
3. Print and then close Ch 26, Ex 13.
4. Close *Open house md* without saving the changes.

chapter summary

- Word is a word processing program that includes some basic database functions. With the database functions, you can alphabetize information, arrange numbers numerically, or select specific records from a data source.
- Word lets you sort text in paragraphs, text in table rows, or records in a data source. You can also select specific records from a data source to be merged with a main document.
- Word can perform these three types of sorts: alphanumeric, numeric, and date.
- Text arranged in paragraphs can be sorted by the first character of the paragraph at the Sort Text dialog box.
- The Sort by option at the Sort Text dialog box has a default setting of *Paragraph*. This default setting changes depending on the text in the document and the options specified at the Sort Options dialog box.
- Text arranged in columns with tabs between the columns can be sorted alphabetically or numerically. Text keyed at the left margin is considered *Field 1*, text keyed at the first tab stop is considered *Field 2*, and so on.
- When sorting text, you can sort on more than one field.
- Use the option Header row in the My list has section of the Sort Text dialog box to tell Word to sort all text in columns except for the headings of the columns.
- Sorting text in columns within tables is very similar to sorting columns of text separated by tabs.
- Records in a data source can be sorted in the same way as text in a table, or use the Sort Ascending and Sort Descending buttons on the Database toolbar.
- Records can also be sorted at the Query Options dialog box with the Sort Records tab selected.
- With options from the Query Options dialog box with the Filter Records tab selected, specific records can be selected for merging with the main document.

commands review

	Mouse/Keyboard
Display Sort Text dialog box	Table, Sort
Display Sort Options dialog box	Table, Sort, Options

check your understanding

Completion: In the space provided at the right, indicate the correct term, command, or number.

1. With the sorting feature, you can sort text in paragraphs, records in a data source, or this type of text. ________________
2. These three types of sorts can be performed by Word's sort feature: alphanumeric, numeric, and this. ________________
3. Sort text in paragraphs at this dialog box. ________________
4. This is the default selection at the Separate fields at section of the Sort Options dialog box. ________________
5. When sorting columns, text keyed at the first tab stop is considered to be this field number. ________________
6. Click this option at the Sort Text dialog box to tell Word not to include the column headings in the sort. ________________
7. With the insertion point positioned in a table, clicking Table, then Sort causes this dialog box to display. ________________
8. You can sort records in a data source as you would a table, or using the Database toolbar, or at this dialog box. ________________
9. Select specific records from a data source to be merged with the main document from this dialog box. ________________
10. To complete the last step to select all customers from a data source that have a balance higher than $500, key **500** at this text box. ________________

skill assessments

Note: Before completing the skill assessments, display the Open dialog box, and then select and delete documents created in chapter 24 that begin Ch 24. You may want to check with your instructor before deleting these documents.

Assessment 1

1. At a clear document screen, create the document shown in figure 26.12.
2. Save the document and name it Ch 26, SA 01.
3. Sort the names (not the title) alphabetically by last name.
4. Save the sorted document again with the same name (Ch 26, SA 01).
5. Print and then close Ch 26, SA 01.

Figure 26.12 • Assessment 1

KENTWOOD SCHOOL DISTRICT

Shing, Linda, Superintendent
Valenzuela, Rodney, Assistant Superintendent
Brennan, Sarah, Curriculum Specialist
Goodrow, Gabriel, Support Specialist
Griffin-Leon, Janet, Information Specialist
Olmsted, David, Newsletter Editor
Long, Christine, Assistant Newsletter Editor

Assessment 2

1. At a clear document screen, create the document shown in figure 26.13. (Set tabs for each column of text in the document.)
2. Save the document and name it Ch 26, SA 02.
3. Sort the columns of text alphabetically by last name in the first column. (*Hint: Select the columns of text but not the title, subtitle, and headings.*)
4. Print Ch 26, SA 02.
5. Sort the columns of text by the date of hire in the third column.
6. Print Ch 26, SA 02.
7. Sort the columns of text alphabetically by the department name and then alphabetically by last name.
8. Save the document again with the same name (Ch 26, SA 02).
9. Print and then close Ch 26, SA 02.

Figure 26.13 • Assessment 2

COLEMAN DEVELOPMENT CORPORATION

New Employees

Employee	**Department**	**Hire Date**
Wilson, Grace	Financial Services	02/03/99
Prada, Craig	Human Resources	04/14/99
McClure, Anthony	Administrative Services	03/10/99
Sok, Neay	Financial Services	02/10/99
Woodhouse, Leanne	Support Services	04/07/99
Tucker, Sandra	Human Resources	03/24/99
Mattila, Diana	Administrative Services	02/17/99

Assessment 3

1. Open Table 02.
2. Save the document with Save As and name it Ch 26, SA 03.
3. Sort the text alphabetically by *State* in the first column of the table. (Make sure no text displays in the Then by text box.)
4. Print Ch 26, SA 03.
5. Sort the text numerically by *1st Qtr.* in ascending order in the second column of the table.
6. Display the Table AutoFormat dialog box and apply a table formatting of your choosing to the table.
7. Save the document again with the same name (Ch 26, SA 03).
8. Print and then close Ch 26, SA 03.

Assessment 4

1. Create a main document for envelopes that has the *Client list ds* data source document attached and then merge the envelope with those records in *Client list ds* with the city *Concord*. Merge to a new document. (*Hint: Begin at the Mail Merge Helper dialog box.*)
2. Save the merged document and name it Ch 26, SA 04.
3. Print and then close Ch 26, SA 04.
4. Close the envelope main document without saving the changes.

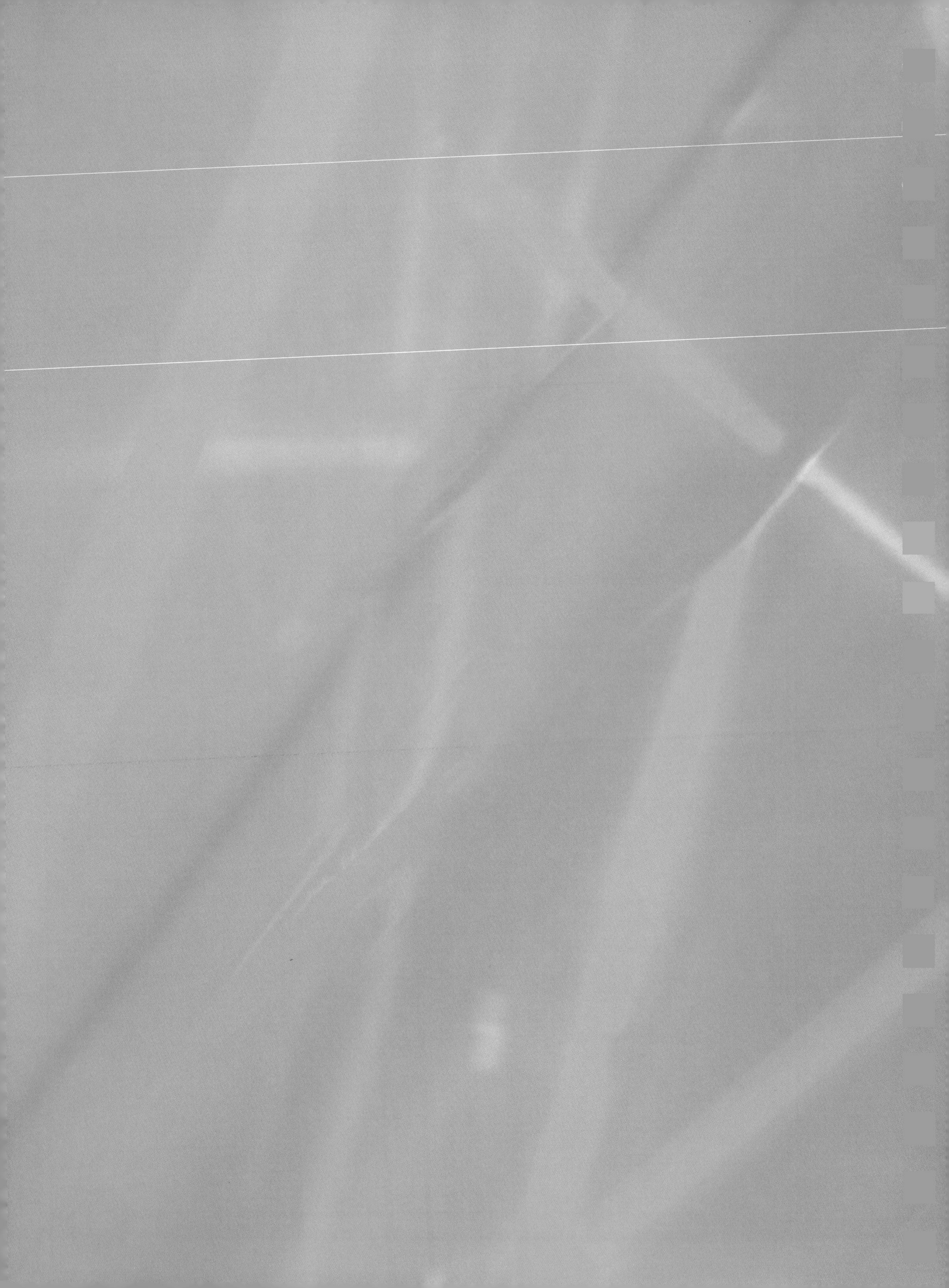

chapter TWENTY-SEVEN

27 Creating Outlines

PERFORMANCE OBJECTIVES

Upon successful completion of chapter 27, you will be able to:

- **Display a document in Outline view.**
- **Create an outline.**
- **Assign headings in an outline.**
- **Collapse and expand outline headings.**
- **Organize an outline.**
- **Number an outline.**
- **Navigate in a document using the Document Map feature.**

Word's outlining feature will format headings within a document as well as let you view formatted headings and body text in a document. With the outlining feature you can quickly see an overview of a document by collapsing parts of a document so that only the headings show. With headings collapsed, you can perform such editing functions as moving or deleting sections of a document.

Word also includes the Document Map feature. This feature is similar to the outlining feature. The Document Map is a separate pane that displays an outline of the document's headings. In Document Map, you can change heading levels and jump to specific headings in a document.

Creating an Outline

To create an outline, you identify particular headings and subheadings within a document as certain heading levels. The Outline view is used to assign particular heading levels to text. You can also enter text and edit text while working in Outline view. To change to Outline view, click the Outline View button at the left side of the horizontal scroll bar, or click View, then Outline. Figure 27.1 shows the Report 01 document as it will appear in exercise 1 with heading formatting applied in Outline view.

Outline View

figure 27.1

Document in Outline View

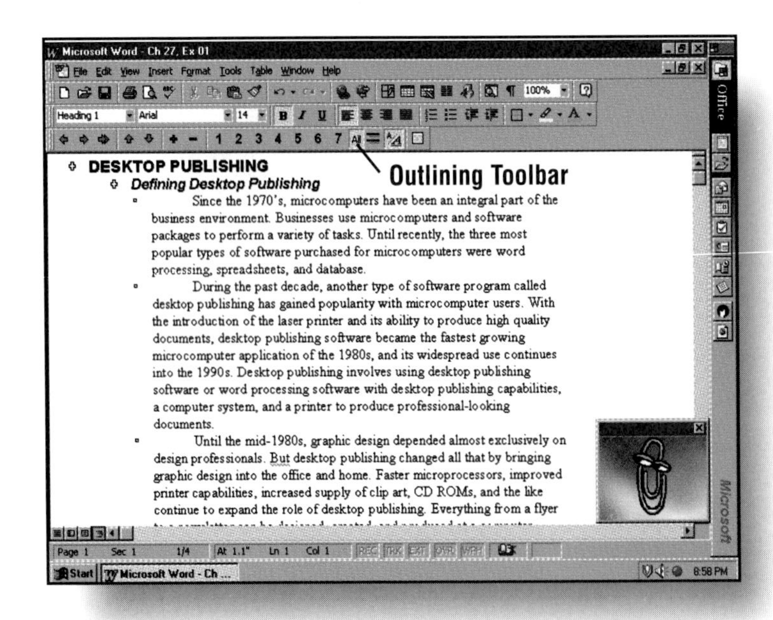

In Figure 27.1, the title DESKTOP PUBLISHING is identified as a first-level heading, the heading *Defining Desktop Publishing* is identified as a second-level heading, and the paragraphs following are normal text.

When a document contains headings and text that have been formatted in the Outline view, each paragraph is identified as a particular heading level or as normal text. Paragraphs are identified by *outline selection symbols* that appear in the selection bar at the left side of the screen. Figure 27.2 describes the three outline selection symbols and what they indicate.

figure 27.2

Outline Selection Symbols

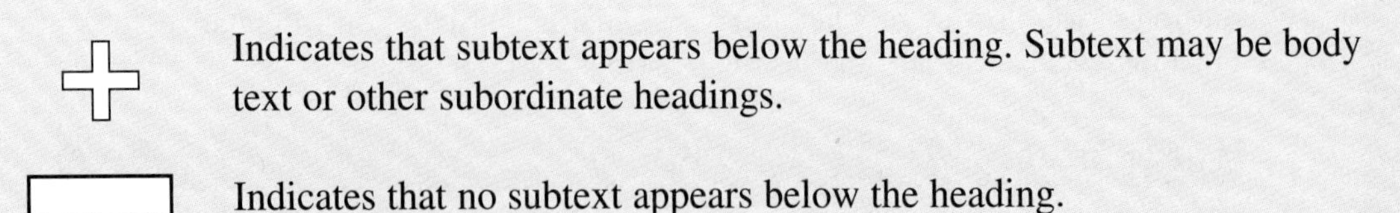

Indicates that subtext appears below the heading. Subtext may be body text or other subordinate headings.

Indicates that no subtext appears below the heading.

Indicates the paragraph is normal text.

The outline selection symbols can be used to select text in the document. To do this, position the arrow pointer on the outline selection symbol next to text you want to select until it turns into a four-headed arrow, and then click the left mouse button.

Assigning Headings

When a document is displayed in Outline view, the Outlining toolbar displays below the Formatting toolbar as shown in figure 27.1. Use buttons on this toolbar to assign various level headings and outline numbers to paragraphs.

When you initially display a document in Outline view, each paragraph is identified as a normal text paragraph. To identify certain paragraphs as heading levels, use the arrow buttons at the left side of the Outlining toolbar. These buttons and their keyboard equivalents are described in figure 27.3 along with the other buttons on the Outlining toolbar.

figure 27.3 *Outlining Toolbar Buttons*

Button	Name	Action
	Promote	Promotes heading (and its body text) by one level; promotes body text to the heading level of the preceding heading.
	Demote	Demotes heading by one level; demotes body text to the heading level below the preceding heading.
	Demote to Body Text	Demotes heading to body text.
	Move Up	Moves selected paragraph(s) to appear before first visible paragraph that precedes selected paragraph(s).
	Move Down	Moves selected paragraph(s) to appear after first visible paragraph that follows selected paragraph(s).
+	Expand	Expands first heading level below currently selected heading.
-	Collapse	Collapses body text into heading, then collapses lowest heading levels into higher heading levels.
1 2 3 4 5 6 7	Show Headings 1 through 7	Displays all headings and text through lowest level button chosen.
All	Show All Headings	Displays all text if some collapsed; displays only headings if all text already expanded.
	Show First Line Only	Switches between displaying all body text or only first line of each paragraph.
	Show Formatting	Displays outline with or without character formatting.
	Master Document View	Changes to Master Document view or back to Outline view. Displays Master Document toolbar to right of Outline toolbar.

Promote

Style

Demote

To change a paragraph that is identified as normal text to a first-level heading, position the insertion point on any character in the text (or select the text), and then click the Promote button on the Outlining toolbar. This applies the Heading 1 style to the paragraph. The Heading 1 style is a style that has been predefined by Word. This style displays in the Style button on the Formatting toolbar. (First button at left side.) The Heading 1 style sets the text in 14-point Arial bold.

To change a paragraph to a second-level heading, position the insertion point anywhere within the text, and then click the Demote button. This applies the Heading 2 style to the text. The Heading 2 style sets text in 12-point Arial bold italic and indents the text one-half inch. Figure 27.4 shows the formatting that is applied for each heading level.

figure 27.4 ***Heading Formatting***

Heading 1	14-point Arial bold
Heading 2	12-point Arial bold italic; indented 0.5 inch from left margin
Heading 3	12-point Arial; indented 1 inch from left margin
Heading 4	12-point Arial bold; indented 1.5 inches from left margin
Heading 5	11-point Times New Roman; indented 2 inches from left margin
Heading 6	11-point Times New Roman italic; indented 2.5 inches from left margin
Heading 7	10-point Arial; indented 3 inches from left margin
Heading 8	10-point Arial italic; indented 3.5 inches from left margin
Heading 9	9-point Arial bold italic; indented 4 inches from left margin

exercise 1

Formatting a Document with Buttons on the Outlining Toolbar

1. Open Report 01.
2. Save the document with Save As and name it Ch 27, Ex 01.
3. Change to the Outline viewing mode by clicking the Outline View button at the left side of the horizontal scroll bar.
4. Promote and demote heading levels by completing the following steps:
   a. Position the insertion point anywhere in the title, *DESKTOP PUBLISHING*, and then click the Promote button on the Outlining toolbar. (*Heading 1* will display in the Style button on the Formatting toolbar.)

b. Position the insertion point anywhere in the heading, *Defining Desktop Publishing*, and then click the Demote button on the Outlining toolbar. (*Heading 2* will display in the Style button on the Formatting toolbar.)
c. Position the insertion point anywhere in the heading, *Initiating the Desktop Publishing Process*, and then click the Promote button on the Outlining toolbar. (*Heading 2* will display in the Style button on the Formatting toolbar.)
d. Position the insertion point anywhere in the heading, *Planning the Publication*, and then click the Promote button on the Outlining toolbar. (*Heading 2* will display in the Style button on the Formatting toolbar.)
e. Position the insertion point anywhere in the heading, *Creating the Content*, and then click the Promote button on the Outlining toolbar. (*Heading 2* will display in the Style button on the Formatting toolbar.)

5. Save the document again with the same name (Ch 27, Ex 01).
6. Print and then close Ch 27, Ex 01.

You can also promote or demote a heading in the Outline view by dragging the selection symbol to the left or right one-half inch. For example, to demote text identified as a Heading 1 to Heading 2, position the arrow pointer on the plus symbol before the Heading 1 text until it turns into a four-headed arrow, hold down the left mouse button, drag the mouse to the right until a gray vertical line displays down the screen, and then release the mouse button.

Complete similar steps to promote a heading. For example, to promote a Heading 2 to a Heading 1, position the arrow pointer on the plus symbol before the Heading 2 text until it turns into a four-headed arrow, hold down the left mouse button, drag the mouse to the left until a gray vertical bar displays with a small square attached, and then release the mouse button.

Another way to demote a heading is to position the insertion point in the heading text, and then click the Demote to Body Text button on the Outlining toolbar.

Demote to Body Text

exercise 2

Demoting Headings in a Document

1. Open Ch 27, Ex 01.
2. Save the document and name it Ch 27, Ex 02.
3. Make sure the Outline viewing mode is on and then demote the heading *Creating the Content* to Heading 3 level by completing the following steps:
   a. Press Ctrl + End to move the insertion point to the end of the document and then scroll up in the document until *Creating the Content* is visible (located toward the end of the document).

b. Position the mouse pointer on the plus symbol that displays before *Creating the Content* until the mouse pointer turns into a four-headed arrow.
c. Hold down the left mouse button, drag the mouse to the right until a gray vertical line displays down the screen, and then release the mouse button.

4. Demote the heading, *Planning the Publication*, to a Heading 3 level by completing steps similar to those in step 3.
5. Save the document again with the same name (Ch 27, Ex 02).
6. Print and then close Ch 27, Ex 02.

Collapsing and Expanding Outline Headings

One of the major benefits of working in the Outline view is the ability to see a condensed outline of your document without all of the text in between headings or subheadings. Word lets you collapse a heading level in an outline. This causes any text or subsequent lower heading levels to disappear temporarily. When heading levels are collapsed, viewing the outline of a document is much easier. For example, when an outline is collapsed, you can see an overview of the entire document and move easily to different locations in the document. You can also move headings and their subordinate headings to new locations in the outline.

The ability to collapse and expand headings in an outline provides flexibility in using Word's outline feature. One popular use of this capability is to move quickly from one portion of a document to another. For example, if you are working at the beginning of a lengthy document and want to move to a particular section, but you cannot remember the name of the heading in that section or the page number on which it is located, switch to the Outline view, collapse the entire outline, position the insertion point in the desired heading, and then expand the outline.

Another popular use of the collapse and expand feature is in maintaining consistency between various headings. While creating a particular heading, you may need to refer to the previous heading. To do this, switch to the Outline view, collapse the outline, and the previous heading is visible.

2

Show Heading 2

To collapse the entire outline, click the Show Heading button containing the number of headings desired. For example, if a document contains three heading levels, clicking the Show Heading 2 button on the Outlining toolbar will collapse the outline so only Heading 1 and Heading 2 text is displayed.

Show All Headings

Click the Show All Headings button to deactivate the button and the document collapses displaying only heading text, not body text. Click the Show All Headings button again to activate it and the document expands to show all heading levels and body text. If you click the Show All Headings button to deactivate it, the document would display as shown in figure 27.5. (The document in figure 27.5 is the document from figure 27.1.) When a heading is collapsed, a gray horizontal line displays beneath it.

27.5

Collapsed Outline

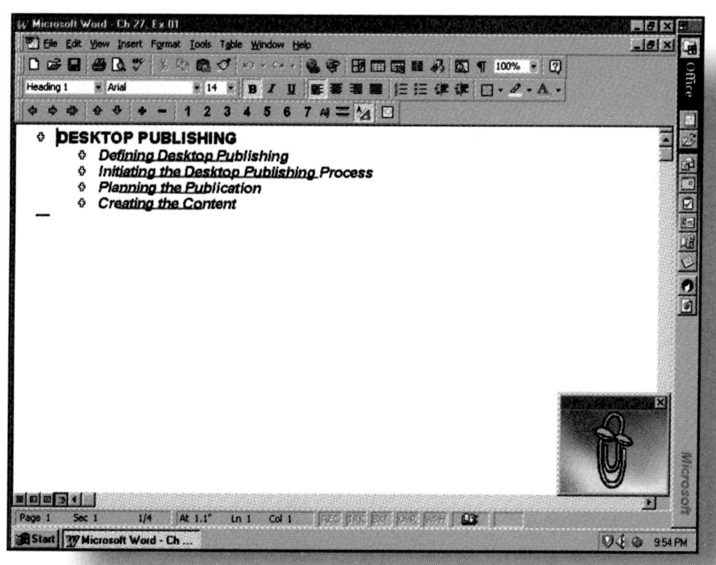

exercise 3

Collapsing an Outline

1. Open Ch 27, Ex 01.
2. Save the document with Save As and name it Ch 27, Ex 03.
3. Make the following changes to the document:
   a. Make sure the document is displayed in the Outline viewing mode.
   b. Click the Show All Headings button on the Outlining toolbar to deactivate it.
   c. With the outline collapsed, select the heading *Defining Desktop Publishing*, and then delete it. (This deletes the heading and all text below the heading.)
4. Save the document again with the same name (Ch 27, Ex 03).
5. Print and then close Ch 27, Ex 03. (This will print the collapsed outline, not the entire document.)

To collapse all of the text beneath a particular heading (including the text following any subsequent headings), position the insertion point within the heading, and then click the Collapse button on the Outlining toolbar. To make the text appear again, click the Expand button on the Outlining toolbar. For example, if you collapsed the first second-level heading shown in the document in figure 27.1, the document would display as shown in figure 27.6.

Collapse

Expand

27.6 Collapsed Second-Level Heading

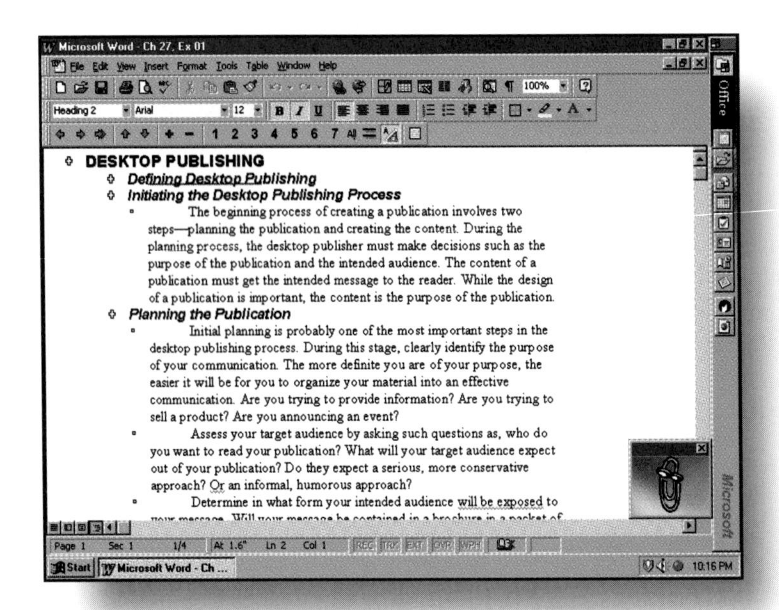

exercise 4

Collapsing and Expanding an Outline

1. Open Report 04.
2. Save the document with Save As and name it Ch 27, Ex 04.
3. Make the following changes to the document:
   a. Change to the Outline viewing mode.
   b. Promote the title *MODULE 3: DESIGNING A NEWSLETTER* to Heading 1.
   c. Demote the heading *Applying Desktop Publishing Guidelines* to Heading 2.
   d. Promote the title *MODULE 4: CREATING NEWSLETTER LAYOUT* to Heading 1.
   e. Demote the heading *Choosing Paper Size and Type* to Heading 2.
   f. Promote the heading *Choosing Paper Weight* to Heading 2.
   g. Promote the heading *Creating Margins for Newsletters* to Heading 2.
4. Collapse and expand the document by completing the following steps:
   a. Position the insertion point anywhere in the title, *MODULE 3: DESIGNING A NEWSLETTER*, and then click the Collapse button on the Outlining toolbar. (This collapses the text in the first module so only the title and heading display.)

b. Click the Expand button to expand the display of the text in the first module.
c. With the insertion point still positioned anywhere in the title, *MODULE 3: DESIGNING A NEWSLETTER*, click the Show Heading 1 button on the Outlining toolbar. (This displays only the two titles.)
d. Click the Show Heading 2 button on the Outlining toolbar. (This displays the titles and headings.)
e. Click the Expand button on the Outlining toolbar.
f. Click the Show First Line Only button on the Outlining toolbar. (This displays only the first line of each paragraph in the first module.)
g. Click the Show First Line Only button to deactivate it.
h. Click the Show All Headings button on the Outlining toolbar to deactivate it. (This displays only the titles and headings in the document.)
i. Select the heading *Choosing Paper Weight* and then delete it.
j. Click the Show All Headings button on the Outlining toolbar to activate it and display the entire document.

5. Save the document again with the same name (Ch 27, Ex 04).
6. Print and then close Ch 27, Ex 04.

Show First Line Only

Organizing an Outline

Collapsing and expanding headings within an outline is only part of the versatility offered by Word's outline feature. It also offers you the ability to rearrange an entire document by reorganizing an outline. Whole sections of a document can quickly be rearranged by moving the headings at the beginning of those sections. The text that is collapsed beneath the headings is moved at the same time.

For example, to move a second-level heading below other second-level headings, you would collapse the outline, select the second-level heading to be moved, and then click the Move Down button on the Outlining toolbar until the second-level heading is in the desired position.

Move Down

If headings are collapsed, you only need to select the heading and move it to the desired location. Any subsequent text that is hidden is moved automatically. You can also move headings in a document by positioning the arrow pointer on the plus symbol before the desired heading until it turns into a four-headed arrow, holding down the mouse button, dragging the heading to the desired location, and then releasing the mouse button. As you drag the mouse, a gray horizontal line displays in the document with an arrow attached. Use this horizontal line to help you move the heading to the desired location.

Moving Headings in a Document

1. Open Ch 27, Ex 01.
2. Save the document with Save As and name it Ch 27, Ex 05.
3. Make the following changes to the document:
   a. With the Outline viewing mode turned on, click the Show Heading 2 button on the Outlining toolbar.
   b. Move *Creating the Content* above *Planning the Publication* by completing the following steps:
      1) Position the insertion point anywhere in the heading *Creating the Content*.
      2) Click once on the Move Up button on the Outlining toolbar.

Move Up

   c. Move the heading *Initiating the Desktop Publishing Process* below *Planning the Publication* by completing the following steps:
      1) Position the arrow pointer on the plus symbol immediately left of the heading *Initiating the Desktop Publishing Process* until it turns into a four-headed arrow.
      2) Hold down the left mouse button, drag the mouse down until the gray horizontal line with the arrow attached is positioned below *Planning the Publication*, and then release the mouse button.
      3) Deselect the text.
4. Save the document again with the same name (Ch 27, Ex 05).
5. Print Ch 27, Ex 05. (Only the title and headings will print.)
6. Click the Show All Headings button on the Outlining toolbar to display the document text, and then close the document.

Numbering an Outline

Headings in an outline can be automatically numbered with options from the Bullets and Numbering dialog box with the Outline Numbered tab selected. If headings in an outline are moved, inserted, or deleted, the headings are automatically renumbered by Word. Heading numbers become part of the document and display in the Normal and Page Layout viewing modes as well as the Outline view.

To number headings in an outline, display the document in the Outline viewing mode, select the document text, and then click Format, then Bullets and Numbering. At the Bullets and Numbering dialog box, click the Outline Numbered tab. At the Bullets and Numbering dialog box with the Outline Numbered tab selected, as shown in figure 27.7, click the desired numbering method, and then click OK.

27.7 *Bullets and Numbering Dialog Box with Outline Numbered Tab Selected*

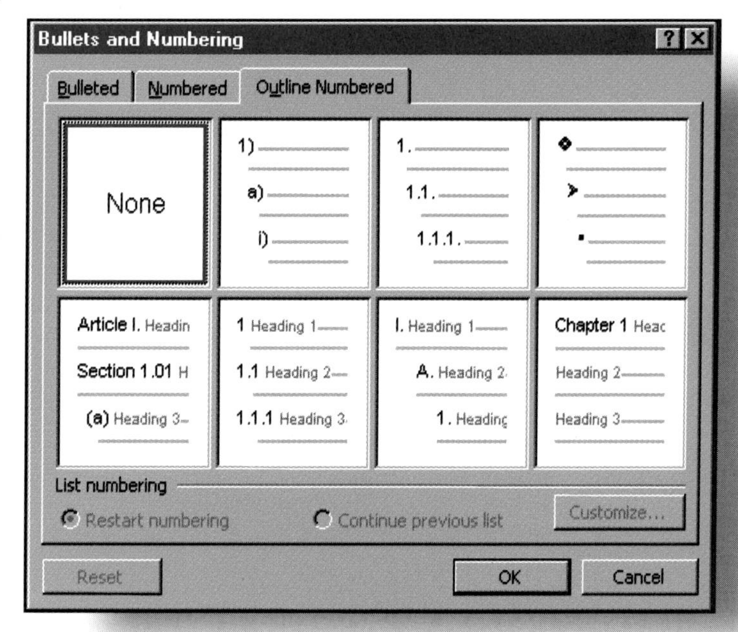

exercise 6

Numbering Headings in an Outline

1. Open Ch 27, Ex 04.
2. Save the document with Save As and name it Ch 27, Ex 06.
3. Make the following changes to the document:
   a. Click the Show Heading 2 button on the Outlining toolbar.
   b. Add numbering by completing the following steps:
      1) Press Ctrl + A to select all text in the document.
      2) Click Format, then Bullets and Numbering.
      3) At the Bullets and Numbering dialog box, click the Outline Numbered tab.
      4) At the Bullets and Numbering dialog box with the Outline Numbered tab selected, click the third numbering option from the left in the bottom row.
      5) Click OK to close the dialog box.
   c. Move the title *MODULE 3: DESIGNING A NEWSLETTER* (and all the headings below it) below the title *MODULE 4: CREATING NEWSLETTER LAYOUT* (and all the headings below it).
   d. Change the module 3 title to module 4 and change the module 4 title to module 3 (since these titles were reversed).

4. Save the document again with the same name (Ch 27, Ex 06).
5. With the document still collapsed, print the document.
6. Close Ch 27, Ex 06.

Document Mapping

Word 97 includes a Document Map feature you can use to navigate easily in a document and keep track of your location within the document. The Document Map displays any headings that are formatted with Word's heading styles (Heading 1 through 9) or outline-level paragraph format. If there are no headings formatted with heading styles or outline levels, Document Map searches for paragraphs that look like headings, such as short lines set in a larger type size. If no headings are found, the Document Map pane is blank.

Document Map

The Document Map is a separate pane that displays the outline of a document. To display the Document Map pane, click the Document Map button on the Standard toolbar. This displays the Document Map pane at the left side of the document as shown in figure 27.8. Figure 27.8 displays the document named Ch 27, Ex 04. Ch 27, Ex 04 contains headings with heading styles applied with buttons on the Outlining toolbar.

figure 27.8 ***Document Map Pane***

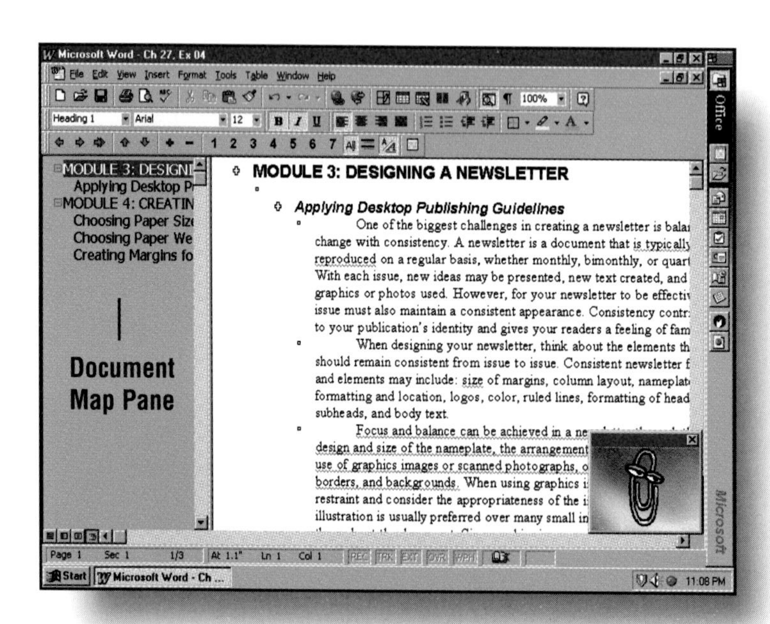

In the Document Map pane in figure 27.8, not all of the heading text is visible. To display the entire heading, position the arrow pointer on the heading and the heading text displays in a yellow box.

In exercise 7, you will display the Document Map for Report 01 and also Report 03. Neither of these documents contain headings that are formatted with Word's heading styles. However, Document Map will search the document and then display the short lines in the Document Map pane.

exercise 7

Displaying the Document Map Pane in a Document

1. Open Report 01.
2. Display the Document Map pane and move to different locations in the document by completing the following steps:
   a. Click the Document Map button on the Standard toolbar.
   b. Click the heading *Creating the Content* that displays in the Document Map pane.
   c. Click the heading *Defining Desktop Publishing* that displays in the Document Map pane.
   d. Remove the Document Map pane by clicking the Document Map button on the Standard toolbar.
3. Close Report 01.
4. Open Report 03.
5. Display the Document Map pane and move to different locations in the document by completing the following steps:
   a. Click the Document Map button on the Standard toolbar.
   b. Click the heading *MODULE 2: PLANNING A NEWSLETTER*.
   c. Click the heading *MODULE 1: DEFINING NEWSLETTER ELEMENTS*.
   d. Remove the Document Map pane by clicking the Document Map button on the Standard toolbar.
6. Close Report 03.

If Word's heading styles have been applied to a document's heading, many of the same options on the Outlining toolbar are available in the Document Map pane. To display the options available, position the arrow pointer on a heading in the Document Map pane and then click the right mouse button. This displays the shortcut menu shown in figure 27.9.

27.9 *Document Map Shortcut Menu*

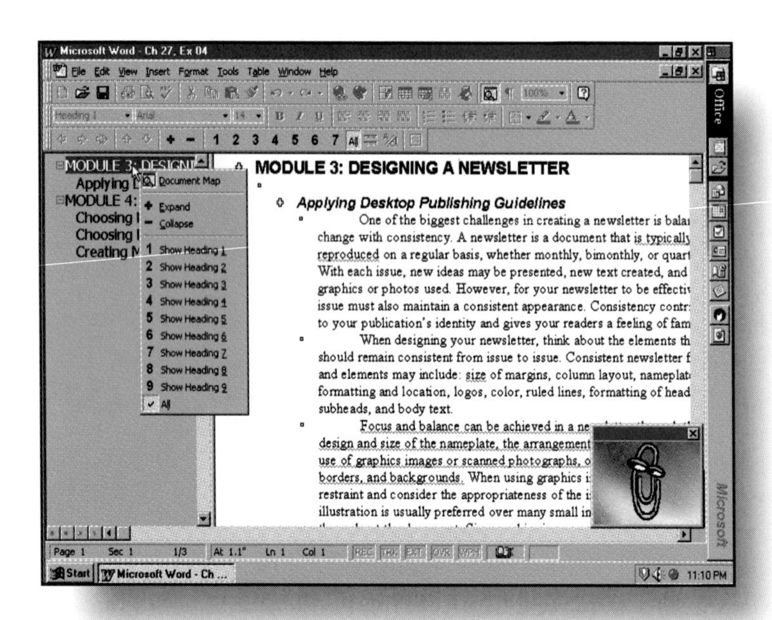

At the shortcut menu, click the desired option. For example, to collapse text within a heading, position the arrow pointer on the heading, click the *right* mouse button, and then click the *Collapse* option at the shortcut menu. This collapses the text so only the heading displays where the insertion point is positioned.

exercise 8

Collapsing and Expanding a Document Using the Document Map Pane

1. Open Ch 27, Ex 04.
2. Display the Document Map pane and collapse and expand the document by completing the following steps:
   a. Click the Document Map button on the Standard toolbar.
   b. Collapse the document so only first-level headings are displayed by completing the following steps:
      1) Position the arrow pointer on the heading, *MODULE 3: DESIGNING A NEWSLETTER,* that displays in the Document Map pane and then click the *right* mouse button.
      2) At the shortcut menu that displays, click the left mouse button on *Show Heading 1*.
   c. Show first- and second-level headings. To do this, position the arrow pointer on either of the two headings in the Document Map pane, click the *right* mouse button, and then click *Show Heading 2* at the shortcut menu.

d. Position the arrow pointer on the heading *Creating Margins for Newsletters* and then click the left mouse button. (This moves the insertion point to that heading in the document window.)
e. Expand the document by positioning the arrow pointer on any heading in the Document Map pane, clicking the *right* mouse button, and then clicking the left mouse button on *All* at the shortcut menu.

3. Remove the Document Map pane by clicking the Document Map button on the Standard toolbar.
4. Close Ch 27, Ex 04.

chapter summary

- Word's outlining feature will format headings within a document as well as let you view formatted headings and body text in a document.
- To create an outline, first identify particular headings and subheadings within a document as certain heading levels. The Outline view is used to assign particular heading levels to text.
- When a document contains headings and text that have been formatted in the Outline view, the paragraphs are identified by one of the *outline selection symbols* that appear in the selection bar at the left side of the screen.
- The outline selection symbols can be used to select text in the document.
- When a document is displayed in Outline view, the Outlining toolbar displays below the Formatting toolbar. Use buttons on the Outlining toolbar to assign various level headings to paragraphs.
- When a paragraph is identified as a first-level heading, the Heading 1 style is applied to that paragraph. This style sets the text in 14-point Arial bold.
- Heading 2 style is applied to a paragraph identified as a second-level heading. This style sets text in 12-point Arial bold italic and indents the text one-half inch.
- The advantage of working in the Outline view is the ability to see a condensed outline of your document without all of the text in between headings or subheadings. Another benefit of working in the Outline view is in maintaining consistency between various headings.
- Word's outline feature offers you the ability to rearrange an entire document by rearranging an outline.
- Headings in an outline can be automatically numbered with options from the Heading Numbering dialog box. If headings in an outline are moved, inserted, or deleted, the headings are automatically renumbered.
- Use the Document Map feature to navigate easily in a document and keep track of your location within a document. The Document Map is a separate pane that displays the outline of a document. Display the Document Map pane by clicking the Document Map button on the Standard toolbar.

commands review

	Mouse/Keyboard
Change to Outline view	Click [icon] at left side of horizontal scroll bar; or click View, Outline
Document Map pane	Click [icon] on Standard toolbar

check your understanding

Matching: In the space provided at the left, write the letter of the term that matches the description. (Terms may be used more than once.)

A	Document Map	F	outline selection symbols
B	Expand	G	Outlining toolbar
C	Heading 1	H	plus symbol
D	Heading 2	I	Show Heading 1
E	Outline Numbered	J	Show Heading 2

_______ 1. This toolbar displays in Outline view below the Formatting toolbar.

_______ 2. This heading number applies 12-point Arial bold italic to text.

_______ 3. This symbol appears in the selection bar at the left side of the screen and indicates that subtext appears below the heading.

_______ 4. This feature will display the outline of a document in a separate pane.

_______ 5. This heading number indents a paragraph 0.5 inch from the left margin.

_______ 6. Click this button on the Outlining toolbar to display only first-level headings.

_______ 7. Automatically number headings in an outline with options from the Bullets and Numbering dialog box with this tab selected.

_______ 8. These appear in the selection bar at the left side of the screen.

_______ 9. Click this Outlining toolbar button to make collapsed text appear.

_______ 10. This heading number applies 14-point Arial bold to text.

skill assessments

Note: Before completing the skill assessments, display the Open dialog box, and then select and delete documents created in chapter 25 that begin Ch 25. You may want to check with your instructor before deleting these documents.

Assessment 1

1. Open Report 03.
2. Save the document with Save As and name it Ch 27, SA 01.
3. Make the following changes to the document:
   a. Change to the Outline viewing mode.
   b. Promote or demote the following titles, headings, or subheadings as identified below:

MODULE 1: DEFINING NEWSLETTER ELEMENTS	=	Heading 1
Designing a Newsletter	=	Heading 2
Defining Basic Newsletter Elements	=	Heading 2
MODULE 2: PLANNING A NEWSLETTER	=	Heading 1
Defining the Purpose of a Newsletter	=	Heading 2

   c. Collapse the outline so only the two heading levels are displayed.
4. Save the document again with the same name (Ch 27, SA 01).
5. Print and then close Ch 27, SA 01. (This will print the collapsed outline, not the entire document.)

Assessment 2

1. Open Ch 27, SA 01.
2. Save the document with Save As and name it Ch 27, SA 02.
3. Make the following changes to the document:
   a. Collapse the outline and then move the module 1 title and the headings below it after the module 2 title and the heading below it.
   b. Renumber the modules (module 2 becomes 1 and module 1 becomes 2).
   c. Move the section on *Designing a Newsletter* below the section on *Defining Basic Newsletter Elements*.
4. With the outline still collapsed, save the document again with the same name (Ch 27, SA 02).
5. Print and then close Ch 27, SA 02.

Assessment 3

1. Open Ch 27, SA 01.
2. Save the document with Save As and name it Ch 27, SA 03.
3. Make the following changes to the document:
   a. Display only level one and level two headings in the document.
   b. Select all the text in the document.
   c. Add numbering to the outline.
   d. Delete the section on *Designing a Newsletter*.
   e. Expand the document.
4. Save the document again with the same name (Ch 27, SA 03).
5. Print and then close Ch 27, SA 03.

chapter TWENTY-EIGHT

Creating Fill-In Forms

PERFORMANCE OBJECTIVES

Upon successful completion of chapter 28, you will be able to:

- **Create a form template.**
- **Fill in a form document.**
- **Print, edit, and customize a form.**
- **Draw a table in a form template.**

Many businesses use preprinted forms that are generally filled in by hand, with a typewriter, or using a computer. These forms require additional storage space and also cost the company money. With Word's form feature, you can create your own forms, eliminating the need for preprinted forms.

In this chapter, you will learn how to create a template document for a form that includes text boxes, check boxes, and pull-down lists. You will learn how to save the form as a protected document and then open the form and key information in the fill-in boxes. You will create basic form documents in this chapter. For ideas on creating advanced forms, please refer to Word's Help guide.

In chapter 11, you learned how to create fill-in fields in a main document. The main document containing fill-in fields also required a data source for other variable information. Creating a form does not require a main document or a data source. The form is created as a template document that contains fill-in fields. Information is keyed in the fields when a document based on the form template is opened.

Creating a Form

In Word, a *form* is a protected document that includes fields where information is entered. A form document contains *form fields* that are locations in the document where one of three things is performed: text is entered, a check box is turned on or off, or information is selected from a drop-down list. There are three basic steps that are completed when creating a form:

1. Create a form document based on a template and build the structure of the form.
2. Insert form fields where information is to be entered at the keyboard.
3. Save the form as a protected document.

Creating the Form Template

A form is created as a template so that when someone fills in the form they are working on a copy of the form, not the original. The original is the template document that is saved as a protected document. In this way, a form can be used over and over again without changing the original form. When a form is created from the template form document that has been protected, information can only be keyed in the fields designated when the form was created.

Figure 28.2 shows an example of a form document created with the form feature. (You will create this form in exercise 1.) You can create forms that contain fields for text, such as the fields *Name:*, *Address:*, *Date of Birth:*, etc., shown in figure 28.2. Forms can also contain check boxes, such as the boxes after *Yes* and *No*, shown in Figure 28.2. Forms can also contain drop-down lists (not used in the form shown in figure 28.2). You will learn about drop-down lists later in this chapter.

Word provides a Forms toolbar with buttons you can use to easily insert a text box, check box, or other form fields into a form template document. To display the Forms toolbar shown in figure 28.1, position the arrow pointer on either the Standard or Formatting toolbar, click the *right* mouse button, and then click *Forms* at the drop-down list. You can also display the Forms toolbar by clicking View, pointing to Toolbars, and then clicking Forms.

figure 28.1 ***Forms Toolbar***

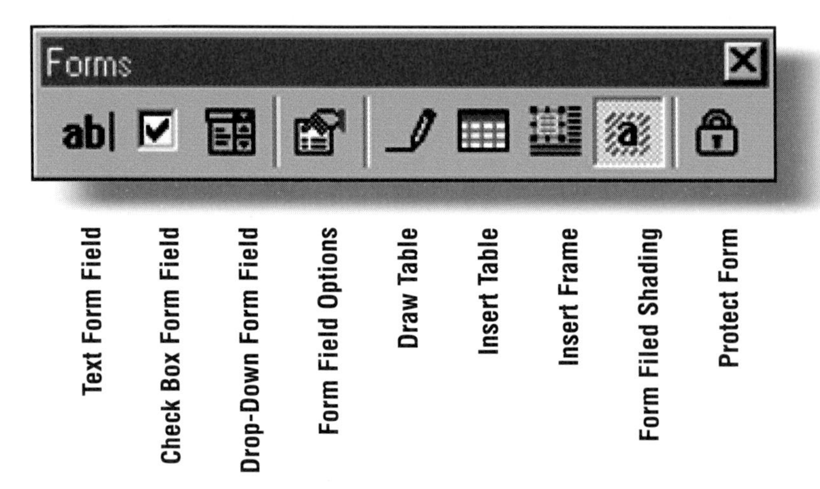

Generally, a form is created based on the default template document (called the *Normal* template). The form is created and then saved as a protected template document. To learn how to create a form document, complete exercise 1.

exercise 1

Creating a Form Document

1. Create the form shown in figure 28.2 as a template document by completing the following steps:
   a. Click File, then New.
   b. At the New dialog box with the General tab selected, make sure *Blank Document* is selected in the list box.
   c. Click Template in the Create New section at the bottom right corner of the dialog box.
   d. Click OK or press Enter.
   e. At the document screen, change the default font to 12-point Times New Roman by completing the following steps:
      1) Click Format, then Font.
      2) At the Font dialog box, click *12* in the Size list box. (Times New Roman should already be selected in the Font list box.)
      3) Click the Default button.
      4) At the question asking if you want to change the default font, click Yes.
   f. Key the beginning portion of the form shown in figure 28.2 up to the colon after *Name:*. After keying the colon, press the space bar once, and then insert a form field where the name will be keyed by completing the following steps:
      1) Turn on the display of the Forms toolbar by clicking View, pointing to Toolbars, and then clicking Forms.
      2) At the Forms toolbar shown in figure 28.1, click the Text Form Field button. (The form field displays as a shaded area surrounded by brackets in the document screen.)

Text Form Field

   g. After inserting the form field, press the Enter key, and then create the remaining text and text form fields as shown in figure 28.2. To create the check boxes after *Yes* and *No*, position the insertion point where you want the check box to display, and then click the Check Box Form Field button on the Forms toolbar.

Check Box Form Field

   h. After the form is completed, protect the document by clicking the Protect Form button on the Forms toolbar.

Protect Form

   i. Turn off the display of the Forms toolbar by clicking the Close button located at the right side of the Forms toolbar Title bar.
2. Save the document with Save As and name it XXX Template Document. (Use your initials in place of the *XXX*.)
3. Print and then close XXX Template Document.

28.2

Exercise 1

LIFETIME ANNUITY INSURANCE APPLICATION

FIRST APPLICANT

Name: [ ]
Address: [ ]
Date of Birth: [ ]
Occupation: [ ]

SECOND APPLICANT

Name: [ ]
Address: [ ]
Date of Birth: [ ]
Occupation: [ ]

1. During the past 3 years, have you for any reason consulted a doctor or been hospitalized?

   First Applicant: Yes ☐ No ☐
   Second Applicant: Yes ☐ No ☐

2. Have you ever been treated for or advised that you had any of the following: heart, lung, nervous, kidney, or liver disorder; high blood pressure; drug abuse, including alcohol; cancer or tumor; AIDS, or any disorder of your immune system; diabetes?

   First Applicant: Yes ☐ No ☐
   Second Applicant: Yes ☐ No ☐

These answers are true and complete to the best of my knowledge and belief. To determine my insurability, I authorize any health care provider or insurance company to give any information about me or my physical or mental health.

FIRST APPLICANT'S SIGNATURE ______________________________

SECOND APPLICANT'S SIGNATURE ______________________________

Filling In a Form Document

After a template form document is created, protected, and saved, the template can be used to create a personalized form document. When you open a form template document that has been protected, the insertion point is automatically inserted in the first form field. Key the information for the data field and then press the Tab key to move the insertion point to the next form field. You can move the insertion point to a preceding form field by pressing Shift + Tab. To fill in a check box form field, move the insertion point to the check box, and then press the space bar. Complete the same steps to remove an X from a check box form field. As an example of how to fill in a form template, complete exercise 2.

exercise 2

Filling in a Template Form Document

1. Create a form with the XXX Template Document form template by completing the following steps:
   a. Click File, then New.
   b. At the New dialog box, double-click the XXX Template Document icon (where your initials display instead of the *XXX*).
   c. Word displays the form document with the insertion point positioned in the first form field after *Name*. Key the name **Dennis Utley** (as shown in figure 28.3), and then press the Tab key or the Enter key to move to the next form field.
   d. Fill in the remaining text and check box form fields as shown in figure 28.3. Press the Tab key to move the insertion point to the next form field. Press Shift + Tab to move the insertion point to the preceding form field. (To insert the X in a check box, move the insertion point to the check box, and then press the space bar.)
2. When the form is completed, save the document and name it Ch 28, Ex 02.
3. Print and then close Ch 28, Ex 02.

28.3

Exercise 2

LIFETIME ANNUITY INSURANCE APPLICATION

FIRST APPLICANT

Name: Dennis Utley
Address: 11315 Lomas Drive, Seattle, WA 98123
Date of Birth: 02/23/59
Occupation: Accountant

SECOND APPLICANT

Name: Geneva Utley
Address: 11315 Lomas Drive, Seattle, WA 98123
Date of Birth: 09/04/62
Occupation: Social Worker

1. During the past 3 years, have you for any reason consulted a doctor or been hospitalized?

   First Applicant: Yes ☐ No ☒ Second Applicant: Yes ☐ No ☒

2. Have you ever been treated for or advised that you had any of the following: heart, lung, nervous, kidney, or liver disorder; high blood pressure; drug abuse, including alcohol; cancer or tumor; AIDS, or any disorder of your immune system; diabetes?

   First Applicant: Yes ☐ No ☒ Second Applicant: Yes ☐ No ☒

These answers are true and complete to the best of my knowledge and belief. To determine my insurability, I authorize any health care provider or insurance company to give any information about me or my physical or mental health.

FIRST APPLICANT'S SIGNATURE SECOND APPLICANT'S SIGNATURE

______________________________ ______________________________

Printing a Form

After the form fields in a form document have been filled in, the form can be printed in the normal manner. In some situations, you may want to print just the data (not the entire form) or print the form and not the fill-in data.

If you are using a preprinted form that is inserted in the printer, you will want to print just the data. Word will print the data in the same location on the page as it appears in the form document. To print just the data in a form, click Tools, then Options. At the Options dialog box, click the Print tab. At the Options dialog box with the Print tab selected, click Print data only for forms in the Options for current document only section (this inserts a check mark in the check box), and then click OK or press Enter. Click the Print button on the Standard toolbar. After printing only the data, complete similar steps to remove the check mark from the Print data only for forms check box.

To print only the form without the data, you would click File, then New. At the New dialog box, select the desired template document in the Template list box, and then click OK or press Enter. With the form document displayed in the document screen, click the Print button on the Standard toolbar, and then close the document.

exercise 3

Printing Only Data in a Form Document

1. Open Ch 28, Ex 02.
2. Print only the data in the form fields by completing the following steps:
   a. Click Tools, then Options.
   b. At the Options dialog box, click the Print tab.
   c. At the Options dialog box with the Print tab selected, click Print data only for forms in the Options for current document only section. (This inserts a check mark in the check box.)
   d. Click OK or press Enter.
   e. Click the Print button on the Standard toolbar.
3. After printing, remove the check mark from the Print data only for forms option by completing the following steps:
   a. Click Tools, then Options.
   b. At the Options dialog box with the Print tab selected, click Print data only for forms in the Options for current document only section. (This removes the check mark from the check box.)
   c. Click OK or press Enter.
4. Close Ch 28, Ex 02 without saving the changes.

Editing a Form Template

When a form template is created and then protected, the text in the template cannot be changed. If you need to make changes to a form template, you must open the template document, unprotect the document, and then make the changes. After making the changes, protect the document again. To unprotect a template document, display the Open dialog box, display the *Templates* folder, display all files, and then open the template document. To unprotect the document, click Tools, then Unprotect Document. Make any necessary changes to the document and then protect it again by clicking Tools, then Protect Document. Save the template document again with the same name.

exercise 4

Editing a Template Form

1. Add the text shown in figure 28.4 to the XXX Template Document form template by completing the following steps:
   a. Click File, then Open.
   b. At the Open dialog box, click the down-pointing triangle to the right of the Look in: text box. From the drop-down list that displays, click the drive where the *Templates* folder is located. (If you have Microsoft Office installed on a hard-drive system, click *(C:)*, double-click *Program Files*, double-click *Microsoft Office*, and then double-click *Templates*. This path will vary if you have only Word installed and not Microsoft Office. If you are using Word on a network system, check with your instructor to determine the location of the *Templates* folder.)
   c. With the *Templates* folder selected, click the down-pointing triangle to the right of the Files of type text box (located at the bottom left corner of the dialog box), and then click *All Files*.
   d. Double-click *XXX Template Document* in the list box (where *XXX* indicates your initials).
   e. With the *XXX Template Document* form template displayed in the document screen, unprotect the document by clicking Tools, then Unprotect Document.
   f. Add the paragraph and the check boxes shown in figure 28.4 to the form.
   g. Protect the document again by completing the following steps:
      1) Click Tools, then Protect Document.
      2) At the Protect Document dialog box, make sure Forms is selected and then click OK.
   h. Save the document with the same name (XXX Template Document).
2. Print and then close XXX Template Document.

3. Return to the drive where your student data disk is located by completing the following steps:
   a. Click File, then Open.
   b. At the Open dialog box, click the down-pointing triangle to the right of the Look in: text box, and then click *3½ Floppy (A:)* (this may vary depending on the drive where your student data disk is located).
   c. Click the down-pointing triangle to the right of the Files of type text box (located at the bottom left corner of the dialog box) and then click *Word Documents*.
   d. Click Cancel.

figure 28.4 ***Exercise 4***

3. During the past 3 years, have you for any reason been denied life insurance by any other insurance company?

First Applicant: Yes ☐ No ☐

Second Applicant: Yes ☐ No ☐

Customizing Form Field Options

A drop-down list, text box, or check box form field is inserted in a document with default options. You can change these default options for each form field. Options at the Drop-Down Form Field Options dialog box can be used to create form fields with drop-down lists.

Creating Form Fields with Drop-Down Lists

When creating form fields for a form document, there may be some fields where you want the person entering the information to choose from specific options, rather than keying the data. To do this, create a form field with a drop-down list. First, display the *Templates* folder, and then open the template document. Unprotect the template document, key the field name, and then click the Drop-Down Form Field button on the Forms toolbar. After inserting the drop-down form field, click the Form Field Options button on the Forms toolbar. This displays the Drop-Down Form Field Options dialog box, as shown in figure 28.5.

Drop-Down Form Field

Form Field Options

Drop-Down Form Field Options Dialog Box

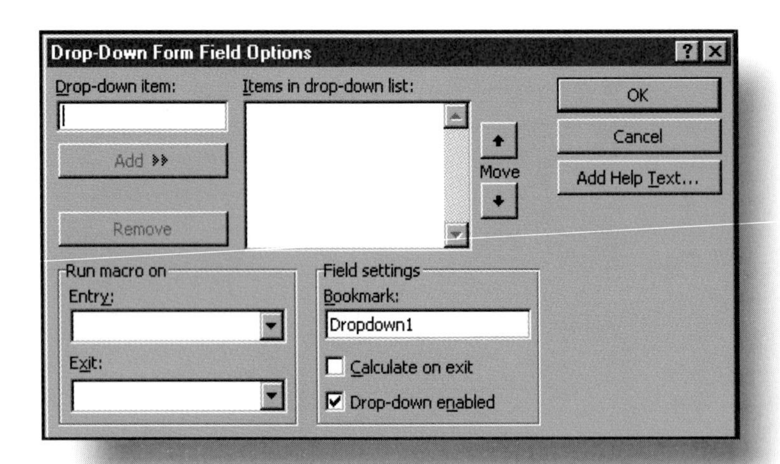

At the Drop-Down Form Field Options dialog box, key the first option you want to display in the drop-down list, and then click the Add button. Continue in this manner until all drop-down list items have been added and then click OK or press Enter to close the Drop-Down Form Field Options dialog box. Protect and then save the template document. A drop-down form field in a form document displays as a gray box with a down-pointing arrow at the right side of the box. You can remove drop-down items at the Drop-Down Form Field Options dialog box by selecting the item in the Items in drop-down list box and then clicking the Remove button.

When filling in a form field in a form template document that contains a drop-down list, position the insertion point in the drop-down form field, and then complete one of the following steps:

- Click the down-pointing triangle at the right side of the form field.
- Press F4.
- Press Alt + down arrow key.

When you choose one of the methods above, a drop-down list displays with the choices for the form field. Click the desired choice, or press the up or down arrow key to select the desired choice, and then press the Enter key.

Changing Text Form Field Options

To change options for a text form field, position the insertion point on the text form field you want to change and then click the Form Field Options button on the Forms toolbar. This displays the Text Form Field Options dialog box shown in figure 28.6.

28.6

Text Form Field Options Dialog Box

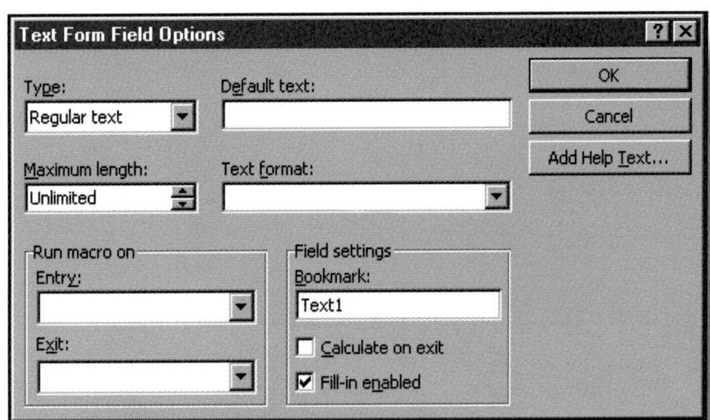

At the Text Form Field Options dialog box, you can change the type of text that is to be inserted in the form field. The default setting at the Type text box is *Regular text*. This can be changed to *Number*, *Date*, *Current date*, *Current time*, or *Calculation*.

If you change the Type option, Word will display an error message if the correct type of information is not entered in the form field. For example, if you change the form field type to *Number* in the Type text box, only a number can be entered in the form field. If something other than a number is entered, Word displays an error message, the entry is selected, and the insertion point stays in the form field until a number is entered.

If a particular text form field will generally need the same information, key that information in the Default text text box. This default text will display in the form field. If you want to leave the default text in the form document, just press the Tab key or the Enter key when filling in the form. If you want to change the default text, key the new text over the default text when filling in the form.

With the Maximum length option at the Text Form Field Options dialog box, you can specify an exact measurement for a form field. This option has a setting of *Unlimited* by default.

Formatting options for text in a form field can be applied with options at the Text format text box. For example, if you want text to display in all uppercase letters, click the down-pointing triangle at the right side of the Text format text box, and then click *Uppercase* at the drop-down list. When you key text in the form field while filling in the form, the text is converted to uppercase letters as soon as you press the Tab key or Enter key. The Text format options will vary depending on what is selected in the Type text box.

Changing Check Box Form Field Options

Check Box form field options can be changed at the Check Box Form Field Options dialog box shown in figure 28.7. To display this dialog box, position the insertion point on a check box form field and then click the Form Field Options button on the Forms toolbar.

28.7 *Check Box Form Field Options Dialog Box*

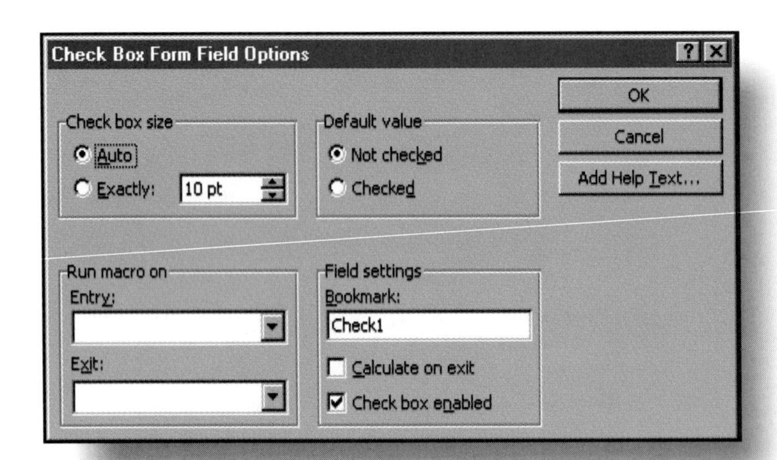

By default, Word inserts a check box in a form template document in the same size as the adjacent text. This is because Auto is selected at the Check box size section of the Check Box Form Field Options dialog box. If you want to specify an exact size for the check box, click Exactly, and then key the desired point measurement in the Exactly text box.

A check box form field is empty by default. If you want the check box to be checked by default, click the Checked option in the Default value section of the dialog box.

exercise 5

Creating a Form with Text Fields, Check Boxes, and Drop-Down Lists

1. Create the form shown in figure 28.8 as a template document named XXX Ch 28, Ex 05 by completing the following steps:
   a. Click File, then New.
   b. At the New dialog box with the General tab selected, make sure *Blank Document* is selected in the list box.
   c. Click Template in the Create New section at the bottom right corner of the dialog box.
   d. Click OK or press Enter.
   e. At the document screen, change the default font to 12-point Times New Roman. (For help on how to do this, see exercise 1, step 1e.)
   f. Turn on the display of the Forms toolbar.
   g. Key the title of the form, *APPLICATION FOR PREFERRED INSURANCE*, centered and bolded. Press the Enter key

twice, turn off bold, and then return the paragraph alignment to left. Key **Date:**, press the space bar once, and then insert a text form field that inserts the current date by completing the following steps:

1) Click the Text Form Field button on the Forms toolbar.
2) Click the Form Field Options button on the Forms toolbar.
3) At the Text Form Field Options dialog box, click the down-pointing triangle at the right side of the Type text box, and then click *Current date* at the drop-down list.
4) Click OK or press Enter to close the Text Form Field Options dialog box.
5) Press the right arrow key to deselect the field and move the insertion point to the right side of the field. (You can also position the I-beam pointer immediately right of the field and then click the left mouse button.)

h. Press the Enter key twice, key **Name:**, press the space bar once, and then create the form text field. Do the same for **Address:** and **Date of Birth:**.

i. Key **Social Security Number:** and then create a text form field that allows a maximum of 11 characters (the number required for the Social Security number including the hyphens) by completing the following steps:

1) Press the space bar once after keying **Social Security Number:**.
2) Click the Text Form Field button on the Forms toolbar.
3) Click the Form Field Options button on the Forms toolbar.
4) At the Text Form Field Options dialog box, select *Unlimited* that displays in the Maximum length text box, and then key **11**.
5) Click OK or press Enter to close the Text Form Field Options dialog box.
6) Press the right arrow key to deselect the field and move the insertion point to the right side of the field. (You can also position the I-beam pointer immediately right of the field and then click the left mouse button.)

j. Press the Enter key twice, key **Gender:**, and then press the Tab key. Create the text and check boxes after *Gender:* as shown in figure 28.8.

k. After creating the check box after *Male*, press the Enter key twice, key **Nonprofit Employer:**, press the space bar once, and then create a drop-down form field with three choices by completing the following steps:

1) Click the Drop-Down Form Field button on the Forms toolbar.

2) Click the Form Field Options button on the Forms toolbar.
3) At the Drop-Down Form Field Options dialog box, key **College** in the Drop-down item text box.
4) Click the Add button.
5) Key **Public School** in the Drop-down item text box.
6) Click the Add button.
7) Key **Private School** in the Drop-down item text box.
8) Click the Add button.
9) Click OK or press Enter to close the Drop-Down Form Field Options dialog box.
10) Press the right arrow key to deselect the field and move the insertion point to the right side of the field. (You can also position the I-beam pointer immediately right of the field and then click the left mouse button.)

l. Press the Enter key twice, key **How are premiums to be paid?**, press the space bar once, and then create a drop-down form field with the choices *Annually, Semiannually,* and *Quarterly* by completing steps similar to those in 1k.
m. Continue creating the remainder of the form as shown in figure 28.8.
n. After the form is completed, protect the document by clicking the Protect Form button on the Forms toolbar.
o. Close the Forms toolbar.

2. Save the document and name it XXX Ch 28, Ex 05. (Use your initials in place of the *XXX*.)
3. Print and then close XXX Ch 28, Ex 05.

figure 28.8 **Exercise 5**

APPLICATION FOR PREFERRED INSURANCE

Date: [ ]

Name: [ ]

Address: [ ]

Date of Birth: [ ]

Social Security Number: [ ]

Gender: Female ☐ Male ☐

Nonprofit Employer: [ ]

How are premiums to be paid? [ ]

1. Will this insurance replace any existing insurance or annuity?
   Yes ☐ No ☐

2. Within the past 3 years has your driver's license been suspended, revoked, or have you been convicted for driving under the influence of alcohol or drugs?
   Yes ☐ No ☐

3. Do you have any intention of traveling or residing outside the United States or Canada within the next 12 months?
   Yes ☐ No ☐

Signature of proposed insured:

______________________________ Date ____________

exercise 6

Filling in a Template Form Document

1. Create a form with the XXX Ch 28, Ex 05 form template by completing the following steps:
   a. Click File, then New.
   b. At the New dialog box, double-click XXX Ch 28, Ex 05 (where your initials are displayed instead of the *XXX*).
   c. Word displays the form document with the insertion point positioned in the *Name:* form field. Fill in the text and check boxes as shown in figure 28.9. (Press the Tab key to move the insertion point to the next form field. Press Shift + Tab to move the insertion point to the preceding form field.) To fill in the form fields with drop-down lists, complete the following steps:
      1) With the insertion point in the drop-down list form field, click the down-pointing arrow at the right side of the text box.

2) Click the desired option at the drop-down list.

2. When the form is completed, save the document and name it Ch 28, Ex 06.
3. Print and then close Ch 28, Ex 06.

Exercise 6

APPLICATION FOR PREFERRED INSURANCE

Date: (current date)

Name: Jennifer Reynolds

Address: 2309 North Cascade, Renton, WA 98051

Date of Birth: 12/18/63

Social Security Number: 411-23-6800

Gender: Female ☒ Male ☐

Nonprofit Employer: Public School

How are premiums to be paid? Quarterly

1. Will this insurance replace any existing insurance or annuity?
   Yes ☒ No ☐

2. Within the past 3 years has your driver's license been suspended, revoked, or have you been convicted for driving under the influence of alcohol or drugs?
   Yes ☐ No ☒

3. Do you have any intention of traveling or residing outside the United States or Canada within the next 12 months?
   Yes ☐ No ☒

Signature of proposed insured:

______________________________ Date __________________

Creating Tables in a Form Template

A table can be very useful when creating a form with form fields. A table can be customized to create a business form such as an invoice or a purchase order. Figure 28.10 shows an example of a form you will create in exercise 7 using the table feature.

exercise 7

Creating a Form Using the Table Feature

1. Create the form shown in figure 28.10 as a template document and name it XXX Ch 28, Ex 07 (where *XXX* are your initials), by completing the following steps:
   a. Click File, then New.
   b. At the New dialog box with the General tab selected, make sure *Blank Document* is selected in the list box.
   c. Click Template in the Create New section at the bottom right corner of the dialog box.
   d. Click OK or press Enter.
   e. At the document screen, change the default font to 12-point Times New Roman.
   f. Display the Forms toolbar.
   g. Click the Draw Table button on the Forms toolbar. Use the buttons on the Tables and Borders toolbar to draw the table lines as shown in figure 28.10.
   h. After drawing the table, close the Tables and Borders toolbar.
   i. Select the cells that will contain the text *Date*, *Description*, *Amount*, and *Ref #* and then click the Center Vertically button on the Tables and Borders toolbar.
   j. Key the text in the cells as shown in figure 28.10. Insert text form fields as shown in the figure. (To insert the three text form fields in the Date column, insert the first text form field and then press the Enter key. This moves the insertion point down to the next line within the cell. Continue in this manner until all three text form fields are inserted. Complete similar steps for the three text form fields in the Description, Amount, and Ref # columns.)
   k. After the table is completed, protect the document by clicking the Protect Form button on the Forms toolbar.
   l. Close the Forms toolbar.
2. Save the document and name it XXX Ch 28, Ex 07. (Use your initials in place of the *XXX*.)
3. Print and then close XXX Ch 28, Ex 07.

Draw Table

Center Vertically

figure 28.10 *Exercise 7*

GOOD SAMARITAN HOSPITAL
1201 James Street
St. Louis, MO 62033
(818) 555-1201

Account Number: [ ]

Invoice Number: [ ] Date: [ ]

Date	Description	Amount	Ref #
[ ] [ ] [ ]	[ ] [ ] [ ]	[ ] [ ] [ ]	[ ] [ ] [ ]

exercise 8

Filling in a Template Table Form

1. Create a form with the XXX Ch 28, Ex 07 form template by completing the following steps:
   a. Click File, then New.
   b. At the New dialog box, double-click XXX Ch 28, Ex 07 (where your initials are displayed instead of the *XXX*).
   c. Word displays the form document with the insertion point positioned in the first form field. Fill in the text and check boxes as shown in figure 28.11. (Press the Tab key to move the insertion point to the next form field. Press Shift + Tab to move the insertion point to the preceding form field.)
2. When the form is completed, save the document and name it Ch 28, Ex 08.
3. Print and then close Ch 28, Ex 08.

figure 28.11

Exercise 8

GOOD SAMARITAN HOSPITAL
1201 James Street
St. Louis, MO 62033
(818) 555-1201

Account Number: 3423-001

Invoice Number: 342 **Date:** 04/30/99

Date	Description	Amount	Ref #
04/13/99	Bed linens	$984.50	5403
04/21/99	Hospital slippers	$204.00	9422
04/23/99	Hospital gowns	$750.25	6645

chapter summary

- You can create your own forms with Word's form feature, thus eliminating the need for preprinted forms.
- A form is created as a template document that contains fill-in fields. Information based on the form template is keyed in the fields when a document is opened.
- A form document contains *form fields* where one of three actions is performed: text is entered, a check box is turned on or off, or information is selected from a drop-down list.
- Three basic steps are involved in creating a form: 1) create a form document based on a template and build the structure of the form; 2) insert form fields where information is to be entered at the keyboard; and 3) save the form as a protected document.
- Create a template document by clicking Template at the New dialog box.

- Word provides a Forms toolbar with buttons you can use to easily insert a text box, check box, or other form field into a form template document.
- After a template form document is created, protected, and saved, the template can be used to create a personalized form document.
- After the form fields have been filled in, the form can be printed in the normal manner, or you can print just the data from the Options dialog box with the Print tab selected.
- When a form template is created and then protected, the text in the template cannot be changed. To edit a template document, you must open the document, unprotect it, make the necessary changes, and then protect the document again.
- Use options at the Drop-Down Form Field Options dialog box to create form fields with drop-down lists.
- Change options for a text form field at the Text Form Field Options dialog box.
- Change check box form field options at the Check Box Form Field Options dialog box.
- Click the Draw Table button on the Forms toolbar and then draw table lines to create a form.

commands review

	Mouse /Keyboard
New dialog box	File, New
Text Form Field Options dialog box	Position insertion point on text form field, then click [button] on Forms toolbar.
Check Box Form Field Options dialog box	Position insertion point on check box form field, then click [button] on Forms toolbar.
Drop-Down Form Field Options dialog box	Position insertion point on drop-down form field, then click [button] on Forms toolbar.

check your understanding

Completion: In the space provided at the right, indicate the correct term, command, or number.

1. Generally, a form is created based on this default template document. ____________
2. A fill-in form can include text boxes, check boxes, and/or these. ____________
3. This is the third basic step performed when creating a form document. ____________

4. Begin creating a template document at this dialog box. ____________
5. To display the Text Form Field Options dialog box, position the insertion point on a text form field, and then click this button on the Forms toolbar. ____________
6. To protect a document, click this button on the Forms toolbar. ____________
7. If you want the user to fill in a form by choosing from specific options, create this type of form field. ____________
8. To fill in a check box form field, move the insertion point to the check box, and then press this key on the keyboard. ____________
9. The default setting for a text form field can be changed to *Number, Date, Current time, Calculation*, or this. ____________
10. This is the default setting for the Maximum length option at the Text Form Field Options dialog box. ____________
11. When filling in a form template document, press this key to move the insertion point to the next form field. ____________
12. If you want text to display in all uppercase letters, first click this at the Text Form Field Options dialog box. ____________
13. This Word feature can be used to create a business form such as an invoice or purchase order. ____________

skill assessments

Note: Before completing the skill assessments, display the Open dialog box, and then select and delete documents created in chapter 26 that begin Ch 26. You may want to check with your instructor before deleting these documents.

Assessment 1

1. Create the form shown in figure 28.12 as a template document named XXX Ch 28, SA 01. Insert text form fields and check box form fields in the document as shown in figure 28.12.
2. Print and then close XXX Ch 28, SA 01.

Figure 28.12 • Assessment 1

GOOD SAMARITAN HOSPITAL

APPLICATION FOR FUNDING

Project Title: [ ]

Department Applying: [ ]

Facility: SFH ☐ LC ☐ SCC ☐

Contact Person(s): [ ]

Check the statement(s) that best describe(s) how this proposal will meet the eligibility criteria:

☐ Improved patient care outcomes

☐ Cost reduction

☐ Improved customer satisfaction

☐ Reduced outcome variation

☐ Compliance with quality standards

Signature	Date
Department	Extension

Assessment 2

1. Create a form with the XXX Ch 28, SA 01 form template. Insert the following information in the form:

   Project Title: Quality Improvement Project
   Department Applying: Pediatrics
   Facility: (check SFH)
   Contact Person(s): Alyce Arevalo
   Check all the statements describing the proposal except *Cost reduction*.

2. When the form is completed, save the document and name it Ch 28, SA 02.
3. Print and then close Ch 28, SA 02.

Assessment 3

1. Create the form shown in figure 28.13 as a template document named XXX Ch 28, SA 03. Customize the table as shown in figure 28.13. Insert text form fields and check box form fields in the table shown in the figure.
2. Print and then close XXX Ch 28, SA 03.

Figure 28.13 • Assessment 3

LIFETIME ANNUITY

PROFESSIONAL LIABILITY INSURANCE APPLICATION

Name: [ ]

Address: [ ]

County: [ ]	**SSN:** [ ]	**DOB:** [ ]
Type of Deduction: ☐ Flat ☐ Participating	**Deduction Amount:** ☐ None ☐ $2,500 ☐ $1,000 ☐ $5,000	

Check if this insurance is to be part of a program.
☐ AANA ☐ AAOMS ☐ APTA-PPS ☐ None

Check your specific professional occupation.

☐ Chiropractor	☐ Medical Technician
☐ Dental Anesthesia	☐ Nurse
☐ Dental Hygienist	☐ Nurse Practitioner
☐ Dietitian/Nutritionist	☐ Occupational Therapist
☐ Laboratory Director	☐ Optometrist
☐ Medical Office Assistant	☐ Paramedic/EMT

Signature:	**Date:**

Assessment 4

1. Create a form with the XXX Ch 28, SA 03 form template. Insert the following information in the form:

   Name: Steven Katori
   Address: 11502 South 32nd Street, Bellevue, WA 98049
   County: King
   SSN: 230-52-9812
   DOB: 11/20/60

   Type of Deduction: (check Flat)
   Deduction Amount: (check $1,000)
   Part of insurance program? (check None)
   Occupation: (check Nurse Practitioner)

2. When the form is completed, save the document and name it Ch 28, SA 04.
3. Print and then close Ch 28, SA 04.

Assessment 5

1. Delete the XXX Template Document form document created in exercise 1 by completing the following steps:
   a. Click File, then New.
   b. At the New dialog box, position the arrow pointer on the *XXX Template Document* template form, and then click the *right* mouse button.
   c. From the pop-up menu that displays, click *Delete*.
   d. At the question asking if you want to delete the document, click Yes.
2. Complete similar steps to delete the other template documents created in this chapter containing your initials.

chapter TWENTY-NINE

29 Creating Tables and Indexes

PERFORMANCE OBJECTIVES

Upon successful completion of chapter 29, you will be able to:

- **Create, compile, and update a table of contents.**
- **Create, compile, and update an index.**
- **Create, compile, and update a table of figures.**
- **Create, compile, and update a table of authorities.**

A book, textbook, report, or manuscript often includes sections such as a table of contents, index, and table of figures in the document. Creating these sections can be tedious when done manually. With Word, these functions can be automated to create the sections quickly and easily. In this chapter, you will learn the steps to mark text for a table of contents, index, table of figures, and table of authorities, and then compile the table or list.

Creating a Table of Contents

A table of contents appears at the beginning of a book, manuscript, or report and contains headings and subheadings with page numbers. Figure 29.1 shows an example of a table of contents.

Table of Contents

TABLE OF CONTENTS

Chapter 1: Trends in Telecommunications **2**

Telecommunications at Work 2
Evolution in Telecommunications 4
Chapter Summary 8
Terminology Review 9
Check Your Understanding 10

Text to be included in a table of contents can be identified by applying a heading style, or text can be marked as a field entry. The advantage to using styles to mark text for a table of contents is that it is quick. The disadvantage is that the headings in the document will display with the formatting applied by the style.

The advantage to marking headings for a table of contents as a field entry is that no formatting is applied to the heading in the document. The disadvantage is that it takes more time to mark headings.

Marking Table of Contents Entries as Styles

A table of contents can be created by applying heading styles to text to be included in the table of contents. When creating a table of contents, there are two steps involved in creating the table of contents:

1. Apply the appropriate styles to the text that will be included in the table of contents.
2. Compile the table of contents in the document.

Normal

Style

Word automatically includes text that is formatted with a heading style in a table of contents. In chapters 25 and 27 you learned that Word contains nine heading styles that can be applied to text. If you have already applied these styles to create an outline, the same headings are included in the table of contents. If the styles have not previously been applied, you can apply them with the Style button on the Formatting toolbar, or with buttons on the Outlining toolbar in the Outline viewing mode. To apply styles for a table of contents, position the insertion point on any character in the text you want included in the table of contents, click the down-pointing triangle to the right of the Style button on the Formatting toolbar, and then click the desired style. Continue in this manner until all styles have been applied to titles, headings, and subheadings in the document.

Compiling a Table of Contents

After the necessary heading styles have been applied to text that you want included in the table of contents, the next step is to compile the table of contents. To do this, position the insertion point where you want the table to appear; display the Index and Tables dialog box with the Table of Contents tab selected, as shown in figure 29.2; make any desired changes; and then click OK. Word compiles the table of contents and then inserts it at the location of the insertion point, with the formatting selected at the Index and Tables dialog box.

29.2 ***Index and Tables Dialog Box with Table of Contents Tab Selected***

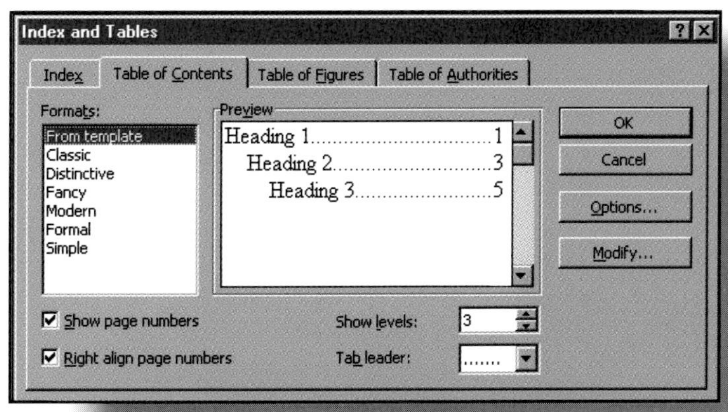

At the Index and Tables dialog box with the Table of Contents tab selected, you can choose from a variety of preformatted tables. These formats are displayed in the Formats list box in the dialog box. When a format is selected, a preview displays in the Preview box. The check boxes at the bottom let you specify how much of the formatting you want applied to text in the table of contents. The page number displays after the text or aligned at the right margin, depending on the formatting selected. The number of levels displayed depends on the number of heading levels specified in the document.

Tab leaders can be added to guide the reader's eyes from the table of contents heading to the page number. To add leaders, click the down-pointing triangle at the right side of the Tab leader text box, and then click the desired leader character from the drop-down list. If leaders are added, the Preview box displays the leaders. Some formats provide leaders.

If you want the table of contents to print on a page separate from the document text, insert a section break that begins a new page between the table of contents and the title of the document. If the beginning of the text in the document, rather than the table of contents, should be numbered as page 1, change the starting page number for the section. A table of contents is generally numbered with lowercase Roman numerals.

exercise 1

Applying Styles and Compiling a Table of Contents

1. Open Report 01.
2. Save the document with Save As and name it Ch 29, Ex 01.
3. Apply heading styles to the title, headings, and subheadings by completing the following steps:
   a. With the insertion point positioned at the beginning of the document, press the Enter key once. (This adds room for the table of contents you will be inserting later.)
   b. Select the entire document and then change the line spacing to single.
   c. Position the insertion point on any character in the title, *DESKTOP PUBLISHING*, click the down-pointing triangle to the right of the Style button on the Formatting toolbar, and then click *Heading 1*.
   d. Position the insertion point on any character in the heading, *Defining Desktop Publishing*, click the down-pointing triangle to the right of the Style button on the Formatting toolbar, and then click *Heading 2*.
   e. Apply the *Heading 2* style to the following headings:
      Initiating the Desktop Publishing Process
      Planning the Publication
      Creating the Content
4. Position the insertion point immediately left of the *D* in *DESKTOP PUBLISHING* and then insert a section break by completing the following steps:
   a. Click Insert, then Break.
   b. At the Break dialog box, click Next page.
   c. Click OK or press Enter.
5. With the insertion point positioned below the section break, insert page numbering and change the beginning number to 1 by completing the following steps:
   a. Click Insert, then Page Numbers.
   b. At the Page Numbers dialog box, click the down-pointing triangle at the right side of the Alignment option, and then click *Center* at the drop-down list.
   c. Click the Format button (in the dialog box, not on the Menu bar).
   d. At the Page Number Format dialog box, click Start at. (This inserts 1 in the Start at text box.)
   e. Click OK or press Enter to close the Page Number Format dialog box.
   f. At the Page Numbers dialog box, click OK or press Enter.
6. Compile and insert a table of contents at the beginning of the document by completing the following steps:

a. Position the insertion point at the beginning of the document (on the new page).
b. Key **TABLE OF CONTENTS**, centered.
c. Press the Enter key once and then change the paragraph alignment back to left.
d. Click Insert, then Index and Tables.
e. At the Index and Tables dialog box, click the Table of Contents tab.
f. At the Index and Tables dialog box with the Table of Contents tab selected, click *Formal* in the Formats list box.
g. Click OK or press Enter.

7. Position the insertion point on any character in the title, *TABLE OF CONTENTS*, and then apply the *Heading 1* style. (This will change the font to 14-point Arial bold and also change the alignment to left.)
8. Insert page numbering in the Table of Contents page by completing the following steps:
   a. Click Insert, then Page Numbers.
   b. At the Page Numbers dialog box, click the Format button.
   c. At the Page Number Format dialog box, click the down-pointing triangle at the right side of the Number format text box, and then click *i, ii, iii, ...* at the drop-down list.
   d. Click Start at. (This inserts *i* in the Start at text box.)
   e. Click OK or press Enter to close the Page Number Format dialog box.
   f. At the Page Numbers dialog box, click OK or press Enter.
9. Check the page break in the document and, if necessary, adjust the page break.
10. Save the document again with the same name (Ch 29, Ex 01).
11. Print the table of contents page. (Check with your instructor to see if you should print the other pages of the document.)
12. Close Ch 29, Ex 01.

Marking Table of Contents Entries as Fields

If you do not want style formatting to be applied to the title, headings, or subheadings in a document but you do want to create a table of contents for the document, mark text for the table as fields. When text is marked for a table of contents, a field code is inserted in the document. (This code should be visible in the document screen. If it is not, click the Show/Hide ¶ button on the Standard toolbar.)

To mark a title in a document for a table of contents, position the insertion point at the beginning of the title, and then click Insert, then Field. At the Field dialog box, shown in figure 29.3, click *Index and Tables* in the Categories list box, and click *TC* in the Field names list box. Position the I-beam pointer inside the Field codes text box to the right of the *TC* and then click the left mouse button. Key the title surrounded by quotation marks followed by **\l1**. The first character after the backslash is a lowercase L and the second character is the number 1. Click OK or press Enter to close the dialog box.

29.3 ***Field Dialog Box***

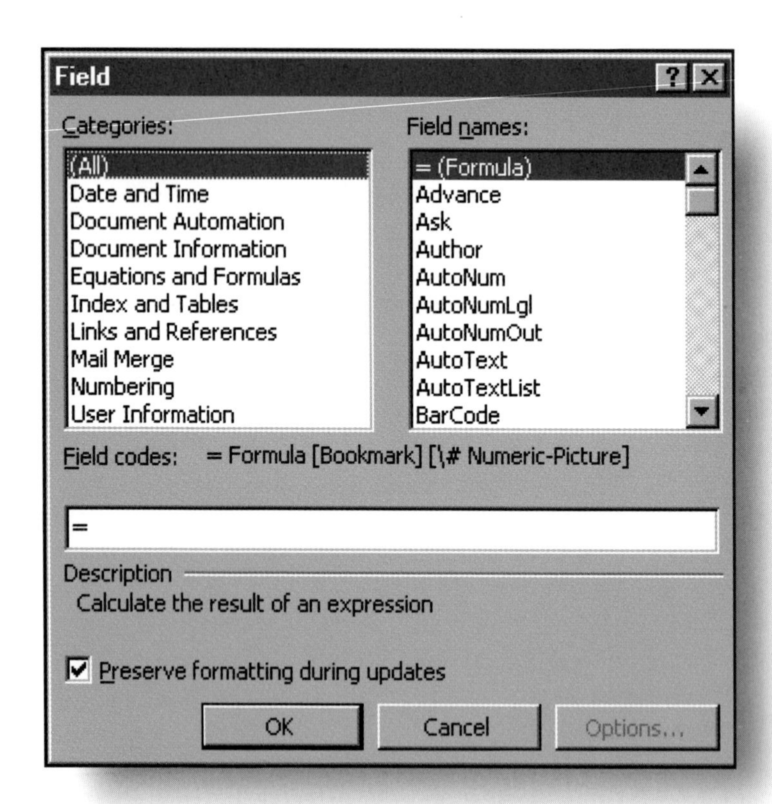

The field code { **TC "*TITLE OF DOCUMENT*"\l1** } (where the document title is inserted between the quotation marks) is inserted at the beginning of the document title. The backslash and the lowercase L are referred to as a *switch*. This switch tells Word that the character after the switch is the heading level for the table of contents. If you were marking a heading for level 2 in the table of contents, you would enter a 2 after the \l switch. After marking text for a table of contents, compile the table of contents as described earlier in this chapter.

exercise 2

Marking Headings as Fields and Then Compiling a Table of Contents

1. Open Report 03.
2. Save the document with Save As and name it Ch 29, Ex 02.
3. Mark the titles and headings as fields for a table of contents by completing the following steps:
   a. With the insertion point positioned at the beginning of the document, press the Enter key once. (This adds room for the table of contents you will be inserting later.)
   b. Position the insertion point at the beginning of the title, *MODULE 1: DEFINING NEWSLETTER ELEMENTS*, and then mark it as a field for the table of contents by completing the following steps:
      1) Click Insert, then Field.
      2) At the Field dialog box, click *Index and Tables* in the Categories list box.
      3) Click *TC* in the Field names list box.
      4) Position the I-beam pointer inside the Field codes text box to the right of the *TC* and then click the left mouse button.
      5) Key **"MODULE 1: DEFINING NEWSLETTER ELEMENTS"\l1**. (The first character after the backslash is a lowercase L and the second character is the number 1.)
      6) Click OK or press Enter. (If the field code is not visible, click the Show/Hide ¶ button on the Standard toolbar.)
   c. Position the insertion point at the beginning of the heading, *Designing a Newsletter*, and then mark it as a field for the table of contents by completing the following steps:
      1) Click Insert, then Field.
      2) At the Field dialog box, click *Index and Tables* in the Categories list box.
      3) Click *TC* in the Field names list box.
      4) Position the I-beam pointer inside the Field codes text box to the right of the *TC* and then click the left mouse button.
      5) Key **"Designing a Newsletter"\l2**. (The first character after the backslash is a lowercase L and the second character is the number 2.)
      6) Click OK or press Enter.
   d. Complete steps similar to those in 3b or 3c to mark the following text as a field with the specified level:

Defining Basic Newsletter Elements	= Level 2
MODULE 2: PLANNING A NEWSLETTER	= Level 1
Defining the Purpose of a Newsletter	= Level 2

4. Position the insertion point immediately left of the { that begins the field code before the title *MODULE 1: DEFINING NEWSLETTER ELEMENTS*, and then insert a section break that begins a new page. (*Hint: Refer to exercise 1, step 4.*)
5. With the insertion point positioned below the section break, insert page numbering at the bottom center of each page of the section and change the starting number to 1. (*Hint: Refer to exercise 1, step 5.*)
6. Compile and insert a table of contents at the beginning of the document by completing the following steps:
   a. Position the insertion point at the beginning of the document (on the new page).
   b. Key **TABLE OF CONTENTS**, centered and bolded.
   c. Press the Enter key once and then change the paragraph alignment back to left.
   d. Click Insert, then Index and Tables.
   e. At the Index and Tables dialog box, click the Table of Contents tab.
   f. At the Index and Tables dialog box with the Table of Contents tab selected, click *Fancy* in the Formats list box.
   g. Click the Options button.
   h. At the Table of Contents Options dialog box, click Table entry fields. (This option is located in the bottom left corner of the dialog box.)
   i. Click OK or press Enter to close the Table of Contents Options dialog box.
   j. Click OK or press Enter to close the Index and Tables dialog box.
7. Insert page numbering on the Table of Contents page at the bottom center. (*Hint: Refer to exercise 1, step 8.*)
8. Check the page breaks in the document and, if necessary, adjust the page breaks.
9. Save the document again with the same name (Ch 29, Ex 02).
10. Print the table of contents page. (Before printing, make sure that hidden text will not print. To do this, click the Options button at the Print dialog box. At the Print dialog box with the Print tab selected, make sure there is no check mark in the Hidden text option.) (Check with your instructor to see if you should print the entire document.)
11. Close Ch 29, Ex 02.

Updating or Replacing a Table of Contents

If you make changes to a document after compiling a table of contents, you can either update the existing table of contents or replace the table of contents with a new one. To update the current table of contents, position the insertion point anywhere within the current table of contents (this causes the table of contents to display with a gray background), and then press F9. (This is the Update Field key.) At the Update Table of Contents dialog box shown in figure 29.4, click Update page numbers only if the changes occur only to the page numbers, or click Update entire table if changes were made to headings or subheadings within the table. Click OK or press Enter to close the dialog box.

figure 29.4 *Update Table of Contents Dialog Box*

If you make extensive changes to the document, you may want to replace the entire table of contents. To do this, position the insertion point anywhere within the current table of contents (this causes the table of contents to display with a gray background), and then click Insert, then Index and Tables. At the Index and Tables dialog box, make sure the Table of Contents tab is selected, and then click OK or press Enter. At the prompt asking if you want to replace the existing table of contents, click Yes.

exercise 3

Updating a Table of Contents

1. Open Ch 29, Ex 01.
2. Save the document with Save As and name it Ch 29, Ex 03.
3. Select the entire document and then change the line spacing to double.
4. Update the table of contents by completing the following steps:
   a. Position the insertion point anywhere within the current table of contents. (This causes the table of contents to display with a gray background.)
   b. Press F9. (This is the Update Field key.)
   c. At the Update Table of Contents dialog box, make sure Update page numbers only is selected, and then click OK or press Enter.

5. Save the document again with the same name (Ch 29, Ex 03).
6. Print the table of contents page. (Check with your instructor to see if you should print the entire document.)
7. Close Ch 29, Ex 03.

Deleting a Table of Contents

A table of contents that has been compiled in a document can be deleted. To do this, select the entire table of contents in the normal manner, and then press the Delete key. When the insertion point is positioned on any character in the table of contents, the entire table of contents displays with a gray background. This does not select the table. To delete the table, you must select it in the normal manner using either the mouse or the keyboard.

Creating an Index

An index is a list of topics contained in a publication, and the pages where those topics are discussed. Word lets you automate the process of creating an index in a manner similar to that used for creating a table of contents. When creating an index, you mark a word or words that you want included in the index. Creating an index takes some thought and consideration. The author of the book, manuscript, or report must determine the main entries desired and what subentries will be listed under main entries. An index may include such items as the main idea of a document, the main subject of a chapter or section, variations of a heading or subheading, and abbreviations. Figure 29.5 shows an example of an index.

figure 29.5 ***Index***

INDEX

A
Alignment, 12, 16
ASCII, 22, 24, 35
  word processing, 39
  data processing, 41

B
Backmatter, 120
  page numbering, 123
Balance, 67-69
Banners, 145

C
Callouts, 78
Captions, 156
Color, 192-195
  ink for offset printing, 193
  process color, 195

D
Databases, 124-129
  fields, 124
  records, 124
Directional flow, 70-71

Marking Text for an Index

A selected word or words can be marked for inclusion in an index. Before marking words for an index, determine what main entries and subentries are to be included in the index. Selected text is marked as an index entry at the Mark Index Entry text box.

To mark text for an index, select the word or words, and then click Insert, then Index and Tables. At the Index and Tables dialog box, click the Index tab. At the Index and Tables dialog box with the Index tab selected, as shown in figure 29.6, click the Mark Entry button. At the Mark Index Entry dialog box, shown in figure 29.7, the selected word(s) appears in the Main entry text box. Make any necessary changes to the dialog box, and then click the Mark button. (When you click the Mark button, Word automatically turns on the display of nonprinting characters and displays the index field code.) Click Close to close the Mark Index Entry dialog box.

figure 29.6

Index and Tables Dialog Box with Index Tab Selected

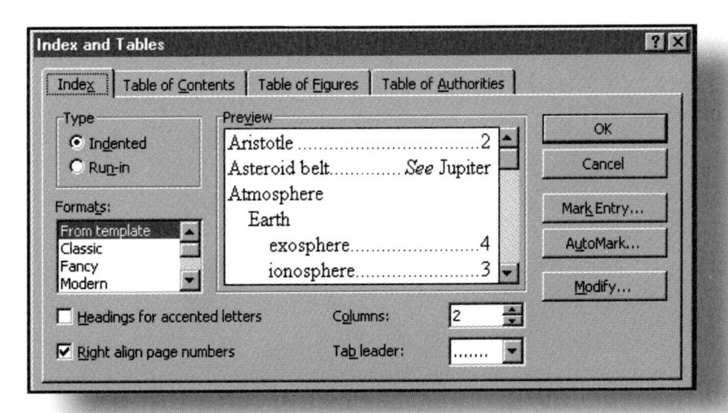

figure 29.7

Mark Index Entry Dialog Box

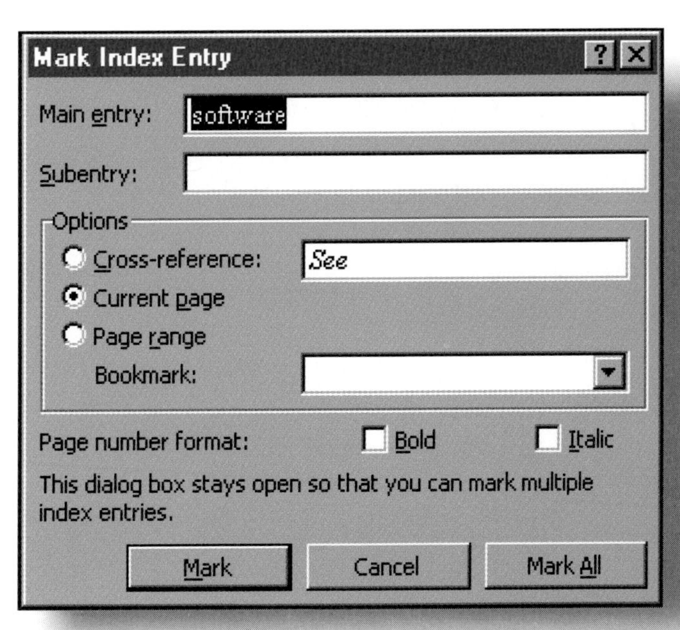

At the Mark Index Entry dialog box, the selected word or words display in the Main entry text box. If the text is a main entry, leave it as displayed. If, however, the selected text is a subentry, key the main entry in the Main entry text box, click in the Subentry text box, and then key the selected text. For example, suppose a publication includes the terms *Page layout* and *Portrait.* The words *Page layout* are to be marked as a main entry for the index and *Portrait* is to be marked as a subentry below *Page layout*. To mark these words for an index, you would complete the following steps:

1. Select *Page layout*.
2. Click Insert, then Index and Tables.
3. At the Index and Tables dialog box, make sure the Index tab is selected, and then click the Mark Entry button.
4. At the Mark Index Entry dialog box, click the Mark button.
5. With the Mark Index Entry dialog box still displayed on the screen, click in the document to make the document active, and then select *Portrait*.
6. Click the Mark Index Entry dialog box Title bar to make it active.
7. Select *Portrait* in the Main entry text box and then key **Page layout**.
8. Click in the Subentry text box and then key **Portrait**.
9. Click the Mark button.
10. Click Close.

The main entry and subentry do not have to be the same as the selected text. You can select text for an index, type the text you want to display in the Main entry or Subentry text box, and then click Mark.

At the Mark Index Entry dialog box, you can apply bold and/or italic formatting to the page numbers that will appear in the index. To apply formatting, click Bold and/or Italic to insert a check mark in the check box.

The Options section of the Mark Index Entry dialog box contains several options, with Current page the default. At this setting, the current page number will be listed in the index for the main and/or subentry. If you click Cross-reference, you would key the text you want to use as a cross-reference for the index entry in the Cross-reference text box. For example, you could mark the word *Monospaced* and cross-reference it to *Typefaces*.

Click the Mark All button at the Mark Index Entry dialog box to mark all occurrences of the text in the document as index entries. Word marks only those entries whose uppercase and lowercase letters exactly match the index entry.

exercise 4

Marking Words for an Index

1. Open Report 01.
2. Save the document with Save As and name it Ch 29, Ex 04.
3. Make the following changes to the document:
   a. Number pages at the bottom center of each page.

b. Set the title, *DESKTOP PUBLISHING*, and the headings, *Defining Desktop Publishing*, *Initiating the Desktop Publishing Process*, *Planning the Publication*, and *Creating the Content*, in 14-point Times New Roman bold.

4. Mark the word *software* in the first paragraph for the index as a main entry and mark *word processing* in the first paragraph as a subentry with *software* as the main entry by completing the following steps:
   a. Select *software* (located in the last sentence of the first paragraph).
   b. Click Insert, then Index and Tables.
   c. At the Index and Tables dialog box, click the Index tab.
   d. Click the Mark Entry button.
   e. At the Mark Index Entry dialog box, click the Mark All button.
   f. With the Mark Index Entry dialog box still displayed, click in the document to make the document active, and then select *word processing* (located in the last sentence of the first paragraph). (You may want to drag the dialog box down the screen so more of the document text is visible.)
   g. Click the Mark Index Entry dialog box Title bar to make it active.
   h. Select *word processing* in the Main entry text box and then key **software**.
   i. Click in the Subentry text box and then key **word processing**.
   j. Click the Mark All button.
   k. With the Mark Index Entry dialog box still displayed, complete steps similar to those in 4f through 4j to mark the *first* occurrence of the following words as main entries or subentries for the index:

      In the first paragraph in the *Defining Desktop Publishing* section:

      spreadsheets = subentry (main entry = *software*)
      database = subentry (main entry = *software*)

      In the second paragraph in the *Defining Desktop Publishing* section:

      publishing = main entry
      desktop = subentry (main entry = *publishing*)

      In the second paragraph in the *Defining Desktop Publishing* section:

      printer = main entry
      laser = subentry (main entry = *printer*)

In the third paragraph in the *Defining Desktop Publishing* section:

design	=	main entry

In the fourth paragraph in the *Defining Desktop Publishing* section:

traditional	=	subentry (main entry = *publishing*)

In the first paragraph in the *Initiating the Desktop Publishing Process* section:

publication	=	main entry
planning	=	subentry (main entry = *publication*)
creating	=	subentry (main entry = *publication*)
intended audience	=	subentry (main entry = *publication*)
content	=	subentry (main entry = *publication*)

In the third paragraph in the *Planning the Publication* section:

message	=	main entry

l. Click Close to close the Mark Index Entry dialog box.
m. Click the Show/Hide ¶ button on the Standard toolbar to turn off the display of nonprinting characters.

5. Save the document again with the same name (Ch 29, Ex 04).
6. Close Ch 29, Ex 04.

Compiling an Index

After all necessary text has been marked as a main entry or subentry for the index, the next step is to compile the index. An index should appear at the end of a document, generally beginning on a separate page. To compile the index, position the insertion point at the end of the document, and then insert a page break. With the insertion point positioned below the page break, key **INDEX** centered and bolded, and then press the Enter key. With the insertion point positioned at the left margin, click Insert, then Index and Tables. At the Index and Tables dialog box, click the Index tab. At the Index and Tables dialog box with the Index tab selected, select the desired formatting, and then click OK or press Enter.

Word compiles the index and then inserts it at the location of the insertion point with the formatting selected at the Index and Tables dialog box. Word also inserts a section break above and below the index text.

At the Index and Tables dialog box with the Index tab selected, you can specify how the index entries will appear. In the Type section, the Indented option is selected by default. At this setting, subentries will appear indented below main entries. If you click Run-in, subentries will display on the same line as main entries.

Word provides seven formatting choices in the Formats list box. When you select an option from this list, the Preview box displays how the index will appear in the document.

By default, numbers are right aligned in the index. If you do not want numbers right aligned, click the Right align page numbers check box to remove the check mark.

The Columns option has a default setting of *2*. At this setting, the index will display in two newspaper columns. This number can be increased or decreased.

The Tab leader option is dimmed for all formats except *Formal*. If you click *Formal* in the Formats list box, the Tab leader option displays in black. The default tab leader character is a period. To change to a different character, click the down-pointing triangle at the right of the text box, and then click the desired character.

exercise 5

Compiling an Index

1. Open Ch 29, Ex 04.
2. Save the document with Save As and name it Ch 29, Ex 05.
3. Compile the index and insert it in the document by completing the following steps:
   a. Position the insertion point at the end of the document.
   b. Insert a page break.
   c. With the insertion point positioned below the page break, key **INDEX** centered and bolded.
   d. Press the Enter key, turn off bold, and then change the paragraph alignment back to left.
   e. Click Insert, then Index and Tables.
   f. At the Index and Tables dialog box, click the Index tab.
   g. At the Index and Tables dialog box with the Index tab selected, click *Classic* in the Formats list box, and then click OK or press Enter.
   h. Select the title *INDEX* and then set it in 14-point Times New Roman bold.
4. Save the document again with the same name (Ch 29, Ex 05).
5. Print the index (last page). (Check with your instructor to see if you should print the entire document.)
6. Close Ch 29, Ex 05.

Creating a Concordance File

Words that appear frequently in a document can be saved as a concordance file. This saves you from having to mark each reference in a document. A concordance file is a regular Word document containing a single, two-column table with no text outside the table. In the first column of the table, you enter words you want to index. In the second column, you enter the main entry and subentry that should appear in the index. To create a subentry, separate each main entry from a subentry by a colon. Figure 29.8 shows an example of a completed concordance file.

29.8 Concordance File

World War I	World War I
Technology	Technology
technology	Technology
teletypewriters	Technology: teletypewriters
motion pictures	Technology: motion pictures
television	Technology: television
Radio Corporation of America	Radio Corporation of America
coaxial cable	Coaxial cable
telephone	Technology: telephone
Communications Act of 1934	Communications Act of 1934
World War II	World War II
radar system	Technology: radar system
computer	Computer
Atanasoff Berry Computer	Computer: Atanasoff Berry Computer
Korean War	Korean War
Columbia Broadcasting System	Columbia Broadcasting System
Cold War	Cold War
Vietnam	Vietnam
artificial satellite	Technology: artificial satellite
Communications Satellite Act of 1962	Communications Satellite Act of 1962

In the concordance file shown in figure 29.8, the text as it appears in the document is inserted in the first column (such as *World War I*, *Technology*, and *technology*). The second column contains the text as it should appear in the index specifying whether it is a main entry or subentry. For example, the text *motion pictures* in the concordance file will appear in the index as a subentry under the main entry *Technology*.

After a concordance file has been created, it can be used to quickly mark text for an index in a document. To do this, open the document containing text you want marked for the index, and then click Insert, then Index and Tables. At the Index and Tables dialog box, click the AutoMark button. At the Open Index AutoMark File dialog box shown in figure 29.9, double-click the concordance file name in the list box.

figure 29.9

Open Index AutoMark File Dialog Box

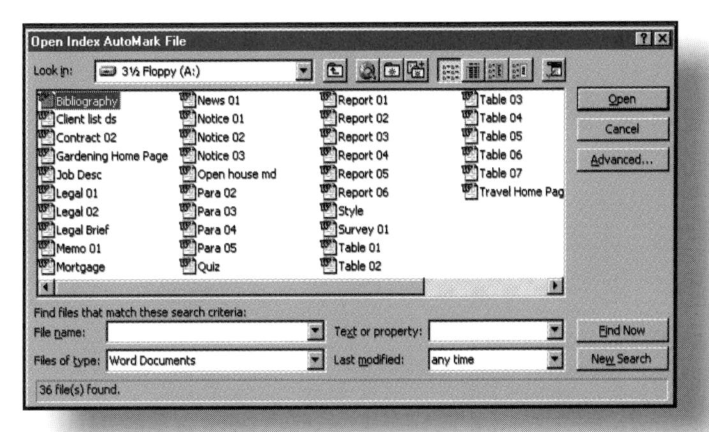

Word turns on the display of nonprinting characters, searches through the document for text that matches the text in the concordance file, and then marks it accordingly. After marking text for the index, insert the index in the document as described earlier.

When creating the concordance file in exercise 6, Word's AutoCorrect feature will automatically capitalize the first letter of the first word entered in each cell. In figure 29.10, you can see that many of the first words in the first column do not begin with a capital letter. Before completing the exercise, consider turning off this AutoCorrect capitalization feature. To do this, click Tools, then AutoCorrect. At the AutoCorrect dialog box click the *Capitalize first letter of sentences* check box to remove the check mark. Click OK to close the dialog box.

exercise 6

Creating a Concordance File

1. At a clear document screen, create the text shown in figure 29.10 as a concordance file by completing the following steps:
   a. Click Table, then Insert Table.
   b. At the Insert Table dialog box, click OK or press Enter. (This inserts a table in the document containing two rows and two columns.)
   c. Key the text in the cells as shown in figure 29.10. (If you did not remove the check mark before the *Capitalize first letter of sentences* option at the AutoCorrect dialog box, the *n* in the first word in the first cell *newsletters* is automatically capitalized Delete the capital *N*, key an **n**, press the down arrow key [this will capitalize it again], and then click the Undo button. You will need to repeat this for each cell entry in the first column that should begin with a lowercase letter.)
2. Save the document and name it Ch 29, Concord File.
3. Print and then close Ch 29, Concord File.

Exercise 6

newsletters	Newsletters
software	Software
desktop publishing	Software: desktop publishing
word processing	Software: word processing
printers	Printers
laser	Printers: laser
design	Design
communication	Communication
consistency	Design: consistency
elements	Elements
Nameplate	Elements: nameplate
Logo	Elements: logo
Subtitle	Elements: subtitle
Folio	Elements: folio
Headlines	Elements: headlines
Subheads	Elements: subheads
Byline	Elements: byline
Body Copy	Elements: body copy
Graphics Images	Elements: graphics images
audience	Newsletters: audience
purpose	Newsletters: purpose
focal point	Newsletters: focal point

If you removed the check mark before the *Capitalize first letter of sentences* option at the AutoCorrect dialog box, you may need to turn this feature back on. To do this, click Tools, then AutoCorrect. At the AutoCorrect dialog box click the *Capitalize first letter of sentences* check box to insert the check mark. Click OK to close the dialog box.

exercise 7

Compiling an Index Using a Concordance File

1. Open Report 03.
2. Save the document with Save As and name it Ch 29, Ex 07.
3. Make the following changes to the document:
   a. Select the entire document and then change the font to 12-point Century Schoolbook.
   b. Set the titles and headings in the document in 14-point Century Schoolbook bold.
4. Mark text for the index using the concordance file by completing the following steps:
   a. Click Insert, then Index and Tables.
   b. At the Index and Tables dialog box, click the AutoMark button.
   c. At the Open Index AutoMark File dialog box, double-click *Ch 29, Concord File* in the list box.
5. Compile and insert the index in the document by completing the following steps:
   a. Position the insertion point at the end of the document.
   b. Insert a page break.
   c. Key **INDEX** bolded and centered.
   d. Press the Enter key, turn off bold, and then return the paragraph alignment to left.
   e. Click Insert, then Index and Tables.
   f. At the Index and Tables dialog box, click the Index tab.
   g. At the Index and Tables dialog box with the Index tab selected, click *Formal* in the Formats list box, and then click OK or press Enter.
   h. Click the Show/Hide ¶ button on the Standard toolbar to turn off the display of nonprinting characters.
   i. Set the title *INDEX* in 14-point Century Schoolbook bold.
6. Check the page breaks in the document and, if necessary, adjust the page breaks.
7. Save the document again with the same name (Ch 29, Ex 07).
8. Print the index (last page). (Check with your instructor to see if you should print the entire document.)
9. Close Ch 29, Ex 07.

Updating or Replacing an Index

If you make changes to a document after inserting an index, you can either update the existing index or replace the index with a new one. To update an index, position the insertion point anywhere within the index (displays with a gray background), and then press F9.

Replace an index in the same manner as replacing a table of contents. To do this, position the insertion point anywhere within the current index (this causes the index to display with a gray background), and then click Insert, then Index and Tables. At the Index and Tables dialog box, make sure the Index tab is selected, and then click OK or press Enter. At the prompt asking if you want to replace the existing index, click Yes.

exercise 8

Updating an Index

1. Open Ch 29, Ex 07.
2. Save the document with Save As and name it Ch 29, Ex 08.
3. Insert a page break at the beginning of the title, *MODULE 2: PLANNING A NEWSLETTER*.
4. Update the index by completing the following steps:
   a. Position the insertion point on any character in the index.
   b. Press F9.
5. Save the document again with the same name (Ch 29, Ex 08).
6. Print only the index. (Check with your instructor to see if you should print the entire document.)
7. Close Ch 29, Ex 08.

Deleting an Index

An index that has been compiled in a document can be deleted. An index is deleted in the same manner as a table of contents. To delete an index, select the entire index using either the mouse or the keyboard, and then press the Delete key.

Creating a Table of Figures

A document that contains figures should include a list (table) of figures so the reader can quickly locate a specific figure. Figure 29.11 shows an example of a table of figures. A table of figures can be created using a variety of methods. The easiest method is to mark figure names as captions and then use the caption names to create the table of figures.

figure 29.11 *Table of Figures*

TABLE OF FIGURES

Creating Captions

There are a variety of methods you can use to create a caption for text. One method you can use to create a caption is to select the text, and then click Insert, then Caption. At the Caption dialog box shown in figure 29.12, make sure *Figure 1* displays in the Caption text box and the insertion point is positioned after *Figure 1*. Key the name for the caption, and then click OK or press Enter. Word inserts *Figure 1 (caption name)* below the selected text.

29.12 ***Caption Dialog Box***

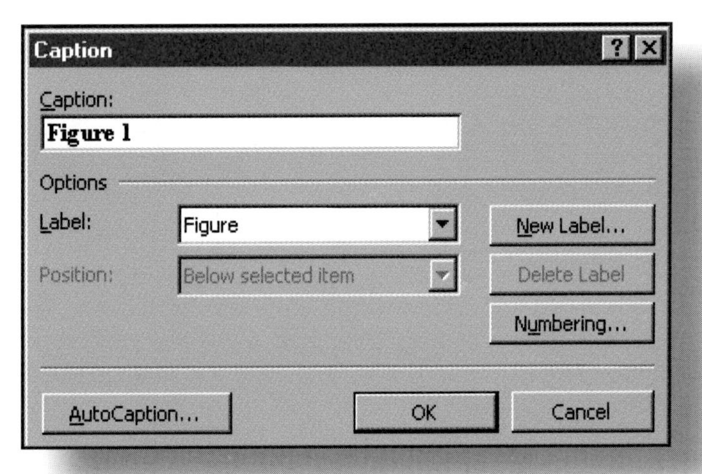

Compiling a Table of Figures

Once figures have been marked as captions in a document, a table of figures can be compiled and inserted in the document. A table of figures is compiled in a document in a manner similar to a table of contents. A table of figures generally displays at the beginning of the document, after the table of contents. To compile a table of figures in a document containing figures marked as captions, position the insertion point at the beginning of the document and then insert a section break that begins a new page. (If the document contains a table of contents, position the insertion point between the table of contents and the title of the document.) Move the insertion point above the section break and then key **TABLE OF FIGURES** bolded and centered. Press the Enter key and then turn off bold and change the paragraph alignment back to left. Click Insert, then Index and Tables. At the Index and Tables dialog box, click the Table of Figures tab. At the Index and Tables dialog box with the Table of Figures tab selected, as shown in figure 29.13, make any necessary changes, and then click OK or press Enter.

29.13 *Index and Tables Dialog Box with the Table of Figures Tab Selected*

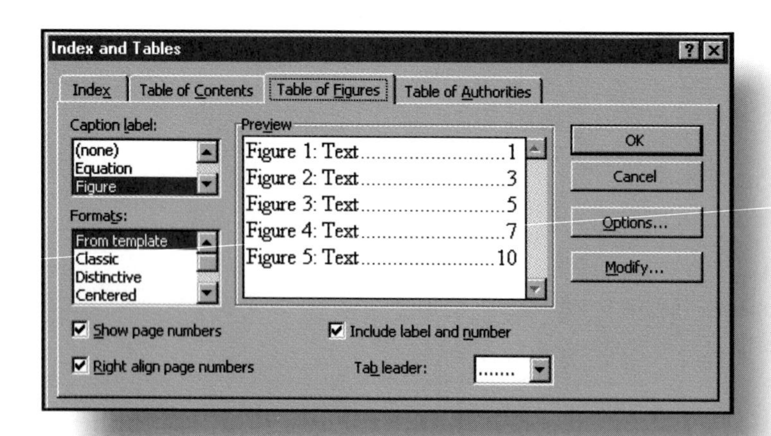

The options at the Index and Tables dialog box with the Table of Figures tab selected are similar to those options available at the dialog box with the Table of Contents tab selected. For example, you can choose a format for the table of figures from the Formats list box, change the alignment of the page number, or add leaders before page numbers.

exercise 9

Creating a List of Figures

1. Open Report 06.
2. Save the document with Save As and name it Ch 29, Ex 09.
3. Add the caption *Figure 1 Basic Hardware* to the bulleted text, and the lines above and below the bulleted text, that displays in the middle of page 2 by completing the following steps:
   a. Move the insertion point to the middle of page 2 and then select the lines and the bulleted text between the two lines.
   b. Click Insert, then Caption.
   c. At the Caption dialog box, press the space bar once, and then key **Basic Hardware**. (The insertion point is automatically positioned in the Caption text box, immediately after *Figure 1*.)
   d. Click OK or press Enter.
4. Complete steps similar to those in 3 to create the caption *Figure 2 Input Devices* for the bulleted text toward the bottom of the second page. (Be sure to include the lines above and below the bulleted text.)

5. Complete steps similar to those in 3 to create the caption *Figure 3 Output Devices* for the bulleted text that displays at the bottom of the second page and the top of the third page (the location may vary slightly). (Be sure to include the lines above and below the bulleted text.)
6. Compile and insert a table of figures at the beginning of the document by completing the following steps:
   a. Position the insertion point at the beginning of the document, press the Enter key, and then insert a page break.
   b. Move the insertion point above the page break and then key **TABLE OF FIGURES** bolded and centered.
   c. Press the Enter key, turn off bold, and then change the paragraph alignment back to left.
   d. Click Insert, then Index and Tables.
   e. At the Index and Tables dialog box, click the Table of Figures tab.
   f. At the Index and Tables dialog box with the Table of Figures tab selected, click *Formal* in the Formats list box.
   g. Click OK or press Enter.
7. Check the page breaks in the document and, if necessary, adjust the page breaks.
8. Save the document with the same name (Ch 29, Ex 09).
9. Print the Table of Figures page. (Check with your instructor to see if you should print the entire document.)
10. Close Ch 29, Ex 09.

Updating or Replacing a Table of Figures

A table of figures can be updated in the same manner as updating a table of contents. To update a table of figures, position the insertion point anywhere within the current table of figures (this causes the table of figures to display with a gray background), and then press F9. (This is the Update Field key.) At the Update Table of Figures dialog box, click Update page numbers only if the changes occur only to the page numbers, or click Update entire table if changes were made to headings or subheadings within the table. Click OK or press Enter to close the dialog box.

If you make extensive changes to the document, you may want to replace the entire table of figures. To do this, position the insertion point anywhere within the current table of figures, and then click Insert, then Index and Tables. At the Index and Tables dialog box, make sure the Table of Figures tab is selected, and then click OK or press Enter. At the prompt asking if you want to replace the existing table of figures, click Yes.

Deleting a Table of Figures

A table of figures that has been compiled in a document can be deleted. A table of figures is deleted in the same manner as a table of contents. To delete a table of figures, select the entire table of figures using either the mouse or the keyboard, and then press the Delete key.

Creating a Table of Authorities

A table of authorities is a list of citations identifying the pages where the citations appear in a legal brief or other legal document. Word provides many common categories under which citations can be organized. Word includes Cases, Statutes, Other Authorities, Rules, Treatises, Regulations, and Constitutional Provisions. Within each category, Word alphabetizes the citations. Figure 29.14 shows an example of a table of authorities.

figure 29.14 *Table of Authorities*

TABLE OF AUTHORITIES

CASES

Mansfield v. Rydell, 72 Wn.2d 200, 433 P.2d 723 (1983) 3
State v. Fletcher, 73 Wn.2d 332, 124 P.2d 503 (1981) 5
Yang v. Buchwald, 21 Wn.2d 385, 233 P.2d 609 (1991) 7

STATUTES

RCW 8.12.230(2) 4
RCW 6.23.590 7
RCW 5.23.103(3) 10

Some thought goes into planning a table of authorities. Before marking any text in a legal document, you need to determine what section headings you want and what should be contained in the sections.

When marking text for a table of authorities, you need to find the first occurrence of the citation, mark it as a full citation with the complete name, and then specify a short citation. To mark a citation for a table of authorities, you would complete the following steps:

1. Select the first occurrence of the citation.
2. Click Insert, then Index and Tables.
3. At the Index and Tables dialog box, click the Table of Authorities tab.
4. At the Index and Table dialog box with the Table of Authorities tab selected, click the Mark Citation button.
5. At the Mark Citation dialog box shown in figure 29.15, edit and format the text in the Selected text box as you want it to appear in the table of authorities. Edit and format the text in the Short citation text box so it matches the short citation you want Word to search for in the document.

6. Click the down-pointing triangle at the right of the Category text box and then click the category from the drop-down list that applies to the citation.
7. Click the Mark button to mark the selected citation or click the Mark All button if you want Word to mark all long and short citations in the document that match those displayed in the Mark Citation dialog box.
8. The Mark Citation dialog box remains in the document screen so you can mark other citations. To find the next citation in a document, click the Next Citation button. (This causes Word to search through the document for the next occurrence of text commonly found in a citation such as *in re* or *v.*)
9. Select the text for the next citation and then complete steps 5 through 7.
10. After marking all citations, click Close.

29.15

Mark Citation Dialog Box

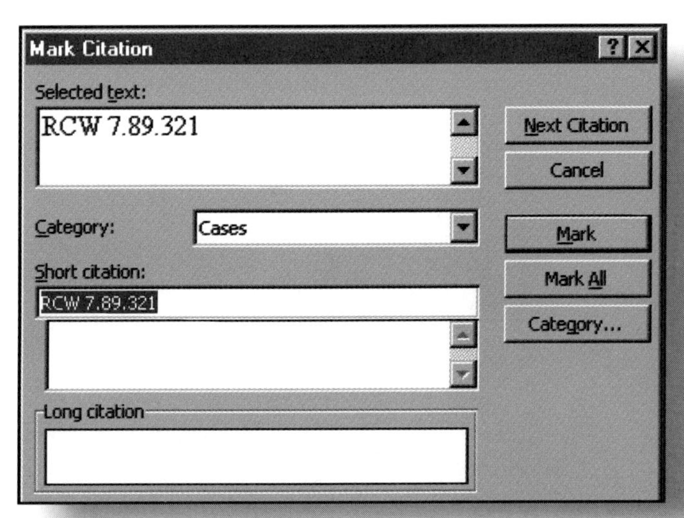

Compiling a Table of Authorities

Once citations have been marked in a document, the table of authorities can be compiled and inserted in the document. A table of authorities is compiled in a document in a manner similar to a table of contents or figures. A table of authorities generally displays at the beginning of the document. To compile a table of authorities in a document containing text marked as citations, you would complete the following steps:

1. Position the insertion point at the beginning of the document and then press the Enter key twice.
2. Position the insertion point at the beginning of the title of the document and then insert a section break that begins a new page.

3. Position the insertion point at the beginning of the document and then key **TABLE OF AUTHORITIES** centered and bolded.
4. Press the Enter key and then turn off bold and change the paragraph alignment back to left.
5. Click Insert, then Index and Tables.
6. At the Index and Tables dialog box, click the Table of Authorities tab.
7. At the Index and Tables dialog box with the Table of Authorities tab selected, choose the desired formatting.
8. Click OK or press Enter.

If you want the table of authorities to print on a page separate from the document text, insert a section break that begins a new page between the table of authorities and the title of the document. If the beginning of the text in the document, rather than the table of authorities, should be numbered as page 1, change the starting page number for the section.

The Index and Tables dialog box with the Table of Authorities tab selected contains options for formatting a table of authorities. The Use passim option is active by default (the check box contains a check mark). When it is active, Word replaces five or more page references to the same authority with *passim*. With the Keep original formatting check box active, Word will retain the formatting of the citation as it appears in the document. Click the Tab leader option if you want to change the leader character.

By default, Word compiles all categories for the table of authorities. If you want to compile citations for a specific category, select that category from the Category drop-down list.

exercise 10

Compiling a Table of Authorities

1. Open Legal Brief.
2. Save the document with Save As and name it Ch 29, Ex 10.
3. Mark *RCW 7.89.321* as a statute citation by completing the following steps:
   a. Select *RCW 7.89.321*. (This citation is located toward the middle of the second page. *Hint: Use the Find feature to help you locate this citation.*)
   b. Click Insert, then Index and Tables.
   c. At the Index and Tables dialog box, click the Table of Authorities tab.
   d. At the Index and Table dialog box with the Table of Authorities tab selected, click the Mark Citation button.
   e. At the Mark Citation dialog box, click the down-pointing triangle at the right side of the Category text box, and then click *Statutes* at the drop-down list.
   f. Click the Mark All button.
   g. Click Close.

4. Complete steps similar to those in 3 to mark *RCW 7.53.443* as a statute citation. (This citation is located toward the middle of the second page.)
5. Complete steps similar to those in 3 to mark *RCW 7.72A.432(2)* as a statute citation. (This citation is located toward the top of the third page.)
6. Complete steps similar to those in 3 to mark *RCW 7.42A.429(1)* as a statute citation. (This citation is located toward the top of the third page.)
7. Mark *State v. Connors*, 73 W.2d 743, 430 P.2d 199 (1974) as a case citation by completing the following steps:
   a. Select *State v. Connors*, 73 W.2d 743, 430 P.2d 199 (1974). (This citation is located toward the bottom of the second page. *Hint: Use the Find feature to help you locate this citation.*)
   b. Click Insert, then Index and Tables.
   c. At the Index and Tables dialog box with the Table of Authorities tab selected, click the Mark Citation button.
   d. At the Mark Citation dialog box, click the down-pointing triangle at the right side of the Category text box, and then click *Cases* at the drop-down list.
   e. Click in the Short citation text box and then key **State v. Connors**.
   f. Click the Mark All button.
   g. Click Close.
8. Complete steps similar to those in 7 to mark *State v. Bertelli*, 63 W.2d 77, 542 P.2d 751 (1971). Enter *State v. Bertelli* as the short citation. (This citation is located toward the bottom of the second page.)
9. Complete steps similar to those in 7 to mark *State v. Landers*, 103 W.2d 432, 893 P.2d 2 (1984). Enter *State v. Landers* as the short citation. (This citation is located toward the top of the third page.)
10. Turn on page numbering and compile the table of authorities by completing the following steps:
    a. Position the insertion point at the beginning of the document and then press the Enter key once.
    b. Position the insertion point immediately left of the *S* in *STATEMENT OF CASE* and then insert a section break that begins a new page.
    c. With the insertion point positioned below the section break, turn on page numbering at the bottom center of each page and change the starting number to 1.
    d. Position the insertion point above the section break and then key **TABLE OF AUTHORITIES** centered and bolded.
    e. Press the Enter key, turn off bold, and then change the paragraph alignment back to left.

f. Click Insert, then Index and Tables.
g. At the Index and Tables dialog box, click the Table of Authorities tab.
h. At the Index and Tables dialog box with the Table of Authorities tab selected, click *Formal* in the Formats list box.
i. Click OK or press Enter.

11. With the insertion point positioned anywhere in the table of authorities, turn on page numbering at the bottom center of each page and change the numbering format to lowercase Roman numerals.
12. Turn off the display of nonprinting characters.
13. Save the document again with the same name (Ch 29, Ex 10).
14. Print the table of authorities. (Check with your instructor to see if you should print the entire document.)
15. Close Ch 29, Ex 10.

Updating or Replacing a Table of Authorities

A table of authorities can be updated in the same manner as updating a table of contents or figures. To update a table of authorities, position the insertion point anywhere within the current table of authorities (this causes the table of authorities to display with a gray background), and then press F9. (This is the Update Field key.) At the Update Table of Authorities dialog box, click Update page numbers only if the changes occur only to the page numbers, or click Update entire table if changes were made to citations in the document. Click OK or press Enter to close the dialog box.

If you make extensive changes to the document, you may want to replace the entire table of authorities. To do this, position the insertion point anywhere within the current table of authorities, and then click Insert, then Index and Tables. At the Index and Tables dialog box, make sure the Table of Authorities tab is selected, and then click OK or press Enter. At the prompt asking if you want to replace the existing table of authorities, click Yes.

Deleting a Table of Authorities

A table of authorities that has been compiled in a document can be deleted. A table of authorities is deleted in the same manner as a table of contents. To delete a table of authorities, select the entire table of authorities using either the mouse or the keyboard, and then press the Delete key.

chapter summary

- Word contains options for automating the creation of a table of contents, index, list, or table of authorities.
- Text to be included in a table of contents can be identified by applying a heading style, or text can be marked as a field entry.
- Two steps are involved in creating a table of contents: apply the appropriate styles to the text that will be included, and compile the table of contents in the document.
- To compile the table of contents, position the insertion point where you want it to appear, display the Index and Tables dialog box with the Table of Contents tab selected, make any desired changes, and then click OK.
- At the Index and Tables dialog box, you can choose from a variety of preformatted tables.
- If you want the table of contents to print on a page separate from the document text, insert a section break that begins a new page between the table of contents and the title of the document. You may need to adjust the page numbering also.
- If you make changes to a document after compiling a table of contents, you can either update the existing table of contents or replace it. An index, a table of figures, or a table of authorities can be updated in the same manner.
- To delete a table of contents, select the entire table of contents, and then press the Delete key. Delete an index, a table of figures, or a table of authorities in the same manner.
- An index is a list of topics contained in a publication and the pages where those topics are discussed. Word lets you automate the process of creating an index in a manner similar to that for creating a table of contents.
- Mark text for an index at the Index and Tables dialog box with the Index tab selected.
- After all necessary text has been marked as a main entry or subentry for the index, the next step is to compile the index so that it appears at the end of the document beginning on a separate page.
- Word provides seven formatting choices for an index in the Formats list box at the Index and Tables dialog box.
- Words that appear frequently in a document can be saved as a concordance file so that you need not mark each reference in a document.
- A concordance file is a regular document containing a single, two-column table created at the Insert Table dialog box.
- A table of figures can be created using a variety of methods. The easiest method is to mark figure names as captions and then use the caption names to create the table of figures.
- A table of figures is compiled in a document in a manner similar to a table of contents and generally displays at the beginning of the document, after the table of contents.
- A table of authorities is a list of citations identifying the pages where the citations appear in a legal brief or other legal document.
- When marking text for a table of authorities, find the first occurrence of the citation, mark it as a full citation with the complete name, and then specify a short citation at the Index and Tables dialog box.
- A table of authorities is compiled in a document in a manner similar to a table of contents or figures. A table of authorities generally displays at the beginning of the document.

commands review

	Mouse/Keyboard
Display Index and Tables dialog box	Insert, Index and Tables
Display Insert Table dialog box	Table, Insert Table

check your understanding

Matching: In the space provided at the left, write the letter of the term that matches the description. (Terms may be used more than once.)

A. Table of Contents
B. Index
C. Table of Figures
D. Table of Authorities
E. Concordance file
F. Index and Tables dialog box
G. Fields
H. Compiling
I. Captions
J. Main entries
K. Subentries
L. Marking

_______ 1. Helps save time when marking text for an index.
_______ 2. Identifies citations in a legal brief.
_______ 3. Generally placed at the end of a document.
_______ 4. This is the next step in creating a table of contents after applying the necessary heading styles.
_______ 5. If included in a document, it usually follows the table of contents.
_______ 6. Generally placed at the beginning of a document.
_______ 7. The easiest way to create a table of figures is to use these.
_______ 8. If you do not want style formatting applied in a document, mark text for the table of contents as these.
_______ 9. Choose a preformatted table of contents at this dialog box.
_______ 10. This is a list of topics contained in a publication.

skill assessments

Note: Before completing the skill assessments, display the Open dialog box, and then select and delete documents created in chapter 27 that begin Ch 27. You may want to check with your instructor before deleting these documents.

Assessment 1

1. Open Report 04.
2. Save the document with Save As and name it Ch 29, SA 01.
3. Make the following changes to the document:
   a. Set the titles and headings in 14-point Times New Roman bold.
   b. Mark titles, headings, and subheadings for a table of contents.
   c. Number the pages at the bottom center of each page.
   d. Compile the table of contents. (Include a title for the table of contents.)
   e. Number the table of contents page at the bottom center of the page. (Change the number to a lowercase Roman numeral.)
4. Save the document again with the same name (Ch 29, SA 01).
5. Print the table of contents page. (Check with your instructor to see if you should print the entire document.)
6. Close Ch 29, SA 01.

Assessment 2

1. At a clear document screen, create the text shown in figure 29.16 as a concordance file.
2. Save the document and name it Ch 29, SA Concord File.
3. Print and then close Ch 29, SA Concord File.
4. Open Ch 29, SA 01.
5. Save the document with Save As and name it Ch 29, SA 02.
6. Make the following changes to the document:
   a. Mark text for an index using the concordance file, Ch 29, SA Concord File.
   b. Compile the index at the end of the document.
7. Save the document again with the same name (Ch 29, SA 02).
8. Print the index. (Check with your instructor to see if you should print the entire document.)
9. Close Ch 29, SA 02.

Figure 29.16 • Assessment 2

NEWSLETTER	Newsletter
newsletter	Newsletter
consistency	Newsletter: consistency
element	Elements
margins	Elements: margins
column layout	Elements: column layout
nameplate	Elements: nameplate
location	Elements: location
logos	Elements: logos
color	Elements: color
ruled lines	Elements: ruled lines
Focus	Elements: focus
balance	Elements: balance
graphics images	Graphics images
photos	Photos
Headlines	Newsletter: headlines
subheads	Newsletter: subheads
White space	White space
directional flow	Newsletter: directional flow
paper	Paper

Assessment 3

1. Open Ch 29, SA 02.
2. Save the document with Save As and name it Ch 29, SA 03.
3. Insert a page break at the beginning of the title, *MODULE 4: CREATING NEWSLETTER LAYOUT*.
4. Update the table of contents and the index.
5. Save the document again with the same name (Ch 29, SA 03).
6. Print the table of contents and then the index. (Check with your instructor to see if you should print the entire document.)

Unit Six

PERFORMANCE ASSESSMENTS

DEMONSTRATING YOUR SKILLS

Assessment one

1. Open Mortgage.
2. Save the document with Save As and name it Unit 6, PA 01.
3. Sort the paragraphs alphabetically by the first word of each paragraph. (After the sorting is completed, delete the hard returns that are moved to the beginning of the document.)
4. Save the sorted document again with the same name (Unit 6, PA 01).
5. Print and then close Unit 6, PA 01.

Assessment two

1. Open Table 07.
2. Save the document with Save As and name it Unit 6, PA 02.
3. Sort the text alphabetically in the first column.
4. Apply the *Colorful 3* table formatting to the table.
5. Save the document again with the same name (Unit 6, PA 02).
6. Print and then close Unit 6, PA 02.

Assessment three

1. Open Report 04.
2. Save the document with Save As and name it Unit 6, PA 03.
3. Make the following changes to the document:
   a. Change to the Outline viewing mode.
   b. Apply Heading 1 and Heading 2 styles to the titles and headings in the document.

c. Collapse the outline so only two heading levels are displayed.
d. Move the module 3 section below the module 4 section and then renumber the modules (3 becomes 4 and 4 becomes 3).
e. Move the heading *Creating Margins for Newsletters* above the heading *Choosing Paper Size and Type*.

4. With the outline still collapsed, save the document again with the same name (Unit 6, PA 03).
5. Print and then close Unit 6, PA 03.

Assessment four

1. Create the table form shown in figure U6.1 as a template document named XXX Unit 6, PA 04 (where your initials are inserted in place of the *XXX*). Customize the table as shown in figure U6.1. Insert text form fields in the table as shown in the figure.
2. Save the document with Save As and name it XXX Unit 6, PA 04. (Use your initials in place of the *XXX*.)
3. Print and then close XXX Unit 6, PA 04.

REDWOOD COMMUNITY COLLEGE
312 South 122nd Street
Mendocino, CA 94220
(707) 555-7880

Name: [ ] **Date:** [ ]

Department: [ ]

Description	Qty.	Cost
[ ] [ ] [ ]	[ ] [ ] [ ]	[ ] [ ] [ ]

Figure U6.1 • Assessment 4

Assessment five

1. Create a form with the XXX Unit 6, PA 04 form template. Insert the following information in the form:

   Name: Ronald Jarvis
   Date: (key the current date)
   Department: Public Relations

   Description: Transfer Brochure
   Qty.: 400
   Cost: $225.00

   Description: Technology Degree Brochure
   Qty.: 250
   Cost: $179.50

   Description: College Newsletter
   Qty.: 2,000
   Cost: $150.50

2. When the form is completed, save the document and name it Unit 06, PA 05.
3. Print and then close Unit 06, PA 05.

Assessment six

1. At a clear document screen, create the text shown in figure U6.2 as a concordance file.
2. Save the document and name it Unit 6, Concord File.
3. Print and then close Unit 6, Concord File.
4. Open Report 04.
5. Save the document with Save As and name it Unit 6, PA 06.
6. Make the following changes to the document:
   a. Mark text for an index using the concordance file, Unit 6, Concord File.
   b. Compile the index at the end of the document.
   c. Mark the title and headings for a table of contents.
   d. Compile the table of contents at the beginning of the document.
7. Save the document again with the same name (Unit 6, PA 06).
8. Print the table of contents and the index. (Check with your instructor to see if you should print the entire document.)
9. Close Unit 6, PA 06.

message	Message
publication	Publication
design	Design
Flier	Flier
letterhead	Letterhead
newsletter	Newsletter
intent	Design: intent
audience	Design: audience
layout	Design: layout
thumbnail	Thumbnail
principles	Design: principles
focus	Design: focus
balance	Design: balance
proportion	Design: proportion
contrast	Design: contrast
directional flow	Design: directional flow

Figure U6.2 • Assessment 6

CREATING ORIGINAL DOCUMENTS

Assessment seven

Situation: You are an administrative assistant at Rockford Medical Center and you have been asked by your supervisor to create a directory with the information displayed below. After creating the directory, sort the text alphabetically by last name. Save the document and name it Unit 6, PA 07. Print Unit 6, PA 07. With Unit 6, PA 07 still open, sort the text numerically by extension, and then save the document with the same name. Print and then close Unit 6, PA 07.

Grogan, Avery	President	2005
Cartagena, Eduardo	Vice President	2012
Gaines, Jessica	Vice President	2056
Klein, Dayna	Vice President	2190
Elmore, Marcus	Vice President	2089
Bevan-Church, Chloe	Director	2971
Sackett, Joel	Director	2702
Lahti, Chandra	Director	2864
Lyons, Melissa	Director	2311
Goelzer, Conrad	Director	2788
Fallstrom, Gregory	Director	2622

Eccles, Rachelle	Director	2541
Lee, Sang	Director	2482
Soileau, Victoria	Director	2766
Oslakovic, Craig	Director	2515

Assessment eight

Situation: You are an administrative assistant in the vocational department at Redwood Community College. You have been asked by your supervisor to create a fill-in form template for advisory committees that contains the following information (you determine the layout of the form and the types of form fields used):

ADVISORY COMMITTEE MEMBER APPLICATION

Committee Requested: Science, Social Studies, Arts, or Health and Fitness

Name:
Company Address:
Telephone:
Job Title:
Years of Experience:
Gender: Male or Female

After creating the form template, save the template document as XXX Unit 6, PA 08. Use the XXX Unit 6, PA 08 form template to create a filled-in form. You make up information to fill in the form fields. After the form is filled in, save it and name it Unit 6, PA 08. Print and then close Unit 6, PA 08.

Assessment nine

1. Display the New dialog box.
2. At the New dialog box, delete the following template form documents:
   XXX Unit 6, PA 04 (where your initials display rather than *XXX*)
   XXX Unit 6, PA 08 (where your initials display rather then *XXX*)
3. Close the New dialog box.

appendix a

Proofreaders' Marks

	Proofreaders' Mark	Example	Revised
#	Insert space	lettertothe	letter to the
℘	Delete	the commands is	the command is
lc /	Lowercase	lc he is Branch Manager	he is branch manager
(cap) or uc ≡	Uppercase	(cap) Margaret simpson	Margaret Simpson
¶	New paragraph	¶ The new product	The new product
no ¶	No paragraph	the meeting. no ¶ Bring the	the meeting. Bring the
∧	Insert	pens, clips (and)	pens, and clips
⊙	Insert period	a global search⊙	a global search.
⊐	Move right	⊐ With the papers	With the papers
⊏	Move left	⊏access the code	access the code
⊐⊏	Center	⊐ Chapter Six ⊏	Chapter Six
∽	Transpose	It is raesonable	It is reasonable
(sp)	Spell out	(sp) 475 Mill (Ave.)	475 Mill Avenue
. . .	Stet (do not delete)	I am very pleased	I am very pleased
⁀	Close up	regret fully	regretfully
ss	Single-space	The margin top ss is 1 inch.	The margin top is 1 inch.
ds	Double-space	ds Paper length is set for 11 inches.	Paper length is set for 11 inches.
ts	Triple-space	ts The F8 function key contains commands	The F8 function key contains commands
bf	Boldface	bf Boldface type provides emphasis.	**Boldface** type provides emphasis.
(ital)	Italics	(ital) Use italics for terms to be defined.	Use *italics* for terms to be defined.

appendix b

Formatting a Memo

The formatting for an interoffice correspondence, referred to as a *memo*, can vary. Microsoft Word 97 offers three memo templates, each with different formatting for the memo headings. Many companies design their own formatting for a memo. In some exercises in this textbook, you will be required to key and format a memo. When asked to format a memo, use the formatting shown below.

Include reference initials at the end of the memo as shown below, along with the document name. The reference initials are indicated by the *XX*. In this textbook, insert your initials instead of the *XX*.

1-inch top margin

DATE: September 30, 1999

ds

TO: Adam Mukai, Vice President

ds

FROM: Carol Jenovich, Director

ds

SUBJECT: NEW EMPLOYEES

ts

Two new employees have been hired to work in the Human Resources Department. Lola Henderson will begin work on October 1 and Daniel Schriver will begin October 14.

ds

Ms. Henderson has worked for three years as an administrative assistant for another company. Due to her previous experience, she was hired as a program assistant.

ds

Mr. Schriver has just completed a one-year training program at Gulf Community College. He was hired as an Administrative Assistant I.

ds

I would like to introduce you to the new employees. Please schedule a time for a short visit.

ds

XX:Memo

appendix c

Formatting a Business Letter

A variety of formatting styles can be applied to a business letter. Some common business letter styles include block style, modified block style, and simplified. In some exercises in this textbook, you will be required to key and format a business letter. When asked to format a business letter, use the block style shown below. Include your initials at the end of the letter, followed by the document name. The business letter shown below is formatted with standard punctuation. Standard punctuation includes a colon after the salutation and a comma after the complimentary close.

2-inch top margin

December 7, 1999

5 Enters (Returns)

Mr. Paul Reinke
Iverson Medical Center
1290 South 43rd Street
Houston, TX 77348

ds

Dear Mr. Reinke:

ds

During the entire month of January, our laser printer, Model No. 34-454, will be on sale. We are cutting the original price by 33 percent!

ds

When you purchased your computer system from our store last month, you indicated an interest in a laser printer. Now is your chance, Mr. Reinke, to purchase a high-quality laser printer at a rock-bottom price. Once you have seen the quality of print produced by a laser printer, you will not be satisfied with any other type of printer.

ds

Visit our store at your convenience and see a demonstration of this incredible printer. We are so confident you will purchase the printer that we are enclosing a coupon for a free printer cartridge worth over $100.

ds

Very truly yours,

4 Enters (Returns)

Gina Cerazzo, Manager

ds

XX: Block Letter

ds

Enclosure

index

d

f

q

r

s

t

photo credits

The following photos are courtesy of:

Page	
2	Intel Corporation (second from top)
129	Hewlett-Packard Company
153	Micron Electronics, Inc.
175	Apple Computer, Inc.
227	Hewlett-Packard Company
245	Frank Pryor/Apple Computer, Inc.
287	Apple Computer, Inc.
317	Hewlett-Packard Company
341	Peter Fox/Apple Computer, Inc.
377	Peter Fox/Apple Computer, Inc.
403	Hewlett-Packard Company
437	Hewlett-Packard Company
465	Hewlett-Packard Company
497	Peter Fox/Apple Computer, Inc.

Word Toolbars: Standard and Formatting

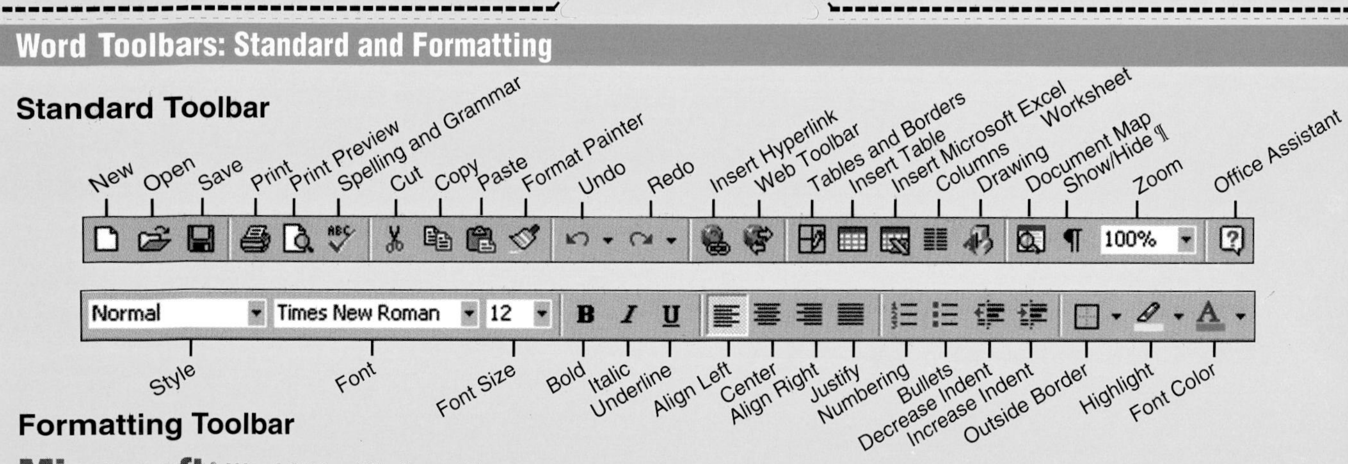

Microsoft® Word 97 for Windows 95

Word Keyboard Shortcuts

Paragraph Formatting		Character Formatting		Other Actions	
Center	Ctrl+E	Bold	Ctrl+B	Cut	Ctrl+X
Right Align	Ctrl+R	Italic	Ctrl+I	Copy	Ctrl+C
Left Align	Ctrl+L	Continuous Underline	Ctrl+U	Paste	Ctrl+V
Justify	Ctrl+J	Word Underline	Ctrl+Shift+W	Repeat	Ctrl+Y or F4
Increase Indent	Ctrl+M	Double Underline	Ctrl+Shift+D	Cancel	Esc
Decrease Indent	Ctrl+Shift+M	Subscript	Ctrl+=	New Line	Shift+Enter
Hanging Indent	Ctrl+T	Superscript	Ctrl+Shift+=	New Page	Ctrl+Enter
Remove Hanging Indent	Ctrl+Shift+T	All Caps	Ctrl+Shift+A	New Column/Split Table	Ctrl+Shift+Enter
Open/Close Space Before	Ctrl+0 (zero)	Small Caps	Ctrl+Shift+K	Optional Hyphen	Ctrl+Hyphen
Single-space Lines	Ctrl+1	Font	Ctrl+D	Nonbreaking Hyphen	Ctrl+Shift+Hyphen
Double-space Lines	Ctrl+2	Point Size	Ctrl+Shift+P	Nonbreaking Space	Ctrl+Shift+Spacebar
1.5 Line Spacing	Ctrl+5	Hidden	Ctrl+Shift+H	Tab Character (table)	Ctrl+Tab
Apply Style	Ctrl+Shift+S	Reset Character	Ctrl+Shift+Z, or Ctrl+Spacebar	Show Nonprinting Characters	Ctrl+Shift+*
Reset to Style	Ctrl+Q				

Microsoft® Word 97 for Windows 95

For complete help on keyboard shortcuts, click the Office Assistant button and type **Keyboard shortcuts**

Word Function Keys

	F1	F2	F3	F4	F5	F6
key only	Help	Move	AutoText	Repeat Last Action	Go To	Next Pane
SHIFT+	**Reveal Formatting**	**Copy Text**	**Change Case**	**Repeat Find/Go To**	**Go Back**	**Previous Pane**
CTRL+		Print Preview	Cut to Spike	Close Document	Restore Window Size	Next Window
CTRL+SHIFT+			Insert Spike		Edit Bookmark	Previous Window
ALT+	**Next Field**			**Exit**		
ALT+SHIFT+	Previous Field	Save				

	F7	F8	F9	F10	F11	F12
key only	Spelling	Extend	Update Field	Menu Bar	Next Field	Save As
SHIFT+	**Thesaurus**	**Shrink Selection**	**Toggle Field Code**	**Shortcut Menu**	**Previous Field**	**Save**
CTRL+	Move Doc Window	Size Doc Window	Insert Field	Max Doc Window	Lock Field	Open
CTRL+SHIFT+	Update Link	Extend (block)	Unlink Field	Activate Ruler	Unlock Field	Print
ALT+	**Find Next Misspelling**		**Toggle All Field Codes**	**Max App Window**		
ALT+SHIFT+			Do Field Click			

Microsoft® Word 97 for Windows 95

For complete help on keyboard shortcuts, click the Office Assistant button and type **Keyboard shortcuts**